The Islamic Near East
and North Africa

The Islamic Near East and North Africa

An Annotated Guide to Books in English for Non-Specialists

David W. Littlefield

1977

LIBRARIES UNLIMITED, INC.

Littleton, Colo.

LIBRARIES UNLIMITED, INC.
P.O. Box 263
Littleton, Colorado 80160

016.956
L 716 i

Library of Congress Cataloging in Publication Data

Littlefield, David W   1940-
    The Islamic Near East and North Africa.

    Includes indexes.
    1. Near East--Bibliography. 2. Africa, North--
Bibliography. I. Title.
Z3013.L58   [DS44]   016.956   76-218
ISBN 0-87287-159-2

TABLE OF CONTENTS

INDIVIDUAL COUNTRIES

ACKNOWLEDGMENTS

The following individuals have contributed to making this *Guide* more useful than it would have been without their help:

Dr. George Atiyeh, Head, Near East Section, Orientalia Division, Library of Congress, reviewed my list in the last stage of writing, made a number of suggestions for additions, and helped me with this project in various other ways. He has been a sounding board for my ideas and opinions for years and a constant source of encouragement and help in my career. I am glad to have the opportunity to express my gratitude publicly.

Dr. Lawrence Marwick, Head, Hebraic Section, Orientalia Division, Library of Congress, has been a friend and source of encouragement for years; he made possible the inclusion of books on the Hebrew language, about which I was totally ignorant.

Dr. John Ruedy, History Department, Georgetown University, discussed with me at length my section on North Africa at an early stage in the project.

Dr. George D. Selim, Near East Section, Orientalia Division, Library of Congress, was of help in selecting works on the Arabic language.

Dr. Karl and Barbara Stowasser of the University of Maryland gave me vital assistance in selecting and annotating works on the Turkish, Persian, and Arabic languages.

Edith Scott, Head, Cataloging Instruction Office, Library of Congress, taught me much of what I know about librarianship, has often discussed with me my ideas on aspects of library service (with fortitude, patience, and good humor), and encouraged me professionally in ways that have had an ultimate influence on this book and its philosophy; she also read and commented on an early version of the "Introduction" and the "How to Use the Guide" section.

Aaron Rosenbaum of *Near East Report* commented on some of my selections concerning Israel and the Arab-Israeli conflict, suggested a few additional items, and caused me to reconsider a number of items I had previously rejected on various other topics.

Daniel Stohlman of the Jewish Theological Seminary Library gave me some valuable hints on Hebrew literature.

Lastly, I wish to pay tribute to two of my professors who have had a decisive influence on me. The late, and very much missed, Dr. Halford L. Hoskins of the School of International Service, The American University, led my most intensive educational experience in the field, and indeed in my academic career; his example and guidance as teacher and human being were of vital importance to me.

Dr. Irfan Shahîd, Professor of Arabic, School of Languages and Linguistics, Georgetown University, showed me what real scholarship is all about, initiated my interest in Koranic and Arabic studies, and helped me develop basic tools with which to pursue these fields. When he finishes his books, they should stand as monuments in their fields.

Both of these men, so different in many ways, have stimulated the minds of their students, in whom they took an active interest as thoughtful teachers, and have encouraged them by recognizing that even neophytes can contribute new ideas and approaches.

INTRODUCTION

This *Guide* is a highly selective list of books chosen from among the best works available: "standard" items, and some not so "standard," which in the compiler's judgment will stimulate the interest of the non-expert reader, will help him to understand various aspects of the region (including Cyprus, Afghanistan, and Mauritania) from ca. 600 A.D. to the present, will meet his basic information needs, and will bibliographically direct his first steps as he moves beyond the material found in the books listed.

The *Guide* is intended to help the library respond to the needs of its readers by enabling it to acquire conveniently and quickly a well-rounded collection of works of permanent value, and to develop its collection to whatever depth is desired in individual topics. Because it is selective, the *Guide* is by no means a comprehensive list of all "standard" works, although such a list can be compiled from the bibliographies listed herein.

There are two main elements in the *Guide*: *First*, a basic collection of books (the numbered items). These works document the major aspects of Near Eastern history and life and represent the main disciplines through which the region is studied. They are the foundations for study, whatever its level of scholarship may be. They are, specifically as indicated in the annotations, the works that any library should purchase and that any student should read first. *Second*, the supplementary listings. These listings are provided in annotations of basic items, and in certain topical subdivisions for which there are no comprehensive systematic works that could be considered basic items. These are intended for the use of readers who wish to pursue specific topics in greater depth. They are generally the standard works that budding specialists must read after their basic studies.

Each section was treated independently of the others when selecting books, in an attempt to cover each topic and discipline systematically within the overall goals of the *Guide*. Therefore, each topic contains basic works for both readers and libraries: some items will not be essential purchases for any but large libraries but should be read by anyone interested in the topic. To facilitate purchase of the most appropriate basic representative works by libraries of various sizes, there is a section of special lists in the appendix of the *Guide*, while the annotations and codes provide additional assistance.

SELECTIVE PROCESS

Working from a list of works tentatively chosen for inclusion, the author sought to ascertain the scientific and educational consensus on which are the best works on each topic by scanning many bibliographies item by item. The bibliographies and footnotes of the individual works were also examined, as were lists and reviews in periodicals such as *Choice*, *Library Journal* (both of which regularly include many books on the region), the *Middle East Journal*, *International*

Journal of Middle East Studies, etc. Simultaneously the shelves and catalogs of the Library of Congress and several local libraries were systematically surveyed for books of interest. In addition, a number of specialists were consulted for additional guidance. The great majority of the items considered were examined, or even read completely, and then annotated. At each stage in the process of completing the list many items were reconsidered and some were reexamined. This process of pre-selection, examination, and final selection continued literally until the day the manuscript was mailed to the publisher; new items were continuously added. In the final stage of writing some items were discovered or reconsidered too late for me to examine them or to locate their bibliographical data; it was deemed to be of greater service to the reader to include these works with incomplete data than to omit them entirely for the sake of completeness and consistency. The data and annotations for some works are incomplete because they arrived at the Library of Congress too late for their cataloging information to be available, or because they appeared in the form of CIP material that did not include galleys or other information from which full annotations could be made. Some forthcoming items were annotated from publishers' catalogs and advertisements (a note to this effect is added to the annotation), and a very few others were annotated on the basis of reviews.

SELECTION CRITERIA

The final selections reflect my professional judgment as continuously formed, modified, or confirmed by the scientific and educational consensus of specialists and by years of practical experience in the multiple roles of student, researcher, generalist, librarian (reference, cataloging, book selection and acquisition), book reviewer, home library builder, and bibliographer. In cases where my judgment differed from the consensus of the relative merits of various works or when a choice had to be made in order to keep the basic list within reasonable bounds, the disputed items have been included as supplementary materials on the grounds that they do have merit and will be expected to appear in any list of this sort.

This list tries to satisfy what the compiler perceives to be a number of basic needs. Most bibliographies have been essentially listings of books considered for inclusion independently of each other. Even when annotated, graded by audience, or limited in number of items, they have provided little or no guidance to the librarian or reader who does not need the whole collection. They usually included many works without critical reconsideration simply because these works were alleged to be "standard" books. Very many bibliographies have not carefully considered the needs of their readership. This *Guide* is intended to be an integrated whole; each book has been considered critically not only for its own sake but in relation to the others. Moreover, I have attempted to provide enough guidance so that each user can determine which individual books meet his particular needs.

I have one basic presupposition concerning the process of introducing the beginner to a program of area studies. Within limits I have allowed it to influence my selection. It seems to me that anyone interested in a region should understand the people: their social structure, customs, daily lives, nature of interpersonal relations, popular psychology, attitudes, world-view, etc.; as much as possible the reader should view things as the people of the region view them. To the extent that maximum empathy is not a continuous, conscious part of every reflection on the area, social and political analysis tends to become invalid. Most people, including many writers, tend to apply their own standards uncritically to other peoples, whose values, categories of thought, and responses to stimuli are quite different from theirs in *form* if not in *essence*; it is necessary to differentiate between what is universal human reaction and what is culturally determined *form* of reaction to stimuli. Therefore, I have included books which I believe help the reader to view the people as they live and die and to gain a feeling for the environment they live in; thus, many travelogues and ethnological studies are included.

In most subject areas I have included available writings by the indigenous peoples—prime historical sources, literary and religious works, political works. One reads these books for the same reasons that one reads Machiavelli and Luther in Renaissance history courses: as representative works, and also as source materials for understanding the psychology of the writers and the ethos of their times.

I have sought to include some of the best nineteenth century travel and other works, of which there are a multitude, to maximize a feel for that era. Only by understanding that background can we understand the nature of the problems facing the region today. The nineteenth century was a period during which a great many changes disturbed and continue to disturb the foundations of the area's traditional existence. By permitting us to compare the situations then and now, nineteenth century travel accounts will help us understand what changes have or have not occurred, the reasons for change or the lack of it, and what changes should or may occur in the future.

Other considerations influenced my selections. I have covered topics of abiding importance, especially those to which public libraries have to respond; thus there are more books on Israel than otherwise might be the case if proportionate coverage for each country were an overriding consideration. I have included some books that are of poor quality but that are all we have on some subjects.

I have included topics and books basic to graduate study—books that a college student ought to read if he intends to specialize in the region. Mastery of the books in this *Guide* should give the student a basic knowledge equivalent to a couple of years of graduate study. If he achieves this before he enters a graduate program, he should be able to benefit much more from his formal studies; most graduate programs have to devote time to basics because few undergraduate schools have regional courses. I have tried to make this *Guide* suitable for use as a basic bibliography for student assignments at the university level.

I have also kept in mind professors in other fields who might want to assign their students collateral readings on the Near East for comparative study, as well as non-specialists who are teaching courses on the region and the libraries that will have to back up those courses.

Generally, these many considerations are not contradictory, but they have combined to determine some choices and omissions that would not be necessary if only a single audience was being served. On the whole, I do not think these decisions have affected adversely any groups of the *Guide*'s intended users.

GAPS IN COVERAGE

This *Guide* covers an area encompassing three continents (Europe, Asia, Africa); three main culture areas (Persian, Turkish, and Arabic); a period of 1400 years; a vast region always in a constant state of flux and subject to outside influences and invasions from many directions by many diverse peoples; 22 independent states. Scholarly interest in the region has been accelerating since the turn of the nineteenth century, and particularly in the twentieth century. Most of the many popular works written about it have been devastatingly faulted by biases and frequent disregard for or ignorance of the facts, while many have been written for polemical purposes—even scholarship has suffered greatly from these factors. Today, local suspicions and even hatred of the West, as well as local politics, have increasingly closed the region to Western scholarship. Furthermore, the region's societies and cultures are so alien to us that empathy is difficult, if not impossible. The vernacular languages, which, except for modern Turkish, are written in an alphabet different from our own, are difficult for us to learn and use as a vehicle of understanding and communication; this fact has drastically reduced the potential number of scholars and others who might help us discover the Near East.

The users of this *Guide* should be aware that this selection of suggested readings must be uneven in coverage because it reflects the adequacies and inadequacies of the literature itself. Many gaps in all fields of knowledge remain to be bridged. In many fields, so few scholarly works have been produced that there is no basis for popular works; many essential subjects inspire too little popular interest to induce the production of popular works even when the scholarship is available. In its various sections, the *Guide* frequently notes lacunae in the literature.

TRANSLATIONS

Many of the greatest works of Western scholarship are written in French or German, which graduate students are expected to know in addition to their vernacular languages. Relatively few of these works have been translated into English. There is a relative paucity of translations from the local languages; while many translations exist, many more basic works remain unavailable except in their original languages. There are very few translations of vernacular secondary works in the various fields, though these would provide introductions that we now lack in English and fill existing gaps until Western scholars come up with books more suited to our special needs.

REPRINTS AND O.P.'S

The burgeoning reprint industry has made available to libraries innumerable out-of-print works that still are considered to be basic. Among these treasures, however, are many books of questionable value. They may have been the best to be had at one time, thus they were, and still are, often quoted in other books and cited in the standard bibliographies; but they have been superseded and now offer nothing to new collections or to libraries filling in gaps. Reprints should be purchased only after careful investigation; it would be much better to decide which "golden oldies" are basic to one's collection and then shop for reprints. Because so many books are being reprinted, I have not hesitated to include many o.p. works. I would not expect recent travelogues to be reprinted, however; thus, while I have included especially good ones from somewhat earlier periods, I have tended to stress those published since 1965 (and particularly from later years), partly because they will retain their validity longer and partly because recent works might well be available from remainder dealers and used book stores.

READING FOR PLEASURE

There are lamentably few books available that both entertain and inform adequately. I have selected from the mass of travel and descriptive books the ones that I judge to be the best of both—or, failing that, the most informative. Several that are not really very informative have been found to be so exceptionally enjoyable that I have included them as well.

SPECIALIZED WORKS

I was sometimes faced with the choice of including an advanced or specialized work not necessarily suited even for larger collections, or leaving a gap in the coverage. In such cases, I chose to fill the gap, indicating the work's specialized nature in the annotation.

MISCELLANEOUS

Occasionally several essentially equal works exist on the same topic, particularly in the case of general, introductory works; I selected the one or two most appropriate to the overall objectives of the *Guide* or simply made an arbitrary choice.

It is virtually impossible for one person to master the literature of all the fields represented herein. Therefore, even utilizing the sources which I have, there are likely to be errors of omission, errors of judgment in my selections, and inadequacies in the annotations. Revision of this *Guide* is anticipated, depending on its reception; therefore, I request anyone so motivated to write to me in care of the publisher with suggestions and comments that might be used to improve the next edition. I am specifically interested in suggestions for appropriate novels, written by Westerners, that have Near East-North African settings or themes, such as historical novels; although I made no attempt to include any in this volume, some of them are quite as valuable as the travelogues in providing a feel for the region. All letters will be answered.

HOW TO USE THIS GUIDE

1. **Entries**: In most cases, LC entries are used, dates being omitted except for pre-20th century authors. When not used as main entries, editors are given in the body of the entry and are included in the index. In some cases LC has used a fuller form of the name than is found on the title page; when the more complete form might be confusing, the additional portions of the name have been bracketed for ease in identification.

2. **Filing Titles**: A romanized vernacular language title in brackets, which is the LC filing title, is provided for translations when that title or a reasonable facsimile is not found in the t.p. title; an Arabic or Persian work is often known by the vernacular title rather than its translated form. Only the English title is found in the index, but the vernacular title can be ascertained by looking the author up in the index. As this problem did not seem to pertain to translations of Hebrew works, I omitted the filing titles of works in that language.

3. **Translators**: I included the name of translator only for pre-1900 and literary works. *Books in Print*, *British Books in Print*, book catalogs, and even bibliographies frequently list books under their translators. In *BIP* and *BBIP*, the entries under the vernacular name are usually so garbled and unrecognizable that searching is much quicker under translator, editor, or title.

4. **Imprints**: The main criterion for selection of particular editions was availability. This presented problems because *BIP*, etc., frequently failed to provide complete imprint information. When no LC card was available for the in-print edition, I was forced to settle for the incomplete information; in some cases only a distributor was listed, which compounded the problem of locating the LC card number. Incidentally, it should be noted that British publishers tend to keep books in print somewhat longer than many American publishers, particularly the more standard items. American publishers often simply put their imprint on books completely produced in the U.K. It was found that whereas many of the books with the American imprint were o.p., the British edition was still available. While I have generally listed the American edition when available, for works published since the inception of the Shared Cataloging program (1965-1966), the LC usually has cards for both British and American editions.

5. **Imprint Date**: When the information is available, the dates of both the new and the old editions are provided, particularly for reprints. For *reissues* I have provided the notation "c. 1955," etc., after the imprint date to convey the fact that this is the original publication date. It is indicated to ease confusion when the date on an LC card is different from the reissue date, so that librarians will know that they can order an LC card for accurate cataloging information and that only the date will have to be changed. Cambridge University Press and Oxford University Press, for example, keep basic works in print through reissue, but LC does not acquire and catalog all reissues.

6. **Cataloging Data**: LC does not acquire for cataloging all editions of each work. When only another edition was currently available, "LC n.a." (LC card not

available) is indicated in the entry, but the classification numbers are provided from previous LC cataloging. It should be noted that due to many recent revisions of the LC classification schedules in BP (Islam), DS (Arab countries, Islamic Empire, Islamic civilization, Near East), and DT (North Africa), in particular, the class numbers of unreprinted older works are out of date; I have made no attempt to supply the new numbers for each item. Reprints cataloged at LC are assigned the most up-to-date classification number.

7. **Miscellaneous**: If no ISBN or DDC number is listed, it was not available. Some books were annotated before LC cards became available from which cataloging information could be taken. In the case of new reprints, I often used the old edition for annotating. Works arriving at LC as CIP copy or having top priority but not having cards available at publication of the *Guide* were often at least in the shelf list, so the classification number was available even though the LC card number and DDC were not.

8. **Collection Size**: In many of the annotations I refer to various collections for which the books might be best suited. This indication is meant to be suggestive only.

> By "*smaller collections*" I mean small town and neighborhood branch public libraries, or collections supporting colleges with only a few hundred students, or perhaps two-year colleges.
>
> "*Medium-sized*" collections includes main public libraries serving smaller cities or regions; college collections serving 1000-2000 students.
>
> "*Larger collections*" refers to public libraries serving medium-sized cities; or to small university or large college collections that could reasonably be expected to have 1,000 books on any major geographical region, but that would not be large enough to have a resident specialist available to aid in collection building, or that do not serve a school large enough to support a full program of Near Eastern studies.

9. **Symbols**:
   P — Public Libraries.
   C — College Libraries.
   S — Students.
   1 — absolutely basic to every collection or reader except as indicated otherwise in the annotation.
   2 — indicates the next book to purchase or read.
   3 — should be purchased or read, but of lower priority.
   No number — the main audience is being indicated, but the book is not of top priority.

When no designation of audience is provided, the choice of the work is a matter for the library or reader depending on need or interest. I have omitted indicators from translations of literary works or primary sources because they do not constitute basic informative works for core collections, but rather are sources for special study to be read mainly after reading the secondary works, or for pleasure. I have indicated the importance or worth of most non-coded works in the annotations. The audience-priority codes are additional aids in book selection on individual topics. When items are coded *both* P1 and P2, or both S1 and S2, P1 is for larger collections, P2 for smaller ones; S1 is for serious readers, S2 for general readers.

B — the bibliography in the work is an excellent guide to further study.

R — the book is suitable for reference even though not necessarily specifically intended for that purpose.

10. If there is no annotation for a numbered item, it is because I was unable to obtain a copy of the book, though I have listed it along with any available bibliographical data because it appeared to be of special value.

11. **Special Lists**: In the special lists at the end of the book, I have included books that I consider to be of permanent value and basic sources of information. I have excluded guide books and most of the travelogues as not being essential to core collections; I excluded individual primary sources—literary works, works of philosophy, theology, medieval histories, etc.—for the same reasons I did not provide codes for them.

12. **Near Eastern Names—Spelling**: The spelling of Near Eastern names and terms is a very difficult problem for the non-specialist, and indeed even for the specialist, since they are written in an altogether different script and particularly since the vowels are not written into the words, nor printed in books. Persian, Arabic, and Ottoman Turkish often pronounce the same Arabic script letter differently, and the vowel sounds of the three languages differ greatly. In Arabic, besides the "standard" written Arabic, which is pronounced in speeches and spoken among educated Arabs from different countries, each country, and often individual communities, has its own dialect, all of which feature a multitude of different pronunciations of both consonants and vowels; these colloquial differences in pronunciation usually carry over at least in part into pronunciation of standard written Arabic words. As a result, Westerners, particularly non-specialists, have written their books using a host of variant spellings of the same words to approximate the vernacular sounds, some of which have no Western equivalents. Naturally, there is a different set of variations for each Western language. There are a number of standard English romanizations, particularly those used by the *Encyclopedia of Islam, International Journal of Near Eastern Studies, Middle East Journal*, and the Library of Congress. The specialized works and general works written by specialists usually use one of these systems.

I have used the LC system for main entries and names in annotations; names in annotations, however, are given without diacritical marks. The rule of thumb one must use to maintain sanity is not to worry about precise spellings of the various names in titles: if there is a resemblance of consonants and their order in two or three names, terms, etc., and careful attempts to pronounce them produce a half-way reasonable facsimile of similarity, the chances are that they are the same, at least with regard to the books in this *Guide* and most modern books. A few examples: al-Ghazali or al-Ghazzali; Ahmadiyah, Ahmadiyya; Koran, Qur'an; caliphate, Khalifate; Muhammad, Mohamed, Mahomet.

The initial prefix "al-" (often westernized as as-, ad-, el-, El ... , Al ... , 'l, etc.) is the article "the"; it is disregarded in filing names romanized by LC (i.e., al-Ghazali files under G). If LC uses as main entry an author's own Westernization of his name that incorporates the article (capitalized), the article is treated as part of his name and filed accordingly.

GENERAL WORKS

I. BIBLIOGRAPHIES

1. Abboud, Peter F. "Arabic Language Instruction," **MESA Bulletin**, v. 5, no. 2 (May 1, 1971), pp. 1-23.
   A commentary on research and teaching of classical, modern standard, and colloquial Arabic, with a useful annotated bibliography that includes dictionaries, textbooks, etc.

2. Adam, André. **Bibliographie critique de sociologie, d'ethnologie et de géographie humaine du Maroc: travaux de langues anglaise, arabe, espagnole et française.** Algiers, Impr. Louis-Jean, 1972. 353p. (Mémoires du Centre de Recherches anthropologiques, préhistoriques et ethnographiques, 20). LC 75-502738.
   Topical arrangement.

3. Adams, Charles J., ed. **A Reader's Guide to the Great Religions.** New York, Free Press, 1965. 364p. index. LC 65-15440. Z 7833.A35. DDC 016.2.
   Bibliographical essays by various authorities. Adams' own essay (Chapter 8) deals with various aspects of Islam. It comments on the value and significance of each book or article, most of which are in English, the rest being in French or German. It provides an excellent start for the serious beginner. It has been updated, with modifications, by Adams' items in *MESA Bulletin*, "The State of the Art, VIII: Islamic Religion": Part I, v. 4, no. 3 (Oct. 1970); Part II, v. 5, no. 1 (Feb. 1, 1971). Most of the English language books are included in this *Guide*.
   See also:
   Geddes, Charles L. **An Analytical Guide to the Bibliographies on Islam, Muhammad, and the Qur'an.** Denver, American Institute of Islamic Studies, 1973. 102p. (Bibliographic Series, No. 3). LC 73-175468. Z 7835.M6A54 no. 3. DDC 016.016297.

4. Alexander, Yonah. **Israel: Selected, Annotated and Illustrated Bibliography.** Gilbertsville, N.Y., Victor Buday, 1968. 116p. index. o.p. LC 68-31763. Z 3476.A43. DDC 016.915694.
   [P1, C1]   Brief, useful entries on a wide variety of subjects, topically arranged. Includes translations of literary works and fairly balanced selection on the Arab-Israeli conflict. Selective, not exhaustive. Though out of date, it is very worthwhile.

5. Atiyah, Aziz Suryal. **The Crusade: Historiography and Bibliography.** Bloomington, Indiana University Press, 1962. 170p. index. LC 62-18368. Z 6207.C97 A8. DDC 016.94018.
   [C2]   Consists mostly of bibliography, with an introduction to each section, an evaluation of primary sources in various languages, and some one-sentence annotations of secondary works. The book is divided by subject and type of material. There are a few very useful comments on gaps in the field and on the quality of the most basic works. Full attention is given to Arabic sources and secondary works. Included also are many helpful background works on the Crusades, and a large section on Islamic history and culture.

6. Atiyeh, George Nicholas. **The Contemporary Middle East, 1948-1973: A Selective and Annotated Bibliography.** Boston, G. K. Hall, 1975. 664p. $49.00. LC 74-19247. ISBN 0-8161-1085-9. Z 3013. A85. DDC 915.6.
   [P1, C1]   About 6,500 books and articles published during this period in English, French, German, Italian, and Spanish, plus a few in Arabic, Persian, and Turkish. Emphasis is on general works, bibliographies, religion, history, politics, social conditions, education, and economic conditions, with a few items on literature and the arts. It covers North Africa, the Near East (excluding Israel, except in terms of the Arab-Israeli conflict, to which a separate section is devoted). Annotations, which range in length from a few lines to a paragraph, deal with each item's contents and importance (when appropriate), with little attempt at evaluation. The

individually numbered items are arranged by general topic, by region (subdivided topically), then by country (subdivided by topic). Basic for larger collections. A single index lists authors, persons, places, and concepts, with cross-references.

See also:

Beirut. Université Saint Joseph. Centre d'Études pour le Monde Arabe Moderne. **Arab Culture and Society in Change: A Bibliography of Books and Articles in English, French, German and Italian.** Beirut, Dar el-Mashreq; distr. New York, Near East Books Co., 1973. 318p. $15.00. LC 73-960590. Z 3013.B43 1973. DDC 016.91'0039'27. Lists 4,954 items, including theses, on all aspects; most entries have one-sentence annotations.

Tel Aviv University. Mekhon Shiloah le-Heker ha-Mizrah ha-Tikhon ve-Afrikah. **A Bibliography of Articles on the Middle East, 1959-1967.** Comp. by Uri Dotan; ed. by Avigdor Levy. Tel Aviv, Shiloah Center for Middle Eastern and African Studies, 1970. 227p. LC 79-953368. Z 3013.D67. Lists 2,902 articles in various languages, including Arabic and Hebrew, arranged topically.

7. **A Basic Bibliography for the Study of the Semitic Languages.** Ed. by J. H. Hospers. Leiden, E. J. Brill, 1973-1974. 2 v. LC 73-181086. ISBN 90-04-03623-7. Z 7049. S5B35.

Volume 2 (108p.) concerns Arabic; Volume 1 (400p.), the other Semitic languages. For each language it lists works on all aspects of the languages and their literatures, as well as works on the cultures, history, and religions of the peoples who spoke them. The unannotated entries are primarily for more recent books and articles, in various languages, with lists of bibliog aphies and journals. For beginners.

8. Bevis, Richard W. **Bibliotheca Cisorientalia: An Annotated Checklist of Early English Travel Books on the Near and Middle East.** Boston, G. K. Hall, 1973. 317p. $29.50. LC 73-0173. ISBN 0-8161-0969-9. Z 3013.B47. DDC 016.9156'04.

An annotated bibliography of English language travel books published before 1914. It is divided as follows: English books (233p.), translations into English (32p.), collections (12p.), biography, criticism, and scholarship on the topic (29p.), bibliography (5p.). Each item has a note on where the book was located by the author and his research assistants in libraries, including the Library of Congress, on three continents. The books listed in this bibliography are vital sources of information on the periods covered, both for their accessibility to English-speaking publics, and because they often constitute the only information available due to the uncertain state of Near Eastern archives (or the complete lack thereof). They record atmosphere, life, conditions, history and politics, and landscapes. Many of them have been or are being reprinted, and librarians should watch for them. A very few of the best are included in the present *Guide*, but many more were omitted due to lack of space.

9. Birge, John Kingsley. **A Guide to Turkish Area Study.** Washington, D.C., Committee on Near Eastern Studies, American Council of Learned Societies, 1949. 240p. LC 50-8773. DR 417.B5. DDC 016.9156.

Brief essays on aspects of Turkey and its life, each of which has a bibliographical essay (to page 143). Includes a 40-page bibliography and a chronology from the Middle Ages to February 1945. Despite its age, it is still quite useful to students.

10. Bodurgil, Abraham. **Ataturk and Turkey: A Bibliography, 1919-1938.** Washington, Library of Congress, 1974. 74p. LC 73-18313. ISBN 0-8444-0112-9. Z 2850.B64. DDC 016.9561.

Lists books and articles concerning the period that have been published to the present time in Western languages (including Slavic). Most items deal with political life, but some cover history, geography, economics, education, religion, and other topics. LC call numbers provided. Subject index.

11. **The Central Middle East: A Handbook of Anthropology and Published Records on the Nile Valley, the Arab Levant, Southern Mesopotamia, the Arabian Peninsula, and Israel.** Ed. by Louise Sweet. New Haven, HRAF Press, 1971. 323p. (Area Survey Series).

$13.00; $7.00pa. LC 70-148033. ISBN 0-87536-107-2; 0-87536-108-0pa. DS 57.C44.
DDC 915.6'03'4.

[C1] A guide for further research. Each of the five chapters has a survey of the region's
geography, populations, society, and the usual ethnological categories, religion, culture, etc.,
with a lengthy annotated, critical bibliography of books, articles and theses in various Western
languages. It is one of the more useful bibliographies listed in this *Guide*; most of the English
language monographs listed in *The Central Middle East* will be found in this *Guide*.

For further guidance see:

Antoun, Richard T. "Three Approaches to the Cultural Anthropology of the Middle
East," **MESA Bulletin**, v. 5, no. 2 (May 1, 1971), pp. 24-53, which contains three
syllabi and a bibliography of 336 items, including books and articles.

Gulick, John, "The Anthropology of the Middle East," **MESA Bulletin**, v. 3, no. 1
(Feb. 15, 1969), pp. 1-14, which comments on a number of books and the subjects
being studied, the approaches taken, etc.

Behn, Wolfgang. **The Kurds, a Minority in Iran: An Annotated Bibliography.** Toronto,
University of Toronto School of Library Science, 1969(?). 28p. LC 74-189283.
Z3369.K87 B43.

12. Clements, Frank. **T. E. Lawrence: A Reader's Guide.** Hamden, Conn., Archon Books,
    1972. 208p. index. $8.50. LC 72-8438. ISBN 0-208-01313-X. Z 8491.5.C57 1973.
    DDC 016.828'9'1208.

A critical annotated bibliography of writings by and about Lawrence of Arabia, describing and evaluating every edition of his works, including dust-jacket blurbs and articles. It
includes books and articles about him, Arab sources, and more general works that refer to him
or provide essential background to his role. Clements omitted the following works (which were
published in time for inclusion and which contain much additional documentation on the
period and on Lawrence's role): Briton Cooper Busch, *Britain, India and the Arabs, 1914-
1921* (University of California Press, 1970); Jukka Nevakivi, *Britain, France and the Arab
Middle East, 1914-1920* (London, Athlone Press, 1969); Sulayman Musa, *al-Harakah
al-ᶜArabiyah* (Beirut, Dar al-Nahar, 1971). Others may also have been omitted, but these are
particularly important since they are based on official British sources only lately open to the
public.

13. Creswell, Sir Keppel Archibald Cameron. **A Bibliography of the Architecture, Arts and
    Crafts of Islam, to 1st January, 1960.** Cairo, American University at Cairo Press, 1961.
    1330 columns. price not reported. **Supplement, January 1960–1 January 1972.**
    Cairo, American University at Cairo Press, 1973. 358 columns. LC 62-3352. Z 5956.
    I8C74. DDC 016.709'17'671.

An exhaustive listing of books and articles in various languages.

14. Davison, Roderic H. "Ottoman History (Post-1789)," **MESA Bulletin**, v. 4, no. 1
    (Feb. 15, 1970), pp. 1-14.

A bibliographical essay listing and commenting on some of the best articles and books on
the subject in various languages, with recommendations on what is needed in the field. Davison
is a well-known specialist.

15. Ettinghausen, Richard. **A Selected and Annotated Bibliography of Books and Articles
    in Western Languages Dealing with the Near and Middle East, with Special Emphasis
    on Mediaeval and Modern Times.** New York, AMS Press, 1974. (Repr. of 1954 ed.).
    137p. index. $10.00. LC 70-180337. ISBN 0-404-56249-3. Z 3013.E8 1974.

[P1, C1] Intended mainly for college and public libraries as a selective guide for academic
reading and preliminary research, it contains 1,972 items, excluding works on language and literature. Most items are briefly annotated; it includes works in various Western languages. The
works listed are "best" books and have a wide range of coverage. It includes 16 pages on the
ancient period. Arrangement is by subject, subdivided by country. Because most items are
o.p., it will be useful for selecting reprints and for ordering books on interlibrary loan. A
good supplement to the present *Guide*.

16. Fatemi, Ali Mohammad S., Abbas Amirie, and Panos Kokoropoulos. **Political Economy of the Middle East; A Computerized Guide to the Literature.** Akron, Ohio, Department of Economics, University of Akron, 1970. 346, 326p. $12.50. LC 77-17252. Z 3013. F3. DDC 016.9156'03'3.

Lists 2,600 books and articles in various languages, of 1958-1970 vintage, on politics, economics, and related subjects. Three approaches to the items are possible: KWIC title index; the entries, which are arranged by subject; author index. Not for most libraries, but good to know about.
See also:
American University of Beirut. Economic Research Institute. **A Cumulation of a Selected and Annotated Bibliography of Economic Literature on the Arabic-Speaking Countries of the Middle East, 1938-1960.** Boston, G. K. Hall, 1967. 358p. LC 73-174059. Z 7165.A67 A57 1967. DDC 016.3309'17'4927.

17. Garsse, Yvan van. **Ethnological and Anthropological Literature on the Three Southern Sudan Provinces: Upper Nile, Bahr el Ghazal, Equatoria.** Vienna, Institut für Volkerkunde der U. Wien, Engelbert Stiglmayr, 1972. 88p. (Acta Ethnologica et Linguistica, No. 29). LC 74-172317. Z5113.G35 1972b. DDC 016.30129'624.

Lists 1,072 books and articles, arranged by author, with subject index. Various languages. Deals with the black African population of the Sudan, Nuer, Azande, etc. While important to the Sudan, as the books on the Sudanese civil war between the North and the South in the Sudan section of this *Guide* will indicate, the black tribes are outside the culture area covered by this *Guide*; therefore, no books on the topic are included.

18. Geddes, Charles L. **An Analytical Guide to the Bibliographies on Modern Egypt and the Sudan.** Denver, American Institute of Islamic Studies, 1972. 78p. (Bibliographic Series, No. 2). LC 72-195113. Z 7835.M6 A54 No. 2. DDC 016.910'031'17671 s.

Describes bibliographies published separately and in books, journals, etc.
See also:
U.S. Library of Congress. European Affairs Division. **Egypt and the Anglo-Egyptian Sudan: A Selective Guide to Background Reading.** By Helen F. Conover. Washington, D.C., Library of Congress, 1952. 26p. LC 52-60008. Z 3656.U55 1952. DDC 016.9162.

Maunier, René. **Bibliographie économique, juridique, et sociale de l'Égypte moderne (1798-1916).** New York, Burt Franklin, 1971. (Repr. of 1918 ed.). 372p. LC 70-122842. ISBN 0-8337-2306-5. Z 3656.M45 1971.

New York. Public Library. **Modern Egypt: A List of Reference to Material in the New York Public Library.** By Ida A. Pratt. New York, Kraus Reprint, 1969. (Repr. of 1929 ed.). 320p. LC n.a. Z 3656.N53 1969.

19. Goell, Yohai. **Bibliography of Modern Hebrew Literature in English Translation.** New York, KTAV Publishing House, 1968. 103p. indices. $12.50. LC 68-59494. ISBN 0-87068-062-5. Z 7070.G57. DDC 016.8924'09005.

[C]   Arranged by author within each genre—anthologies, poetry, prose, drama, essays, children's literature—with author indices in English and Hebrew, and a supplement. It covers only the post-Haskalah period and is based "almost solely" on the holdings of the Jewish National and University Library in Jerusalem. Contains listings from a wide variety of books and periodicals, including many that should be readily available on interlibrary loan.

20. Hale, Gerry A. "Maps and Atlases of the Middle East," **MESA Bulletin,** v. 3, no. 3 (Oct. 15, 1969), pp. 17-39.

Lists various kinds of maps and atlases, plus mapping agencies, with comments on problems and gaps.

21. Hill, Roy Wells. **A Bibliography of Libya.** Durham, England, Durham Colleges in the University of Durham, Department of Geography, 1959. 100p. (Research Papers Series No. 1). o.p. LC 61-40975. Z3971.H5.

Books and articles in various languages, topically arranged. No index or item numbers. One of a number of bibliographies in the series on the region.

22. Kabeel, Soraya M. **Selected Bibliography on Kuwait and the Arabian Gulf.** Kuwait, Libraries Department, Kuwait University, 1969. 104p. (Bibliographic Series, No. 1). LC 70-17777. Z3453.P33K3. DDC 016.9153'6.

Lists 1,300 books and articles: 39 pages on the Persian Gulf, 19 pages on Kuwait, 6 pages on Bahrain, 5 pages on Oman, 1 page on Qatar. Under each country entries are arranged topically, with *see also* references under each topic to more general works. Index includes titles, authors, subjects.

23. Khalidi, Walid, and Jill Khadduri. **Palestine and the Arab-Israeli Conflict: An Annotated Bibliography.** Beirut, Institute for Palestine Studies, 1974. 736p. index. ca. $25.00. LC n.a. Z3479.R4 K45.

Lists 4,580 books, articles, pamphlets, theses, and dissertations in French, German, Russian, and particularly Arabic, Hebrew, and English, on all aspects. Sections cover Israel, Zionism, aspects of Jewish history; international aspects, including the involvement of European countries and the United States; the Palestinian and Arab attachment to Palestine and Jerusalem; the United Nations; Arab states' policies; the individual wars. Includes materials published from 1880 to 1971. The index lists titles, authors, and persons who are subjects of works. Entries are arranged in 104 subject divisions. Quinquennial supplements are envisioned. Beautifully produced. Annotations, which are usually one to four lines long, note contents, important opinions, backgrounds of authors. Translation into various languages is indicated for many of the items. One of the most extensive bibliographies available.

24. "Language Tapes, Records and Correspondence Courses in Middle Eastern Languages," **MESA Bulletin,** v. 7, no. 2 (May 1, 1973), pp. 32-39.

25. Lawless, Richard I. **A Bibliography of Works on Algeria Published in English since 1954.** Durham, University of Durham Centre for Middle Eastern and Islamic Studies, 1972. 39p. (University of Durham. Centre for Middle Eastern and Islamic Studies. Occasional Papers Series, No. 1). $3.00pa. LC 73-158010. ISBN 0-903011-02-6. Z 3681.L38. DDC 016.9165.

26. Le Gassick, Trevor J. "Literature in Translation–Modern Arabic," **MESA Bulletin,** v. 5, no. 1 (Feb. 1, 1971), pp. 26-38.

Comments on individual works and their current availability; includes non-fiction works in translation.
See also:
Alwan, Mohammed Bakir, "A Bibliography of Modern Arabic Fiction in English Translation," **Middle East Journal,** v. 26, no. 2 (Spring, 1972), pp. 195-200; "A Bibliography of Modern Arabic Poetry in English Translation," **Middle East Journal,** v. 27, no. 3 (Summer, 1973), pp. 373-381. These two articles are attempts at exhaustive listings.

27. London. University. School of Oriental and African Studies. **Historical Writing on the Peoples of Asia. Volume 4, Historians of the Middle East.** Ed. by Bernard Lewis and P. M. Holt. London, Oxford University Press, 1962. 519p. index. $14.00. LC 61-4093 rev. ISBN 0-19-713528-5. DS 32.5.L6. DDC 950.072.

Papers by top specialists. Part I (270p.) treats Arabic, Persian, and Turkish historiography from the Middle Ages to the present. Part II (120p.) deals with European historical writing during the same period. Part III (60p.) treats modern Near Eastern historians, and Part IV covers a variety of general themes. Treatment, while extensive, is not systematic or comprehensive because of the nature of the work, which originated in a conference. Some items are fairly general, others quite specific. For a comprehensive, systematic guide, *see* Sauvaget (item 38). *Historians of the Middle East*, however, discusses much of the extant literature and the problems of the sources, so it is quite illuminating to the budding specialist or to someone interested in comparative historiography. It also contains much general information needed to put in context the works discussed, which often reveals much about the history of the periods covered.

28. Macro, Eric. **Bibliography on Yemen and Notes on Mocha.** Coral Gables, Fla., 1960. 63p. LC 60-9009. Z 3028. Y4 M3. DDC 016.95332.

Thirty pages of bibliography (894 books and articles in various languages, including Arabic) and 30 pages of descriptive notes on one of Yemen's main cities.

29. Mayer, Leo Ary. **Bibliography of Moslem Numismatics, India Excepted.** 2nd enl. ed. London, Royal Asiatic Society, 1954. 283p. LC 57-18156. PJ 408.06 n.s. vol. 35 1954.

30. **The Middle East and Islam, A Bibliographical Introduction.** Ed. by Derek Hopwood and Diana Grimwood-Jones. Zug, Switzerland, Inter Documentation Co.; distr. New York, International Publications Service, 1972. 368p. (Bibliotheca Asiatica, 9). $25.00. LC 72-85349. ISBN 3-85750-003-4. Z 3013.M48. DDC 016.9156'03.

A collection of bibliographies on various countries and topics (such as the various literatures, Islam, etc.), in which a number of authorities list the (approximately) 50 books in all relevant languages, including vernaculars, that they believe a basic *research* collection should have. The aim originally was to set up a university library from scratch on the basis of the scientific and educational consensus. For most collections it is not very useful as a buying guide because there is much foreign language material and because much of the rest is too advanced. However, larger collections will find it useful for increasing the depth of their collections and for locating translations of standard works not currently available in English, while students can use it as a guide for interlibrary borrowing. Unfortunately, no bibliographic data are provided to aid in acquisitions.

See also:

Field, Henry. **Bibliography on Southwestern Asia.** Coral Gables, University of Miami Press, 1953- . LC 53-9439. Z 3013.F5. Deals with anthropogeography, zoology, and botany. Maps. Seven or eight cumulations, none published in the last decade.

Selim, George Dimitri. **American Doctoral Dissertations on the Arab World, 1883-1968.** Washington, D.C., Library of Congress; for sale by Superintendent of Documents, U.S. Government Printing Office, 1970. 103p. LC 79-607590. Z 3013.S43. DDC 016. 91003'174'927. A new edition is in the press.

31. **Middle East and North Africa: A Bibliography for Undergraduate Libraries.** By Harry N. Howard and others. Williamsport, Pa., Bro-Dart Publishing Co., 1971. 80p. (Foreign Area Materials Center. Occasional Publication No. 14). o.p. LC 72-151801. Z 1009.N54 No. 14 [Z 3451]. DDC 016.915. [910'.03'08 s].

[P1, C1] The 1,192 items are arranged by subject and separately by author, covering the ancient period to the present. Entries are *not* annotated, but each item is graded A, B, or C, according to whether it is necessary for all collections, necessary to back up courses, or necessary to back an area studies program. LC numbers are provided. Out-of-print items are so indicated. Entries give location of reviews in such periodicals as *Choice, Middle East Journal, LJ,* as well as in various disciplinary journals and the *American Universities Field Staff Bibliography.* Includes various materials in Western languages, including periodicals, though most of the items are in English. Many of the items are of interest mainly to colleges and universities with very extensive programs that allow considerable specialization at the undergraduate level. A useful supplement to the present *Guide* both for categories excluded from it and for building in greater depth.

See also:

Alexander, Yonah. **The Middle East: Selected and Annotated Bibliography.** Gilbertsville, N.Y., Victor Buday, 196-?. LC cataloging n.a.

32. **Middle East Journal.** Quarterly. Middle East Institute, 1761 N. Street, N.W., Washington, D.C. 20036. $10.00. LC 48-2240. DS 1. M5.DDC 956.

[P1, C1, S1] The best source of current bibliography in all languages, it has not only a large section of full-length and shorter reviews, but lists of forthcoming and recent books and lists of articles and book reviews in other periodicals. In this respect it provides full coverage of most of the important regional and other journals, all of which are of great assistance to anyone trying to keep up with the literature. Occasionally publishes a special bibliography on a topic such as Arabic literature in translation. An issue contains three or four articles on the contemporary

Near East (i.e., 1945 to the present); many of these are reports on current conditions, but many are substantial items that remain standard sources for years. There is also a lengthy chronology. The *Journal* is the single most important periodical on the region for non-specialist collections. A 20-year cumulative index has been published. The Middle East Institute is associated with top scholars in the field. It publishes books, a bi-weekly newsletter of items from the vernacular regional press (*Monitor*), reports of its annual conferences, and annotated bibliographies of recent books every year or two.

33. Middle East Studies Association of North America. New York University, Hagop Kevorkian Center for Near Eastern Studies, Washington Square, New York, N.Y. 10003.

This is the top American organization of scholars specializing in the various fields of Near Eastern studies, with worldwide ties. It publishes two journals:
Middle East Studies Association of North America Bulletin, 3x/yr. LC 68-130933. DS 41.M533. DDC 956'0072. To members only. This is the single most useful periodical for the teacher, because it covers the entire field and has syllabi, special bibliographies, state-of-the-art summaries in fields such as Islam, anthropology, literature, language, history, etc. Also includes information on the MESA annual conference and other conferences of Near Eastern organizations, schools, etc.; available scholarships; Near Eastern programs at universities and colleges; summer programs; Ph.D. dissertations; forthcoming works by members; etc. MESA's other publication is:
International Journal of Middle East Studies. quarterly. $18.00. Cambridge University Press, 32 East 57th St., New York, New York 10022. LC 79-15777. DS41.I55. DDC 915.6'03'305. Membership in MESA, which is $30.00, includes the *Bulletin* and *IJMES. IJMES* contains articles and book reviews strictly for the specialist.

34. Nasri, Abdel Rahman. **A Bibliography of the Sudan, 1938-1958**. London, Oxford University Press, 1962. 171p. o.p. LC 63-772. Z 3711.N3. DDC 016.9624.

Supplements Richard Leslie Hill, *A Bibliography of the Anglo-Egyptian Sudan, from the Earliest Times to 1937* (London, Frank Cass, 197-?. 213p. $14.00. LC n.a.). Lists 2,763 books and articles, etc., in various languages, including Arabic, arranged topically with subject and author indices.

35. Patai, Raphael. **Jordan, Lebanon and Syria: An Annotated Bibliography**. New Haven, HRAF Press, 1957. 289p. (Behavior Science Bibliographies). o.p. LC 57-13286. Z 3013.P3. DDC 016.9569.

36. [Pearson, J. D.] London. University. School of Oriental and African Studies. Library. **Index Islamicus, 1906-1955: A Catalogue of Articles on Islamic Subjects in Periodicals and Other Collective Publications**. London, Mansell Information/Publishing Ltd., 1972. (Repr. of 1958 ed.). 897p. index. LC n.a. ISBN 0-7201-0282-0. Z 7835.M6L6. DDC 016.9156. Supplements: 1956-1960, Cambridge, England, W. Heffer, 1962. 316p.; 1961-1965, Cambridge, England, W. Heffer, 1967. 342p.; 1966-1970, London, Mansell, 1972. 384p. ISBN 0-7201-0282-0; 1971-1972, London, Mansell, 1973, ISBN 0-7201-0285-5.

The 1971-1972 Supplement is the first annual supplement; it is issued in paperback, with a quinquennial cumulation promised. (*BIP* lists the first four volumes available from International Publications Service in New York for $110.00.) Compiled from an exhaustive list of periodicals, Festschriften, congress proceedings, etc., this basic bibliography includes all the fields of Islam and Islamic civilization—art, science, literature and language, education; history, geography, ethnology, archaeology, epigraphy, numismatics, of the Islamic countries of North Africa, the Near East, Central Asia, India and Pakistan. Arranged topically, with author index. Most collections will not want this item, but all serious students should know that it exists, and libraries backing Near East programs must have it.

37. Saba, Mohsen. **English Bibliography of Iran**. Tehran[?], Centre for Studies and Research on the Iranian Civilization, 196-?. 313p. index. LC 78-221539. Z3366.S23. DDC 016.9155.

Topically arranged, partly annotated; includes articles and books, all subjects. Also a 49-page history of Iranology in English. Author index only.

Other useful items include:

Bartsch, William H. **The Economy of Iran, 1940-1970: A Bibliography.** Durham, University of Durham, Centre for Middle Eastern and Islamic Studies, 1971. 114p. LC 72-179546. ISBN 0-903011-00-X. Z 7165.I66 B37. DDC 016-3309'55'05.

Elwell-Sutton, Laurence Paul. **A Guide to Iranian Area Study.** Ann Arbor, Mich., published for the American Council of Learned Societies by J. W. Edwards, 1952. 235p. LC 52-4643. DS 254.5.E4. DDC 915.5. Brief introductory essays on aspects of Iran, each of which has a bibliographical essay; includes 52-page chronology and 818-item bibliography.

Nawabi, Y. M. **A Bibliography of Iran: A Catalogue of Books and Articles on Iranian Subjects, Mainly in European Languages.** Tehran, printed at Khajeh Press, 1969– . LC 74-151275. Z 3366.N38. DDC 016.9155'03.

Saba, Mohsin. **Bibliographie française de l'Iran: bibliographie méthodique et raisonnée des ouvrages français parus depuis 1560 jusqu'à jours.** 3rd ed. Tehran, Université de Tehran, 1966. 297p. LC n.a. Z 3366.S2 1966. DDC 016.9155.

United States. Library of Congress. General Reference and Bibliography Division. **Iran: A Selected and Annotated Bibliography.** Comp. by Hafez F. Farman. New York, Greenwood Press, 1968. (Repr. of 1951 ed.) 100p. LC 68-55131. Z 3366.U53 1968. DDC 016.9155'03. A most useful item that describes and sometimes evaluates works in various languages.

Wickens, G. M., Roger M. Savory, and W. J. Watson. **Persia in Islamic Times: A Practical Bibliography of Its History, Language and Culture.** Montreal, McGill University, 1964.

Wilson, Sir Arnold Talbot. **A Bibliography of Persia.** Oxford, Clarendon Press, 1930. 253p. LC 30-33355. Z 3366.W74. DDC 015.55.

38. Sauvaget, Jean. **Introduction to the History of the Muslim East: A Bibliographical Guide.** Based on the 2nd ed. as recast by Claude Cahen. Berkeley, University of California Press, 1965. 252p. o.p. LC 64-25271. Z 3013.S314.

[C1] The basic bibliographic guide for more advanced students and builders of comprehensive collections. It lists works in Western and vernacular languages in bibliographical essays on various topics, including history, civilization, and religion. Key periodical articles are also included in the listings. A basic work helpful in purchasing reprints and translations, and for ordering books on interlibrary loan.

39. Schlüter, Hans. **Index Libycus: A Bibliography of Libya, 1957-1969, with Supplementary Material, 1914-1956.** Boston, G. K. Hall, 1972. 305p. $19.50. LC 72-2779. ISBN 0-8161-0939-7. Z 3971.S36. DDC 016.9161'2.

Supplements and expands Hill (item 21). It includes books and articles published during the period in various languages; it is selective, particularly for the sections on archaeology, geology, economics, and politics. Topically arranged, with author index.

40. Stevens, John Harold, and Russell King. **A Bibliography of Saudi Arabia.** Durham, University of Durham, Centre for Middle Eastern and Islamic Studies, 1973. 81p. (University of Durham. Centre for Middle Eastern and Islamic Studies. Occasional Papers Series, No. 3). $4.50pa. LC n.a. ISBN 0-903011-04-2.

Lists 1,100 European and English language books and articles published between 1900 and 1970, topically arranged. No index.
See also:

Geddes, Charles L. **Analytical Guide to the Bibliographies on the Arabian Peninsula.** Denver, American Institute of Islamic Studies, 1974. 50p. (Bibliographic Series, No. 4). LC 74-162911. Z 7835.M6A54 no. 4 [Z 3026.A1]. DDC 016.191009'17'671 s.

United States. Library of Congress. Near East Section. **The Arabian Peninsula: A Selected, Annotated List of Periodicals, Books and Articles in English.** New York, Greenwood Press, 1969. (Repr. of 1951 ed.). 111p. LC 68-55135. Z 3026.U53 1969. DDC 016.9153.

41. Suzuki, Peter. **Social Change in Turkey since 1950: A Bibliography of 866 Publications.** College Park, European Division, University of Maryland (Heidelberg, High Speed Press Center), 1969. 108p. price n.a. pa. LC 70-495419. Z 7165.T9S9. DDC 016.3091'561.

Books, dissertations, and articles from many sources in various languages, especially Western, on social, cultural, and economic conditions and change in Turkey, and a wide range of other relevant topics. Alphabetical listing only. No indices.

See also:

Beeley, Brian W. **Rural Turkey: A Bibliographic Introduction.** Ankara, Hacettepe University Institute of Population Studies, 1969. 120p. LC 72-256019. Z 7165.T9B43. DDC 016.3091'561. Books, articles, chapters of books, reports, and theses in various languages, including English and Turkish.

42. Tamkoç, Metin. **A Bibliography on the Foreign Relations of the Republic of Turkey, 1919-1967, and Brief Biographies of Turkish Statesmen.** Ankara, Middle East Technical University, Faculty of Administrative Sciences, 1968. 248p. index. (Publication No. 11). LC 79-11439. Z 2857.R4T3. DDC 016.327561.

Topical arrangement. Various languages, mostly Turkish—two chapters contain works in Western languages. The biographies are of presidents, prime ministers, and foreign ministers.

43. U. S. Library of Congress. General Reference and Bibliography Division. **North and North East Africa: A Selected Annotated List of Writings, 1951-1957.** By Helen Conover. New York, Greenwood Press, 1968. (Repr. of 1957 ed.). 182p. index. LC 68-55132. Z 3501.U57 1968. DDC 016.96.

Includes 346 items—books, articles, and pamphlets—in Western languages, each with a lengthy annotation. Covers Morocco, Algeria, Tunisia, Libya, Egypt, Sudan, Ethiopia, Eritrea, Somaliland. Each country is subdivided by several broad topics. Not for purchase by most collections because it is limited to publications appearing during a very limited period, but it is worth knowing about.

44. Weiker, Walter F. "Modern Turkish Studies," **MESA Bulletin**, v.3, no. 3 (Oct. 15, 1969), pp. 1-16.

This bibliographic essay on the state of the art provides many useful references from a wide variety of sources, including books, articles, and dissertations on all aspects of twentieth century Turkey, except culture.

45. Wilber, Donald Newton. **Annotated Bibliography of Afghanistan.** 3rd ed. New Haven, Conn., Human Relations Area Files Press, 1968. 252p. index. (Behavior Science Bibliography). $11.00. LC 68-22209. ISBN 0-87536-226-5. Z 3016.W5 1968. DDC 016.91581.

Lists 1,600 items, many of which are very carefully if briefly annotated. Arranged by topic: general, geography, history, social organization and institutions, political structure, economy, language and literature, art and archaeology. Includes books and articles in Western, Slavic and vernacular languages.

See also:

Asia Society. Afghanistan Council. **Recent Books about Afghanistan: A Selected, Annotated Bibliography, 1968-1973.** New York, Asia Society, 1973. 19 leaves. LC n.a. Partly annotated, intended to supplement Wilber. Includes some novels, juvenile literature, films, and records.

46. Windfuhr, Gernot L., and John R. Workman. "Literature in Translation—Iranian Into English," **MESA Bulletin**, v.7, no. 1 (Feb. 1, 1973), pp. 9-41.

An essay on the state of the art and a listing of 334 books and periodical items, including secondary works on Persian literature, both classical and modern. Also includes items from other related languages (such as Kurdish and Pashto), as well as folk literature.

II. REFERENCE WORKS

An **Area Handbook** is available for each country covered in this *Guide*; each is listed in the appropriate section. An **Area Handbook**, which is a basic reference work for the non-specialist, contains information from the public record, articles, and books, on all aspects of the country, including society, geography, education, culture, the press, women, government and politics, foreign relations, public information, the economy (including labor, monetary systems and fiscal policy), internal security and public order, history, etc. Included are maps and tables, as well as extensive bibliographies of books and articles in English, and an index. They are updated at five-year intervals (approximately); usually the updating involves complete rewriting, but sometimes new chapters are simply added, particularly if there is an important development (such as the establishment of a new type of regime) that requires a new edition out of normal sequence. An example is the *Afghanistan Handbook*, which was reissued with new introductory chapters outlining the changes made and the current situation. The **Area Handbooks** are produced for the Department of the Army by Foreign Area Studies, The American University, Washington, D.C.; occasionally individual handbooks are contracted out to other organizations. All are available from the Superintendent of Documents, U.S. Government Printing Office, Washington, D.C. 20402; each order should include the GPO catalog number (which is D 101.22) plus the DA PAM number shown in the entry—the number remains the same for each edition of the **Handbook**—e.g., *Area Handbook for Afghanistan*, D 101.22:550-65. The Library of Congress now catalogs them under the individual in charge of the volume, rather than by name of the organization producing them. In this *Guide* they shall be entered under the title *Area Handbook for . . .* , with the LC main entry indicated in brackets immediately following the title.

It should be noted that while the **Handbooks** are sufficiently reliable for most readers, they do contain factual errors and are conservatively written, avoiding any controversial statements. Thus, while they are extremely useful as handy references for a multitude of purposes, when accuracy of fact and interpretation of data are important, any material cited should be checked in independent sources. Each college library should have a complete set and should retain old editions.

No further annotation will be given for individual **Area Handbooks** in this *Guide*.

47. Bacharach, Jere L. **A Near East Studies Handbook, 570-1974.** Seattle, University of Washington Press, 1974. LC 74-14547. ISBN 0-295-95329-2; 0-295-95361-6pa. DS 61.B3. DDC 956'.002'02.

[P1, C1, S1] An absolutely essential reference work for all but perhaps small public libraries, intended for more serious readers and students. It omits North Africa west of Egypt. It contains lists with dates of dynasties; separate lists of individual rulers, prime ministers, presidents, etc., by country or region; genealogies of rulers, Imams, and key Arab tribes; a list of twentieth century abbreviations commonly found in the literature; an historical atlas of some 30 maps; a glossary of vernacular terms; a conversion table for Hijri (Islamic calendar)—Christian era dates; an extensive historical chronology; and indices.

48. Bosworth, Clifford Edmund. **The Islamic Dynasties: A Chronological and Genealogical Handbook.** Edinburgh, University Press; distr. Chicago, Aldine Publishing Co., 1967. 245p. bibliog. indices. (Islamic Surveys, 5). $6.00. LC 67-17613. ISBN 0-202-15009-7. DS 36.85.I8 no. 5. DDC 909'.09'176'7.

[P1, C1, S1] Divided geographically, this book provides lists and dates of the rulers of each dynasty from North Africa and Spain to India, with a brief resume of the history and place in the Muslim world of each. Hijri and Christian dates are given for each ruler. An extremely useful reference book.

49. Djambatan Uitgeversbedrijf, N.V., Amsterdam. **Atlas of the Arab World and the Middle East.** New York, St. Martin's Press, 1960. 60p., incl. 40p. of maps. gazetteer. o.p. LC MAP60-313. G1785.D5 1960a. DDC 912.66.

This general atlas provides a multicolored map of each country or major region, indicating chief towns and cities, railroads, and main roads; main geographical features are indicated by shading. Small maps show climate, irrigation, population, and economics, and there are diagrams of the main cities. Included are several maps of the whole region from North Africa to Iran depicting the same information. The main virtue of the *Atlas* is that it is specialized and compact enough to assist the general reader who needs to locate places as he is reading books on the twentieth century. The more advanced reader will want to refer to *The Times Atlas of the World* or *National Geographic Atlas of the World*, which are infinitely more detailed, but cumbersome. For quick reference when detail is not necessary.

50. **Encyclopedia of Islam.** New ed. Leiden, E. J. Brill, 1954– (in process, issued in fascicles). LC 61-4395. DS 37.E523. DDC 956.003. First ed.: **The Encyclopaedia of Islam: A Dictionary of the Geography, Ethnography and Biography of the Muhammadan Peoples.** Leiden, E. J. Brill, 1913-1936. LC 26-2691 rev. DS 37.E5.

A comprehensive encyclopedia of all aspects, including religion, history, culture. Includes country and city histories, and biographies. By leading Orientalists from all parts of the world. The second edition is currently into "K" and seems slated to proceed for another decade or more. Some of the new articles are inferior to the old ones despite advances in research. The old edition's French and German versions contain articles not in the English. The new edition has many more articles than the first. For the majority of readers, most of the articles are too scholarly and specialized. The biographies provide most available facts but are too often short on material illuminating the subject's importance and all too often fail to provide much information on individual works of writers. Many articles rightly reflect our uncertainties about their subjects but too often confuse the reader by getting into scholarly arguments. A basic reference tool for the serious student. The articles are arranged according to *vernacular* terms, using a German-based romanization system.

51. Hazard, Harry W., comp. **Atlas of Islamic History.** 3rd rev. ed. Princeton, N.J., Princeton University Press, 1954. 49p. gazetteer. (Princeton Oriental Studies, v. 12). o.p. LC 54-9020. PJ 25.P7 vol. 12 1954 [G 1786.S1H3 1954].

Contains 19 pages of three-color (plus black and white) outline maps that show the situation and changes made in the political boundaries from the seventh through the twentieth centuries (by century). Opposite each map is an outline of the history of the century covered, noting chief rulers, current rulers of each country, region and changes, temporary and permanent, attempted invasions, raids, etc. Separate maps of the whole region cover geographical features, the Crusades (with an outline of the Crusades, their leaders, main battles, nationalities of the Crusaders at each period, etc.); the Ottoman Empire, with an outline on the opposite page of the conquests and losses in each area of the Empire; and two pages of maps of Central and South Asia and the Far East to show the development and status of Islam in those regions. There is also a conversion table for Muslim and Christian dates, from A.H. 1 to A.H. 1395 (1975). A basic book.
See also:
Reichert, Rolf. **A Historical and Regional Atlas of the Arabic World.** Salvador, Bahia, Centro de Estudos Afro-Orientais, Universidad de Bahia, 1969. 204p. LC 73-653906. G 1030.R4 1969. DDC 911'.174'927.

52. Hurewitz, Jacob Coleman. **The Middle East and North Africa in World Politics: A Documentary Record.** 2nd ed., rev. and enl. New Haven, Conn., Yale University Press, 1975– . 3v. LC 74-83525. DS 42.H782 1975. DDC 956. Vol. 1: **European Expansion, 1535-1914.** $30.00. ISBN 0-300-01294-2. Vol. 2: **Anglo-French Supremacy, 1914-1945.** Vol. 3: **Anglo-French Withdrawal and Soviet-American Rivalry, 1945-1975.** First ed.: **Diplomacy in the Near and Middle East: A Documentary Record, 1535-1956.** New York, Octagon Books, 1972. (Repr. of 1956 ed.). 2v. $27.50. LC 72-2494. ISBN 0-374-94056-8. DS 42.H782 1972. DDC 956.

[P1, C1, S1]   A collection of key diplomatic and related documents, arranged chronologically, concerning Near Eastern relations with Russia, Europe, and the United States. Each item has an introduction and bibliographical notes for further reading. This is a basic work for any decent collection. Smaller collections may find the first edition sufficient, since the essential introductory documents are there, but the second edition has many more items, besides being more up to date. Another important documentary work, though much more specialized, is Higgins, Rosalyn, *United Nations Peacekeeping, 1946-1967: Documents and Commentary* (London, Oxford University Press, 1969-[1970]. 3v. LC 76-39893. ISBN 0-19-214975-X (v.1). JX 1981.P7H5. DDC 341.6). Volume 1 concerns the Middle East–UNTSO, UNEF, Lebanon, Yemen.

53. Khalil, Muhammad, ed. **The Arab States and the Arab League: A Documentary Record.** Beirut, Khayats, 1962. 2v. (1724p.). index. price n.a. LC NE 63-705. DS 36.2.K45.

[P1, C1]   Volume 1 consists of key twentieth century constitutional and political documents arranged by country, including the North African states. Volume 2 consists of documents on Arab unity, inter-Arab relations, Arab League resolutions, bilateral agreements between various Arab states; relations with other countries, including World War I era documents and post-World War II security agreements, proposals, and pacts; communiques; U.N. resolutions on Palestine, Libya, Algeria, etc. A basic reference work.

54. Magnus, Ralph H., ed. **Documents on the Middle East.** Washington, D.C., American Enterprise Institute for Public Policy Research, 1969. 232p. (United States Interests in the Middle East). $3.00pa. LC 75-93191. DS 42.M3. DDC 327.56'073.

A handy collection of documents and statements of various kinds, mainly on U.S. policy and relations in the region, including a few dating in the pre-World War II era, but mostly from the post-War period: mutual security agreements and policies, US-Arab relations, the Northern Tier States, Palestine conflict, the June War and its aftermath. By no means comprehensive but useful to have when reading the appropriate books in this *Guide*.

55. Mansoor, Menahem. **Political and Diplomatic History of the Arab World, 1900-1967: A Chronological Study.** Washington, D.C., NCR Microcard Editions, 1972. 7v. LC 72-184866. ISBN 0-910972-09-5. DS 62.8.M35. DDC 320.9'17'4927.

Five volumes of chronology and two volumes of indices. Intended to be the first tool in a huge documentation project that ultimately is supposed to include dozens of volumes of documents, a biographical dictionary, etc.; it is also useful on its own. Basic faults in implementation and organization of the indices make it hard to use at times, but it is an essential work for large reference collections and students wishing to research specific periods of time in any detail.

56. al-Marayati, Abid A., comp. **Middle Eastern Constitutions and Electoral Laws.** New York, Praeger, 1968. 483p. (Praeger Special Studies in International Politics and Public Affairs). o.p. LC 67-25237. LC class: LAW. DDC 342'.56.

A collection of the constitutions and electoral laws in effect in 1967-1968. For earlier documents, the basic work is Davis, Helen Clarkson (Miller), *Constitutions, Electoral Laws, Treaties of State in the Near and Middle East*, 2nd ed. (New York, AMS Press, 1970. [Repr. of 1953 ed.]. 551p. $15.00. LC 79-99886. ISBN 0-404-01995-1. LC class: LAW. DDC 342'.56.)

57. **The Middle East: A Political and Economic Survey.** 4th ed. Ed. by Peter Mansfield. London, Oxford University Press, 1973. 591p. tables. index. $19.95. LC 73-159442. DS 44.M5 1973. ISBN 0-19-215933-X. DDC 915.6'03'4.

[P1, C1]   After a general introduction to the history and current situation of the area, there is a series of general essays by various authorities on aspects of the area's politics. Included are items on the origins of the Palestine problem, Arab political movements, U.S.-Near East relations, oil, and cultural trends, for a total of 135 pages. Then follow country surveys, each of which discusses politics, international relations, history, economic history, resources, policies, industries, etc. A standard work for years, this fourth edition is quite useful. It does not include North Africa. A basic reference work.

58. **The Middle East and North Africa, 1973-1974.** 20th ed. London, Europa Publications; distr. New York, International Publications Service, 1973. 872p. $30.00. annual. LC 48-3250 rev. 2. DS 49.M5 20th 1973/1974.

[P1, C1] The basic reference work on the contemporary region, including North Africa and Cyprus. It contains sections on specific topics: the year's events, Arab-Israeli conflict 1967-1973; the Jerusalem question; Palestinian Arab organizations; oil, including a list of the oil companies and their ownership; Suez Canal; religions. Part II is a systematic survey of regional organizations, including local U.N. agencies and their organization, statistics, and activities; the Arab League; CENTO, EEC relations; Federation of Arab Republics and other indigenous groupings, including OAPEC, OPEC, etc. Part III consists of individual country surveys covering history; government organization, with summaries of constitutions; statistics; economy and finance; diplomatic representation; lists of publishers, periodicals, and newspapers, with their editors; education, including lists of universities; bibliography. There is a 105-page "Who's Who" section, and a section of general information such as calendars, weights, etc. Also, a list of worldwide research institutions that study the region, with their addresses, publications, etc.

Other annual reference works include:

Middle East Annual Review. The Middle East Review Co., Ltd., Great Chesterford, Essex CB 10 1NR England. $8.15 plus postage. LC 75-642848. HC 410.7.A.M517. DDC 330.9'56'04. Based on material prepared by the Economist Intelligence Unit.

Middle East Record. Tel Aviv, Israel Universities Press, for Shiloah Center for Middle Eastern and African Studies. LC 63-48859. DS 63.M58. First published for 1960 and 1961, then resumed for 1967 and 1968. Each volume is a massive topical treatment of diplomatic, political, and economic aspects of the region, arranged chronologically under each topic, with references to the sources, including books and periodicals in many languages, including Arabic and Hebrew. Too much for most libraries, but a must for serious students.

59. Průsěk, Jaroslav, ed. **The Dictionary of Oriental Literatures.** New York, Basic Books, 1974? 3v. $35.00. LC 73-82742. Vol. III, **West Asia and North Africa.** Ed. by Jiri Becka. 213p. LC n.a. ISBN 0-465-01649-9. PJ 31.D5. DDC 808.8.

[P1, P2, C1] Prepared by the Oriental Institute in Prague, supervised by and written in part by American and European scholars, including some top names in the field. This volume covers all eras, including the ancient and modern, and the literatures of all languages, including the Soviet East (Georgian, Turkic, Tatar, etc.) and Armenian. However, most of the ancient literatures (Assyrian, ancient Egyptian, Biblical Hebrew) are represented by only a very few entries, the Soviet East literatures by only a few main figures. The main literatures covered are Persian, Turkish, Arabic and Armenian; excludes modern Israeli literature. The (signed) entries are mainly biographies, with a few items on aspects of literature, and some non-literary writers of great importance are included—al-Ghazali, etc. Each article provides some biographical data, information on key works, some criticism of the writer and individual works, notes on his importance, bibliographical notes on translations and secondary works. Length ranges from a paragraph to a page or more, but most entries are within the half-column to full-column range. A very useful work for the non-specialist, it will provide information on most writers represented in this *Guide.*

60. Ronart, Stephen, and Nandy Ronart. **Concise Encyclopedia of Arabic Civilization: The Arab East.** New York, Praeger, 1960. 589p. o.p. LC 60-10553. DS 215.R6. DDC 915.3. **The Arab West.** New York, Praeger, 1966. 410p. o.p. LC 66-13401. DT 173.R6. DDC 910.03174927. (Listed in Blackwell's Middle East Catalog No. 989 at £10.00 and £9.00.)

[P1, C1] Brief, alphabetically arranged, carefully researched and written articles on people, places, concepts, organizations, history, and Islamic civilization and religion, with surveys of the individual countries. For the general reader. An absolutely basic work for all but small public libraries.

61. Shimoni, Yaacov, and Evyatar Levine, eds. **Political Dictionary of the Middle East in the 20th Century.** Supplement ed. by Itimar Rabinovich and Haim Shaked. Rev. ed. New York, Quadrangle, 1974. 510p. illus. $6.95pa. LC 76-175628. ISBN 0-8129-0482-6. DS 61.S52 1974. DDC 320.9'56'04.

[P1, C1, S1]   Each article is written by an Israeli specialist. It includes country surveys, many biographies, and various topics in Near Eastern political history and international relations, such as the Arab-Israeli wars, United Nation's role in them, United States and Russian relations with the region, etc. North Africa is given but passing attention. Extensive cross-referencing between articles. The separate supplement (85p.) to the original edition of 1972 brings the work up to date. It continues articles from the first edition and contains many new items, including the Yom Kippur War of 1973, new biographies, and continuations of the country histories. Articles with continuations are marked in each part so the user knows when to refer to the other. Despite its underlying Israeli perspective, which at times influences the selection of facts and their interpretation, the book is sufficiently reliable to be considered a basic work for all libraries.

Another work is:

Heravi, Mehdi, ed. **Concise Encyclopedia of the Middle East.** Washington, D.C., Public Affairs Press, 1973. 336p. $12.00. LC 73-82012. DS 43.H47. DDC 915'.6'03'03.

An erratically selected group of articles by various authorities, it stresses the twentieth century but has some entries on the earlier periods beginning with Muhammad. At times useful for items not treated or not treated separately in Shimoni (especially biographies and some historical events). A low priority item.

III. GENERAL WORKS

62. Beaumont, Peter, Gerald H. Blake, and J. Malcolm Wagstaff. **The Middle East: A Geographical Study.** New York, John Wiley, 1975. bibliog. illus. index. price n.a. LC 74-28284. DS 49.7.B36 1975. DDC 330.9'56'04.

First covers general topics: relief, geology, soils, climate, water, evolution of the landscape; rural land use; population; cities and towns (development, characteristics); economic development problems, industry and trade; petroleum; political geography. Then follow country surveys, from Libya to Iran. For each country emphasis is on a historical problematic approach to a particular aspect of the economy—agriculture, land use, industrialization, etc., so that treatment of the countries is not systematic and consistent. Despite this, the book is a useful supplement to the other geographies in this *Guide*.

63. Brice, William C. **South-West Asia.** London, University of London Press, 1966. 448p. bibliog. illus. maps. index. (A Systematic Regional Geography, v. 8). LC 67-75420. G 126.U67 vol. 8. DDC 915.6.

Part I treats systematically the geography of the whole area—physical aspects, climate, flora and fauna, ethnology, economy, historical geography. Part II deals with the main regions—Asia Minor, Armenian Plateau, Iranian Plateau, Levant, Arabia, Mesopotamia. Each is subdivided by subregion; natural and climatic features of each are discussed, as are ethnology, trade routes, rivers, etc., with indications of manmade changes such as dams, irrigation systems, etc., and their impact. Part III deals with the social and economic geography of the separate states: Turkey, Cyprus, Iran, Afghanistan, Syria, Lebanon, Israel, Jordan, Iraq, and Arabia. It generalizes on the economy, state economy activities, agriculture, industries, and resources of each country. The emphasis throughout the book is on human movement and active interaction with the geography; because of this approach, one can readily surmise the potential of and limitations on past and future interaction between man and land, and can readily imagine why human movement assumed the particular patterns it did. The book is a useful reference for information on the geographical aspects of a region's history and conditions—but *not* for specific information, since everything is given in general terms. The many maps and the text allow one to visualize the routes of trade and conquest, etc., which makes this book essential for larger collections. Specific information is to be found in Cressey (item 65) and Fisher (item 66).

64. Clarke, John Innes, and W. B. Fisher, eds. **Populations of the Middle East and North Africa: A Geographical Approach.** New York, Africana Publishing Corp., 1972. 432p. bibliog. index. $19.50. LC 72-80410. ISBN 0-8419-0125-2. HD 3634.8.C57 1972b. DDC 301.32'9'56.

[B] This is a collection of essays by geographers on the individual countries of the region. They present the latest figures and trends concerning population growth and distribution, urbanization, migration, communal organization, rural population, and fertility. Some items include economic and social notes and examine the relationship of demographic trends to economic developments. It can be expected to retain its validity for a few years. Since most of the information clusters around the mid-1960s, one should expect data on the 1970s to be available soon, but there is no guarantee that the new data will be presented in such convenient form. The chapter bibliographies are excellent. Not conveniently usable as a reference work.

65. Cressey, George Babcock. **Crossroads: Land and Life in Southwest Asia.** Philadelphia, J. B. Lippincott, 1960. 593p. bibliog. illus. index. (The Lippincott Geography Series). o.p. LC 60-11518. DS 49.7.C7. DDC 915.6.

[P1, C1, S1] A basic textbook on the geography of the Near East. It treats the Near East as a whole for all topics: the peoples and their history and demographic patterns; the land (geology, land forms, earthquakes, sand dunes, climate); rivers; land use (arable land, tenancy patterns and types); crops; livestock, forests, mineral resources; oil; international contacts (communications, trade, history, and political problems). Cressey then treats the individual countries, covering all aspects except culture: history, peoples, problems, main cities, economy. It has innumerable excellent and informative photos and maps. To be read after Longrigg (item 69).

66. Fisher, William Bayne. **The Middle East: A Physical, Social and Regional Geography.**
6th ed., completely rev. and reset. London, Methuen; distr. New York, Barnes & Noble, 1971. 571p. bibliog. maps. index. $21.00. LC 78-597190. ISBN 0-416-09140-7. DS 49.F56 1971. DDC 915.6.

[P1, P2, C1, S2] The standard geography of the region, including Egypt, Sudan, and Libya. It begins with a general description of the physical aspects, geology, climate, soils, and vegetation (97p.). This is followed by 93 pages on the peoples, languages, sects, social groups (nomads, town-dwellers, etc.); historical geography (his history is quite oldfashioned and error-prone), with indications of current problems and political conditions. The next 67 pages treat economic life in general, oil, resources, and industry. The rest of the book deals with the individual countries: physical geography, main regions, land use and crops, irrigation, land reform, pastoralism, industry, people, communications and towns, ports, minerals. Fisher is valuable for the specific information he provides about specific areas and topics. Brice (item 63) provides the general context for all this, while Cressey (item 65) provides an overview of all aspects of the region, with many more very useful photos than the other books, as well as terminology and information on specific phenomena (such as sand dunes) that is not found in the other works in this *Guide.* Longrigg (item 69) is a general introduction for all readers unacquainted with the region, and it should be read first for orientation. Despite the considerable overlap of all these books, each is sufficiently different in approach and specifics to warrant purchase by all college and most other collections.

67. Hourani, Albert Habib. **Minorities in the Arab World.** London, Oxford University Press, 1947. 140p. index. o.p. LC 47-6840. DS 39.H6. DDC 323.156.

[P1, C1] This is an extremely useful outline which, despite its age, is the best book we have on the subject; it excludes North Africa. Hourani discusses the statistics and origins of the various groups, their status, roles and development, the nineteenth and twentieth centuries (especially since World War I). He includes a country-by-country survey, with notes on the influence of Western intervention in minority-majority relations, which has had important effects to this day. It nicely brings together widely dispersed information in a meaningful form, which is a great help in understanding the recent importance of minority groups in the region.

68. Khadduri, Majid, and Herbert J. Liebesny. **Law in the Middle East.** Only Vol. 1 published: **Origin and Development of Islamic Law.** Washington, D.C., Middle East Institute, 1955. 395p. bibliog. glossary. index. o.p. LC 55-2903. LC class: LAW. DDC 340.095.

Articles by various experts: constitutional organization, early and later development; sources of the law; Shiite theories; family law; transactions, penal law, judicial organization; Islamic law under the Ottoman Empire; international law; development of the capitulations; conflict in international law between Islamic and modern law, and between the laws of various religions. A useful supplement to Schacht (item 540).
See also:
Liebesny, Herbert J. **The Law of the Near and Middle East: Readings, Cases and Materials.** Albany, State University of New York Press, 1974. 301p. bibliog. index. LC 74-22046. ISBN 0-87395-256-1; 0-87395-257-X (microfiche). LC class: LAW. DDC 340'.0956. Sections on the concepts of Islamic jurisprudence, legal reforms in the nineteenth and twentieth centuries, comparative law (Muslim and modern Middle Eastern), etc., in selected topics: marriage, inheritance, contracts and torts, penal law, procedure. Includes commentary on most items. The bibliography is very useful.

69. Longrigg, Stephen Hemsley. **The Middle East: A Social Geography.** 2nd ed. Chicago, Aldine Publishing Co., 1970. 291p. bibliog. illus. index. $7.95; $3.45pa. LC 75-91722. ISBN 0-202-10008-1; 0-202-10013-8pa. DS 44.L56. DDC 309.1'56.

[P1, S1] A general work by a foremost scholar with long experience in the region (the Sudan and North Africa are excluded). It presents the sweep of history as background to the current situation; discussions of the peoples, sects, and minority groups are followed by individual country surveys of the geography, economics, population, and communications. Then follow general essays on public life, society and culture, agriculture and industry, and oil. A first book, particularly for smaller collections.

70. Rivlin, Benjamin, and Joseph S. Szyliowicz, eds. **The Contemporary Middle East: Tradition and Innovation.** New York, Random House, 1965. 576p. bibliog. index. $9.95. LC 64-18229. ISBN 0-394-30461-6. DS 57.R77.

[P1, C1, S1] The best selection of readings on the region, by various Western authorities and a few Near Eastern writers, including political leaders. It includes the Islamic background, Western penetration, Islamic modernism; nationalism; social, political and economic modernization; ideology; the Near East in world politics; God, women, youth; economic planning and population control. A good eye-opening perspective for beginners and a good resource book for general collections. A useful supplementary collection, which includes articles and chapters from books, some of which are found in this *Guide*, is Jacob M. Landau, *Man, State and Society in the Contemporary Middle East* (New York, Praeger, 1972. 532p. $13.50. LC 78-159412). It excludes Turkey, Iran, Afghanistan, Sudan, and North Africa.

Other very useful collections of articles and readings that provide much important material include:

Gendzier, Irene L., ed. **A Middle East Reader.** New York, Pegasus, 1969. 473p. bibliog. LC 70-91615. DS 62.8.G45. DDC 320.9'56.

Laqueur, Walter Ze'ev. **The Middle East in Transition: Studies in Contemporary History.** Freeport, N.Y., Books for Libraries Press, 1971. (Repr. of 1958 ed.). 513p. LC 70-156676. ISBN 0-8369-2367-7. DS 63.L36 1971. DDC 320.9'56'04.

Nolte, Richard H. **The Modern Middle East.** New York, Atherton Press, 1963. 218p. LC 63-18181. DS 42.4.N6. 1963. DDC 915.6.

Thompson, Jack Howell, and Robert D. Reischauer, eds. **Modernization of the Arab World.** Princeton, N.J., Van Nostrand, 1966. 249p. LC 67-548. DS 63.T49. DDC 915.6.

IV. HISTORY AND POLITICS

A. GENERAL

71. Armajani, Yahya. **The Middle East, Past and Present.** Englewood Cliffs, N.J., Prentice-Hall, 1970. 432p. bibliog. illus. index. $8.95. LC 77-76315. ISBN 0-13-581579-7. DS 62.A73. DDC 956.

[P1, C1, S1] This introductory history textbook, by a Persian Christian, has been criticized by at least one eminent specialist, who went so far as to say that there were so many mistakes in it that it would have been better if it had not been published at all; the same specialist recommended Fisher (item 74) instead. However, that reviewer failed to mention that there was not and is not currently available another general introduction that demonstrates such thoughtful concern for the beginner. Everything is explained, including much terminology. The book is fairly evenly proportioned in its coverage, and tries to relate past to present to make the whole more meaningful. Religious and cultural aspects are covered, while Iran is given much more space than in Fisher—perhaps Armajani slightly overdoes it. Armajani is readable. He does make mistakes, and his romanization of vernacular terms is utterly chaotic. However, the reader will not come away grossly misled in most cases, and he should get more from it than from many other works because of its method of exposition.

Two general histories quite useful to the beginner are:

Hottinger, Arnold. **The Arabs, Their History, Culture and Place in the Modern World.** Berkeley, University of California Press, 1963. 344p. illus. LC 64-1108. DS 62.H8233. DDC 953.

Kirk, George Eden. **A Short History of the Middle East from the Rise of Islam to Modern Times.** 7th ed. New York, Praeger, 1964. 340p. LC 64-25427. DS 33.K57 1964. DDC 309.156. A standard brief history, three-fifths of which covers the period from 1918 to the early 1960s.

72. Brockelmann, Carl. **History of the Islamic Peoples.** Tr. from German. With a review of events, 1939-1947, by Moshe Pearlmann. New York, Capricorn Books, 1960. 582p. bibliog. index. (CAP Giant, 204). $2.95pa. LC A66-41. ISBN 0-399-50107-X. DS 38.B72 1960. DDC 953.

[P1, C1, S1] A factual, deadly dull, basic work, encyclopedic in detail, on the Near East and North Africa from Muhammad's time to 1947. It crams into its finely printed pages most of the historical facts that anyone would ever need to know. The only material on cultural matters consists of descriptions of some key buildings. Despite its title, it contains nothing on the other Islamic countries in Africa and Asia.

73. **The Cambridge History of Islam.** Ed. by P. M. Holt, Ann K. S. Lambton, and Bernard Lewis. Cambridge, England, Cambridge University Press, 1970. 2v. bibliog. indices. $39.00. LC 73-77291. ISBN 0-521-07567-X (v.1); 0-521-07601-3 (v.2). DS 35.6.C3. DDC 910.03'176'7.

[P1, P2, C1, S1] Essays by top experts on the history of the Islamic countries and their civilization, rather than a history of the religion of Islam. Volume 1 covers the Near East systematically from pre-Islamic Arabia through the twentieth century, including Central Asia. Concluding chapters discuss Islam in the Soviet Union, communism in the Near East; the political impact of the West; economic and social change. Volume 2 discusses the non-Near Eastern regions India and Pakistan, including the breakdown of traditional Muslim society, religion and culture; Southeast Asia, which includes both religious and political history; Africa and the Muslim West, including North Africa, Sudan, West Africa, Spain, and Sicily. The rest of the second volume deals with general aspects: the geographical setting; sources of Islamic civilization; economy, society and institutions; law and justice; religion and culture; mysticism; revival and reform in Islam; Arabic, Persian, Turkish, and Urdu literatures; art and

and architecture; science, philosophy, warfare, and the transmission of learning and literary influence to Europe. One of the first books for most collections. A similar work by top scholars is: Spuler, Bertold. *The Muslim World: A Historical Survey.* Tr. from German. (Leiden, E. J. Brill, 1960– . LC A61-1030. DS 38.S643).

74. Fisher, Sydney Nettleton. **The Middle East: A History.** 2nd ed., rev. and enl. New York, Knopf, 1969. 749p. bibliog. index. $13.95. LC 68-24673. ISBN 0-394-42882-X. DS 62.F5 1969. DDC 956.

[P1, C1, S1, B] This is the standard textbook on the subject, from the appearance of Islam to the present. It emphasizes the period since the foundation and expansion of the Ottoman Empire, with much attention to Ottoman institutions. Treatment is basically factual. The chapter bibliographies have not been completely brought up to date since the basic cut-off date, 1967. A basic book, which may be said to complement Hitti (item 88) in matters historical. It completely ignores cultural aspects.

75. Hodgson, Marshall G. S. **The Venture of Islam: Conscience and History in a World Civilization.** Chicago, University of Chicago Press, 1975. 3v. 532, 609, 469p. bibliog. illus. index. $60.00. LC 73-87243. ISBN 0-226-34677-3(set); 0-226-34678-1 (v.1); 0-226-34680-3 (v.2); 0-226-34681-1 (v.3). LC cataloging n.a.

[P1, C1, S1] A major interpretation of Islamic history and civilization in all its aspects from Muhammad to modern times, which offers a perspective quite different from the usual. The author seeks to suggest the dynamics, nature, and interaction of politics, economics, society, government, and the religious-intellectual-legal complex, and the development and relation to the rest, of the various cultural manifestations. While basic facts are provided, emphasis is on analysis. Volume 1 deals with the history and civilization to the tenth century, including the nature and growth of Islamic law and the relation of the various schools to society; the reasons the law developed as it did; growth of the other Islamic sciences–Hadith, history, Muslim personal piety, role of the Qur'an, theology, philosophy, their nature, origin and development. The volume begins with an introduction to Islamic studies and to Hodgson's methodology. Volume 2 treats the history and formation of the international political order–the economic, social, ideological bases of the various regimes, and their cultures; rise of the Turkish states in Iran and the Eastern Empire. Also covered are institutions, socio-political organization, social order, mercantile interests, military power, liberty; a socio-economic interpretation of the geographical and climatic aspects of the period's history; the poor and common man; village-urban life and political influence systems; the maturing of the intellectual traditions, literatures; Mongols and their aftermath; visual arts; expansion of Islam into Indonesia and Africa; and history to the end of the fifteenth century. Volume 3 discusses the sixteenth century to modern times. Part 1 deals in sweeping terms with the history, culture, spirit, economy and structure of the Safavid, Ottoman, and Indian Timurid empires, and then the eighteenth century as the setting for the onslaught of the West. This is treated in the second section, "The Islamic Heritage in the Modern World." Hodgson analyses the Western surge to prominence through the changes in its life and civilization, and he explains why Asia did not keep pace. Also covered are the imposition of the Western order on India, Egypt and other Eastern nations, and the influence process; reasons why the East reacted as it did, the nature of that reaction; the new Middle Eastern culture and "modernism"; Turkish reform, revival of Islamic heritage in the Arab lands, new Arabic literature; Zionism and the Arab reaction; Muslim India; independence; Islamic cosmopolitanism. Throughout, the reader's understanding is aided by maps, chronological, genealogical and related tables; the footnotes often provide thumbnail critiques of standard and other books; each volume has an index, a glossary, and a selective annotated bibliography. The approach is broad and utilizes what we know of the processes of civilization's various manifestations. It tries to broaden the reader's outlook and help him view the whole and its parts from a variety of approaches, to sensitize and train him to look beyond his own cultural perspective, and beyond the traditional methods of studying Islamic civilization. A fascinating, stimulating work to be read (and reread at each stage of study) by anyone who has a functional acquaintance with the subject. Good to use with the *Cambridge History of Islam* (item 73).

76. Holt, Peter Malcolm. **Egypt and the Fertile Crescent, 1516-1922: A Political History.**
Ithaca, N.Y., Cornell University Press, 1966. 337p. bibliog. index. $8.50; $2.45pa.
LC 66-18429. ISBN 0-8014-0189-5; 0-8014-9079-0pa. DS 63.H62 1966a. DDC 956.

[P1, C1, S1] An excellent history of the Near East under Ottoman rule, emphasizing internal politics rather than international relations, though the latter are discussed when relevant to the main subject. A careful work, basic to any collection, and a must for students.

77. McNeill, William Hardy. **The Rise of the West: A History of the Human Community.**
Chicago, University of Chicago Press, 1963. 829p. illus. maps. index. $9.95. LC 63-13067.
ISBN 0-226-56143-7. CB 59.M3. DDC 901.9. Paperback: A Phoenix Book, P 385.
$4.25. ISBN 0-226-56144-5.

[P1, C1, S1] An outstanding synthesis of world history in which a significant quantity of material on the Islamic Near East and Islam is put into the perspective of worldwide historical and intellectual currents. It shows the interplay of the Near East with Asia and Europe as no other book does, and it does so in a most comprehensible manner for anyone with a background in European history. The author assumes that the reader has such a background, but no background in the other regions, which are treated in a more elementary fashion, is needed. Basic information and explanations for everything are provided, but with a great deal of sophistication. A truly stimulating book, basic for any college and larger public library.

78. Stavrianos, Leften Stavros. **The Balkans since 1453.** New York, Holt, Rinehart, World,
1958. 970p. bibliog. index. (Dryden Editions). $15.75. LC 58-7242. ISBN 0-03-
009685-5. DR 36.S83. DDC 949.6.

[C1, S1] This history of the Balkans includes a great deal of information on the Ottoman Empire, its history and institutions, and the individual peoples of the region. Only the first 215 pages deal with the period to 1815; the next 330 pages cover 1815 to 1914; the rest of the book, through 1956. It covers international and intra-Balkan diplomacy, international and internal developments, with notes on the economy and society of the area. It puts nicely into perspective many elements of the "Eastern question." It is useful not only for its material on the Balkans and the Empire, but for the Balkan perspective of the Ottoman system, treatment of the various peoples, how the millet system worked, and how Turkey lost the Balkan provinces.

B. TO 1800

79. Arnold, Sir Thomas Walker. **The Caliphate.** New York, Barnes & Noble, 1966. (Repr.
of 1924 ed.). With a chapter by Sylvia Haim. 267p. index. o.p. LC 66-1500. DS 236.
A7 1966. DDC 320.91767. (BIP lists a 1965 ed., London, Routledge & Kegan Paul,
$9.95. ISBN 0-7100-1027-3.)

Covers the history of the Caliphate: the concept, the theological and legal aspects; the Abbasid dynasty; the figurehead Caliphs in Cairo in the late medieval period; the assumption of the title by independent dynasties; the Ottomans and the Caliphate; the Mughals in India. There are appendices on various aspects of the idea and on the use of the term Khalifah and the title "Sultan." It is the standard work, written just after the Caliphate was abolished in Turkey. Haim's new chapter gives more detail on the abolishment and its aftermath, as well as the debate in the Near East and India about the future of the Caliphate. A basic work on a key topic.

80 Atiyah, Aziz Suryal. **Crusade, Commerce and Culture.** Gloucester, Mass., Peter Smith,
1969. (Repr. of 1962 ed.). 280p. bibliog. index. $5.50. LC 70-10643. ISBN 0-8446-
0463-1. D 160.A8 1969. DDC 940.1'8.

[C1] This is a study in East-West relations. It views the Crusades as an attempt by Europe to solve the "Eastern question," tracing East-West relations before the Crusades, including Alexander's invasions, Byzantine-Arab relations, Christian pilgrimage to the Holy Land. It treats the sweep of the Crusades and their nature, and the results; it then covers the Muslim counter-Crusade, Muslim propaganda and views (including Arab efforts), and then the Turkish onslaught, including the capture of Constantinople. The book also discusses the romance of medieval commerce in the Levant, including cultural interchange, particularly the rise of Arab culture, though it does not treat the transmission of Eastern culture to Europe as much as might be desired. An interesting book for the general reader with a fairly good background.

81. al-Balādhurī, Ahmad ibn Yahyā (d. 892). **The Origins of the Islamic State**, being a translation from Arabic . . . of **Kitāb Futūh al-Buldān**, by Philip K. Hitti and Francis Clark Murgotten. New York, AMS Press, 1973. (Repr. of 1916-1924 ed.). 2v. index. $32.50. LC 76-82247. ISBN 0-404-51163-5. DS 38.2.B313. DDC 909'.0974'927.

This famous history, a prime source on its period, is a typical example of early medieval Islamic historiography, which utilized an anecdotal method. It is rather hard reading because of the style of writing and compilation, but it is important for the historical data and for the material on the government and life of the times, the Islamic lore current and considered important at the time, taxation, etc. Beginning with Muhammad the Prophet, it covers the early conquests and the Caliphate, including the conquest of Spain, North Africa, and Iran, and the terms of surrender of these areas. It was a basic source for many succeeding histories.

82. Benveniste, Meron. **The Crusaders in the Holy Land.** New York, Macmillan, 1972. 408p. illus. indices. $12.95. LC 70-180293. D 182.B44 1972. DDC 915.694'4'033.

[P1] A popular description of the Holy Land during the time of the Crusades as seen in the relics of the period: a description of the land and people as manifested in the antiquities left by the Crusaders. It attempts to describe all such remains. It discusses the individual cities and towns; the countryside, fortifications, churches, and monasteries; the Frankish way of life; life in Palestine and Jerusalem, including laws, history, markets, construction. Actually a historical geography, it is a fascinating work for the general reader.

Another work is:

Smail, R. C. **The Crusaders in Syria and the Holy Land.** New York, Praeger, 1974. 232p. bibliog. index. $12.50. LC 72-79511. LC cataloging n.a.

83. Bosworth, Clifford Edmund. **The Ghaznavids: Their Empire in Afghanistan and Eastern Iran, 994-1040.** Beirut, Librairie du Liban; distr. Mystic, Conn., Lawrence Verry, 1972. (Repr. of 1963 ed.). 331p. index. $8.50. LC n.a. DS 228.7.B6 1972. DDC 955.02.

A history of the Turkish dynasty that established a high civilization in the northeastern corner of the Islamic Empire. The emphasis is on the civilization, administration, army, and society, with chapters on the rise of the Seljuq Turks, their struggle with the Ghaznavids, and the latter's final defeat. There is much information on the economy and other aspects of the province of Khurasan and its capital Nishapur during the period. In addition, the book includes much information on broader aspects of the history of the period as context that will be helpful to more advanced students. Bosworth does not provide a detailed account of the rise, reign, and conquests of the dynasty's founder, Mahmud, because this, he says, is adequately covered in: Muhammad Nazim, *The Life and Times of Sultan Mahmud of Ghazna* (New Delhi, Munshiram Manoharlal; distr. Columbia, Mo., South Asia Books, 1971. Repr. of 1931 ed. $8.00. LC 78-927021. DS 288.7.N39 1971. DDC 954.02'2'0924). Nazim is far too detailed for college students. Bosworth should be in larger collections.

84. Gabrieli, Francesco, comp. **Arab Historians of the Crusades.** Selected and tr. from the Arabic sources. Tr. from Italian. London, Routledge & Kegan Paul, 1969. 398p. bibliog. index. (The Islamic World). ₤4.50. LC 78-435858. ISBN 0-7100-2874-1. D 151.G313 1969b. DDC 909.07.

[C1] This interesting book contains selections from 17 medieval Arab authors, roughly treating the first 200 years of the Crusades, through the fall of Acre. It is arranged to portray the whole through Muslim eyes and to reveal the method and style of Muslim historiography. It will be eye-opening for most readers.

85. Glubb, Sir John Bagot. **The Great Arab Conquests.** Englewood Cliffs, N.J., Prentice-Hall, 1964. 384p. 35 maps. index. $8.00. LC 64-12094. DS 232.G55 1964. DDC 953.

Utilizing original Arabic and Western secondary sources, the ex-commander of Jordan's Arab Legion has written in popular style a military history of the period from the time of Muhammad and his campaigns to the end of the first wave of the Muslim conquests (654), with additional material on the civil wars of the reign of Uthman, the third Caliph, and the fourth, Ali, as well as the latter's struggle with Mu'awiyah, his successor and the first Umayyad Caliph, through the renewal of the conquest movement and Mu'awiyah's death in 680. Glubb often uses his personal experiences in military activity in the region, his knowledge of the Bedouins, whom he led for decades, and parallels from various eras of Arab history to make our image of these campaigns and Bedouin fighting methods more vivid. Rather too detailed for the uninitiated, but quite interesting to one with some idea of the period's history. Glubb wrote three more volumes, which span the history of the Islamic Empire to 1463: *The Empire of the Arabs* (1965. 384p.), on further conquests, Umayyads, and Abbasids, to 861; *The Course of Empire: The Arabs and Their Successors* (1966. 424p.), on the Islamic Empire from Spain to Armenia, 865-1145; *The Lost Centuries: From the Empires to the Renaissance of Europe, 1145-1463* (1967. 511p.), from the defeat of the Crusades to the fall of Constantinople. (All Prentice-Hall, all o.p. The four volumes were originally published in England and may still be available there.) None of the four books is decently written, but Glubb tries in amateur fashion to cover the sweep of Muslim history in the Middle Ages with some intelligence and a certain vividness; he utilizes many stories from the Arabic chronicles. He tries to impart an understanding of the conditions and attitudes of the various dynasties and their actions, by means of comparison with the same period in Europe, as well as other devices to overcome the usual Western attitudes and value judgments that might keep readers from viewing events with an open mind. The dozens of maps in each volume are most useful. The books are more detailed than smaller public libraries may need, depending on their readership. Despite the deluge of names and dates, the books are relatively easy to read, if at times somewhat boring, and are a painless, if not always reliable, introduction to a decisively important era of history. Therefore, they are a useful addition to larger public and even college collections.

86. Hitti, Philip Khûri. **The Arabs: A Short History.** 5th ed. New York, St. Martin's Press, 1968. 211p. index. $5.95. LC 68-57929. DS 223.H48 1968. DDC 909'.09'74927. Paperback: London, Macmillan, 1968. (Papermac 234). $0.65. LC 70-401353. ISBN 0-333-03590-9.

[P1] A well-written, very interesting popular general history of the Arabs, their society and civilization, and their contribution to the West, including their transmission of ancient Greek civilization. It will be a revelation to the general reader, and may awaken a deep interest in the subject, as it did for the author of this *Guide* and some of his acquaintants.

87. Hitti, Philip Khûri. **Capital Cities of Islam.** Minneapolis, University of Minnesota Press, 1973. 176p. bibliog. illus. index. $7.95. LC 72-92335. ISBN 0-8166-0663-3. DS 38.3.H58 1973. DDC 910'.031'7671.

[P] Hitti, well-known popularizer of Arab history, has written three further popularizations (cf. items 179, 195) based on item 88, for public libraries and the totally uninitiated reader. They are interesting and enjoyable to read. Each handles its subject matter in a different way, from a different perspective. There is, of course, some overlapping of material in these works, but this in no way vitiates their utility, since they reinforce and complement each other. They should not form part of a core collection, but they warrant purchase as supplementary works. This volume views main points of Arab history and civilization by focusing on six main capital cities: Mecca, Medina, Damascus, Baghdad, Cairo, and Cordova. Each served as capital of all or part of the Islamic Empire during a "golden age" of Islamic history and culture. Hitti gives the history of the city and main events of its era; notes on its main buildings; excerpts from early and pre-twentieth century travellers who visited the city; indications of its cultural importance, including famous figures who lived there, and a few miscellaneous facts about the city.

88. Hitti, Philip Khûri. **History of the Arabs from Earliest Times to the Present.** 10th ed. New York, St. Martin's Press, 1970. 822p. illus. index. $12.50; $8.95pa. LC 74-102765. DS 37.7.H58 1970. DDC 953.

[P1, P2, C1, S1] The standard work, covering the period mainly from Muhammad's time to the Turkish conquest of Egypt in 1517, with material on the pre-Islamic period and the Ottoman Empire. It is a veritable encyclopedia in narrative form of the history and civilization of the Islamic Middle East, North Africa and Spain during the Middle Ages. It discusses many classical books in all fields as part of the written artifacts of that civilization. It is essential for all but the smallest collections. It has more detail than the average reader will want, but it is an indispensable resource for libraries serving educated readers who might want more than a cursory survey but who do not need to know everything. The student who masters Hitti has a good start in the field. Despite its formidable appearance, what with diacritical marks on the innumerable Arabic names that rush through it and its sheer bulk, it is relatively easy to read and is quite comprehensible, so no reader should be put off by its appearance.

89. Ibn al-Furāt, Muhammad ibn ᶜAbd al-Rahīm. **Ayyubids, Mamelukes and Crusaders: Selections from the Tārikh al-Duwal wa'l-Mulūk.** Text ed. and tr. by U. and M. C. Lyons. Cambridge, England, W. Heffer, 1971. 2v. £11.50. LC 77-879125. ISBN 0-85270-058-X (v.1); 0-85270-059-8 (v.2). DS 38.7.I242. DDC 962'.02.

This interesting history covers the period 1244-1277, especially the period after 1260, which was the period of the Sultan Baybars and his battles against the Crusaders, and the appearance of the Mongols. It is a basic source for the era, being a typical example of Arab writing of the time, and providing an excellent example of the subjective Muslim perspective, which much resembles the one-sided outlook of contemporary Christian sources. Only for large collections that have sizeable or comprehensive representative holdings on the period. Volume 1 contains the Arabic text, and Volume 2 the introduction and translation; only the latter volume is necessary.

90. Ibn al-Qalānisī, Abū Yaᶜlā Hamzah ibn Asad (d. 1160). **The Damascus Chronicle of the Crusades.** Extracted and tr. from Arabic by H. A. R. Gibb. London, Luzac; distr. Totowa, N.J., Rowman & Littlefield, 1967. (Repr. of 1932 ed.). 368p. indices. $8.50. LC n.a. D 152.I252. DDC 940.18.

An official of Damascus records his first-hand observations and the accounts of other witnesses, using documents of his time. The book is in the form of annals; it is rather dry, but it is our best and oldest source for the period 1097 to 1159. It features detailed accounts of battles, some of which are exceedingly interesting.
See also:
Usāmah ibn Murshīd ibn Munqidh (1095-1158). **An Arab-Syrian Gentleman and Warrior in the Period of the Crusades: Memoirs of Usāmah ibn-Munqidh (Kitāb al-Iᶜtibār).** Tr. from Arabic by Philip K. Hitti. Beirut, Khayats, 1964. (Repr. of 1929 ed.). 265p. index. LC 65-7849/CD.DS 97.U7 1964. DDC 915.691. Interesting account, by a member of the Syrian elite, of his experiences with anecdotes, stories of holy men, cures, hunting experiences, battles, etc., from 1138 to 1164.

91. Ibn Khaldūn (1332-1406). **[Kitāb al-ᶜIbar. al-Muqaddimah]. The Muqaddimah: An Introduction to History.** Tr. from Arabic by Franz Rosenthal. Abridged and ed. [from the 3 vol. ed.] by N. A. Dawood. Princeton, N.J., Princeton University Press, 1969. 465p. index. (Bollingen Series, 160). $3.45pa. LC 72-8164. D 16.7.I2333 1969. DDC 901.9. **The Muqaddimah: An Introduction to History,** by Ibn Khaldūn. 2nd ed. Princeton University Press, 1967. 3v. (Bollingen Series, 43). $35.00. LC 58-5608. ISBN 0-691-01754-9.

The Muqaddimah is one of the most famous works of medieval Islam, being a theory of history, society, politics and civilization, and one of the more interesting works to come from a medieval civilization. Ibn Khaldun sought to fill a gap in Greek-Muslim philosophy: a pragmatic science of man based on the philosophical theories and methodology known to his time, but probing deeper and seeking the causes of events and the nature of the processes of history. His premise is that one must know man to know history. He procedes to posit a theory of man's existence covering all aspects of human behavior and endeavor, including the end or purpose of man and society. Understanding history, he says, one can then best act in accordance with reality and the nature of things, which is the most appropriate manner. In many respects, Ibn Khaldun's ideas and theories are surprisingly "modern"; it appears that he had relatively little influence on his successors, unfortunately. Larger collections will want the complete work, but smaller libraries should at least have the abridgment. Most students can be satisfied with the shorter form, which is highly recommended for public libraries.

92. Mahdi, Muhsin. **Ibn Khaldun's Philosophy of History: A Study in the Philosophic Foundation of the Science of Culture.** Chicago, University of Chicago Press, 1964. 325p. bibliog. index. (A Phoenix Book, P. 167). $4.25pa. LC 64-23414. ISBN 0-226-50183-3. D 116.7.I3M3 1964. DDC 901.

A presentation, analysis, and critique of the theories propounded in *The Muqaddimah* and their structure; it should be purchased by any library owning the subject work (item 91). It tells something of the book and its author and will make Ibn Khaldun's ideas more meaningful, particularly since Mahdi presents his examination in the context of the ideas of which Ibn Khaldun's were a part, and indicates the significance of his new construction, as well as his positions regarding earlier thinking and philosophy. It examines the philosophic foundation and principles of the new science of civilization and history, showing Ibn Khaldun's intent and method of argumentation. It also provides the reader with further information on Islamic philosophy, Islamic historiography and its relation to religion and philosophy, and the background to Ibn Khaldun's work and attitude toward history. The book assumes considerable reader background.

93. Lewis, Archibald R. **Naval Power and Trade in the Mediterranean, A.D. 500-1100.** New York, Johnson Reprint Corp., 1970. (Repr. of 1951 ed.). 271p. bibliog. index. $12.00. LC n.a. D 128.L4. DDC 940.

A very useful overview of medieval naval and economic history. It discusses the background for trade, including the political and basic economic aspects; it notes changes in these factors over time and indicates the power relations between the various empires. It provides a good general perspective on the period, despite any modification in its conclusions by the vast amount of additional research on the era that has accumulated since it was first published. It concludes with the period during which the West achieved naval and commercial domination of the Mediterranean Sea and surveys the history and main factors of that rise in relative power. An interesting book for readers with a good general background in European and Islamic history.

94. Lewis, Bernard. **The Arabs in History.** London, Hutchinson; distr. New York, Humanities Press, 1965. 199p. bibliog. index. $5.00. LC n.a. DS 223.L4. DDC 910.909174927. Paperback: Harper Torch Book, TB 1029. $1.95. ISBN 0-06-131029-8.

[P1, C1, S1] This brief overview of Arab history for the beginner, by a foremost Arabist, very nicely puts everything into perspective in a balanced, readable form. Basic for all readers and collections.

95. Margoliouth, David Samuel. **Lectures on Arabic Historians.** New York, Burt Franklin, 1972. (Repr. of 1930 ed.). 160p. $15.00. LC 72-82293. ISBN 0-8337-2214-X. DS 38.16.M37 1972. DDC 909'.04'927072024.

This work is inadequate and out of date, but it is a readable account by a well-known scholar. It discusses the idea and development of Arab historiography, the materials used, its predecessors, the forms of the various works and their nature. It is a useful introduction to the period up to the tenth century. Includes a final lecture on the later classical historians to the fifteenth century. The reprint price is blatant robbery and the book is not *that* good.

The major work on the subject is Rosenthal, Franz, *A History of Muslim Historiography*, 2nd ed. (Leiden, E. J. Brill, 1968. 656p. LC 68-113306. D 198.2.R67 1968). About a third consists of an introduction to the various types of histories and "philosophies" written during the medieval period and the intent of history; the rest consists of translations and Arabic texts of various complete or partial works on historiography as an Islamic science.

96. Masʿūdī (d. 956?). **[Murūj al-Dhahab]. El-Masʿūdī's Historical Encyclopedia, Entitled Meadows of Gold and Mines of Gems.** Tr. from Arabic by Aloys Sprenger. London, Oriental Translation Fund of Great Britain and Ireland, 1841. 2v. (Oriental Translation Fund, No. 54). o.p. LC n.a. PK 408.06.

This classic basic source, written by a widely travelled Muslim intellectual, deals with the geography of the known world; the Israelite kings as mentioned in the Koran; pre-Islamic prophets; events to Muhammad's time; the Hindus, their history and religion; the seven climates, the seas and their tides; great rivers; China, the Caucasus, Bulgaria; ancient history including the Assyrians, Alexander, the Greeks and Romans; Sudan; the Slavonians, Franks, and Italians; Arabs and Arabia, and Arab folk-lore; the various religious calendars. It also covers Muhammad and the history of the Islamic Empire to the time of the Abbasid Caliph al-Mutiʿ (946-974). A fascinating book, enhanced by the translator's very extensive notes. A basic book for larger collections.

See also:
Khalidi, Tarif. **Islamic Historiography: The Histories of Mas^cūdi.** Albany, State University of New York Press, 1975. bibliog. LC n.a. ISBN 0-87395-282-0. DS 37.5.M35 K45.

97. Mayer, Hans Eberhard. **The Crusades.** Tr. from German. London, Oxford University Press, 1972. 339p. bibliog. index. $10.25; $3.95pa. LC 72-193660. ISBN 0-19-873015-2; 0-19-87316-0pa. D 157.M3813. DDC 940.1'8.

[C1, S1] A scholarly but quite readable outline history, mainly from the European perspective. A useful introduction.

98. Niẓām al-Mulk (1018-1092). **The Book of Government, or Rules for Kings: The Siyàsat-nàma or Siyar al-Mulk.** Tr. from Persian by Hubert Drake. New Haven, Yale University Press, 1960. 259p. bibliog. index. (UNESCO Collection of Representative Works. Rare Masterpieces of Philosophy and Science). o.p. LC 60-1744. JC 49.N43 1960a. DDC 354.55.

[C] Written by a man who was the chief minister for two Seljuq rulers (for over 30 years), the book provides a wealth of general and often very specific advice for rulers on religious life, handling of the people and officials; how various officials should run their offices (tax collectors, judges); how peasants should be treated, etc. Also included are the training of pages, conduct of audiences, titles; exposing heretics; and keeping everyone in his proper place. Final chapters provide historical episodes from which lessons may be drawn. A basic work on kingship, political practice, and the courts of the period.

99. Oldenbourg, Zoé. **The Crusades.** Tr. from French. New York, Pantheon Books, 1966. 650p. bibliog. index. $8.95. LC 65-10013. ISBN 0-394-42073-X. D 158.04. DDC 909.07. Paperback: Ballantine Books (U8004). $1.25.

[P1] This story of the first three Crusades reads like a novel and is continuously interesting. The author seeks to set the scene in its social, religious, and political aspects and transport the reader to the era by making him appreciate fully its life, thought, and general mood. An effort is made to treat the Muslim side. Well worth reading. For public libraries.

100. Owen, Roger, and Thomas Naff, eds. **The Muslim World in the 18th Century.** London, Frank Cass; distr. Portland, Ore., International Scholarly Book Services, 1975 (forthcoming). ca.300p. LC n.a. ISBN 0-7146-3003-9. LC cataloging n.a.

Original contributions by various specialists concerning the central Ottoman administration, its relations with the provinces, economy and society, religion and the arts (from catalog blurb). In view of our small knowledge about the period, this work should be a basic source for some time to come.

101. Peters, Francis E. **The Harvest of Hellenism: A History of the Near East from Alexander the Great to the Triumph of Christianity.** New York, Simon and Schuster, 1971. 800p. bibliog. index. (A Clarion Book). $4.95pa. LC 74-116509. ISBN 0-671-20659-1pa. DS 57.P46. DDC 939.

[P1, C1, S2] While this history of the period from the 4th century B.C. to the 4th century A.D. does not even cover the era up to the coming of Islam and is far too detailed for many readers, it is most useful for background to the intellectual and cultural currents which, in their age of decline, are the immediate backdrop to the coming of Islam. McNeill (item 77) will be adequate for most, but deeper understanding may be sought in the detail provided by Peters.

102. Prawer, Joshua. **The Crusaders Kingdom: European Colonialism in the Middle Ages.** New York, Praeger, 1972. 587p. bibliog. index. $18.50. LC 72-77069. D 182.P68 1972. DDC 915.694'03'3.

A description of all aspects of the Kingdom, rather than a history: political and class structure, the Jews, role of the Church; pilgrims and pilgrimages; Oriental church; military orders; military arts and science; fortifications; economic life and commerce; the arts. Concluded by a synthesis of Prawer's findings and analysis from the perspective of the Crusades as a colonial movement. For larger collections.

103. Prawer, Joshua. **The World of the Crusaders.** New York, Quadrangle Books, 1972. 160p. illus. index. $8.95. LC 72-83624. ISBN 0-297-99537-5. D 157.P7 1973. DDC 909.07.

[P] An interesting popular work which outlines the Crusades' history, the situation in Europe and the Levant. The bulk of it deals with the Kingdom of Jerusalem—aspects of life, government, chivalry, and the orders; castles, warfare, commerce. A popularization of (item 102).

104. Runciman, Steven. **A History of the Crusades.** Cambridge, England, Cambridge University Press, 1951 (reissued regularly). 3v. bibliog. indices. $15.50/vol. LC 51-10801. D 157.R8. DDC 940.18. Paperback: Harper & Row, 1964-1967. Harper Torchbooks, The Academy Library: v.1 TB 1143. o.p.; v.2 TB 1243. $3.45; v.3 TB 1298. o.p. Also, Penguin Peregrine Books. £0.75. v.1: 0-14-021379; v.2: 0-14-055051-8; v.3: 0-14-055052-6.

[P1, C1, S2] The most extensive English work, emphasizing the European perspective. It utilizes only those Arabic sources that have been translated into European languages; many of those were inadequately translated and presented in non-scholarly fashion in the main source collections. It will be the standard work until Setton (item 108) is completed.

105. Saunders, John Joseph. **A History of Medieval Islam.** London, Routledge & Kegan Paul, 1965. 219p. bibliog. index. $7.00. LC n.a. ISBN 0-7100-2077-5. DS 223.S25 1965. DDC 956.

[P1, C1, S1] An excellent general introduction to the history of the Islamic Empire, containing an outline of the facts with much generalization and interpretation; it never goes beyond the understanding of the general reader. A first book that makes the entire period intelligible as few others can.

Other works on the period include:

Assaad, Sadik A. **The Reign of al-Hakim bi Amr Allah (386/996-411/1021): A Political Study.** Beirut, Arab Institute for Research and Publishing, 1974. 209p. $8.00. LC cataloging n.a.

Aziz Ahmad. **A History of Islamic Sicily.** Edinburgh, University of Edinburgh Press, 1975; Chicago, Aldine Publishing Co., 1975 (forthcoming). (Islamic Surveys, No. 10).

Dixon, Abd al-Ameer Abd. **The Umayyad Caliphate, 65-86/684-705 (A Political Study).** London, Luzac, 1971. 222p. bibliog. index. LC 70-879403. ISBN 0-7189-0149-5. DS 38.5.D59. DDC 953'.02.

Muir, Sir William (1819-1905). **The Caliphate: Its Rise, Decline, and Fall.** New and rev. ed. by T. H. Weir. New York, AMS Press, 1975. (Repr. of 1924 ed.). 633p. bibliog. illus. index. LC 74-180365. ISBN 0-404-56305-8. LC cataloging n.a. The standard history for students until the past few years. Based on traditional sources, it is still useful.

Shaban, M. A. **The Abbasid Revolution.** Cambridge, England, Cambridge University Press, 1970. 181p. bibliog. LC 75-112474. ISBN 0-521-07849-0. DS 76.4.S44 1970. DDC 955'.9'02.

Shaban, M. A. **Islamic History, A.D. 600-750 (A.H. 132): A New Interpretation.** Cambridge, England, Cambridge University Press, 1971. 196p. bibliog. LC 79-145604. ISBN 0-521-08137-8. DS 38.5.S5. DDC 909'.09'7671. A controversial interpretation of selected aspects of early Islamic history, it is quite interesting for the more advanced reader.

al-Tabari (838?-923). **The Reign of al-Mu^ctasim (833-842).** Tr. from Arabic by Elma Marin. New Haven, American Oriental Society, 1951. 142p. bibliog. LC 51-8818. DS 234.T313. DDC 953.

Wellhausen, Julius (1844-1918). **The Arab Kingdom and Its Fall.** London, Curzon Press; distr. Totowa, N.J., Rowman & Littlefield, 1973. 591p. LC 73-764. ISBN 0-87471-174-6. DS 38.5.W4513 1973. DDC 953'.02. The standard work on the Omayyad period.

Bowen, Harold. **The Life and Times of ᶜAlī b. ᶜĪsā, the Good Vizier.** New York, AMS Press, 1975. (Repr. of 1928 ed.). 420p. illus. bibliog. LC 77-180320. ISBN 0-404-56215-9. DS 38.4.A53B68 1975. DDC 909'.09'7671[B]. A good portrait of the office of vizier (wazir).

106. Saunders, John Joseph. **The History of the Mongol Conquests.** London, Routledge & Kegan Paul, 1971. 275p. bibliog. index. $9.75. LC 72-883985. ISBN 0-7100-7073-X. DS 19.S27. DDC 950'.2.

[B, C1, S1] An excellent, well-researched and well-documented survey and analysis of the wave that swept the East and devastated Europe and the Near East during the Middle Ages. It also discusses the pre-Mongol Turks as background. It is the most recent general work on the subject. Written for the uninitiated educated general reader, it maintains a good balance of manageable quantities of detail and discreet generality. It includes useful discussions of the sources that will guide the reader seeking further information.

107. Saunders, John Joseph. **The Muslim World on the Eve of Europe's Expansion.** Englewood Cliffs, N.J., Prentice-Hall, 1966. 146p. bibliog. (A Spectrum Book. The Global History Series). o.p. LC 66-23442. DS 38.S36. DDC 909.09767.

A collection of excerpts on the fifteenth and sixteenth century Near East and Islamic world, including Africa, and the first contacts with the West, from primary and secondary works. Each selection is preceded by a brief introduction. It is not informative on specifics, but it introduces the reader to source materials, while the secondary excerpts discuss important points. For college libraries.

108. Setton, Kenneth Meyer, ed. **A History of the Crusades.** Madison, University of Wisconsin Press, 1969– . ca. 6v. bibliog. maps. index. v.1 and 2 only, $15.00 each vol. LC 68-9837. ISBN 0-299-04831-4(v.1); 0-299-04841-1(v.2). v.1-3 only, $25.00 each. ISBN 0-299-06670-3(v.3). D 157.S482. DDC 940.1'8.

[C2] A comprehensive systematic history consisting of chapters by various authorities. Each volume includes significant chapters on the history of the Islamic Empire at the time, and the Crusades from the Muslim standpoint. The maps are excellent. Volume 1 covers the first 100 years, volume 2 the period 1189 to 1311. A major work, which belongs in larger college collections.

109. Stewart, Desmond Stirling. **Early Islam.** New York, Time, Inc., 1967. 192p. bibliog. illus. index. (Great Ages of Man). o.p. LC 67-27863. D 199.3.S86. DDC 915.6.

[P1, C1] The history of the expansion of Islam and the medieval Islamic Empire; the basic tenets of Islam; highlights of Islamic civilization. The well-written text, useful bibliography, and especially the many excellent black and white and color illustrations of the architecture and minor arts of Islam make this a good first book for smaller libraries and the general reader.

110. Von Grunebaum, Gustave Edmund. **Classical Islam: A History, 600-1258.** Tr. from German. Chicago, Aldine Publishing Co., 1970. 243p. bibliog. index. $6.00. LC 78-75049. ISBN 0-202-15016-X. DS 38.3.V6413 1970b. DDC 909.09'767.

[C2, S2] An excellent general interpretation of the religious, cultural, political, social, and historical forces of the era as they interacted to influence the course of medieval Islamic history. This history is traced in its various stages, with much attention given to the relationships of the Islamic Empire to other empires, to Europe, and to the Eastern peoples. This book is less straight history than Saunders (item 105), which should be read first. Von Grunebaum was one of the top experts when the book was written, and it may be said to represent the culmination of his thinking after a lifetime of study. A basic book.

C. MEDIEVAL SPAIN UNDER THE MUSLIMS

111. Burckhardt, Titus. **Moorish Culture in Spain.** Tr. from German. New York, McGraw-Hill, 1972. 219p. bibliog. illus. index. $12.95. LC 73-148981. ISBN 0-07-008923-X. DP 103.B8713. DDC 914.6'06'927.

[P2, C1] A fairly comprehensive work which includes the sciences, religion, art and architecture, literature; chivalrous love as its concept developed among Spanish-Arab poets and other writers; recreation, philosophy, faith and science; Sufism; Moorish culture in Toledo and Granada. The photos and diagrams are quite useful. A brief, general introduction.

112. Chejne, Anwar G. **Muslim Spain: Its History and Culture.** Minneapolis, University of Minnesota Press, 1974. 559p. bibliog. index. $24.50. LC 73-87254. ISBN 0-8166-0688-9. DP 103.C35. DDC 914.6'03'2.

[B, P1, P2, C1, S1] The basic work on the subject, based on all available sources, which constitute but a part of what will eventually be usable for further research. The first 109 pages provide a survey of the history of the eight-century Muslim era. The rest of the 411-page text section discusses aspects of society and particularly the civilization: the social tensions existing in Muslim Spain; government and administration; the process by which Muslim civilization developed, including transfer from the Eastern Islamic Empire; education; Arabic and linguistic studies; literature; courtly love; history, geography and travel; the religious sciences; philosophy and mysticism; architecture, minor arts, and music; natural sciences; the Islamic legacy in Europe and its transmission. The 62 pages of notes and the 45-page bibliography are exceptionally useful and make this a handbook for further study. The author covers a vast range of material and successfully relates Spanish-Arabic civilization to the mainstream of Islamic civilization by constant references to Eastern works. He discusses the nature of the various fields of activity, tells why they developed as they did, and provides many details on important works and the writers and their world. A must for all libraries and students. The historical section is the book's weak point, and a detailed work on that subject is still necessary.

One aspect of considerable interest is discussed in:

Ashtor, Eliyahu. **The Jews of Muslim Spain.** Tr. from Hebrew. Philadelphia, Jewish Publication Society of America, 1973– . 2v. illus. LC 73-14081. ISBN 0-8276-0017-8 (v.1). DS 135.S7A8.

113. Dozy, Reinhart Pieter Anne (1820-1883). **Spanish Islam: A History of the Moslems in Spain.** Tr. from French. London, Frank Cass, 1972. (Repr. of 1913 ed.). 769p. bibliog. index. (Islam and the Muslim World, No. 12). $30.00. LC 72-196546. ISBN 0-7146-2128-5. DP 102.D7 1972. DDC 946'.004'927.

A political history to the latter part of the eleventh century. This is the standard work; however, the eleventh to fifteenth centuries have not been studied sufficiently even today, so most works deal with that period in an extremely inadequate fashion. In addition to a wealth of detail and some generalities and analysis, Dozy includes innumerable anecdotes about events, people, and society, taken from the primary sources. An interesting book even for the general reader. An up-to-date work in English is needed for any decent collection. The best work available is Evariste Lévi-Provençal, *Histoire de l'Espagne Musulmane* (Paris, G.-P. Maisonneuve et Larose, 1967. 3v.), of which it is said that it is unlikely anyone can say much more on the subject unless vast new primary sources are discovered; should a translation become available, it should be purchased by most collections.

114. Imamuddin, S. M. **A Political History of Muslim Spain.** Rev. and enl. ed. Dacca, Pakistan, Najmah Sons, 1969. 394p. bibliog. illus. LC 70-930354. DP 103.I4 1969. DDC 946'.02.

A factual account with some general discussion, this is the most recent detailed work in English. It is a useful, if very boring, introductory outline. Includes material on the Moriscos and a separate chapter on the Muslim administration. Not original research, but synthetic; weak where the research has been weak, especially for the latter period. For larger collections.

115 al-Maqqari, Aḥmad ibn Muhammad (d. 1631/1632). **The History of the Mohammedan Dynasties in Spain.** Extracted from the **Nafhu-t-tîb Min Ghusni-l-Ibni-l-Khattîb,** and tr. with notes by Pascual de Gayangos. New York, Johnson Reprint Co., 1969. (Repr. of 1840 ed.). 2v. $95.00. LC n.a. DP 101.M213.

Nafh al-Tib is a basic Arabic source for Muslim Spanish history and culture, especially Spanish-Arabic literature, being basically a compilation of material from other works arranged in chronological order. The first half consists of a history of Muslim Spain through the Christian *reconquista* and biographies of Muslim scholars in Spain, and Andalusian Muslim scholars who went East; the second half of the book is a biography of the great statesman Ibn al-Khatib. This translation omits the biography of Ibn al-Khatib, the biographies of the scholars who left Spain, and certain other material. The work begins with an extensive geographical and cultural description of Spain, with material on the structure and organization of the administration, literature and other written works produced there, and a history of the successive dynasties, with much on Cordova. It is larded with anecdotes on events and persons. A most interesting portrait of medieval Spain.

116. Watt, William Montgomery, and Pierre Cachia. **A History of Islamic Spain.** Edinburgh, Edinburgh University Press; distr. Chicago, Aldine Publishing Co., 1966. 210p. (Islamic Surveys, 4). $7.95. LC 66-2646. ISBN 0-202-15005-4. DS 36.85.I8 No. 4. DDC 946.02. Paperback: Garden City, N.Y., Doubleday, 1967. (Anchor Books A601).

[P1, C1, S1] An interpretive outline of the history of the Arab and Berber Muslims in Spain, with chapters on Arabic literature, Islamic civilization, and the intellectual artifacts of the era, and with brief, suggestive comments on their influence on Europe, particularly in the field of European Romantic and epic literature. Watt raises many questions that have yet to be answered definitely because there is much research yet to be done. It should be read after Hitti (item 88) and before Chejne (item 112).

D. 1800 TO THE PRESENT

We lack a good comprehensive work on the history of the nineteenth century. Despite the vast amount of research that remains to be done, a creditable work for students and the general reader could be produced with the material we have.

117. Antonius, George. **The Arab Awakening: The Story of the Arab National Movement.** Beirut, Lebanon, Librairie du Liban, 1970. 471p. index. LC n.a. DS 63.A5. DDC 950. Paperback: New York, Capricorn Books, 1965. (Repr. of 1946 ed.). 471p. (A Capricorn Book, CAP 118). $2.45. LC n.a. ISBN 0-399-50024-3.

[P1, C1, S1] The classic work on the growth of Arab nationalism and the independence movement from its genesis in the latter nineteenth century through the post-World War II and mandate periods. It details the history of the Arab secret societies, Arab resistance to the Turks, the Arab Revolt, Lawrence, the MacMahon-Husayn correspondence (which is included in the documentary appendix) as well as the other European dealings with the Arabs; the Peace Conference, the Mandates, and post-War developments throughout the area east of Egypt, including the development of the Palestine problem. It is the first well-researched account and remains the basic work today; it is detailed and comprehensive. It is outdated by new sources and research into those sources, but the new data have not been synthesized. This book is essentially a polemic: a plea to the conscience of the liberal English-speaking world against the French and the Zionists; it is a basic source of information, but it represents the authoritative Arab version of the events covered.

An essential collection of scholarly essays on the subject for more detailed study is:

Dawn, C. Ernest. **From Ottomanism to Arabism: Essays on the Origins of Arab Nationalism.** Urbana, University of Illinois Press, 1973. 212p. $8.95. LC 72-88953. ISBN 0-252-00202-4. DS 63.6.D38. DDC 320'5'4'09174927. Dawn is a long-time student of the topic; these items, which have been published previously, are based on solid research in the Arabic sources.

118. Be'eri, Eliezer. **Army Officers in Arab Politics and Society.** Tr. from Hebrew. New York, Praeger, 1970. 514p. tables. bibliog. index. o.p. LC 68-54318. SBN 269-67062-9. DS 62.8.B413.A70. 1970. DDC 322'4.

This work presents background, history, and analysis of coups and politics in the Arab countries (excluding the four North African countries), free officer movements, etc. It then analyzes and generalizes about the social origins and motivations of the officer classes in each country and their ideologies; the structure of the military governments and societies, etc. It adds much to Hurewitz (item 122), to which it is complementary. Be'eri is an Israeli and his Israeli biases, which border on the anti-Arab, are evident in a variety of ways. It is otherwise grievously faulted as well, but however much these faults vitiate the book's reliability, it is still well worth reading. Be'eri and Hurewitz are useful primarily as additional sources of information on Arab politics and government. Part of the origin of both books lies in the search for a theory of the military coups that seized control of so many Third World nations, and the resulting fad among political scientists who sought to fit facts and generalities in their usual disciplinary procrustean beds. The attempt at a scientific approach is valid, of course, but as far as this observer can see little has come of the effort, at least with regard to the Near East— few additional monographs have been written on the subject. One of the problems is that we have so few sources to work with, and field work to obtain substantive information is difficult, if not impossible, to arrange in these countries. Therefore, speculation is a must; it often goes too far, but it somehow has been found acceptable in academia. Another problem is that many of the political scientists have studied theory and perhaps history, but they show no appreciation of the basic factor in these countries—the people, whatever class. However much lip-service they pay to social processes, they usually do not have the necessary background in ethnology, anthropology, and sociology as applied to the region to make valid judgments about Near Easterners' motivations and actual political dynamics. This is a gross generality to make about a group of scholars, but the notable exceptions such as Waterbury (item 1075) somehow seem to prove the adequacy of this rule of thumb. Students must be aware of this when reading the political science works listed in this *Guide.* The most detailed historical study is Haddad, George Meri, *Revolutions and Military Rule in the Middle East* (New York, Robert Speller, 1965-1973. 3v. LC 65-20537. ISBN 0-8315-0060-3[v.2]. DS 63.H26. DDC 320.9'56'04). Volume 1, which concerns Turkey, Iran, and Afghanistan, and volume 3, dealing with Egypt, Sudan, Yemen, and Libya are thin and offer little. However, volume 2, which treats Iraq, Syria, Lebanon and Jordan, offers much information rarely, if at all, available anyplace else, and a wealth of detail. But beware of his value judgments and his opinions of the ancient regime, of which he was a member.

119. Conference on the Beginnings of Modernization in the Middle East in the Nineteenth Century, University of Chicago, 1966. **Beginnings of Modernization in the Middle East: The Nineteenth Century.** Ed. by William R. Polk and Richard L. Chambers. Chicago, University of Chicago Press, 1968. 427p. bibliog. notes. index. (Publications of the Center for Middle Eastern Studies, No. 1). $12.75. LC 68-16712. ISBN 0-226-67425-8. DS 42.C6. DDC 309.1'56.

A collection of interesting papers by top experts on social, political, ideological, and cultural changes in the nineteenth century, noting the effects of Western intervention and penetration as colonial powers. They also deal with economics, urbanization, the processes and history of the Westernizing movements, and the position of women. Several of the 20 items are sufficiently general in nature to be most helpful to college collections, but most are rather technical for the beginner. There is little else available conveniently; they fill in some gaps in existing general works, and they indicate some of the directions of current research on this fascinating subject.

120. Haim, Sylvia G., ed. **Arab Nationalism: An Anthology.** Berkeley, University of California Press, 1974. (Repr. of 1962 ed.). 255p. bibliog. (California Library Reprint Series, 55). $12.75. LC n.a. ISBN 0-520-02645-4. DS 63.H27. DDC 956.

[P1, P2, C1, S1]   The best single work on the origin and history of Arab nationalist ideology, with a 72-page introduction that is the best survey available. Also included are 20 basic Arab statements, most translated from Arabic. It should be noted that these are all statements from the older "liberal" generation. They are relevant, but much less directly so now than previously, because the old ideas have not produced anything concrete, and Leftist-Marxist ideology has increasingly come to dominate the debate. These older "liberal" and "conservative" versions are now important but retreating, even vestigial, residues in what is now a transitional period. To be read in conjunction with Hourani (item 121) and Khadduri (item 126). A basic work for public and college collections.

See also:

Nuseibeh, Hazem Zaki. **The Ideas of Arab Nationalism.** Port Washington, N.Y., Kennikat Press, 1972. (Repr. of 1956 ed.). 227p. LC 78-153234. ISBN 0-8046-1544-6. DS 38.N87 1972. DDC 320.5'4'09174927.

121. Hourani, Albert Habib. **Arabic Thought in the Liberal Age, 1798-1939.** London, Oxford University Press, 1962. 403p. bibliog. index. o.p. LC 63-185. JA 84.A6H6. DDC 320. 953. Paperback: (Oxford Paperbacks, 197). $3.75. LC 70-595206. ISBN 0-19-285039-3.

[P1, P2, C1, S1] Putting his material into its historical context, Hourani details the modernization of Arab thinking, particularly political ideas—in their legal, religious, ethnicist, and sociological manifestations. He traces the adoption of Western ideas, the specific content of those ideas, the approaches each writer used, the background for the specific reactions of each and the ideas that resulted; the lives of the writers. This book provides the details for the generalities found in Lewis (item 127) and Sharabi (item 135), etc. A basic work for readers with background obtained from general works listed in this *Guide*, including Rosenthal (item 539), and for all but the smallest collections.

See also:

Abu-Lughod, Ibrahim. **Arab Discovery of Europe: A Study in Cultural Encounters.** Princeton, N.J., Princeton University Press, 1963. 188p. LC 62-21102. PJ 25.P7 no. 22 [DS 63.A25 1963]. DDC 956. A study of the nineteenth century Arab travellers to Europe, their reactions, the Western books translated into Arabic, books written about Europe. A basic source on the process by which European civilization infiltrated the Arab world.

Kerr, Malcolm H. **Islamic Reform: The Political and Legal Theories of Muḥammad cAbduh and Rashīd Riḍā.** Berkeley, University of California Press, 1966. 249p. LC 65-24177. LC class: LAW. DDC 340.

al-Husry, Khaldun Sati. **Three Reformers: A Study in Modern Arab Political Thought.** Beirut, Khayats, 1966. 176p. bibliog. LC NE 66-1117. JC 49.H35. DDC 320.01. Deals with al-Ṭahṭāwi, Khayr al-Din al-Tūnisi, and al-Kawākibi.

122. Hurewitz, Jacob Coleman. **Middle East Politics: The Military Dimension.** New York, Octagon Books, 1974. (Repr. of 1969 ed.). 550p. bibliog. LC 73-22034. ISBN 0-374-94059-2. DS 62.8.H8 1974. DDC 320.9'56'04. Paperback: Praeger University Series, U-660. $3.95. LC 68-30937.

[C1, S2] A history of Near Eastern politics emphasizing the military participation in government—coups, Arab-Israeli conflict, arms races. It begins with generalities on the background: the Islamic legacy, European ruling styles and their influence on politics and armies in the region. Then follows a survey of individual countries, followed by more generalities such as the military and social change processes and U.S. policy options. Much that is negative might be said about this work, particularly its origin in an academic ivory tower environment—i.e., it is not based on field work but relies on the literature and various other sources, and it shows this clearly—and its lack of profundity. However, it brings together much information and supplements the usual textbooks. To be used in conjunction with Be'eri (item 118).

123. Ismael, Tareq Y. **Governments and Politics of the Contemporary Middle East.** Homewood, Ill., Dorsey Press, 1970. 495p. bibliog. index. (The Dorsey Series in Political Science). $10.50. LC 78-112831. DS 62.8.I83. DDC 320.9'56.

[P1, C1, S1] An introductory work that includes a number of chapters written by well-known, highly qualified authorities. Introductory chapters treat the legacies of Islam and nationalism; current ideological trends (nationalism, socialism, communism) and modernization. The rest of the book consists of chapters on individual countries. It does *not* include North Africa. There is some material on non-political government activities, especially economic and social policy; as in most books, the formal governmental structures and administration are treated insufficiently or ignored altogether, since the emphasis is on political history. The chapter bibliographies are quite useful. It is well paired up with Peretz (item 130), though either book will serve as well by itself. A basic book.

124. Karpat, Kemal H., ed. **Political and Social Thought in the Contemporary Middle East.** New York, Praeger, 1968. 397p. bibliog. index. $10.00; $3.95pa. LC 68-4168. JA 84. N18K3 1968. DDC 320.9'56.

A collection of Arabic (296 p.), Turkish (77 p.), and Persian (16 p.) writings on nationalism, Islamic modernism and socialism; Arab socialism and its relationship to nationalism; communism and capitalism and the Arab left; Arab unity and ideology; Turkish ideology, Ataturkism, and nationalism. Each item has an introduction, as does each main section. Most items are of 1959-1963 vintage, and thus represent only a brief period; with regard to the Arab selections in particular, one cannot determine whether these items represent the honest ideas of the writers or Egyptian and other propaganda and government doctrines, especially since they were written during a period of intense ideological inter-Arab propaganda. This problem of representativeness somewhat limits the book's usefulness, though it does suggest the published ideas of the period. It is to be purchased and used only along with other collections or more representative material, and general works on the subjects included.
See also:

Binder, Leonard. **The Ideological Revolution in the Middle East.** New York, Wiley, 1964. 287p. LC 64-17132. DS 63.B5. DDC 320.956. Essays on various aspects, for the advanced student.

Hanna, Sami A., and George H. Gardner. **Arab Socialism: A Documentary Study.** Leiden, E. J. Brill, 1969. 418p. LC 72-416099. HX 434.A6H34. DDC 335'.009171'65. Scholarly substantive essays by the authors, plus several translations of basic works from Arabic.

Agwani, Mohammed Shafi. **Communism in the Arab East.** New York, Asia Publishing House, 1969. 259p. bibliog. LC 72-17772. HX 435.A6A68. DDC 335.43'09171'65.

Laqueur, Walter Ze'ev. **Communism and Nationalism in the Middle East.** New York, Praeger, 1957. 375p. bibliog. index. LC 58-3256. DS 63.L35 1957. DDC 956.

Salama, A. M. Said. **Arab Socialism.** By Abdel Moghny Said. New York, Barnes & Noble, 1972. 136p. LC 73-163868. ISBN 0-06-496069-2. HX 442.S245 1972B. DDC 335'. 00917'4927.

125. Kerr, Malcolm H. **The Arab Cold War: Gamal ᶜAbd al-Nāṣir and His Rivals, 1958-1970.** 3rd ed. London, Oxford University Press, 1971. 166p. (Galaxy Book GB 358). $1.95pa. LC 74-171045. ISBN 0-19-501475-8. DS 63.1.K47 1971. DDC 320.9'174'927.

[P1, P2, C1, S1] A standard work (by a leading Arabist) for the general reader and student. It traces inter-Arab relations chronologically, in sweeping, general terms. A basic work which, though less detailed, can be considered a sequel to Seale (item 930); it should be read after a more general work.

126. Khadduri, Majid. **Political Trends in the Arab World: The Role of Ideas and Ideals in Politics.** Baltimore, The Johns Hopkins Press, 1970. 298p. index. $11.00; $3.00pa. LC 79-112361. ISBN 0-8018-1122-8; 0-8018-1440-5pa. JA 84.A6K5. DDC 320.9'174'927.

[P1, P2, C1, S1] An introductory survey of main currents in Arab political thought emphasizing nationalism, socialism, communism, Arab socialism, constitutionalism and democracy, and Islam as a socio-political order. Each topic is subdivided into subtrends. Key thinkers are discussed in a clear style comprehensible to the general reader. Khadduri covers some material found in other works listed in this *Guide*, but he treats it more concisely and includes additional material. To be read after the appropriate chapters of general works such as Ismael (item 123). Unfortunately, the book's coverage stops about 15 years short of where it should have, particularly since there is little or nothing of substance available on the period leading into the present, which is a transitional phase of Arab thought. Khadduri virtually ignores the new left, non-Baathist socialism, and the reams of books on socialism that appeared in Egypt in the 1960s.

This book should be read strictly for its discussion of the ideas, which were mainly those of the intellectuals and not of the masses or the practicing politicians, who were primarily motivated by other considerations, such as self-interest. Since there is no discussion of the mundane factors, it is impossible for the author to weigh adequately the actual relative importance of the ideas as moving factors in the region, and he makes no attempt to do so. This is a typical failing on the part of most books in the field, partly because precise information is so difficult, if not impossible, to come by. This is especially true since politicians are not going to admit that their behavior deviates from the ideal or allow outsiders to have material that could be used against them. Even if some indication of the non-ideological factors was available in specific form, it would be hard to measure the influence of each factor, relative to the others. Despite the fact that this should be obvious, and that without this measurement one's political analysis is inadequate, the disciplinary works in the field do not admit it, so the student must constantly be conscious of the fact that the image of Near Eastern politics he will have after reading most of the works in this *Guide* is a grossly distorted caricature of reality.

127. Lewis, Bernard. **The Middle East and the West.** Bloomington, Indiana University Press, 1964. 160p. bibliog. index. $5.50. LC 64-10830. ISBN 0-253-15270-4. DS 63.L44. DDC 956. Paperback: Harper Torch Books, The Academic Library, TB 1274. $1.95. ISBN 0-06-131274-6.

[P1, C1, S1] After defining the Near East in terms of its geography, history, religion, languages and cultures, Lewis masterfully suggests the Western impact on the region and its reaction: the quest for independence; ideas of patriotism and nationalism; the Islamic reaction; reform and modernism; the involvement of the Near East in world affairs. An effective and stimulating evocation of the processes involved in the intellectual changes that occurred as the area began to enter the modern world. To be read after one of the introductory works such as Ismael (item 123) and before works such as Hourani (item 121) and Khadduri (item 126). For all libraries and students.

Lewis is illuminated by Hans Kohn's classic works. The famous student of nationalism was a journalist in the region during the 1920s, and he makes vivid to the general reader the problems and processes of modernization and Westernization, the rise and nature of nationalism, and the imperialism to which nationalism was a reaction.

See also:

Kohn, Hans. **Western Civilization in the Near East.** New York, Columbia University Press, 1936. 329p. LC 37-23489. CB 251.K62.

Kohn, Hans. **A History of Nationalism in the East.** Grosse Pointe, Mich., Scholarly Press, 1969. (Repr. of 1929 ed.). 476p. LC 77-5655. D 463.K63 1969. DDC 320.9'5.

Kohn, Hans. **Nationalism and Imperialism in the Hither East.** New York, Howard Fertig, 1969. (Repr. of 1932 ed.). 339p. LC 68-9622. D 463.K6453 1969. DDC 956.

128. Lutskii, V. B. **Modern History of the Arab Countries.** Tr. from Russian. Moscow, Progress Publishers, 1969. 422p. LC 72-485278. DS 62.4.L8713.

This posthumously compiled composite work by a foremost Russian expert deals mainly with the period of the latter eighteenth century through 1918. It is the only full-length, systematic treatment of the period that concentrates on internal developments, though the international events that most Western histories stress are also discussed, particularly when the economic and other impact of European "imperialism" is dealt with. Generally the selection and presentation of the facts is reasonably straightforward, except that there is much information on economics and social relations, a predictable Marxist interest. The Marxist orientation does not operate as a straitjacket but in fact offers the reader a different perspective, which is often helpful. The book is not laden with jargon and is written in a manner that makes it accessible to the general reader who has read Holt (item 76). Though variously faulted and demanding careful critical reading, it may be considered a basic work for the more serious reader.

129. Macdonald, Robert W. **The League of Arab States: A Study in the Dynamics of Regional Organization.** Princeton, N.J., Princeton University Press, 1965. 407p. bibliog. index. $12.00; $2.95pa. LC 65-10832. ISBN 0-691-03034-0; 0-619-00003-4pa. DS 36.2.M3. DDC 341.18.

This is the only English work on the League. It covers its decision-making processes, activities, functions of its various organs, administrative organization (both theory and reality); policy-making and execution; programs (including trade and other economic aspects); cultural, social, and technological programs; collective security and dispute settlement; interaction with other international activities and organizations. Not a very sophisticated study, and it is rather general, in addition to which the author does not include a systematic study of the League's history; all this limits its usefulness, but we have nothing else.

130. Peretz, Don. **The Middle East Today.** 2nd ed. New York, Holt, Rinehart and Winston, 1971. 496p. bibliog. index. $9.95. LC 73-135127. ISBN 0-03-085556-X. DS 62.8.P45 1971. DDC 915.6.

[P1, C1, S1] The standard survey of the twentieth century Near East by a well-known specialist and educator, used as a college textbook but useful for any student. After initial chapters on nineteenth century background and general aspects of history, ideology, etc., the various countries are discussed individually. May usefully be read in conjunction with Ismael (item 123). Excludes North Africa (but includes Egypt).

131. **Political Dynamics in the Middle East.** Ed. by Paul Y. Hammond and Sidney S. Alexander. New York, American Elsevier Publishing Co., 1972. 666p. index. (The Middle East: Economic and Political Problems and Prospects). $19.50. LC 71-161688. ISBN 0-444-00110-7. DS 63.1.P65. DDC 320.9'56'04.

[P1, C1, C2, S1, S2] An excellent collection of Rand-Resources for the Future studies by top expert , analysing the background and contemporary politics, with a strong emphasis on prognosis of the prospects for the 1970s. Mainly analytical in nature, the essays are a first-rate, stimulating, and very knowledgeable supplement to the standard systematic works. They include studies of individual countries, the Arab-Israeli conflict, and aspects of international relations of the region. The emphasis on problems and policy alternatives renders the book somewhat ephemeral for smaller collections, but it is a useful addition to larger collections and a must for collections backing up courses on the twentieth century and for students of the period.

132. Polk, William Roe. **The United States and the Arab World.** 3rd ed. Cambridge, Mass., Harvard University Press, 1975. 478p. bibliog. index. (The American Foreign Policy Library). $15.00. LC 74-80440. ISBN 0-674-92718-4. DS 39.P64 1975.

[P1, C1, S1] This book is a good description and history of the Arab countries, emphasizing the twentieth century, with much on the nineteenth century and on the social-political-intellectual-economic forces operating in the region. It is concluded by a 90-page section containing the history of U.S. policy, a critique of recent policy, and suggested guidelines for the future. An able interpretation by a top Arabist and ex-State Department official. The partly annotated bibliography is quite useful.
Other useful works include:

Beling, Willard A. **Pan-Arabism and Labor.** Cambridge, Mass., Harvard University Press, 1960. 127p. bibliog. LC 60-15082. HD 6800.5.B4. DDC 331.88094.

Izzedin, Nejla Mustapha. **The Arab World: Past, Present and Future.** Chicago, Henry Regnery, 1954. 412p. LC 53-9624. DS 49.I9. DDC 953.

Kimche, Jon. **The Second Arab Awakening.** New York, Holt, Rinehart and Winston, 1970. 288p. LC 76-80364. ISBN 0-03-081852-4. DS 62.8.K54 1970b.

Kimche, Jon. **Seven Fallen Pillars: The Middle East, 1915-1952.** New York, Praeger, 1953. 439p. LC 53-5307. DS 62.K52. DS 953. Kimche is a long-time observer of Near Eastern affairs, and his books are quite interesting reading for all.

Koury, Enver M. **The Patterns of Mass Movements in Arab Revolutionary Progressive States.** The Hague, Mouton, 1970. 308p. LC 76-110953. HN 766.A8 K65. An application of current political and sociological theories to the Arab world; a hash with little internal or theoretical coherence, insufficiently thought out, but useful nonetheless as food for thought for the knowledgeable non-expert.

Special attention is deserved by two collections of essays by Elie Kedouri:

The Chatham House Version and Other Middle Eastern Studies. New York, Praeger, 1970. 488p. LC 72-97184. DS 62.4.K4 1970b. DDC 956.

Elie Kedouri. **Arabic Political Memoirs and Other Studies.** London, Frank Cass; distr. Portland, Ore., International Scholarly Book Services, 1974. 327p. LC 73-93913. ISBN 0-7146-3041-1. DDC n.a. Both collections focus on twentieth century regional politics, including the politics of individual countries, and European diplomatic activities. They are based on original sources and are well documented—indeed, they are most useful sources of bibliographic items for the student. They are written with a fairly sharp bite, reflecting Kedouri's jaundiced view of things; he delights in debunking the cherished assumptions of the Near Eastern Studies establishment. Many of the items deal with subjects of considerable interest. These two books are to be treasured by the advanced student in need of facts, or the initiated student in need of stimulation, for the sheer pleasure of the enlightening reading they offer.

An interesting work for the general reader on the kings of Arabia, Jordan, and Iraq is:

Morris, Jan. **The Hashemite Kings.** New York, Pantheon, 1959. 208p. LC 59-8585. DS 247.H46 M6. DDC 956.9.

133. Sachar, Howard Morley. **The Emergence of the Middle East, 1914-1924.** New York, Alfred A. Knopf, 1969. 518p. bibliog. index. $12.50. LC 76-79349. ISBN 0-394-44754-9. DS 62.9.S23 1969. DDC 956.

[B, P1, C1, S1] An interesting, well-written survey of World War I and the post-War period during which the political geography and socio-political-economic dynamics of the modern Near East were shaped. The best work for the general reader and beginning student, detailing battles, politics, and diplomacy. It generally avoids the usual historical controversies, and it is not technical in its scholarship. The 31-page bibliography is very useful. It should be noted that Sachar has his own conclusions with which some will disagree. Also, the book has various methodological falws and a tendency to let style overcome strict accuracy in its statements of cause-effect relations and other generalities. However, this in no way detracts from its qualities as a fascinating introduction to a most important period.

The British Foreign Office records and other documents for the period were opened only in the late 1960s, and they have revealed much that was only speculated on previously. The following books provide more details on the diplomacy of the period; the most recent ones are based on British archives.

Busch, Briton Cooper. **Britain, India and the Arabs, 1914-1921.** Berkeley, University of California Press, 1971. 522p. bibliog. LC 71-132421. ISBN 0-520-01821-4. DS 63.2.G7 B85 1971. DDC 327.42'056.

Friedman, Isaiah. **The Question of Palestine, 1914-1918: British-Jewish-Arab Relations.** London, Routledge & Kegan Paul, 1973. 433p. bibliog. LC 73-179574. ISBN 0-7100-7622-3. DS 125.5.F73. DDC 956.94'001.

Kedourie, Elie. **England and the Middle East: The Destruction of the Ottoman Empire, 1914-1921.** London, Bowes & Bowes, 1956. 236p. bibliog. LC 56-4094. DR 588.K4. DDC 327.420956.

Klieman, Aaron S. **Foundations of British Policy in the Arab World: The Cairo Conference of 1921.** Baltimore, Johns Hopkins Press, 1970. 322p. bibliog. LC 73-103613. ISBN 0-8018-1125-2. DS 63.2.G7K58. DDC 327.42'056.

Nevakivi, Jukka. **Britain, France and the Arab Middle East, 1914-1920.** London, Athlone, 1969. 284p. LC 77-400670. ISBN 0-485-17113-9. DS 63.2.G7N4 1969. DDC 327.42'056.

Zeine, Zeine N. **The Emergence of Arab Nationalism: With a Background Study of Arab-Turkish Relations in the Near East.** 3rd ed. Delmar, N.Y., Caravan Books, 1973. 192p. LC 76-39576. ISBN 0-88206-000-7. DS 63.6.Z44 1973. DDC 327.496'1'056.

Zeine, Zeine N. **The Struggle for Arab Independence: Western Diplomacy & the Rise and Fall of Faisal's Kingdom in Syria.** Beirut, Khayat's, 1960. 297p. LC A 61-142. DS 98.Z4.

Two books from the perspective of the Ottoman Empire and Central Powers are:

Trumpener, Ulrich. **Germany and the Ottoman Empire, 1914-1918.** Princeton, N.J., Princeton University Press, 1968. 433p. bibliog. index. LC 68-10395. DD 120.G3 T7. DDC 327.43'0561. Based on German archives, this is a detailed study of various aspects, mainly from a German perspective; topical treatment, not straight chronological narrative.

Weber, Frank G. **Eagles and Crescent: Germany, Austria and the Diplomacy of the Turkish Alliance, 1914-1918.** Ithaca, Cornell University Press, 1970. 284p. bibliog. LC 70-109339. ISBN 0-8014-0566-1. D 566.W37. DDC 327.43'0561.

134. Sachar, Howard Morley. **Europe Leaves the Middle East, 1936-1954.** New York, Alfred A. Knopf, 1972. 752p. bibliog. index. $15.00. LC 72-2157. ISBN 0-394-46064-2. DS 63.S2. DDC 956'.03.

[P1, C1, S1] A survey of the history and politics of the period in which the positions of Britain and France in the region began to decline, emphasizing British-French policies rather than local Near Eastern politics. It discusses the rise of local nationalist resistance, the threats posed by Russia and the Axis, World War II battles, and the circumstances governing the development of British-French positions, the implementation of their policy, and the process of withdrawal after World War II. It has much on the Palestine conflict, treating it in a generally fair and useful manner that helps the reader understand the problem. An extremely well-written and interesting comprehensive account basic for all collections, and a must for students who have read one or more of the general introductions to twentieth century Near Eastern history. The same general comments on the author's approach and methods apply to this book as to item 133.

Other essential books on the period are:

Hirszowicz, Łukasz. **The Third Reich and the Arab East.** Tr. from Polish. London, Routledge & Kegan Paul, 1966. 403p. LC 66-73886. DS 63.2.G4H53. DDC 327.43056.

Survey of International Affairs, Wartime Series. London, Oxford University Press, 0000. LC 25-22280 rev. 3. D 442.S8. Vol. 2, **The Middle East in the War,** by George Kirk. 1952. Vol. 5, **The Middle East, 1945-1950,** by George Kirk. 1954.

135. Sharabi, Hisham Bashir. **Arab Intellectuals and the West: The Formative Years, 1875-1914.** Baltimore, The Johns Hopkins Press, 1970. 139p. index. $7.95. LC 78-108384. ISBN 0-8018-1142-2. DS 36.8.S5 1970. DDC 001.2'09'174927.

[C2, S2] An interpretive essay on the Arab response to the penetration of Western civilization and ideas: the challenge and response; Islamic reformism; Christian intellectualism and Western nationalism and socialism; Muslim secularism; the political manifestations of these responses. It explores the ideas, the mechanics of penetration, the individuals and the psychology of their response; it does so more analytically and with different emphases, as well as more briefly, than Hourani (item 121) and Khadduri (item 126).

136. Sharabi, Hisham Bashir. **Nationalism and Revolution in the Arab World (The Middle East and North Africa).** Princeton, N.J., D. Van Nostrand, 1966. 176p. bibliog. (New Perspectives in Political Science). $2.95pa. LC 66-1254. ISBN 0-442-07525-1. DS 38.S44. DDC 320.9174927.

[P1, C1, S1] A handbook on the ideology, politics, and institutions of the Arab world, and an extremely useful glossary of Arabic political and ideological terminology (103 p.). The rest of the book is a collection of brief excerpts from statements, speeches, and constitutions, which illustrate the author's points. Includes Arabism and Islam, the heritage of European domination, the systems of power that have developed in the region; the coups d'état; socialism and revolutionism; revolutionary ideology. A useful introduction that is still relevant despite being somewhat out of date.

137. Stewart, Desmond Stirling. **The Middle East: Temple of Janus.** London, H. Hamilton, 1972. 432p. bibliog. index. £4.00. LC n.a. ISBN 0-241-02135-9. DS 62.4.S73. DDC 956.

The author is a well-known popularizer of Near Eastern subjects, a translator of Arabic literature into English, and a journalist of wide contacts and experience in the Near East. The book deals with Egypt from the time the Suez Canal opened (1869), the Ottoman Empire, British rule in the region, and the Arab-Israeli conflict. The aim, apparently, is to suggest and evoke the feel of key currents in the flow of modern Near Eastern history; it does so with an inconsistent degree of detail on the various subjects dealt with. It is not comprehensive in its historical coverage, and for the most part it just mentions in passing subjects such as Iraq, Syria, and the French role. It is thoroughly interesting and extremely well written. There are many vignettes and impressionistic images of key individuals such as the Egyptian kings, Nasser, Ataturk, the British viceroys in Egypt and Iraq, Lawrence, Gertrude Bell, etc., which put them into sharp perspective. Worth reading in conjunction with other works. It suggests ideas that help the reader understand other countries, which are hardly touched on but which participated in and were swept by the forces treated herein. For the initiated reader.

V. INTERNATIONAL RELATIONS

There are a number of glaring lacunae in this field which libraries should fill when the necessary books become available. A number of specialized works exist, but we still need general treatments of nineteenth and twentieth century British and French policy (there is no detailed study of French policy, while the works on twentieth century British policy and relations are stopgaps). We need more detailed works on Russian and Soviet dealings with the region. American relations are given considerable attention in this *Guide.* The information that Americans have on this important subject should be as complete as possible, since this is where a knowledge of the region directly relates to them and to their welfare. Unfortunately, there is no comprehensive work on our relations with the region since 1939; we need a book on our relations during the 1960s and a much better book on the 1950s than we have. Books on relations of individual countries in the region are found in the country listings, except that all books on U.S. relations with individual countries are located in Section V (E–United States Relations).

A. GENERAL

138. Anderson, M. S. **The Eastern Question, 1774-1923: A Study in International Relations.** London, Macmillan, 1966. bibliog. index. (Papermacs). £2.25pa. LC 66-13896. ISBN 0-333-03781-2. D 371.A43 1966. DDC 949.6.

[B, P1, C1, S1] This is the best survey of the extremely complex story of European diplomacy and war in the Near East, and the Near Eastern aspects of intra-European rivalries. It is hard reading, but it rewards careful study because the material is well organized and effectively presented. The extensive bibliography makes it a good handbook for research. A basic book for college libraries and all students.

See also:

Daniel, Norman. **Islam, Europe and Empire.** Edinburgh, Edinburgh University Press, 1966. 619p. bibliog. illus. LC 65-22498. DS 63.D3. DDC 301.29'1767'04. European attitudes toward the Near East and Islam, including political and religious views, the discovery of the ancient Near Eastern antiquities, etc.

Hoskins, Halford Lancaster. **British Routes to India.** New York, Octagon Books, 1966. (Repr. of 1928 ed.). 494p. LC 66-22691. HF 3508.I6 H6 1966. DDC 380.09. A detailed history of British interests in the region and their political, economic, and exploration activities from the eighteenth century to the latter nineteenth century, including the international politics and concerns for the communications with the Empire in India. Emphasizes the role and development of the various means of communication–Suez Canal, Euphrates river boats, overland routes, telegraph, railroads. Interesting to all readers.

Boahan, A. Adu. **Britain, the Sahara and the Western Sudan, 1788-1861.** Oxford, Clarendon Press, 1964. 268p. LC 64-54602. DT 356.B57. DDC 327.420661. Expeditions to Timbuctoo and sub-Maghreb regions; the slave trade; role of British consuls in Tunis, etc.; how interest in the region percolated among the British public.

Marlowe, John. **Perfidious Albion: The Origins of Anglo-French Rivalry in the Levant.** London, Elek, 1971. 323p. bibliog. LC 73-886510. ISBN 0-236-15425-7. DS 62.9.M37. DDC 327.42'044. A detailed diplomatic history for advanced students; too often, however, the details overpower one's sense of the whole.

139. Fitzsimons, Matthew A. **Empire by Treaty: Britain and the Middle East in the Twentieth Century.** Notre Dame, Ind., University of Notre Dame Press, 1964. 235p. index. $6.00. LC 64-15439. ISBN 0-268-00088-3. DS 63.2.G7F5. DDC 327.42056.

[C1, S2]   Covers British relations with the region after World War I, to 1958, with an epilog to the early 1960s. Neither profound nor definitive, it is a useful survey of British attempts to secure Britain's position in an era of declining power and influence, in the face of an increasingly dominant regional nationalism actively opposed to Western presence. Based on the press, parliamentary documents, and secondary sources, it fills a gap, providing more detail than Monroe (item 145), but it needs replacement by a more deeply researched and up-to-date work.

140. Howard, Harry Nicholas. **The Partition of Turkey: A Diplomatic History, 1913-1923.** New York, Howard Fertig, 1966. (Repr. of 1931 ed.). 486p. bibliog. $14.50. LC 66-24347. DR 584.H6 1966. DDC 956.101.

[P1, C1, S2]   Still the standard work on the subject. It includes background, economic aspects, alliances of Turkey and her entrance into World War I on Germany's side, Balkan diplomacy, the Lausanne Conference, and much on the European diplomacy involved. The vast amount of more recent research has not been synthesized in a work to supersede it, though this probably could be done fairly readily. It is so detailed that Anderson (item 138) should be read first for orientation. For the general reader, Sachar (item 133) will suffice, though it puts less emphasis on diplomacy.
  A study based on extensive research is:

Helmreich, Paul C. **From Paris to Sèvres: The Partition of the Ottoman Empire at the Peace Conference of 1919-1920.** Columbus, Ohio State University Press, 1974. 376p. bibliog. index. LC 73-12812. D651.T9 H44. ISBN 0-8142-0170-9.

141. Ismael, Tareq Y. **The Middle East in World Politics: A Study in Contemporary International Relations.** Syracuse, N.Y., Syracuse University Press, 1974. 297p. bibliog. $12.00; $5.00pa. LC 73-16637. ISBN 0-8156-0101-8; 0-8156-0102-6pa. DS 62.8.I84. DDC 327.56.

[P1, C1, S1]   A basic text which updates Lenczowski (item 144) and others. It covers the relations of Britain, France, the USSR, China, Africa, and the U.S. with the Near East; the U.N. and the region; internal sources of Near Eastern foreign policy; the region as a subordinate system in global politics. Chapters, a few of which are written by other scholars, contain some historical background but deal mainly with the post-1945 period. It is unfortunate that there is no chapter on the Near East in Third World politics, nor detailed chapters on the pre-1945 period. The quality of the chapters varies; topics are handled in an inconsistent manner, and some of the chapters are disappointing. However, the book brings together basic topics and is a useful introduction to the subject.
  See also:

Beling, Willard A. **The Middle East: Quest for an American Policy.** Albany, State University of New York Press, 1973. 347p. LC 73-4281. ISBN 0-87395-228-6; 0-87395-229-4 (microfiche). DS 119.7.M472 1973. DDC 327.73'056.   Fourteen excellent essays providing a variety of disciplinary and theoretical approaches to the international relations and interactions of the region, with main emphasis on the Arab-Israeli conflict. Several chapters (fewer than half) deal with U.S. policy, though all deal with *factors* the U.S. faces in formulating its policy.

Masry, Youssef el. **The Arab Role in Africa.** By J. Baulin [pseud.]. Baltimore, Penguin Books, 1962. 143p. LC 62-51100 rev. DT 176.M34. DDC 961.

Khalili, Joseph E. **Communist China's Interaction with the Arab Nationalists Since the Bandung Conference.** New York, Exposition Press, 1970. 121p. LC 73-126369. ISBN 0-682-47115-1. DS 63.2.C5K5. DDC 327.51'0174'927.

A textbook similar in form to Ismael's is:

Marayati, Abid A. **International Relations of the Middle East.** Cambridge, Mass., Schenckman Publishing Co., 1975 (forthcoming).

142. Laqueur, Walter Ze'ev. **The Soviet Union and the Middle East.** New York, Praeger, 1959. 366p. bibliog. index. o.p. LC 59-7304. DS 63.2.R9L3. DDC 327.47056.

  The standard work on the subject for the period 1917-1958. It deals mainly with Soviet attitudes toward the region as manifested in Russian writings, how they developed, their relation to communist theory, internal debates on the proper policy toward the Third World countries, Soviet press reactions and views, regional diplomacy, and the politics of international forums. Laqueur's sources are from the public record, and the depth of his discussion varies, sometimes remaining superficial. Its account and evaluation of Russian-Middle Eastern diplomatic and other relations is not detailed enough, partly because of insufficient sources (though Laqueur could have done more with available material); it does not provide what most readers will want. But it is the best we have for the period.

143. Laqueur, Walter Ze'ev. **The Struggle for the Middle East: The Soviet Union and the Middle East, 1958-1970.** Baltimore, Penguin Books, 1972. 267p. $1.65pa. LC 72-169359. ISBN 0-14-021393-7. DS 63.2.R9L32 1972. DDC 327.47'056.

[P1, C1, S1]   A systematic survey (using Russian, Arabic, and other sources) of Russian relations with the individual countries of the region, including foreign aid and ideological aspects. The treatment and analysis are superficial, but the outline of facts and trends is most useful. There is much more about events in the Near East than in (item 142) and less on internal Russian ideological discussions. There is also a chapter on communism in the Arab countries, and much on the oil factor. A good introduction for the general reader, its usefulness is enhanced by the documentary appendix, which occupies a third of the volume and which includes statements by Near Eastern leaders and local communists, press articles, and material from Russian sources. Research is based strictly on public record sources. A more detailed work is necessary and librarians should watch for such works.

See also:

Freedman, Robert Owen. **Soviet Policy toward the Middle East since 1970.** New York, Praeger; 1975. ca.200p. bibliog. LC 74-31504. ISBN 0-275-05920-0. DS 63.2.R9F7. DDC 327.47'056. To Nixon's resignation.

Klieman, Aaron S. **Soviet Russia and the Middle East.** Baltimore, Johns Hopkins Press, 1970. 107p. LC 71-128822. ISBN 0-8018-1192-9. DS 63.2.R9K55. DDC 327.47'056. A brief essay for general readers.

The Soviet Union and the Middle East: The Post-World War II Era. Ed. by Ivo J. Lederer and Wayne S. Vucinich. Stanford, Calif., Hoover Institution Press, 1974. 302p. LC 72-87716. ISBN 0-8179-1131-9. DS 63.2.R9S63. DDC 327.47'056. Among the most important of these essays are Waterbury's on Russia and North Africa, Safran's on Russia and Israel, and Vucinich's on Soviet studies on the Middle East, an exhaustive listing and commentary of Russian works on the region that is quite important for students who know Russian.

Lenczowski, George. **Soviet Advances in the Middle East.** Washington, D.C., American Enterprise Institute for Public Policy Research, 1972. 176p. LC 78-186300. DS 63.2.R9L43. DDC 327.47'056.

Smolansky, Oles M. **The Soviet Union and the Arab East under Khrushchev.** Lewisburg, Bucknell University Press, 1974. 326p. LC 73-2890. ISBN 0-8387-1338-6. DS 63.2. R9S55. DDC 327.47'107'4927.

Spector, Ivor. **The Soviet Union and the Muslim World, 1917-1958.** Seattle, University of Washington Press, 1959. 328p. LC 59-2232. DS 63.2.R9S65 1959. DDC 327.47'056.

The U.S.S.R. and the Middle East. Ed. by Michael Confino and Shimon Shamir. New York, Halstead Press, 1973. 441p. LC 73-2735. ISBN 0-470-16832-3. DS 63.2.R9U19 1973. DDC 327.47'056. Includes several solid chapters of hard information on communism in various Arab countries.

McLane, Charles B. **Soviet-Middle East Relations.** London, Central Asian Research Centre; distr. New York, Columbia University Press, 1973. (Soviet-Third World Relations, Vol. 1). 126p. $15.00. LC 73-179968. ISBN 0-231-03779-1. DS 63.2.R9M3 1973b. DDC 327.47'056. The record of Russian relations with the Near East and North Africa, consisting of basic data taken mainly from Russian sources. Each country of the region is treated separately; several pages of general discussion are followed by chronological tables of political, economic, and cultural relations. Unfortunately, only the month of each recorded incident is provided. Covers the period 1955 to 1970, with a few earlier items. A most useful reference work for larger collections.

McLaurin, Ronald D. **The Middle East in Soviet Policy.** Lexington, Mass., Lexington Books, 1975. 200p. bibliog. LC 74-31715. ISBN 0-669-98285-7. DS 63.2.R9M33. DDC 327.47'056. A generalized, topical survey whose conclusion is that there is little to worry about with regard to Russian domination of the region.

144. Lenczowski, George. **The Middle East in World Affairs.** 3rd ed. Ithaca, N.Y., Cornell University Press, 1967 (c.1962). 723p. bibliog. index. $12.50. LC 62-16343. ISBN 0-8014-0255-7. DS 62.L53 1967. DDC 956.

[P1, C1, S1] The standard textbook on the twentieth century Near East and its international relations in the context of domestic politics to 1960. A systematic history with relatively little analysis, by a well-known member of the "old school" of "Cold War" specialists. The book is quite useful as an introductory survey of events and reference book, but its explanations of events are not reliable, partly because of the conventional wisdom and presuppositions that color the author's generalities and his too frequent uncritical acceptance of official lines, and partly because of the lack of basic sources. The author failed to edit grammatically the transitional passages between additions made in successive editions; the updated material was simply added, and the previous text remained unmodified. If he could not even correct his tenses, we must at least suspect an insufficient concern with the accuracy and selection of his material and a lack of care in drawing his conclusions. A basic book because nothing has replaced it. Updated to some extent by Ismael (item 141).

See also:

Dib, Georges Moussa. **The Arab Bloc in the United Nations.** Amsterdam, Djambatan, 1956. 128p. LC A57-2326. JX 1977.2.N4D48. DDC n.a.

Afifi, Muhammad al-Hadi. **The Arabs and the United Nations.** London, Longmans, 1965. 202p. bibliog. LC 65-961. DS 39.A35. DDC n.a.

145. Monroe, Elizabeth. **Britain's Moment in the Middle East, 1914-1956.** Baltimore, The Johns Hopkins Press, 1963. 254p. bibliog. index. (Britain in the World Today). o.p. LC 63-18821. DS 63.2.G7M6 1963. DDC 327.42056. Paperback: London, Chatto and Cape Services, 1963. 256p. £1.25. ISBN 0-7011-0580-1.

[C1, S1] A useful general survey and interpretation of British policy and diplomacy. It is evenly balanced in its coverage of the periods, but it is opinionated. A basic work because we lack a more scholarly, well-documented book. Fitzsimons (item 139) is complementary.

See also:

Cumming, Henry Harford. **Franco-British Rivalry in the Post-War Near East: The Decline of French Influence.** London, Oxford University Press, 1938. 229p. bibliog. LC 39-4117. D 465.C8.

146. Pennar, Jaan. **The U.S.S.R. and the Arabs: The Ideological Dimension, 1917-1972.** New York, Crane-Russak Co., 1973. 180p. $9.75. LC 73-81254. ISBN 0-8448-0216-6. DS 63.2.R9P46. DDC 327.47'017'4927.

[C1, S1] This book discusses the Soviet-Arab ideological relationship, particularly during the 1960s and 1970s. It surveys the origins of Arab communism and early Soviet thinking on the Arab world and national liberation movements; recent history of the Arab communists, including those in Algeria, Sudan, Egypt and the Eastern Arab states; Egypt's "non-capitalist" path and Egypt's treatment of its communists; the Syrian and Iraqi Baath parties and their relations with Russia; the forms of Arab socialism and Russian attitudes toward them. The book summarizes a number of other works listed in this *Guide*, being based on the standard secondary works and Russian and Arab sources, and it will serve smaller libraries adequately.

147. Ro'i, Yaacov. **From Encroachment to Involvement: A Documentary Study of Soviet Policy in the Middle East, 1945-1973.** New York, Halstead Press, 1974. 616p. bibliog. index. LC 74-19460. ISBN 0-470-73150-8. DS 63.2.R9R64. DDC 327.47'056.

Covers 116 topics, many of which are provided with two or three documents from various sources; chronologically arranged. Each item has an introduction by Ro'i providing the general and immediate background to the topic or item, with frequent quotes from other Soviet documents, responses by the U.S. and other nations involved, and a few references for further reading; many items have postscripts noting reactions to the statement. The footnotes provide further explanations and details, as well as sources of additional documents. Includes communiques, statements, diplomatic notes, speeches, articles from *Pravda* and other press articles, and some writings and statements by Middle Easterners. It does not contain treaties and similar documents, the most important of which will be found in Hurewitz (item 52). The book contains a wealth of information and is a basic handbook on the subject. A study based on this type of material may be found in: Yodfat, Aryeh, *Arab Politics in the Soviet Mirror* (New York, Halstead Press, 1973. 332p. LC 73-156684. ISBN 0-7065-1268-5. DS 63.2.R9Y62 1973. DDC 301.15'43'3209174927).

148. Williams, Ann. **Britain and France in the Middle East and North Africa, 1914-1967.** New York, St. Martin's Press, 1968. 194p. illus. bibliog. (The Making of the Twentieth Century). LC 68-26561. DS 63.W47. DDC 909'.09'74927082.

This is a very brief treatment that hardly does justice to the subject (and particularly to the French relationship), even for an introduction intended for the general reader. But it is the only such work available.

B. RED SEA REGION

149. Abir, Mordechai. **Oil, Power and Politics: Conflict in Arabia, the Red Sea and the Gulf.** London, Frank Cass; distr. Portland, Ore., International Scholarly Book Services, 1974. 209p. $12.50. LC n.a. ISBN 0-7146-2990-1. DT 39.A23 1974.

A study of the local and international politics of Saudi Arabia, Southern Arabia, the geopolitical importance of the Red Sea and the way in which it is involved in world and regional politics, and the conflicts in the Horn of Africa—the Eritrea-Ethiopia problem and its relation to international and inter-Arab politics. Included are excellent discussions of the internal situation in Saudi Arabia, South Yemen, and Somalia; the relations between Sudan and Ethiopia; American, Russian, and Chinese involvement; the relationship of the whole situation to the Arab-Israeli conflict; and a judicious prognosis for the future. A very relevant book for more advanced students of the Near East and international relations; it has much material not conveniently available elsewhere. The many footnotes are quite useful.

For further information on Somalia, which is an important focal point in the Red Sea region, which has made headlines due to the Russian presence there, and which has recently become a member of the Arab League, see:

Area Handbook for Somalia [Kaplan, Irving]. 1969. DAPAM 550-86. LC 73-607519. DT 401.K33. DDC 309.1'67'73.

Lewis, I. M. **The Modern History of Somaliland: From Nation to State.** New York, Praeger, 1965. 234p. (Asia-Africa Series). LC 65-14183. DT 401.L4. DDC 967.73.

150. Marston, Thomas E. **Britain's Imperial Role in the Red Sea Area, 1800-1878.** Hamden, Conn., Shoestring Press, 1961. 550p. bibliog. o.p. LC 61-13336. DS 63.2.G7M3.

Based on British documents, this work stresses the period 1832 to 1878. It discusses events in the region and the development and implementation of British policy (particularly from the local perspective, rather than London's) in Arabia, Aden, Yemen, and Abyssinia. An excellent discussion and case study of the problems of British policy formulation stemming from the dual handling by the Indian Office (then the East India Company) and the Foreign Office, and their lack of unity of purpose and coordination, which sometimes created great confusion. There is much discussion of events outside the region as they related to British policy there, and a treatment of domestic British influences on policy. For more comprehensive collections.

C. INDIAN OCEAN

151. **The Indian Ocean, Its Political, Economic and Military Importance.** Ed. by Alvin J. Cottrell and R. M. Burrel. New York, Praeger, 1972. 457p. index. (Praeger Special Studies in International Politics and Public Affairs). $25.00. LC 72-79543. DS 335.I5 1972. DDC 320.9'182'4.

Conference papers by specialists on shifting power balances; politics and economics of natural resources (oil, minerals, agriculture, fishing, manufacturing); international trade routes, transportation organization; geopolitics; military-strategic aspects. Topics specifically on the Near East include the Persian Gulf, the Arabian Peninsula and adjacent islands; Red Sea and Suez; local conflicts; the USSR and U.S. presence; the Horn of Africa and its local conflicts, and great power interests there; Ethiopia and the Indian Ocean. It also includes the perspectives of Australia, Indonesia, South Asia, South Africa; the India-Pakistan conflict. Finally it treats great power interests; the present state of the Indian Ocean, including recent major power moves and the significance of sea power; the Japanese, Chinese, British, and French perspectives. A timely discussion containing a wealth of information and analysis basic to policy evaluation and formulation. Mainly for more comprehensive collections.

152. Toussaint, Auguste. **History of the Indian Ocean.** Tr. from French. Chicago, University of Chicago Press, 1966. 292p. bibliog. index. $6.00. LC 65-20964. ISBN 0-226-80887-4. DS 335.T613 1966. DDC 909.09667.

A general history from earliest times to the 1950s, which treats politics and trade, geography, naval science and its influence on the course of events, European contacts, explorations, and trade relations. It relates a wide range of events in readable language, putting them into a perspective different from what most readers are accustomed to. The author is quite interested in regional unity and cooperation and notes some of the measures taken over the years to increase unity. A good book for general background on a region that is in the process of becoming a major focus of great power rivalry, and to which the Persian Gulf, Suez Canal, and Red Sea are vital as power fulcra.

D. PERSIAN GULF (ARABIAN GULF)

153. Kelly, John Barrett. **Britain and the Persian Gulf, 1795-1880.** Oxford, Clarendon Press, 1968. 911p. bibliog. index. $41.00. LC 68-100230. ISBN 0-19-821360-3. DS 326.K4 1968. DDC 327.42'053'6.

A massive study that provides extensive background to each topic discussed, to show why Britain took each step it did in the Gulf. It also provides the context of the Eastern Question and of Britain's relations with European countries, and it describes specific actions in the Gulf, British relations with Iran and India, and the formation of British policy. It includes British actions in dealing with the Arabian slave trade. A first-rate book that is a mine of information on an important topic. Probably too detailed for all but comprehensive collections. A similar work on a later period is Busch, Briton Cooper. *Britain and the Persian Gulf, 1894-1914.* Berkeley, University of California Press, 1967. 432p. LC 67-24120. DS 326.B83. DDC 327.42053'6.

154. Marlowe, John. **The Persian Gulf in the Twentieth Century.** New York, Praeger, 1962. 280p. bibliog. index. o.p. LC 62-13490. DS 326.M3. DDC 955.

A factual survey of the political history of the countries around the Gulf and the British rule therein. Quite useful for putting a wide variety of facts into perspective, especially from the British point of view. It covers general historical background to 1914; World War I and post-War era; oil, 1900-1939; rise of the modern Persian Gulf governments after World War I; World War II; the post-World War II era (which takes up almost one half the book). Duplicates information found in other books listed in this *Guide*, but it provides a good orientation to Persian Gulf affairs.

155. Wilson, Sir Arnold Talbot (1884-1940). **The Persian Gulf: An Historical Sketch from the Earliest Times to the Beginning of the Twentieth Century.** 2nd impr. London, George Allen and Unwin, 1954. 327p. bibliog. index. £3.00. LC 55-30846. ISBN 0-04-953003-8. DS 326.W5 1954.

An old book, originally published at the turn of the century, but the only one available. Arnold cites the ancient and medieval sources extensively, and he deals at length with European entry and expansion into the region, with information on trade and the context of local history and politics. There are chapters on the Persian Gulf pirates, slave trade, and the growth of the Arab emirates. It is useful mainly as background to works on the nineteenth and twentieth centuries but is well written and interesting to read for its own sake.

E. UNITED STATES RELATIONS

156. Badeau, John Stothoff. **The American Approach to the Arab World.** New York, Harper & Row, 1968. 209p. index. (Policy Books of the Council on Foreign Relations). $4.95. LC 67-22494. ISBN 0-06-010188-1. DS 63.2.U5 B32. DDC 327.56'073. Paperback: Harper Colophon Books, CN 412. $2.95. ISBN 0-06-090412-7.

[P1, C1, S1] Badeau, a scholar who lived in the Arab world for years, discusses U.S. policy needs with regard to the Arabs. He helps the reader understand some of the forces in the Arab world and their interaction with U.S. interests, perspectives, and past policy on Israel, oil, the "Cold War," etc. Although one may disagree with some of his views and analyses, the book is essential. U.S.-Arab relations are often given short shrift because of the American sympathy for Israel and the widely held negative stereotypes of the Arabs that condition American outlook. Badeau offers a very useful (if sometimes biased) corrective to this view of the Arabs, which should be read by anyone even slightly interested in the Near East.

157. Campbell, John Coert. **Defense of the Middle East: Problems of American Policy.** Rev. ed. New York, Praeger, 1961. 400p. bibliog. index. pa. o.p. LC 60-9110. DS 63.2.U5C3 1960.

[B, P1, C1, S1] A "Cold War" account of U.S. relations with the Near East, U.S. policy and diplomacy, from World War II to 1959 (160p.). The rest of the volume takes up a series of problems such as military strategy, bases and military aid; alliances; economics and policy; the U.S. and the changing Middle East; the Arab-Israeli conflict. Though out of date, it provides the only lengthy narrative survey we have; it also affords a view of the "Cold War" that will be valuable in giving perspective to readers who have not lived through the era. A basic introduction, with a very useful annotated bibliography.

158. Daniel, Robert L. **American Philanthropy in the Near East, 1820-1960.** Athens, Ohio University Press, 1970. 322p. bibliog. index. $10.50. LC 77-81451. SBN 8214-0063-0. DS 63.2.U5D35. DDC 301.29'56'073.

[P1, C1, S1] The U.S. has a long tradition of philanthropy in the region. Although this philanthropy was originally an auxiliary to missionary activity, it ultimately evolved apart from attempts to convert Eastern Muslims and Christians to American Christianity. Covering Malta, Greece, the Balkans, Syria, and Turkey, the book discusses the missionary activities, the impact of the various efforts—which sought to change the technology and culture of the area and to train native leaders to continue the work, as well as to meliorate conditions generally, especially in time of disaster. It also discusses relations with Eastern Christians; the American individuals who took part; educational and publishing activities (including the local independent colleges and schools); medical work; the Near East Foundation; problems of local nationalism and political conflicts with the U.S. and how they affected the philanthropic effort; agricultural work; relations with local governments. A basic work on U.S.-Near East relations, it contains a mine of information.

159. DeNovo, John A. **American Interests and Policies in the Middle East, 1900-1939.** Minneapolis, University of Minnesota Press, 1963. 447p. bibliog. index. $11.50. LC 63-21129. ISBN 0-8166-0302-2. DS 63.2.U5D4. DDC 327.73056.

[P1, C1, S1] This is a deeply researched, detailed history that treats the foundation and implementation of U.S. policy and the more important commercial, humanitarian, and cultural activities of Americans in the period before the U.S. became a significant actor in the region. It includes the partition of the Ottoman Empire after World War I. This is the only such work available; a few other more recent works treat the subject briefly and in general terms, but they are usually based in great part on DeNovo. There is an increasing number of works that treat in more detail individual topics dealt with in this book, a few of which are included in this *Guide*; more can be expected, and librarians should watch for them. In the book, DeNovo promises a sequel, but to date the publisher has not received a manuscript.

160. Evans, Laurence. **United States Policy and the Partition of Turkey, 1914-1924.** Baltimore, The Johns Hopkins Press, 1965. 437p. bibliog. index. (The Johns Hopkins University Studies in Historical and Political Science. Series LXXXII [1964] No. 2). $12.00. LC 65-11660. ISBN 0-8018-0192-3. H31.J6 ser. 82, no. 2. [E 183.8.T8E9]. DDC 956.102.

This is a study of the formulation and implementation of U.S. policy during World War I and especially during the Peace Conference, as well as the final settlement with Turkey. It includes much on the diplomacy with France, Britain, and Turkey; the question of war aims; the mandate system; Arab and Zionist cases; the self-determination issue; King-Crane Commission; Treaty of Sèvres; the United States and the mandatory regimes; U.S. relations with independent Turkey; and the Lausanne Conference. It is rather specialized, dry reading, but it will fill a gap in the coverage of the period until something better is available. For larger collections.

161. Field, James A. **America and the Mediterranean World, 1776-1882.** Princeton, N.J., Princeton University Press, 1969. 485p. bibliog. index. $13.50. LC 68-11440. ISBN 0-691-04590-9. DS 63.2.U5F47. DDC 327.56'073.

[P1, C1, S1] A deeply researched, well-written, fascinating account that actually deals more with the Near East and North Africa (the Barbary pirates, etc.) than with Mediterranean Europe. It traces the domestic, cultural, religious and economic influences that sparked official and private U.S. interest in the area, and renders a detailed account of those interests and the history of American missionary activity, commerce, diplomacy, and naval activity, with ample attention given to the individuals who took part in events there. A basic work for the student and good reading for the more educated general reader.

162. Finnie, David H. **Pioneers East: The American Experience in the Middle East.** Cambridge, Mass., Harvard University Press, 1967. 333p. bibliog. illus. index. (Harvard Middle Eastern Studies, 13). $9.50. LC 67-20875. ISBN 0-674-66900-2. DS 48.F5. DDC 915.6'04.

This is the fascinating story of the Americans in the Near East—Constantinople, Egypt, Palestine, Lebanon and Syria, Iran and Mesopotamia—through the 1840s. They were missionaries, naval and military officers, diplomats, and technicians hired by area governments. Their lives, motives and reasons for being there, their problems, and anecdotes about activities and adventures are colorfully described in an informal style that is good reading for its own sake. It is based on original sources. The main emphasis is on why the Americans were there; with the exception of a few key figures the accounts are not detailed, but they give a good idea of the problems and conditions the Americans encountered. To a great extent the book uses as its focus the travel books of John Lloyd Stephens (item 463).

163. Hall, Luella J. **The United States and Morocco, 1776-1956.** Metuchen, N.J., Scarecrow Press, 1971. 1114p. map. $25.00. LC 71-142233. ISBN 0-8108-0338-0. E 183.8.M8H3. DDC 327.73'0449'49.

A massively detailed and documented history based on U.S. archives documents, the press, and secondary works. The ample material on U.S.-Moroccan relations is buried in a mass of detail on Moroccan history, and inter-European and U.S.-European diplomacy which directly and indirectly bore on Morocco and the course of its relations with the United States. The author explains *everything*, sometimes in overwhelming detail, particularly for the period 1894 to 1912. Coverage is uneven. Emphasis increases with the lateness of the period until just before World War II, which is discussed in much less detail than the 1900-1912 period. Unfortunately, the chapter on the post-World War II period is of minimal usefulness, due to lack of available source material. It should be noted that while there is much on internal history of the country, it is taken mainly from a relatively few secondary works, or, for earlier periods, from U.S. diplomatic reports as well. The student will have to judge the reliability of the various parts of the book on the basis of the sources cited in the hundreds of notes. The only comprehensive work on the topic.

164. Harris, George Sellers. **Troubled Alliance: Turkish-American Problems in Historical Perspective, 1945-1972.** Washington, D.C., American Enterprise Institute for Public Policy Research; Stanford, Calif., Hoover Institution on War, Revolution and Peace, Stanford University, 1972. 262p. bibliog. illus. index. (AEI-Hoover Policy Study, 2; Hoover Institution Studies, 33). $8.50; $4.50pa. LC 72-83379. E 183.8.T8H3. DDC 301.29'56'1073.

Based on Turkish and Western documents, press and secondary sources, this extremely useful study includes the origins and carrying out of the Marshall Plan in Turkey, NATO, U.S. activities and aid in Turkey, and the development of problems in U.S.-Turkish relations during the 1960s, in the context of Turkish politics. Specific topics include the Cyprus problem; rise of anti-Americanism in Turkey; military cooperation problems in the context of United States, Western, and Soviet strategy and other military changes; development assistance problems. Several documents are appended. The bibliography is quite useful. A basic work.

See also:

Howard, Harry Nicholas. **Turkey, the Straits and U.S. Policy.** Baltimore, The Johns Hopkins Press, 1975. 352p. bibliog. LC 74-6826. ISBN 0-8018-1590-3. D 465.H66. DDC 327.73'0561. Diplomatic history of U.S. involvement in the question, imbedded in a mass of background material. Most of the text deals with the period 1914-1946: World War I interallied agreements; Peace Conference; Montreux Convention (1933-1939); Turkey's entry into World War II; 1945-1946 debates between the United States, Russia, Britain, etc.; 1950s-1970s.

165. **Soviet-American Rivalry in the Middle East.** Ed. by J. C. Hurewitz. New York, Praeger, 1969. 250p. bibliog. index. $8.00; $2.95pa. LC 78-75238. DS 63.2.R9S6 1969. DDC 327.1'0956.

[P1, C1, C2, S2] Conference papers by top specialists. They discuss various aspects of the military competition and arms levels, the military balance, arms transfers and controls, the 6th Fleet and U.S. diplomacy, military factors in regional instability. Also covered are economic competition in the 1970s (declining U.S. involvement, Soviet trade and aid); regional economics in the 1970s; cultural rivalry (U.S. and USSR efforts); and internal regional contests. Another topic is the quest for stability—alliances, systems, and trends; British and French roles; Russian search for security; persistence of regional quarrels. Most of the essays are general and analytical rather than factual or historical; each outlines and generalizes on the external and internal factors that influence and are influenced by the activities of the great powers. Each stresses problems and policy-making, with much prognostication and speculation on the future. Much of the material is still relevant, and thus the book is an essential complement to the historical works listed in this *Guide*.

166. Tibawi, Abd al-Latif. **American Interests in Syria, 1800-1901: A Study of Educational, Literary and Religious Work.** Oxford, Clarendon Press, 1966. 333p. bibliog. index. $11.25. LC 66-69456. ISBN 0-19-821355. BV 3200.T5. DDC 266.023095691.

This well-researched work traces the history of the American Protestant missionary work that culminated in the establishment of schools (one of which became American University of Beirut) and Arabic printing presses (in the discussion of the books they produced). Based on archives and missionary sources, the main emphasis is on the American Board of Commissioners for Foreign Missions. It details at length the problems faced—financial, cultural, political, personnel, debate over whether to stress work with Eastern Christians or Muslims; progress and failures; philosophy and policy; relations with the Ottoman government. It details changes made under the Board of Foreign Missions of the Presbyterian Church when that body took over, adjustments made to changing local conditions, and competition by other denominations. There are appendices on American diplomatic, exploration, and archaeological activities. Tibawi discusses the role of native Christians, who were treated as less than equal by the Americans, and he constantly evaluates the actual influence of the American efforts in the Arab "renaissance"—much less than has been claimed, he says, though still significant. An important aspect of U.S. relations with the region, a basic work for larger collections.

167. Trask, Roger R. **The United States Response to Turkish Nationalism and Reform, 1914-1939.** Minneapolis, University of Minnesota Press, 1971. 280p. bibliog. index. $11.50. LC 74-153505. ISBN 0-8166-0613-7. E 183.8.T8T7 1971. DDC 327.561'073.

This study of Turkish-U.S. relations treats a variety of subjects independently without integrating them. Two introductory chapters treat U.S. relations to 1914 and 1914-1923; the bulk of the book deals with the remaining period. Topics include diplomacy regarding resumption of diplomatic relations after the Treaty of Lausanne; U.S. attitudes toward the Kemalist revolution; Turkish nationalism and various problems arising due to nationalist sensitivities; commercial relations; U.S. investments and technical aid; U.S. educational, social, cultural, and philanthropic activities, and the basis for good relations that they helped foster; status of U.S. citizens in Turkey; U.S., Turkey, and international politics, 1923-1939. A leit-motif of the book is the change in the American image of the "terrible Turk" to a more favorable attitude. A useful survey, it concludes that the U.S. took a constructive view and did not let problems detract from its positive efforts to improve relations, which provided a solid foundation for relations for years to come.

See also:

Gordon, Leland J. **American Relations with Turkey, 1830-1930: An Economic Interpretation.** Philadelphia, University of Pennsylvania Press, 1932. 402p. LC 32-4426. HF 3114.G6.

168. **United States Interests in the Middle East.** Washington, D.C., American Enterprise Institute for Public Policy Research, 1968. 132p. (Special Analysis, 17). $3.00pa. LC 68-58174. DS 63.2.U5A8. DDC 301.29'56'073.

[P1, C1, S1] A brief introductory presentation of the development and status of U.S. politico-strategic, economic, and cultural interests in the region, with a final chapter on the conditions and prospects for peace in the area. The first chapter outlines the area's international relations and U.S. policy; chapter two discusses the economic importance of the area to the United States and the West as a whole, with notes on the economic situation in each country and its prospects. Chapter three surveys the history of U.S. cultural and educational activities, both private and official. The next chapter summarizes U.S. interests, the forces affecting regional stability, and the problem of the status quo with regard to U.S. interests. A summary of the conventional view, particularly that held in the 1950s and earlier 1960s, which is still fairly common but which has lately been subject to increasing questioning. For all libraries.

See also:

Gibert, S. P. **U.S. Security Interests in the Persian Gulf.** New York, Crane-Russak Co., 1975. LC n.a. ISBN 0-8448-0324-3.

169. Wright L[enoir] C[hambers]. **United States Policy Towards Egypt, 1830-1914.** New York, Exposition Press, 1969. 270p. bibliog. (An Exposition-University Book). $7.50. LC 78-83503. ISBN 0-682-46945-9. E 183.8.E3 W7 1969. DDC 327.62'073.

A general history of U.S. interests in Egypt in the political, economic, and cultural fields, and the course of our relations. After a survey of the first 30 years, the author discusses Egypt and the Civil War; Americans in the Egyptian military; U.S.-European relations regarding the mixed courts and other European controls over and interference in Egyptian affairs which affected its international relations; the U.S. and the Egyptian debt; U.S.-Egyptian trade; missionaries in Egypt, their religious and educational activities; U.S. reaction to the British occupation in 1882; the U.S. and the Suez Canal. A useful work with extensive notes and bibliography.

170. Yeselson, Abraham. **United States-Persian Diplomatic Relations, 1883-1921.** New Brunswick, N.J., Rutgers University Press, 1956. 252p. bibliog. index. o.p. LC 56-7614. E 183.8.I55Y4 1956. DDC 327.730955.

This book begins with the 1856 treaty of friendship, U.S. missionary activities and background information on active U.S. interest in Iran (which began with the first legation there in

1883 as a result of dangers to the missionaries). It then details U.S. interests and the variations in State Department and Congressional attention, vain Iranian efforts to secure U.S. aid against Russian and British interference in her affairs; U.S. reactions to British-Russian rivalry in Iran and the activities of U.S. diplomats there; reaction to the 1905-1906 Revolution and its aftermath; activities of U.S. citizens and dangers to them; the Shuster mission, Iranian efforts to gain U.S. advisors and aid, and Shuster's expulsion; World War I and the Peace Conference and reactions to the plight of Christians in Iran; reaction to the Anglo-Persian agreement and Soviet tactics there; U.S. advisors after World War I; oil diplomacy. A most useful, informative, and interesting book based on official archives, it does not get bogged down in an overabundance of detail.

A short overview for the general reader is:

Heravi, Mehdi. **Iranian-American Diplomacy.** Brooklyn, Theodore Gaus' Sons, 1969. 161p. bibliog. LC 71-96255. E 183.8.I55 H4. DDC 327.55'073.

VI. BIOGRAPHY

There are no general modern biographical dictionaries *per se* for any period. The appropriate works in the **Reference Works** section (pp. 30-34) do contain many biographies. Biographical dictionaries abound in the vernacular literatures, particularly in the classical period, which has a long tradition of collective biography (but not individual, except for Muhammad)—Hadith authorities, ulama, judges, notables, etc.

Two of the best known classical dictionaries have been translated or are in the process of translation:

> Ibn Khallikān (1211-1282). **Ibn Khallikan's Biographical Dictionary.** Tr. from Arabic by Bn. Mac Guckin de Slane. Beirut, Librairie du Liban, 1970. 4v. LC 79-22299. D 198.3.I 2433. DDC n.a.

> Ibn sa^cd, Muḥammad (784-ca.845). **Kitab al-Tabaqat al-Kabir.** Tr. from Arabic by S. Moinul Haq. Karachi, Pakistan Historical Society, 1967– . LC SA 68-10265. BP 70.I 3213. DDC 297'0922.

While most libraries would have little use for these works, students will find them of interest as documents in Islamic civilization, and also as sources of information. *The Encyclopedia of Islam* (item 50) contains many biographies and is more useful for most students than these classical works. See also Biography sections under Islam and individual countries.

A. GENERAL

171. Adelson, Roger. **Mark Sykes: Portrait of an Amateur.** London, Jonathan Cape, 1975. 336p. bibliog. illus. LC 75-317645. ISBN 0-224-01070-0. DA 574.S85A63.

Presents the life and involvements of the Englishman known to students of the region as co-author of the Sykes-Picot Agreement, by which Britain and France apportioned the Eastern Arab provinces of the Ottoman Empire between them during World War I. In straightforward fashion the author depicts this fascinating individual's life, character, background, and ideas, his activities in British politics, and his British government and private activities concerning the Near East. Despite its importance in the literature and Arab political consciousness, the Sykes-Picot Agreement is given only more or less passing notice as but one incident of many in Sykes' involvement with the region, which included a long-term contact with Picot. A useful, interesting book based on original sources. It is good reading for its own sake as well as an excellent contribution to Near East studies.

172. Brodie, Fawn McKay. **The Devil Drives: A Life of Sir Richard Burton.** New York, W. W. Norton, 1967. 390p. bibliog. index. $6.95. LC 66-18069. ISBN 0-393-07374-2. G 246.B8B7. DDC 910.0942.

[P] This is the most recent and best biography of the Orientalist, adventurer, ethnographer, pornographer, and explorer who mastered over two dozen languages and myriad disguises in order to dissolve into the native masses of the countries he lived in. He reported to the world what it was like inside, often much to the world's disgust. He knew India, visited the Muslim holy cities, Mecca and Medina, explored Africa and just missed finding the source of the Nile, translated Oriental classics into English, and variously astounded the world and enriched our knowledge of the East. This biography is well written, well researched, and uses its sources intelligently; it is sensible and balanced and does not emphasize the sensational, though it offers enough to whet the appetites of the most jaded thrill-seeker (without in the slightest satisfying him!).

173. Burgoyne, Elizabeth. **Gertrude Bell, From Her Personal Papers.** London, Ernest Benn; distr. Mystic, Conn., Lawrence Verry, 1958-1961. 2v. index. $10.00. LC 58-3415 rev. DA 566.9.B39B8. DDC 920.7.

This book consists mainly of extracts from her letters and diaries, with connecting passages and explanatory notes by the editor. Volume 1 concerns the earlier and longer period of her life. Volume 2, covering the period 1914-1926, constitutes a fascinating basic source on British policy and administration in Iraq, the creation of the Iraqi government, and native Iraqi politics. The letters include a mass of knowledgeable reflections on personalities (especially for the period after 1918), as well as notes on her personal activities. Readers should have a considerable knowledge of the period before dipping into this volume.

174. Cleveland, William L. **The Making of an Arab Nationalist: Ottomanism and Arabism in the Life and Thought of Satiᶜ al-Husri.** Princeton, N.J., Princeton University Press, 1971. 211p. bibliog. (Princeton Studies on the Near East). $8.50. LC 78-155961. ISBN 0-691-03088-X. DS 61.52.H87C55. DDC 320.5'4'0924 [B].

Husri was the man who systematized Arab nationalist ideology and gave it a philosophical and "scientific" basis. The first 80 pages deal with his life as father of Ottoman, then Iraqi and Syrian education, his work in inculcating Ottoman loyalty, then Arab exclusivism through articles and the school systems he headed. The rest of the book treats his theories, methodology, inspirations and motives. Unfortunately, the book does not document his influence as an Arab nationalist ideologue.

175. Ehrenkreuz, Andrew S. **Saladin.** Albany, State University of New York Press, 1972. 290p. bibliog. index. $10.00. LC 78-161443. ISBN 0-87395-095-X. DS 38.4.S24E34. DDC 962'.02'0924 [B].

[C1] This revisionist biography, based on careful use of original sources, strips the romance from Saladin's life, by means of plodding and usually dry factual presentation and analysis. Saladin (Salah al-Din in Arabic) was, according to the author, *not* an "Islamic" hero seeking to strengthen the cause of the religion, but rather a dynasty-maker; he did relatively little against the Crusaders, actually avoiding decisive combat, for the most part. It is a controversial book, but it is well worth having, since Saladin is viewed as a romantic figure by Westerners, who should read this corrective. It is one of only a very few serious works on Saladin, and it is informative in a broader sense concerning the Islamic Empire.

176. Grafftey-Smith, Sir Laurence. **Bright Levant.** London, John Murray, 1970. 295p. illus. index. £3.00. LC 73-549933. ISBN 0-7195-2069-X. DS 63.2.G7G7. DDC 327.42'056.

Very interesting, witty, often revealing memoirs of 40 years of British foreign service in the Near East: Egypt, Arabia, Mosul, Iraq, Albania, but mainly Egypt. Informative, often entertaining comments on life, politics, British-native relations, with many anecdotes on events and personalities. Good thumbnail sketches and pungent observations on many British and Arab figures.

177. Graves, Philip Perceval. **The Life of Sir Percy Cox.** London, Hutchinson, 194- ? 350p. o.p. LC A41-3395. DA 566.9.C67G7.

A remarkable British colonial administrator-linguist-Orientalist-naturalist who came to the Near East in the British Service, via India and Somalia: Muscat, 1899; Bushir, Iran, 1904-1914; Mesopotamia in the latter part of World War I; Iran, 1919-1920; Iraq, 1920-1921; the Cairo Conference. There is much information on the events in which Cox took part—partly as filler because there is little information on Cox, partly because the events are so complex that much explanation is necessary. The book will be of interest to many readers because of this information, even if the man is not brought to the fore as much as one might wish. It gives a fair account of Cox's interest in nature; his relations with others (rather rosily portrayed by the admiring writer); his personality, method of operation, and duties; his exploration of the countries he worked in. Emphasizes the period to 1923, with a brief chapter on the final years, 1923-1937. A very sympathetic portrayal. It is hoped that someone like John Marlowe will publish a really good biography; but this one, if reprinted, will do until something better is available.

178. Haslip, Joan. **Lady Hester Stanhope.** Geneva, Heron Books, 1970. (Orig. pub. in 1934). 327p. illus. (Women Who Made History). LC 77-575640. DA 536.S8H35 1970. DDC 915.68 [B].

A typical Haslip biography of the eccentric Englishwoman who defied English society in her youth and then defied danger to travel among the tribesmen of the Near East. There she became a legend for her courage in facing down tyrants on behalf of "her" people, her pride, her horsemanship, and finally her raging temper and eccentricity, when she set up a "court" among the Druses in Lebanon and became known as a "Queen." Her reputation was so widespread that she is mentioned in a number of the travel books of the day, when a visit to her home was quite an accomplishment (cf. Kinglake, item 460). She died in grimy poverty. One will not learn much about the Near East, but she is a fascinating character not ill-served by this biography.

179. Hitti, Philip Khūri. **Makers of Arab History.** New York, St. Martin's Press, 1968. 268p. index. $6.95. LC 68-20139. D 198.3.H5. DDC 920'.009176'7. Paperback: Harper & Row, 1971. (Harper Torch Books, TB 1548). $2.75. ISBN 0-06-131548-6.

[P3] In this perspective of the history of the Islamic Empire, Dr. Hitti presents the lives and achievements of key political and intellectual figures and the events and intellectual currents of which they were a part and which they greatly influenced. He treats Muhammad; the second Caliph Umar; the fifth Caliph, Mu'awiyah; Abd al-Rahman of Islamic Spain; the Abbasid Caliph al-Ma'mun; the founder of the Fatimids, Ubaydallah al-Mahdi; and Saladin. Then the intellectual leaders: al-Ghazzali; the key figure in Islamic law, al-Shafi^{c}i; the first Islamic philosopher, al-Kindi; Avicenna (Ibn Sina); Averroes (Ibn Rushd); and Ibn Khaldun. This latter section contains more material on the personal lives of the subjects than does the former, covering their ideas and their importance as well. The book is interesting and non-technical, and the amount of detail is quite manageable. An enjoyable way to learn basic information.

180. Keddie, Nikki R. **Sayyid Jamāl ad-Dīn "al-Afghānī": A Political Biography.** Berkeley, University of California Press, 1972. 479p. bibliog. index. LC 74-159671. ISBN 0-520-01986-5. BP 80.A45K43. DDC 297'.092'4 [B].

al-Afghani is an enigmatic figure about whom there has been much speculation and debate since the late nineteenth century. He is credited with being a seminal figure in the process of Islamic modernization. He sought to bridge traditional Islam and the modern West—to bring Islam into the mainstream of modern civilization without sacrificing the Islamic essence of his people, while seeking to make them politically independent of the West. Keddie, using available Arabic, Persian, Urdu, French, and English documents, and other materials, tries to indicate al-Afghani's ideas, aims, and methods, to record the known details of his life and career, and to assess his influence. Much of the book is devoted to setting the record straight and to settling aspects of the debates, which is done in a scholarly fashion; thus the book is hard reading for the uninitiated, but it contains much useful information about his era.

181. Khadduri, Majid. **Arab Contemporaries: The Role of Personalities in Politics.** Baltimore, The Johns Hopkins Press, 1973. 255p. index. $8.95. LC 72-12576. ISBN 0-8018-1453-7. DS 39.2.A2K48. DDC 320.9'17'4927.

[C3] Discussed are Aziz Ali al-Misri, Nuri al-Sa^{c}id, and Nasser as military politicians; professional politicians (Hajj Amin al-Husayni, King Faysal of Arabia, Bourguiba, Kamil al-Chadirchi, Kamal Junblat and Khalid Bakdash); and intellectual politicians (Ahmad Lutfi al-Sayyid, Muhammad Husayn Haykal, Michel Aflaq). The author knew each personally. Each is labelled as an idealist, extremist, realist, traditionalist, or combination. Each chapter outlines the life, career, and goals of its subject; it describes and evaluates sympathetically his methods, achievements, and failures. The volume is intended to be a companion to (item 126). The problem with this book, as with most of this author's other works listed in this *Guide*, is that his generalities and attempts at analysis are conventional, even banal, and too often uncritical, even when he attempts "criticism." Thus the reader is left hanging, if not necessarily misled. This book on key figures in Arab politics powders over the warts, even when they are visible, and too many of his assessments are unhelpful. Interesting, but of low priority.

182. Marlowe, John. **Late Victorian: The Life of Sir Arnold T. Wilson.** London, Cresset Press, 1967. 418p. bibliog. illus. index. o.p. LC 67-77978. DA 566.9.W53M3. DDC 942.083'0924.

[C] Wilson was one of the brilliant British soldier-statesman-Orientalists who spent decades in the Near East, beginning in Iran in 1908, where he immersed himself in the country while working in the British consulate. He served in Iraq during World War I, to 1921, as Cox's (item 177) assistant, engaging in mutual antagonisms with Lawrence and Gertrude Bell, who were as brilliant, confident, and independent as he was. The book has much on British rule in the region, British policy, A.T.'s ideas and fascinating life; the Iraq rebellion of 1920; Iran, 1921-1926; Wilson's books on the region, including his memoirs, *SW Persia: A Political Officer's Diary, 1907-1914, Loyalties: Mesopotamia, 1914-1917, Mesopotamia, 1917-1920: A Clash of Loyalties,* and *The Persian Gulf* (item 155); life in England and Parliament 1933-1939, where he was something of a radical; and his death on an RAF bombing mission over Europe, 1940. An excellent and informative book on a fascinating man. The three volumes of memoirs are extremely interesting works for the reader who has some background on the era, and are highly recommended as good, highly informative reading.

183. Sim, Katherine. **Desert Traveller: The Life of Jean Louis Burckhardt.** London, Victor Gollancz, 1969. 447p. bibliog. illus. £3.00. LC 79-442522. ISBN 0-575-00310-3. DS 61.7.B8S5. DDC 915.6'04.

[P] A fascinating narrative, based mainly on the subject's works, of the life of the intrepid scholar and explorer who journeyed through the Middle East discovering Petra, the Great Temple of Rameses II at Abu Simbel, and other now well-known ancient sites. He made the pilgrimage to Mecca in disguise and penetrated the Nubian desert. The book describes his self-education and intensive preparations for his exciting ventures. Great reading for the general public.

184. Storrs, Sir Ronald (1881-1955). **The Memoirs of Sir Ronald Storrs.** New York, AMS Press, 1973. (Repr. of 1937 ed.). 563p. index. (Mid-East Studies). $32.50. LC 77-180678. ISBN 0-404-56337-6. D 469.G7S75 1973. DDC 325'.342'0924. [B]

[C1] *Orientations* is the better-known title of this memoir of the British Orientalist, soldier, and colonial administrator, which covers the period 1881 to 1932. It describes his experiences in Cairo in the first decade of the twentieth century, with accounts of events and personalities, the British administration there, Egyptian society and politics, and Kitchner in Egypt. Also covered are World War I in the Near East; British policy and conditions during this period; relations with the Arabs, negotiations with Amir Abdullah of Arabia and with Sherif Husayn, culminating in the famous Husayn-McMahon Correspondence; Baghdad, 1917; Egypt, 1917; Palestine through the 1920s, as administrator; Palestine's internal politics, Jewish-Arab relations, OETA, Zionist attitudes and activities, and Arab views; and Christian activities in Palestine. There are chapters on Lawrence, on Storrs' work in Cyprus, with a description of that country, and on Enosis and its politics. Of considerable value for its information on the period and for the vividness of his first-hand account of many very important events. A basic source, fascinating reading.

185. Waterfield, Gordon. **Layard of Nineveh.** London, John Murray, 1973. 535p. illus. index. £3.25. LC 64-4433. ISBN 0-7195-0812-6. DS 70.88.L3W3. DDC 942.08'1'0924 [B].

[P, C] Another remarkable Victorian adventurer, who at 22 went to live among the reputedly ferocious Bakhtiary tribe of Persia and at 28 excavated Nineveh. Layard, who was a Turcophile, become involved in British politics after the finish of his archaeological career. He served a long stint in the foreign service, in Spain, and for several years in the 1870s was ambassador to the Ottoman Empire. The book details his travels, summing up his travel books. It describes his discoveries, his political and diplomatic views and career, travels during the Crimean War and his criticism of government actions there, and his career in the House of Commons. A most interesting book, with much information on the life, politics, and diplomacy of the Near East.

B. LAWRENCE OF ARABIA

186. Aldington, Richard. **Lawrence of Arabia: A Biographical Enquiry.** London, Collins, 1969 (c.1955). 448p. bibliog. illus. index. ₤2.10. LC 74-449223. ISBN 0-00-211467-4. D 568.4.L45A6 1969. DDC 940.4'15'0924.

Aldington undertakes to demolish the myth of Lawrence, by making a systematic, point-by-point examination of every facet of his life and career, everything he said about himself, and statements made by others. In short, he uses most of what we know about Lawrence to show that Lawrence consistently and consciously exaggerated or covered up to his benefit the reality and quality of everything he did, for pathological emotional reasons; this is the main theme of the whole book, which also concludes that Lawrence was a homosexual. His military exploits, which are examined in detail, were not only duplicated but were surpassed by other Englishmen in Arabia; they were not only exaggerated as to their importance, but were not really important at all. While a resounding corrective to the legend was needed, Aldington writes in a spirit of blind hostility, with the self-indulgent value judgments that intrude constantly. His often deliberately twisted interpretations and his many irrelevant, spiteful interjections may cause the critical reader to reject the entire book out of hand. Unfortunately, it is our only such work. It is comprehensive, and it must be read by serious readers of the other biographies. In using the standard sources, Aldington was able to come up with much support for his many convincing points, which necessitate a thorough review and reinterpretation of everything we know about Lawrence. Aldington was a prolific professional writer of many biographies and literary works on a multitude of subjects. We can assume that such a writer, however excellent his work, has not given a subject like Lawrence the years of objective research and pondering necessary to gain a broad and detailed knowledge of the subject's life and times, and to develop the balance, insight, and perspective needed for a proper evaluation of a human being. For the professional writer, a selling point is necessary; in the case of Lawrence, there are many controversial points that could be crassly exploited to produce a best seller. Aldington exploited the points he wanted to just as crassly as Lowell Thomas did in creating the legend.

187. Armitage, Flora. **The Desert and the Stars.** New York, Holt, 1955. 318p. bibliog. index. o.p. LC 55-9223. D 568.4.L45A68. DDC 923.542.

A straightforward if admiring account of the life of Lawrence of Arabia, which in a final chapter attempts to refute Aldington (item 186).

Another popular work, copiously illustrated with photos and paintings is:

Brent, Peter Ludwig. **T. E. Lawrence.** London, Weidenfeld & Nicolson, 1975. 232p. bibliog. (Great Lives). LC 74-32436. D 568.4.L45B7 1975. DDC 940.4'15'0924 [B].

A psychological interpretation is:

Mack, John E. **A Prince of Our Disorder: The Life of T. E. Lawrence.** Boston, Little, Brown, 1975 (forthcoming). bibliog. index. LC n.a. ISBN 0-316-54232-6. LC cataloging n.a. Mack, professor of psychiatry at Harvard Medical School, attempts to understand Lawrence from a basically sympathetic but not apologetic perspective. Although it is not a detailed factual recital, it includes much information in the form of corrections of conventional knowledge, based on interviews with relatives and acquaintances, the secondary literature, and original documents (not just bowdlerized published collections). Discusses the literary influences on Lawrence's outlook and concludes that Lawrence *did* have a major role in the Arab revolt; refutes Aldington at many points.

188. Knightly, Phillip, and Colin Simpson. **The Secret Lives of Lawrence of Arabia.** New York, McGraw-Hill, 1970. 333p. bibliog. illus. index. $8.95. LC 71-105951. ISBN 0-07-035120-1. D 568.4.L45K55 1970. DDC 940.4'15'0924.

Using new sources, the authors present new information and views on controversial aspects of Lawrence's life. They challenge Aldington and they provide much on Lawrence's life after the War, which most books do not deal with adequately; on his masochism, his friendship with Mrs. Bernard Shaw, his post-War military life; and on his role as a British agent before the War. Not a comprehensive work, and the definitive work is yet to come, but a necessary supplement to the other works listed in this *Guide.*

189. Lawrence, Thomas Edward, 1888-1935. **The Seven Pillars of Wisdom: A Triumph.**
Garden City, N.Y., Doubleday, 1966 (c.1935). 622p. $10.00. LC 65-29662. ISBN
0-385-04423-2. D 568.4.L4 1966. DDC 940.415.

Lawrence's classic account of the Arab revolt during World War I and the Arabs as he
saw them. Still great reading whether or not one cares about the charges, made with considerable justice, that it is not an entirely accurate account. Still sufficiently popular that its Dell
paperback edition (now o.p.) has gone through multiple printings. Lawrence became a legend
when he was publicized by Lowell Thomas in wildly romantic terms. This legend and some
controversial aspects of his life, as well as the fact that those aspects must forever remain a
mystery, have contributed to a continuing interest in Lawrence.

Other works by Lawrence currently in print include:

The Essential T. E. Lawrence. Ed. by David Garnett. Viking Compass, C 141. $1.65pa.
ISBN 0-670-00141-4.

The Mint. Norton Library. $1.95pa. ISBN 0-393-00196-2.

Minorities. Ed. by J. M. Wilson. Doubleday. $10.00. ISBN 0-385-07001-2.

Evolution of a Revolt: Early Post War Writings. Ed. by S. and R. Weintraub. Pennsylvania State University Press. $7.50. ISBN 0-271-73133-8.

190. Liddell Hart, Sir Basil Henry. **Colonel Lawrence: The Man Behind the Legend.** New
York, Dodd, Mead, 1935. 406p. maps. index. LC 36-300. D 568.4.L45L5 1935.
DDC 940.4153. (Blackwell's List No. 989 lists: **T. E. Lawrence in Arabia and After,**
1971. (Repr. of 1936 ed.). £9.00; £0.90pa.)

The military history of Lawrence and the Arab revolt, well written by a reknowned
expert in military science who was an admiring friend of the subject, with only a little on the
pre- and post-World War I periods. A most interesting book for the general reader. It complements the other works in this *Guide*, which deal only briefly or unsystematically with the
military aspect. Cf. Aldington's account (item 186).

191. Mūsá, Sulaymān. **T. E. Lawrence: An Arab View.** By Suleiman Mousa. Tr. from Arabic.
London, Oxford University Press, 1966. 301p. bibliog. o.p. LC 66-73739. D 568.4.L45M8.
DDC 940.4150924.

This account from the Arab perspective seeks to show that Lawrence's role in the Arab
Revolt was far overplayed by the West, when in actuality the Arabs did most of it themselves.
Not a particularly impressive book in its scholarship and methodology, but it reflects the
current view in the Arab world. A useful example of the special pleading characteristic of so
many Arabic works of history, but a point that deserves attention.

VII. CIVILIZATION

See also the "Civilization" sections under individual countries.

A. GENERAL

192. Farrukh, Omar A. **The Arab Genius in Science and Philosophy.** Tr. from Arabic by
John B. Hardie. Washington, D.C., American Council of Learned Societies, 1954. 161p.
(Near Eastern Translation Program, No. 10). LC 55-1238 rev. B741.F33. DDC 189.3.

A typical Arab view of medieval Islamic civilization still propounded today in book after
book; the title indicates the gist of the book. Europe's nineteenth century discovery of the
Near East included medieval Arabo-Islamic civilization, which one school of thought, at least,
praised highly. In a period when the West was impinging on Islamic culture, Muslims found such
praise a great ego boost, especially when Europeans traced the source of their own renaissance
to contacts with Islamic civilization and learning in Spain, Sicily, etc., as some did. As the Arabs
discovered their own "lost" civilization, to a significant extent through the efforts of Europeans, they developed much pride in it for its own sake, not just as a defense against Western
civilization. Nowadays, though Arab scholars are still using Western scholarship, they rely more
on themselves to study their heritage—using methods gained from Europe, which in turn
Europe had learned from Islam, as Farrukh might put it. Farrukh is a product of the early
transition stage from dependence to more self-assured scholarly independence.

193. Goitein, Solomon Dob Fritz. **Jews and Arabs: Their Contacts Through the Ages.** 3rd ed.,
rev. New York, Schocken Books, 1974. 263p. bibliog. index. $10.00; $2.95 pa. LC
74-9141. ISBN 0-8052-3567-1; 0-8052-0464-4pa. DS 135.T8 G 57 1974. DDC
301.29'17'671.

[P] A book for the educated general reader by one of the greatest Hebraicists-Arabists, who
has done extensive work on the subject. Dealing first with the pre-Islamic period, he demolishes
the myth of semitic brotherhood so glibly used by many writers and apologists, and then
details the realities of Jewish-Muslim relations during the Middle Ages. He covers the problem
of Jewish status in the Islamic Empire and Jewish cultural development during the same era.
Even for readers not interested in Jewish-Muslim relations, Goitein presents a fascinating,
informative picture of medieval Jewish life and culture which is in fact the book's main
emphasis; indeed, this emphasis will disappoint those interested in more detail on Jewish-
Muslim relations. The last few pages concern the modern conflict, stressing the rebirth of two
peoples, which he says is the basis for the conflict; he does not go into any detail on the conflict itself.

194. Goitein, Solomon Dob Fritz. **A Mediterranean Society: The Jewish Communities of the
Arab World as Portrayed in the Documents of the Cairo Geniza.** Berkeley, University of
California Press, 1967-ca. 1975. 3v. bibliog. notes. index. LC 67-22430. D 199.3.G58.
DDC 915.6'09'74924. Vol. 1: **Economic Foundations.** 1967. 550p. 100p. notes. 60p.
indices. $17.25. ISBN 0-520-00484-1; Vol. 2: **Community.** 1971. $20.00. ISBN
0-520-01867-2; Vol. 3: **Daily Life and the Individual.** 1975 (forthcoming).

[C2, S3] This massive, deeply researched work concerns mainly the Cairo Jewish community
and its relationship with the medieval Muslim world around it. It is based primarily on a treasure
house of contemporary documents discarded in a room in a Cairo synagogue because it was
believed wrong to destroy writings in Hebrew characters (in this case Arabic language written
in Hebrew script). Goitein has studied these priceless documents for decades, and the result,
integrated with a thorough study of all other sources, is a work with so much information on
the Islamic world, including its economics, that it is an invaluable source for all good Near
Eastern collections, particularly since it deals with all aspects of life. Volume 1 discusses the

documents; the Mediterranean scene during the period 969-1250; the groups of working people; finance and commerce (including the characteristics of the merchant class and the way business was carried on, commodities, trade routes, and prices); travel and seafaring. Volume 2 deals with the Jewish community, including its organization; education; the political class; interfaith relations; communal jurisdiction (including courts, law, and procedures); the state; Jewish-Muslim government relations; documentary appendices. Volume 3 will cover housing, clothing, food and daily routine; the family; the Mediterranean mind.

195. Hitti, Philip Khûri. **Islam: A Way of Life.** Minneapolis, University of Minnesota Press, 1970. 188p. bibliog. index. $6.50. LC 78-104054. ISBN 0-8166-0569-6. D 199.3.H57 1970. DDC 910.03'176'7. Paperback: New York, Henry Regnery, 1971. (Gate 6155). $1.95.

[P]   Another of Hitti's popularizations. Rather than being an exposition of the Islamic way of life as such, it is an introduction to Muhammad's life and Islam's teachings, and it is a brief history of Islamic civilization—the sects, philosophy, science, literature, etc.

196. Ibn al-Nadim, Muḥammad ibn Isḥāq (fl. 987). **The Fihrist of al-Nadim: A Tenth-Century Survey of Muslim Culture.** Ed. and tr. by Bayard Dodge. New York, Columbia University Press, 1970. 2v. (1149p.). bibliog. index. $40.00. LC 68-8874. ISBN 0-231-02925-X. Z 7052.I213. DDC 910.03'175'927.

A scholar and book dealer, the author wrote an immense catalog of all books known to him after much searching, with information on their authors, contents, and subjects. This is probably the single most important document in the history of Islamic civilization through the tenth century. It is arranged topically, then by author. It is a mine of information on all aspects of tenth century knowledge and literary activity, and the times as reflected in books and the lives of the writers. In some areas it is our main or only source of information—for example, see his account of an early version of the Arabian Nights, and some of the Islamic and other religious sects of the time. It is an important source in the history of Islamic philosophy and for information on the process by which Greek philosophy and science entered Islamic civilization. Dodge further assists the student with voluminous informative notes, a glossary, and a 204-page biographical dictionary, which identifies each individual and gives classical and other sources of further information on him, and his location in the *Fihrist.*

197. Kaykāvūs ibn Iskandar ibn Qābūs, ᶜUnṣur al-Maᶜālī (1021/1022-1098/1099). **Qābūs-nāma. (A Mirror for Princes).** Tr. from Persian by Reuben Levy. New York, E. P. Dutton, 1951. 265p. bibliog. index. o.p. LC 51-11112 rev. BJ 1678.P3K33 1951a. DDC 170.02232.

A book of practical counsel by a Persian prince to his son, who is slated to be his successor, emphasizing moral percepts and rules of conduct. It covers everything: the basics of religion, cultivation of the mind, recreation, enjoyment of life, the sciences, how to buy slaves, court conduct (both as King and courtier), duties of the king and his vizier, economics. It contains many illustrative anecdotes and quotations from poetry. Aside from being a good example of a common genre of literature, it provides many details that illuminate court life and outlook of eleventh century Iran.

198. Lewis, Bernard, comp. **Islam, from the Prophet Muhammad to the Capture of Constantinople.** New York, Walker & Co., 1975?. bibliog. glossary. index. (The Documentary History of Western Civilization Series). $12.50 per vol. LC cataloging n.a. ISBN 0-8027-2023-4 (v.1); 0-8027-2055-2 (v.2). Paperback: Harper Torchbooks, $3.95 per vol. LC 72-7229. ISBN 0-06-138924-2 (v.1); 0-06-138925-0 (v.2). DS 36.855.L48 1974. DDC 910'.031'7671.

An interesting collection of translations by the compiler. Many of these are here translated for the first time, mainly from medieval Arabic, but also from Persian, Turkish, and even Hebrew texts. Each item is preceded by an introduction. Two-thirds of Volume 1 present accounts of events in the history of the Islamic Empire; 50 pages deal with the concepts of government, statecraft, and administration; the rest of the volume covers war, military arts, conquests, and peace terms. Volume 2 treats religion, law, society, economics, ethnic groups and minorities, and humor. Rather than being a systematic collection of fundamental documents, the book seeks to provide the more advanced student with additional source material through which he can develop a greater feel for the currents, styles, and modes of thought of Islamic civilization as reflected in our available sources.

199. Levy, Reuben. **The Social Structure of Islam, Being the Second Edition of The Sociology of Islam.** Cambridge, England, Cambridge University Press, 1962. 536p. bibliog. index. $15.50; $4.95pa. LC (1957 ed.) A 57-3647. ISBN 0-521-09182-9. HN 40.M6L4.

[P1, P2, C1, S1] A formal systematic survey of the Islamic institutions of the medieval period: social classes, women, children, law, moral sentiments, and ethics; Islamic customs and secular law; the Caliphate, political institutions, and the administration; military organization; Islamic cosmology and the theory of creation. It is a detailed, comprehensive manual of the theory and practice of the religious, ethical, political, philosophical, social, and legal structures of Islamic civilization, containing a wealth of information and using and defining a great deal of Arabic vocabulary. A basic book for all serious students, and a must for all but the smallest collections. It should be read before any other work on Islamic law, because it deals with many of the basic concepts and provisions of the law throughout.

200. Mez, Adam, 1869-1917. **The Renaissance of Islam.** Tr. from German. New York, AMS Press, 1974. 538p. $27.00. LC 70-180361. ISBN 0-404-56293-0. DS 36.85.M4913 1974. DDC 910'.031'7671.

[C2] A classic work on the civilization of the tenth century Muslim world, including all aspects of life: government, culture, economics, classes of society, religion and its organization, festivals, communications, science, etc. There are many quotations and details not found in the other works listed in this *Guide.* An interesting and very useful mosaic image of Islam's "golden age." A basic work.

201. Nasr, Seyyed Hossein. **Science and Civilization in Islam.** Cambridge, Mass., Harvard University Press, 1968. 384p. bibliog. index. $10.00. LC 68-25616. ISBN 0-674-79305-6. Q 125.N17. DDC 509'.1767. Paperback: New York, New American Library (Plume, Z 5005). $3.50.

[P1, P2, C1, S1] A history of Islamic science and its key figures. It describes the various fields—medicine, alchemy, physics, cosmology, geography and natural history, mathematics, astronomy, science of man—relating each as pursued and expounded by the scientists to the Islamic view of the world it reflected. Following a chapter on the influence of Islamic alchemy on the West is a longish section dealing with philosophy, theology-philosophy conflict, and the Gnostic (Sufi) tradition. The first 90 pages concern the basis of Islamic civilization, the universal men who were the key scientists and who were major philosophers and theologians as well, and the teaching system and educational institutions that produced them. The book is written in non-technical language, which makes even the more abstract and analytical portions intelligible for the less initiated reader. A most informative and interesting book, basic for colleges and students.

202. Rosenthal, Erwin Isak Jacob. **Judaism and Islam.** New York, Thomas Yoseloff, 1961. 154p. bibliog. index. (Popular Jewish Library). o.p. LC 61-13935. BP 173.J8R6. DDC 297.

[C] A general work for the general reader. It tries to suggest the Jewish elements and influences in various aspects of Islam, with comparisons of the two faiths, including theology, the Koran, Hadith, and law. The first section goes so far as to suggest that Islam is *dependent* on Judaism. Most of the book describes Judaism's development and manifestations under medieval Islam, including philosophy, theology, ethics, poetry, scholarship, etc., noting Muslim influences thereon and parallels between Islam and Judaism during that period. Complements Goitein (item 193).

203. Schacht, Joseph, and C. E. Bosworth, eds. **The Legacy of Islam.** 2nd ed. Oxford, Clarendon Press, 1974. 530p. bibliog. illus. index. $11.95. LC 74-195528. ISBN 0-19-821913-X. DS 36.85.S3. DDC 909.

[P1, C1] This new edition of the standard work has chapters by various top authorities on the history of Islamic studies and the image of Islam in the West; Islam as a force in the Mediterranean world and Europe's interaction with Islam; Islam in Africa, India, Central Asia, and Indonesia; politics and war—theory, practice, and history. These are chapters and treatments not found in the old edition. Also, economics, art and architecture, literature, philosophy and theology, law, the sciences and music, all of which are organized somewhat differently in the new edition, reflecting new approaches. The old edition's chapters on Spain and Portugal and on the Crusades have been dropped. This book is a useful supplementary reading representing recent scholarship; students might do well to compare the two editions. Also, cf. Arnold, Sir Thomas Walker, and Alfred Guillaume, *The Legacy of Islam* (Oxford, Clarendon Press, 1952. [Repr. of 1931 ed.]. 416p. illus. LC 31-34509. D 199.3.A7).

For smaller libraries, Hitti's *History* of the Arabs will be quite sufficient. More advanced students should find Peters' *Allah's Commonwealth* more meaningful because it synthesizes and relates everything and often gives more detail.

Another introduction is:

Savory, Roger M., ed. **Introduction to Islamic Civilization.** Cambridge, England, Cambridge University Press, 1975 (forthcoming). LC 74-25662. ISBN 0-521-20777-0; 0-521-09948-Xpa.

Other works on Islamic civilization are:

Dunlop, D. M. **Arab Civilization to A.D. 1500.** New York, Praeger, 1971. 368p. LC 72-125397. DS 36.855.D85 1971b. DDC 910'.03'17671. Treats the subject in such a manner that it is almost a series of bibliographical essays on the classical Arabic writings in each field.

Faris, Nabih Amin, ed. **The Arab Heritage.** New York, Russell & Russell, 1963. (Repr. of 1944 ed.). 279p. LC 63-8362. DS 215.F3 1963. DDC 915.3.

Gibb, Hamilton Alexander Rosskeen. **Studies in the Civilization of Islam.** Ed. by S. J. Shaw and W. R. Polk. Boston, Beacon Press, 1962. 399p. LC 62-7195. D 199.3.G5. DDC 915.6. Key articles on various aspects of history and civilization by one of the top Orientalists; most of them are standard works in the field. Many can be appreciated by only slightly initiated readers.

Hell, Joseph. **The Arab Civilization.** Tr. from German. Cambridge, England, W. Heffer, 1926. 128p. bibliog. LC 26-22004. DS 215.H4.

Unity and Variety in Muslim Civilization. Ed. by Gustave E. Von Grunebaum. Chicago, University of Chicago Press, 1963. (Repr. of 1955 ed.). 385p. LC has 55-11191. DS 38.V6 [1955]. DDC 915. Aspects of Islamic civilization, plus items on Islam in Indonesia, tropical Africa, Turkey, medieval Spain, North Africa, Iran.

Studies in Islamic Cultural History. Menasha, Wis., American Anthropological Association, 1954. 60p. (Comparative Studies in Cultures and Civilization, No. 2). (American Anthropological Association. Mémoire No. 76). LC 54-4261. GN 2.A22 No. 76. [D 199.3.V65] DDC 915. Important essays.

Von Grunebaum, Gustave Edmund. **Islam: Essays in the Nature and Growth of a Cultural Tradition.** New York, Barnes & Noble, 1961. 206p. LC 61-66666. D 199.3.V62 1961a. DDC 915.6. Important essays by a top Orientalist.

Young, Theodore Cuyler, ed. **Near Eastern Culture and Society: A Symposium on the Meeting of East and West.** Princeton, N.J., Princeton University Press, 1951. 250p. LC 54-13881. PJ 25.P7 Vol. 15 [DS 38.Y6]. DDC 915. Thirteen essays on Near East-Western relations. The first six dwell on Western studies—history and prospects—of Islamic art, science, religion, and literature. The last seven concern East-West interaction in the cultural and diplomatic realms. Useful for beginners, particularly the first group.

204. Schroeder, Eric. **Muhammad's People; A Tale By Anthology: The Religion and Politics, Poetry and Violence, Science, Ribaldry & Finance of the Muslims from the Age of Ignorance Before Islam and the Mission of God's Prophet to Sophistication in the Eleventh Century, a Mosaic Translation.** Porter's Landing, Freeport, Me., Bond Wheelwright Co., 1955. 838p. bibliog. indices. $7.50. LC 54-10621. D 199.3.S42. DDC 950.

[P1, C1, S1] A remarkable collection of lore from classical Islamic literature for the edification of the reader, which, in entertaining fashion, opens a window on Islamic civilization and history.

There are anecdotes about kings and heroes from classical histories, poetry, stories and ribaldry about the classes of society; religious literature; Sufism. It gives a clear idea of the style and type of writing, and insight into the audiences for whom the selections were originally written. A basic work.

205. Stewart-Robinson, J. **The Traditional Near East.** Englewood Cliffs, N.J., Prentice-Hall, 1966. 183p. (A Spectrum Book). o.p. LC 66-28107. DS 42.4.S75. DDC 910.091767.

A collection of interesting and stimulating articles on issues in the history of the Islamic Empire and its civilization for the reader with a basic general knowledge. It covers two interpretations of Islamic history; items on the role of the Turks in Islam; Persian-Arab relations; the individual in Islamic law; is the Caliph a Pope?; the rise of Islamic philosophy; and literary tendencies.

206. al-Tanūkhī, al-Muḥassin ibn ᶜAlī, 940?-994. [Nishwār al-Muḥāḍarah wa-Akhbar al-Mudhākarah.] The Table-Talk of a Mesopotamian Judge. Tr. from Arabic by D. S. Margoliouth. London, Royal Asiatic Society, 1922. 2v. LC 46-33483 rev. PJ 408.07 v. 27-28. [PJ 7741.T3N5].

Interesting anecdotes and narratives of miscellaneous facts and material that give much insight into the author's times and civilization, through what he heard and witnessed, concerning government, history, officials, and economics. An interesting, often entertaining source on the Islamic Empire. Volume 1 is Arabic text; Volume 2, the translation.

207. Tritton, Arthur Stanley. **The Caliphs and Their Non-Muslim Subjects: A Critical Study of the Covenant of Umar.** London, Frank Cass; distr. Portland, Ore., International Scholarly Book Services, 1970. (Repr. of 1930 ed.). 240p. bibliog. index. $13.00. LC 72-185326. ISBN 0-7146-1996-5. DS 36.9.D47T74 1970. DDC 910'.031'7671.

A factual statement of available data on the life and treatment by Muslims of Christians and Jews in the Islamic Empire, with comments on the Covenant attributed to Umar, the second Caliph, concerning the status of these groups. Coverage is topical: government service, religious buildings, church and state, Arab Christians; religious practices, particularly public ceremonies and bell-ringing; dress codes, persecutions, social conditions; medicine and literature; holy ground; taxation. There is much on the restrictions on minority activities, variations in their treatment, the extent to which the Covenant was observed, and its legal aspects. Tritton concludes that the position of the minorities was not secure, though their members often occupied high positions in the Muslim governments. Too detailed and technical for most collections, but it concerns an often-asked question, and it is still one of the best treatments of the subject available.

208. Von Grunebaum, Gustave Edmund. **Medieval Islam: A Study in Cultural Orientation.** 2nd ed. Chicago, University of Chicago Press, 1953. 378p. index. $6.75; $3.45pa. (Phoenix Book, P69). LC 53-9941. ISBN 0-226-31024-8; 0-226-31025-6pa. D 199.3. V64 1953. DDC 950.

[P1, C1, S1, S2] This is an attempt to explore Islam's self-view, its structure, institutions, social structure, values and ideals, and the relationship of the Muslim and Christian worlds. It deals with revelation in Islamic thought; Islamic piety and religious life, religious poetry, asceticism; law and state and their meaning to Islam and Muslims; Arab-non-Arab rivalries; human ideals (man, in religion, literature); reverence for knowledge; polite education (*adab*); literature; and varieties of history and their nature. This is an illuminating work by an outstanding Orientalist; it is basic for college and larger public libraries. Not for the beginner, since a general background is assumed.

209. Watt, William Montgomery. **The Influence of Islam on Medieval Europe.** Edinburgh, Edinburgh University Press; distr. Chicago, Aldine Publishing Co., 1972. 125p. bibliog. (Islamic Surveys, 9). $5.50. LC 70-182902. ISBN 0-202-15022-4. DS 36.85.I8 No. 9 [CB 251]. DDC 910'.031'17675 [914'.03'1].

Lectures on the interaction of Europe and Islam during the Middle Ages—intellectual, material, historical. One aspect discussed is Islam's role in the awakening of Europe, particularly the self-awareness and rise of Christian confidence which led to the Crusades. Fine for the general reader well acquainted with European history, though elementary and too brief for the reader more knowledgeable of the Islamic world. In effect, it summarizes information found in greater detail in Hitti (item 88).

See also:

Daniel, Norman. **The Arabs and Mediaeval Europe.** London, Longman, 1975. 378p. bibliog. illus. index. (Arab Background Series). £7.50. LC 73-93276. ISBN 0-582-78045-4. LC cataloging n.a.   A variety of details and generalizations illustrating and documenting the range of relations between the Islamic and European worlds of the eighth to the fourteenth centuries. Taken from European sources and depicting only the European perspective, it shows the state of Europe's knowledge of the Arabs and Islam and its attitudes towards them, its reactions to the relations, and its misunderstandings, with comments on feelings and experiences shared by both Europeans and Arabs. Includes daily relations of Crusaders with the Muslims, religious polemics, passage of Arab science to Europe, aspects of the relationship found in European literature, and many comments on European writings of various kinds. For the reader with some background, but very difficult reading due to the author's style.

Daniel, Norman. **Islam and the West: The Making of an Image.** Edinburgh, Edinburgh University Press, 1960. 443p. LC 60-4951. BP 172.D3. DDC 297.

B. ART

See also the "Civilization" sections under individual countries.

210. Arnold, Sir Thomas Walker. **Painting in Islam: A Study of the Place of Pictorial Art in Muslim Culture.** New York, Dover Publications, 1965. 159p. illus. index. $3.00. LC 65-12451. ISBN 0-486-21310-2. ND 198.A7 1965. DDC 759.956.

Discusses Islamic hostility to pictorial art in its religious life: theological attitudes; the destruction of many manuscripts in the historic sacks of cities; origins of painting in the Muslim world; the painter and his manner of working the subject matter; Islamic religious art (such as pictures of Muhammad or Ali); the prophets; portraits; the expression of emotion in the paintings. An interesting work, one of few available in any language on the subject. Useful for those who have read one of the basic introductions listed in this *Guide*; not a comprehensive introductory work itself.

211. Creswell, Keppel Archibald Cameron. **A Short Account of Early Muslim Architecture.** Beirut, Librairie du Liban, 1968. (c.1958). 330p. bibliog. illus. index. $8.40. LC 72-253234. NA 380.C73 1968. DDC 723'.3.

[C1]   This standard work on the subject, by a foremost expert, covers the period through the end of the ninth century. It treats the details of individual buildings and the origins and influence of various styles, with discussions of the theories and literature on the subject. It includes selected buildings from North Africa and Spain but excludes Iran, Turkey, and India since they had no major Islamic structures at this early date. The text is followed by 72 pages of illustrations.

212. Grabar, Oleg. **The Formation of Islamic Art.** New Haven, Conn., Yale University Press, 1973. 233p. bibliog. 131 illus. index. $17.50. LC 72-75193. ISBN 0-300-01505-4. N 6260.G69.

[B, C2]   The development of Islamic art from the seventh to the tenth centuries: a stimulating interpretive essay that seeks to explore the process by which a distinctive style blossomed. It explores the symbolic aspects, Islam's attitude toward art, Islamic religious and secular art, decoration, and the author's conclusion about the process. This is not a systematic history and presentation of specific works of art. It requires some general background on the reader's part in history and art. It is an important study in Islamic civilization from a particular perspective, helps make meaningful much of what the reader will learn from other books, and suggests ideas that the student should consider in his further reading, both on art and on other aspects of Islamic civilization. Basic for larger collections. The critical bibliographical essay is quite helpful.

See also:

The Islamic City and Its Role in Art. Ed. by A. Hutt. London, Luzac, 1975?.

213. Grube, Ernst J. **The World of Islam.** New York, McGraw-Hill Book Co., 1967. 176p. bibliog. index. (Landmarks of the World's Art). o.p. LC 66-19271. N 6260.G77. DDC 704.948'9'7.

[P1, C1, S1] A chronological or topical treatment, whichever is more appropriate to the particular subject being discussed, on medieval Islamic art. It has an adequate text that is useful for the general reader, but the main reason for purchasing this oversized volume is the magnificent colored plates that dominate the book (105 color plates, 101 black and white illustrations). It should be in all libraries; it is hoped that the publisher will reissue it.

214. Jairazbhoy, Rafique Ali. **An Outline of Islamic Architecture.** New York, Asia Publishing House, 1972. 338p. bibliog. illus. index. $16.00. LC 73-166250. ISBN 0-210-31156-8. NA 380.J34. DDC 723'.3.

[B, P1, C1] A country-by-country account, with a chapter on "How Islamic architecture transformed the face of Europe." It covers India, Turkey, and Iran, as well as the rest of the Near East and North Africa, and it includes the historical context. A useful introduction, with 189 plates and textual illustrations.

215. Kühnel, Ernst. **Islamic Art and Architecture.** Tr. from German. Ithaca, N.Y., Cornell University Press, 1966. 200p. bibliog. illus. index. $9.50. LC 66-19223. ISBN 0-8014-0238-7. N 6260.K7783 1966. DDC 704.94897.

[P1, C1, S2] A systematic introductory survey from the beginnings through the Ottoman period, covering some key buildings, plus items in the minor arts, styles, motifs, etc. Its aim is to orient the reader to the main characteristics of each type of art during the various periods in each main region, rather than to survey famous art works. Thus it deals mainly in generalities, and should be read in conjunction with works detailing individual items. Basic.

216. Kühnel, Ernst. **The Minor Arts of Islam.** Tr. from German. Ithaca, N.Y., Cornell University Press, 1971. 255p. bibliog. 206 illus. index. $10.00. LC 75-110331. ISBN 0-8014-0563-7. NK 1674.K813 1971. DDC 709'.176'71.

An introduction to the "minor" arts—painting, metal work, carpets, books and manuscript illuminations, pottery, glass and crystal, ivory work. Arranged by type of work, subdivided by period. A handbook for museum employees, collectors, and dealers. The author discusses styles, details found rarely or commonly, schools, techniques, style distribution, degree of rarity, and forgeries. This work provides the beginner with a useful perspective and much information not found in other introductions. Generalities rather than individual pieces are the author's main interest, though famous items are well represented as examples.

217. New York. Metropolitan Museum of Art. **A Handbook of Muhammadan Art.** By Maurice Sven Dimand. 3rd rev. and enl. ed. New York, Metropolitan Museum of Art; distr. Greenwich, Conn., New York Graphic Society, 1958 (c.1944). bibliog. illus. o.p. LC 58-2391. NK 720.N4 1958. DDC 745.

This basic outline is arranged by type of art, subdivided by area-period-school. It covers the minor (non-architectural) arts: wall and miniature painting; calligraphy and illumination; bookbinding; sculpture in stone and stucco; wood carving, ivory, and bone carving; metalwork, ceramics, glass, and crystal; textiles and carpets. The text describes and details the significance of individual pieces in the Museum, and other items as well. It requires supplementary reading such as Kühnel (item 216) for general and specific characteristics of the art, as well as works with color illustrations, since its hundreds of illustrations are in black and white.

218. Rice, David Talbot. **Islamic Art.** New York, Praeger, 1965. 286p. bibliog. illus. $8.50. LC 65-10179. ISBN 0-275-41720-4. N 6260.R53 1965. DDC 704. 94897. Paperback: $3.95. ISBN 0-275-70310-X.

[C1] A general history for the uninitiated presented chronologically and by region. The author is not a specialist in the field, and one eminent specialist has cautioned his readers against the book. However, as a commonly available and not grossly misleading orientation, it is useful for public libraries and the general reader. Covers the period through sixteenth century Iran and the Ottoman Empire, omitting India. A great many of the 249 photos are in color.

219. Ry van Beest Holle, Carel J. du. **Art of Islam.** Text by Carel J. Du Ry. New York, H. N. Abrams, 1971. 263p. bibliog. illus. index. (Panorama of World Art). LC 72-92914. ISBN 0-8109-8014-2. N6260.R914.

[P1, C1, S1] A general introduction covering basically the same material as other works in this *Guide*. The color plates that grace nearly every page are, on the whole, the best that the annotator has seen, and there are many more of them. When the items depicted are those used to illustrate similar books, the photos in this book are usually from a different angle and generally give a greater feel for the reality of the piece than do the illustrations in the other books. A most rewarding and enjoyable book.

VIII. LANGUAGE AND LITERATURE

Except for the most recent works, Near Eastern literatures are quite different in their conception from Western literature, their form, and much of their content. The uninitiated enters a new world and needs a complete reorientation in order to get his bearings. Unfortunately, the tools for such a reorientation are few and those that do exist are quite inadequate. Though much research has yet to be done, and works for the scholar are relatively few, still, enough work has been done so that large single volumes could be prepared for each literature. Translations of literary works are also relatively few, and they are widely scattered, mainly in periodicals. A sizeable anthology could readily be compiled for each literature with little trouble. We almost totally lack general works on the modern literatures, and we are almost as bad off for the period since 1400. When this type of material is published, it must be considered essential for most libraries. As for the languages, we can make do for the most part, but there is much work still to be done on dictionaries, grammars, etc.

A. GENERAL

220. Arberry, Arthur John. **Aspects of Islamic Civilization as Depicted in the Original Texts.** New York, A. S. Barnes, 1964. 408p. o.p. LC 65-24575. BP 89.A7 1964b. DDC 910. 03'176'7. Paperback: Ann Arbor, University of Michigan Press, 1967. 409p. (Ann Arbor Paperbacks, AA 130). $2.95. ISBN 0-472-06130-5.

[P1, C1, S1] Selections from the many translations of key Persian and Arabic works made by the late famous Orientalist. The collection represents an excellent cross-section of types and styles of Islamic belles-lettres and popular religious literature, mainly from the medieval period. Each piece has an introduction. Included is a bibliography of the translator's works. A basic book.

221. Chraibi, Driss. **Heirs to the Past.** Tr. from French. London, Heinemann, 1972. 106p. pa. LC 73-150065. ISBN 0-435-090079-X. PZ4.C552 He. DDC 843'.9'14.

A novelette by an outstanding Algerian author who writes in French. The theme of the novelette is the conflict of modern European civilization versus traditional faith.

222. Hillelson, Sigmar, ed. **Week-End Caravan.** 2nd ed. London, W. Hodge, 1947. 352p. bibliog. LC 48-12573. PJ 409.H5 1947. DDC 890.82.

Anthology of prose and verse translations from Arabic, Persian, and Turkish, and of passages relating to the Islamic countries by Western writers. Arranged by topic—harem, natural and unnatural history, magic and the jinn, the nursery, detectives, travellers' tales. A delightful book that gives the Western reader an excellent idea of what many medieval "adab" works were like.

223. Ibrāhīm, Ṣunᶜ Allāh. **The Smell of It and Other Stories.** Tr. from French. London, Heinemann, 1971. 118p. (African Writers Series, 95). £1.50; £0.50pa. LC 72-193283. ISBN 0-435-90633-X; 0-435-90095-1pa. PZ4.I135 Sm. [PJ 7838.B7173 T53]. DDC 892.7'3'6.

Five interesting stories originally written in French by a North African writer.

224. Kritzeck, James, ed. **Anthology of Islamic Literature from the Rise of Islam to Modern Times.** New York, Holt, Rinehart and Winston, 1964. 379p. bibliog. o.p. LC 63-11871. PJ 7694.E1K7. DDC 808.89. Paperback: New York, New American Library, 1966. 352p. (A Mentor Book, MT 666). $0.75.

[P1, C1, S1] A wide variety of interesting and sometimes entertaining excerpts from poetry and prose, including non-fiction works in various fields such as theology, to 1800. Each selection has a short introduction. Most selections are well-known pieces, by a variety of translators, and are fairly representative.

225. Kritzeck, James, comp. **Modern Islamic Literature from 1800 to the Present.** New York, Holt, Rinehart and Winston, 1970. 310p. bibliog. $10.00. LC 66-10269. ISBN 0-03-053685-5. PJ 409.K7. DDC 892.7'08'005. Paperback: New York, New American Library, 1972. (Mentor Books MJ 1166). $1.95.

[P1, C1, S1] A wide variety of literary and non-literary writings by Muslim authors from all over the Muslim world. Most of the items do not reflect Islamic themes, but many are interesting to read; when they are read with other works, they offer some entrance into the variety of the non-Western world, its ideas, milieux, and people. Each selection has a brief introduction. For public libraries.

226. Najib Ullah. **Islamic Literature: An Introductory History with Selections.** New York, Washington Square Press, 1973. 442p. bibliog. index. o.p. LC 63-1613. PJ 807.N3.

[P1, C1, S1] Arabic, Turkish, and Persian literature from Islam to recent times, with many translations, especially poetry. The first 211 pages cover Arabic, including non-belletristic works; pages 216-365 cover Persian literature; and pages 370-428, Turkish literature. The latter two include only belles-lettres. The only such work in English, it is essential for all libraries.

227. New York University Near Eastern Round Table, 2d., 1968-1969. **Modern Near East: Literature and Society.** Ed. by C. Max Kortepeter. New York, Center for Near Eastern Studies, New York University, 1971. 83p. $1.95. pa. LC 72-181640. PJ 310.N4. DDC 890.

Four essays on aspects of Arabic, Turkish, Persian, and Hebrew literature and society.

228. Nicholson, Reynold Alleyne. **Studies in Islamic Poetry.** Cambridge, England, Cambridge University Press, 1969. (Repr. of 1921 ed.). 300p. index. (Cambridge University Press Library Editions). $17.50. LC 70-103805. ISBN 0-521-07779-6. PJ 827.N5 1969. DDC 892.7'1'34.

Part I (42 pages) consists of Persian court poetry. It is a translation of parts of Muhammad CAwfi's *Lubab al-A.bab*, which has many different samples of poetry, with Nicholson's comments on the types and content of the poetry. Part II (165 pages) consists of *Luzumiyat* of Abu al-CAla' al-MaCarri, the blind premier poet of the tenth century. It is reflective poetry, with some running commentary and an introduction. The rest contains the Arabic text of MaCarri's poetry. A useful addition to larger collections.

229. Nicholson, Reynold Alleyne, tr. **Translations of Eastern Poetry and Prose.** New York, Greenwood Press, 1969. (Repr. of 1922 ed.). 200p. bibliog. index. $10.00. LC 74-90154. ISBN 0-8371-2301-1. PJ 418.N5 1969. DDC 808.81.

[P1, C1] Thirty-two authors are represented, mainly poets and mainly Arab. Some Persian and some non-belletristic works are included, such as history. A useful collection for smaller college and public libraries.

230. Ortzen, Len, comp. and tr. **North African Writing.** Tr. from French. London, Heinemann Educational Books; distr. New York, Humanities Press, 1970. 134p. bibliog. (African Writers Series, 73). $1.75. LC 71-475404. ISBN 0-435-90073-0. PZ 1.073 No. DDC 843'.008.

Short stories by Algerian, Moroccan, and Tunisian authors writing in French: Muhammad Dib, Driss Chraibi, Hacene Farouk Zehar, Ahmed Sefrioui, Mouloud Feraoun, Assia Djebar, Malek Haddad, Kateb Yacine, etc. Includes useful introductions on the lives, works, and background of the authors and their times. Much reflection in the stories on the French occupation period, the problems of the Frenchified Algerians, French-native relations, etc. Most interesting and enjoyable reading.

B. ARABIC LANGUAGE (GENERAL)

231. Chejne, Anwar G. **The Arabic Language: Its Role in History.** Minneapolis, University of Minnesota Press, 1969. 240p. bibliog. illus. index. $6.75. LC 68-16314. ISBN 0-8166-0516-5. PJ 6075.C5. DDC 492.7'09.

[P1, C1, S1]   The main emphasis in this fairly interesting book is the position the language has occupied in society and the role it has in building the modern nation-state. It discusses the religious significance of Arabic as the language of the Koran and its subsequent role in various fields. There is a basic introduction to the characteristics of the language for the totally uninitiated reader, and to the history of its codification, standardization and philological studies, its development and decline. Also covered are the revival of literary Arabic in modern times, largely as a result of the West's penetration and both direct and indirect influences; the modern leaders of the linguistic movement and their main students; problems and proposals concerning the reform of the language and its script. The book goes into some detail on the medieval studies because of their importance: the fields of study; the need to interpret the Koranic language for religious reasons; Arabic in the hands of non-Arab Muslims who had to learn it for religious purposes and because it became the language of civilization and the royal courts; the Greek translation movement; schools of philological study and their arguments; Arabic's role in the educational curriculum and branches of science. Also, the spread of education and journalism and resulting stylistic developments; the Arab academies for language study and coining of new words; Arabic versus Western languages; and government policy on the use of Arabic. A useful introduction for the general reader.

C. ARABIC WRITTEN LANGUAGE
(MODERN STANDARD AND CLASSICAL)

232. Ba^clabakkī, Munīr. **al-Mawrid. A Modern English-Arabic Dictionary.** Beirut, Dar al-Ilm lil-Malayin, 1967. 1090p. $15.00. LC NE 67-1799. PJ 6640.B34.

[C1]   For written, not spoken Arabic. Like all English-Arabic dictionaries currently available, this is more useful for Arabic-speakers working with English; native speakers of English must use an Arabic-English dictionary in order to use the English-Arabic dictionaries, because the multiple Arabic terms and phrases provided for each English word are not individually defined as to their precise meanings, nuances and usages; nor are the examples and phrases fully translated or explained. Ba'albaki is the "best buy" available—others have fewer words or are outdated or much more expensive. This is another area in which the interests of the student have been neglected—if Cassell can produce readily usable English-German and other dictionaries, surely the Arabists can also do the same thing. Ba'albaki is beautifully printed on good paper and adequately bound.

233. Beeston, Alfred Felix Landon. **Written Arabic: An Approach to the Basic Structures.** Cambridge, England, Cambridge University Press, 1968. 117p. indices. $11.00; $3.95pa. LC 68-18342. ISBN 0-521-07081-3; 0-521-09559-Xpa. PJ 6307.B4. DDC 492.7'5.

Intended for mature readers seeking a basic knowledge of modern Arabic as a tool for reading works in their particular disciplines, it is a systematic survey with cross-referencing for review and reference. Basically clear, but requires concentration. It should be used with a reference grammar, and with diligence can be used without a teacher, though a teacher or other informant would be most helpful.

234. Caspari, Carl Paul (1819-1892). **A Grammar of the Arabic Language.** Tr. from German, and edited with numerous additions and corrections, by W[illiam] Wright. 3rd ed. Rev. by W. Robertson Smith and M. J. de Goeje. Cambridge, England, Cambridge University Press, 1967. 2v. in 1. $7.95pa. LC 68-75078. PJ 6305.C5 1967. DDC 492.7'5.

The most detailed Arabic reference grammar, for advanced students, containing the Arabic grammatical terminology. Mainly classical Arabic, whereas Haywood and Nahmad (item 237) is essentially modern standard Arabic. For larger collections. It should be noted that this book is generally known as "Wright."

235. Cowan, David. **An Introduction to Modern Literary Arabic.** Cambridge, England, Cambridge University Press, 1958. 205p. $10.50; $4.45pa. LC 58-14739. ISBN 0-521-09240-X. PJ 6307.C6. DDC 492.78242.

An elementary introductory textbook. Although it is not very good methodologically (it follows the traditional format: grammar lesson, examples, vocabulary, two-way exercises) and it lacks both indexes and glossaries, it usefully supplements the other grammars listed in this *Guide*, providing simpler explanations of some basic points and additional examples. No key for the exercises.

236. Hava, J. G. **Arabic-English Dictionary.** Beirut, Catholic Press, 1963. LC n.a. for this ed. PJ 6640.H3 1963.

A student's dictionary for classical Arabic.

237. Haywood, John A., and H. M. Nahmad. **A New Arabic Grammar of the Written Language.** London, Percy Lund, Humphries, 1964 (c.1962). 687p. index. $15.00; key $3.00. LC 62-6908. ISBN 0-674-60851-X; Key 0-674-50300-7. PJ 6307.H36 1964. DDC 492.78242.

Although this was allegedly intended to be a learning grammar, it is very poor as a beginner's text. However, it is the only work that presents grammar systematically and does not overwhelm the beginner with details useful only to the most advanced student; therefore, it is indispensable as a *reference* grammar.

238. Lovell, Emily Kalled. **A Reference Handbook for Arabic Grammar.** Tempe, Ariz., Lovell, 1974. 195p. index. LC 74-82909. PJ 6307.L6. DDC 492'.7'5. (Order from E. K. Lovell, Box 26013, Tempe, Arizona 85282.)

An alphabetical listing of aspects of modern standard Arabic, using Arabic terms in cases where there is no English equivalent. Each term and usage is explained, with examples. A most convenient aid for less advanced students who are using one of the standard texts, either conventional or aural-oral method, who have at least an elementary knowledge of basic grammatical terminology, alphabet, and basic concepts. It is a good source for review and further explana..on of usage, and it will help in composition. Unfortunately, the index is not sufficiently detailed, so the student must have some idea of what he is looking for and how it is classified grammatically. The Arabic script is cursive, not typed or printed.

239. Madina, Maan Zilfo. **Arabic-English Dictionary of the Modern Literary Language.** New York, Pocket Books, 1973. 791p. $2.50pa. LC n.a. ISBN 0-671-78656-3.

This pocket dictionary is basically an abridgement and rearrangement of Wehr (item 240); it will satisfy most needs—at a vast price difference. There is no paperback English-Arabic dictionary.

240. Wehr, Hans. **A Dictionary of Modern Written Arabic.** Ed. by J. Milton Cowan. Ithaca, N.Y., Spoken Language Service, 1971. (Repr. of 1961 ed.). $40.00. 1110p. LC 73-159677. ISBN 0-87950-000-X. PJ 6640.W43 1971. DDC 492.7'321.

The basic Arabic-English dictionary. It should be noted that any reader wishing to use any of the Arabic dictionaries in print today must know Arabic word structure fairly well. Entry is by root—from which various words are derived using prefixes, infixes, and suffixes according to generally standard patterns—rather than by individual words as in Persian and Turkish dictionaries, languages that are not based on an expandable root structure. This means that the reader who wants to look up an inscription on a postage stamp or figure out the meaning of an Arabic poster in a press photo cannot decipher the text simply by using the dictionary. Only libraries backing up Arabic courses or serving communities that have extensive need for this type of dictionary should pay the high price. Collections that have infrequent need for an Arabic-English dictionary can be satisfied with Madina (item 199). A new edition of Wehr, which is supposed to be much more complete, is near completion and should be published in the not-too-distant future.

D. ARABIC SPOKEN DIALECTS
("COLLOQUIAL" ARABIC)

1. Egyptian

We are in desperate need of an Egyptian-English, English-Egyptian dictionary.

241. Mitchell, T. F. **Colloquial Arabic: The Living Language of Egypt.** London, English
Universities Press, 1962. 240p. (The Teach Yourself Books). $3.50. LC 66-6303.
PJ 6779.M48 1962.

A brief handbook on the spoken language. Pocket-sized and cloth, it is arranged
topically from the simple to the more complex, with no exercises. Half the book consists
of a wide range of practical terms and phrases arranged by topic—travel, human body, post
office, etc.—and these phrases serve as additional grammatical examples. Romanized, not in
Arabic script. A solid, useful, convenient work that can be used to make basic communication
possible in a relatively short time. Anyone using it should have available some recording of
basic Egyptian phrases (even if not from this book) so that he can start off with a reasonable
facsimile of the correct pronunciation.

242. Mitchell, T. F. **An Introduction to Egyptian Colloquial Arabic.** London, Oxford University Press, 1956. 285p. o.p. LC 56-14549. PJ 6779.M5. DDC 492.779.

A textbook for students, arranged in conventional form—lessons, with grammar,
examples, two-way translation exercises, a key to each exercise, and two-way lexicons.

243. Tewfik, Laila Younis, Richard S. Harrell, and George D. Selim. **Lessons in Colloquial
Egyptian Arabic.** Rev. ed. Washington, D.C., Georgetown University Press, 1963.
1v. (various paging). (Georgetown University, Institute of Languages and Linguistics.
Arabic Series, 2). o.p. LC 64-2973 rev. PJ 6779.T4 1963. DDC 492.779.

An intermediate text for those with a beginning course behind them, featuring useful
phrases and grammar, but no vocabularies.

2. Iraqi

244. Clarity, Beverly E., Karl Stowasser, and Ronald G. Wolfe, eds. **A Dictionary of Iraqi
Arabic: English-Arabic.** Washington, Georgetown University Press, 1964. 202p.
(Institute of Languages and Linguistics, Georgetown University. Arabic Series,
No. 6). $6.00. LC 65-1782. PJ 6826.C5. DDC 492.779.

Transliterated Arabic terms, not in Arabic script, so that anyone can use it. An example
of an Iraqi sentence with English translation is given for each word and each use of the word.

245. Erwin, Wallace M. **A Basic Course in Iraqi Arabic.** Washington, D.C., Georgetown Uni-
versity Press, 1969. 389p. index. (Institute of Languages and Linguistics, Georgetown
University. The Richard Salde Harrell Arabic Series, No. 11). $6.50. LC 79-19390.
PJ 6823.E68. DDC 492.7'7.

An oral-aural approach: dialogues, grammar and extensive drills; Iraqi-English,
English-Iraqi glossaries.

246. Erwin, Wallace M. **A Short Reference Grammar of Iraqi Arabic.** Washington, D.C.,
Georgetown University Press, 1963. 392p. (Institute of Languages and Linguistics,
Georgetown University. Arabic Series, No. 4). $6.00. LC 65-1653. PJ 6823.E7.

A systematic outline of the phonology, morphology, and syntax of Baghdadi Arabic,
for students who have already had an introductory course.

247. Woodhead, Daniel, and Wayne Beene. **Dictionary of Iraqi Arabic: Arabic-English.**
Washington, D.C., Georgetown University Press, 1967. 509p. (School of Languages
and Linguistics. Richard Slade Harrell Arabic Series). $6.00pa. LC n.a. ISBN
0-87840-02-10.

Arabic words in transliteration, not Arabic script, so anyone can use it. One English phrase or term is given for each Arabic item, with an Arabic sentence translated into English to illustrate each usage of an item.

3. Moroccan

248. Abdel-Massih, Ernest J. **A Course in Moroccan Arabic.** Ann Arbor, Center for Near Eastern and North African Studies, University of Michigan, 1970. 449p. index. LC 72-24170. PJ 6770.M6 A25. DDC 492.7'9.

A beginning textbook, using the oral-aural approach, in the conversational colloquial language. It is organized into basic learning units, with extensive drills and texts and a Moroccan-English vocabulary.

249. Harrell, Richard S. **A Short Reference Grammar of Moroccan Arabic.** With an appendix of texts in urban Moroccan Arabic by Louis Brunet. Washington, D.C., Georgetown University Press, 1962. 263p. (Institute of Languages and Linguistics, Georgetown University. Arabic Series, No. 1). $6.00pa. LC 64-1550. PJ 6763.H3. DDC 492.779.

A systematic grammar for those who have had an introductory course. There are no exercises or glossaries, but there is a wealth of examples. The dialect of Fez, Rabat, and Casablanca.

250. Harrell, Richard S. **Dictionary of Moroccan Arabic: Arabic-English.** Washington, D.C., Georgetown University Press, 1966. 268p. (School of Languages and Linguistics. Richard Slade Harrell Arabic Series). $6.00pa. LC n.a. ISBN 0-87840-02-9.

Arabic words in transliteration, one English word or phrase per Arabic item, with an Arabic sentence (translated into English) to explain or exemplify each usage.

251. Sobelman, Harvey, and Richard S. Harrell. **A Dictionary of Moroccan Arabic: English-Arabic.** Washington, D.C., Georgetown University Press, 1963. 228p. (Institute of Languages and Linguistics, Georgetown University. Arabic Series, No. 3). $6.00pa. LC 64-2927. PJ 6767.S6. DDC 492.779.

Colloquial language dictionary, one Arabic word for each English word, with an Arabic sentence translated into English exemplifying each usage. Not in Arabic script, so anyone can use it.

4. Syrian

252. Cowell, Mark W. **A Reference Grammar of Syrian Arabic (Based on the Dialect of Damascus).** Washington, Georgetown University Press, 1964. 587p. index. (Institute of Languages and Linguistics, Georgetown University. Arabic Series, No. 7). $6.50. LC 65-1652. PJ 6813.C6. DDC 492.77.

A systematic work for the more advanced student, it can also be used by a beginner. It has cross-references for review, but no exercises, though it has many examples.

253. Sa'id, Majed F., and Frank Rice. **Eastern Arabic.** Beirut, Khayats, 1960?

A useful systematic introduction for the beginner.

254. Stowasser, Karl, and Moukhtar Ani. **A Dictionary of Syrian Arabic (Dialect of Damascus): English-Arabic.** Washington, D.C., Georgetown University Press, 1964. 269p. (Georgetown University, School of Languages and Linguistics. Arabic Series, No. 5). $5.00pa. LC 65-3789. PJ 6816.S8. DDC 492.79.

A dictionary of colloquial vocabulary and expressions. The Arabic phrases and expressions listed for each English term are translated to make the Arabic usage clear. Not in Arabic script, so anyone can use it.

E. ARABIC LITERATURE

1. History and Criticism

255. Gibb, Sir Hamilton Alexander Rosskeen. **Arabic Literature: An Introduction.** 2nd rev. ed. Oxford, Clarendon Press, 1963. 182p. bibliog. $4.25. LC 63-2995. ISBN 0-19-815108-X. PJ 7510.G5 1963. DDC 892.709. Paperback: Oxford University Press, 1974. (Oxford Paperbacks, 332). $2.50. ISBN 0-19-881332-5.

[P1, C1, S1] This is a brief introduction by the late dean of Western Arabists; it nicely sums up the genres, context, and content of Arabic literature. It gives attention to other types of writing, but not to the extent that Nicholson, Goldziher, and Lichtenstadter (items 262, 256, 261), do. It covers a great deal of the basic material in an easy-to-read style that somewhat masks the great scholarship underlying it. The first or second book to read, it contains little on the period 1517-1800, and three pages on the period since 1800. A basic book.

256. Goldziher, Ignac (1850-1921). **A Short History of Classical Arabic Literature.** Tr. from Hungarian. Hildesheim, George Olms Verlagesbuchhandlung, 1966. 172p. index. LC 68-76129. PJ 7510.G6313. DDC 892.7'09.

[C2, S2] This is a veritable handbook of Arabic civilization as reflected in written intellectual artifacts. It traces the rise, nature, significance, and individual authors and works of the fields covered by Arabs and Arabic-writing intellectuals down to the seventeenth century. Included are belles-lettres, philology, Islam, science, and history. It often becomes an annotated bibliography of key works, but it explains well the circumstances in which the material developed. One of the first books to read. Gibb (item 255) and Nicholson (item 262) are of much higher priority for purchase, since Goldziher overlaps them greatly, while Hitti (item 88) and Chejne (item 231) also provide the reader with much of the information not found in Gibb and Nicholson. Goldziher's concise, factual, descriptive rendering and his mode of expression sometimes bring his material into more meaningful focus for the reader, and his perspective is somewhat different.

257. Haywood, John A. **Modern Arabic Literature, 1800-1970: An Introduction with Extracts in Translation.** New York, St. Martin's Press, 1972. 306p. bibliog. index. $10.95. LC 72-83417. PJ 7538.H3 1972. DDC 892'.7'09005.

[C1, S1] A hastily written volume divided as follows: 25 pages on the classical heritage, genres and styles; 50 pages on the latter eighteenth century and three-fourths of the nineteenth century; 80 pages on the latter nineteenth century through 1920; 45 pages of very spotty coverage of the period 1920-1960. There follow twelve longish prose extracts; poetry is interspersed throughout the text. Hardly a good book, but a must purely because we are desperate for anything we can get, and it is unique.

See also:

Khouri, Munah Abdallah. **Poetry and the Making of Modern Egypt (1882-1922).** Leiden, E. J. Brill, 1971. 210p. bibliog. LC 72-856581. PK 8210.K5. DDC 892.7'1'0093. Relation of poetry to other genres of literature, its times, the influence of the introduction of the periodical press; propaganda and psychological values of poetry. Role in social change and development of Egyptian self-concept, and reformation of Arabic language and its literature. Translations and original texts illustrate the author's points.

258. Kilpatrick, Hilary. **The Modern Egyptian Novel: A Study in Social Criticism.** London, Ithaca Press, for the Middle East Centre, St. Antony's College, 1974. 254p. bibliog. (St. Antony's Middle Eastern Monographs, No. 1). $10.00. LC n.a. ISBN 0-903729-04-0.

A study of the development of social criticism in Egyptian fiction 1914-1968, emphasizing the period since World War II. Includes coverage of relations between individuals and groups, people and government institutions; character development; the authors' approaches to their subjects; the issues raised; solutions if any, offered by the authors; thematic development. Part I is a chronological treatment, while Part II discusses and compares the treatment of various social themes—politics, government, women, rural and urban conditions, the intellectual and society, education. Pages 198 to 247 contain synopses of the novels. Included are a number of the novels included in this *Guide.* One of the few English works on Arabic fiction. See also:

Sakkūt, Hamdī. **The Egyptian Novel and Its Main Trends from 1913 to 1952.** Cairo, The American University in Cairo Press, 1971. 165p. bibliog. index. LC 73-149196. PJ 8212.S22 1971. DDC 892.7'3'03. Mainly individual authors and plot summaries with critique of their key works. Little information on the real significance of each novel in the Egyptian literary movement.

Semah, David. **Four Egyptian Literary Critics.** Leiden, E. J. Brill, 1974. 219p. LC 74-168637. ISBN 90-04-03841-3. PJ 7538.S4. DDC 892'.7'09. Discusses al-ᶜAqqād, Haykal, Taha Husayn, Muhammad Mandur.

259. Landau, Jacob M. **Studies in the Arab Theater and Cinema.** Philadelphia, University of Pennsylvania Press, 1958. 290p. bibliog. index. $10.00. LC 56-12588. ISBN 0-8122-7188-2. PN 2960.A67L3. DDC 792.0956.

[C] Beginning with the early background—passion plays and shadow plays—Landau traces the development of Arabic drama and theater. He covers the Europeans' import of their own plays and theater, Arabic translations of European plays, the creation of a native Arabic drama, and then theaters and local troupes. He discusses the main actors, government financial encouragement, schools of dramatic arts, and the position of the theater in Arabic culture. He also discusses the plays and their themes and genres, key playwrights, censorship, and finally the development of the cinema and its stars and directors, government use of movies, etc. Although not up to date or complete, it is the only thing we have and is a most useful introduction. It includes a list of Arabic plays from 1848 to 1956.

260. Lasater, Alice E. **Spain to England: A Comparative Study of Arabic, European and English Literature of the Middle Ages.** Jackson, University Press of Mississippi, 1974. 230p. bibliog. index. LC 73-94277. ISBN 0-87805-056-6. PN 671.L3.

Beginning with a brief summary of intellectual life in Muslim Spain, the author seeks to suggest, in this interesting synthesis of the available literature, the Arabic-Muslim influence on European and English literature: lyric poetry, its forms and themes; visions of the afterlife found in literature; tales and fables; romances. The treatment is general rather than detailed and factual, though a goodly number of specific examples are provided as evidence. The subject has only begun to be researched, and, as the author states, the book only scratches the surface. Nevertheless, for the general reader it is interesting and revealing, while for the serious student it is a good general orientation and source of ideas for further study. For most college collections.

261. Lichtenstadter, Ilse. **Introduction to Classical Arabic Literature, with Selections from Representative Works.** New York, Twayne, 1974. 352p. bibliog. index. (Introductions to World Literature). $8.95. LC 73-8070. ISBN 0-8057-3111-3. LC cataloging n.a.

[P1, P2, C1, S1] A useful introduction to the various fields of Arabic writing, not merely belles-lettres, with selections from each genre. We still lack a thorough discussion of belles-lettres for this period.

262. Nicholson, Reynold Alleyne. **A Literary History of the Arabs.** Cambridge, England, Cambridge University Press, 1969. 506p. bibliog. index. $17.50; $4.95pa. LC 72-401710. ISBN 0-521-09572-7. PJ 7510.N5. DDC 892.7'09.

[P1, C1, S1] The most important of the very few English language general works. Itself a work of high literary quality, it deals with medieval Arabic writing in general and contains a great deal of historical background information—it more properly might be viewed as an introduction to Islamic civilization. It is, however, an interesting book. Because it has many quotations from poetry and other works, and because it is unique, it is a must for all libraries. We still lack a good introduction to the subject, and we need a volume on medieval belles-lettres and one on modern literature.

A more specialized work worth reading is:

Hamori, Andras. **On the Art of Medieval Arabic Literature.** Princeton, N.J., Princeton University Press, 1974. 199p. bibliog. LC 73-2484. ISBN 0-691-06264-1. PJ 7541.H34. DDC 892'.7'1309.

263. Nykl, Alois Richard. **Hispano-Arabic Poetry and Its Relations with the Old Provencal Troubadours.** New York, Hispanic Society of America, 1970. (Repr. of 1946 ed.). 416p. index. $8.00. LC n.a. PJ 7755.N8. DDC 892.7109.

[C] A chronological treatment attempting a comprehensive survey of the whole field, plus a 40-page indication of the contacts between the love poetry and the early Aquitanian troubadours. For each period the author deals with individual poets, giving their background, their famous works, the genres they worked in, in their reputations according to various medieval writers, anecdotes preserved about each, and, most importantly, copious translations of the poetry. The book is a systematic listing, with no attempt made at narrative presentation. The poetry itself is quite interesting to read, and one can find much of interest to students of European literature, on which the Hispanic-Arab poets had considerable influence.

2. Collections

264. ʿAbd al-Wahhāb, Fārūq, comp. **Modern Egyptian Drama: An Anthology.** Minneapolis, Bibliotheca Islamica, 1974. 493p. LC 72-94939. ISBN 0-88297-005-4. PJ 7694.E5 A2.

After a 31-page introduction are readable translations of four very interesting pieces: Tawfiq al-Hakim's *The Sultan's Dilemma*; Mikhail Romon's *The New Arrival*; Rashad Rushdy's *A Journey Outside the Wall*; and Yusuf Idris' *The Farfoors.*

265. Abū Tammām Ḥabīb ibn Aws al-Ṭā'ī (fl. 808-842). **al Washiyyat al Hamasa al Sugra: An Anthology of Wild Ones.** Tr. from Arabic by Arthur Wormhoudt. Oskaloosa, Iowa, William Penn College, 1974. 97p. (An Arab Translation Series, 14). LC cataloging n.a.

A classical anthology of early Arabic poetry, mainly pre-Islamic.

266. Arberry, Arthur John. **Arabic Poetry: A Primer for Students.** Cambridge, England, Cambridge University Press, 1965. 174p. $10.95; $4.95pa. LC 65-11206. ISBN 0-521-09257-4cl. PJ 7692.E3 A7. DDC 892.71008.

Thirty-one poems by as many poets, consisting of Arabic text and unrhymed translation on opposite pages. The poets are mainly from the medieval period, with a few from the pre-Islamic era, and only three who lived well into the twentieth century. There is a 27-page general introduction and notes on each poem, with biographical notes on the poets. Not a terribly good selection, but convenient until something better is available.

267. Arberry, Arthur John. **Modern Arabic Poetry: An Anthology with English Verse Translations.** London, Taylor's Foreign Press, 1967. 70, 76p. (Cambridge Oriental Series, No. 1). $9.50. LC 67-105223. PJ 7655.A7. DDC 892.7'1'008.

The rhymed, verse translations are rendered in old-style English—thee, thou, wast, etc. Poems that use the classical conventions of Arabic poetry (which persisted until modern times and only recently have been phased out), are appropriately rendered by this translation, though the usage in translations of modern-style poems is less appropriate. Not a good collection, but there is little else available.

268. Aruri, Naseer Hasan, and Edmund Ghareeb, eds. **Enemy of the Sun.** Washington, Drum and Spear Press, 1970. xlviii, 141p. (Poets of Liberation Series). $2.50pa. LC 73-136966. ISBN 0-87782-500-9. PJ 7810.P3 A7. DDC 892'.7'1608.

Translations of modern Palestinian Arabic poetry by well-known writers, portraying the tragedy of the flight of the Palestinians from their homes in what is now Israel; the refugees and the Palestinian diaspora; the commandos as the heroes of the desperate; love for Palestine and despair at being outcasts; resistance and hope. The poets include Mahmud Darwish (an Israeli Arab), Rashid Husayn, Samih al-Qasim, Nizar Qabbani, Fadwa Tuqan, and others.

Some of them live in Israel, and they express frustration, grief, anger at the Israelis, and at the United States for helping Israel. Poetry has been, from time immemorial, a basic medium of communication for the Arabs, who "worship" their language and poetry; thus, this Palestinian poetry is quite significant in the community of refugees at various levels. It is important that Americans be aware of it, and this anthology accomplishes that objective effectively.

269. Howarth, Herbert, and Ibrahim Shukrallah. **Images from the Arab World: Fragments of Arab Literature, Translated and Paraphrased.** London, The Pilot Press, 1944. 143p. indices. LC 44-51566. PJ 7796.E1H6. DDC 892.7082.

An interesting and entertaining collection of miscellaneous literary, religious, and non-fiction fragments from a wide variety of sources, both classical and modern.

270. Ibn Saʿīd, ʿAlī ibn Mūsá al-Maghribī. **[Rayāt al-Mubarrizīn].** Moorish Poetry. A translation of **The Pennants,** an Anthology Compiled in 1243 by the Andalusian Ibn Saʿīd, by A. J. Arberry. Cambridge, England, Cambridge University Press, 1953. 198p. index. o.p. LC 53-9497 rev. PJ 7694.E3I2. DDC 892.71082.

Spanish Arabic poetry included in a representative anthology compiled at the height of the Andalusian Arabic poetic movement. A good addition to representative collections.

271. Johnson-Davies, Denys, ed. and tr. **Modern Arabic Short Stories.** London, Oxford University Press, 1967. 194p. $6.00. LC 67-87750. ISBN 0-19-416858-1. PJ 7694.E8J6.

Twenty representative short stories from various countries, with biographical notes on the authors. A thoroughly enjoyable, well-translated selection.

272. Khouri, Mounah A., and Hamid Algar. **An Anthology of Modern Arabic Poetry.** Berkeley, University of California Press, 1974. 252p. bibliog. $12.00; $2.95pa. LC 77-189220. ISBN 0-520-02234-3; 0-520-02898-8pa. PJ 7695.E3K48. DDC 892'.7'1608.

Arabic and English on opposite pages. The only bilingual collection other than Arberry (item 267) of twentieth century poetry. The 80 poems, by 35 writers, include a few Syro-Americans such as Gibran, Rihani, and Naimy, several Egyptian modernists, and mainly contemporary representatives of the free verse movement from various countries. This poetry flows in the mainstream of world literature and is not tied to Arab-Islamic civilization as are the classicists and neo-classical poets who are represented in Arberry. Includes a section of biographical notices. Quite enjoyable to read for its own sake.

273. Lyall, Sir Charles James (1845-1920). **Translations of Ancient Arabian Poetry, Chiefly Pre-Islamic.** With introd. and notes. London, Williams & Norgate, 1930. 52, 142p. index. LC 46-37737. PJ 7796.E3L9 1930. DDC 892.71082.

Rhymed verse translations, with a 52-page introduction and notes on each of the 50 poems.

274. Manzalaoui, Mahmoud, ed. **Arabic Writing Today: The Short Story.** Berkeley, University of California Press, 1968. 407p. bibliog. $8.50. LC n.a. ISBN 0-520-01800-1. PJ 7695.E8M3. DDC 892.7'3'608.

Prefaced by a general introduction, this is a collection of 30 stories written mainly by Egyptians; each has a separate introduction. Translation by various Egyptians and two Englishmen, it is a joint effort by a Committee of the American Research Center in Egypt, which is translating various genres of Arabic literature into English. The English style is adequate. The items do not overlap Johnson-Davies (item 271). The stories reveal much about Egypt.

275. Monroe, James T. **Hispano-Arabic Poetry: A Student Anthology.** Berkeley, University of California Press, 1974. 402p. LC 72-103925. ISBN 0-520-01692-0. PJ 8414.M6.

Following a very useful 71-page introductory history and discussion of Arabic poetry in Spain and the types of poetry, there are 43 poems, with original Arabic texts and translations on opposite pages.

276. **[Mu^{c}allaqàt]. The Seven Odes: The First Chapter in Arabic Literature.** Tr. by A. J. Arberry. New York, Macmillan, 1957. 258p. index. o.p. LC 57-13803 rev. PJ 7642.E5A7. DDC 892.71.

An excellent translation of the seven most famous pre-Islamic Arabic poems, with a general introduction and epilog that are quite interesting and informative. Each poem has an extensive introduction, with notes on earlier translations and on the poets. Long extracts from the poems are found in Arberry (item 220), which will be sufficient for smaller collections.

277. Mufaḍḍal ibn Muḥammad, al-Ḍabbī, comp. (8th cent.). **The Mufaḍḍaliyāt: An Anthology of Ancient Arabian Odes.** Ed. by Charles James Lyall. Oxford, Clarendon Press, 1918-1921. 3v. LC 22-9421. PJ 7643.A2 1921.

Typical pre-Islamic Arabic poetry by many poets in one of the most famous of the classical anthologies. A scholarly edition, Vol. I has the Arabic text, Vol. II the translation, and Vol. III the index. College libraries need only the translation; actually, a more up-to-date version would be preferred. Pre-Islamic poetry is important both in its own right and as source material on Arabia and the Arabic language before Islam; also, it greatly influenced the poetry and language of succeeding generations. It was treasured the way most cultures value their "classics," and was quoted in medieval books on many subjects just as nineteenth century British writers threw in lines from "the Bard" or Tennyson. This book was a standard collection as Palgrave's *Golden Treasury* was to Victorians. (Arabic poetry was also quoted in Persian and Turkish literature much as Virgil and Homer were in Britain and the United States.)

278. Wilson, Epiphanius Wilson, ed. (1845-1916). **Oriental Literature: The Literature of Arabia.** Freeport, N.Y., Books for Libraries Press, 1971. (Repr. of 1900 ed.). 141p. (Play Anthology Reprint Series). $9.75. LC 71-174763. ISBN 0-8369-8229-0. PJ 7601.L5 1971.

Contains a prose version of the *Romance of Antar*, 42 pages of various classical poems, and excerpts from the *Arabian Nights*.

3. Classical Authors to 1800

279. Abū al-^{c}Alā', al-Ma^{c}arrī (973-1057). **The Luzumiyat of Abu'l-Ala.** Selected from his **Luzum Ma La Yalzam** and **Suct uz-Zand,** and first rendered into English by Ameen Rihani. New York, James White, 1918. 100p. o.p. LC 19-3290. PJ 7796.E9A24.

A pleasant verse translation (by a famous Lebanese-American writer) of the blind poet's poetic musing, sharp criticism of hypocrites, and comments on life. Includes a brief introduction on the poet and his verse, and notes on the individual quatrains.

280. Abū al-^{c}Alā, al-Ma^{c}arrī (973-1057). **Risālat ul Ghufrān: A Divine Comedy.** Tr. from Arabic by G. Brackenbury. Cairo, al-Maaref Printing and Publishing House, 1943. 159p. LC 49-43706. PJ 7701.A15 A713. DDC 892.71.

This famous work by the blind tenth century poet is an allegorical trip to Heaven. It includes conversations with the ancient Muslim poets, who tell how they came to Heaven and what they did to be saved; also discussing repentance and the true acknowledgment of God. Part III describes at length the joys of Paradise. Part IV describes the limbo of the Jinn, while part V describes Hell and includes conversations with the pre-Islamic poets and Satan himself. Finally the narrator returns to Paradise where he has a conversation with Adam. Its parallels with Dante are intriguing. It includes many excerpts from Arabic poetry. A basic work for literature collections should a reprint become available.

281. Abū al-^{c}Alā', al-Ma^{c}arrī (973-1057). **Saqt al Zand, The Spark from the Flint.** Tr. from Arabic by Arthur Wormhoudt. Ann Arbor, published on demand by University Microfilms, 1972. 125p. (An Arab Translation Series, No. 2). LC cataloging n.a.

Early poems of the blind poet.

282. Abū Nuwās (ca. 756-ca. 810). **The Diwan of Abu Nuwas al Hasan Ibn Hani al Hakami.** Tr. from Arabic by Arthur Wormhoudt. Ann Arbor, Mich., Published on demand by University Microfilms, 1974. 235p. Lc cataloging n.a.

The major Abbasid poet who lived under the caliphs Harun al-Rashid and his son Amin. He specialized in wine-songs, savage satire, and gross obscenity.

283. Abū Tammām Ḥabīb ibn Aws al-Ṭā'ī (fl. 808-842). **The Diwan of Abu Tammam Habib ibn Aus al Tai.** Tr. from Arabic by Arthur Wormhoudt. Oskaloosa, Iowa, William Penn College, 1974. 184p. (An Arab Translation Series, No. 11). LC cataloging n.a.

A distinguished Abbasid poet who is famous more for his classic anthology of Arabic poetry, the *Hamasah*, than for his own creations.

284. cAntarah ibn Shaddad, al-cAbsī. **Diwan Antara ibn Shaddad Ibn Qurad al 'Abs; Diwan Laila Akhyaliyya.** Tr. from Arabic by Arthur Wormhoudt. Ann Arbor, Mich., published on demand by University Microfilms, 1974. 128p. LC cataloging n.a.

Antarah, who was one of the pre-Islamic *Mu'allaqāt* poets, is also the hero of a medieval Arabic romance. Laila Akhyaliyya was an Umayyad poetess whose poems are laments for her dead lover.

285. Arabian Nights. **The Thousand and One Nights; Or, Arabian Nights Entertainments.** Tr. by Edward William Lane. New York, Charles Scribner's Sons, 1930. 1388p. LC 30-26609. PJ 7715.L3 1930. DDC 892.73. o.p. **[Arabian Nights]. The Portable Arabian Nights.** Ed. with an introd. by Joseph Campbell. New York, Viking Press, 1952. 786p. $5.50; $2.95pa. LC 52-7413. ISBN 0-670-13002-8; 0-670-01059-6pa. PJ 7715.P3. DDC 892.73 [398.21]. Arabian Nights. **The Arabian Nights' Entertainments; Or, The Book of a Thousand Nights and a Night.** A Selection . . . from the . . . translation by Richard F. Burton . . . chosen and arranged by Bennett A. Cerf, and are printed complete and unabridged with many of Burton's notes. New York, The Modern Library, 1932. 823p. LC 32-28027. PJ 7715.B8 1932b. o.p.

[C1] The Arabian Nights is a compilation of folk-tales, fables, and fairy stories from a wide variety of sources—Near East, India and peripheral regions—which entered Arab mass culture over the centuries during which the Islamic Empire had a worldwide trade and other contacts. Put together in Mamluk Egypt, they reflect the popular culture—material culture, superstitions, ideals, realities—of the era. These stories were told in the market places by raconteurs down through the nineteenth century. Lane's translation is well written in archaic English and is very entertaining. Cerf's edition contains an extensive portion of Burton's translation, which is one of the standard renditions. Burton's notes were extensive and were a mine of ethnological and other information. Larger libraries should purchase a complete edition when one is available. Campbell's Portable edition is an abridgement of John Payne's translation; most of the stories are abridged or summarized, a couple of dozen being given in full.

The only monograph in English about the Arabian Nights is Gerhardt, Mia Irene, *The Art of Story-Telling: A Literary Study of the Thousand and One Nights* (Leiden, E. J. Brill, 1963. 500p. bibliog. index. LC 67-7224. PJ 7737.G4. DDC n.a.). The lengthy bibliography includes translations, disciplinary works, background readings, as well as works on the *1001 Nights*. Written from the viewpoint of the European reader of translations it discusses the origin, contents, texts, and translations of the work, and gives a literary analysis of the various types of stories—travel, fairy, crime, learning, wisdom and piety, and love stories. For the initiated reader.

286. Badīc al-Zamān al-Hamadhānī (969-1008). **The Maqāmāt of Badīc al-Zamān al-Hamadhānī.** Tr. from Arabic, with an introd. and notes by W. I. Prendergast. London, Curzon Press; distr. New York, Humanities Press, 1973. (Repr. of 1915 ed.). 190p. $8.00. LC 74-162001. ISBN 0-7007-0029-3. PJ 7750. B3 M33 1973. DDC 892.7'8'3407.

The Maqamat are brief anecdotal pieces in rhymed prose connected thematically through the devices of a common character and a common narrator. Extensive notes explicate the text, while the introduction discusses the author and the genre, which was very popular during the tenth and eleventh centuries. (For further comment, cf. al-Hariri, item 288). The present work is one of the most famous in the genre, and some of the author's anecdotes are quite entertaining. A basic work for representative collections. This work and that of al-Hariri in their heavily annotated scholarly editions as listed in this *Guide* provide considerable insight into the cultural life of the medieval period, by revealing what the educated and literati were expected to have as general knowledge, and what intellectual entertainments they indulged in.

287. Bidpai. Arabic version. Kalilah wa-Dimnah. Syriac. **Kalilah and Dimnah; Or, the Fables of Bidpai.** An English translation of the later Syriac version by I. G. N. Keith-Falconer. Amsterdam, Philo Press, 1970. (Repr. of 1885 ed.). 320p. LC 79-570615. ISBN 90-6022-254-7. PN 989.I5B4 1970. DDC 892.7'1'32.

An early example of Arabic prose literature, which was translated in the eighth century by the Persian Ibn al-Muqaffa^C from middle Persian, and was a milestone in the development of Arabic prose writing. For most readers, the value of the translation is that it allows them to read some typical Arabic medieval literature.

288. al-Hariri (1054-1122). [al-Maqāmāt]. **The Assemblies of Hariri.** Tr. from Arabic by Thomas Chenery. Farnborough, England, Gregg International Publishers, 1969. 2v. (Oriental Translation Fund Publications, new series, 9-10). £10.00. LC 72-875638. ISBN 0-576-03582-3. PJ 408.06 n.s. v. 9-10 1969. DDC 892.7'1'34.

al-Hariri composed exceedingly refined literary essays in rhymed prose. Their object was style rather than content, and they consisted of anecdotes with some semblance of a unifying theme. Unfortunately, most of the work assumes a detailed knowledge of Arabic and Islamic culture, and the pieces abound in allusions that cannot be translated but can only be explained in long notes, which occupy half of each volume. The allusions and the heavily loaded vocabulary were part of the art, which is thus extremely difficult for the uninitiated to appreciate. However, as this was an extremely important and famous work, it must be included in representative collections. For additional comment, see item 286.

289. Ibn Hazm, ^{C}Ali ibn Ahmad (994-1064). [Ṭawq al-Ḥamāmah]. **A Book Containing the Risāla Known as The Dove's Neck-Ring, about Love and Lovers.** Tr. from Arabic by A. R. Nykl. Paris, Librairie Orientaliste Paul Geuthner, 1931. 74, 244p. bibliog. o.p. LC 33-3387 rev. 3. HQ 19.I213. DDC 892.78.

This critical translation also contains a long introduction on the historical background, Ibn Hazm's biography, the poetry in his book, the relationship of Spanish-Arabic poetry to Spanish and French poetry. The book itself is a manual of courtly love, its pleasures and problems. Larded with illustrative anecdotes and poetry, it deals with the origins and types of love; lovers' communications and secrecy; the characteristics and qualities of lovers; their vices, such as faultfinding; slanderers and other outsiders who interfere with love's progress; meetings of lovers, faithfulness, behavior in separation, death, perversions, virtue, the Islamic ideal and legal aspects; the excellence of continence. This is no Arabic *Kama Sutra*, for there is nothing on sexual technique. A document in the history of medieval courtly love and a piece of good Arabic literature. Arthur John Arberry also has a translation. Neither version has been reprinted to date. Nykl is a specialist on Muslim Spain and its literature.

290. Imru' al-Qays (fl. 530). **The Diwan of Imrū al Qais ibn Hujr ibn Kinda ibn Qahtạn; Diwan al Khirniq bint Badr ibn Hiffạn Akhbar Sulaik.** Tr. from Arabic by Arthur Wormhoudt. Oskaloosa, Iowa, William Penn College, 1974. 74p. LC cataloging n.a.

A top pre-Islamic poet, one of whose poems was included in the *Mu^{C}allaqat*. He is thought to be one of the great innovators of poetic themes and figures of speech that later became standard.

291. Jāḥiẓ, ^{C}Amr ibn Baḥr (d. 868 or 869). **The Life and Works of Jāḥiẓ; Translations of Selected Texts.** By Charles Pellat. Tr. from French. Berkeley, University of California Press, 1969. 286p. (The Islamic World). $8.75. LC 69-12475. ISBN 0-520-01498-7. PJ 7745.J3A26. DDC 892.7'8'3408.

[C1] An excellent representative selection from one of the greats of classical Arabic literature. His works covered a wide range of topics, all written in a literary form, including theology, polemics, zoology, belles-lettres, etc. His works include all types of Arabic writing of the time and reveal much about tenth century Islamic society and civilization. The selections, which are well translated (by Pellat into French, then into English), are interesting and instructive and are a good introduction to the author.

292. Jarir ibn ^cAṭiyah (d. 728?). Naqā'iḍ Jarir wa-al Farazdaq]. The Naqaith of Jarir and al Farazdaq. Tr. from Arabic by Arthur Wormhoudt. Ann Arbor, Mich., published on demand by University Microfilms, 1974. 175p. LC cataloging n.a.

Jarir and Farazdaq were two Umayyad poets who engaged in a vituperation contest. The extant remnants of this contest became one of the more famous collections of Arabic poetry, because of the poets' skills. It is said that the qualities of the two rivals were debated with the most intense partisanship even by common soldiers, much as people today root for one or the other of two first-string quarterbacks on a football team. Some of it is rather vulgar.

293. Khansā' bint ^cAmr (d. ca. 645). Diwan al Khansa. Tr. from Arabic by Arthur Wormhoudt. Ann Arbor, Mich., published on demand by University Microfilms, 1971. 108p. LC cataloging n.a.

A pre-Islamic poetess reknowned for her elegies to her slain brothers.

294. Labīd ibn Rabī^cah (ca. 560-ca. 661). The Golden Ode. Tr. by William R. Polk. Photos by William J. Mares. Chicago, University of Chicago Press, 1974. xxi, 177p. illus. LC 73-85248. ISBN 0-226-46717-1. PJ 7696.L3M8 1974.

A translation of one of the most famous pre-Islamic Arabic poems, which was included in the *Mu^callaqāt*. Each line is accompanied by the Arabic original, a commentary, and an excellent photograph. The photos clearly indicate the imagery used by Labid and help the reader comprehend the meaning and atmosphere of the poem. The work illuminates many other pre-Islamic poems as well, which is important for users of this *Guide*. (Cf. item 644, which is a description of the trip taken by Polk and Mares to prepare this book.)

295. Mutanabbī, Abū al-Ṭayyib Aḥmad ibn al-Ḥusayn (915 or 916-965). Poems of al-Mutanabbi: A Selection, with introd., tr., and notes by A. J. Arberry. Cambridge, England, Cambridge University Press, 1967. 155p. bibliog. £3.40. LC 67-79534. ISBN 0-521-04038-8. PJ 7750.M8A6 1967. DDC 892.7'1'3.

[C1] Arabic text, with English translation on opposite pages, of poems by the great Arab poet. The helpful notes explain much that is obscure in the texts. Arberry's translations of the 26 poems do not try to be poetic, but rather are fairly literal renditions. The complete *Diwan* has been translated by Arthur Wormhoudt: *The Diwan of Abu Tayyib Ahmad ibn al Husain al Mutanabbi* (Oskaloosa, Iowa, William Penn College, 1971. 244p. o.p. LC 72-177472. PJ 7750.M8A28 1971). A revised edition is in preparation.

296. al-Tha^cālibī, ^cAbd al-Malik ibn Muḥammad (961 or 962-1037). The Laṭā'if al-Ma^cārif of Tha^cālibī; the Book of Curious and Entertaining Information. Tr. with an introd. and notes by C. E. Bosworth. Edinburgh, Edinburgh University Press; distr. Chicago, Aldine Publishing Co., 1968. 164p. bibliog. index. $15.00. LC 68-22847. ISBN 0-202-15011-9. AG 90.I8T53. DDC 001.2.

A non-book of miscellaneous, variously useful information compiled for officials and courtiers of the Eastern Islamic Empire: odd bits of information to spice conversation and letters, in accordance with the norms of the author's era. It includes famous firsts, nicknames, family traditions, anecdotes, information on Muhammad and his tribe, rulers, unusual incidents, etc., etc. Sometimes quite entertaining. Too much for all but the most comprehensive collections, but a rare translation of a common type of literature, which offers insight into elite concerns and manners of the time.

4. Modern Authors since 1800

297. ᶜAbd al-Ṣābūr, Ṣalāḥ. **Murder in Baghdad. [Ma'sāt al-Ḥallāj]. Prize-Winning Verse Play in Two Acts.** Tr. by Khalil I. Semaan. Leiden, E. J. Brill, 1972. xx, 76p. LC 72-193465. PJ 7804.S3M313. DDC 892'.7'26.

This play was patterned after Eliot's *Murder in the Cathedral.* al-Hallaj, a famous Sufi martyr, was executed during the Abbasid period for his uncompromising religious beliefs, which, although they inspired the masses, ran counter to those of the contemporary government and religious authorities. (Cf. Schimmel, item 558.)

298. Barakat, Halim Isber. **Days of Dust.** Tr. from Arabic by Trevor Le Gassick. Wilmette, Ill., Medina University Press International, 1974. xxxviii, 179p. LC 74-77249. ISBN 0-914456-09-1. PZ 4.B227Day3. [PJ 7816.A67] DDC 892'.7'36.

A novel of the 1967 Arab-Israeli War.

299. al-Bayātī, ᶜAbd al-Wahhāb. **Lilies and Death.** Tr. from Arabic by Mohammed Bakir Alwan. Baghdad, al-Adib Printing Press, 1972. 80p. pa. LC 74-154002. PJ 7816.A92L5. DDC 892'.7'16.

Poems by a top Iraqi poet.

300. Darwish, Mahmūd. **Selected Poems.** Introduced and translated by Ian Wedde and Fawwaz Tuqan. Cheadle Hulme, Carcanet Press Publishing; distr. Chester Springs, Pa., Dufour Editions, 1973. 88p. LC 74-167709. ISBN 0-85635-064-0; 0-85635-065-6pa. PJ 7820.A8A27. DDC 892'.7'16.

Darwish, in exile from Palestine, lives in Cairo. This work represents a variety of themes, many rooted in the poet's longing for Palestine and the trauma of its loss; also some of the poems are on Cuba. Another selection is: *Splinters of Bone, Poems* (Tr. by B. M. Bennani. Greenfield Center, N.Y., Greenfield Review Press, 1974. 42p. LC 74-25797. ISBN 0-912678-17-8. PJ 7820.A7A23. DDC 892'.7'16.

301. Ghānim, Fatḥī. **The Man Who Lost His Shadow.** By Fathy Ghanem. Tr. from Arabic by Desmond Stewart. Boston, Houghton Mifflin, 1966. 352p. o.p. LC 66-11227. PZ 4.G429 Man 2.

By an Egyptian author, the novel takes place in the early 1950s in Cairo; the plot is important for its own sake, but it also gives glimpses of life in Cairo among the various middle-upper classes.

302. Gibran, Kahlil.

This Lebanese immigrant, who has periodically been the object of sentimental fads in the United States and whose books are perennial bestsellers regardless of fads, was also acclaimed in the Arab world, for he wrote both in Arabic and in English. The following are translations of his works from Arabic. The first work listed is very representative of Christian Arabic literature of the late Ottoman period and of Lebanese society.

Spirits Rebellious. [al-Arwāh al-Mutamarridah]. New York, Knopf, 1948. LC 48-7942. BR 1616.G5.

Tears and Laughter. New York, Philosophical Library, 1949. LC 49-3948. PJ 7741. G 54 T42.

Nymphs of the Valley. New York, Knopf, 1948. LC 48-5471. PZ3.G347.

Prose Poems. New York, Knopf, 1934. LC 35-2233. PJ 7741.G54A24.

A Tear and a Smile. New York, Knopf, 1950. LC 50-5761. PJ 7741.G54T392.

Thoughts and Meditations. New York, Citadel Press, 1960. LC 60-15449. PJ 7826.I2T5.

Secrets of the Heart. New York, Wisdom Library, 1971. LC 72-176717. PJ 7826. I2A233 1971.

A Voice of the Master. New York, Citadel Press, 1958. LC 58-13334. PJ 7826.I2V6. DDC 892.78.

The Broken Wings. New York, Citadel Press, 1957. LC 57-11769. PJ 7826.I2B7. DDC 892.73.

A Self-Portrait. New York, Citadel Press, 1959. LC 59-14062. PJ 7826.I2Z54. DDC 892.76.

A Treasury of Kahlil Gibran. New York, Citadel Press, 1951. LC 51-10021. PJ 7741.G54A23.

A Second Treasury of Kahlil Gibran. New York, Citadel Press, 1962. LC 62-10221. PJ 7826.I2A23.

Biographical:

Beloved Prophet: The Love Letters of Kahlil Gibran and Mary Haskell, and Her Private Journal. Ed. by Virginia Hilu. New York, Knopf, 1972. 450p. LC 70-79342. ISBN 0-394-43298-2. PS 3513.I25Z54 1972. DDC 811'.5'2[B].

Visions of Life as Expressed by the Author of the Prophet. The Letters of Kahlil Gibran and Mary Haskell. Ed. by Annie Salem Otto. Houston?, A. S. Otto,? 1970. 677p. LC 71-119616. PS 3513.I25Z54 1970. DDC 811'.5'2.

Naimy, Mikhail. **Kahlil Gibran: A Biography.** New York, Philosophical Library, 1950. 267p. LC 50-12146. PJ 7741.G54Z8. DDC 928.1. Naimy, an outstanding Lebanese writer, was a close friend of Gibran's.

Hawi, Khalil S. **Kahlil Gibran: His Background, Character and Works.** Beirut, American University of Beirut, 1963. LC n.a.

Sherfan, Andrew Dib, comp. **A Third Treasury of Kahlil Gibran.** Secaucus, N.J., Citadel Press, 1975. 434p. $8.95. LC 73-90950. ISBN 0-8065-0403-X. Contains *Mirrors of the Soul*, edited by Joseph Sheban, which has selections from Gibran with commentary on his life and work; *The Wisdom of Gibran*, edited by Joseph Sheban, which is a selection of quotations from his works, arranged alphabetically by subject; and Joseph P. Ghougassian's *Kahlil Gibran, Wings of Thought*, on his life and work.

The most recent and exhaustively researched and detailed work on Gibran is:

Gibran, Jean, and Kahlil Gibran. **Kahlil Gibran, His Life and World.** Boston, New York Graphic Society, 1974. 442p. illus. $12.50. LC 73-80368. ISBN 0-8212-0510-2. PJ 7826.I2Z615. Many new details on his life, with many photographs of the poet and his friends. Has next to nothing on his work and ideas, though much on the process of writing.

303. al-Ḥakīm, Tawfīq. **[Uṣfūr min al-Sharq]. Bird of the East.** Tr. from Arabic by W. Bayly Winder. Beirut, Khayats, 1966. 169p. LC 71-16764. PJ 7828.K52U813. DDC 892.7'3'5.

An autobiographical novel written in 1937 by a leading Egyptian writer. The main theme is the similarities and differences between East and West, in which the Islamic element in al-Hakim's heritage comes to the fore, though it is overlaid with Western culture. It reveals Near Eastern views of Western civilization, and the problems of life and adjustment of an Easterner in a Western environment—in this case, Paris.

304. al-Ḥakīm, Tawfīq. **Fate of a Cockroach: Four Plays of Freedom.** Selected and tr. from Arabic by Denys Johnson-Davies. London, Heinemann Educational Books; distr. New York, Humanities Press, 1973. 184p. (African Writers Series, 117). $3.00pa. LC 73-164698. ISBN 0-435-90117-6. PJ 7828.K52A25 1973. DDC 892.725.

Four plays by the Egyptian playwright who was a pioneer in Arabic drama. The themes are man's love of freedom and refusal to give up in adversity; the conflict between traditional life and customs and the freedom from their deadening effects that education brings; freedom of choice for the ruler; freedom through pursuing the middle way. They comment on life, sometimes with ascerbic satire, sometimes tragically. Very entertaining.

305. al-Ḥakim, Tawfiq. [Yawmiyāt Nā'ib fi al-Aryāf]. **Maze of Justice.** Tr. from Arabic by A. S. [Abba] Eban. London, The Harvill Press, 1947. LC 48-11710 rev. PZ 3.H12758 Maz. DDC 892.73.

An autobiographical novel of the human aspects of relations between government and governed—both officials and peasants are described very revealingly. A critique of the lack of integrity displayed by officials. Humorous, but very biting, with suggestions for combating this problem. The author, an Egyptian, was a lawyer in the countryside for a period of time and was involved in the problem.

306. al-Ḥakim, Tawfiq. [Yā tāli' al-Shajarah]. **The Tree Climber: A Play in Two Acts.** Tr. from Arabic by Denys Johnson-Davies. London, Oxford University Press, 1966. 87p. (A Three Crowns Book). $1.50. LC 67-77355. ISBN 0-19-418521-4. PJ 7828.K52Y283. DDC 892.72'6.

A most entertaining, often amusing play about a murder; it will appeal to many readers. Like most of al-Hakim's works, it has broad appeal; although it sets the scene in Egypt and evokes local color, it deals more with universalisms.

307. Ḥaqqi, Yaḥyā. **The Saint's Lamp and Other Stories.** Tr. from Arabic by M. M. Badawi. Leiden, E. J. Brill, 1973. 90p. (Arabic Translation Series of *The Journal of Arabic Literature*, v. 2). fl. 16pa. LC 73-164418. ISBN 90-04-03605-9. PJ 7828.Q7S2. DDC 892'.7'35.

A selection of outstanding short stories by a well-known Egyptian author. They are significant for their art and their study of Muslim society and culture. They will be particularly interesting to the general reader with some knowledge of the Near East, but any educated reader might enjoy them.

308. Ḥusayn, Muḥammad Kāmil. [Qaryah Zālimah]. **City of Wrong: A Friday in Jerusalem.** Tr. from Arabic with an introd. by Kenneth Cragg. London, G. Bles, 1960. 225p. o.p. LC NE 61-49. BP 172.H813 1960. DDC 232.963. Paperback: New York, Seabury Press, 1966. (A Seabury Paperback, SP 28). o.p. LC 66-22992.

This is a fictional account by an outstanding Egyptian Muslim intellectual of Good Friday and its meaning. Whereas Muslim doctrine through the ages has simply denied Christ's crucifixion because the Koran says that he was not really crucified and that someone else died in his place, Husayn goes beyond this and studies the event of Christ's condemnation by his own community. The point is the *will* to crucify him: the moral encounter of good and evil, and man's rejection of the Christ. The specific point is "the appeal beyond conscience to the collective in human affairs, the wrong of man's slavishness to communal interest and the inability of religion or law to save man from his tragic rebellion against the truth of conscience unless . . . religion and law . . . are properly related to truth in the capacity of servants not masters" (Introd., p. xiv). Husayn uses this as the vehicle for a critique of Islam, deploring the act in specifically Muslim terms and posing the question of how far the "consensus" of the Islamic community can go in justifying and rationalizing wrong done by the community as a whole. ("Consensus" is an important Muslim concept involving the idea of a sacred community under God's guidance and the belief that since God guides the community, he will not allow it to commit error.) This includes the sin of displacing God by a loyalty to some other, false, absolute principle such as nationalism, race, creed, trade, etc. In killing Christ, man slew his conscience and extinguished the light of his life. There is much more in this parable, for Muslim and Christian alike—love, violence, truth, the meaning of Christ, etc. It is a fascinating work, and very thought-provoking. It received a strong reaction in the Muslim world when it was originally published in Egypt.

309. Maḥfuẓ, Najib. **God's World: An Anthology of Short Stories.** Tr. from Arabic by Akef Abadir and Roger Allen. Minneapolis, Bibliotheca Islamica, 1973. 240p. (Studies in Middle Eastern Literatures, No. 2). $8.00pa. LC 73-79201. ISBN 0-8297-006-2.

Selected from various collections by the famous Egyptian novelist, according to what the editors-translators think are the main themes of Mahfuz's production in this genre. An interesting selection well translated. Good reading.

310. Maḥfūẓ, Najib. **[Zuqqāq al-Midāq]. Midaq Alley, Cairo.** Tr. from Arabic by Trevor Le Gassick. Beirut, Khayats, 1966. 319p. pa. LC 73-161190. PZ 3.M2784 Mi 1. [PJ 7846.A46Z46]. DDC 892'.7'36.

One of the most popular novels of the outstanding Egyptian writer. Set in an alley which actually exists, it reveals the lives of the people living there during World War II, in an often humorous manner. Great reading.

311.   Somekh, Sasson. **The Changing Rhythm: A Study of Najib Maḥfūẓ's Novels.** Leiden, E. J. Brill, 1973. 241p. bibliog. index. (Studies in Arabic Literature: Supplements to *The Journal of Arabic Literature*, v. 2). fl. 64.00. LC 73-174560. ISBN 90-04-03587-7. PJ 7846.A549Z88. DDC 892'.7'36.

After a 34-page introduction on the development of the Egyptian Arabic novel, and a 25-page chapter on Muhfuz's life, the book discusses his novels through 1966–their intent, style, structure, themes, characters–and offers a critique. A final section treats his more recent works, and an appendix has plot outlines of each novel through 1966. The only English work on the outstanding Egyptian writer.

312. al-Muwaylihi, Muḥammad. **A Study of Hadith ᶜĪsā Ibn Hishām, Muḥammad al-Muwaylihi's View of Egyptian Society during the British Occupation.** With an introd. and English translation of the 3rd ed. by Roger M. A. Allen. Albany, State University of New York Press, 1974. 10 sheets. bibliog. index. fiche, LC 74-3054. ISBN 0-87395-088-7. microfiche PZ3. [PJ 7850.U9]. DDC 892'.7'35.

The first quarter of the book includes a biography of the author, who was a member of the elite during the last quarter of the nineteenth century and a sometime journalist who spent some time in Europe; the literary background to his genre and style; the history of the text and a literary appreciation of the book, as well as the image of Egyptian society reflected in the book. This work is intended to be fictionalized "fact," and it describes and satirizes the political elite of Egypt and members of the various classes, with detailed criticisms of their philosophies and behavior, and their vain efforts at a mechanical imitative type of Westerniza-tion; the processes of justice, corruption, morals of the clerics, etc. The narrator is sitting in a graveyard, when up from a nearby tomb pops a Pasha from the time of Muhammad Ali; 'Isa proceeds to show him the sights. The contrasts between the old and the "new" Egypt are noted by the characters and provide a take-off point for often lengthy expositions of condi-tions in the author's time. A most interesting, often enjoyable book in a good translation. For larger collections and for students with some background on the period.

313.   Naimy, Mikhail. **A New Year: Stories, Autobiography and Poems.** Tr. from Arabic by J. R. Perry. Leiden, E. J. Brill, 1974. 92p. (Arabic Translation Series, v. 3). fl. 16.00. pa. LC 74-179426. ISBN 90-04-03915-5. PJ 7852. A5A26. DDC 882'.7'8509.

Selections from two of this top Arab writer's periods: the first two decades of the 1900s, and the 1950s.

314.   Saᶜīd, ᶜAlī Aḥmad. **The Blood of Adonis; Transpositions of Selected Poems of Adonis (Ali Ahmed Said).** By Samuel Hazo. Pittsburgh, University of Pittsburgh Press, 1971. 54p. (Pitt Poetry Series). $4.95; $2.50pa. LC 70-134490. ISBN 0-8229-3213-X; 0-8229-5220-3pa. PJ 7862.A519A24. DDC 892.7'1'6.

Selected poems by the winner of the Syria-Lebanon Award of the International Poetry Forum, in an approved translation.

315.   Ṣāliḥ, Ṭayyib. **[Mawsim al-Hijrah ilā al-Shamāl]. Season of Migration to the North.** Tr. from Arabic by Denys Johnson-Davies. London, Heinemann Educational Books; distr. New York, Humanities Press, 1970. 169p. (African Writers Series, 66). $4.50; $2.00pa. LC 75-433646. ISBN 0-435-90630-5. PZ4.S163 Se. [PJ 7862.A564]. DDC 892.7'3'6.

An excellent Arabic novel by a Sudanese writer. It is the story of a young man who returns to the village from studying in the West and who constantly compares the two lives he has led. It reveals much of village life and the problems of a transitional man. Excellent reading.

316. Ṣāliḥ, Ṭayyib. **The Wedding of Zein and Other Stories.** Tr. from Arabic by Denys Johnson-Davies. London, Heinemann Educational Books; distr. New York, Humanities Press, 1969. 120p. (African Writers Series, 47). $1.75pa. LC 68-59635. PZ 4.S163 We. [PJ 7862.A564]. DDC 892.7'3'6.

Two short stories and a novelette by an outstanding Sudanese writer; they provide insight into Sudanese village life.

317. Sharkawi, A. R. [al-Ard]. **Egyptian Earth.** Tr. from Arabic by Desmond Stewart. London, Heinemann; distr. Thompson, Conn., Interculture Associates, 1962. 250p. $2.00pa. LC 62-45305. ISBN 0-88253-121-2. PZ4.S53 Eg.

A profound novel of village life seen through the eyes of a 12-year-old boy. Shows peasant resistance to a tyrannical government decree that threatens their ruin, and the problems and process of activating a servile, passive, traditional society. Excellent reading. By a well-known Egyptian writer.

318. Ṭāhā Ḥusayn (1889-1973). [al-Ayyām]. **V. 1: An Egyptian Childhood, the Autobiography of Taha Husayn.** Tr. from Arabic by E. H. Paxton. London, George Routledge, 1932. 168p. o.p. LC 32-25481 rev. 2. DT 107.2.T3A33. DDC 916.2. **V. 2: The Stream of Days, A Student at the Azhar.** Tr. from Arabic by Hilary Wayment. London, Longmans, 1948. 134p. o.p. LC 60-37052. DT 107.2.T3A332 1948. DDC 916.2.

Volume 1 deals with the childhood of the blind Egyptian writer. It suggests, in a very beguiling fashion and with a gentle wit, his arrival at awareness of the world and his experiences. It is an impressionistic evocation rather than a systematic narrative. The Arabic original is a literary masterpiece to which the translation cannot possibly do justice, but it is good reading for anyone and gives interesting glimpses into Egyptian country life. Volume 2 suggests the author's experiences in his early education at the great Muslim university in Cairo and reveals much about that institution and student life at the turn of the century. It also gives glimpses of the process by which Western civilization infiltrated Egyptian intellectual life. A third volume exists only in Arabic.

319. Cachia, Pierre. **Ṭāhā Ḥusayn: His Place in the Egyptian Literary Renaissance.** Totowa, N.J., Rowman and Littlefield, 196-? (Repr. of 1956 ed.). 260p. $6.50. LC 65-6290. PJ 7864.A35 Z6. (*Br.B.inPr.* lists Luzac, 1956 ed., £1.50.)

When he died in 1973, the blind writer was the dean of Egyptian if not all Arabic letters. He had written novels, studies, and other works, and had engaged in a myriad of activities which entitled him to the sobriquet; he was a major intellectual force in Egypt and the Arab world. Cachia's book traces the author's life, ideas, and activities in the context of the times he lived in and critically analyses his approach, achievements, and impact, not only in literature, but in literary criticism, education, and modernism in Egypt.

F. PERSIAN LANGUAGE

320. Elwell-Sutton, Laurence Paul. **Elementary Persian Grammar.** Cambridge, England, Cambridge University Press, 1963. 223p. index. $12.50; $6.95pa. Key: 1966. $1.95. LC 63-24608 rev. ISBN 0-521-09206-Xpa. PK 6235.E53. DDC 491.558242.

A traditional grammar arranged for beginning students: lesson, vocabulary, two-way translation exercises. Includes English-Persian, Persian-English glosses. Not very good, but useful nonetheless as one of few of its kind.

321. Hayyim, Sulaymān. **The Shorter Persian-English Dictionary, Treating 30,000 Words and Idioms Used in Modern Persian.** 3rd ed. rev. and enl. Tehran, Y. Beroukhim, 1967 (c. 1958). 814p. LC 73-171942. PK 6379.H34 1967. DDC 491'.55'321.

We are very poorly equipped with good Persian dictionaries, but this one will be adequate for most purposes. More extensive ones with more terms (by the same author) were published by the same company. The companion volume is *The Shorter English-Persian*

Dictionary Treating Some 40,000 of the Commonest and the Most Essential English Words and Idioms for Use by Iranian Students of the English Language. 2nd ed., rev. and enl. Tehran, Y. Beroukhim, 1968 (c. 1953). 751p. LC 73-171940. PK 6379.H34 1968. DDC 491'.55'321.

322. Lambton, Ann Katherine Swynford. **Persian Grammar.** Cambridge, England, Cambridge University Press, 1967 (c. 1953). 275p. indices. $12.50; $2.95pa. Key: $2.95. LC 60-4244. ISBN 0-521-09124-1. PK 6235.L35. DDC 491.555.

A traditional approach, more advanced and much more detailed than Elwell-Sutton (item 320), but generally better, with grammar lesson, vocabulary and two-way exercises in each lesson. No glossary. For the beginner without a teacher, Elwell-Sutton is a useful supplement because of its somewhat different explanations and exercises and its glosses. Lambton published a separate glossary which unfortunately was not paired up with this book in any of its editions; rather than spend money on her glossary, purchase a student's dictionary, which will be much more useful. Both Lambton and Elwell-Sutton demand much concentration because of their methods of exposition.

323. Mace, John. **Teach Yourself Modern Persian.** New York, David McKay, 1963. 264p. (Teach Yourself Series). $4.00. LC n.a. PK 6235.M27. DDC 491.558242.

An excellent introduction, which is better than Lambton (item 322) for beginners. However, Lambton will be needed after Mace.

324. Obolensky, Serge, K. Y. Panah, and F. K. Nouri. **Spoken Persian.** Ithaca, N.Y., Spoken Language Services, 1973. 2v. $8.00 (v.1); $6.00 (v.2). LC 73-15155. ISBN 0-87950-295-9. PK 6235.O3. DDC 491'.55'82421.

One of the best introductions, using the oral-aural approach.

G. PERSIAN LITERATURE

1. History and Criticism

325. Arberry, Arthur John. **Classical Persian Literature.** London, George Allen & Unwin; distr. New York, Hillary House Publications, c/o Humanities Press, 1967 (c. 1958). 464p. bibliog. index. $11.00. LC 65-7435/CD. PK 6406.A7. DDC 891.5509.

[P1, C1, S1] The basic English language introduction to the medieval age of Persian literature—the tenth to the fifteenth century. It suggests the origins of the rise of Persian literature and the historical context in which this occurred. It then deals with periods and individual authors, providing biographical notes on each principal author and discussing the nature of the genres in which they worked, the qualities of their craft and important individual works, and the conditions under which they worked. Unlike many of the usual histories of Oriental literature, Arberry sticks to belles-lettres unless some unusual reason dictates otherwise, and he includes many quotations, particularly from poetry. The reader should begin with Levy (item 330) before reading Arberry, because Arberry assumes some basic knowledge of the civilization and literature. An interesting book for college students.

326. Browne, Edward Granville (1862-1926). **A Literary History of Persia.** Cambridge, England, Cambridge University Press, 1964-1969. 4v. bibliog. indices. $14.50/v. LC 30-15417. PK 6097.B72.

[P1, C1, C2, S1, S2] This is the standard history of Persian literature. Though it was first published early in the twentieth century, it has not been surpassed as a source of information and quotations. It covers the pre-Islamic period in the first third of Volume 1, then concentrates on the Islamic period, to 1924; the twentieth century period is covered only briefly. It has a broad definition of literature, which includes history, theology, and other subjects about which Persians wrote; it does cover belles-lettres fully. The detailed discussions of non-literary works are extremely valuable because there is relatively little material about them in English monographic works. Browne discusses the lives of the authors and their main works, sometimes providing outlines of works on which little or nothing had been written previously. Unfortunately he has a tendency to merely hint at some very important topics that had been well covered in the secondary literature (to which he makes explicit reference). He also provides some notion of the historical background. An absolutely essential work for any decent collection; it is useful for reference and interesting to read.

327. **Iran: In Celebration of the 2500th Anniversary of the Founding of the Persian Empire by Cyrus the Great.** Ed. by Javad Haidari. New York, St. John's University, 1971. 191p. (Review of National Literatures, V. 1, no. 1). LC 73-30828. PK 6406.I7. DDC 891'.5.

Essays on aspects of Persian literature and its impact on Europe (late nineteenth-twentieth century trends); Persian literature and national identity (the classical writers, with samples of their works); Matthew Arnold's *Sohrab and Rustam* and its Persian original (an episode from Firdawsi's *Shahnamah*), and the *Shahnamah*'s impact on Europe; Fitzgerald's *Rubaiyat of Omar Khayyam* and the fad it sparked in England and the United States; Goethe's *West-Easterly Diwan* and its Persian mysticism; *Ta'ziyah* (Persian passion plays); Persian medieval popular romances; a bibliographical essay on Persian literature and translations into Western languages. An eye-opening, stimulating collection that both the beginner and the advanced student will appreciate. For larger public and most college collections, though not a high priority item.

The story of the translation of Persian poetry into English and its impact on English and American literature—adaptations, translations, critical works, etc.—is told in Yohannan, John D., *Persian Poetry in England and America: A 200 Year History* (Delmar, N.Y., Caravan Books, 1975. bibliog. [Persian Studies Series, 3]. LC n.a. ISBN 0-88206-006-6). The massive bibliography of the translations and other works is most helpful.

328. Ishaque, Muhammad. **Modern Persian Poetry.** Calcutta, Mohammad Israil, 1943. 226p. bibliog. index. LC 44-43809. PK 6418.I7.

Originally a University of London doctoral thesis written in the 1930s, this book covers the rise of modern poetry; the poets' language, including changes from the classical period, European loan words, and attempts to purify the language of foreign elements; metres; verse forms; themes. It deals very briefly with each of 80 poets individually, then generalizes for the whole. It discusses the classical and modern verse forms and includes many quotations, with translations. Too specialized for most readers, but there is nothing else at all in English.

329. Kamshad, Hassan. **Modern Persian Prose Literature.** Cambridge, England, Cambridge University Press, 1966. 226p. bibliog. index. $10.95. LC 66-10041. PK 6423.K3. DDC 891.553309.

This book deals with "imaginative prose" of the twentieth century. Providing the historical context of the times, the author discusses main authors and their lives and works; he notes the main themes, authors' motivations, trends in the literature, and the significance of each author in the whole picture. This occupies 136 pages. The remaining 81 pages deal with Sadiq Hidayat, the main writer of the period. Rather than being a general treatise, it is essentially a listing of authors. Essential because it is the unique work on the subject.

330. Levy, Reuben. **An Introduction to Persian Literature.** New York, Columbia University Press, 1969. 194p. index. (UNESCO Introductions to Asian Literatures. Persian Heritage Series). $7.50. LC 68-8876. ISBN 0-231-03177-7. PK 6406.L38. DDC 891.5'509.

[P1, C1, S1] A brief elementary outline containing generalities on Persian prose and poetry and brief treatments of key figures, as well as translations. The main emphasis is the medieval period, though a few major writers after 1500 are discussed. The first work to read. Appended is a useful list of Persian works in translation, including non-literary works.

331. Rypka, Jan. **History of Iranian Literature.** Tr. from Czech. Ed. by Karl Jahn. Dordrecht, D. Reidel Publishing Company, 1968. 929p. bibliog. index. LC 68-95715. PK 6097. R913. DDC 891.5.

After a 66-page introduction on pre-medieval Iranian literature and languages, the book deals with the history of Persian literature through the twentieth century (to page 418). A

60-page section treats very concisely the non-literary writing to the end of the eighteenth century. A 120-page section discusses Tajik literature. There are 100 pages on folk literature; a brief section on Persian literature in India; and a 100-page bibliography of books and articles in many languages, including Persian and Slavic. The treatment is mainly topical, partly by period, and interpretive-analytical rather than factual and chronological, as Browne is. It probes the background, including the social-political-historical factors, and discusses the nature, types, and content of the literature and its various genres, including key works of many writers, about whom there is considerable material. No translations are provided as examples. For the reader who has a background from Browne (item 326), etc., and who has done selected reading in the translations listed in this *Guide*, Rypka will be enlightening, as well as a stimulus to further and deeper study. For the Westerner, it indicates the extent and nature of Soviet bloc studies of Eastern literatures.

2. Collections

332. Arberry, Arthur John. **Immortal Rose: An Anthology of Persian Lyrics.** London, Luzac, 1948. 174p. o.p. LC 49-29548. PK 6449.E5 A7. DDC 891.551082.

   Arberry's verse translations of classical ghazals (lyric poems) by six greats: Sanai (1080-1150), Attar (1130-1230), Rumi (1207-1273), Saadi (1184-1292), Hafiz (1320-1389), whose poems occupy about a third of the book, and Jami (1414-1492). Pleasant reading.

333. Arberry, Arthur John. **Persian Poems: An Anthology of Verse Translations.** New York, E. P. Dutton, 1954. 239p. bibliog. index. (Everyman Library, No. 996). LC 54-11396. PK 6449.E5 A73. [AC 1.E8 No. 996]. DDC 891.551082.

   Poems by 25 poets, including some from the modern era, by 25 translators. They are arranged by type—quatrains, lyrics, odes, didactic poems, idylls, epics. Included are brief biographical notices on the poets, and somewhat longer notes on the translators. A pleasant collection for its own sake, as well as a basic collection of important classic works.

334. Chodzke, Alexander Borejko (1804-1891). **Specimens of the Popular Poetry of Persia, As Found in the Adventures and Improvisations of Kurroglu, the Bandit-Minstrel of Northern Persia, and in the Songs of the People Inhabiting the Shores of the Caspian Sea.** Orally collected and tr. with philological and historical notes. New York, Burt Franklin, 1971. (Repr. of 1842 ed.). 592p. (Burt Franklin Research & Source Works Series, 642. Essays in Literature and Criticism, 119). $25.00. LC 74-153024. ISBN 0-8337-0563-6. PK 6449.E7C5 1971. DDC 398.2'0955.

   The first 344 pages contain a connected prose version of the popular adventures of the outlaw-hero; the adventures reflect the values and lives of the common people. These tales, which were collected over eleven years of residence in the area, have come down over the centuries and are still popular. The rest of this valuable work contains prose translations of songs of the Astrakan Tatars, Kalmuks, Turkmans, Persian Turks, and Caspian Sea peoples, concluding with a short section of vernacular texts.

335. Hasan, Hadi, tr. **A Golden Treasury of Persian Poetry.** Delhi, The Publication Division, Ministry of Information and Broadcasting; distr. Columbia, Mo., South Asia Books, 1966. 228p. (A National Book Trust Book). $4.00. LC SA67-4132. PK 6449.E5H3. DDC 891.5'5'1008.

   Pieces of Persian poetry by 81 authors of various eras through the twentieth century, from Iran and India; the selection includes a variety of styles and themes.

3. Individual Authors

336. Āl Aḥmad, Jalal. [**Mudir-i Madrasah**]. **The School Principal: A Novel.** Tr. from Persian by John K. Newton. Minneapolis, Bibliotheca Islamica, 1974. 144p. (Studies in Middle Eastern Literatures, No. 4). $5.00pa. LC 74-80599. ISBN 0-88297-008-9. PK 6561.

A work of social criticism by a leading Persian writer (d. 1969) who was a leader of the non-establishment intelligentsia. It explores problems of Iran's school system. Some of his writings, including this work, have been banned for a period of time.

337. Bābā-Ṭāhir (11th cent.). [Tarānah-hā]. The Lament of Bābā Tāhir. Persian text; tr. by Elizabeth Curtis Benton. Ed. by Y. Jamshidi pur. Tehran, 1963. 116p. illus. LC 68-37115. PK 6550.T3 1963.

Poems by a medieval poet whose simple, often mystical lines have retained much of their popularity today.

338. Bābā-Ṭāhir (11th cent.). The Rubāiyyāt of Bābā Tāhir Oryan of Hamadān. Tr. from Persian by Mehdi Nakosteen. Boulder, University of Colorado Press, 1968. 54 leaves. LC 67-23561. PK 6550. T3 1968. DDC 891.5'5'11.

Half the book is an introduction to the life, literature, and times of the poet. It includes the Persian text and a translation that reads well.

339. Bighāmī, Muḥammad Ibn Aḥmad. [Dārāb nāmah]. Love and War; Adventures from the Firuz Shāh nāma of Sheikh Bighami. Tr. from Persian by William J. Hanaway. Delmar, N.Y., Scholars Facsimiles & Reprints, 1974. 208p. (UNESCO Collection of Representative Works. Persian Heritage Series, 19). LC 74-6039. ISBN 0-8201-1126-0. PK 6451. B53 D3213 1974. DDC 891'.55'31.

A medieval epic and love story about a Persian prince's search for his dream girl, a Yemeni princess. It combines adventure, fairy tales, and intrigue. This translation, which is a delight to read, is an abridgement of the original, which ran to as much as several volumes. It is sufficiently enjoyable that the reader will continually be frustrated by the frequent bracketed summaries of omitted adventures, which whet his appetite because many of them seem to be even more interesting than some of the episodes that are included in their complete form.

340. Fakhr al-Din Gurjani (fl. 1048). Vis and Ramin. Tr. from Persian by George Morrison. New York, Columbia University Press, 1972. 357p. (Persian Heritage Series, UNESCO Collection of Representative Works). $15.00. LC 70-169960. ISBN 0-231-03408-3. PK 6451.F28V53. DDC 398.22'0955.

An eleventh century romantic epic narrative poem in prose translation. It has parallels with, and may have been a model for, the story of Tristan and Isolde, the Celtic tale. An enjoyable work in an adequate translation.

341. Farīd al-Dīn ᶜAṭṭār (13th cent.). The Conference of the Birds, Mantiq ut-Tayr: A Philosophical Religious Poem in Prose. Berkeley, Shambala, 1971. 147p. (The Clear Light Series). $2.50. LC n.a. ISBN 0-87773-031-8. PK 6451.F4M28.

A prose translation (from the French) of a famous classical Persian Sufi allegorical poem by one of the most illustrious Persian poets before the great Jalal al-Din Rumi (items 349-352). The poem provides a wide range of wisdom on how to live a spiritual life. A popular version.

342. Firdawsī. The Epic of Kings: Shah-nama. Tr. from Persian by Reuben Levy. London, Routledge & Kegal Paul, 1973. 423p. (Persian Heritage Series. UNESCO Collection of Representative Works). ₤5.00. LC n.a. ISBN 0-7100-1367-1. PK 6456.A1L4 1973. DDC 891.5'511.

The *Shahnamah* is the national epic of Iran and was the first major medieval Persian literary work. It recounts the legends of Iran starting from creation, and the exploits of its semi-mythical kings, with flights of fancy, supernatural beings, etc. This translation is a prose version by an expert Persianist. Some of the repetitive and other passages have been omitted or abbreviated for readability. The translation of this series of stories about heroes and battles flows smoothly and excitingly, and the reader will find it most interesting. The work is important today because Iran is looking back into this period as part of its search for a self-image; it was important in the past because it helped spark a Persian cultural renaissance independent of Arab, though not of Islamic, culture in the tenth century A.D. A basic work.

343. Ḥāfiẓ (14th cent.). **Hafiz of Shiraz: Thirty Poems.** Tr. by Peter Avery and John Heath-Stubbs. London, John Murray, 1952. 66p. (Wisdom of the East Series). o.p. LC 52-4924. PK 6465.Z31A9. DDC 891.551.

Readable renderings with a brief introduction.

344. Ḥāfiẓ (14th cent.). **Fifty Poems of Ḥāfiẓ: Texts and Translations.** Collected by Arthur J. Arberry. Cambridge, England, Cambridge University Press, 1947. 187p. o.p. LC 47-6020. PK 6465.Z31A7. DDC 891.551.

Persian and English, parallel texts, with introduction and notes.

345. Ḥāfiẓ (14th cent.). **Poems from the Diwan of Hafiz.** Tr. from Persian by Gertrude Bell. London, William Heinemann, 1928. 175p. o.p. LC 28-23565. PK 6465.Z32B4 1928.

Excellent translations of poems written by one of Iran's greatest poets, rendered into latter nineteenth century but very readable verse by the famous Orientalist. Includes an 81-page introduction and 30 pages of notes.

346. Hidāyat, Ṣādiq (1903-1951). [Buf-i Kūr]. **The Blind Owl.** By Sadegh Hedayat. Tr. from Persian by D. P. Costello. New York, Grove Press, 1957. 130p. o.p. LC 58-6702. PZ 4.H633 Bl 4. DDC 891.553. Paperback: 1958. $1.25. ISBN 0-394-17445-3.

A novelette by one of Iran's outstanding writers. Educated in Europe, Hidayat returned to Iran and wrote some 30 volumes, mainly of short stories. He returned to Paris in 1951 and killed himself the same year. A retranslation of the book, bracketed by studies of the author, his influence, the contents and sources (literary and cultural) of the book, and its structure is found in Iraj Bashiri's *Hedayat's Ivory Tower: Structural Analysis of the Blind Owl* (Minneapolis, Manor House, 1974. LC 73-620244. PK 6561. H43 B833. DDC 891.55'3'3). Bashiri says that the main sources of the book are Rilke's *Notebooks of Malte Laurids Brigge*, the Indian *Buddha-carita*; and Kafka. Bashiri's conclusions are controversial but most interesting. The only English monograph on Hidayat.

347. Hidāyat, Ṣādiq (1903-1951). **Sadeq's Omnibus: A Collection of Short Stories.** Tr. by Siavosh Danesh. Teheran, Mahre Danesh Publications, n.d. 115p. LC 73-200655. PK 6561.H43A24. DDC 891'.55'33.

Six stories by Iran's greatest modern writer. The translator's English is not perfect, nor is his style the best, but it is readable. The book is worth having since there is almost nothing else available; however, it does not do justice to the stories.

348. ʿIrāqī, Fakhr al-Dīn Ibrāhīm (d. 1289?). **The Song of Lovers (ʿUshshāq-nāma)** by ʿIrāqī. Ed. and tr. into English by Arthur J. Arberry. London, published for the Islamic Research Association by Oxford University Press, 1939. 84, 100p. index. o.p. LC 49-44136. PK 6477.I7U8 1939. DDC 895.551.

A "mystical, philosophical" treatise in verse on divine love and love of God, which is very readable and comprehensible. Includes Persian text.

349. Jalāl al-Dīn Rūmī, Mawlānā (1207-1273). [Fīhi mā Fīhi]. **Discourses of Rumi.** Tr. from Persian by A. J. Arberry. London, John Murray, 1961. 276p. ₤.50. LC 61-40019. ISBN 0-7195-1194-1. BP 188.2.J313. DDC 297.4. Paperback: New York, Samuel Weiser. $3.50. ISBN 0-87728-179-3.

Rumi was one of the most influential Sufi poets and a great Persian stylist. This work consists of what might be called table-talk on aspects of Sufism and Rumi's ideas. They are documents that are basic to understanding his poetry, especially his great work, *The Masnavi.* The *Discourses* are difficult to read but are an interesting example of a top Muslim mind at work. They deal with aspects of daily and spiritual life and contain much for any thoughtful, searching reader, since not all the material is specifically Islamic in nature. There is no comprehensive study of Rumi in English. One useful work is Iqbal, Afzal, *The Life and Work of Muhammad Jalal-ud-Din Rumi*, 3rd rev. ed. (Lahore, Institute of Islamic Culture, 1974. 306p. BP 189.7.M42 I65 1974. DDC n.a. Annemarie Schimmel is preparing a study of his poetry and thought; she discusses Rumi at length in item 558.

350. Jalāl al-Dīn Rūmī, Mawlānā (1207-1273). **Mystical Poems of Rumi, First Selection, Poems 1-200.** Tr. from Persian by A. J. Arberry. Chicago, University of Chicago Press, 1968. 203p. bibliog. (Persian Heritage Series, No. 3. UNESCO Collection of Representative Works). o.p. LC 68-29935. PK 6840.E5A7. DDC 891.5'5'11. Paperback: 1974. (A Phoenix Book, P 584). $2.95. ISBN 0-226-02468-7.

A selection from Rumi's vast output, being basically literal translations that are presented as prose sentences. Copious notes illuminate the texts, which are not particularly enjoyable or easy reading but are essential for knowing something about the author, who had a tremendous influence and is still popular. He was the most famous of the Persian Sufi poets.

351. Jalāl al-Dīn Rūmī, Mawlānā (1207-1273). **Rumi, Poet and Mystic (1207-1273): Selections from His Writings.** Tr. from Persian with introd. and notes by Reynold A. Nicholson. London, George Allen and Unwin; distr. New York, Hillary House, 1950. 190p. (Ethical and Religious Classics of the East and West, No. 1). $8.00. LC 51-32475 rev 2. PK 6480.E5N5 1950. DDC 891.551.

Excellent translations of mainly Sufi religious poetry. It has much to offer the general reader aside from its value as an example of this great poet's work.

352. Jalāl al-Dīn Rūmī, Mawlānā (1207-1273). **[Masnavi]. Tales from the Masnavi.** Tr. from Persian by A. J. Arberry. London, George Allen and Unwin; distr. New York, Crane-Russak, 1961. 300p. (UNESCO Collection of Representative Works. Persian Series). $5.75. LC 61-66200 rev. ISBN 0-8448-0589-0. PK 6481.M8E52 1961. DDC 891.551.

A prose translation of the original rhymed couplets. The stories are Sufi teaching parables; each concludes with the moral of the tale. The *Masnavi* is Rumi's masterwork. Also, by the same translator, *More Tales from the Masnavi* (London, George Allen and Unwin, 1963. 252p. LC 63-24201. PK 6481.M8E52 1963. DDC 891.551).

353. Niẓāmī Ganjavī (1140 or 1141-1202 or 1203). **The Haft Paikar (The Seven Beauties), Containing the Life and Adventures of King Bahrām Gūr, and the Seven Stories Told by His Seven Queens.** Tr. from Persian with a commentary by C. E. Wilson. London, Probsthain, 1924. 2v. (Probsthain's Oriental Series, v. 12-13). o.p. LC 24-30342. PK 6501.H43W5.

A verse translation of one of the major works of one of the greatest Persian Sufi poets, who was even until lately immensely popular in Turkey as well as Iran. It relates the adventures of the semi-legendary Emperor Bahram Gur, interspersed with philosophical musings.

354. Niẓāmī Ganjavī (1140 or 1141-1202 or 1203). **[Laylī va Majnūn]. Laili and Majnún.** From the Persian of Nizami, by James Atkinson. New York, Johnson Reprint Corp., 1969. (Repr. of 1836 ed.). 162p. $10.00. LC n.a. PK 6501.L33A8.

The tragic pre-Islamic Arabian story of *Majnun Layla* found its way into the other Near Eastern literatures. It was treated masterfully in Nizami's poem and is presented in this enjoyable Victorian translation, which belongs in all representative collections.

Another version:

The Story of Layla and Majnun. Tr. from Persian and ed. by Rudolf Gelpke; English version in collaboration with E. Mattin and G. Hill. Oxford, Cassimer, 1966. 221p. LC 66-74639. PK 6501.L33G4 1966. DDC 891.5511.

355. Niẓāmī Ganjavī (1140 or 1141-1201 or 1203). **[Iskandar-nāmah]. The Sikander Nāma, E Bara; Or, Book of Alexander the Great.** Tr. from Persian, with notes by Captain Henry Wilberforce Clarke. London, W. H. Allen, 1881. 831p. LC 44-25727 rev. PK 6501.I84C5.

Alexander became a legendary figure in Near Eastern Islamic classical literature. Nizami's famous epic poem blends the figure of Alexander with Solomon and other legendary characters, and features Alexander's exploits and much philosophical speculation. This is a "prose" translation arranged in verse stanzas. Surely too much for most libraries, but it should be in the most comprehensive representative collections.

356. Omar Khayyam. **Rubaiyat. The 1st and 4th Editions in English Verse by Edward FitzGerald.** New York, Crowell, 1964. 80p. PK 6513.A1 1964. LC 64-20696. DDC 891.55.

Curiously, Khayyam is known in Iran as a mathematician, and his poetry was virtually unknown until FitzGerald's version swept Europe. Another FitzGerald edition is: *The Rubayyat of Omar Khayyam: Life and Love in One of the World's Most Famous Poems in the Classic Translation of Edward FitzGerald* (Kansas City, Hallmark Editions, 1967. 59p. LC 67-17906. PK 6513.A1 1967. DDC 891.5'5'11).

Other translations include the following:

The Original Rubaiyyat of Omar Khayyam. A New Translation with Critical Commentaries. By Robert Graves and Omar Ali-Shah. Tucson, Ariz., Omen Press, 1972 (c. 1967). 86p. bibliog. LC 72-90287. PK 6156.G7 1972. DDC 891'.55'11.

The Wisdom of Omar Khayyam: A Selection of Quatrains. Tr. from Persian by Eben Francis Thompson. New York, Philosophical Library; distr. Book Sales, 1967. 1v. (unpaged). LC 67-6842. PK 6516.T62. DDC 891.5'51'1.

Omar Khayyam: A New Version Based Upon Recent Discoveries. By Arthur J. Arberry. London, John Murray, 1952. 159p. LC 52-1013. PK 6516.A1 1952. DDC 891.551.

The only substantive book on Khayyam in English is:

Dashti, Ali. **In Search of Omar Khayyam.** Tr. from Persian by L. P. Elwell-Sutton. New York, Columbia University Press, 1971. 276p. bibliog. index. LC 77-168669. ISBN 0-231-03188-2. PK 6525.D313 1971b. DDC 891'.55'11. A Persian scholar seeks to understand the man, his personality, and his work, and to determine which quatrains attributed to him are actually his. A highly technical work beyond most readers, but it is all we have.

357. Sa^cdi. **Morals Pointed and Tales Adorned: The Bustān of Sa^cdi.** Tr. from Persian by G. M. Wickens. Toronto, University of Toronto Press, 1974. xxviii, 316p. (Persian Heritage Series, No. 17). $20.00. LC cataloging n.a. ISBN 0-8020-1840-8.

The great Persian poet's first dated work, and one of the most popular classical works, of which many verses have become quoted as proverbs. It is a collection of interesting, well-told stories of various kinds, including much wisdom on politics, government, the good life, love, and the virtues.

358. Sa^cdi. **The Gulistan; Or, Rose Garden of Sa^cdi.** Ed. and tr. from Persian by Edward Rehatsek. London, George Allen and Unwin, 1964. 265p. £3.75. LC 65-53451. ISBN 0-04-891026-0. PK 6541.G2R4 1965a. Paperback: Capricorn Books (CAP 125). o.p. ISBN 0-388-50101-0.

One of the most famous Persian literary works, this is an example of *adab*, or courtly literature, which is not strictly literary but seeks to impart wisdom in an entertaining manner, in high literary style. An introduction that traces the history and problems of translation, and another on the book itself, are most enlightening. Enjoyable reading for its own sake. It should be noted, as both a caution and a come-on, that it is not for the delicately inclined, but rather for the non-puritan who would enjoy the *Decameron*. However, it is not grossly written, and its racy humor is often delicious.

359. [Marzuban-nāmah]. **The Tales of Marzuban.** Tr. from Persian by Reuben Levy. New York, Greenwood Press, 1968. (Repr. of 1959 ed.). 254p. $11.50. LC 68-8337. ISBN 0-8371-0162-X. PJ 939.M3 1968. DDC 398.21'0935.

A classical collection of fables, anecdotes, etc., in which the main characters are portrayed as animals, fishes, birds, fairies, etc. The stories are told by a prince who seeks to impart moral doctrine and much practical wisdom, and they are written in Persian court literary style. Interesting reading.

H. TURKISH LANGUAGE

360. Alderson, Anthony Dolphin, and Fahir İz. **The Concise Oxford Turkish Dictionary.** Oxford, Clarendon Press, 1959. 807p. $9.50. LC 59-16894. ISBN 0-19-864109-5. PL 191.A55. DDC 494.3532.

The standard Turkish-English, English-Turkish dictionary for students. An abridgement of H. C. Hony's *A Turkish-English Dictionary* (Oxford University Press, 1950) and Fahir İz and H. C. Hony's *An English-Turkish Dictionary* (Oxford University Press, 1952), both of which are quite out of date and thus of questionable priority for most colleges as separate purchases. Turkish vocabulary is constantly changing. The language is still developing rapidly, since it began to adjust to the modern world only in the nineteenth century, and more particularly after Ataturk came to power after World War I. Therefore, an up-to-date dictionary should be obtained as soon as one becomes available.

361. İngilizce-Türkçe **Redhouse Sözlüğü-Redhouse English-Turkish Dictionary.** Istanbul, Redhouse Yayinevi; distr. New York, William S. Heinmann, 1974. 1152p. $25.00. LC n.a. PL 191.R5 1974. DDC 494.3532.

362. Lewis, Geoffrey L. **Turkish Grammar.** Oxford, Clarendon Press, 1967. 303p. index. $8.50. LC 68-75910. ISBN 0-19-815375-9. PL 123.L4. DDC 494'.35'5.

A systematic survey and reference grammar with many examples, but without exercises or vocabulary lists. Organized topically with no gradation or lesson organization. For the more advanced student. Primarily for written Turkish. The best work of its kind.

363. Mardin, Yusuf. **Colloquial Turkish.** New York, Dover Publications, 1961. 288p. (Trubner's Colloquial Manuals). $4.00pa. LC 63-2250. ISBN 0-486-20983-0. PL 139.M3. DDC 494.358242.

An excellent introduction for the beginner.

364. **Turkish-English Dictionary.** 2nd ed. Istanbul, Redhouse Yayinevi; distr. New York, William Heinmann, 1974. 1292p. $25.00. LC n.a. PL 191.R55 1974. DDC 494'.35'22.

The best Turkish-English dictionary. It is "based largely" on the work of 1890 by James Redhouse but has been brought up to date; thus, it includes modern Turkish words as well as Ottoman. Entries are in the modern roman script, followed by the words in the Ottoman (modified Arabic) script, which enhances its usefulness.

365. U.S. Foreign Service Institute. **Turkish: Basic Course.** By Lloyd B. Swift and Selman Ağrali. Washington, D.C., Department of State; available from Superintendent of Documents, U.S. Government Printing Office, 1966-1970. 2v. $2.25/vol. pa. LC 68-67108. PL 127.U55. DDC 494'.35'8242.

An oral-aural conversational course divided into gradual study units, with dialogues, grammatical notes and extensive examples and drills. Turkish-English, English-Turkish glossaries.

I. TURKISH LITERATURE

1. History and Criticism

366. Andrews, Walter G. **Introduction to Ottoman Poetry.** Minneapolis, Bibliotheca Islamica, 1975 (forthcoming). (Studies in Middle Eastern Literatures). $12.00pa. LC 74-27615. ISBN 0-88297-012-7. LC cataloging n.a.

367. Bombaci, Alessio. **La Letteratura Turca.** Milan, Sansoni-Academia, 1969. 528p. bibliog. index. (Le Letterature nel mondo). LC 70-496480. PL 205.B6 1969.

[P1, C1, S1] A survey reaching back into the pre-Islamic period, which includes some material besides belles-letters—a time-honored custom among historians of Turkish, Persian, and Arabic literature. It covers key individual authors, with some attention to historical background and general aspects such as Arabic and Persian influences, themes, genres, language, mysticism in poetry, etc. There is a brief final section on Mongol literature. By no means exhaustive, it is one of the few general works available in any Western language. A translation has been announced and when it is available, Bombaci and Halman will be the only general works on the topic in English.

368. Halman, Talat Sait. **A History of Turkish Literature.** Minneapolis, Bibliotheca Islamica, ca. 1975.

[P1, C1]   No further information available.

369. Martinovich, Nicholas N. **The Turkish Theatre.** New York, Benjamin Blom, 1968. (Repr. of 1933 ed.). 125p. bibliog. $12.50. LC 68-20241. PL 271.E5M3 1968. DDC 894'.35'200.

A discussion of Turkish popular theater: *Orta Oiunu*, plays performed in public squares, similar to the classical Greek mime and Italian *commedia dell'arte*, with a description of the places in which they are performed, characters, etc.; *Meddah*, storytelling by mimicry, usually by individuals, in the marketplace, at parties, celebrations, etc.; *Karagöz*, puppet theater, with descriptions of the puppets, themes, characters, etc. Included are seven texts illustrating the three types. Interesting and informative.

370. **Turkey: From Empire to Nation.** Ed. by Talat Sait Halman. Jamaica, N.Y., St. John's University, 1973. 142p. (Review of National Literatures). LC 77-126039. PL 205.H3.

Essays by various authors on aspects of Turkish literature: classical, modern; the theater; poetry; image of the Turks in Elizabethan drama; historiography of Turkish literature in Turkish and Western languages. A useful, though by no means comprehensive, survey for college libraries.

2. Collections

371. Gibb, Elias John Wilkinson, ed. and tr. (1857-1901). **Ottoman Literature: The Poets and Poetry of Turkey.** Tr. with introd. and biog. notes. With Arabian, Persian and Hebrew poems and a special introd. by Theodore P. Ion. New York, Gordion Press, 197-?. (Repr. of 1901 ed.). 351p. index. $17.00. LC n.a. ISBN n.a. PL 271.E3G5. DDC 894. 3510822.

One of the few books of translations from Ottoman Turkish (which was written in modified Arabic script and had much Persian and Arabic vocabulary). It consists of a 32-page introduction, 164 pages of translations, 54 pages of biographies of poets, followed by notes to the poems. Includes a Hebrew poem, *The Love Song of King Suleiman*, and 46 pages of miscellaneous Arabic and Persian poems. Gibb was the outstanding Western student of Turkish literature, his major work being the six-volume *History of Ottoman Poetry*.

372. Halman, Talat Sait. **Modern Turkish Drama: An Anthology of Plays in Translation.** Minneapolis, Bibliotheca Islamica, 1975? $8.00pa.

Translations of four modern plays by various translators.

373. **The Literary Review** (Winter, 1960-61). Teaneck, N.J., Fairleigh-Dickinson University. LC 59-65170. AP 2.L6377. DDC 051.

This number contains modern Turkish prose and poetry translations.

374. Toygar, S. Behlül, comp. **Fifteen Turkish Poets, 75 Poems.** Istanbul, Iskender Matbaasi, 1969. 207p. LC 79-242850. PL 271.E3T6.

Turkish and English on opposite pages. For each poet there is a biographical introduction and several poems. Emphasizes the late-nineteenth and twentieth century poets. The translations are not the best but are suggestive; since there are so few Turkish works translated into English, we are desperate for anything we can get.

375. **Turkish Literature, Comprising Fables, Belles-Lettres, and Sacred Traditions.** Tr. into English by Epiphanius Wilson. Freeport, N.Y., Books for Libraries Press, 1970. (Repr. of 1901 ed.). 462p. (Play Anthology Reprint Series). $25.00. LC 77-111117. ISBN 0-8369-8120-X. PL 271.E1 T8 1970. DDC 894'.35'08.

A variety of popular fables, a nineteenth century play, classical poetry, and popular tales. One of very few collections of Ottoman Turkish literature.

3. Individual Authors

376. Dağlarca, Fazil Hüsnü. **Seçme Şiirler-Selected Poems.** Tr. from Turkish. Pittsburgh, University of Pittsburgh Press, 1969. 195p. (Pitt Poetry Series, 46). $4.50; $2.50pa. LC 69-12329. ISBN 0-8229-3176-1; 0-8229-5204-1pa. PL 248.D3A6 1969. DDC 894'.35'13.

Turkish and English texts on opposite pages. By the International Poetry Forum winner.

377. Fuzūli, Mehmet. **Leylā and Majnūn.** Tr. from Turkish by Sofi Huri, with a history of the poem, notes and bibliography by Alessio Bombaci. London, George Allen and Unwin; distr. New York, Crane-Russak Company, 1970. 350p. bibliog. index. (UNESCO Collection of Representative Works. Turkish Series). $12.75. LC 73-853172. ISBN 0-8448-0625-0. PL 248.F95L43. DDC 894'.35'12.

Fuzuli was one of the greatest Turkish poets. Bombaci's introduction presents his life, and discusses his works (which were written in Turkish, Persian, and Arabic). In treating his poetry, Bombaci includes some of his lyric poems, with notes on his themes, style, and exposition, and then traces the history of the legend of Majnun Layla (cf. Nizami, item 354), citing excerpts from the Arabic version and Nizami's Persian poem; he finally treats Fuzuli's version, discussing its place in Turkish literature, structure, style, etc. (112 pages). The rest of the book contains the translation. This version is a mystical interpretation of the story, which becomes an allegory, and thus there are philosophical asides throughout. For larger collections.

378. Hikmet, Nâzim (1902-1963). **The Day Before Tomorrow, Poems.** Tr. from Turkish by Taner Baybars. Oxford, Carcanet Press; distr. Chester Springs, Pa., Dufour Editions, 1972. 45p. $6.00; $2.50pa. LC 72-185817. ISBN 0-902145-43-6; 0-85635-006-0pa. PL 248.H45A22 1972. DDC 894'.3'513.

By one of Turkey's outstanding modern writers, who has also written plays and a novel.

379. Hikmet, Nâzim (1902-1963). **The Moscow Symphony and Other Poems.** Tr. from Turkish by Taner Baybars. Chicago, Swallow Press, 1971. 64p. bibliog. (Poetry Europe Series, 13). o.p. LC 73-118823. PL 248.H45A217 1971. DDC 894'.35'13.

380. Hikmet, Nâzim (1902-1963). **Selected Poems.** Tr. from Turkish by Taner Baybars. London, Jonathan Cape; distr. New York, Grossman Publishers, c/o Viking Press, 1967. 93p. $3.50; $1.50pa. LC 68-91439. ISBN 0-670-37208-0; 0-670-37209-9pa. PL 248.H45A22. DDC 894'.35'13.

381. Kalyoncu, Güngör Dilmen. **The Ears of Midas: A Verse Play (Midas'in Kulaklari).** Tr. from Turkish by Carolyn Graham. Ankara, Ankara Universitesi Basimevi, 1967. 89p. LC 77-256430. PL 248.K228M513. DDC 894'.35'2'3.

By a young Turkish playwright. Apollo gives Midas the ears of an ass as a punishment for having judged Pan the best musician in a contest; but Midas nullifies the punishment by becoming vain and proud of the ears. Entertaining reading.

382. Kanik, Orhan Veli (1914-1950). **I Am Listening to Istanbul; Selected Poems.** Tr. from Turkish with an introd. by Talat Sait Halman. New York, Corinth Books, 1971. 94p. $6.50; $3.50pa. LC 74-156854. ISBN 0-87091-063-9; 0-87091-062-0pa. PL 248.K23A25. DDC 894'.35'13.

By an outstanding Turkish poet.

383. **[Kitab-i-Dede Korkut]. The Book of Dede Korkut: A Turkish Epic.** Tr. by Faruk Sümer, Ahmet E. Uysal, and Warren S. Walker. Austin, University of Texas Press, 1972. 23, 212p. bibliog. $7.50. LC 72-3214. ISBN 0-292-71501-3. PL 248.K5E57. DDC 398.2'2'0958.

An Orghuz (Turkoman) epic which is held to be among the greatest pieces of Turkish literature—indeed, the Turkish national epic. A collection of stories about heroes and war, it reflects medieval Turkish life and values and is a valuable source on Turkish society. A basic work that makes interesting reading.

384. Yaşar Kemal. **[Ince Memed]. Memed My Hawk.** Tr. by Edouard Roditi. New York, Pantheon Books, 1961. 371p. $6.95. LC 60-11761. ISBN 0-394-43576-1. PZ4.K318 Me.

An adventure novel by one of Turkey's outstanding writers. It reveals much about peasant life and problems in the Taurus Mountains. Good reading.

385. Yaşar Kemal. **[Ortadirek]. The Winds from the Plain.** Tr. by Thelda Kemal. New York, Dodd, Mead, 1969. 286p. o.p. LC 72-75200. PZ4.K318Wi 4. [PL 248.K43]. DDC 894'.353'3.

A novel of village life, with much detail and insight into the peasant way of thinking and approach to life.

J. HEBREW LANGUAGE

386. Alcalay, Reuben. **The Complete Hebrew-English Dictionary.** Tel-Aviv, Massadah Publishing Company, 1964. 2884 columns. LC HE66-1319. PJ 4833.A42 1965. DDC n.a.
(BIP lists a 2-volume edition published by Hartmore House; distr. Bridgeport, Conn., Associated Booksellers. $19.95/vol.).

The best such work available. It has one English word or phrase for each Hebrew word or expression, facilitating quick reference.

387. Ben-Yehuda, Ehud, and David Weinstein. **Ben-Yehuda's Pocket English-Hebrew, Hebrew-English Dictionary.** New York, Washington Square Press, 1966. 306, 320p. $1.25pa. LC 62-55263 (in Hebrew). PJ 4833.B35. DDC 492.432.

A basic student's dictionary. One major defect that should be noted is that a significant number of the neologisms coined by the chief editor's father, the great exponent and revitalizer of Hebrew as a modern language, have been included instead of the Israeli Hebrew terms actually used; these neologisms are no longer relevant, and their inclusion here can lead to frustrating errors when one is translating into Hebrew. For all libraries. A more recent paperback is: Siven, Reuben, and Edward A. Levenston, *The New Bantam-Megiddo Hebrew & English Dictionary* (New York, Bantam Books, 1975. 399, 294p. $1.95. LC n.a.).

388. Blumberg, Harry, and Mordecai H. Lewittes. **Modern Hebrew: A First Year Course in Conversation, Reading and Grammar.** Rev. ed. New York, Hebrew Publishing Company, 1963. 450p. indices. o.p. LC 64-34784. PJ 4567.B652.

An elementary grammar, with extensive exercises and glossaries.

389. Levenston, Edward A., and Reuben Sivan. **The Megiddo Modern Dictionary: English-Hebrew.** Tel-Aviv, Megiddo Publishing Company, 1966. 1267p. LC HE66-1735. PJ 4833.L55. DDC 492.432.

One of the best dictionaries available, it has one Hebrew word or phrase for each English word or expression for quick reference.

390. Rosen, Haiim B. **A Textbook of Israeli Hebrew.** 2nd corrected ed. Chicago, University of Chicago Press, 1966. indices. $10.00. LC 66-31274 rev. ISBN 0-226-72602-9. PJ 4567.R6 1966. DDC 492.48242.

The best introduction for college students and educated readers. It includes conversational, Biblical and modern written Hebrew, with texts for reading and some exercises. Rather technically and dryly written, and somewhat difficult to use because of its organization and method of exposition, but very broadly informative on the language. It includes a useful vocabulary (but no glossary, so a dictionary is a necessity).

K. HEBREW LITERATURE (ISRAELI)

1. History and Criticism

391. Halkin, Simon. **Modern Hebrew Literature, from the Enlightenment to the Birth of Israel; Trends and Values.** New York, Schocken Books, 1970. 238p. LC 71-110610. PJ 5017.H3 1970. DDC 892.4'09.

The author views literature as a mirror reflecting the major socio-historical forces in Jewish life. The book is couched in sweeping generalities, with but brief mention of individual writers as examples. Most of the book concerns Palestinian literature. It discusses the characteristics of the literature, its content, themes, approaches, and moods. There is much material on poetry. It treats the holocaust, Zionism, religious motifs and the "quest for faith," among other themes. It concludes with a biographical section that notes the significance, type of literature, and names of some individual works of each author. Partly helpful when combined with other works in this *Guide*, but it provides no real information for the uninitiated to sink his teeth into.

392. Kohansky, Mendel. **The Hebrew Theater: Its First Fifty Years.** New York, KTAV Publishing House, 1969. 306p. illus. LC 70-81145. PN 2919.K6. DDC 792'.095694.

A history, covering areas outside Palestine and Israel, with much on Habimah, one of the chief companies, and material on the plays themselves, and the training process.
See also:
Shakow, Zara. **The Theater in Israel.** New York, Herzl Press, 1963. 144p. illus. LC 64-13489. PN 3035.S5. Includes some history and much on the state of the art, but deals mainly with the individual theaters and troupes.

393. Rabinovich, Isaiah. **Major Trends in Modern Hebrew Fiction.** Chicago, University of Chicago Press, 1968. 288p. LC 68-15035. ISBN 0-226-70132-8. PJ 5029.R3. DDC 892.4'3'509.

Includes authors such as Mendele Mokher Sefarim, Shalom Aleichem, Itzhak Leib Peretz, Feierberg, Gnessin, Brenner, Zeitlin, Shoffman, Berdichevsky, Berkovitz, Hazaz, Agnon. Many are not Palestinians. The book discusses the characteristics of each writer, his role in literature, etc., but provides no information on his life, except in a biographical section at the end of the book. Another case in which appreciation of the writer utterly wins out over usable information. The uninitiated reader who reads it before reading the individual works will find them prejudged in his mind, in terms of another person's perspectives and opinions.

394. Ribalow, Menachem. **The Flowering of Modern Hebrew Literature: A Volume of Literary Evaluations.** Ed. and tr. by Judah Nadich. New York, Twayne Publishers, 1959. 394p. bibliog. $7.50. LC 59-8385. PK 5020.R44. DDC 892.409.

Critical essays and excerpts: Bialik, Tchernihovsky, Shneur, Fichman, Shimoni, Hameiri, Shalom, Agnon, Shoffman, Shoham. Most of the writers spent at least part of their lives in Palestine-Israel. An interesting book.

395. Silberschlag, Eisig. **From Renaissance to Renaissance.** New York, KTAV Publishing House, 1973-197-? 2v. v.1: $15.00. LC 72-5817. ISBN 0-87068-184-2. PJ 5017.S39. DDC 892.4'09.

[P1, C1, S1] A history of nineteenth and twentieth century Hebrew literature. Only Volume 1 has been published; Volume 2 will include Israeli literature.

396. Wallenrod, Reuben. **The Literature of Modern Israel.** New York, Abelard-Schuman, 1956. 253p. bibliog. index. (Ram's Horn Books). o.p. LC 56-12168. PJ 5020.W3. DDC 892.409.

This book is one of very few on Israeli literature in English. It goes back to the waves of Aliyah (immigration) to Palestine, including Diaspora Hebrew writers who influenced Israeli literature. It discusses the authors and their works, the types of mood expressed, subjects covered. Treatment is mainly general, seeking to characterize the literature; some, but very few, individual works are mentioned. The stress is on comparisons with previous writers, changes in mode and manner, motifs, authors' ideas and worldviews. There is little on the lives and backgrounds of individual writers and their eras. One must have a fairly thorough knowledge of each author's works to understand the book.

397. Yudkin, Leon Israel. **Escape into Siege: A Survey of Israeli Literature Today.** London, Routledge and Kegan Paul, 1974. 197p. bibliog. index. (The Littman Library of Jewish Civilization). £3.75. LC n.a. ISBN 0-7100-7924-9. DDC 892.409006.

Contains chapters on Bialik's poetry, Agnon's short stories, Yizhar; the hero in flight; new directions in Israeli fiction; A. Appelfeld; the Israeli writer and the holocaust; Israeli poetry—Gilboa, Amihai, and Zach; new wave in Israeli poetry; consciousness of self in the current Israeli novel. Rather than a systematic survey, this is an impressionistic series of essays that indicate some of what may be found in Israeli literature and that raise some questions. As such, it is less an introduction than a device for interesting the general reader.

2. Collections

398. Birman, Abraham, comp. **An Anthology of Modern Hebrew Poetry.** New York, Abelard-Schuman, 1968. 320p. bibliog. index. o.p. LC 68-16350. SBN 200-71419-8. PJ 5059. E3 B5. DDC 892.4'08.

Translations only, with a 95-page introduction. Includes some authors not represented in Mintz (item 400). Individual poems overlap sometimes with Mintz, but Birman also includes different poems for each poet commonly represented.

399. Burnshaw, Stanley, T. Carmi, and Ezra Spicehandler, eds. **The Modern Hebrew Poem Itself, from the Beginnings to the Present: Sixty-Nine Poems in a New Presentation.** New York, Schocken Books, 1966. 220p. (A Schocken Folio). $3.95pa. LC 66-26731. ISBN 0-8052-2815-2pa. PJ 5038.B8 1966. DDC 892.41008.

Each poem has the text in Hebrew script, with transliteration and translation, then an analysis of the poem and information on the author, written by a critic. Includes notes on the translators-critics. A most interesting book.

400. Mintz, Ruth Finer, ed. **Modern Hebrew Poetry: A Bilingual Anthology.** Berkeley, University of California Press, 1966. 54, 371p. $7.95; $2.50pa. LC 65-19246. ISBN 0-520-00867-7; 0-520-00868-5pa. PJ 5059.E3M53. DDC 892.41008.

Following a long introduction on the authors and their works and on Hebrew literature in general as it relates to the poetry, the bulk of the book consists of Hebrew texts and translations on opposite pages. Includes Bialik, Tchernichovsky, Fichman, Shimoni, Schneour, Uri Greenberg, Shlonsky, T. Carmi and others.

401. **Modern Hebrew Literature.** Ed. with introduction and notes by Robert Alter. New York, Behrman House, 1975. 398p. bibliog. (Library of Jewish Studies). LC cataloging n.a. ISBN 0-87441-218-8.

Translations of short stories by key writers, including some non-Palestinians. Each story has a two- to four-page introduction on the life and art of the writer, and a discussion of the story.

402. Penueli, Shmuel Yeshayahu, and A. Ukhmani, eds. **Anthology of Modern Hebrew Poetry.** Jerusalem, Institute for the Translation of Hebrew Literature and Israel Universities Press; distr. New York, Daniel Davey & Co., 1966. 2v. (431p.). LC HE67-1643. PJ 5059.E3P4.

English only, by a variety of poets and translators. Includes a brief general introduction, and a short introduction on each poet.

403. Penueli, Shmuel Yeshayahu, and A. Ukhmani, eds. **Hebrew Short Stories: An Anthology.** Tel-Aviv, Institute for the Translation of Hebrew Literature, and Megiddo Publishing Company, 1965. 2v. £4.20 (*BBIP*). LC HE66-779. PZ 1.P38 He.

English only. Each author has a brief introduction. Includes some non-Palestinian-Israeli writers and motives. Enjoyable stories that suggest aspects of life in Israel and the shtetl.

404. Rabikovitz, Dalia. **The New Israeli Writers: Short Stories of the First Generation.** New York, Funk and Wagnalls, 1969. 319p. (Sabra Books). o.p. LC 69-13467. SBN 87631-006. PZ1.R115 Ne. DDC 892.4'3'608.

Fourteen stories by various authors and translators, including stories reflecting the Arab-Israeli conflict.
See also:

P.E.N., Israel, 1974, A Collection of Recent Writing in Israel. Ed. by Richard Flantz. Tel-Aviv, Israel P.E.N. Centre, 1974. 167p. LC cataloging n.a. Short stories, poems and a few essays from the last five years.

3. Individual Authors

405. Agnon, Samuel Joseph (1888-1970). **The Bridal Canopy.** Tr. by I. M. Lask. New York, Schocken Books, 1967. 389p. $5.95; $2.95pa. LC 67-14955. ISBN 0-8052-3020-3; 0-8052-0182-3pa. PZ 3.A2733 Br 5.

A famous novel of Eastern European Jewish folk life in the early 1800s, by a top writer. Good reading.

406. Agnon, Samuel Joseph (1888-1970). **A Guest for the Night.** Tr. from Hebrew by Misha Louvish. New York, Schocken Books, 1968. 485p. $6.95. LC 68-13723. ISBN 0-8052-3091-2. PZ 3. A2733 Gu.

A novel originally published in Hebrew in 1939.

407. Agnon, Samuel Joseph (1888-1970). **Twenty-One Stories.** Ed. by Nahum N. Glatzer. New York, Schocken Books, 1970. 287p. $6.50; $2.95pa. LC 71-108902. ISBN 0-8052-3350-4; 0-8052-0313-3pa. PZ 3.A 2733 Tu 3. [PJ 5053.A4]. DDC 892.4'3'5.

A very entertaining collection that includes a postscript on Agnon's life, his works and their translations, and the individual stories in the book.

408. Bialik, Hayyim Nahman (1873-1934). **Complete Poetic Works.** Tr. from Hebrew. New York, Histadruth Ivrith of America, 1948- . LC 48-21808. PJ 5053.B5A33. DDC 892.41.

Selected Poems. Ed. by Israel Efros. New York, Bloch Publishing Company for Histadruth Ivrith of America, 1965. 243p. LC 66-454. PJ 5053.B5A24 1965. DDC 892.415.

Bialik Speaks: Words from the Poet's Lips, Clues to the Man. By Mordecai Ovadyahu. Tr. from Hebrew. Ramat Gan, Israel, Massada, 1969. 192p. LC 72-951573. PJ 5053. B5M4813. DDC 892.4'1'5.

One of the greatest modern Hebrew poets.

409. Hazaz, Hayim. **Mori Sa^cid.** Tr. from Hebrew by Ben Halpern. New York, Abelard-Schuman, 1956. 340p. LC 56-7618. PZ3.H338 Mo.

A novel of the Yemenite Jews who settled in Israel.

410. Kaniuk, Yoram. **Adam Resurrected.** Tr. from Hebrew by Seymour Simckes. New York, Atheneum, 1971. 370p. LC 76-124962. PZ4.K165 Ad. [PJ 5054.K326]. DDC 892.4'3'6.

The Acrophile. Tr. from Hebrew by Z. Shapiro. New York, Atheneum, 1961. 182p. LC 61-5238. PZ4.K165 Ac 2.

Himmo, King of Jerusalem. Tr. from Hebrew by Y. Shechter. New York, Atheneum, 1969. 246p. LC 68-9824. PZ4.K165 Hi. [PJ 5054.K326]. DDC 892.4'3'6.

Novels.

411. Kishon, Ephraim. **Blow Softly in Jericho.** Tr. from Hebrew by Yohanan Goldman. New York, Atheneum, 1970. 237p. $6.50. LC 75-119913. ISBN 0-689-10339-5. PJ 5054. K5B6. DDC 892.4'8'607.

Short humorous pieces by one of Israel's best-known humorists, who has also written short stories and a novel (*The Fox in the Chickencoop: A Satirical Novel.* Tel-Aviv, Bronfman Publications, 1971). Other works published in English include: *Noah's Ark, Tourist Class, So Sorry We Won, Unfair to Goliath,* and *Woe to the Victors,* all published by Atheneum.

412. Kovner, Abba. **A Canopy in the Desert, Selected Poems.** Tr. from Hebrew by Shirley Kaufman, with Ruth Adler and Nurit Orchan. Pittsburgh, University of Pittsburgh Press, 1973. 222p. (Pitt Poetry Series. Pitt Paperback, 76). $8.95; $3.95pa. LC 73-169597. ISBN 0-8229-3260-1; 0-8229-5232-7pa. PJ 5054.K6C3. DDC 892.4'1'6.

Winner of the International Poetry Forum. This selection contains items from various works reflecting on Jewish history and the experience in Europe; prayer poems; the Israeli experience.

413. Maletz, David. **Young Hearts: A Novel of Modern Israel.** Tr. from Hebrew by Solomon N. Richards. New York, Schocken Books, 1950. 237p. LC 50-7276. PZ3.M2928 Yo.
A novel of kibbutz life.

414. Oz, Amos. **Elsewhere, Perhaps.** Tr. from Hebrew by Nicholas de Lange. New York, Harcourt Brace Jovanivich, 1973. 309p. $7.95. LC 73-8628. ISBN 0-15-18374-5. PZ 4.O 989 E1. DDC 892.4'3'6.
A novel by one of Israel's outstanding young writers.

My Michael. Tr. from Hebrew by Nicholas de Lange. New York, Alfred A. Knopf; distr. New York, Random House, 1972. 287p. $6.95. LC 70-171158. ISBN 0-394-47146-6. PZ4.O 989 My. DDC 892.4'3'6.
A novel.

Touch the Water, Touch the Wind. New York, Harcourt Brace Jovanovich, 1974. $6.95. LC 74-12178. ISBN 0-15-190873-7. PZ4.O989 To. DDC 892.4'3'6.

Oz is one of Israel's leading young novelists.

415. Yaari, Yehudi. **[Ka-or Yahel]. When the Candle Was Burning.** Tr. from Hebrew by Menahem Hurwitz. London, Victor Gollancz, 1947. 227p. o.p. LC 48-12841. PZ 3.Y104 Wh. DDC 892.43.
A novel of Russian pogroms and immigration to Palestine, and early Zionist life there.

416. Yizhar, S. **Midnight Convoy and Other Stories.** Tr. from Hebrew. Jerusalem, Institute for the Translation of Hebrew Literature, 1969. 273p. LC 76-13636. PZ3.Y6 Mi. [PJ 5054.Y55].
Short stories on the 1948-1949 War.

IX. SOCIETY

A. GENERAL

417. Arfa, Hassan. **The Kurds: An Historical and Political Study.** London, Oxford University Press, 1966. 178p. bibliog. index. $7.75. LC 66-73170. ISBN 0-19-215150-9. DS 51.K7 A8. DDC 909.0749159.

A former Iranian Chief of Staff and diplomat traces the history of the Kurds in Turkey, Iran, and Iraq from earliest times, concentrating on a country-by-country political survey that illuminates recent events in Iraq. Included are some personal notes by the author, who fought the Kurds in Iran. A useful, not unsympathetic account; one of few available on the Kurds. Edgar O'Ballance has written an account of the Kurdish War in Iraq: *The Kurdish Revolt, 1961-1970* (London, Faber and Faber, 1973. £2.95. LC 73-173758. ISBN 0-571-09905-X. DS 51.K7022 1973). It gives the history of the Kurds in the twentieth century as background, details the military actions and indicates the political aspects of the Kurdish effort to attain independence and the Iraqi attempts to quash the rebellion, which has welled up once again and has been the subject of press articles in Spring 1974.

See also:

Eagleton, W. **The Kurdish Republic of 1946.** London, Oxford University Press, 1963. 142p. LC 63-2313. DS 318.E2. DDC 955.05.

Ghassemlou, A. Rahman. **Kurdistan and the Kurds.** Prague, Czechoslovakia Academy of Sciences, 1965. 304p. LC 65-85590. DS 51.K7 G513. The historical, cultural and social background to the Kurdish problem; the nineteenth and twentieth centuries, economic background; a Marxist analysis of the political problem.

418. Baer, Gabriel. **Population and Society in the Arab East.** New York, Praeger, 1964. 275p. bibliog. o.p. LC 63-18535. HN 767.5.B213. DDC 309.156.

[P1, P2, C1, S1] A systematic handbook of sociological factors in Egypt, Syria, Lebanon, Iraq, Arabia, Sudan and Jordan. It covers demography; women and family; religious and ethnic communities; cc nmunal structure; Bedouin life, society, and relations to the state; peasants, land reform; the village, its society and institutions; cities, their development, structure, society and institutions; class structure, etc. Although it is dated, it is still a most useful introduction; it provides a wealth of basic information for reference and for further study. A basic work, which we hope will be reprinted or issued in a new edition.

419. Berger, Morroe. **The Arab World Today.** Garden City, N.Y., Doubleday, 1962. 480p. bibliog. index. o.p. LC 62-7601. DS 63.B43. DDC 956.Paperback: Doubleday Anchor Book. A 406. $2.50. ISBN 0-385-01001-X.

[P1, C1, S1] A sociologist details the social, psychological, and anthropological aspects of life in the Eastern Arab countries, describing social and family structure and pressures on the individual; mores, customs, values, and the problems of urbanization and modernization. He devotes much space to political aspects as well: nationalism, socialism, and anti-Westernism. The book is popularly written, in non-technical language, and is an excellent introduction which contributes greatly to our understanding of the events and the people. For all readers.

See also:

Prothro, Edwin Terry, and Lutfy Najib Diab. **Changing Family Patterns in the Arab East.** Beirut, American University of Beirut, 1974. 240p. LC 73-85671. HQ 525.A7P76. DDC 301.42'0917'4927.

420. Berque, Jacques. **The Arabs, Their History and Future.** Tr. from French. New York, Praeger, 1964. 310p. index. o.p. LC 64-19954. DS 218.B413. DDC 915.3.

[C2, S2, S3] This is a terribly difficult book by a first-rate French sociologist who has had much experience in the Arab world. It is difficult not because it is technical, but because it is a suggestive, vague *evocation* of the Arab, instead of a mere description, and it assumes a solid background on the part of the reader. It deals often and effectively with intangibles of Arab behavior—the Arab "mind," the "irrational," which is so hard to put into words. It focuses on the sweep of things, attitudes, points of interaction, movements that are hard to pin down. But it is a landmark work; it will severely tax the student's knowledge, sensitivity, and intellect, and it will reward him immensely.

421. Bill, James A., and Carl Leiden. **The Middle East: Politics and Power.** Boston, Allyn and Bacon, 1974. 350p. bibliog. $12.95. LC 74-2709. DS 62.8.B53. DDC 301.5'92'0956.
[B, C1, S2] A general comparative study of the socio-political dynamics of the region, including North Africa. It discusses political development and modernization, Islam's ability to adjust to change, and Islamic modernization; politics of social stratification, various kinds of group structures and their processes; authoritarian patrimonial leadership and its socio-political processes; leadership and the challenge of change (illustrated by the cases of Abdul Aziz Ibn Saud, Nasser, and Reza Shah); tradition and change; bureaucracy; military and the role of violence, including assassination and terrorism; ideology. Each topic is discussed in depth: structures and how they operate in both their traditional and their transitional forms; patterns of change, the nature of the system; the heritage going back to Muhammad to illustrate continuity and change. A very useful study, which renders a full exposition of the factors operating in Near Eastern politics. These factors are usually discussed briefly and superficially in introductory chapters of the standard textbooks. For all college collections and advanced students. It is also useful for its discussions and applications of recent theories, and for its inclusion of disciplinary works in the bibliography.
See also:
Dekmejian, R. Hrair. **Patterns of Political Leadership: Egypt, Israel, Lebanon.** Albany, State University of New York Press, 1975. 400p. bibliog. LC 74-20940. ISBN 0-87395-291-X; 0-87395-292-8 microfiche. JQ 1758.A91D44. DDC 301.44'92'0956. A comprehensive study of cabinet leadership groups, with a profile of each country's political elites, social backgrounds, characteristics, attitudes, and behavior. It tests some hypotheses on sources, recruitment patterns, cohesion, strategies, tenure, and disposition of these leaders. Much factual information.

422. Bois, Thomas. **The Kurds.** Tr. from French. Beirut, Khayats, 1966. 159p. bibliog. LC 67-66415. DS 51.K7B613. DDC 915.66'7'03.
[C1] A general work on this Near Eastern people that inhabits Turkey, Iraq and Iran; the Kurds' war with the Iraqi government has frequently been in the American press. The book treats Kurdish history, personal life, social life and customs, religion, recreation, family and marriage, social structure, literature, health, medicine, funeral customs, superstitions, and the development of Kurdish nationalism. A good introduction, with a brief but useful bibliography, on a topic about which little has been written. Treatment is entirely general; it has little specific data on the Kurds in the individual countries.

423. Cohen, Hayyim J. **The Jews of the Middle East, 1860-1972.** Tr. from Hebrew. New York, John Wiley, 1973. 213p. bibliog. index. (A Halstead Press Book). $12.50. LC 73-9236. ISBN 0-470-16424-7. DS 135.L4C6413. DDC 301.45'19'24056.
A brief survey of the history of the Jews in Turkey, Iran, Iraq, Syria and Lebanon, Egypt, Yemen, and Southern Arabia. Arrangement is topical: political changes, demographic evolution, economic transformations, education, social changes. Covers status, conditions, relations with Muslims, pogroms, and social life and customs. Since little research has been done, this is necessarily a sketchy, generalized outline that provides basic information as a basis for further study. There is little on Zionism in these countries.

424. Coon, Carleton Stevens. **Caravan: The Story of the Middle East.** Rev. ed. New York, Henry Holt, 1958. 386p. bibliog. illus. $10.00. LC 58-13740. ISBN 0-03-005105-3. (Reprint: Huntington, N.Y., R. E. Krieger Pub. Co., 1976. $12.00. ISBN 0-88275-393-2.)
[P1, C1, S1] An introductory survey of the peoples of the area from Morocco to Afghanistan, their history, culture, anthropo-geography, social organization, languages, religions, and historical dynamics. It has notes on common features and differences, and it provides a wealth of

general information in non-technical language. It is somewhat out of date and at times simplistic, and some of the author's theories have been challenged, but it imparts an overall knowledge of the basics, and a feel for the area, as well as providing basic vernacular terminology. The author's many personal observations make an interesting subject fascinating. A basic book for all readers.

See also:

Hardy, Michael James Langley. **Blood Feuds and the Payment of Blood Money in the Middle East.** Beirut, 1963. 106p. LC 65-2275. LC class: LAW.

Kamell, Michael W. **The Middle East: A Humanistic Approach.** Elizabeth, N.J., Andrews Publishing Company, 1973. 352p. bibliog. LC 73-80509. DS 57.K3. DDC 915.6'03'4.
A work for the beginner emphasizing the life of the people, stated in general terms. Discusses languages, religion, family, legends and customs, birth and death ceremonies, the arts, education, Islamic civilization, status of women, effects of oil wealth. No politics or history.

425. Fisher, Sydney Nettleton, ed. **Social Forces in the Middle East.** Ithaca, N.Y., Greenwood Press, 1968. (Repr. of 1955 ed.). 282p. bibliog. index. $15.00. LC 68-23289. HN 660.8.A8F5 1968. DDC 309.1'56.
[C3, S2] Top experts have written general essays on various social groups—farmers, military officers in politics, Israeli immigrants, Bedouins, intellectuals, economic planners, bazaar merchants, entrepreneur class, villagers, and industrial workers. Though the book is quite out of date in some specifics and in the relative unsophistication of the methods used, it is general and non-technical enough to serve as an introduction for non-specialists, and it is still accurate enough to provide much perspective on the area. It discusses the role in society of each group, social change within each, its problems in performing its role, problems in dealing with change, and the problems of modernizers in dealing with the group when they try to make changes that affect that group's interests. The essays also note changes already taking place. The price is rather high for its degree of usefulness.

426. **From Madina to Metropolis: Heritage and Change in the Near Eastern City.** Ed. by Leon Carl Brown. Princeton, N.J., Darwin Press, 1973. illus. index. (Princeton Studies on the Near East). $16.95. LC 76-161054. ISBN 0-87850-006-5. HT 147.N4F76. DDC 301. 36'3'0956.
[C3] Eleven fascinating essays, well written in non-technical language by top specialists in a variety of fields, on the history, problems, and processes of urban change and planning in the Near East and North Africa. They treat various aspects of planning, mainly from a historical perspective, either in terms of the broad sweep of history, or for brief periods in specific regions. Included are pieces on the Ottoman Empire, Kuwait, Morocco, Herat, Cairo, Beirut, Omdurman, and the traditional Muslim city in general. A most welcome volume in a very sparse literature, with 111 extremely interesting illustrations, plans, drawings and useful chapter bibliographies. The essays contain much general information and raise searching questions. Suitable for larger collections and more advanced students in a variety of fields.

See also:

Berger, Morroe, ed. **The New Metropolis in the Arab World.** New York, Octagon Books, 1974. (Repr. of 1963 ed.). 254p. LC 73-16877. ISBN 0-374-90609-2. HT 147.5.B4 1974. DDC 301.36'3'09174927. Conference papers.

The Islamic City: A Colloquium. Ed. by Albert H. Hourani and S. M. Stern. Philadelphia, University of Pennsylvania Press, 1970. 222p. LC 75-105944. ISBN 0-571-09085-0. D 199.3.I789. DDC 301.3'64'091767.

Lapidus, Ira Marvin. **Muslim Cities in the Later Middle Ages.** Cambridge, Mass., Harvard University Press, 1967. 307p. bibliog. LC 66-21339. JS 61.L3. DDC 301.3'64'091767.

Fabritskii, Bentsian Borisovich. **Khiva.** Leningrad, Aurora Art Publishers, 1973. 206p. LC cataloging n.a.   This interesting collection of colored photos of the Uzbek Muslim desert city provides in its cumulative effect an excellent feel for the atmosphere of this type of city all over the region: the style of architecture, etc., and the barrenness of its existence, which makes the inhabitants rely solely on what they themselves can create.

427. Halpern, Manfred. **The Politics of Social Change in the Middle East and North Africa.**
Princeton, N.J., Princeton University Press, 1963. 431p. index. (A Rand Corporation
Research Study). $13.50; $2.95pa. LC 63-12670. ISBN 0-691-03051-0; 0-691-00006-9pa.
HN 660.8.H2. DDC 309.156.

[P1, C1, S1] A general theoretical–but readable and not too technical–account and analysis
of aspects of change in the Near East and North Africa: changing social structure, ideology,
and the range of political choices; nationalism; communism; the Muslim Brethren; political
modernization (the army, political parties, unions); bureaucracy and the problems of change,
including political stability; regional rivalries; international politics. It is partially out of date
and is less sophisticated than present disciplinary theories and techniques, and some of its
ideas are no longer accepted; nevertheless, it puts together much material that will help orient
the student, particularly since many of its theoretical propositions and topics of discussion are
still relevant. Its discussion of these subjects has not been surpassed for the region.

Three significant works for advanced students are:

Nieuwenhuijze, Christoffel Anthonie Olivier van. **Social Stratification and the Middle
East: An Interpretation.** Leiden, E. J. Brill, 1965. 84p. bibliog. LC 66-4102. HN 660.8.
A8N5. DDC 301.440956.

Nieuwenhuijze, Christoffel Anthonie Olivier van. **Sociology of the Middle East: A Stock-
taking and Interpretation.** Leiden, E. J. Brill, 1971. 819p. LC 72-178015. HN 660.8.
A8N54. DDC 309.1'56. A massive disciplinary work stated in generalizations, not
factual detail. It is so generalized that one reviewer wondered whether it has any use at
all. To be referred to by advanced students as food for thought.

Nieuwenhuijze, Christoffel Anthonie Olivier van. **Development: A Challenge to
Whom? An Essay on the Present State and the Next Stage in Development Studies, with
Special Reference to Sociology, and with Examples from the Middle East.** The Hague,
Mouton, 1969. 203p. LC 70-86204. HD 82.N53. DDC 338.9'001.

428. Hamady, Sania. **Temperament and Character of the Arabs.** New York, Twayne
Publishers, 1960. 285p. bibliog. index. $7.50. LC 60-9942. DS 218.H18. DDC
136.4956.

[C1, S1] An oft-quoted work on the Arab psyche: emotions, feelings, reactions, interrelationships; attitude toward the state and authority, class system, tradition, religion, and
superstitions; etiquette, values, loyalties, ideals, and identifications; mental and intellectual
qualities and functioning. This is a collection of generalities, based partly on the literature as
indicated in the extensive notes, and partly on the author's experience and personal observations. Most of her statements must be considered hypotheses, particularly those on thought
and psychological processes. Many of her points on behavior can be noted in the ethnological
and sociological works listed in this *Guide*; much in this book overlaps with material found in
Berger (item 419), which is for most readers a more useful book. Hamady's is one of the first
works to treat the subject comprehensively and it is a useful orientation. However, a barrel of
salt is a necessary side dish since she is a Western-educated scholar from the Druse elite; Druse-
Arab relations are such that Druses served in the Israeli army from the first. Thus she writes
as an outsider with a potential bias. An interesting work for the knowledgeable student is
Patai, Ralphael, *The Arab Mind* (New York, Scribner, 1973. 376p. LC 72-11120. ISBN
0-684-13306-7. DS 36.77.P37 1973. DDC 301.29'17'4927). Patai is rather too old-fashioned
in some of his ideas, and he often appears to be trying to prove a point (whose validity is sometimes questionable), but the book is a source of ideas and stimulation. Another work that is
intended for the general reader but that must also be read with a barrel of salt (although it has
much useful and interesting material), is Laffin, John, *The Arab Mind Considered: A Need for
Understanding* (New York, Taplinger, 1975. 180p. index. $8.95. LC 75-5042. ISBN 0-8008-
0294-2). The author claims long and intensive experience in the region, and uses personal
experiences, an abundance of Arabic language material, and the usual secondary sources, including Hamady, to illustrate his points and show what Arab writers say about themselves. Main
topics include Arab popular and classical culture, shame, women and sex attitudes; violence in
Arab life and history; the Arabs view themselves; military rule; attitudes toward Israel and
the West; There is no evidence of polemical intent. See also AlRoy (item 859).

429. Joseph, John. **The Nestorians and Their Muslim Neighbors: A Study of Western Influence on Their Relations.** Princeton, N.J., Princeton University Press, 1961. 281p. bibliog. index. o.p. LC 61-7417. DS 39.J6.

The Nestorians were also called Assyrians, and most of them lived in Iran. After a general introduction on their history and status under Muslim rule, the book deals with the European missionary movements that tried to convert them; their political problems; the imposition of Western interests, enthusiasms, romantic feelings, and values on the situation in trying to force Iran to improve the Nestorians' political situation; great power attempts to use them and other minorities as pawns in their struggle for influence in the Near East; their expulsion from Iran during and after World War I; resettlement in Iraq and the international and local aspects of their massacre in Iraq; the situation during and after World War II; the causes of local tensions between Muslims and Assyrians. A valuable contribution to our understanding of Near Eastern minority problems, and one of the few books on the subject in any language.

430. Lerner, Daniel. **The Passing of Traditional Society: Modernizing the Middle East.** New York, Free Press; distr. Riverside, N.J., Macmillan Company, 1964 (c. 1958). index. 466p. $8.95; $2.45pa. LC 64-57470/CD. HN 660.8.L43 1964. DDC 309.156.

[C2, S2] A basic survey, based on extensive field work, which delves into the process of change and transition. It explores many individual factors and their manifestations in various Near Eastern countries, including the media, leadership, and the various groups and classes of people. The material is ground-breaking rather than definitive, and the conclusions need revising and rethinking, but it is a useful source of ideas. A basic book.

431. Lutfiyya, Abdulla M., and Charles W. Churchill. **Readings in Arab Middle Eastern Societies and Cultures.** New York, Humanities Press, 1970. 733p. index. $11.50pa. LC 69-19116. DS 36.8.L35. DDC 309.1'174'927.

[P1, C1, S1, S2] A collection of previously published articles and excerpts from books on Arab society, its traditional life and social change: social organization, culture, institutions; stratification; the family, urban life; role of communication. For all but smallest college collections. Most of the items are of pre-1960s vintage, but this does not vitiate its utility since most of the material has not been superseded. The material is scattered in a wide range of periodicals and out-of-print books; this volume makes it available in very convenient form.

432. Patai, Raphael. **Golden River & Golden Road: Society, Culture and Change in the Middle East.** 3rd enl. ed. Philadelphia, University of Pennsylvania Press, 1969. 560p. index. $15.00; $5.95pa. LC 70-84742. ISBN 0-8122-7289-7; 0-8122-1009-3pa. DS 57.P3 1969. DDC 915.6'03.

[C2, S2] Anthropological studies of the peoples and social institutions of the region. Topics include "The Middle East as a Culture Continent"; cousin marriage, Bedouin-peasant dichotomy, women, sex mores, dual organization, towns; role of religion, socio-cultural determinants of nationalism; dynamics of Westernization and regional reactions to it. Not a comprehensive work, it is too often overdrawn and over-generalized, and it is definitely for the more advanced reader. Useful, however, because it does generalize for the entire region, and it offers a variety of perspectives, besides being one of the few general works on the subject.

433. Pierce, Joe E. **Understanding the Middle East.** Rutland, Vt., Charles E. Tuttle, 1971. 232p. bibliog. illus. index. $6.25. LC 70-158787. ISBN 0-8048-0670-5. DS 57.P53 1971. DDC 915.6.

[P1, C1, S1] A pocket-sized introduction (for public libraries) to the people of the region; it will be of interest to general reader and student alike. The author, an anthropologist who lived for seven years in Turkey (cf. item 989) uses his own experiences extensively as well as other studies to help us understand what makes the people "tick." Topics include the pluralistic nature of society; virginity values; honor; types and dynamics of power structures, leadership, and families; the relations of the people to their governments; tribe-state relations; the supernatural; ceremonies of life; hospitality; material culture; aspects of traditionalism and change. Much emphasis is put on helping the reader comprehend the differences between Near Eastern and Western life and ways of thinking. Pierce does not hesitate to give his own opinions, some of which are most interesting. A first book.

434. **Rural Politics and Social Change in the Middle East.** Ed. by Richard Antoun and Iliya Harik. Bloomington, Indiana University Press, 1972. 498p. bibliog. (International Development Research Center. Studies in Development, No. 5). $13.50. LC 77-180485. ISBN 0-253-39505-4. DS 57.R87. DDC 309.1'56'04.

[C2, S2] An important collection of conference papers and comments by other participants on a rarely discussed subject. After five articles on the state of the art and the existing literature, which indicate gaps in research and suggest new approaches and questions, there follow 11 papers on specific aspects as studied in individual communities in a variety of countries, including Morocco, Tunisia, Turkey, Iran, Egypt, Lebanon, and the Near East as a whole. Covered are topics such as local political processes, the relationship of local to national activities and processes, rural migration, land use, politics and economics; social class-family structure and politics; political and economic change and reform. The essays study barriers to change, methods of change, and the relation of these to current structures, as well as how the structures and customs are changing. Much information is to be found in this book, and for the budding specialist somewhat advanced in the discipline, it will be very stimulating and useful, particularly since it applies a variety of approaches. For larger collections.

435. Shiloh, Ailon, ed. **Peoples and Cultures of the Middle East.** New York, Random House, 1969. 453p. bibliog. index. $9.95. LC 68-25342. ISBN 0-394-30473-X. HN 660.8. A8S53. DDC 309.1'56.

[P1, C1, S1, S2] A useful collection of articles and selections from books by various authorities, which seeks to present a comprehensive view and basic data on ethnic groups in the various areas; life of the various classes and population groups, including peasants and nomads; social stratification; population dynamics—health, family, child rearing, youth. It also covers cultural change and conservatism in bureaucracies, medicine, and approach to problem solving. A useful supplementary source for basic, smaller collections.

436. **Society and Political Structure in the Arab World.** Ed. by Menahem Milson. New York, Humanities Press, 1973. 338p. (The Van Leer Jerusalem Foundation Series). LC 73-85037. ISBN 0-391-00258-9. DS 62.8.S65 1973. DDC 320.9'17'4927.

Eight interesting interpretive essays by Israeli specialists on the social basis for and aspects of the politics of Egypt, Syria, Palestine (pre-1948), Jordan, Tunisia, Sudan, all treated individually, the Arab military coups, and nomadic social organization. Rather than being formal social or political analysis, the essays treat their subjects from a historical perspective, with indications of the influence of social dynamics on political systems and their operation. They are very informative, and several offer some new hard data; their cumulative effect, aside from their information, is to sensitize the reader to the approach and to suggest questions he should ask himself when reading straight political history. For larger collections and more advanced students with a good historical background.

437. Sweet, Louise Elizabeth. **Peoples and Cultures of the Middle East.** Garden City, N.Y., Natural History Press, 1970. 2v. bibliog. $4.50/vol. pa. LC 74-89112. ISBN 0-385-00378-1 (v.1); 0-385-07792-0 (v.2). HN 660.8.A8S9. DDC 309.1'56.

[P1, P2, C1, S1] An excellent basic collection of ethnological and sociological articles and excerpts from books. For all but the smallest libraries.

438. Thornburg, Max Weston. **People and Policy in the Middle East: A Study of Social and Political Change as a Basis for United States Policy.** New York, W. W. Norton, 1964. 249p. o.p. LC 64-10575. HN 660.8.T47. DDC 309.156.

[S1] The late Thornburg, an oil engineer who worked for years in the region, uses his wide and deep knowledge to suggest vividly and clearly to the layman the dynamics of Near Eastern social and political life and change. He investigates the psychology of the whole and how this relates to local reaction to the process, and he discusses the mechanics of attempted planned and externally initiated changes of many kinds. Why are the reactions so often negative and dysfunctional? How have policy-makers and planners erred? What can they do to elicit positive, functional reactions? What can and should the United States do? These questions the book seeks to answer, at least in part; although it was written a decade ago, it is still one of the more illuminating books on the subject and a must for beginning students.

B. WOMEN

To date there have been no good comprehensive works on women in the region. Many of the books in the previous section (Society, General) have information on the position of women and their daily lives, as do the works in the Society sections under individual countries. Most of the material concerns traditional and lower-class women. The following are some additional items that contain a wide variety of information and descriptions:

438a. Amine, Rhoda Gordon (Lingard). **Seven Years in the Sun.** London, Robert Hale, 1959. 192p. LC 60-50308.A62. DDC 916.2.
Egypt.

438b. Cooper, Elizabeth. **The Women of Egypt.** London, Hurst and Blackett, 1914. 380p. LC 14-16468. HQ 1792.C6.

All aspects of the life of women from various classes: the author's first-hand observations. Also other matters.

438c. Cooper, Elizabeth. **The Harem and the Purdah: Studies of Oriental Women.** Detroit, Gale Research Company, 1974. LC 68-23147. ISBN 0-8103-3167-5. HQ 1170.C77 1974. DDC 301.41'2'095.
Egypt, Bedouins, India, China, Burma, Japan.

438d. Dolinger, Jane. **Behind Harem Walls.** London, Alvin Redman, 1960. 195p. illus. LC n.a. HQ 1170.D6.

Personal experiences of an American woman among Moroccan women, describing their ways of life. Mainly upper class; the transition from old to new ways.

438e. Hansen, Henny Harald. **Daughters of Allah: Among Moslem Women in Kurdistan.** Tr. from Danish. London, George Allen and Unwin, 1960. 191p. LC 60-50612. HQ 1779. K8 H33. DDC 915.667.

438f. Khan, Mazhar ul Haq. **Purdah and Polygamy: A Study in the Social Pathology of the Muslim Society.** Peshawar Cantt, Pakistan, Nashiran-e-Ilm-o-Taraqiyet, 1972. LC n.a. HQ 1170.K44.

A critique of Purdah and harems by a Muslim. which concludes that Purdah (seclusion of women) has had a disastrous effect on Muslim family, society, and individuals, both psychologically and intellectually, including men and women.

438g. Van Ess, Dorothy. **Fatima and Her Sisters.** New York, John Day, 1961. 187p. LC 60-15743. DS 215.V28. DDC 301.4209567.
Arabia.

438h. Woodhall, Ruth Frances. **Moslem Women Enter a New World.** New York, AMS Press, 1975. (Repr. of 1936 ed.). 432p. LC 75-180309. ISBN 0-404-56334-1. HQ 1170.W625 1975. DDC 301.41'2.

438i. Woodhall, Ruth Frances. **Study of the Role of Women, Their Activities and Organizations in Lebanon, Egypt, Iraq, Jordan and Syria, October, 1954-August, 1955.** New York, International Federation of Business and Professional Women, 1956. 95p. LC 57-3585. HQ 1730.W6. DDC 396.

438j. Woodhall, Ruth Frances. **Women and the New East.** Washington, D.C., Middle East Institute, 1960. 436p. illus. LC 60-51147. HQ 1170.W64. DDC 396.095.

Turkey, Iran, Pakistan, Afghanistan, Indonesia, India, based on visits to each country, interviews, etc., 1956-1957: education, health, moral life, economic role, political and legal status, women's organizations. By country.

X. EDUCATION

Despite the importance of the subject, very little has been written on it.

439. Dodge, Bayard. **al-Azhar, A Millenium of Muslim Learning.** Washington, D.C., Middle East Institute, 1974. 239p. bibliog. index. $7.95. LC 74-181623. LG 511.C45D6 1974. DDC 378.6216. Paperback: 1961. $2.50. LC 61-65458.

A history of the Mosque-university, which has been the center of Muslim Orthodox scholarship and education for 1000 years. The history of the university is given in the context of its times, because it had a central place in culture, society, and politics. The book includes a history of the buildings and the library, the role it played, and finally its modern reorientation, organization, and curriculum. The author, who occupied an important place in the history of the American University of Beirut, was an old Middle East hand and used Arabic sources for his book.

440. Dodge, Bayard. **Muslim Education in Medieval Times.** Washington, D.C., Middle East Institute, 1962. 119p. bibliog. index. $3.75pa. LC 63-144. LA 99.D6. DDC 377.

A narrative description of the cultural activities and institutions, education organization, curriculum, process of scholarship and learning (not just formal education), and why they developed as they did. There are two appendices. One summarizes the contents of al-Bukhari's *al-Jami^c al-Sahih* (a canonical collection of Hadith) to show the importance of the various subjects covered in the book; the other summarizes the contents of al-Shafi^{c}i's *Kitab al-Umm*, a foremost codification of Islamic law, to show topics that occupied a central place in medieval Muslim education. The book includes much on the development of the Islamic religious sciences (not just how they were taught), and the history of educational theory. Actually, it contains rather more on intellectual life than on the educational institutions *per se*). For the uninitiated reader the names flow by unintelligibly, but the book provides much information and is interesting to read.

441. Nakosteen, Mehdi Khan. **History of Islamic Origins of Western Education, A.D. 800-1350, with an Introduction to Medieval Muslim Education.** Boulder, University of Colorado Press; distr. Boulder, Colorado Associated University Press, 1964. 361p. bibliog. index. $8.95. LC 63-22473. ISBN 0-87081-015-4. LA 99.N3. DDC 370.956.

[B, C1, S2] The first 71 pages deal with education, its scope, institutions and libraries. There is a list and a discussion of Muslim works on education, with an annotated bibliography of 25 directly related works and 40 works with information on education, and other educational treatises, plus a list of lost works. Included also is a chapter on Sa'di's theory and reflections; chapters on Islamic scholarship; transmission to the West of Islamic science and thought, with tables and chronologies. Various appendices list translations of Greco-Hellenistic works into Syriac, Arabic, etc.; authors and educational works in Ibn Nadim's *Fihrist*; a list of authors with information on the works and lives of Muslim scholars in the sciences, history, geography, medicine, philosophy, theology. It also lists the translators from Arabic to Latin, Hebrew, Spanish, and Catalan, and some of the works they thus transmitted to Europe. A mine of information which is in effect a handbook for researchers. For larger collections.

442. Qubain, Fahim Issa. **Education and Science in the Arab World.** Baltimore, The Johns Hopkins Press, 1966. 539p. bibliog. index. $15.00. LC 65-26182. ISBN 0-8018-0541-4. LA 1101.Q3. DDC 378.00917165.

The main interest of this work is to make a "survey of the extent and quality of the science training establishment and scientific manpower resources of the Arab countries." It includes North Africa. It describes and evaluates these resources, first giving a general discussion of the educational system as background, then making comparisons between the individual countries. There is much information and discussion of higher education, in general and with regard to the individual sciences, in each country. Also: research organizations, planning agencies, manpower availability, etc. Much emphasis on the quality of education, foreign institutions in each country, and foreign study by Arab students. Though out of date, it is the only comprehensive work and still has some validity today.

443. Szyliowicz, Joseph S. **Education and Modernization in the Middle East.** Ithaca, N.Y., Cornell University Press, 1973. 512p. bibliog. index. $19.50. LC 72-12292. ISBN 0-8014-0758-3. LA 1045.S99. DDC 370.19'3'0956.

[C2, S3]   The first 178 pages treat the background: Near Eastern educational environment, traditional education, the nineteenth century introduction of modern education into the area. The next 70 pages treat the creation of the modern systems. The rest of the book details the systems and problems, dynamics and prospects of education in Egypt, Turkey, and Iran, with some generalizations on the other states. The author points out that the problems are essentially the same in the other countries. There is no detailed account of the structures of the systems, but rather indications of their magnitudes, human aspects, psychology, processes, philosophies, and various measures taken during recent times, all pointing to the author's conclusions as to their successes, failures, and prospects. His conclusions are terribly depressing. A basic work, since it is all we have. However, considering its great cost in relation to the relatively little hard data it contains, it is a marginal work for most collections that do not have a particular interest in the subject.

See also:

Matthews, Roderic Donald, and Matta Akrawi. **Education in Arab Countries of the Near East: Egypt, Iraq, Palestine, Transjordan, Syria, Lebanon.** Washington, D.C., American Council on Education, 1949. 584p. illus. index. LC 49-50272. LA 1045.M3. DDC 370.956. Surveys each country's government agencies, laws, teacher qualifications, curricula, systems, faculty, etc. No attempt is made at evaluation—it tells how the system *should* work, not whether it actually meets its goals.

XI. ECONOMY

Except for oil and some specialized subjects, and a few works on individual countries, relatively little has been written; in particular, there are few comprehensive works on the modern period. The research on earlier eras has hardly begun. See also the **Economy** sections under individual countries.

A. GENERAL

444. Clawson, Marion, Hans H. Landsberg, and Lyle T. Alexander. **The Agricultural Potential of the Middle East.** New York, American Elsevier Publishing Company, 1971. 312p. maps. statis. tables. index. (Middle East Economic & Political Problems and Prospects). $19.50. LC 79-135058. ISBN 0-444-00093-3. S470.N4C55. DDC 630'.956.

[P1, C1, C2, S1] The first 109 pages of this oversized, double-columned book describe various aspects of current agriculture: soils, climate, water resources; land and water use, and management; inputs such as machinery, fertilizer, pesticides; possibilities of regional cooperation; manpower; farms and their management; crops, livestock; economic aspects; marketing and trade; rural communities and agricultural services. The next 60 pages discuss the potential for development, factors and problems, and what needs to be done to accomplish this development, followed by 40 pages that provide much detail on soil types and water supply. The rest consists of statistical tables on all aspects. It does not include general country surveys. The book combines a wealth of basic information, generalities, comparisons between countries, comments on statistical data available and its inadequacies, and careful analysis. It is the best book in English on the subject as a whole despite its special emphasis, and it is a basic work for all but small collections. To be read after the general geographies.

445. **Economic Development and Population Growth in the Middle East.** Ed. by Charles A. Cooper and Sidney S. Alexander. New York, American Elsevier Publishing Company, 1972. 620p. $19.95. LC 71-158633. ISBN 0-444-00107-7. HC 410.7.E35. DDC 338.956.

[C3] Covers Egypt, Israel, Lebanon, Jordan, Iraq, Syria, and the Arabian Peninsula, treating in part the direct and indirect implications of the human factor. Most of the essays discuss the policy needs of the countries in most aspects of their economies. There are some descriptions of economic conditions and structures, but the emphasis is on planning, problems, and trends, particularly those the authors think to be the central features and problems, which sometimes differ from country to country, but which in many cases are common to all of them. Population *per se* is not the main interest, though it is discussed in several individual essays. Projections into the future are important parts of each presentation. While the book is not a systematic study or a presentation of data, it does have much useful information and food for thought for students of economic policy and developmental economics. Probably too much for most collections, depending on what courses they support.

446. Economist Intelligence Unit, Ltd., London. **The Middle East and North Africa.** Prepared by the Economist Intelligence Unit, Ltd., and the Cartographic Department of the Clarendon Press. London, Oxford University Press, 1970. (Repr. of 1960 ed.). 135p. bibliog. stat. tables. maps. gazetteer. $15.00; $6.00pa. LC 72-189768. ISBN 0-19-519146-3. G 1785.E2 1970. DDC 912'.13309'5604.

[P1, C1, S1] Includes 17 pages of fairly detailed shaded topographical-political maps and 47 pages of outline maps depicting climatic factors, geology, various economic aspects (minerals, oil, resources and facilities, soils, agricultural products, communications, industries, population). Then follow 55 pages of statistics, mostly tabular, on many aspects of the economy, and finally a 15-page gazetteer. This volume is extremely useful, not only for its economic data, which of course is now very much out of date, but for the maps and gazetteer, which are often useful for general reference. North Africa, while covered in this volume, is updated in the *Africa* volume of the same series. When a revised edition of the present work is published, it should be purchased; it will be very useful for comparison purposes to have both editions.

447. Hershlag, Zvi Yehuda. **Introduction to the Modern Economic History of the Middle East.** Leiden, E. J. Brill; distr. New York, Humanities Press, 1964. 419p. bibliog. appendices. index. $22.00. LC 65-37559. HC 412.H4.

[P1, C1, C2, S1, S2]   A general history, especially for the period 1800-1950, covering the main events, actions, and patterns that form the background to the contemporary situation. Basic information is provided, with many generalities concerning trends, a fair amount of documentation, and a useful bibliography. A good general overview, but too superficial, partly because so much research remains to be done. The book continually notes the interrelations of politics, economy, society, and problems of developmental growth. Includes 105 pages of documents. To be read in conjunction with Issawi (item 448). If the choice must be made, purchase Issawi and a general work on the twentieth century.

448. Issawi, Charles Philip, comp. **The Economic History of the Middle East, 1800-1914: A Book of Readings.** Chicago, University of Chicago Press, 1966. 543p. bibliog. index. $12.50. LC 66-11883. HC 412.I784. DDC 330.956.

[C1, S2]   Contains 62 readings from a variety of sources, most of them translated from Western and vernacular languages; it includes contemporary secondary and primary sources, official and unofficial reports, and the best from twentieth century scholars. Each item has an introduction by Issawi. Covers the Ottoman Empire, Iraq, Syria, Arabia, Egypt, and Sudan; arrangement is by country. Issawi has also prepared a separate volume on Iran (item 750). The items have been selected, arranged and introduced to form a comprehensive, coherent treatment on all aspects of the various economies. A basic source book containing a wealth of information about a subject on which research has hardly begun.

449. Kermani, Taghi T. **Economic Development in Action: Theories, Problems and Procedures as Applied to the Middle East.** Cleveland, World Publishing Company, 1967. 236p. index. (World Series in Economics). o.p. LC 67-11436. HC 410.7.K4. DDC 330.956.

The major development theories are summarized and an outline of the basic economic structure of the region is presented, after which the author discusses the various problems of economic development: population, capital formation, regional obstacles, institutional-governmental factors, and the government role in the economy, planning, agricultural development policies, and industrial growth. He also reviews United States aid policies and the obstacles that reduce the effectiveness of such aid. Treatment is mostly general, though it gets somewhat technical at times. Useful in support of a course on economic development and regional economics.

450. Preston, Lee E. **Trade Patterns in the Middle East.** Washington, D.C., American Enterprise Institute for Public Policy Research, 1970. 96p. (United States Interests in the Middle East). $3.00pa. LC 75-134959. HF 3760.8.P73. DDC 382'.09'56.

A brief survey and analysis of inter-country trade relations, focusing on real commodity trade, not capital flows and currency problems. It discusses the directions of trade, both outside the region and between countries of the area, composition of trade, problems of trade imbalances, foreign aid, possibilities for regional integration, past and present trends and future potential, the interrelationship of trade and development. There is a separate chapter on Israel, and an in-depth case study of Egypt by Karim A. Nashashibi. Of the many statistical tables, most concern the years 1958 and 1966, provided for purposes of comparison and for elucidation of the trends discussed. Written so the non-specialist with some background in economics can understand it, it is one of few monographs on the subject. Useful for larger college collections.

The following works will also add to the reader's image of the economic situation and dynamics in the region:

Amin, Galal A. **The Modernization of Poverty: A Study in the Political Economy of Growth in Nine Arab Countries, 1945-1970.** Leiden, E. J. Brill, 1974. 124p. bibliog. LC 74-196110. ISBN 90-04-03969-4. HC 498.A68. DDC 330.9'17'4927. A survey and analysis; the politics of saving and investment, including planning, education, nationalism; a critique of economic distribution and income inequality in the current period of the new elites; over-urbanization.

Bonné, Alfred. **State and Economics in the Middle East: A Society in Transition.** 2nd ed. rev. London, Routledge and Kegan Paul, 1955. 452p. index. LC 55-1832. HN 663. B6 1955. DDC 309.156. A general interpretation and presentation of basic economic dynamics and characteristics, their processes and evolution, all sectors. General characteristics of government, attitudes towards the various forms of economic activity, including Islamic teachings. Popular psychology, bars to economic advancement. Not a source of statistical and factual information, but useful for orientation. Written in non-technical language.

Budig, Hars J., and Mehmet Suer. **Middle East and North Africa Markets Review.** Epping, Gower Economic Publications. annual. LC 74-640571. HC 410.7.ATM48. DDC 330.9'56'04.

Conference on Middle Eastern Affairs, 17th, Washington, D.C., 1963. **The Developmental Revolution: North Africa, the Middle East, and South Asia.** Ed. by William R. Polk. Washington, D.C., Middle East Institute, 1963. 269p. LC 64-1070. HD 82.C5744 1963a. DDC 309.22082. More generalities than hard fact, but many of the papers are quite interesting; scope is broader than just economics.

Ellis, Howard Sylvester. **Private Enterprise and Socialism in the Middle East.** Washington, D.C., American Enterprise Institute for Public Policy Research, 1970. 126p. bibliog. LC 75-133604. HC 410.7.E43. DDC 330.956. Basic economic information; discussion of the form of socialism, if any; country's approach to economic problems and prospects. Covers Egypt, Iraq, Turkey, Lebanon, Iran.

Islam and the Trade of Asia: A Colloquium. Ed. by Donald Sidney Richards. Philadelphia, University of Pennsylvania Press, 1970. 266p. LC 70-120112. ISBN 0-8122-7619-1. HF 3760.8.Z7A8. DDC 382'.09176'7105. One of few books on medieval economic history of the region.

De Somogyi, Joseph. **A Short History of Oriental Trade.** Hildesheim, Olms, 1968. 281p. bibliog. LC 68-104659. HF 3764.D45. DDC 382'.095.

Kanofsky, Eliyahu. **The Economic Impact of the Six-Day War: Israel, the Occupied Territories, Egypt, Jordan.** New York, Praeger, 1970. 451p. bibliog. LC 78-122083. HC 410.7.K3. DDC 330.9569. Has much basic information on the economics of the countries involved.

El Mallakh, Ragaei. **Economic Development and Regional Cooperation: Kuwait.** Chicago, University of Chicago Press, 1968. 265p. bibliog. index. LC 68-20512. HC 497.K8E4. DDC 330.953'67. How Kuwait uses its oil money at home and abroad, especially the other Arab countries, with special treatment of the Kuwait Fund for Arab Economic Development; problems of planning and balanced growth.

Meyer, Albert Julius. **Middle Eastern Capitalism, Nine Essays.** Cambridge, Mass., Harvard University Press, 1959. 161p. LC 59-14040. HC 412.M4. DDC 330.956.

Studies in the Economic History of the Middle East: From the Rise of Islam to the Present Day. Ed. by M. A. Cook. London, Oxford University Press, 1970. 526p. LC 72-495272. ISBN 0-19-713561-7. HC 410.7.S84. DDC 330.956. Important conference papers; half are on the period to 1800, the rest on the period thereafter. They cover a wide variety of topics.

B. OIL

451. Longrigg, Stephen Hemsley. **Oil in the Middle East, Its Discovery and Development.** 3rd ed. London, Oxford University Press, 1968. 519p. index. $12.00. LC 67-114585. ISBN 0-19-214965-2. HD 9576.A2L6 1967. DDC 338.2'7'2820956.

Covers the period to 1966, treating the development of the companies, exploration, historical-political-economic context; leases, laws, company relations with producer countries; royalty agreements and negotiations; pipelines, terminals, and refineries. There is no great detail on the actual exploration, nor on the "romance" of it all, nor is there material on personalities as found in Mosley (item 452). It is strictly a factual account with few political details, though there are a few generalities on political aspects. It presents a lot of detail on the development of the individual fields and the companies involved. There are 261 pages that deal with the period to 1953, the rest cover to 1966. Really a reference work, not an introductory work for the general reader, who should read first Schwadran (item 454). Mainly for larger collections, though it is a basic work on the subject. Most collections can be satisfied with Schwadran.

452. Mosley, Leonard. **Power Play: Oil in the Middle East.** New York, Random House, 1973. 457p. bibliog. index. $10.00. LC 73-13789. ISBN 0-394-47050-8. HD 9576.N36.M65 1973. DDC 338.2'7'2820956. Paperback: Baltimore, Md., Penguin Books, 1974. $2.95. LC n.a. ISBN 0-14-003908-2.

[P1, C1, S1] A British journalist has prepared this fascinating, popularly written introduction to the history of Near Eastern oil development. It will provide even specialists with useful background. It is mainly the story of the international wheeling and dealing of an interesting bunch of characters, most of whom acted for monetary reasons. It also discusses the roles of Western governments at various times of crisis and competition, as well as the reactions and actions of the Arab rulers. Much information and many anecdotes are presented concerning the personalities involved—Gulbankian, Ibn Saud, J. Paul Getty, the Shah of Iran, and many others. It is thin in places, but it gives a good idea of how things were done and what was involved. Basically responsible, not too polemical, and fairly balanced. It should be noted, however, that there are too many errors of simple fact, and the author apparently intended to write a quotable book; thus, he makes many charges, statements, and speculations reflecting on the parties' motives and cause-effect relations, which he does not support with facts. And he asks loaded questions. Still, a basic work.

Another useful work of a popular nature is Stork, Joe, *Middle East Oil and the Energy Crisis* (New York, Monthly Review Press, 1975. 326p. index. LC 74-7786. ISBN 0-85345-335-7. HD 9576.N36S73. DDC 338.2'7'2820956). This is a moderate radical view opposed to the oil companies. It traces the development of the industry, its role in the region and the process by which it gained control of the region's oil and eliminated competition, exploiting its position to raise profits; the role of the government and the cozy relations between government and companies, including the placing of oil people in key official positions; the struggle of the Near Eastern countries to gain increased control and royalties; the political background throughout the twentieth century to the present, emphasizing the post-World War II era; the 1973 situation; relation to the international financial and general economic situation—Western Europe, the United States and the Third World. Only in the last 50 pages does a specifically radical perspective appear; the rest is based on extensive research in thoroughly respectable public record sources. Useful as a general orientation, it clarifies some of the more technical aspects of pricing and the interrelationships of actors and factors that most books have trouble explaining to the totally uninitiated.

453. Schurr, Sam H., and Paul T. Homan. **Middle Eastern Oil and the Western World: Prospects and Problems.** New York, American Elsevier Publishing Company, 1971. 206p. index. (The Middle East: Economic and Political Problems and Prospects). $19.50. LC 72-135059. ISBN 0-444-00094-1. HD 9576.N36S36. DDC 338'2'7'2820956.

Totally relevant to the study of the present situation, providing basic information on the nature and dynamics of Western dependence on Middle Eastern oil; facts and figures, and projections to 1980. Much discussion of alternative sources of soil, such as shale oil, and their prospects.

454. Shwadran, Benjamin. **The Middle East, Oil and the Great Powers.** Jerusalem, Hebrew Universities Press; distr. New York, John Wiley, 1974. 630p. bibliog. index. (A Halstead Press Book). $20.00. LC 73-10181. ISBN 0-470-79000-8. HD 9576.N36S54 1974. DDC 338.2'7'2820956.

[P1, C1, S1] A history of the oil industry and oil politics through March 1973. It excludes North Africa. Emphasis is on the interaction between the great powers, the oil companies, and the local governments; negotiations for concessions, the local structures of the concessionaires and concessions; terms of concessions, which are often summarized at length, including price-royalty-tax formulas; international politics of Near Eastern oil and roles played by individual countries in backing up their oil companies. Includes facts and figures on production and revenues by governments and companies, political and economic background of the positions of producer countries in negotiating, and their use of oil revenues. Also, material on pipelines, transportation, refineries, gas use. Treatment is chronological by country; each discussion concludes with a section on recent developments and prospects. There is a final section on regional collective instrumentalities such as OPEC; conclusions on the importance of oil and its revenues for the region; great power policies and objectives, and the implications of events in the area; outlook for the future. It includes extensive bibliographical and informative notes. This work is extremely useful in explaining recent events, particularly the actions of the producing countries with regard to prices and cutbacks. Notably lacking is a significant discussion of the relation of the Arab-Israeli conflict to oil production in the future; in the few lines the author does devote to the subject, he irresponsibly dismisses out of hand, for the flimsiest of reasons, the possibility of an oil cutback impact on Western-Arab-Israeli interrelations; thus, he utterly fails the reader with respect to a very important subject. The first book to read or purchase; the other works listed in this *Guide* are basic, but supplementary.

See also:

Mikdashi, Zuhayr M. **The Community of Oil Exporting Countries: A Study in Governmental Cooperation.** Ithaca, N.Y., Cornell University Press, 1972. 239p. bibliog. LC 71-38287. ISBN 0-8014-0690-0. HD 9560.5.M54. DDC 338.2'7'2820611. History, structure and activities of OPEC and much on the Organization of Arab Petroleum Exporting Countries. Written so the non-expert reader can comprehend it.

Penrose, Edith Tilton. **The Large International Firm in Developing Countries: The International Petroleum Industry; with a Chapter on the Oil Industry in Latin America by P. R. Odell.** London, Allen and Unwin, 1968. 311p. bibliog. LC 68-141024. HD 69.I7P4. DDC 338.8'8.

455. Stocking, George Ward. **Middle East Oil: A Study in Political and Economic Controversy.** Nashville, Tenn., Vanderbilt University Press, 1970. 485p. bibliog. index. $15.00. LC 73-115095. ISBN 0-8265-1156-2. HD 9576.N36S7. DDC 338.2'7'2820956.

This excellent study devotes 117 pages to the pre-1950 period, the remainder of the book to the period thereafter. It is the history of the concession grants, negotiations, issues involved, the Organization of Petroleum Exporting Countries; economic factors, pricing and costs, prospects and problems for the future. In most cases the political context is indicated. It is well written in non-technical language, and it provides needed details without overwhelming the reader as Longrigg (item 451) does. It provides more material on the most recent period than Shwadran does, especially details on negotiations and cost-price issues. It will provide the reader with much of the background he needs to understand what is happening today; it complements Longrigg, Shwadran, and Mosley.

XII. DESCRIPTION AND TRAVEL

A. GENERAL

456. Hamilton, Paul. **Seas of Sand.** London, Aldus Books, 1971. 191p. illus. (Aldus Encyclopedia of Discovery and Exploration). o.p. LC 72-180229. SBN 490-00230-7. DS 204.5.H35 1971. DDC 953'04.

A brief, fascinating history of exploration and travel in Arabia, North Africa and the Sahara to Niger. The innumerable illustrations (mostly colored) are marvelous. Excellent for public libraries.

457. Henderson, Harry Will. **The Arab Middle East.** New York, Thomas Nelson, 1970. 224p. bibliog. illus. index. LC 77-99438. DS 44.H42. DDC 915.69'03'4.

Description and travel with historical notes and many illustrations. The book devotes much attention to the Arab-Israeli conflict, and it attempts to be fair in explaining the Arab view. For the uninitiated general reader.

458. Ibn Batuta (1304-1377). **[Tuḥfat al-Nuzzār]. Travels in Asia and Africa, 1325-1354.** Tr. and selected by H. A. R. Gibb. New York, A. M. Kelley, 1969. (Repr. of 1929 ed.). 398p. illus. indices. (The Broadway Travellers). (*BIP* lists an ed. distr. by British Book Center, $15.00.). LC 73-93906. SBN 678-06523-3. G490.I2 1969. DDC 915'.04'2.

[C1, S3] The narrative of the author's travels throughout the Islamic Empire, India, West Africa, China, and Indonesia, in which the people and places are described vividly. He was a Muslim cleric who made the pilgrimage and then travelled just for the sake of travelling. He devotes much attention to religious matters, and reveals much about religious life during the period. A most interesting book. The abridgement is sufficient for smaller libraries, but larger libraries should get the three-volume set instead.

See also:

Ibn Batuta (1304-1377). **[Tuḥfat al-Nuzzār]. The Travels of Ibn Batuta, 1325-1354.** Tr. from Arabic by H. A. R. Gibb. Cambridge, England, Cambridge University Press, 1958- . 3v. (The Hakluyt Society, works. 2d series, No. 110, 117, ___). £4.00 (v.3 only). LC 58-1319. G 161.H2 2d ser., No. 110, etc. [G370.I23].

459. Ibn Jubayr, Muḥammad ibn Aḥmad (1145-1217). **The Travels of Ibn Jubayr; Being the Chronicle of a Mediaeval Spanish Moor Concerning His Journey to the Egypt of Saladin, the Latin Kingdom of Jerusalem, and the Norman Kingdom of Sicily.** Tr. from Arabic by R. J. C. Broadhurst. London, Jonathan Cape, 1952. 430p. index. o.p. LC 53-23033 rev. DS 46.I 213. DDC 915.3. (Also, ed. by William Wright. New York, AMS Press, 1973. $9.50. LC 77-173005. ISBN 0-404-03480-2. DS 36.6. I26 1973. DDC 910'.031'767.)

[C1, S3] The trip, which occurred in 1183-1185, is recounted in a fascinating detailed description of the lands visited, their buildings, monuments, the people and their activities, clothes, behavior; the pyramids, Alexandria's lighthouse; Mecca, Medina. The author, a pious Muslim, reflects on what he saw, including the religious and other significance of the journey and experiences. The book is very instructive and adds a vivid touch of life to study of the era: you are there. A basic work.

460. Kinglake, Alexander William. **Eothen.** Lincoln, University of Nebraska Press, 1970. (Repr. of 1904 ed.). 371p. (A Bison Book, 509). $2.50. LC 71-93107. ISBN 0-8032-5711-2. DS 48.K5 1970. DDC 915.6.

A classic of Near Eastern travel (1834-1835), marvelously humorous and irreverent, but most perceptive of the people and their lives. It has descriptions of local clothing and food; the

Greek Church; Istanbul, Cyprus, Smyrna; his visit with Lady Hester Stanhope in Beirut (cf. Haslip, item 178); Palestine; Bedouin life; Cairo. The author includes a continuous trenchant commentary on the English way of life as he compares it and its practitioners with Oriental ways; these comments make the book that much more entertaining.

461. Searight, Sarah. **The British in the Middle East.** New York, Atheneum, 1970. 215p. bibliog. illus. index. (A Social History of the British Overseas). o.p. LC 79-77744. DS 63.2.G7S4 1970. DDC 301.29'42'056.

The story of the British adventurers, statesmen, businessmen, and archaeologists in the Near East and their activities, in the context of British expansion into the area. It is a fascinating book about the romance of the British discovery of the Near East, but it has virtually no *social* history, which would be quite a separate topic requiring a tremendous amount of research and a massive tome. Because so much space is devoted to the travellers who wrote books about their experiences, it serves as an annotated bibliography of many classic travelogues. A delightful book with 52 pages of marvelous illustrations.

462. Stark, Freya.

Freya Stark was another of the British Victorian women who went to the Near East and became an Orientalist; she first arrived there in 1927. She was a prolific letter writer and also wrote many travel books on the places she lived in and visited. Most of the books are fairly interesting, though not necessarily very informative, and they are quite uneven in quality. All but one of the books annotated below are volumes in her autobiography, which consist to a great extent of her letters to a wide variety of individuals, with connecting commentary. The many illustrations in each book are uniquely interesting and well selected. Ms. Stark was a camera buff, and if she really wants to make a contribution to the field she should publish a huge rotogravure volume of these marvelous pictures, which capture the people and geography of the Near East as few published illustrations have. Some of them have been published in *Space, Time & Movement in Landscape* (London, Her Godson, 1969. 167p. LC 79-449077. DS 44.5.S7. DDC 915.6'04).

See also:

Letters from Syria. London, John Murray; distr. Levittown, N.Y., Transatlantic Arts, 1942. illus. index. $6.95. LC 43-3012. ISBN 0-7195-1323-5. DS 98.S76. (*BBIP* has £1.00.) Records her first two years in the region, in Syria and Lebanon.

Beyond Euphrates, Autobiography, 1928-1933. London, John Murray, 1951. 341p. illus. index. £1.50. LC 51-8441. ISBN 0-7195-1328-6. DS 51.B3S76 1951. DDC 915.67. 1928-29 in Canada; Baghdad, 1929; Iran, 1929-1931; Baghdad, 1932-1933.

The Coast of Incense, Autobiography, 1933-1939. London, John Murray, 1953. 287p. illus. index. £1.50. LC 53-36749. ISBN 0-7195-1329-4. DS 247.H32S8. DDC 915.3. Hadramawt, 1933-1935; Iraq, 1935-1937; Huraidha, Aden, 1937-1938; Greece-Syria, 1938-1939.

East Is West. London, John Murray; distr. Levittown, N.Y., Transatlantic Arts, 1945. 218p. illus. index. $6.95. LC 45-11113. ISBN 0-7195-1324-3. DDC 915.6. A narrative, not an autobiography volume, which discusses her experiences and the political and social conditions in Yemen, and Aden, Egypt, Palestine-Syria-Jordan, and Iraq, as a British agent during the War. A useful discussion of the politics of the area and particularly of the British activities there.

Dust in the Lion's Paw; Autobiography, 1939-1946. London, John Murray, 1961. 296p. illus. index. £1.50. LC 62-3879. ISBN 0-7195-1334-0. D 766.S77 1961. DDC 828.912. While there is some overlap of material treated in *East Is West*, the treatment is quite different and much additional information is provided. She left Iraq in the latter part of 1943 and travelled through the United States and Canada as part of a British propaganda effort to explain British policy in the Middle East, particularly with regard to the Palestine problem. Her account of this trip and her many speeches is extremely interesting. The latter part of the book covers her travels to England in 1944 and to India and Italy in 1945.

This series of books presents to the reader much on the Near East and its important personalities, politics, the common people, and the British presence, life, and policies there. They offer many insights rarely found elsewhere, and are excellent for the reader who wants to absorb the atmosphere of the place.

A new edition of her letters is being edited by Lucy Moorhead: *Letters [of] Freya Stark* (Salisbury, Compton Russell, 1974- . V. 1: *The Furnace and the Cup, 1914-30* (£6.50. LC 75-322361. DS 49.S758. DDC 915.6'04'0924.

463. Stephens, John Lloyd (1805-1852). **Incidents of Travel in Egypt, Arabia Petraea and the Holy Land.** Ed. with an introd. by Victor Wolfgang von Hagen. Norman, Oklahoma University Press, 1970. 54, 473p. $9.95. LC 69-10624. ISBN 0-8061-0886-X. DS 48.S84 1970. DDC 915.

Stephens, an American lawyer, began travelling in 1936 for his health, and ended up staying in the Near East for over a year. This is one of the most interesting and best-written travelogues in this *Guide*. The author makes sharply perceptive observations about the region and its people and his experiences. He provides a very manageable degree of detail, and a humane but somewhat irreverent humor touches his whole perspective. A quarter of the book concerns Palestine and the Holy Places of Christendom, about which he is mildly and gently irreverent. A real joy to read, and a good way to soak up atmosphere.

464. Villiers, Alan [John]. **Sons of Sinbad: An Account of Sailing with the Arabs in Their Dhows in the Red Sea, around the Coasts of Arabia and to Zanzibar and Tanganyika; Pearling in the Persian Gulf; and the Life of the Shipmasters, the Mariners and Merchants of Kuwait.** New York, Charles Scribner's Sons, 1969. (Repr. of 1940 ed.). 414p. illus. o.p. LC 69-17039. G 525.V5 1969. DDC 910.9'16'67.

[P] Villiers' fascinating, exceptionally well-written account of his adventures in the late 1930s. He describes the dhows, their construction and sailing; all aspects of life aboard and in port; the ports visited; the food, the trade, and the people. Informative in a specialized subject, but fun to read.

465. Volney, Constantin Francois Chasseboeuf, comte de. (1757-1820). **Travels through Syria and Egypt in the Years 1783, 1784, and 1785; Containing the Present Natural and Political State of These Countries, Their Productions, Arts, Manufactures and Commerce; with Observations on the Manners, Customs and the Government of the Turks and Arabs.** Tr. from French. New York, Johnson Reprint Corp., 1973. (Repr. of 1787 ed.). 2v. illus. (Middle East Reprint). $35.00. LC 72-14229. ISBN 0-384-64890-8. DS 47.V8 1973. DDC 915.691.

An exceptionally well-written, perceptive account of Egypt, Syria, Lebanon, and Palestine, which constitutes one of our basic sources for the period: the conditions of the region, its contemporary history, structure and dynamics of the political and social system, with descriptions of the lives of the people. The account of the political system and ruling class is extensive and highly informative; it includes an excellent account of the Mamlukes in Egypt, their military service, and the quality of the army. Also, detailed accounts of the minority groups, their origins, behavior and existence. An exceedingly interesting book for any reader, basic for larger collections.

B. GUIDEBOOKS

See also the Guidebooks sections under individual countries.

466. Berrett, Lamar C. **Discovering the World of the Bible.** Provo, Utah, Young House, 1973. 701p. illus. maps. bibliog. index. $14.95; $10.95pa. LC 72-80275. ISBN 0-8425-0598-9; 0-8425-0599-7pa. DS 43.B43. DDC 220.9'1.

A travel guide to the Bible land countries: Cyprus, Egypt, Greece, Turkey, Iraq, Israel, Italy, Jordan, Lebanon, Syria. It covers the regions where there are sites of interest to Christians, and the non-Christian points of interest in these regions of each country. It cites Biblical passages relating to the places described, and the events that occurred there. The most detailed descriptions and historical notes are of Biblical, post-New Testament Christian and

Crusades, and ancient sites and antiquities, the others being mentioned mainly in passing. Of use only to Christians because of its criterion for selection; those interested in a more general tour should refer to other guidebooks. Even Christian travellers will need another standard guide, because the practical information on facilities, official formalities, exchange, etc., is totally lacking. Not for armchair travellers.

467. **Fodor's Islamic Asia: Iran. Afghanistan.** New York, McKay, 1973– .
    671 p. illus. maps. index. $12.95. LC 74-641031. ISBN 0-679-00043-7. DS 254.F642. DDC 915.

    A typical Fodor guide. Iran occupies 302 pages; Afghanistan, 182 pages; and Pakistan, 168 pages.

468. **The Middle East: Lebanon-Syria-Jordan-Iraq-Iran.** Paris, Hachette, 1965. maps. index. (Hachette World Guides). (*BBIP* lists £4.50.) LC 66-54176. DS 43.M6813.

    A detailed travel guide, with practical information that covers communications and transport as well as other areas. Covers Jerusalem along with the other countries. Includes itineraries, detailed descriptions of sights and the geography, with brief historical notes and guides to museums. Not particularly interesting to armchair types, except perhaps in conjunction with travelogues to make the latter more meaningful. Check for later editions and *Fodor*, etc., before relying exclusively on this one, since the tourist information is out of date.
    See also:

    Shawker, Kay. **Complete Reference Guide to the Arab Middle East: Lebanon, Syria, Jordan, Egypt [and] Iraq.** New York, Pan American Airways, 1967. 191 p. illus. LC 67-19408. DS 43.S5. DDC 915.6'04. A handy orientation, though out of date.

XIII. RELIGION
(GENERAL AND CHRISTIANITY, DRUSES)

469. Arberry, Arthur John, ed. **Religion in the Middle East.** Cambridge, England, Cambridge University Press, 1969. 2v. bibliog. index. $37.50. LC 68-21187. ISBN 0-521-07400-2. BL 1600.A7. DDC 200'.956.

[C1] A comprehensive survey by various authorities (only two of them Muslim!) on Judaism (four items), Christianity and its many sects and denominations, and Islam, followed by a section of five stimulating interpretive essays on the interaction of the three faiths. It deals mainly with the modern period, but some essays provide background on the preceding periods. The section on Islam surveys the main branches and sects, and in addition surveys Islam as it is found in the various regions of the world, including the USSR, Africa, the Balkans, etc. A very informative work, but the essays often demand careful reading to pick bits of useful information from them because the data are not presented systematically; treatment is inconsistent from essay to essay. The section on Judaism deals not at all with its principles, but with its current status and modern history and development, Israeli Judaism, the Oriental communities past and present, and the Jews of Yemen. The section on Christianity is mainly historical, with some suggestion of the modern lives and dynamics of the various sects as well as specific information on the current situation. Near Eastern early Christianity and its history, spread, development and influence are touched on only lightly. Other religions are ignored altogether. Not for quick reference; the bibliography is irresponsibly sorry. The set exhibits many of the worst features of the multi-author composite work, and rather few of its advantages. A basic work for larger collections.

Another useful work is:

Cooley, John K. **Baal, Christ and Mohammad: Religion and Revolution in North Africa.** New York, Holt, Rinehart and Winston, 1965. 369p. bibliog. LC 64-21922. BL 2462.C6. DDC 209.61. A popular history, more than half of which deals with the post-medieval period. Not theology or internal politics, but rather the interaction of Christianity and North African history. Interesting and informative.

470. Arpee, Leon. **A History of Armenian Christianity, from the Beginning to Our Own Time.** New York, The Armenian Missionary Association, 1946. 386p. bibliog. index. o.p. LC 46-778. BR 1100.A7. DDC 281.62.

This work traces the origin of the Church, the translation of the Bible, early doctrinal writings, the history of the Church in the context of Armenian national history; monasticism, the saints, the Paulicians; relations with Rome and the Greeks, the controversies; devotional writers; the period of Muslim domination; the Cilician period; persecutions; Roman Catholic missionary efforts; Protestant evangelism; the period of the Turkish massacres, 1915-1923. Not a completely objective work, but it has most of the basic information readers might need, and it is one of the few works available.

471. Attwater, Donald. **The Christian Churches of the East.** Milwaukee, Bruce Publishing Company, 1947-48. 2v. bibliog. illus. index. o.p. LC 47-28901. BX 320.A78. DDC 281.9.

[P1, C1] Volume 1 discusses the Churches in communion with Rome: the Byzantine Rite and its various branches (Italo-Greeks, Ukrainians, Yugoslavs, Melkites, Greeks, Russians, etc.); the Alexandrian Rite (Copts and Ethiopians); Antiochene Rite (Syrians, Maronites, Malankanese); Armenian Rite; Chaldean Rite; it also deals with Eastern monasticism. Volume 2 first discusses the Orthodox Church in general, then deals with the various patriarchates—Constantinople, Alexandria, Antioch, Jerusalem, Moscow, Serbia, Rumania, and the other Greek Churches in Cyprus, Sinai, Greece; other Orthodox churches in Bulgaria, Georgia, Japan, Finland, Poland,

the Orthodox in America. It also covers the Nestorians, Coptic and Ethiopian Monophysites, the Monophysite Alexandrian Rite; Jacobites of Syria and Malabar; the Armenian Monophysites. A final chapter discusses the possibilities for the reunion of the East. For each group, Attwater presents the liturgies and various ritual and other practices, history and current situation, organization, theology, numbers, vestments and equipment, calendars, eucharist forms and theory, etc.; the priesthood. The presentation is systematic and consistent, so that comparison between groups can be readily made, even when the author does not make it himself, as he frequently does. The book, intended for Catholics, presents a plea for understanding of the Eastern Churches; it assumes the reader has some knowledge of basic issues. However, this does not at all hamper non-Catholics' getting full value from it. A good reference work, written in popular style, which can be read straight through.
      See also:

Atiyah, Aziz Suryal. **A History of Eastern Christianity.** London, Methuen, 1968. 486p. LC 68-97975. BX 103.2.A8. DDC 281.

Zernov, Nicholas. **Eastern Christendom: A Study of the Origin and Development of the Eastern Orthodox Church.** New York, Putnam, 1961. 326p. LC 61-5715. BX 320.2.Z45 1961. DDC 281.9.

472. Dick, Ignace. **What Is the Christian Orient?** Tr. from French. Westminster, Md., The Newman Press, 1967. 176p. o.p. LC 66-28936. BX 106.2.D513. DDC 281'.5.

[P1, C1, S1] A popular explanation for Catholics in an ecumenical age. It deals in very general terms with the origins and development of the various Churches, the reasons for various splits; the liturgical families, cultural languages; the Church in the Arab world; the Byzantine world. Each of the branches is discussed, as are the historical aspects of the schisms, and the meaning to Catholics of the Christian Orient. A useful introduction for the general reader, it masterfully sorts out the various branches, a most confusing matter for the beginner. To be read before Arberry (item 469).

473. Fortescue, Adrian (1874-1923). **The Lesser Eastern Churches.** New York, AMS Press, 1972. (Repr. of 1913 ed.). 468p. illus. index. $22.50. LC 79-168124. ISBN 0-404-02517-X. BX 106.F67 1972. DDC 281.

[C1] This classic, standard reference work covers the Nestorians, the Copts, Ethiopians, Jacobites and Malabar Christians, and the Armenians. In each case there is a detailed discussion of the doctrines; history and development from earliest times; current conditions and existence; rites and practices, customs, vestments, churches, liturgies, organization, and priesthood. While not completely helpful for the present day, it does have a wealth of relevant information, and is useful for comparison with Attwater (item 471), who provides information on the Churches for a later period. It does offer information and detail not in Attwater or Arberry (item 469).

474. Fortescue, Adrian (1874-1923). **The Orthodox Eastern Church.** Freeport, N.Y., Books for Libraries Press, 1971. (Repr. of 1920 ed.). 451p. index. $16.75. LC 70-179520. ISBN 0-8369-6649-X. BX 320.F6 1971. DDC 281.9.

[C1] The Eastern Orthodox Church, a history from early times; Rome and the Eastern Churches; the Byzantine faith and rites; the pre-Schism period, the Great Schism; the Orthodox Church since then; the reunion councils; the Crusades and the Byzantine Church; theology; relations with the Turks. The Church in Fortescue's time: constitution, hierarchy, theology, rites, vestments, calendar, music, liturgy, the sacraments. A general introduction written for Catholics, but not polemical. The same comments apply to this as to item 472.

475. Makārim, Sāmī Nasīb. **The Druze Faith.** Delmar, N.Y., Caravan Books, 1974. 153p. bibliog. index. $10.00. LC 73-19819. ISBN 0-88206-003-1. BL 1695.M33. DDC 297'.85'09.

The Druzes are a "heretical" esoteric offshoot of Isma'ili Shiism. They are centered in Syria and Lebanon and play an important role in local and national politics in these countries. Their relations with the other Muslims are sufficiently bad that they have served with the Israeli army, unlike Israeli Arabs (there is a sizeable group of Druzes in Israel). Their faith is a "secret" religion. The "primary purpose of this book is to introduce the Druze layman to his faith." It is written from a Druze viewpoint. The first 39 pages survey the origins and history of the movement. The next section presents basic theology: God and the universe, the physical world, good and evil; man's soul and body; reincarnation; God and man; man seeking unity with the One and his comprehension of God; Imams; heaven and hell. It then covers the commandments and the seven pillars, the allegorical interpretation of the pillars, and the equality of men before God. It is concluded by several prayers, a chronology, discussions of domestic relations law, men's relations with other man, and a glossary of Arabic terms. It does not deal with the ethnic-communal life of the people. Another source is Hitti, Philip K., *The Origins of the Druze People and Religion, with Extracts from Their Sacred Writings* (New York, AMS Press, 1969. (Repr. of 1928 ed.). 80p. LC n.a. DS 94.8.D8 H5 1969).

See also:

al-Najjār, ᶜAbd Allāh. **The Druze: Millennium Scrolls Revealed.** Tr. from Arabic. [n.p.], American Druze Society, Committee on Religious Affairs, 1973. 215p. LC n.a. BL 1695.N3. A somewhat apologetic discourse on theology and history by a member of the sect. Read Makarim and Hitti first.

476. Meinardus, Otto Friedrich August. **Christian Egypt: Faith and Life.** Cairo, American University in Cairo Press, 1970. 513p. indices. LC 75-962975. BX 136.2.M45.

A general discussion of the modern Coptic Church. Topics include names used by Copts and tattoo identification marks; the Copts in the nineteenth and twentieth centuries; selected issues of theology—sources of theological authority, including scriptures, Church Fathers, the Canons through the ages, saints and relics, with an inventory of the relics found in various Churches, and other issues. It also treats folk religion, including healing ministry, feast days, mysticism, the supernatural; issues of Coptic ethics, including personal status laws, marriage, contraception, female circumcision; issues in Church outreach—relations with the Ethiopian and Nubian Churches, African missions, etc. It includes material on early and modern Coptic relations with the government and apostasy. Probably too detailed for most collections, but it contains a wealth of information.

477. Waterfield, Robin Everard. **Christians in Persia: Assyrians, Armenians, Roman Catholics and Protestants.** New York, Barnes & Noble, 1973. 192p. bibliog. illus. index. $11.75. LC 73-171090. ISBN 0-06-497488-8. BR 115.I7W37 1973b. DDC 275.5.

[C] A general history which covers the Nestorians and early Persian Christianity, Christianity under Islam, and Nestorian missionary work in the eastern areas, including India and China; the decline of the Nestorians and their contacts with Rome. Also, Roman Catholic missionaries from the sixteenth century on, and the coming of the orders; European influence and the orders' missionary work, including nineteenth and twentieth century efforts; the Protestant missions, mainly nineteenth and twentieth century; the Americans; Christian evangelism among the Jews; Anglicans and missions among the Assyrian (Nestorian) Christians; Presbyterian missions; English Church Missionary Society efforts. A useful book for the general reader.

XIV. ISLAM

A. GENERAL WORKS

478. Ali, Ameer (1849-1928). **The Spirit of Islam: A History of the Evolution and Ideals of Islam, with a Life of the Prophet.** London, Methuen, 1967. (Repr. of 1922 ed.). 515p. bibliog. index. (University Paperbacks, UP 107). 27/6. LC 68-97979. BP 161.A335 1967. DDC 297. (*BIP* lists a cloth ed.: Hillary House; distr. New York, Humanities Press. $8.00).

[C1, S2] Ali was one of the Indian Islamic reformers who sought to interpret Islam in modern terms to make it relevant to the times. This controversial book was a defense against Western attacks on Islam by missionaries and Western Orientalists, and Western condescension toward Islamic culture, as well as an effort to bring Muslims who were being completely absorbed into Western civilization back into the Muslim fold. The author compares Islam favorably with Christianity and Judaism and shows that Islam really has an uplifting attitude—not only toward women and slavery, but in its political and scientific spirit. He points out how great Islam was in stimulating civilization: it did so in the past and can do so again. A similar approach is taken with regard to the life and behavior of Muhammad. Ali's arguments and method are still widely used today by Muslim writers.

See also:

Alatas, Hussein Syed. **The Democracy of Islam: A Concise Exposition with Reference to Western Political Thought.** The Hague, van Hoeve, 1956. LC cataloging n.a.

Ali, Syed Ahmad. **Economic Foundations of Islam: A Social and Economic Study.** London, Longmans, 1964. 203p. LC SA66-4219. HB 125.A2A75 1964.

al-Ghazzāli,Muhammad. [Min huna na^clam]. **Our Beginning in Wisdom.** Tr. from Arabic. New York, Octagon Books, 1975. (Repr. of 1953 ed.). 162p. LC 75-14135. ISBN 0-374-90114-7. BP 64.E3 K453413 1975. DDC 297.

Iqbal, Sir Muhammad. **The Reconstruction of Religious Thought in Islam.** Lahore, Muhammad Ashraf, 1962. 205p. LC SA 65-5047. BP 161.I7 1962. A basic work of great influence which tries to reinterpret the understanding of Islam for the twentieth century in light of modern philosophy and science.

Kamal, Ahmad. **The Sacred Journey, Being a Pilgrimage to Mecca: The Traditions, Dogma and Islamic Ritual that Govern the Lives and Destiny of the More Than Five Hundred Million Who Call Themselves Muslims . . .** New York, Duell, Sloan and Pearce, 1961. 108, 115p. LC 61-6920. BP 181.K3. DDC 297.38. Devotional compendium of prayers and legends. Arabic and English.

Khalid, Muhammad Khalid. [**Min Huna Nabda'**]. **From Here We Start.** Tr. from Arabic. Washington, D.C., American Council of Learned Societies, 1953. 165p. LC 54-836 rev. DT 70.K5. DDC 976.2.

Khan, Sir Muhammad Zafrullah. **Islam, Its Meaning for Modern Man.** New York, Harper and Row, 1962. 216p. bibliog. LC 62-11131. BP 161.2.K47. DDC 297.

479. Arnold, Sir Thomas Walker. **The Preaching of Islam: A History of the Propagation of the Muslim Faith.** New York, AMS Press, 1974. (Repr. of 1896 ed.). 388p. bibliog. index. LC 72-180319. ISBN 0-404-56214-0. BP 50.A7 1974. DDC 297'.09.

[C2] An as yet unsurpassed history of Islam's spread throughout the world, through conquest, conversion, and trade, up to the nineteenth century. It includes material on the Christians under Muslim rule, Christian conversion to Islam, and the methods of Muslim missionary work. The book includes material on India, Africa, Indonesia, China, the Balkans, and Spain. Arnold's analysis of why people converted to Islam in the Middle Ages is mostly speculation, mainly from lack of specific evidence. We know more about various aspects of this subject today, but the new findings still have not been synthesized in a monograph. A basic work.

480. ^cAzzām, ^cAbd al-Raḥmān. **The Eternal Message of Muḥammad.** Tr. from Arabic by Caesar E. Farah. New York, New American Library, 1965. 254p. index. (A Mentor Book, MT 634). $0.75pa. LC n.a. BP 161.2.A 993. DDC 297.

[P1, C1, S1] A typical exposition of Islamic ideals for modern Muslims by the first Secretary General of the League of Arab States. It exemplifies attempts by the moderate traditionalists, using the same mode of argument as many other similar works, to define the meaning of Islam and the life, attitude, and ideals it signifies for the good Muslim. ^cAzzām tries to strengthen the faith of the modern Muslim (World War II era), in the face of the challenges of the twentieth century. He attempts to reconcile Islam with the new era by emphasizing the process of interpretation, showing that Islam calls for the "Western" ideals that are accepted by his times and that he believes to be traditionally Islamic. These ideals include racial and social equality, justice, freedom; toleration for other faiths. ^cAzzām universalizes the message; he deals with traditional topics such as the life of the Prophet and its meaning; basic Islamic dogmas; the right life; Muslim brotherhood; the modern Islamic state, its meaning and purpose for life; and the importance of Islamic law. The book also discusses Islam and international relations, waging war, dissemination of the message to the Christians. ^cAzzām comments on the Islamic approach to colonialism, class struggle; racial and national strife; the waning of spiritual forces and waxing of materialism and corruption in today's world; Islam as the bulwark of civilization due to the spiritual and moral basis of Islamic civilization. A basic book.

481. Bell, Richard. **The Origin of Islam in Its Christian Environment.** London, Frank Cass; distr. Portland, Ore., International Scholarly Book Services, 1968. (Repr. of 1926 ed.). 221p. index. (Islam and the Muslim World, No. 10). $8.50. LC 68-112517. ISBN 0-7146-1977-9. BP 172.B45 1968. DDC 261.2.

Bell begins with the Eastern Church and its role and existence in Arabia and the Fertile Crescent, how it got there, and its form as it existed there. The "effect in creating the atmosphere in which Islam took shape" is more Christian than Jewish, but, Bell says, the specific influences on Islam are more Jewish than Christian. The book covers the evidences of Christianity in Arabia in pre-Islamic poetry. It discusses Muhammad as an independent religious leader who sought out information on the other scriptures and was influenced thereby; these influences are manifested in the Koran. To Bell, Muhammad consciously created Islam, a view which no Muslim, who views Islam as God's direct work, can accept. Bell also treats Muhammad's attitude toward Christianity; the Christians in the neighboring countries at the time of the Arab conquests and the conversions to Islam; Christian influences in early Islam after Muhammad's death, including influences on the early biographies of the Prophet.

See also:

Geiger, Abraham. **Judaism and Islam.** New York, KTAV Publishing House, 1970. (Repr. of 1898 ed.). 170p. LC 71-79491. ISBN 0-87068-058-7. BP 134.J4G4313 1970. DDC 297'.197'2.

Torrey, Charles Cutter. **The Jewish Foundation of Islam.** New York, KTAV Publishing House, 1968. (Repr. of 1933 ed.). 164p. LC 67-18817. BP 173.J8T6. DDC 297'.197'2.

482. Burton, Sir Richard Francis (1821-1890). **Personal Narrative of a Pilgrimage to Medinah & Mecca.** Ed. by Isabel Burton. New York, Dover Publications, 1964. (Repr. of 1893 ed.). 2v. illus. index. $3.50/vol. LC 64-18842. ISBN 0-486-21217-3 (vol. 1); 0-486-21218-1 (vol. 2). DS 207.B964 1964. DDC 915.38.

A detailed account of the famous traveller's pilgrimage in disguise, at the risk of his life. It is highly informative about conditions and customs of the time, the pilgrimage itself as it had been carried on through the centuries, Islamic education, descriptions of the buildings, the characteristics of the people, etc. It is written in a brisk, highly literate, and easy-to-read style with brusque commentary. Burton's quick perception and his ability to describe things most vividly make this a very entertaining as well as educational work. Included also are the accounts of Ludovicus Vertomannus (1503), Joseph Pitts (1680), and Giovanni Finati (1814), three of the other few Westerners to see the Muslim Holy Cities from which Christians are excluded on pain of death. A basic work for public and college libraries.

483. Cragg, Kenneth. **The Call of the Minaret.** New York, Oxford University Press, 1964. 376p. bibliog. index. (A Galaxy Book, GB 122). $3.50pa. LC n.a. ISBN 0-19-500709. BP 172.C65. DDC 297.

[P1, C1, S1, S2]   The first half of this book is a superb introduction to Islam, and particularly to its chief beliefs and religious life. Cragg tries to make clear the meaning to Muslims of the Koran; the doctrine of God in his various aspects and attributes; prayer and religious life, and the various ritual actions; the conception of the Good Society, including state, family, marriage, etc. The second half deals with the problems of Christian missionary work: taking Islam seriously; problems of the Muslim world today and the Muslim desire to be understood; techniques for understanding Muslims; the best missionary approach—service and self-example, rather than preaching—with more or less specific suggestions as to what the Christians can do to impress Muslims; past Christian-Muslim relations and their influence on current relationships. A very important chapter, "The Call to Interpretation" indicates Muslim beliefs about Christianity, including Muslim belief in the non-crucifixion of Christ, and how Christians should respond; it covers a wide variety of Muslim-Christian issues. A basic work for college and larger public libraries.

484. Cragg, Kenneth. **Counsels in Contemporary Islam.** Edinburgh, Edinburgh University Press; distr. Chicago, Aldine Publishing Company, 1965. 255p. bibliog. index. (Islamic Surveys, 3). $7.95. LC 65-4825. ISBN 0-202-15002-X. DS 36.85.I8 No. 3.

[P1, C1, S1]   An excellent study of Islamic reaction to the modern world from the latter nineteenth century through the 1950s. It provides information on key figures and movements and helps the reader to understand some of the turmoil in the Muslim world. It covers the debates and the movement that became the Pakistan Movement and led to the partitioning of India; the debates on Islam in Pakistan today and discussion on the various approaches to the renewal of Islam; Muhammad Abduh, Muhammad Rashid Rida, and Mustafa Abd al-Raziq in Egypt; Islam and state—concensus and community; the Muslim intelligentsia, including Taha Husayn, Muhammad Husayn Haykal, Ahmad Amin, Manfaluti, Khalid Muhammad Khalid, and others in Egypt; North Africans such as Malek Bennabi; conservative movements like the Muslim Brotherhood (Egypt) and Pakistan's Jamayat al-Islami; attitudes toward new interpretations of the Koran and how to achieve consensus; Mawlana Azad and Indian Islam; A. A. A. Fyzee; Turkey's significance; Ahmadiyya; recurrent themes. Though it gets technical at times, it is a basic work, to be read before Smith (item 499).

485. Cragg, Kenneth. **The Dome and the Rock: Jerusalem Studies in Islam.** London, SPCK; distr. Naperville, Ill., Alec R. Allenson, 1964. 262p. bibliog. index. $8.00. LC 64-5677. ISBN 0-281-00409-9. BP 161.2.C7. DDC 297.

[C1]   Cragg continues his fruitful exposition of Islam to the Christian world by describing and interpreting many aspects of Islamic worship: prayer, fasts, feasts, pilgrimage; the relationship of Islam to daily life, including sex and marriage, childhood; Islam and the arts; the natural order and Islam's view of it; idols, Islam and superstition; the religious calendar; Islam's devotion and meaning. It makes constant references to Christianity, the aim being to sensitize Christian missionaries for a close relationship with Islam: "by knowing and explaining Islam . . . [to] better arouse and inform a Muslim discovery of Christ." Cragg wants Christianity to "meet" Islam, to encourage mutual discovery. A very informative book that views a side of Muslim life not usually observed, let alone appreciated.

486. Cragg, Kenneth. **The House of Islam.** Encino, Calif., Dickenson Publishing Company, 1975. 145p. bibliog. index. (The Religious Life of Man). $3.95pa. LC 74-83949. ISBN 0-8221-0139-4. BP 161.2.C72. DDC 297.

[P2, C1]   A stimulating, interpretive introduction to Islam, emphasizing the meaning and significance of Muhammad, the Koran, Islamic law, liturgical aspects, the Islamic community, and the various sects, as well as the modern existence of Islam and the problems confronting it. To be read after Gibb (item 488) and Rahman (item 498). For the educated initiated reader.

487. Farah, Caesar E. **Islam: Beliefs and Observances.** 2nd ed. Woodbury, N.J., Barron's Educational Series, 1970. 306p. bibliog. gloss. index. $6.00; $2.50pa. LC 72-135505. ISBN 0-8120-6022-9; 0-8120-0277-6pa. BP 161.2.F3 1970. DDC 297.

[B, P1, C1, S1] A sympathetic introduction for the general reader, covering pre-Islamic Arabia, Muhammad, the Koran and its theology, obligations of Muslims; institutions, orthodoxy, sects, Sufism; modern Islamic reform and modern sects; Islam around the world. Useful annotated bibliography.

488. Gibb, Hamilton Alexander Rosskeen. **Mohammedanism, an Historical Survey.** 2nd rev. ed. London, Oxford University Press, 1969. 160p. bibliog. index. (Oxford Paperbacks University Series, Opus 17). $1.95. LC 78-518140. ISBN 0-19-888017-0. (*BIP* has 0-19-500245-8). BP 50.G5 1969. DDC 297'.09.

[P1, C1, S1] The second work one should read, being an interpretation and summary statement by the late dean of Anglo-American Arabists. The first book to read would be Guillaume or Farah (item 490 or 487).

489. Goldziher, Ignaz. [**Muhammenanische Studien**]. **Muslim Studies.** Tr. from German. Chicago, Aldine Publishing Company; distr. Albany, State University of New York Press, 1966-1971. 2v. $8.00 (v.1); $12.00 (v.2). LC 72-11731. ISBN 0-87395-234-0 (v.1); 0-87395-235-0 (v.2). BP 25.G6143. DDC 297.

A classic in Islamic studies. One of the most important of the studies, which takes up most of the second volume, concerns the development of the Hadith (Islam's oral traditions of the Prophet) and Hadith science; it is technical and outdated, but still a basic introduction to the Hadith materials, which has not been superseded. Also included are items on saint worship, Persian-Arab relations, the Arab tribes and Islam, etc. Many of the items are too specialized for college students, but they are interesting, and Volume 2 is a must. Excellent examples of good scholarship and scholarly method. It should be noted that Muslims completely reject Goldziher's view that the Hadith do not emanate from the time of Muhammad, but from the period after his death when canonical justification was needed for legal and theological decisions on matters that had not come up during the Prophet's lifetime (cf. annotations in the Hadith section of this *Guide*).

490. Guillaume, Alfred. **Islam.** Baltimore, Penguin Books, 1961. 210p. bibliog. index. (A 311). $1.35pa. LC A55-7737. ISBN 0-14-020311-7. BP 161.G87. DDC 297.

[P1, C1] A straightforward introduction for the totally uninitiated reader, and the first book one should read.

491. Jeffery, Arthur, ed. **Islam: Muhammad and His Religion.** New York, Liberal Arts Press, 1958. 252p. bibliog. (The Library of Religion, No. 6). pa. o.p. LC 58-9958. BP 161.J4. DDC 297.082.

[P1, C1, S1] A selection of texts and brief quotations illustrating basic aspects of Islam: Koranic, Hadith, and other passages on Muhammad; the Koran—quotations from and about it; faith and doctrines, duties; spiritual and devotional life. Each section has a brief introduction. A first work for all collections (cf. item 502).

492. Jeffery, Arthur, ed. **A Reader on Islam: Passages from Standard Arabic Writings Illustrative of the Beliefs and Practices of Muslims.** 'S-Gravenhage, Mouton; distr. New York, Humanities Press, 1962. 678p. bibliog. glossary. index. (Columbia University Publications in Near and Middle East Studies, Ser. A, 2). $15.50. LC 62-52447. BP 20.J4. DDC 297.8.

[C2] This excellent source book contains many passages from the Koran, Hadith, Muhammad's biography, creeds and confessions, theological writings, prayers and sermons. The selections are quoted at length to give an idea of the mode of reasoning and expression, the nature of Islamic religious literature, etc. The length of the extracts limits the number of selections included so that only a tiny fraction of the vast literature is presented; but the book is very informative on basic matters and is a worthy supplement to the shorter collections, as well as to the individual works listed in this *Guide*.

493. Macdonald, Duncan Black (1863-1943). **The Religious Attitude and Life in Islam.** New York, AMS Press, 1970. (Repr. of 1909 ed.). 317p. index. $10.00. LC 70-121277. ISBN 0-404-04125-6. BP 165.M23 1970. DDC 297.

[C3, S3] This book deals with the contacts of Muslims with the unseen, in religious and daily life, with particular emphasis on the great Sufi-Sunnite theologian al-Ghazali, and the internal and hidden side of life. It includes the nature of prophecy (noting that Muhammad is not one of the great Semitic prophets) and how it reveals the unseen; soothsayers, Jinn, and poets in Arabia; soothsaying in general, with much from Ibn Khaldun on the subject; dreams and intercourse with the unseen; saints, geomancy, number divination, and Islamic magic; demons and spirits; the ascetic-ecstatic life of Sufism; and a myriad of similar topics. For most collections it is too advanced, particularly because of its detailed emphasis on al-Ghazali, but it is one of few works on the subject, which is still a vital part of living Islam today. The book warrants inclusion in larger collections.

494. Morgan, Kenneth William, ed. **Islam, the Straight Path: Islam Interpreted by Muslims.** New York, Ronald Press, 1958. 453p. bibliog. index. $6.00. LC 58-9807. BP 161.M63. DDC 297.

[P1, C1, S2] Eleven Muslim scholars, many of them well known to Western Islamicists, write on aspects of Islam and its origins, including the basic beliefs and laws; mystical and rationalist interpretations, Shiism, Islamic culture; Islam in the various major areas—Africa, India, Indonesia; the early history of Islam. Naturally, the essayists present a view of Islam they would like the Christian world to know. It duplicates much of what is found in the general works listed in this *Guide.* However, there are significant differences of feeling, nuance, emphasis, etc., so that this book gives a sense of the traditionally oriented modern Muslim's feelings and conceptions of his own religion and its strengths. It should also be noted that much of the same type of presentation is made in Arabic works aimed at Muslims; thus, this book presents an authentic expression of at least part of what is taught by Muslims in their own languages.

495. Nasr, Seyyed Hossein. **Ideals and Realities of Islam.** New York, Hillary House, c/o Humanities Press, 1966. LC n.a. BP 165.N28 1967. DDC 297. Paperback: Boston, Beacon Press, 1972. (Beacon Paperback, 439). $3.95. LC 72-1917. ISBN 0-8070-1131-2.

[P2, C1] Partly introductory, partly original interpretive essays by an outstanding Persian Sufi Muslim scholar. The essays cover Islam, the last religion; the place and meaning of the Koran; Muhammad's significance; the Hadith, the religious law, Sufism; Shiism and Sunnism. A well-written, scholarly Muslim viewpoint, highly recommended for smaller as well as comprehensive collections, and for students with a couple of introductory works behind them.

496. Padwick, Constance Evelyn. **Muslim Devotions: A Study of Prayer-Manuals in Common Use.** London, SPCK; distr. Naperville, Ill., Alec R. Allenson, 1961. 313p. index. $10.50. LC 61-4824. ISBN 0-281-00786-1. BP 188.5.P3. DDC 297.3.

[C1, S3] One of the only English works of any kind on the daily prayer of the Muslim masses. It discusses prayer, its meaning, terminology, types of prayers, and other aspects of the subject, amply illustrated with texts. It also covers saint cults, the Shiites, and the worship of God the creator; and it has much information concerning devotions and worship. There is little on the physical details, and nothing on the preparatory ablutions. It contains a mine of bibliographical information. The prayer is a little-known side of Islam despite its basic nature. Usually Westerners think of Muslim prayer as meaningless physical motions in the mosque, muezzins calling from their minarets, or robed individuals kneeling on their carpets. We find in this book that there is an intense devotional life quite comparable in many ways to Christian devotions and prayers, sometimes expressed in very similar fashion. This book deals with the people, which most works on Islam do not; even though it is a systematic scholarly work, through the weight of its examples and material, it often touches the reader.

497. Peters, Francis E. **Allah's Commonwealth: A History of Islam in the Near East, 600-1100 A.D.** New York, Simon and Schuster, 1974. 800p. bibliog. index. $19.95. LC 73-18733. ISBN 0-671-21564-7. BP 55.P47. DDC 910'.03'7671.

[P1, P2, C1, S1] An extremely useful and interesting history of Islamic intellectual life. Set against the background of the history of the times, it reveals the interaction of Islam and the politics of the Islamic Empire, as well as the interaction of Islam with the other civilizations with which it came in contact. It begins with the pre-Islamic period, the rise of Muhammad and his message. The book then suggests the political history and dynamics of the spread of the Islamic community; the theological encounter with Christianity, which resulted in the rise of Islamic intellection; polemicism, ultimately theology and philosophy; and the rise of the sects in Islam and their political aspects. It also covers the development of the Islamic sciences, the reception of Hellenism, and the process by which it occurred; the non-religious sciences, particularly as part of the Hellenistic-Islamic synthesis; and literature. For the reader who is familiar with the introductory works on Islamic theology-philosophy and Hitti (item 88), this is a basic work that will help him understand Islamic thought, its origins, basic ideas, development, etc.; it beautifully demonstrates how they fit into the whole picture. Coverage of belles-lettres is neither systematic nor comprehensive, but their nature is well indicated. Names and ideas flow ceaselessly through the book, but each is relevant to the discussion, and careful study of each page will be well repaid by its illumination of a wide range of material, particularly as the reader passes on to further study, which will be pursued with greater facility than if the book had not been available. For all college and larger public libraries.

498. Rahman, Fazlur. **Islam.** New York, Holt, Rinehart and Winston, 1966. 271p. bibliog. index. (History of Religion Series). $8.95. LC 66-13499. ISBN 0-03-058090-0. BP 161.2.R29. DDC 297. Paperback: New York, Doubleday, 1968. (Anchor Book A641). $2.50. ISBN 0-385-61794-4.

[P1, P2, C1, S1] Written by an outstanding Muslim scholar, this is by far the best general introduction on Islam for the reader with some background (e.g., from reading items 487 and 490). By no means apologetic for Islam, Rahman provides a reasoned, scholarly Muslim perspective that Western readers can find little fault with on *any* grounds. A basic book.

499. Smith, Wilfred Cantwell. **Islam in Modern History.** Princeton, N.J., Princeton University Press, 1957. 317p. index. $12.50. LC 57-5458. ISBN 0-691-03030-8. BP 38.S56. DDC 297. Paperback: New York, New American Library. (A Mentor Book, MY 1108). $1.25.

[C1, S2] This is a profound study of the problems and processes of Islam's adjustment to the modern world, based on a deep, wide-ranging knowledge of the vernacular literatures and personal experience in the region. It treats individually the Arabs, Turkey, Pakistan, and India. It discusses the various Muslim reactions, from traditionalism and defense of old ways, to efforts at reinterpretation, interaction with nationalism; the ambivalent reaction to Western civilization; the role, rewriting, and interpretation of history; key issues such as the Muslim state, secularization, and the reasons for Islam's weakness. It analyses the adjustment effort in terms of what Smith views as the needs of the Muslim peoples, and the successes, weaknesses, and failures of the various approaches. Smith discusses individual writers and groups, the relationship of the process to politics and to the needs and reactions of the masses, and psychological aspects of the situation. A sympathetic treatment addressed to Muslims and Westerners; not a comprehensive survey of the whole range of issues being discussed. A basic book for more advanced readers and college collections.

Other works on Islam of considerable interest and usefulness are:

Gibb, Sir Hamilton Alexander Rosskeen, ed. **Whither Islam? A Survey of Modern Movements in the Moslem World.** New York, AMS Press, 1973. (Repr. of 1932 ed.). 384p. LC 73-180338. ISBN 0-404-56263-9. BP 163.G54 1973. DDC 297.

Gibb, Sir Hamilton Alexander Rosskeen, ed. **Modern Trends in Islam.** New York, Octagon Press, 1972. (Repr. of 1942 ed.). 141p. LC 76-159188. ISBN 0-374-93046-5. BP 163.G5 1972. DDC 297.

Keddie, Nikki R., ed. **Scholars, Saints and Sufis: Muslim Religious Institutions in the Middle East since 1500.** Berkeley, University of California Press, 1972. 401p. LC 77-153546. ISBN 0-520-02027-8. BP 185.S36. DDC 297'.0956. Ten essays deal with the Ulama, a subject of great importance that has only recently been studied seriously; the others deal with popular Islam. Most essays stress the nineteenth and twentieth centuries. Very important for advanced students, and extremely interesting.

Proctor, Jesse Harris, ed. **Islam and International Relations.** New York, Praeger, 1965. 221p. LC 65-12192. BP 173.5.P7. DDC 297.

Rosenthal, Erwin Isak Jakob. **Islam in the Modern National State.** Cambridge, England, Cambridge University Press, 1965. 416p. bibliog. LC 66-13638. BP 173.6.R6.

von Grunebaum, Gustave Edmund. **Modern Islam: The Search for Cultural Identity.** Berkeley, University of California Press, 1962. 303p. LC 62-17178. DS 57.V6. DDC 915.6. A very important collection of essays dealing with key issues, and a good source of bibliography. For the advanced student.

500. Von Grunebaum, Gustave Edmund. **Muhammadan Festivals.** New York, Henry Schuman, 1958. 107p. index. o.p. LC 58-4109. BP 186.V6 1958. DDC 297.

[P2, C1, S2] A background to and description of Muslim prayer, pilgrimage, the fast of Ramadan and its feasts; Mawlid al-Nabi (Muhammad's birthday); saintly festivals, 10th of Muharram (the death of Husayn ibn Ali). For general readers.

501. Westermarck, Edvard Alexander. **Pagan Survivals in Mohammedan Civilization.** London, Macmillan, 1933. 190p. index. o.p. LC 34-29127. GR 360.M6W35. DDC 398.30964.

Drawing heavily on item 1084 and secondary literature on other countries, the book treats the Jinn, evil eye, curses, barakah; Berber and Roman survivals in Islamic ritual. For each topic, Westermarck discusses theory and practice, with specific examples, and its various aspects, as well as parallels in the pre-Islamic period. He seeks to generalize for the whole Arab world. It should be noted, however, that he is interested in popular Islam, not in what we usually think of as Islamic civilization. A useful orientation to be read before the more detailed works on the individual countries that are included in this *Guide.*

502. Williams, John Alden, ed. **Islam.** New York, George Braziller, 1961. 256p. index. (Great Religions of Modern Man). $4.00. LC 61-15500. ISBN 0-8076-0165-9. BP 161.2.W5. DDC 297.082. Paperback: Washington Square Press, $0.75.

[P1, C1, S1] Another introductory collection of basic illustrative texts: Koran, Hadith concerning Muhammad, the founding of the community, Muhammad's position as founder, legislator and guide; Islamic law in its various aspects; Sufism; theological excerpts emphasizing the chief thinkers rather than the ideas; extracts from the "dissidents"—Shiites, Kharijites. Each item has a one- to three-paragraph introduction that puts it in perspective. Williams and Jeffery (item 491) are complementary. For all collections.

503. Zwemer, Samuel Marinus (1867-1952). **Studies in Popular Islam: A Collection of Papers Dealing with the Superstitions and Beliefs of the Common People.** London, Sheldon Press, 1939. 148p. bibliog. illus. o.p. LC 39-30400. DS 38.Z83. DDC 297.

[C2] Zwemer discusses the "undertow" of the tides of modern Islam: rosary in prayer; use of the 99 names of God; black stone of the Ka^cbah; sword of Muhammad and Ali; Muslim "clock" and calendar, and Koran's influence on them; the familiar spirit (each person has a double, who is the offspring of Satan) and its influence in ritual and other aspects of life; hair, fingernails and beard; translations from the Koran, including their history; the issue of the "illiterate" prophet; Hadith as relating the word of God rather than Muhammad; worship of Adam by angels—the Hebrew origins of a Koran story. A useful and most interesting book.

B. REFERENCE WORKS

504. Hughes, Thomas Patrick. **A Dictionary of Islam, Being a Cyclopedia of the Doctrines, Rites, Ceremonies and Customs, Together with the Technical and Theological Terms of the Muhammadan Religion.** Delhi, Oriental Publishers; distr. Columbia, Mo., South Asia Books, 1974. (Repr. of 1885 ed.). 750p. bibliog. $18.50. LC n.a. BP 40.H8 1973.

[P1, C1, S1] One of the most useful reference works on Islam, particularly for the uninitiated reader. It covers the technical terms of most Islamic sciences, but in non-technical language. It will serve as a dictionary of Koranic terms and as an index to Koranic verses, since most articles cite the relevant verses, as well as appropriate Hadith. Covers as well other aspects of Arab-Islamic civilization, such as language and history of Arabic lexicology, Muslim houses; contains many brief biographies. Includes an index of items in Arabic script. Most readers will find this more useful than the much more technical and advanced *Shorter Encyclopedia of Islam* (item 505), but all libraries should have both.

505. **Shorter Encyclopedia of Islam.** Ed. by H. A. R. Gibb and J. H. Kramers. Ithaca, N.Y., Cornell University Press, c. 1953. 671p. $24.50. LC 57-59109. ISBN 0-8014-0150-X. DS 37.E52. DDC 297.03.

[P1, C1, S1, S2] Articles on Islam extracted from the first edition of the *Encyclopedia of Islam* (which, despite its title, is a comprehensive work on all aspects of Islamic, Arabic, Persian, and Turkish studies). The *Shorter Encyclopedia* covers concepts, individuals, Koranic figures, Islamic institutions, sects, important shrines and holy cities, Islamic law, theology and philosophy, technical terms. A basic work for any collection that goes beyond the elementary. Most of the articles are technical, written by specialists and intended for other specialists or at least for users with a considerable background on Islam. Some are virtually unintelligible to the uninitiated reader.

C. MUHAMMAD, THE PROPHET

506. Andrae, Tor, Bishop (1885-1947). **Mohammed, the Man and His Faith.** Freeport, N.Y., Books for Libraries Press, 1971. (Repr. of 1936 ed.). 274p. $12.00. LC 79-160954. ISBN 0-8369-5821-7. BP 75.A57 1971. DDC 297'.63 [B]. Paperback: New York, Harper and Row, 1960. (Harper Torchbooks/The Cloister Library, TB 62). o.p. LC 60-5489. BP 75.A57 1960. DDC 922.97.

[P2, C1, S1] A highly sympathetic interpretation of Muhammad as prophet, emphasizing the psychological aspects of the religious experience. Andrae notes aspects of the Arabian background, especially the currents of religious thought at the time; he makes numerous comparisons with phenomena in Christianity and other religions that prove the authenticity of Muhammad's religious experiences as manifested and recorded in the Koran. He notes key incidents in the Prophet's life that are important to Muslims and presents some of their religious implications. He probes at some length Muhammad's personality and character, mainly with favorable results. An interesting book, it nicely complements Watt (item 509), which omits Muhammad's character and personality from its considerations.

507. Majlisī, Muḥammad Bāqir ibn Muḥammad Taqī (1627 or 1628-ca. 1699). **The Life and Religion of Mohammad, As Contained in the Sheeah Traditions of the Hyât-ul-Kuloob.** Tr. from Persian by Rev. James L. Merrick. Boston, Phillips, Samson, 1850. 453p. index. o.p. LC 50-45969 rev. BP 75.M152.

A Shiite biography of the Prophet, containing lore about his miracles and anecdotes from Shiite as well as Sunnite sources. Important because of its theological views, both implied and expressed, especially those concerning Muhammad's appointment of Ali (the first Shiite Imam and fourth Caliph) as his successor; this designation is a cardinal point with the Shiites, who believe that the first three Caliphs usurped Ali's rightful position as direct successor to Muhammad. Seventy-two pages of notes. Too much for most collections, but a good example of a typical devotional biography. Fairly easy reading, though extremely detailed.

508. Rahnamā, Zayn al-ᶜAbidin. **Payambar: The Messenger, by Zeinolabedin Rahnema.** Tr. from Persian by L. P. Elwell-Sutton. Lahore, Shaykh Muhammad Ashraf, 1964- . 3v. LC SA66-6886. BP 75.R27413.

A popular biography by a Muslim, translated by a well-known Persianist; it is based firmly on the traditional sources but is written like a novel. A readable blending of traditional lore, which reveals the Muslim's view of his Prophet in full detail, it includes many instances of the situations in which Koranic verses were revealed to Muhammad. For most collections. For the student, it is an excellent way of becoming familiar with the names and personalities that flow through traditional Islamic literature. To be read after Watt (item 509) and Hitti (item 88) through the period of the Umayyad Caliphate. The basic source on the life of the Prophet is Ibn Ishaq's eighth century *Sirat Rasūl Allāh*, available in a translation of Ibn Hishām's ninth century rescension, which is the version that has survived, by Alfred Guillaume: *The Life of Muhammad* (Lahore, Oxford University Press, Pakistan Branch, 1970. 813p. pa. LC 55-12845. BP 75.I25). It is a compendium of accounts from the Hadith and other early sources, legends, with much poetry, far too detailed for most readers, but basic for serious study.

Other examples of Muslim devotional works on the Prophet are:

Jairazbhoy, Qasim Ali. **Muhammad "A Mercy to All the Nations."** London, Luzac, 1937. LC cataloging n.a.

Sarwar, Hafiz Ghulam. **Muhammad, The Holy Prophet.** Lahore, Muhammad Ashraf, 1964. 410p. LC SA 65-4532. BP 75.S35 1964.

Shibli Numani, Muhammad. **Sirat al-Nabi.** Tr. from Urdu. Karachi, Pakistan Historical Society, 1970. 547p. LC 76-931697. BP 75.S4846. The first 101 pages present a useful detailed discussion of the sources of the Prophet's life and a critique of many previous works (from earliest times), including some European works. The rest is a biography based on classical sources. It treats some aspects of Muhammad's life in light of contemporary Arabian conditions. It often gets too technical for most readers, but it nicely reveals the facets of his life that are of particular interest to Muslims.

Siddiqui, Abdul Hameed. **The Life of Muhammad.** Lahore, Islamic Publications, 1969. 410p. LC 77-930763. BP 75.S495. DDC 297'.63 [B].

509. Watt, William Montgomery. **Muhammad, Prophet and Statesman.** London, Oxford University Press, 1974. 250p. bibliog. index. (A Galaxy Book, GB 409). $2.95pa. LC 74-163338. ISBN 0-19-881078-4. BP 75.W33 1974. DDC 297'.63 [B].

[P1, C1, S1] The best biography of the Prophet, it provides many more details, systematically and chronologically, than the other secondary books in this *Guide*. It emphasizes the socio-economic background of Arabia rather than the psychology of religious experience, as Andrae does (item 506). Watt attempts to explain many of the incidents, both religious and biographical, found in the Koran in terms of society and politics, and he examines Muhammad's role in relation to these elements in the life of his era. The development of the Koranic conceptions and the details of Islam are treated, though not systematically and mainly for the early period of Muhammad's call. The Koranic religious law as it developed after the Hijrah is ignored. The first book on Muhammad to be read after a general introduction to Islam.

Other useful Western biographies are:

Buhl, Frants Peder William. **The Life of Muhammad.** Tr. from German. Heidelberg, Quelle & Meyer, 1955. LC cataloging n.a.

Dermengham, Emile. **The Life of Mahomet.** Tr. from French. London, George Routledge, 1930. 352p. LC 30-18759. BP 75.D42. Popularly written, from traditional sources.

Muir, William. **The Life of Muhammad from Original Sources.** A new and rev. ed. by T. H. Weir. New York, AMS Press, 1975. (Repr. of 1923 ed.). 556p. LC 78-180366. ISBN 0-404-56306-6. BP 75.M8 1975.

Rodinson, Maxime. **Mohammed.** Tr. from French. New York, Pantheon Books, 1971. 360p. LC 69-20189. ISBN 0-394-47110-5. BP 75.R5713 1971. DDC 297'.63 [B].

D. KORAN

510. Bell, Richard. **Bell's Introduction to the Qur'an.** Completely rev. and enl. by W. Montgomery Watt. Edinburgh, Edinburgh University Press; distr. Chicago, Aldine Publishing Company, 1970. 258p. bibliog. index. (Islamic Surveys, 8). $7.95. LC 77-106474. ISBN 0-202-15006-2. DS 36.85.I8 No. 8.

[P1, C1, S1] This is the basic introduction to Islam's Holy Book. It gets technical at times, but there is nothing better, and it is quite good. Bell was a foremost student of the Koran, and Watt is a top scholar on both the Book and the Prophet. Watt has much improved Bell's version, has updated various concepts, and has provided additional information and topics. It covers the historical background, Muhammad's prophetic experience, a history of the text, its internal form, style, development of the revelation, and kind of material form in which it occurred; the chronology of the delivery of the verses; doctrines; Muslim and Western scholarship, with discussions of theories of various scholars, especially Bell. It discusses at length Arabic terminology. A basic book.

Other useful works on a variety of subjects are:

Ahmad, Bashiruddin Mahmud, hazrat mirza. **Introduction to the Study of the Holy Quran.** Tr. from Urdu. London, London Mosque, 1949. 446p. LC 52-1519. BP 130. 4.A3. DDC 297.

Baljon, Johannes Marinus Simon. **Modern Muslim Koran Interpretation, 1880-1960.** Leiden, E. J. Brill, 1961. 135p. LC A62-357. BP 130.45.B3. Deals especially with India and Pakistan.

Bravmann, M. M. **The Spiritual Background of Early Islam: Studies in Ancient Arab Concepts.** Leiden, E. J. Brill, 1972. 338p. LC 73-154917. BP 163.B63. DDC 297'.1. Technical scholarly articles basic to serious study of early Islam and pre-Islamic Arabic poetry.

Cragg, Kenneth. **The Event of the Qur'an: Islam in Its Scripture.** London, George Allen and Unwin, 1971. 208p. LC 72-179748. ISBN 0-04-297024-5. BP 130.C67. DDC 297'. 1226'6. Aspects of the phenomenon of the Qur'an in its setting; its meaning, means of expression, process of deliverance to Muhammad.

Cragg, Kenneth. **The Mind of the Qur'an: Chapters in Reflection.** London, George Allen and Unwin, 1973. LC 73-160303. ISBN 0-04-297030-X. BP 130.4.C7. DDC 297'.1226. The impact of the Qur'an on its people, and its active spiritual and intellectual possession of and by its people—its interpretation, levels of meaning for Muslims, etc. Both Cragg books are strictly for those who have mastered most of the books on Islam and the Qur'an in this *Guide*. They are intellectually very demanding—but commensurately rewarding.

Izutsu, Toshihiko. **Ethico-Religious Concepts in the Qur'an.** Rev. ed. Montreal, Institute of Islamic Studies, McGill University; McGill University Press, 1966. 284p. LC 66-16860. BP 134.E8I9 1966. DDC 297.1228.

Izutsu, Toshihiko. **God and Man in the Koran: Semantics of the Koranic Weltanschauung.** Tokyo, Keio Institute of Cultural and Linguistic Studies, 1964. 242p. bibliog. LC 67-77345. BP 134.G6I9. Both Izutsu books are excellent studies in the terminology and theology of the Koran, and both are very informative examples of fruitful methods of Koran study.

Jansen, J. J. G. **The Interpretation of the Koran in Modern Egypt.** Leiden, E. J. Brill, 1974. 116p. LC n.a.

Jeffery, Arthur. **The Foreign Vocabulary of the Qur'an.** Baroda, Oriental Institute, 1938. 311p. bibliog. LC AC 40-1079. PK 2971. G3 no. 79. DDC 892.7. Non-Arabic terminology, obviously current in Meccan Arabic, has implications regarding intellectual and religious currents of Muhammad's time, into which the Koran fits.

Jeffery, Arthur. **The Qur'an as Scripture.** New York, R. F. Moore Company, 1957. 103p. LC 52-10808. BP 130.J42. DDC 297.

Jomier, Jacques. **The Bible and the Koran.** Tr. from French. Chicago, Henry Regnery, 1967. 120p. LC 67-4326. BP 134.B4J613 1967. DDC 297'.122.

Koran. English and Arabic. **The Meaning of the Quran.** By Abu A'la Maududi. Lahore, Islamic Publications, 1967- . LC SA 68-18614. BP 104.8.M313. English Koran, with commentary by the well-known Pakistani Orthodox Muslim writer.

Roberts, Robert. **The Social Laws of the Quran: Considered and Compared with Those of the Hebrew and Other Ancient Codes.** London, Curzon Press, 1971. LC 72-187212. LC class: LAW. DDC 340.5'9.

511. **[Koran]. The Koran Interpreted.** By Arthur J. Arberry. New York, Macmillan, 1964. 350, 358p. $4.95pa. LC 64-9828. BP 109.A7 1964. DDC 297.12.

[P1, C1, S1] This is the best English translation of Islam's Holy Book. However, it is rather literal and literary, leaving the reader to struggle with ambiguities and uncertainties in meaning. These problems are encountered mainly when the reader tries to read it for its detail, in order to interpret the text theologically, etc., or when the reader tries to use it as a pony for the original Arabic. In such cases, several texts must be used.

512. **[Koran]. The Meaning of the Glorious Koran: An Explanatory Translation.** By Mohammed Marmaduke Pickthall. New York, New American Library, 197- ? 464p. index. (A Mentor Religious Classic, MW 1195). $1.50pa. LC n.a. BP 109.P5. DDC 297. (*BIP* lists a cloth ed., distr. New York, Orientalia. $10.00. ISBN 0-87902-182-9.)

[P1, C1, S1] A readable "interpretation" (i.e., translation) by an English convert to Islam. While Arberry is the best generally, it is often obscure, and Pickthall is a useful supplement. Other translations include:

Koran. English. **The Koran: A New Translation.** By N. J. Dawood. Baltimore, Penguin Books, 1961. 427p. LC cataloging n.a.

Koran. English and Arabic. **The Quran: The Eternal Revelation Vouchsafed to Muhammad, the Seal of the Prophets: Arabic Text with New Translation.** By Muhammad Zafrulla Khan. New York, Praeger, 1971. 53, 673p. LC 77-134449. BP 109.K48 1971. DDC 297'.1224.

Koran. English. **The Qur'an.** Tr., with a critical re-arrangement of the Surahs, by Richard Bell. Edinburgh, T. & T. Clark, 1937-39. 2v. LC 38-20150 rev. BP 109.B4. DDC 297. Bell and Dawood both rearranged the Surahs (chapters), and Dawood even some verses, seeking to present a chronologically accurate text. The original compilation of the chapters was basically mechanical in arrangement—from longest to shortest; even medieval Muslim exegetes recognized that the traditional arrangement broke up the order in which the verses had been received, which order was often significant for interpretation, so these two English versions, though not traditional, are not heretical.

513. Watt, William Montgomery. **Companion to the Qur'ān.** New York, Hillary House; distr. New York, Humanities Press, 1967. 355p. bibliog. $9.50. LC 68-70820. BP 130.4.W34. DDC 297'.1227.

[P1, C1, S1, S2] Basically an annotation of Arberry's translation (item 435), this work offers clarifications and alternative readings, as well as background notes and other information that greatly help the reader interpret the Arberry text. We still lack a full, scholarly commentary in English on the *Koran* that utilizes all present knowledge, including comparative Semitics, history of pre-Islamic Arabia, and notes on classical Muslim commentaries. Such a work is utterly essential, but it would be quite technical and probably beyond most college students, even if they knew Arabic. On the other hand, such a work would enable us to see more clearly what the *Koran* is really all about, what is implied in its passages, what knowledge is assumed by the speaker, etc. There are really very few decent books about the *Koran*, as the lack of books in this *Guide* will indicate. Most books deal with special topics or argue for particular points of view on a variety of subjects, and they have not yet been synthesized. For an introduction to the *Koran*, see Watt-Bell (item 510).

E. HADITH

514. Guillaume, Alfred. **The Traditions of Islam: An Introduction to the Study of the Hadith Literature.** Beirut, Khayats, 1966. (Repr. of 1924 ed.). 184p. bibliog. index. LC 66-6587 rev. 2. BP 135.G8 1966. DDC 297.124.

[P1, C1, S1] Still the only general introduction in English for the uninitiated reader. It is a general history and discussion of the nature, literature, and study of the oral traditions of the Prophet Muhammad, which have become almost canonical in religious authority. Includes special excursus concerning Muhammed in the traditions, the Caliphate in the Hadith, etc., with a purely illustrative selection from the number one collection, the *Sahih* of al-Bukhari. The classic work on Hadith by a Western scholar, which should be read after the secondary works in this section, is Goldziher (item 489).

Other works on the Hadith include:

Juynboll, G. H. A. **The Authenticity of the Tradition Literature: Discussions in Modern Egypt.** Leiden, E. J. Brill, 1969. 171p. LC cataloging n.a.

Wensinck, Arendt Jan. **A Handbook of Early Muhammadan Tradition Alphabetically Arranged.** Leiden, E. J. Brill, 1927. 268p. LC 27-12713. BP 135.W4.

515. al-Ḥakim al-Nīsābūrī, Muḥammad ibn ᶜAbd Allāh (933-1014). **An Introduction to the Science of Tradition, Being al-Madkhal ilā Maᶜrifat al-Iklil.** Ed. with introd., tr., and notes by James Robson. London, Royal Asiatic Society of Great Britain and Ireland; distr. Luzac, 1953. 54, 48p. (Oriental Translation Fund Publications. New ser., v. 39). o.p. LC 64-44497. PJ 408. 06 n.s. vol. 39.

Includes Arabic text. Discusses the early collections of Hadith and particularly the criteria for judging sound and unsound traditions. These criteria involve the line of transmitters of Hadith, according to their authoritativeness—these oral traditions of and about the Prophet and his companions and their immediate successors were passed down orally from memorizer to memorizer, scholar to scholar, and became a most important basis for Islamic law. The authenticity of each tradition was judged on the basis of the reliability of the memorizers and the number of gaps in the line of transmission, which was traced back to the initial witness of the event described in the tradition. This book is the introduction to the author's collection of Hadith.

516. Muslim ibn al-Ḥajjāj al-Qushayrī (ca. 821-875). **Sahih Muslim: Being Traditions of the Sayings and Doings of the Prophet Muhammad as Narrated by His Companions and Compiled under the Title al-Jami'-us-Sahih by Imam Muslim.** Tr. by 'Abdul Hamid Siddiqi. Lahore, Sh. Muhammad Ashraf; distr. Columbia, Mo., South Asia Books, 1971-1973. 3v. $30.00. LC 72-930977.

[C3] An adequate translation of the second most prestigious canonical collection of Hadith, with hundreds of often very informative explanatory footnotes. Arranged by topic. The translation omits the chains of transmitters (except for the ultimate authority or two of each item), which made the original texts difficult to read. The thousands of traditions deal with hundreds of questions on all aspects of daily and religious life, which were raised when the Prophet himself was no longer available for decision, and record the recollections of those around Muhammad as to what he did in similar cases, to serve as an indication as to what was the proper belief and behavior and as precedent for future decisions. This translation makes available to the general reader a source that provides great insight into the times of Muhammad and his immediate successors, and a basic document as important as the *Koran* itself in studying Islam.

Another English translation of a standard collection is:

al-Khaṭīb al-Tibrīzī, Muḥammad Ibn ᶜAbd Allāh (fl. 1337). **Mishkāt al-Maṣābih.** Tr. by James Robson, Lahore, Shaikh Muhammad Ashraf, 1960-1965. 4v. in 5. (1453p.). LC SA66-8109. BP 135.A2K435.

517. al-Nawawī (1233-1377). **[Riyāḍ al-Ṣāliḥin]. Gardens of the Righteous—Riyadh as-Salihin of Imam Nawawi.** Tr. from Arabic by Muhammad Zafrullah Khan. New York, Rowman and Littlefield, 1975. LC n.a. BP 135.A2 N363 1975.

[P1, C1] A selection of about 1,800 Hadith from several classical collections, especially al-Bukhari and Muslim, arranged by topic. One of the most widely known collections, it is very typical of the concise compilations made for students and lesser scholars by a great medieval Muslim scholar. A basic work.

518. Siddīqī, Muḥammad Zubayr. **Hadith Literature, Its Origin, Development, Special Features and Criticism.** Calcutta, Calcutta University; distr. Columbia, Mo., South Asia Books, 1961. 211p. index. $7.50. LC SA63-370. BP 135.S5.

[C2, S1] An orthodox Muslim view of its origin and development, with a critique and refutation of the Western scholarly views that are offensive to orthodox Muslims. It discusses the main collections, reasons for the development of the Hadith and how they came to survive, the Hadith sciences and their standard works, Muslim methods of Hadith criticism, and the tradition collectors themselves, including a list of the 123 main ones and biographies. A useful work on an important subject.

F. THEOLOGY AND PHILOSOPHY

519. al-Ash^{c}ari, ^{c}Ali ibn Isma^{c}il (873?-935?). al-Ibanah ^{c}an Uṣul ad-Diyanah. (The Elucidation of Islamic Foundations.) A translation from Arabic with introd. and notes by Walter C. Klein. New York, Krause Reprint Corporation, 196-? (Repr. of 1940 ed.). 143p. bibliog. indices. $8.00pa. LC n.a. BP 166.A733. DDC 397.

This work of the famous theologian is a polemical assortment of arguments intended to provide ammunition for rebuttals by the orthodox against unorthodox writers. In fairly comprehensible form it provides the author's basic views on various issues. The 42-page introduction is useful.

520. al-Ash^{c}ari, ^{c}Ali, ^{c}Ali ibn Isma^{c}il (873?-935?). [al-Luma^c]. The Theology of al-Ash^{c}ari: The Arabic Texts of al-Ash^{c}ari's Kitab al-Luma^c and Risalat Istihsan al-Khawḍ fi ^{c}Ilm al-Kalam. With briefly annotated translations and appendices containing material pertinent to the study of al-Ash^{c}ari. Tr. by Richard J. McCarthy, S. J. Beirut, Imprimerie Catholique, 1953. 275, 109p. bibliog. index. LC 58-42943. BP 161.A7 1953. DDC 297.

al-Ash^{c}ari was the founder of the chief school of thought in Islamic scholastic theology. He legitimized the use of the rational method in theology and actually founded Islamic scholasticism, by resolving a number of troublesome questions. Unfortunately, few of his works have survived. These two are general "popular" works explicating some of his main ideas. *Istihsan* justifies the use of Kalam (rational method used by Muslim philosophers, which theologians previously had condemned) in theology. The appendices contain an abridgement of Ibn ^{c}Asakir's apologia for Ash^{c}arism, and two creeds from two of his works presented for purposes of comparison in parallel columns. A basic work.

521. Averröes (1126-1198). Tahafut al-Tahafut (The Incoherence of the Incoherence). Tr. from Arabic by Simon Van den Bergh. London, Luzac, 1954. 2v. (E. J. W. Gibb Memorial, N. S., 19). (UNESCO Collection of Great Works. Arabic Series). LC 55-4157. PJ 709.G62 vol. 19 [B753.G33T533].

A systematic rebuttal of al-Ghazali's *Incoherence of the Philosophers* (item 529). Volume 1 is the text, Volume 2 the notes. This is considered to be the key source for understanding Averroes' philosophy and theology, being an exposition of his basic ideas written late in life. A very technical work for advanced students and the largest collections.

Other translations of his works include:

The Philosophy and Theology of Averroes, Tractata. Tr. from Arabic by Mohammad Jamil-ur-Rehman. Baroda, A. G. Widgery, 1921. 308p. LC 35-22532. B 749.A4E55.

On the Harmony of Religions and Philosophy. Tr. with introd. and notes, and an extract from Kitab al-Kashf ^{c}An Manahij al-Adilla, by George F. Hourani. London, Luzac, 1961. 128p. LC 63-5506. PJ 709.G62 v. 21 [B 749.F22E54]. There are also several commentaries on the Greek philosophers.

522. Avicenna (980-1037). Avicenna on Theology. Selected and tr. by A. J. Arberry. London, John Murray, 1951. 82p. index. (The Wisdom of the East Series). o.p. LC 51-11811. B 751.A4 E5. DDC 189.3.

Contains extracts from the medieval philosopher's autobiography, his biography by his pupil al-Juzjani, and various of the master's writings concerning the nature of God, predestination, prophecy, prayer, and the after-life. A useful, readable addition to textual source collections (cf. items 585, 586, 590).

Other translations include:

A Compendium on the Soul. Tr. from Arabic by Edward Abbott Van Dyck. Verona, Italy, Stamperia di N. Paderno, 1906. 94p. LC 6-39840. B 751.04 E2.

Avicenna's Psychology: An English Translation of Kitab al-Najat, Book II, Chapter VI with Historico-Philosophical Notes . . . by F. Rahman. London, Oxford University Press, 1952. 127p. bibliog. LC 52-3818. B751.N33R3. DDC 189.3.

Morewedge, Parviz. **The Metaphysica of Avicenna (ibn Sina): A Critical Translation-Commentary of the Fundamental Arguments in Avicenna's Metaphysica in the Dānish nāma-i ^cAlā'i (The Book of Scientific Knowledge).** New York, Columbia University Press, 1973. 336p. LC 73-1464. ISBN 0-231-03597-7. B 751.Z7M67. DDC 189'.5.

The Life of Ibn Sina: A Critical Edition and Annotated Translation. By William E. Gohlman. Albany, State University of New York Press, 1974. LC 73-6793. ISBN 0-87395-226-X. B 751.A5 S5 1974.

523. al-Dawānī, Jalāl al-Dīn Muhammad ibn As^cad (15th cent.). **[Lavāmi^c al-Ishrāq]. Practical Philosophy of the Muhammadan People, Exhibited in the Professed Connexion with the European, So as to Render Either an Introduction to the Other; Being a translation of the Akhlāk-i-Jalāly, the Most Esteemed Ethical Work of Middle Asia.** From the Persian of Pakir Jāny Muhammad Asaad (with references and notes) by W. F. Thompson. London, Oriental Translation Fund of Great Britain and Ireland, 1839. 69, 496p. (Oriental Translation Fund). LC 11-14052 rev. PJ 408.06. [B 753.D32E7].

A treatise on Islamic ethics—personal and political—covering the virtues and vices; equity; acquiring the virtues; cure of mental diseases; why man requires a home; home economics (in the mid-twentieth century sense!); management of wives and children; parental rights; management of domestics; affection. Also covers the State—classes of society, government of the Kingdom, conduct of rulers; friendship; and the proprieties of relations with other men. Some of the topics covered are different from those covered in other treatises listed in this *Guide.*

524. Donaldson, Dwight Martin. **Studies in Muslim Ethics.** London, SPCK; distr. Naperville, Ill., Alec R. Allenson, 1953. 304p. bibliog. index. $9.00. LC 53-3598. ISBN 0-281-01159-1. BJ 1291.D65. DDC 170.

[C2] In Islam there is relatively little formal literature on philosophical ethics. Instead, the ideas are expressed by a wide variety of methods, forms, and types of works for wider audiences than just philosophers. Donaldson deals with early Arab virtues and the literature in which they were expressed; the Koran; principles found in the Hadith; philosophical ethics; Ibn Miskawayhi's manual of ethics, *Fi Tahdhib al-Akhlaq* (item 533); al-Ghazali's ideas; Sufi ethics; modern interpretation. This scholarly work is the only systematic detailed book on the subject in English.

525. Fakhry, Majid. **A History of Islamic Philosophy.** New York, Columbia University Press, 1970. 427p. index. (Studies in Oriental Culture, No. 5). $15.00. LC 71-110144. ISBN 0-231-03231-5. B 741.F23 1970. DDC 181'.07.

[P1, C1, S1] A general introduction to key figures and trends in Islamic philosophy, with some reference to theology, particularly as it relates to the rise of philosophy; Sufism; illuminationism; the religion's reaction to Islamic theology and its yield of great figures in Islamic thought. It concludes with a brief chapter on the modern period. The reader should have some background in philosophy before turning to this book, as far as the concepts and ideas go, but the general reader will find information on how Islamic philosophy came about and the dynamics of Islamic civilization. As a result, this book, the best in the field, is worth perusing, even if the reader is not interested in philosophy *per se.* A mastery of Watt (item 545) will help the reader benefit from Fakhry.

526. al-Fārābī. **Alfarabi's Philosophy of Plato and Aristotle.** Tr. from Arabic with introd. by Muhsin Mahdi. New York, Free Press of Glencoe, 1962. 158p. index. (Agora Editions). o.p. LC 62-11856. B753.F33P53. DDC 180. Paperback: Cornell University Press, 1969. (C.P. 72). $1.95. ISBN 0-8014-9072-3.

al-Farabi's own views are given in the first section, "The Attainment of Happiness"; there is a brief section called "The Philosophy of Plato" and a long section on the philosophy of Aristotle. Not representative of Islamic philosophy as such, but basic for the study of al-Farabi. Probably too specialized for any but the most comprehensive collection (cf. item 587).

527. al-Fārābī. **Fusūl al-Madanī; Aphorisms of the Statesman.** Ed. with English tr., introd. and notes by D. M. Dunlop. Cambridge, England, Cambridge University Press, 1961. 208p. (Oriental Publications, No. 5). o.p. LC 61-2289. PN 6277.A7F3, 1961. DDC 892.78.

Presents al-Farabi's ideas on politics and related matters: happiness and its pursuit; characterizations of rulers and states falling short of the ideal; the virtuous ruler; wisdom; conduct of life; family; knowledge and its types and virtues. Many of the "aphorisms" are half a page or more in length. It is actually a philosophical work dealing with justice and injustice, soul, intellect, human nature, etc., as part of the theory of political philosophy. Contains Arabic text and translation.

528. al-Ghazzālī (1058-1111). **The Faith and Practice of al-Ghazālī.** Tr. from Arabic by W. Montgomery Watt. London, George Allen and Unwin; distr. New York, Orientalia, 1967. (c. 1953). 155p. index. (Ethical and Religious Classics of East and West). $3.75. LC 53-8071. ISBN 0-87902-060-1. B753.G33M83. DDC 189.3.

[C2] Translations of two works by the Muslim master: 1) *Munqidh Min al-Dalal (Deliverance from Error)*, which is his spiritual autobiography as a Sufi; 2) *The Beginning of Guidance*, which is the introduction to *Ihya' ᶜUlum al-Din* (item 532). Two basic works in a readable version (cf. items 592, 595, 596).

529. al-Ghazzālī (1058-1111). **al-Ghazali's Tahafut al-Falasifah.** Tr. from Arabic by Sabih Ahmad Kamali. Lahore, Pakistan Philosophical Congress; distr. New York, Orientalia, 1963. 267p. bibliog. index. (Pakistan Philosophical Congress Publication No. 3). $6.00. LC SA-3167. ISBN 0-87902-054-7. B 753.G33T33 1963.

al-Ghazzali's *The Incoherence of the Philosophers* is a polemic which denies that philosophy provides all necessary knowledge, or indeed any knowledge at all, of God: logic cannot prove religion, which is unknowable. A basic document in Islamic philosophy and theology (cf. item 521).

530. al-Ghazzālī (1058-1111). **[Kīmiyā-yi Saᶜādat]. The Alchemy of Happiness.** Tr. from Hindustani by Claud Field. London, John Murray; distr. New York, Orientalia, 1964. (orig. 1910). (Wisdom of the East). 115p. $1.50. LC A10-1752. ISBN 0-87902-055-5. B 753.G33A2.

Sufi religious life: knowledge of self, God, this world and the next world; music; poetry and dancing as aids in religious life; self-examination; recollection (*dhikr*) of God and the saints; the role of marriage as help or hindrance to satisfactory religious life; the characteristics of the good life; love of God and tests of sincerity.
Another translated work of the master:
Ghazālī's Book of Counsel for Kings. [Naṣīhat al-Mulūk]. Tr. by F. R. C. Bagley. London, Oxford University Press, 1964. 197p. LC 64-56118. JC 393.A3 G453. DDC 321.61.

531. al-Ghazzālī (1058-1111). **The Book of Knowledge, Being a Translation with Notes of the Kitāb al-ᶜIlm of al-Ghazzālī's Ihyā' ᶜUlūm al-Din.** By Nabih Faris. Lahore, Sh. Muhammad Ashraf; distr. New York, Orientalia, 1970. (orig. 1962). 236p. $5.95. LC SA 63-707. ISBN 0-87902-106-3. B 753.G33I33 1962.

The first book of the first quarter of al-Ghazzali's masterwork (item 532). It deals with the value of learning, instruction, and knowledge; evaluation of the branches of knowledge; the science of religion; polemics and theology (*kalam*); the proprieties of student-teacher relations (duties and etiquette); the evils of knowledge; determining the distinguishing features of the learned man; the nature of intellect. A basic work.
Other portions of the *Ihya'* have been translated into English as follows:
Book 2. The Foundations of the Articles of Faith. Tr. by N. A. Faris. Lahore, Muhammad Ashraf, 1963. 144p. LC SA64-2381. BP 177.G513.

Book 3. The Mysteries of Purity. Tr. by N. A. Faris. Lahore, Muhammad Ashraf, 1966. 96p. LC 70-932940. BP 184.4.G47132 1966.

Book 4. Worship in Islam. Tr. by Edwin Elliott Calverly. Madras, The Christian Literature Society for India, 1925. 242p. LC 36-17930 rev. BP 184.3.G513.

Book 5. **The Mysteries of Almsgiving.** Tr. by N. A. Faris. Beirut, American University of Beirut, 1966. 96p. LC 77-3240. Repr.: Lahore, Sh. Muhammad Ashraf, 1974.

Book 9. **Ghazali on Prayer.** Tr. Kojiro Nakumara. Tokyo, University of Tokyo, Institute of Oriental Culture, 1973. 134p. LC 73-178046. BP 184.3.G513 1973. DDC 297'.4'3.

Book 33. **Al-Ghazali's Book of Fear and Hope.** Leiden, E. J. Brill, 1962. 104p. LC 68-37118. BP 166.3.G4813. DDC 297'.2.

532. al-Ghazzali (1058-1111). **The Revival of the Religious Sciences: A Translation of the Arabic Work Ihya' cUlum al-Din.** By Bankey Behari. Farnham, Surrey, England, Sufi Publishing Company, 1972. xliv, 432p. £2.50. LC n.a. ISBN 0-900217-03-0. B753. G33I43 1972.

An abridged translation of the magnum opus of one of the greatest Muslim thinkers. It is to a great extent a Sufi work, most of this abridgement being comprised of Part 4. "The Pathway to Salvation." Many portions of the massive work have been translated into English by a variety of scholars in many countries, and they warrant acquisition by larger collections (cf. item 531). This is the single most important work in the process of uniting Islamic scholastic theology and mysticism, revivifying Islamic theology and bringing formal intellectualism into contact with living, spiritual religion; basing the practical implications of theology and mysticism, as well as keeping them in balance on a thorough grounding of religious morality—purification against vice; and giving a spiritual basis to the legal aspects of Islam and Islamic pragmatism. In this work, in other words, al-Ghazali gave Islam that total balance of all aspects of religion and religious life that keeps a religion alive and on an even keel when maintained; when that balance is lost and one aspect comes to be emphasized dogmatically over the others by some devotees, other aspects are stressed, in reaction, with like fanaticism by other members of the faith, and the religion falters because it loses its basic unity and essence.

533. Ibn Miskawayh, Ahmad ibn Muhammad (d. 1030). **The Refinement of Character.** A tr. from Arabic of **Tahdhib al-Akhlaq,** by Constantine K. Zurayk. Beirut, American University of Beirut; distr. New York, Syracuse University Press, 1968. 221p. index. $8.00. LC 78-258655. ISBN 0-8156-6012-X. BJ 1291.I2713.

One of the few treatises on philosophical ethics, emphasizing moral discipline.

534. Ibn Tufayl, Muhammad ibn cAbd al-Malik (d. 1185 or 1186). **Ibn Tufayl's Hayy ibn Yaqzan, A Philosophical Tale.** Tr. with introd. and notes by Lenn Evan Goodman. New York, Twayne Publishers, 1972. 246p. $6.50. LC 74-169633. B 753.I53R53 1972. DDC 181.

This is a readable translation of a classic work on Islamic philosophy and mysticism, in the form of an allegory about a man who grows up alone from infancy on an island and discovers the way to union with God. Goodman has written a 91-page introduction that analyses the work, and has 70 pages of very informative notes on the text, which cover a wide range of material.

See also:

Hawi, Sami S. **Islamic Naturalism and Mysticism: A Philosophic Study of Ibn Tufayl's Hayy Yaqzan.** Leiden, E. J. Brill, 1974. 282p. LC 74-171187. ISBN 90-04-03812-4. B753.I53R643. DDC 181'.07.

535. Lerner, Ralph, and Muhsin Mahdi, eds. **Medieval Political Philosophy: A Source Book.** Ithaca, N.Y., Cornell University Press, 1972. (c. 1963). 532p. bibliog. index. (Cornell Paperbacks. Agora Paperback Editions). $4.95. LC 72-4326. ISBN 0-8014-9139-8. JA 82.L4 1972. DDC 320.9'02.

Twenty-five selections, each with an introduction. Included are ten Muslim writings by al-Farabi, Avicenna, Averroes, etc.; five Jewish writings, particularly Maimonides; and ten selections from Christian sources (Aquinas, Bacon, Dante, etc.).

536. Macdonald, Duncan Black. **Development of Muslim Theology, Jurisprudence and Constitutional Theory.** New York, Russell & Russell, 1965. (Repr. of 1903 ed.). 386p. index. $9.00. LC 65-18818. ISBN 0-8462-0647-1. BP 161.M3 1966. DDC 297.

[P1, C1, S1] A history of the principles of government, law, and theology in Islam, particularly the formal theories. Outdated, but an expert description and analysis. It is elementary enough to facilitate understanding by a beginner, and it has not been completely superseded as a good introduction to a complicated subject.

537. Muḥammad ᶜAbduh (1849-1905). **[Risālat al-Tawḥid]. The Theology of Unity.** Tr. from Arabic by Kenneth Cragg and Ishaq Musa'ad. New York, Hillary House; distr. New York, Humanities Press, 1966. 164p. index. $6.25. LC 66-70498. BP 166.M7513. DDC 297.2.

A key work from the main figure in the movement to modernize Islam in Egypt, it was an instrument in his attempt to revivify Islam on a solid basis, to shed rigid traditionalism, and to reassert the oneness of God in all its absoluteness against the competition of Western ideas. For more comprehensive collections (cf. Adams, item 583).

538. al-Rāzī, Fakhr al-Dīn Muḥammad ibn ᶜUmar (1149 or 1150-1210). **Imām Rāzī's ᶜIlm al-Akhlāq.** English tr. of his **Kitāb al-Nafs wa'l-Rūḥ wa Sharḥ Quwāhumā,** with introd. and commentary by Saghir Ḥasan Maᶜṣūmi. Islamabad, Pak., Islamic Research Institute; distr. Columbia, Mo., South Asia Books, 1969. 334p. index. $5.75. LC 72-930000. BJ 1291.R3513.

One of the few extant formal philosophical works on ethics, covering the universal ethical principles and the nature of man's various appetites. Includes an introduction on the life and importance of the great polygraphic author.

539. Rosenthal, Erwin Isak Jacob. **Political Thought in Medieval Islam: An Introductory Outline.** Cambridge, England, Cambridge University Press, 1958. 323p. index. ₤2.80. LC 58-14799. JA 82.R6. DDC 320.95.

[P1, C1, S1, S2] A basic survey of the ideas on government and the Caliphate, law and religion by political writers and philosophers. It discusses Ibn Khaldun's theory, the Platonic legacy, and the individual philosophers: al-Farabi, Avicenna, Avempace (Ibn Bajja), Averroes (Ibn Rushd), al-Dawwani, etc. Emphasis is on philosophical, ethical, moral, and religious aspects; the place of political thought in Islamic philosophy; and the connection between religion and politics in Islam. The connection between religion and politics is a vital point in understanding Islamic theory, because Islam is all-embracing: the Caliphate is partly a religious office; Islamic law comprehends both positions in prayer and sales transactions, to give but two examples. This book is a necessary introduction to works on the modern period such as Hourani (item 121), Aziz Ahmad (item 573), etc., because there is a great deal of continuity in the Muslim concerns about religion and government.

540. Schacht, Joseph. **An Introduction to Islamic Law.** Oxford, Clarendon Press, 1964. 304p. bibliog. glossary. index. $10.25. LC 64-6944. ISBN 0-19-825161-0. LC class: LAW. DDC 348.97.

[B, P1, C1] The initial 111-page section on the history of Islamic law is one of the best introductions. The rest of the book is a systematic outline: the "roots" of Islamic law, or methods of interpretation; persons, property, obligations, contracts, family, inheritance, and marriage; penal law and procedure; the nature of Islamic law. Extremely useful for its extensive definitions and use of the Arabic legal vocabulary. A basic work, but technical for the reader unfamiliar with legal concepts, and very hard to read. To be read after Levy (item 199). It should be noted that Schacht's views on the development of the Hadith and law often are rejected by and indeed are offensive to Muslims. This is because they are based on older Western approaches and perceptions as well as on Christian prejudices, rather than Muslim conceptions, which are often governed more by faith and tradition than Western-style skepticism and critical study. Schacht also appears to state his conclusions and some of his declarations too strongly, with the result that some points are overemphasized, while some still-open questions are answered as though a definite statement were possible. The basic work on classical Islamic law. On modern Islamic law,

Asaf Ali Asghar Fyzee's *Outlines of Muhammadan Law* (3rd ed. London, Oxford University Press, 1964. 509p. LC 64-57146, LC class: LAW) is the best treatment, utilizing as examples cases from Muslim courts of India and Pakistan.

Other works of particular note are:

Anderson, J. N. D. **Islamic Law in the Modern World.** New York, New York University Press, 1959. 106p. LC 59-13110. LC class: LAW.

Coulson, Noel James. **Conflicts and Tensions in Islamic Jurisprudence.** Chicago, University of Chicago Press, 1969. 126p. LC cataloging n.a.

Coulson, Noel James. **A History of Islamic Law.** Edinburgh, Edinburgh University Press; distr. Chicago, Aldine Publishing Company, 1964. 264p. bibliog. LC n.a. ISBN 0-202-15004-6. DS 36.85.I8 no. 2. Not a systematic history, but it tries to deal with the nature of Islamic law, its gaps and its conflicts with secular law.

Khadduri, Majid. **War and Peace in the Law of Islam.** Baltimore, Johns Hopkins Press, 1955. 321p. LC 55-8427. BP 175.J5K45. A basic work, particularly on Islamic society's relations with other societies.

Maḥmaṣāni, Ṣubḥi Rajab. **Falsafat al-Tashri^c fi al-Islām: The Philosophy of Jurisprudence in Islam.** Tr. by F. J. Ziadeh. Leiden, E. J. Brill, 1961. 217p. bibliog. LC class: LAW. LC 65-89328.

al-Marghināni, ^{c}Ali ibn Abi Bakr (d. 1196 or 1197). **The Hedaya; Or, Guide, A Commentary on the Mussulman Laws.** Tr. by Charles Hamilton. Lahore, Premier Book House, 1963. 783p. LC 70-7142. LC class: LAW. DDC 340.

Ramadan, Said. **Islamic Law: Its Scope and Equity.** London, P. R. Macmillan, 1961. 171p. LC 61-19100. LC class: LAW. By a leading member of the Muslim Brotherhood (Egypt).

al-Shāfi^{c}i, Muḥammad ibn Idris (767 or 768-820). **Shāfi^{c}i's Risāla.** Tr. by Majid Khadduri. Baltimore, Johns Hopkins Press, 1961. 376p. bibliog. LC 61-13203. LC class: LAW. DDC 348.97.

Schacht, Joseph. **The Origins of Muhammadan Jurisprudence.** Oxford, Clarendon Press, 1950. 348p. bibliog. LC 51-9528. LC class: LAW. DDC [347.0953] 349.53. A detailed, technical work for more advanced readers.

541. Sharif, Mian Mohammad, ed. **A History of Muslim Philosophy, with Short Accounts of Other Disciplines and the Modern Renaissance in Muslim Lands.** Wiesbaden, Otto Harrassowitz; distr. New York, International Publications Service, 1963-1966. 2v. (1792p.). bibliog. index. $65.00/vol. LC 68-114939. B 741.S468. DDC 181'.07. (Also: London, Luzac, 1964-1966. 2v. £12.00/vol. LC n.a.)

A systematic survey consisting of chapters by various authorities, mostly Muslims, from Pakistan and the Near East, plus a few Western specialists. The first 984 pages cover theology and philosophy, the rest cover the arts, literature, historiography, law, the sciences. The final 400 pages cover the modern period and the influence of Islamic thought on the "renaissance" in the Muslim countries, including India-Pakistan, the Near East, and North Africa, with a 130-page index. Most of the chapters on theology and philosophy deal with individual thinkers, their lives, works, ideas, and significance. Too much for beginners, but useful for students acquainted with Western philosophy, and with works in this *Guide*. All but larger collections should probably purchase Fakhry (item 525), Macdonald (item 536) and Watt (item 545), as well as other items, though Sharif provides more detail and is generally more comprehensive.

542. al-Taftāzāni, Mas^{c}ud ibn ^{c}Umar (1322-1389?). [Sharḥ al-^{c}Aqā'id al-Nasafiyah]. **A Commentary on the Creed of Islam. Sa^{c}d al-Din al-Taftāzāni on the Creed of Najm al-Din al-Nasafi.** Tr. with introd. and notes by Earl Edgar Elden. New York, Columbia University Press, 1950. 187p. bibliog. index. o.p. LC 50-5160 rev. BP 161.N363T34. DDC 297.

Typical of a long theological commentary on a text, which in this case is a brief creedal statement of the basic beliefs and doctrines. It illuminates the classical Muslim style of exposition and is a useful text in Ash^{c}arite Islamic theology.

543. Tritton, Arthur Stanley. **Muslim Theology.** London, Luzac, 1947. 218p. bibliog. index. (James G. Forlong Fund, V. 23). o.p. LC 48-13392. BP 161.T7. DDC 297.

[C2] An outline survey: Koran, sects, stages in the development of theology, basic issues, the Mu^ctazilites and their doctrines and philosophical approach; reaction against Mu^ctazilite rationalism and the period and trends up to the development of the orthodox position. Also, the period to al-Ghazali (eleventh-twelfth century). There is little generalization about trends except in brief introductions to the individual thinkers'; ideas on specific subjects. There are also notes on their ideas in areas not covered by other writers. It is hard going for the general reader because of its conciseness and lack of narrative flow, but it is the most systematic treatment we have. It should be read after the introductory works in this *Guide.*
Another very useful work is:

Nasr, Seyyed Hossein. **An Introduction to Islamic Cosmological Doctrines: Conceptions of Nature and Methods Used for Its Study by the Ikhwān al-Ṣafā', al-Birūni, and Ibn Sinā.** Cambridge, Mass., Belknap Press of Harvard University Press, 1964. 312p. bibliog. LC 64-13430 rev. B 745.C6 N3. DDC 113.

544. al-Ṭūsi, Naṣir al-Din ibn Muḥammad (1201-1274). [Akhlāq-i Nāṣiri]. **The Nasirean Ethics.** Tr. from Persian by G. M. Wickens. London, George Allen and Unwin, 1964. 352p. bibliog. index. (UNESCO Collection of Representative Works). o.p. LC 67-4066. BJ 1291.T7813.

[C1] One of the outstanding works of its kind, which, better than other less systematic items, offers "a conspectus of most of the significant moral and intellectual occupations of the medieval Islamic world." It is one of the few systematic works written on philosophical ethics in the medieval period, most others being on more specific topics or written in more popular, semi-literary fashion. A basic book.

545. Watt, William Montgomery. **Islamic Philosophy and Theology.** Edinburgh, Edinburgh University Press; distr. Chicago, Aldine Publishing Company, 1962. 196p. bibliog. index. (Islamic Surveys, 1). $5.50. LC 62-51017. ISBN 0-202-15010-0. DS 36.85.I8 No. 1. DDC 181.947.

[P1, P2, C1, S1] The origins, growth, and ideas of the intellectual and theological aspects of Islam, until the nineteenth century. Most of the book is devoted to the period until the thirteenth century, with a chapter on Iranian Shiism, one on the period to 1900, and a few pages on the modern era. Much discussion of the heterodox as well as orthodox tendencies and schools of thought, the Hellenistic background, and the key figures. A useful introduction to be read before Fakhry (item 525); comprehensible to the educated general reader. A basic book.

546. Wensinck, Arent Jan (1882-1939). **The Muslim Creed, Its Genesis and Historical Development.** London, Frank Cass; distr. Portland, Ore., International Scholarly Book Services, 197-? (Repr. of 1932 ed.). 304p. bibliog. index. $12.50. ISBN 0-7146-1997-3. BP 161. 1.W4 19. DDC 297.2.

[C2] The first 100 pages consist of an introduction to Islamic theology and its development. The rest is made up of texts of and commentary on catechismic creeds, which illustrate and explain basic Islamic dogmatics in reasonably non-technical language. The reader will need a background on the subject from the basic works listed in this *Guide.* Once he has that, Wensinck's texts and explanations will fill in gaps, particularly on subjects (such as eschatology) that are not discussed in detail in the general works, which deal mainly with more theoretical and semi-philosophical aspects. These creeds are statements written to program the faiths and beliefs of the non-cleric, and they reflect the problems and emphases of the troubled times and the threats to the faith that they were intended to combat.

547. Williams, John Alden, comp. **Themes of Islamic Civilization.** Berkeley, University of California Press, 1971. 382p. bibliog. index. $11.75. LC 78-107659. ISBN 0-520-01685-8. BP 20.W53. DDC 910.03'176'71.

[C1, S3] Certain "themes and archetypal ideas" of Islam that have "moulded Muslim minds and found expression in institutions"; these selections express the convictions behind them. Topics include the community; the perfect ruler; the will of God (Shari^cah, or religious law and duties) and man-God relations; the expected deliverer (Mahdi); jihad (holy war); friends of

God (Sufism). Each topic has selections from various sects and viewpoints and from various eras, including the modern reformers. An excellent work for more advanced students and for medium-sized to larger collections.

G. SUFISM

The main body of literature in English on Sufism consists of translations, selections of translations, and secondary works describing the history and doctrines of Sufism in its medieval, classical age, as well as the modern manifestations and the brotherhoods in various countries. These works comprise most of the material listed in this section. The secondary literature is primarily by scholars, mainly British Orientalists. The works of Idries Shah, and others not included here, are the labor of modern Sufis who seek to impart an understanding of Sufism to the general public by offering it as an alternative, sometimes the only method of personal development. Shah's works listed here are but a sampling of his many similar works, most of which are available in paperback as well as cloth bindings.

548. Abun-Nasr, Jamil M. **The Tijaniyya: A Sufi Order in the Modern World.** London, Oxford University Press, 1965. 204p. bibliog. index. $7.25. LC 65-9539. ISBN 0-19-214932-6. BP 189.7.T5A3. DDC 297.8.

A Moroccan order originating in the late eighteenth century, the Tijaniyya spread throughout North Africa, West Africa, and even into the Near East, including Turkey. The author treats first the life of the founder, then the order's doctrines and way of life. Its branches were active in politics in North Africa, where they cooperated with the French, and in West Africa, where they conquered territory and set up states in Senegal, Mali, Mauritania and Niger. The book traces the order's history under the French occupation in West Africa and Tijaniyya's infiltration into the Near East, and discusses its relations with other Muslims. Useful as a case study of Islam's role in modern history, religion, and politics in the region, and as a study of North African Islam.

549. Arberry, Arthur John. **Sufism: An Account of the Mystics of Islam.** New York, Harper and Row, 1970. 141p. (Harper Torchbooks, TP 1531). $1.60pa. LC n.a. Cataloging for 1951 ed.: LC 51-11267. BP 189.A7. DDC 297. (*BIP* lists a 1956 cloth ed.: distr. New York, Humanities Press. $5.50.)

[P1, C1, S1] An introduction to classical medieval Sufism for the non-specialist with a basic background in Islam, by a foremost Orientalist. It covers the development of Sufism, its theory, orders, practice, and literature. A basic work.

550. Birge, John Kingsley. **The Bektashi Order of Dervishes.** Totowa, N.J., Rowman and Littlefield, 1965. (Repr. of 1937 ed.). 291p. bibliog. illus. index. $12.50. LC n.a. BP 189.7.B4B5. DDC 297. (Also, Mystic, Conn., Lawrence Verry, 1965. $13.75.)

A scholarly general work on this important Turkish Sufi order, which originated in the thirteenth century. Birge first traces the history of the order, which, along with the other orders, was abolished during Ataturk's regime. Then he discusses the doctrines and beliefs, and the differences between this order and other Sufis, particularly the notable Shiite aspects, including devotion to Ali and the Imams; rites and practices, ceremonies; relation of Bektashism to other faiths, from which it absorbed many elements. It has many quotations from Bektashi poetry and other religious texts, illustrations and discussions of their symbols. An important book for more comprehensive collections.

551. Brown, John Porter (1814-1872). **The Darvishes; Or, Oriental Spiritualism.** London, Frank Cass; distr. Portland, Ore., International Scholarly Book Services, 1968. (Repr. of 1927 ed.). 496p. index. (Islam and the Muslim World, No. 5). $14.50. LC 68-114037. ISBN 0-7146-1980-9. BP 189.2.B74 1968. DDC 297'.4.

This is an exceptionally detailed account of the Sufi dervishes, based on diligent field work. It contains a systematic description of the beliefs, customs, clothing, ceremonies, etc., of the various Sufi orders. It also deals with the saints, Persian darvishes, Sufism in Iran, and Shiite Sufism. It includes a Turkish Shiite biography of Ali and has many translations from Persian, Turkish, and Arabic sources. It is a mine of information, though probably too detailed for most collections. Works of love like this one are some of our chief primary sources for the study of the conditions of their times, and they are often much more readable than the more recent scholarly works. They supplement the vernacular works, which so rarely exist in Western translations, and they fill in details and provide perspective as only the non-participant observer can.

552. Gilsenan, Michael. **Saint and Sufi in Modern Egypt: An Essay in the Sociology of Religion.** Oxford, Clarendon Press, 1973. 248p. bibliog. index. $15.25. LC 74-157832. ISBN 0-19-823181-4. BP 189.7.S5G55. DDC 297'.4.

One of the few books on contemporary popular Islam (as opposed to formal, establishment orthodox religion). It focuses on the Sufi brotherhood Hamidiyah Shadhiliyah, which is the most heavily structured brotherhood (particularly in Egypt, where it centers around the Nile Delta and Cairo). The author discusses the founder of the brotherhood and his image as a saint among the various classes of people who adhere to the group. Also, the role and practice of the feast day of the Saint; the structure and rules of the order and its branches; its controls and sanctions (the means by which unity, discipline, and order are maintained, including internal activities, politics, and punishments); social ethics and recruitment of members; attitude toward the world—which is negative; ritual, particularly the *dhikr*, or congregational services; conclusions as to the current social role and relationships of the brotherhood. Although the book systematically presents basic information on the order, the stress throughout is on a psychosocial analysis of its importance for its members, on various aspects of the order's beliefs and practices, on its relation to changes occurring in Egyptian society.

Another source on Sufism in Egypt is:

McPherson, Joseph Williams. **The Moulids of Egypt (Egyptian Saint Days).** Cairo, Ptd. N. M. Press, 1941. 351p. illus. LC A42-4680. BP 189.3.M3. DDC 297. Origins, significance of individual celebrations in Cairo, etc., and information for travellers wishing to view them. A fascinating contribution to the study of popular Islam in the 1930s.

553. al-Hujvīrī, ⁽Alī ibn ⁽Usmān (d. ca. 1072). **The Kashf al-Maḥjūb, the Oldest Persian Treatise on Ṣufiism.** New ed. tr. by Reynold A. Nicholson. London, Luzac, 1936. 443p. index. LC 52-47746. BP 189.H783 1936. DDC 297. (*BIP* lists a 1967 ed.: distr. Mystic, Conn., Lawrence Verry. $10.00.)

The author's purpose was to expound and explain the whole Sufi system—doctrines and practices, regulations, etc. The book includes 105 pages of biographies of famous Sufis. It deals with faith, Sufi sects, gnosis, union with God, purification, prayer. Also, fasting, pilgrimage, companionship, Sufi phraseology and terms; audition, poverty, dress, blame from the community; repentance, contemplation, etiquette, and ethics; rules for marriage and celibacy; *Koran* recitation, poetry and other aspects of aural aid in worship. A basic work.

554. Ibn al-⁽Arabī, Muḥyi al-Dīn (1165-1240). **The Tarjumán al-Ashwáq, a Collection of Mystical Odes.** Tr. from Arabic by R. A. Nicholson. London, Royal Asiatic Society, 1911. 155p. index. (Oriental Translation Fund, New Series, Vol. 20). o.p. LC 44-2477. PJ 408.06 n.s. vol. 20 [PJ 7741.I15T3]. DDC 44-2477.

Sufi poetry by one of the foremost Sufi authors, most of whose works are religious and philosophical prose. This edition contains an introduction, the Arabic text, and English translation, with commentaries on each poem. Probably too much for college collections unless they have a special interest. Landau (item 588) has some excerpts, which is sufficient for most libraries and students (cf. items 584 and 590).

555. al-Kalābādhī, Muhammad ibn Ibrāhīm (10th cent.). **The Doctrine of the Ṣufīs [Kitāb al-Ta⁽arruf li-Madhhab Ahl al-Taṣawwuf].** Tr. from Arabic by Arthur John Arberry. Cambridge, England, Cambridge University Press, 1935. 173p. index. o.p. LC 36-30455. BP 189.K3413. DDC 297. (*BIP* lists a 1966 ed.: distr. New York, Orientalia. $2.75. ISBN 0-87902-195-0.)

A treatise that became "an authoritative textbook on Ṣufī doctrine." This is the third most esteemed work, partly because its main purpose is to show that Sufism is orthodox and not heretical, as many orthodox Muslims had charged. The book had a great influence on the ultimate acceptance of Sufism by orthodox Islam. It contains much on Islamic orthodox dogma. It covers Sufi theology, theory, and the ideas behind their practice: poverty, piety, humility, fear of God, sincerity, love, union, ecstasy, remembrance; gnosis; God's various types of warnings to the Sufis and his favors to them, as well as other topics. A basic work for larger collections.

556. **[Nasreddin Hoca]. The Pleasantries of the Incredible Mulla Nasrudin.** By Idries Shah. London, Jonathan Cape, 1968. 218p. £2.25. LC 78-373323. ISBN 0-224-61311-1. PJ 248.N3A27. DDC 398.22'0956. Paperback: New York, E. P. Dutton, 1972. $1.75. ISBN 0-525-47306-8.

The Hoca (hoja, khojah) is the subject of innumerable anecdotes throughout the Near East, most of them aimed at imparting bits of wisdom, particularly in matters of personal life and human relations. Many of them are quite funny. Shah presents this collection culled from tradition as an entertaining means of teaching the Sufi approach. A delightful addition to any collection.

557. Nicholson, Reynold Alleyne. **The Mystics of Islam.** London, Routledge and Kegan Paul, 1966. (Repr. of 1914 ed.). 184p. bibliog. index. LC 64-57340/CD. ISBN 0-7100-1892-4. BP 189.N49 1966. DDC 297'.4'2.

[P1, C1, S2]   After an introduction on the origins of Sufism, the author treats the Sufi path, illumination and ecstasy; gnosis; divine love, saints and miracles; the unitive state. Illustrated with copious extracts from Sufi writers and poets. Throughout Nicholson makes comparisons with Buddhist concepts. A useful introduction to the higher forms and doctrines, not to its popular aspects. Complementary to Arberry (item 549).

558. Schimmel, Annemarie. **Mystical Dimensions of Islam.** Chapel Hill, University of North Carolina Press, 1975. 514p. bibliog. $14.95. LC 73-16112. ISBN 0-8078-1223-4. BP 189.2.S34. DDC 297'.4.

[B, P1, P2, C1, S1]   The best general work on classical Sufism for students who have read Arberry and Nicholson, by a foremost scholar of the subject. It covers earliest times to the nineteenth century, emphasizing India for the later period. Simply and clearly in the course of a very readable, smooth-flowing narrative, the author introduces a great range of Arabic terminology, concepts, and much information on many Sufi writers, saints, and orders. She imparts the spirit and nature of many aspects of the Sufi experience. She discusses at great length the vast literature of Sufism, from formal treatises to poetry and folk-lore—origin, form, contents, nature, ideas found in each individual work, with some quotations. Besides presenting readably a vast quantity of information, which most scholarly tomes would make a dreadful burden, the author discusses a wide variety of scholarly and other writing on the subject, to such an extent that the book is an excellent handbook for further serious study. It should be noted that the book is not arranged in a formal systematic manner; it discusses individuals and topics when appropriate, within a basically chronological and geo-cultural framework. A basic work for all students of Islam and Near Eastern literature.

559. Shah, Idries, Sayed. **The Sufis.** Garden City, N.Y., Doubleday, 1971. 451p. glossary. (Anchor Books, A 765). $2.50pa. LC n.a. ISBN 0-385-07966-4. BP 189.S38. DDC 181.5.

[P2, C1, S1]   This introduction to the Sufi way attempts to suggest the nature of the Sufi approach. It includes much on the history of Sufism, material on its manifestations in Western literature, and introductions to and citations from its most important thinkers. It also explains the symbolic nature of Sufi literature in considerable detail. The educated reader will be surprised at the interaction of Sufism and medieval Christianity, and at the modern manifestations and interactions that Shah describes. The book offers much food for thought and insights on Islam and Western civilization, and it is generally fascinating reading. Sometimes it appears that Shah goes too far in claiming Sufi influence, but somehow the wide-ranging breadth of Shah's claims with regard to Sufism's influence on Western civilization makes the book that much more stimulating. For all but the smallest collections.

560. Shah, Idries, Sayed. **Caravan of Dreams.** London, Octagon Press, 1968. 207p. £1.75. LC 76-353266. PN 6071.S85S48 1972. DDC 398.2'0956. Paperback: Baltimore, Penguin Books, 1972. (A Penguin Book, 3409). $1.00. LC 71-171351. ISBN 0-1400-3409-9.

A collection of teaching stories, anecdotes, fables, and proverbs, as well as personal experiences and reflections by Shah: "A Red Sea Journey," and "Pilgrimage to Mecca."

561. Shah, Idries, Sayed. **Thinkers of the East.** London, Jonathan Cape, 1971. 208p. £2.10. LC 76-578911. ISBN 0-224-61912-8. PN 6701.S85S52 1972. DDC 181'.5. Paperback: Baltimore, Penguin Books, 1972. (A Penguin Book, 3410). $1.00. LC 79-171353. ISBN 0-1400-3410-2.

More teaching stories and anecdotes. These items, which make up most of Shah's more recent books, are intended to stimulate reflection on life's truths and wisdom, despite the fact that many are quite humorous. Sufism, which is partly a method of perception, involves a thinking, reflecting discipline of the mind. It is a long process of experience much like the process of educating a child in the ways of the world: a constant interaction with stimuli results in the development of predilections that reflect the continuum of the interactive environment in which the child finds himself. This continuum can be controlled and directed in a meaningful fashion. For an adept, the Sufi way is also a guided continuum and interactive environment in which he is always involved and through which he develops. These tales, anecdotes, and stories are chosen to provide the reader with an interactive environment that will lead him toward a certain approach and type of thinking.

562. Shah, Idries, Sayed. **The Way of the Sufi.** New York, E. P. Dutton, 1969. 287p. $6.95; $1.95pa. LC 71-92615. ISBN 0-525-23038-6; 0-525-47261-4pa. BP 189.S388. DDC 297'.4.

Consists mostly of excerpts from the classical authors; excerpts from the works of four major orders (Chishti, Qadiri, Suhrawardi, and Naqshabandi); and various other materials. The 35-page introduction, "The Study of Sufism in the West," is quite useful; it describes the various Western interpretations and approaches, both scholarly and mystical, and the problems of arriving at its true essence. The essay embodies a critique of what has been done so far, with indications of Sufism's modern influence. Concludes with a 15-page section of bibliographical notes, which contain much useful information.

563. Smith, Margaret. **Readings from the Mystics of Islam.** Totowa, N.J., Rowman and Littlefield, 1973. (Repr. of 1950 ed.). 144p. $8.50; $3.25pa. LC n.a. BP 189.23.S64. DDC 297.4.

[C1, S2] Standard, representative selections of Arabic and Persian Sufi writings by the greats of the medieval period; it nicely supplements secondary works on the subject.

564. Trimingham, John Spencer. **The Sufi Orders in Islam.** Oxford, Clarendon Press, 1971. 333p. bibliog. glossary. index. $10.50; $2.95pa. ISBN 0-19-826524-7; 0-19-501662-9pa. LC 77-582513. BP 189.T7. DDC 297.4.

[B, C3] The most detailed formal, systematic work on the mystic orders that have dominated much of Islamic life for centuries. It treats their organization, doctrines, ritual, and ceremonies; the role of Sufism in Islam and Islamic society; and modern Sufism. There are tables showing the relationships and history of the various orders, a very extensive bibliography, and a long glossary of Arabic terms that will be an invaluable aid to the student and researcher. It is a good handbook for further study. As this work is rather technical, beginners should first read works like Arberry (item 549), Nicholson (item 557), and Schimmel (item 558).

H. SHIITES

Shiism is the official religion of Iran, and the sect of half of Iraq's population; it is widespread in India and Pakistan, where its members debate theology very intensely with various orthodox groups and other sects. The Shiites had a considerable importance during the Middle Ages and were embroiled in politics to an extent that upset the peace of *sunnite* (orthodox) governments. They ruled Egypt for a while as the Fatimids (the Ismaili Shiite sect whose modern head is the Agha Khan); they ruled Yemen (Zaidi sect) before the Republic of Yemen was created; other Shiite minority communities are embroiled in Syrian and Lebanese politics today. Our material on the Shiites is all too scanty despite their importance, so librarians should watch for additional works in the future.

565. Donaldson, Dwight Martin. **The Shiite Religion: A History of Islam in Persia and Irak.** London, Luzac, 1933. 393p. bibliog. index. o.p. LC 33-31230 rev. BP 195.S5D6. DDC 297.

[P1, C1, S1] This is the only general work in English; the author is a Western scholar of long residence at Mashhad, the largest Shiite shrine in Iran. Main Shiite differences with orthodox Islam include veneration of Ali as the rightful successor to Muhammad as Caliph, and the descent of the religious authority of Muhammad to Ali and the latter's descendents, the Imams, of which Ali is the first of a total of 12; belief in the disappearance of the last Imam, who will return as the Mahdi, or messiah. Donaldson discusses the question of the Imamate, the question of religious succession, the traditions that rose around Muhammad, Ali, and the various Imams, and the historical events concerning them. The lives, traditions, and significance of the individual Imams are surveyed, and anecdotes concerning each are related. Also discussed are aspects of Shiite history, the collections of Shiite Hadith, the sinlessness of prophets and Imams, prophets and Imams as mediators between God and man, and modern sects of Shiism. The book is out of date and inadequate in various respects, but it is basic because of its uniqueness.

Another source is:

Hollister, John Norman. **The Shi'a of India.** London, Luzac, 1953. LC 54-32595. BP 195.S5H6. Begins with a good introduction on the topic in general.

566. Hasan and Husain (Persian Miracle Play). **The Miracle Play of Hasan and Husain, Collected from the Oral Tradition.** Tr. by Sir Lewis Pelley. Westmead, Farnborough, England, Gregg International Publishers, 1970. (Repr. of 1879 ed.). 2v. £14.00. LC n.a. PJ 6470. H34E5 1970.

The murder of Husayn, son of the first Shiite Imam Ali, and himself the third Imam, at Kerbala, Iraq, in 680 is celebrated on the tenth of the Islamic month of Muharram by the Shiites with a popular outpouring of grief that approaches hysteria. Part of the event is the performance of passion plays (ta^cziyah) that depict the slaughter of Husayn, his family and followers in gruesome detail. The plays are an essential part of popular Shiism, particularly in Iraq and Iran. Pelley has brought a large body of the Ta^cziyah plays together. The book is a basic source on Shiism that belongs in larger collections.

567. Ibn al-Muṭahhar al-Ḥillī, al-Ḥasan ibn Yūsuf (1250-1325). **al-Bâbu'l-Ḥâdi ^cAshar; A Treatise on the Principles of Shi^cite Theology.** With Commentary by Miqdâd-i-Fâdil al-Ḥillī. Tr. from Arabic by William McElwee Miller. London, Royal Asiatic Society, 1928. 104p. index. (Oriental Translation Fund, n.s., Vol. 29). LC 46-33484 rev. PJ 408.06 n.s. vol. 29 [BP 195.S5I2].

A Shiite creed with commentary, which has been used as a textbook by Shiites. One of our few sources on the subject in English. Discusses Allah's positive and privative qualities, his justice; prophecy, Imamate, eschatology. A defensive-reaffirmative work which refers to Sunnite and other theological schools and indicates some of the differences between them and the Shiites. A basic work.

568. Ibn Bābawayh, Muḥammad ibn ^cAlī (d. 991 or 992). **A Shiite Creed.** A translation of Risālatu'l-I^ctiqàdat, by Asaf A. A. Fyzee. London, Oxford University Press, 1942. 144p. indices. LC 47-43961 rev. BP 193.I213. DDC 297.

By one of the foremost scholars of the Shiite religion, one of whose collections of Hadith became a canonical authority for his denomination, this "creed" covers all aspects of Shiite theology—God, creation, soul, death, after-life; Koran and the prophets; infallibility of the prophets; the Mahdi and Imamate; the fate of evildoers; the descendants of Ali. A basic work intelligible to a reader with some background. Most useful for comparing Sunnite and Shiite doctrines.

569. Lewis, Bernard. **The Assassins: A Radical Sect in Islam.** New York, Basic Books, 1968. 166p. illus. index. o.p. LC 68-10967. BP 195.A8L4 1968. DC 297'.822.

After an introductory chapter on the Western discovery of the Assassins during the Crusades and the growth of research on the subject in the nineteenth and twentieth centuries, Lewis discusses their Ismailite origins (the Ismailites are a Shiite sect). He briefly notes Ismailite history and theology, their evangelizing and secret "cell" system of organization; the Fatimid (Ismailite) Caliphate in Egypt; the Druze succession and Nizari offshoot, and Ismailite revival in the form of the fanatic Assassins in Iran in the eleventh century. He details their spread from Iran, the historical conditions in which they diffused into Syria, through Iraq; the murders they committed; and the Crusade period, not long after which they were destroyed as a power. An interesting book on a generally obscure but fascinating subject.

See also:

Lewis, Bernard. **The Origins of Isma'ilism: A Study of the Historical Background of the Fatimid Caliphate.** New York, AMS Press, 1974. (Repr. of 1940 ed.). LC 74-180357. ISBN 0-404-56289-2. BP 195.I5L4 1974. DDC 297'.822.

570. al-Sharif al-Rāḍi, Muḥammad ibn al-Ḥusayn, supposed author (969 or 970-1016). **Nahjul Balagha: Sermons, Letters and Sayings of Hazrath Ali.** Tr. from Arabic by Syed Mohammed Askari Jafery. 2nd ed. Karachi, Khorasan Islamic Centre, 1971. 568p. bibliog. LC 77-932559. BP 193.1.A2S513 1971. DDC 297'.81'0924 [B].

[C3] One of the five chief Hadith collections of the Shiites, for whom Ali is a main figure after Muhammad. A 99-page introduction gives a biography of Ali and the compiler of the collection, and miscellaneous information. Most of the book consists of sermons on a multitude of subjects. Each item has a brief introduction by the translator. A basic text.

571. al-Ṭabāṭabā'i, Muhammad Ḥusayn. [Shiʿah dar Islām]. Shiʿa Islam. Ed. and tr. with introd. and notes by Seyyid Hossein Nasr. Albany, State University of New York Press, 1974. bibliog. LC 74-8289. ISBN 0-87395-272-3; 0-87395-273-1 (microfiche). BP 193.5.T3213. DDC 297'.82.

[P1, C1, S1] Nasr indicates that this is the first in a series of translations of Shiite sources. The second will be al-Tabataba'i's book on the Koran, and the last an anthology of the sayings of the Imams. al-Tabataba'i is a typical traditional Muslim scholar who was asked to write two books in the trilogy. This general work is an authentic Shiite exposition, addressed in fact to his fellow Shiites, rather than to Westerners. As such it is not an objective presentation but is sometimes polemical and sometimes obscure (due to his assumptions of knowledge on the part of the reader and omissions of steps in his arguments). He is trying in part to persuade Shiites in the truth of their faith, which he seeks to fortify. The book opens with the rise of Shiism: Ali and the Umayyad takeover of the Caliphate, the theological reasons for the separate roads taken by Sunnism and Shiism; theological attitudes toward the Umayyad Caliphate; the organization of the Shiite movements; conditions under the Abbasids. The branches of Shiism; Shiite theology—Hadith and Koran; interpretation of these basic documents; use of reasoning, philosophy; key figures such as Hilli, al-Tusi, Mulla Sadra; Shiite Sufism (mysticism). Also, specific aspects of theology such as God, God and man, Muhammad and prophethood, eschatology, the Imamate, and the lives of the Imams. Unfortunately, it does not provide detailed accounts of theological points such as eschatology, in which Western readers would have great interest, nor of the lives of the Imams or the ideas of the main thinkers. Readers should refer first to a general introduction to Islam and Donaldson (item 565). We still need a systematic, comprehensive treatment for an understanding of Shiism.

I. REGIONAL

572. Aziz Ahmad. **An Intellectual History of Islam in India.** Edinburgh, Edinburgh University Press; distr. Chicago, Aldine Publishing Company, 1969. 226p. bibliog. illus. index. (Islamic Surveys, 7). $5.75. LC 69-16010. ISBN 0-202-15014-3. DS 36.85.I8 no. 7. DDC 915.4'0976'7.

[C1] The first section summarizes the history of Islam in India: Sunnism, the Shiite sects; the messianic movements, including Ahmadiyya; Sufism; folk religion; and Muslim education, through the modern period. Most of the rest takes up the religious strains of the literatures, including religious works, histories, and belles-lettres, with a discussion of the Arabic, Persian and Urdu literatures and regional vernacular literatures, and a section on Islamic fine arts. One needs only the most superficial knowledge of publishing trends in Pakistan and India to realize how profound is the influence of Islam and medieval Islamic culture and history even today. This book is not only a contribution to one's knowledge of the wider horizons of Islam, but a useful addition to knowledge of the Subcontinent.

573. Aziz Ahmad. **Islamic Modernism in India and Pakistan, 1857-1964.** London, Oxford University Press, 1967. 294p. bibliog. index. $7.25. LC 67-96907. ISBN 0-19-214955-5. BP 63.I42 A9. DDC 915.4'03.

[C2] This fascinating book deals with landmarks of religious and political thought, mainly through discussions of the individual thinkers. The religious and the political are often inextricably intertwined, but the emphasis varies with the individual, his political situation, and his background. The topic and this book are important because even today some of the hottest religious and religio-political controversy in the Muslim world originates from Pakistan and, to a lesser extent, India. The debate encompasses the form of the state, law reform, theology, the validity of the Koran and the Hadith, and reformism versus traditionalism; it often involves bitter sectarianism. Some of the arguments parallel those taken up in the Near East, and in the past there was a significant interaction of ideas that has continued to some extent today between the Near East and Subcontinent. The arguments to a great extent symbolize and, indeed, discuss explicitly the problem of how to approach the modern world, from a particular perspective: the integrity and validity of extant religion and its compatability with modern civilization. A basic book, to be read after Rosenthal (item 539). Two excellent works complement Ahmad and each other, though strictly speaking they are marginal to the purposes of this *Guide.* Wilfred Cantwell Smith, *Modern Islam in India* (Lahore, Pakistan, Sh. Muhammad Ashraf; distr. Columbia, Mo., South Asia Books, 1969. (Repr. of 1946 ed.). $8.50) is a penetrating, stimulating discussion of the modernist movements and Muslim politics; it does not provide a guide to the key figures and literature as Ahmad does, nor a systematic political history, but suggests, through the use of sweeping generalities and lengthy analysis, the thrust of the various tendencies. It helps the reader understand the ideas and their influence on politics, and the background to the Pakistan movement, as well as the current debate; Smith relates the whole to social conditions, structures, and dynamics. Peter Hardy's *The Muslims of British India* (Cambridge, England, Cambridge University Press, 1972. LC 77-184772. ISBN 0-521-08488-1; 0-521-09783-5pa.) is an interesting detailed account of Muslim politics from 1857 to 1947, the development of Muslim communal consciousness, the theological movements and reform efforts, key individuals, their works and ideas, and their role in the political history of India.

574. Bennigsen, Alexandre, and Chantal Lemercier-Quelquejay. **Islam in the Soviet Union.** New York, Praeger, 1967. 272p. bibliog. index. o.p. LC 67-13872. BP 63.R8 1967. DDC 332'.1'0947.

This is not an account of the religion of Islam and its history in Russia and the Soviet Union, but the political history of Russia's Muslims in the twentieth century: Muslims in the revolution, Soviet nationalities policy and administrative reform, Communism and Islam, and the offensive against Islam. The last third deals with Soviet Islam today, including the religion, the Muslim family and Russian attempts to destroy it, modern conditions and survivals from pre-Soviet life, problems of national consciousness and Russian influence, the relation of the Muslim intelligentsia to Soviet society, particularly as a group that is hostile to socialism. The authors see a potential for the rise of Muslim activism and an increasing importance for the Russian Muslims.

575. Canaan, Taufik. **Mohammedan Saints and Sanctuaries in Palestine.** London, Luzac, 1927. 331p. index. (Luzac's Oriental Religions Series, Vol. 5). o.p. LC 34-13102. BP 65.P3C3. DDC 297.

This is a general treatment of the shrines, their characteristics, structure, location, inscriptions, types of sanctuaries, stories and folklore which grew up about them; holy springs, stones, trees, spirits associated with them and the shrines, rites and practices, processions and festivals, healing properties, vows, oaths, votive objects such as lamps and candles; system of upkeep and volunteerism in caring for shrines; sacrifices, songs; cultus of the saints, their characteristics and miracles; saint-man relations; kinds and lists of saints. A scholarly but readable work of considerable interest, it treats the subject in general terms rather than cataloging the names and locations of the saints and shrines and the specifics of each cult. A basic study on popular Islam and Islam in Palestine.

576. Hasluck, Frederick William (1878-1920). **Christianity and Islam under the Sultans.** New York, Octagon Books, 1973. (Repr. of 1929 ed.). 2v. (877p.). bibliog. index. $37.50. LC 72-13668. ISBN 0-374-93747-8. BP 63.T8H3 1973. DDC 200'.9561.

This is a very detailed account of Islamic popular and folk religion and folklore, and its relation to and with Christianity. Hasluck systematically treats first the shrines used by Christians and Turks, and those of each used by the other. He details the various heterodoxies, pagan cultus and saints of various kinds and their miracles. He also describes closely the Bektashi (Sufi) sect, aspects of popular Christianity, popular traditions about places, people and things, and other customs, to a lesser extent. It is mainly factual and descriptive, rather than general and analytical, rather resembling a handbook intended to serve as the foundation for further research. Too much for most colleges, but it has a wealth of information that is at best difficult to find elsewhere.

577. Ja'far Sharif. **Islam in India; Or, the Qārūn-i-Islam, the Customs of the Musalmāns of India, Comprising a Full and Exact Account of Their Various Rites and Ceremonies from the Moment of Birth to the Hour of Death.** New York, Humanities Press, 1972. (Repr. of 1921 ed.). 374p. index. $13.50. LC 73-160700. ISBN 0-7007-0015-3. BP 63.I4J2813 1972b. DDC 297'.0954.

Written originally in the early nineteenth century, it deals with the Deccan Muslims. It is exceedingly minute in detail, treating birth, death, initiation, birthdays, marriage, prayer, saints and cultus, festivals, magic, amulets, games, costume and jewelry, food, etc. Strictly concerned with ethnological details and popular beliefs, it has nothing on theology or orthodox beliefs and actions. A good example of interaction of Islam and daily life among the masses, and the difference between popular forms and scholastic orthodoxy. Useful for making comparisons with popular Islam in the Near East-North African countries.

578. Lavan, Spencer. **The Ahmadiyah Movement: A History and Perspective.** Delhi, Manohar Book Service; distr. Columbia, Mo., South Asia Books, 1974. 220p. bibliog. index. $9.00. LC 74-901627. BP 195.A5L38 1974. DDC 297'.8.

The first recent scholarly study of the origins of this heterodox sect of Islam. The sect originated in India (Punjab) in the latter nineteenth century and, through increasing missionary activity, has become a force to be reckoned with in various parts of the world—there are mosques in England, the United States, and other countries. Ahmadiyya (to use the LC subject heading) took an active part in Indian-Pakistani politics, engaged in extensive polemics with Christians, other Muslims, and other religions. This book deals with the founder, Mirza Ghulam Ahmad, his religious career and ideas, his claim to be the promised messiah and Mahdi; the doctrine concerning Christ's appearance and death in Kashmir; his polemics with Christian, Hindu, and other Muslims; his role in the attempt to modernize Islam; and the defense of Islam in general against Hindu polemics. It also covers the history of the organization and its role in Indian politics, and Ahmadiyya's methods. The period covered is 1876 to 1936. Unfortunately, there is no material on its spread and status to the present time, but the book is basic for an understanding of the present movement.

579. Trimingham, John Spencer. **The Influence of Islam upon Africa.** New York, Praeger, 1968. 159p. bibliog. index. (Arab Background Series). $6.00. LC 68-26872. BP 64.A1T7. DDC 297.096.

[C1] A general discussion of the historical process of Islam's influence as a religious culture on Africans. Opening with a history of Islam's penetration, it treats the factors in Islam's spread—trade and nomadism—as well as the factors that influenced pagans to accept Islam; changes that occur in accepting Islam; belief, ritual, institutions, social and political structure; legal system; economic life. It describes the religious life, comparing black African accommodations of Islam to the various societies and other differences with orthodox and Arab Islam. It concludes with a chapter on African Islam as it faces the challenge of entering the twentieth century, including the issue of secularism. The author concludes that, at the present, secularism is costing Islam its support and position because it confers on its adherents the benefits that Islam used to confer. It should be noted that Trimingham has been somewhat outdistanced by recent research, which has burgeoned of late, and thus he is definitely not the last word. However, this new material has not been synthesized as yet into a single general work that could truly supersede this book or the author's other works.

Two additional sources are:

International African Seminar, 5th, Zaria, Nigeria, 1964. **Islam in Tropical Africa.** Ed. by I. M. Lewis. London, Oxford University Press, 1966. 470p. bibliog. LC 66-75503. BP 64.A4.S82 1964. DDC 301.4529706.

Kritzeck, James, and William H. Lewis, eds. **Islam in Africa.** New York, Van Nostrand-Reinhold, 1969. 339p. bibliog. LC 68-24666. BP 64.A1K7. DDC 297'.096. Both volumes consist of rather specialized essays.

580. Trimingham, John Spencer. **Islam in East Africa.** Oxford, Clarendon Press, 1964. 198p. index. $7.50. LC 64-6991. ISBN 0-19-826520-4. BP 64.A4E27. DDC 297.09676.

A survey of the historical background, the features of Islam in this particular region, Islamic organization (including differences among the various groups in the area), the details of religious and ritual life from birth to death; sects, popular religion and its pre- and post-Islamic elements, including magic and animism; Islamic society, the relationships of Islam to Bantu institutions and application of Islamic law; influence of Islam on material culture. It also includes a discussion of Islam in the modern states, its problems (such as education, social questions, and changes in the economy), and its future prospects.

581. Trimingham, John Spencer. **Islam in West Africa.** Oxford, Clarendon Press, 1959. 262p. $9.00. LC 59-1238. ISBN 0-19-826511-5. BP 64.A4W4. DDC 297.0966.

A basic work that analyzes the dynamics of Islam's multifaceted influence on all aspects of life in animist Africa, the interaction and mutual influence of animism, Islam, and Western civilization. Covers the supernatural, ideas of human personality, God, man's nature and destiny; Islamic institutions, including calendar, cultus, clerical training, influence of the Pilgrimage, and the Arabic language; the religious orders, etc. It treats at length the local pagan religions, the influence of Islam on social structures; life cycle and rites, social life, and Islam's influence on material culture. The author's other books on African Islam include a history of the particular region under Islam; for West Africa, however, he has prepared a separate volume on that subject: *A History of Islam in West Africa* (London, Oxford University Press, 1970 [Oxford Paperbacks, 223]).

The major work on the subject will likely be:

Willis, John Ralph, ed. **Studies on the History of Islam in West Africa.** London, Frank Cass; distr. Portland, Ore., International Scholarly Book Services, 1975 (forthcoming). 3v. ISBN 0-7146-1737-7. Volume 1 is a history of the penetration and spread of Islam; volume 2 deals with the evolution of Islamic institutions; and volume 3 covers the Arabic literature that resulted, in the context of West African religious and intellectual environment [annotation from catalog blurb].

582. Trimingham, John Spencer. **Islam in the Sudan.** London, Frank Cass; distr. Portland, Ore., International Scholarly Book Services, 197- ? (Repr. of 1949 ed.). 280p. index. $8.50. LC n.a. BP 64.S8T7. DDC 297.09624.

This scholarly work begins by describing the land and the people and tracing the history of the Sudan from early times to the present. It covers the introduction of Islam to the area and discusses Sudanese orthodox Islam, popular religious beliefs and practices (including saint worship), Mahdism, the religious orders, Islamic contacts with paganism, and the influence of Western ideas on Sudanese Islam. Emphasis is on the Arab North, where most Muslims are. A most useful survey.

J. BIOGRAPHY

583. Adams, Charles Clarence. **Islam and Modernism in Egypt: A Study of the Modern Reform Movement Inaugurated by Muhammad ᶜAbduh.** New York, Russell & Russell, 1968. (Repr. of 1933 ed.). 283p. bibliog. index. $8.00. LC 68-25061. BP 80.M8 A63 1968. DDC 297'.61'0924.

This book deals mainly with ᶜAbduh, his life and doctrines. It includes discussions of Rashid Rida, ᶜAbduh's disciple, Rida's modernist periodical *al-Manar*, and some of the younger modernists. ᶜAbduh was a key figure in the movement to make Islam strong through making it compatible with modern—i.e., Western—civilization, which was being brought into Egypt in the latter third of the nineteenth century. He occupied responsible positions in Egypt, after having spent some years in Europe, working in part with al-Afghani on the latter's short-lived but very influential journal in Paris. ᶜAbduh figures prominently in many of the works listed in this *Guide*, and for smaller collections these general works, such as Hourani (item 121) will suffice. However, Adams is more systematically inclusive and will be useful for larger collections.

584. Affifi, Abul Ela. **The Mystical Philosophy of Muḥyid Din-Abnul ᶜArabī.** New York, AMS Press, 1974. (Repr. of 1939 ed.). 213p. bibliog. indices. $12.00. LC 77-180312. ISBN 0-404-56305-1. B 753.I24 A35 1974. DDC 189'.5.

[C2] A somewhat technical work that discusses the philosophical aspects of Ibn al-ᶜArabi's thought. It treats his ontology (metaphysical theory of reality); logos (prophets, Muhammad, saints, the perfect man, prophecies); epistemology (psychology, reason, knowledge and mysticism); religion (ethics and aesthetics, universal religion, punishment and reward, good and evil, eschatology, love and beauty); and the sources of his system. Ibn ᶜArabi wrote no single work that presented his entire system, but the author pieces together his structure from his many extant works. Not only is this a relatively rare work on the subject and therefore a must for larger collections, but it reflects an outline of the problems and topics of Islamic theology and is thus broadly useful for students. It uses and defines some of Ibn ᶜArabi's Arabic terminology.

A profound study is:

Corbin, Henry. **Creative Imagination in the Sufism of Ibn 'Arabi.** Tr. from French. Princeton, N.J., Princeton University Press, 1969. 406p. LC 68-20869. ISBN 0-691-09852-2. B 753.I24 C63. Consists of 101 pages of general introduction to his works and ideas, method, etc., then a study of his "theophonic imagination," and 103 pages of notes. For advanced students.

585. Afnan, Soheil Muhsin. **Avicenna, His Life and Works.** London, George Allen and Unwin; distr. New York, Humanities Press, 1958. 298p. bibliog. index. $7.25. LC 58-3795. B 751.Z7 A6. DDC 189.3.

[C1] A good general discussion for the educated general reader, dealing with the great philosopher's background (preceded by a general historical essay and material on tenth century Iran) and then his work in logic, metaphysics, psychology, religion, medicine, and the natural sciences. There are two concluding chapters on Avicenna's influence in the East and West.

586. Corbin, Henry. **Avicenna and the Visionary Recital.** Tr. from French. New York, Pantheon Books, 1960. 423p. bibliog. index. (Bollingen Series, 66). o.p. LC 59-5335. B 751.R63C623. DDC 189.5.

A discussion, with translations, of Avicenna's mystical "recitals" or allegorical tales, outlining "a phenomenology of the Avicennan symbols in their Iranian context." The "recitals" are: *Hayy ibn Yaqzan*, *Recital of the Bird*, and *Salaman and Absal*, which were written in Persian. Included is a translation of a Persian commentary on *Hayy ibn Yaqzan.* Corbin puts Avicenna in his intellectual context, both philosophical and theological, and discusses his influence in Iran and Europe. An interesting, important work for the advanced student.

587. Hammond, Robert. **The Philosophy of Alfarabi, and Its Influence on Medieval Thought.** New York, Hobson Book Press, 1947. 55p. bibliog. index. o.p. LC 47-5674. B 753. F34H3. DDC 189.3.

The medieval philosopher's logic, metaphysics, cosmology and psychology, ethics, politics, etc. Comparisons of al-Farabi and St. Thomas Aquinas utilize parallel passages from the two thinkers' writings. A readable introduction.

588. Landau, Rom. **The Philosophy of Ibn ᶜArabi.** London, George Allen and Unwin, 1959. 126p. index. (Ethical and Religious Classics of East and West). o.p. LC A60-3317. B 753.I24L3. DDC 181.947.

[C1] A general treatment of the great Sufi philosopher-theologian, his place in Islam and his ideas, followed by discussions of some of his individual works and brief quotations from them. The last 30 pages consists of excerpts from *Tarjuman al-Ashwaq* (item 554).

589. Lings, Martin. **A Sufi Saint of the Twentieth Century: Shaikh Ahmad al-ᶜAlawi, His Spiritual Heritage and Legacy.** 2nd ed., rev. and enl. Berkeley, University of California Press, 1971. 242p. bibliog. index. $8.75; $2.95pa. LC 71-182282. ISBN 0-520-02174-6; 0-520-02486-9pa. BP 80.A54L5 1971b.

One of the few biographies of an Islamic figure, written for the general reader. Shaykh Ahmad al-ᶜAlawi was an Algerian who lived from 1869 to 1934. Lings describes Sufism, presents the Shaykh's autobiographical notes, and gives texts on his life from those who knew him. He then outlines the Shaykh's ideas and provides extracts, with comments, from his writings. The book provides insights into the role of the saints from a different perspective than the general works on Sufism or the ethnological studies.

590. Nasr, Seyyed Hossein. **Three Muslim Sages: Avicenna–Suhrawardi–Ibn ᶜArabi.** Delmar, N.Y., Caravan Books, 1975. (Repr. of 1964 ed.). 185p. bibliog. index. pa. LC 75-14430. ISBN 0-88206-500-9. BP 70.N36 1975. DDC 297'.6 [B].

[C1] The three Muslim thinkers are important in their own right and as representatives of three main schools in Islamic thought: the philosopher scientists, the illuminationists, and the Sufis. Nasr traces their lives and discusses their works, predecessors, successors, the school that each founded, and their general significance. An excellent, very interesting, non-technical introduction to these important figures.

591. Sartain, E. M. **Jalāl al-Din al-Suyūṭi.** Cambridge, England, Cambridge University Press, 1975 (forthcoming). 2v. LC n.a. ISBN 0-521-20633-2 (set); 0-521-20547-6 (v.1); 0-521-20546-8 (v.2).

The first volume, which is in English, consists of a study of al-Suyuti (1445-1505) and his times: his life and personality, his studies and debates with Egyptian scholars, his public life, the relationship of his autobiography (the Arabic edition of which is the object of this set) to the tradition of Arabic biography and autobiography. It also covers the late Mamluk period in Egypt, with an account of academic life and the system of education, and it provides commentary on the Arabic text. al-Suyuti was an orthodox Muslim scholar who wrote on many subjects aside from religion, including history. This autobiography is one of very few written by medieval figures. Volume 2 consists of the Arabic text of the autobiography, based on new manuscripts. [This annotation based on dust jacket blurbs.]

592. Smith, Margaret. **al-Ghazāli, the Mystic: A Study of the Life and Personality of Abū Ḥāmid Muḥammad al-Ṭūsi al-Ghazāli, Together with an Account of His Mystical Teaching and an Estimate of His Place in the History of Islamic Mysticism.** London, Luzac, 1944. 247p. bibliog. index. o.p. LC 45-6554. B 753.G34S6. DDC 921.9.

His life and the opinions of others (including his contemporaries) about him, his style, poetry, personal life (104 pages); Part II treats his mystical teaching, including his sources: God, how to become united with God; mystic path and life; love. Also, his influence on Islam and Sufism and on the Sufi orders; on medieval Christian mysticism; St. Thomas Aquinas, Dante, and Pascal. Concludes with a summary of his teaching and contributions to Sufi doctrines. An interesting book, it is not too technical for the reader with some background. It contains more about the man than Watt (item 595), which is the most recent biography.

See also:

Sherif, Mohamed Ahmed. **Ghazali's Theory of Virtue.** Albany, State University of New York Press, 1975. 205p. (Studies in Islamic Philosophy and Science). LC 71-38000. ISBN 0-87395-206-5; 0-87395-207-3 (microfiche). B 753.G34 S54. DDC 179'.9.

al-Ghazali's ethical thought as shown in his extensive treatment of the virtues and their relation to each other and to the ends of life. Very little has been written on this subject in general or with regard to individual writers in Islam.

593. Smith, Margaret. **An Early Mystic of Baghdad: A Study of the Life and Teaching of Hārith B. Asad al-Muḥāsibī, A.D. 781-A.D. 857.** New York, AMS Press, 1973. (Repr. of 1935 ed.). 311p. bibliog. index. $16.50. LC 76-180379. ISBN 0-404-56324-4. BP 80.M83S6 1973. DDC 297'.896'30924 [B].

His life (of which little is known), his disciplines, his writings, and the sources of his ideas. His teaching on psychology; the theology of asceticism; sin; repentance and mortification; grace and the virtues; the life of prayer; mysticism—gnosis, union with God, fellowship, the beatific vision. Also, his influence and critics; influence on the Ash^cation and later Sufis. Smith believes he influenced Avicenna, al-Hujviri, Suhrawardi, and Ibn al-^cArabi; al-Ghazali admits that al-Muhasibi influenced him. Smith also concludes that, at least indirectly, through the works of the figures named above, al-Muhasibi influenced medieval Spanish, Jewish, and Christian mysticism. An interesting book, one of few books on Islamic figures.

594. Smith, Margaret. **Rābi^ca the Mystic & Her Fellow-Saints in Islam, Being the Life and Teachings of Rābi^ca al-^cAdawiyya al-Qaysiyya of Baṣra, Together with Some Account of the Place of the Woman Saints in Islām.** Amsterdam, Philo Press, 1974. (Repr. of 1928 ed.). 219p. bibliog. indices. o.p. LC n.a. ISBN 90-6022-490-6. BP 80.R3S6 1974.

Part I treats her life, Part II her teachings and writings, and Part III (94 pages) the women saints and women in Islam. Based on original sources. The subject was one of the most famous Sufi saints, and the most famous woman saint; she was known for her extreme asceticism and doctrine of pure love for God.

595. Watt, William Montgomery. **Muslim Intellectual: A Study of al-Ghazzali.** Edinburgh, Edinburgh University Press; distr. Chicago, Aldine Publishing Company, 1963. 214p. bibliog. index. $7.95. LC 63-2894. ISBN 0-202-15012-7. B 753.G34W3. DDC 181.947.

This work studies the man and his work in the context of his times and the intellectual currents in philosophy and theology in which his ideas flowed. With a very full background, which often overshadows the material on the man, Watt discusses al-Ghazzali's backlash against philosophy, his introduction of logic to theology, his contacts with Ismailism and his defense of Sunnism; his critique of Sunnite theology and his Sufi connection. Also treated is the place of the intellectual in Muslim society. The excess of background material in the various fields in which the master worked will be useful to the reader not well grounded in the introductory works included in this *Guide*, but unfortunately there is too little information about the man. A basic work because it is intelligible to the general reader.

596. Zwemer, Samuel Marinus (1867-1952). **A Moslem Seeker after God: Showing Islam at Its Best in the Life and Teaching of al-Ghazali, Mystic and Theologian of the Eleventh Century.** New York, Fleming H. Revell, 1920. 302p. bibliog. o.p. LC 20-20655. BP 80.G3Z8.

The great thinker's life and teaching presented in the context of his times, with descriptions of the cities he lived in, utilizing quotations from medieval writers, and many quotations from al-Ghazali. An interesting book which complements Watt (item 595) and Smith (item 592) in various respects.

INDIVIDUAL COUNTRIES

XV. AFGHANISTAN

A. GENERAL WORKS

597. **Area Handbook for Afghanistan.** [Smith, Harvey Henry]. 4th ed. 1974. 56, 453p.
(DA PAM 550-65). $6.40. LC 73-600084. DS 352.S55 1974. DDC 915.81.

[B, C1]   See the annotation at the head of Section II (page 30).

598. Clifford, Mary Louise. **The Land and People of Afghanistan.** Rev. ed. Philadelphia,
J. P. Lippincott, 1973. 159p. illus. index. (Portraits of the Nations Series). LC 72-13178.
ISBN 0-397-31461-2. DS 351.5.C56 1973. DDC 915.81'03'4.

[P]   A sympathetic, straightforward history and description of the country, with much on the
lives of the people, Islam, etc. For younger readers and uninitiated general readers.

599. Dupree, Louis. **Afghanistan.** Princeton, N.J., Princeton University Press, 1973. 760p.
appendices. bibliog. illus. index. $22.50. LC 76-154993. ISBN 0-691-03006-5.
DS 351.5.D86.

[C1, S1]   The standard work on the country. The first 54 pages deal with the geography,
flora and fauna, etc. The next 200 pages treat in depth the people, whom the author has
studied for a quarter of a century, most of the time at first-hand: ethnic groups, language,
religion, folklore and music; settlement patterns; villagers, townsmen, nomads; life cycles
and customs, including all aspects of daily life. This is followed by 160 pages on the history
(to 1880), which suggests in general terms the sweep of events. The rest deals with the period
to 1972, with an epilog on the immediate background to the coup of 17 July 1973, which
founded the Republic of Afghanistan. The section on the modern period includes material
on development efforts, problems and prospects, U.S.-U.S.S.R. competition; socio-political
reforms, and the press. Dupree's treatment of the last two decades is made especially vivid and
meaningful by his personal observations on current conditions and events, including foreign
relations, the Pushtunistan issue, education, student activities and politics, and the economy.
There are many charts covering topics such as social and political structures, newspapers, lists
of cabinets, historical chronology, and an appendix on musical instruments. A basic book.
   See also:
   Afghanistan, Some New Approaches. George Grassmuck and Ludwig W. Adamec, with
   Frances H. Irwin, editors. Ann Arbor, Center for Near Eastern and North African
   Studies, University of Michigan, 1969. 405p. LC 72-11212. DS 352.A335. DDC 915.
   81'03. Essays on ethnography, literature, and politics, a chronology (1747-1968), and
   a bibliography (pp. 339-405).

600. Dupree, Louis, ed. **Afghanistan in the 1970's.** New York, Praeger, 1974. 266p. (Praeger
Special Studies in International Economics and Development). LC 73-9059. ISBN
0-275-28745-9. DS 351.5.D87. DDC 915.8'1'034.

Essays by various authorities on the recent history, peasant-tribal society, search for
national unity; 1964 constitution and politics to 1974; foreign relations, economic development, nomadism, women; university students and politics, education, archaeology and arts,
music. Most of the essays are general and interpretive, written just after the king was ousted
and the country was declared a republic. While there is no information on the republic, the
essays relate past developments to the current situation and suggest the nature of the problems
and prospects facing the new regime. Any general reader interested in the country will want to
read the book. Most libraries, however, should consider it a low priority item because it is
essentially an ephemeral interim report, even though a few of the items are of lasting value.

601. Weston, Christine (Goutiere). **Afghanistan.** New York, Scribner's, 1962. 162p. illus. index. (A World Background Book). $4.95. LC 62-15498. ISBN 0-684-13488-8. DS 352.W4. DDC 915.81.

[P1, C1] A sympathetic introduction to the history of the country and life of the people, illuminated by the author's personal experiences and observations. Simply written, very well illustrated, and quite informative. A first book, for the general reader.

Another useful introduction for the general reader based on the author's personal observation is:

Watkins, Mary Bradley. **Afghanistan, Land in Transition.** Princeton, N.J., Van Nostrand, 1963. 262p. bibliog. illus. index. LC 63-23685. DS 352.W3.

602. Wilber, Donald Newton, et al. **Afghanistan, Its People, Its Society, Its Culture.** 2nd ed. New Haven, Conn., Human Relations Area File Press, 1962. 320p. bibliog. $10.00. LC 62-18167. ISBN 0-87536-921-9. DS 356.W5 1962. DDC 915.81.

[P1, C1] A general work on the country, its history, government, customs, geography, people and society, religion, culture, media, economy, health, trade, foreign relations. Unfortunately outdated, so for most libraries the *Area Handbook . . .* (item 597) will suffice, though Wilber in some ways is supplementary. A better combination is the *Area Handbook . . .* and Dupree (item 599).

B. HISTORY AND POLITICS

603. Adamec, Ludwig W. **Afghanistan's Foreign Affairs to the Mid-Twentieth Century; Relations with the USSR, Germany and Britain.** Tucson, University of Arizona Press, 1974. 324p. bibliog. index. $13.00; $7.95pa. LC 73-86450. ISBN 0-8165-0388-5; 0-8165-0459-8pa. DS 357.5.A63. DDC 327.581.

[P1, C1, S1, S2] A detailed account of the intricate role played by this strategically important country in the rivalry between Britain, Russia, and Germany. It covers the powers' direct role in Afghani politics, and the political history of the country during the period 1900-1946, with a few pages on the post-war period. Based on U.S., British, and German archives, and material found in Russia and Afghanistan, this book illuminates many aspects of the country's history during the period, particularly the pre-World War II era. A basic work, for all but the smallest collections. A must for serious students who have read Fraser-Tytler (item 604) as background orientation.

See also:

Adamec, Ludwig. **Afghanistan, 1900-1923: A Diplomatic History.** Berkeley, University of California Press, 1967. 245p. LC 67-24832. DS 357.5.A6 1967. DDC 327.581.

604. Fraser-Tytler, Sir William Kerr. **Afghanistan: A Study of Political Developments in Central and Southern Asia.** 3rd ed. London, Oxford University Press, 1967. 362p. bibliog. index. $7.75. LC 67-88066. ISBN 0-19-215930-5. DS 356.F7 1967. DDC 958.1.

[P1, C1, S1, S2] A careful, interesting account and interpretation of the country's history since 1747, with a brief introduction to the history from ancient times. It includes a lucid account of the triangular British-Afghan-Indian relationship, with analysis of the failures and successes of British policy. In the chapters on the "Great Game"–British-Russian-Persian-Afghan relations during the nineteenth century–the author stresses the international aspects over the confused internal history. The second and third editions essentially maintained the original text, correcting certain points, adding bibliographical items, and adding chapters bringing the story up to 1964. One of the best books on the subject, which supplements Dupree (item 599).

See also:

Bilgrami, Asghar H. **Afghanistan and British India, 1793-1907: A Study in Foreign Relations.** New York, Sterling Publishers, 1972. 360p. LC 73-900164. DS 357.6.G7B54. DDC 327.42'0581.

Fletcher, Arnold. **Afghanistan, Highway of Conquest.** Ithaca, N.Y., Cornell University Press, 1965. 325p. bibliog. LC 65-17709. DS 356.F57. DDC 958.1.

Kakar, M. Hasan. **Afghanistan: A Study in International Political Developments, 1880-1896.** Kabul, 1971. 318p. LC 72-182717. DS 365.K3. DDC 958.1.

Rastogi, Ram Sagar. **Indo-Afghan Relations, 1800-1900.** Lukhnow, Nav-Jyoti Press, 1965. 256p. LC SA 65-10313. DS 357.5.R3.

605. Gregorian, Vartan. **The Emergence of Modern Afghanistan: Politics of Reform and Modernization, 1880-1946.** Palo Alto, Calif., Stanford University Press, 1969. bibliog. index. $17.50. LC 69-13178. SBN 8047-0706-5. DS 361.G68. DDC 958.1.

[B, C2, S2]   An exhaustively researched study with a monumental bibliography (66 pages) and 92 pages of critical notes. The first 128 pages provide background, mainly on the nineteenth century to 1880, including the international context, European encroachment and the image of Europe in Afghanistan, and the effect of the two Afghan wars, which is a very useful summary in itself. "Modernization" is interpreted broadly, including legal and social reform, reform of the military and the economy; and there is much on the political history and administration, institutions, health, journalism, foreign relations, modernist Islam and religious controversy, education, communications, and cultural activities. This is not a detailed political history loaded with names and internal political struggles, but it emphasizes the rulers' actions. A basic work to be read along with a systematic political history.
See also:

Newell, Richard S. **The Politics of Afghanistan.** Ithaca, N.Y., Cornell University Press, 1972. 236p. LC 78-176487. ISBN 0-8014-0688-9. DS 369.4.N44. DDC 320.9'581'04. General interpretation and analysis, with little factual material, escept in the historical and economic sections. It covers the politics, economy, institutions, recent history in terms of political development, and problems and prospects. Excellent critical bibliography.

Griffiths, John Charles. **Afghanistan.** New York, Praeger, 1967. 179p. LC 67-19582. DS 361.G7. DDC 915.81'03'4. A general work whose main value is its attempt to cut through Western value judgments such as the "democracy" criterion, anti-communism, etc., in treating the political system and the country's relations with Russia.

606. Poullada, Leon B. **Reform and Rebellion in Afghanistan, 1919-1929: King Amanullah's Failure to Modernize a Tribal Society.** Ithaca, N.Y., Cornell University Press, 1973. 318p. bibliog. index. $14.50. LC 72-12291. ISBN 0-8014-0772-9. DS 369.P68 1973. DDC 958.1'04.

A formal presentation and analysis of an important period in the country's modern history. Based on field research, interviews, Pushto and other sources, including British documents. It begins with the nature of tribal politics and power and the influence of the structure and dynamics of this factor on Afghani politics, incorporating some background history to help the reader understand a source of the failure of the reform effort. Also, the "molding of Amanullah" which made him a reformer, with a general assessment of his character. Then the reforms and stages of implementation, social aspects and implications, change in government structure, the new constitution, etc., including the reform laws; army reforms and their relation to tribal politics; religious reforms; economy, including taxes and finance; the failure. The second half of the book details the tribal revolt and ultimate tribal domination of the country, with a political analysis of the rebellion. Also, Russian and British relations as external pressures on events; finally, the lessons and author's conclusions on the effort and errors made by Amanullah. Complements Stewart (item 607).

607. Stewart, Rhea Talley. **Fire in Afghanistan, 1914-1929: Faith, Hope and the British Empire.** Garden City, N.Y., Doubleday, 1973. 614p. bibliog. index. $17.95. LC 70-171321. ISBN 0-385-087242-X. DS 369.S73. DDC 958.1'04'0920.

An exceptionally well written and very interesting narrative based on British documents, concerning the reign of King Amanullah, the first royal reformer of the Afghans, and the British role, as Amanullah sought to make his country modern and independent. The book details his reforms and travels abroad, reaction to the reforms, the tribal rebellion that resulted, and his disposition and exile. It begins with the development of Amanullah's reforming interest and his early life, as well as his accession to the throne. A fast-moving book which will be enjoyed by the general reader and which the student will find useful. Complemented by Poullada (item 606), which will give the reader a much deeper understanding of the events that Stewart relates in such detail.

608. Sykes, Sir Percy Molesworth. **A History of Afghanistan.** New York, AMS Press, 1975. (Repr. of 1940 ed.). 2v. bibliog. index. LC 78-179245. DS 356.S8 1975. DDC 958.

[P1, C1] A general history from ancient times to 1933 (the accession of King Zahir). Volume 2 begins with the first Afghan War (1838). It includes anecdotes, battles, and some brief cultural notes. It is our most detailed English work, inadequate in various respects, but still a useful outline if one wants more detail than is given in the other works in this *Guide.* It is also useful for reference.

C. BIOGRAPHY

609. Adamec, Ludwig W. **Historical and Political Who's Who of Afghanistan.** Graz, Akademische Druck- und Verlagsanstalt, 1974.

[C1] No other information available.

610. ᶜAbd al-Raḥmān Khān, Amir of Afghanistan. **The Life of Abdur Rahman, Amir of Afghanistan.** Ed. by Sultan Mahomed Khan. Tr. from Persian. London, John Murray, 1900. 2v. illus. index. LC 1-27174. DS 366.A13.

Abdur Rahman has been called the founder of modern Afghanistan, since he was the first ruler to seek to modernize the country. The first volume treats his life, commencing with his early public and military career (1858). He assumed the throne in 1880. He discusses his wars and experiences before becoming king, then his administration and the conditions of Afghanistan in 1880; Volume 2 covers his wars to secure the country and expand its boundaries; economic policies and reforms; administrative changes, daily life; Anglo-Afghan relations and the Durand line; setting the final boundaries. He treats at length his ideas on the country's future and the policies that he and his successors should pursue, including relations with Russia and England.

611. Singh, Ganda. **Ahmad Shah Durrani: Father of Modern Afghanistan.** London, Asia Publishing House, 1959. 457p. bibliog. index. LC 60-34852. DS 359.2.S5. DDC 923.1581.

Ahmad Shah was born about 1722, and his early life is virtually unknown. He first comes to the fore in history shortly after Nadir Shah of Iran was assassinated, which left the rule of Afghanistan open. Ahmad Shah was elected Shah and the Afghanis declared themselves independent. Ahmad Shah united Afghanistan and fought a long series of wars with India over the area now known as Pakistan. Most of the text (to page 347) is devoted to his constant battles inside and out of the country. He died in 1772. The final chapter discusses his person, character, and achievements. The rest of the book consists of 11 appendices—civil administration; military administration; mints and coins; relations with the British East India Company in India; genealogy; successors and descendants; the Sikhs, who fought him continuously; chronology; calendar; discussion of individual original sources on which the text is based; a partly annotated bibliography.

D. CIVILIZATION

612. Ali, Muhammed, professor of history, Habiba College, Kabul. **A Cultural History of Afghanistan.** Lahore, Punjab Educational Press, 1964. 255p. illus. LC 73-12752. DS 354.A42. DDC 915.81'03.

The author has prepared a general survey which includes some material on contemporary writers. The only such work available, but cursory and superficial..From ancient times to the modern period.

E. SOCIETY

613. Spain, James William. **The Way of the Pathans.** Karachi, Oxford University Press, 1972. 190p. illus. index. LC n.a. DS 432.P4S63 1972.

An interesting miscellanea of material that was not suitable for the formal study the author was researching when he went to the border area between Afghanistan and Pakistan to study the Pathan tribesmen who have caused such instability in that area. He presents much historical background and discusses the lives of the people, their mores, beliefs, Pathan women. The book includes many anecdotes told by the people, and some of their poetry. The author's scholarly work is: *The Pathan Borderland* (The Hague, Mouton, 1973. 293p. LC 65-8640. DS 432.P4S58).

See also:

Jones, Schuyler. **Men of Influence in Nuristan: A Study of Social Control and Dispute Settlement in Waigal Valley, Afghanistan.** London, N.Y., Seminar Press, 1974. 299p. illus. LC 73-9482. ISBN 0-12-785393-6. DS 354.6.K3 J66. DDC 309.1'58'1.

F. DESCRIPTION AND TRAVEL

614. Elphinstone, Mountstuart (1779-1859). **An Account of the Kingdom of Caubul.** 3rd ed. Karachi, Oxford University Press, 1972. (Repr. of 1815 ed.). 2v. illus. (Oxford in Asia Historical Reprints). RS 125. LC 73-930062. DS 352.E5 1972. DDC 915.81'03'3.

One of the earliest systematic accounts of Afghanistan, this classic work describes the geography, court, people, flora and fauna, and other aspects of the country at great length and in minute detail. It remains one of our basic sources for the period. It has never been surpassed. Other works imparting the flavor of the period and providing considerable information are:

Burnes, Sir Alexander (1805-1841). **Travels into Bokhara Together with a Narrative of a Voyage on the Indus.** 4th ed. Karachi, Oxford University Press, 1973. (Repr. of 1834 ed.). 3v. LC 73-930469. DK 873.B9 1973. DDC 915. Interesting travels and adventures in Afghanistan, Bokhara, and the Indus Valley by a British agent who describes the people and country, governments, etc. Entertaining and informative. Burnes was killed in Afghanistan.

Masson, Charles. **Narrative of Various Journeys in Balochistan, Afghanistan, and the Punjab.** Karachi, Oxford University Press, 1974. (Repr. of 1842 ed.). 3v. LC 74-930533. ISBN 0-19-577160-5. DS 352. M27 1974. Includes description of life there from 1826 to 1838.

615. King, Peter Michael. **Afghanistan: Cockpit in High Asia.** New York, Taplinger Publishing Company, 1966. 224p. illus. index. LC 67-19694. DS 352.K47 1967. DDC 915. 81'04'4.

A very interesting and informative travelogue that gives a good feel for many aspects of the country's life—society, people, government, foreign relations; some historical notes; nomads, customs, superstitions, politics. Much is based on firsthand experience, but the author emphasizes his comments on the country rather than his own experiences.

616. Konishi, Masatoshi. **Afghanistan.** Tokyo and Palo Alto, Kodansha International, 1969. 146p. illus. maps. (This Beautiful World, Vol. 7). $2.75pa. LC 69-16367. ISBN 0-87011-0071-8. DS 352.K62. DDC 915.81'022'2.

[P1] Magnificent views of the buildings, country and its people, all in color. Brief background notes included. A good supplement to other works in this *Guide.* For all libraries.

617. Trautman, Kathleen. **Spies Behind the Pillars, Bandits at the Pass.** New York, David McKay, 1972. 244p. $6.95. LC 74-185128. ISBN 0-679-50293-9. DS 352.T68. DDC 915.8'1'044.

[P] The interesting and often amusing adventures of the wife of an American USIA officer in Kabul: how she got settled and adjusted to the country, her relations with the people, including the foreign community. She describes her travels around the country and the life she observed. Not terribly informative, but good reading. An excellent account of a teacher's stay and travels in the country is: Klass, Rosanne, *Land of the High Flags: A Travel-Memoire of Afghanistan* (New York, Random House, 1964. 319p. LC 64-20030. DS 354.K55. DDC 915.81).

G. GUIDEBOOKS

618. Dupree, Nancy Hatch. **An Historical Guide to Afghanistan.** Kabul, Afghan Tourist Organization; distr. New York, International Publications Service, 1971. 333p. bibliog. illus. index. (Afghan Tourist Organization. Publication No. 5). $8.50. LC 78-131379. DS 351.D87 1971. DDC 915.81'04'4.

A travel guide arranged by itineraries and prepared by a long-time resident of the country. Though Fodor's *Islamic Asia* is still needed for further information, this one includes much practical information in addition to historical background, folklore and legends (some of which are told at length), and archaeological notes. Mainly for prospective travellers, rather than the armchair variety, but it contains a wealth of interesting material, including data on the people. It is very nicely produced (in Japan) and pocket-sized. See also Fodor (item 467) for practical information. Much of Fodor's historical information is based on Dupree.

XVI. ARABIAN PENINSULA

A. GENERAL WORKS

619. **Area Handbook for the Peripheral States of the Arabian Peninsula.** [Stanford Research Institute]. 1971. 201p. (DA PAM 550-92). $4.55. LC 76-608679. DS 247. A14 S78. DDC 915.36.

[B, C1, S1]   See the annotation at the head of Section II (page 30).

620. Dickson, Harold Richard Patrick. **The Arab of the Desert: A Glimpse into Badawin Life in Kuwait and Saudi Arabia.** London, George Allen and Unwin; distr. New York, Barnes and Noble, 1959. 664p. glossary. illus. index. $21.00. LC 63-22943 rev. DS 219.B4D5 1959. DDC 915.3.

A detailed account of all phases of the life and material culture of the Bedouin by a British agent in Kuwait who lived with them for many years. The book relates some of his first-hand experiences, with innumerable illustrations, including drawings and descriptions of Bedouin tents and equipment. It also contains proverbs, tales; general ethnological material; information on medicine, customs, daily life, and flora and fauna. It is one of the most detailed systematic treatments as of the author's time (the 1930s), and it is still a basic work today. An anthropological study that deromanticizes the usual image of the Bedouins is Cole, Donald Powell, *Nomads of the Empty Quarter: The Āl Murrah Bedouin of the Empty Quarter* (Chicago, Aldine Publishing Company, 1975. 179p. illus. (Worlds of Man: Studies in Cultural Ecology). $10.00; $3.45pa. LC 74-18211. ISBN 0-202-01117-8; 0-202-01118-7pa. DS 219.B4C67. DDC 301.45'19'35).

621. Doughty, Charles Montagu (1843-1926). **Travels in Arabia Deserta.** London, Jonathan Cape, 1964. 2v. glossary of Arabic words. illus. £4.50. LC 65-8191/CD. ISBN 0-224-60971-8. DS 207.D73 1964. DDC 915.3'04'4. **Travels in Arabia Deserta.** An abridgement by Edward Garnett. Gloucester, Mass., Peter Smith, 1968. (Repr. of 1931 ed.). 349p. $4.00. LC 68-2007. DS 207.D73 1968. DDC 915.3'04'4.

The classic work on Arabia. In the late nineteenth century Doughty disguised himself (after a long period of preparation) and lived among the Bedouin, of whose lives and ways of thinking he provides a minute description in this massive work. He records his personal experiences and thoughts during the time, and also describes village life, in a quaint but readable style that will absorb the reader. Smaller collections can be satisfied with the abridgement, while large collections should have both.

622. Halliday, Fred. **Arabia without Sultans.** Baltimore, Penguin Books, 1974. 572p. LC 75-305136. ISBN 0-14-621818-1. DS 227.H25. DDC 953'.05. U.S. ed.: Vintage Books (pa.). LC 74-29336. ISBN 0-394-71592-2. DS 227.H25 1975. DDC 953'.05.

A Marxist interpretation of events in the various countries of the Arabian Peninsula. Aspects of the historical, geographical, and political and international background are presented; U.S. policy is discussed. Emphasis is on the struggle of the working and lower classes against the ruling classes. Unfortunately, Halliday freely applies leftist value judgments, labels, and assumptions in his presentation of facts and interpretations. He does this so blatantly that the whole treatment is badly skewed, and he makes many undocumented assertions of a highly controversial nature. The book is clearly a polemic, rather than a scholarly analysis from a certain perspective, and is not to be taken at face value. However, it has several virtues: it brings together much information otherwise scattered, and it is more up to date than most books, which makes it useful as a supplementary work. It also serves to acquaint readers with an approach, outlook, terminology, and ideas of the left in the region, which will help prepare him for reading leftist works produced there. It briefly treats Saudi Arabia, but it treats at length North and South Yemen, Oman (including the war in Dhofar against leftist rebels), and the other Persian Gulf states. Also treated (in less detail) are the roles of Iran, the great powers, and China.

623. Holden, David. **Farewell to Arabia.** London, Faber and Faber, 1966. 268p. bibliog. illus. index. LC 66-73872. DS 244.53.H57. DDC 953.05.

A reporter's personal impressions, with historical and political background (1950s-1960s) of all states of the Peninsula. Oriented around the withdrawal of British power from the area, it discusses new forces, development, changes, and contradictions as traditional and modern ways clash and overlap.

624. Palgrave, William Gifford (1826-1888). **Narrative of a Year's Journey through Central and Eastern Arabia (1862-1863).** Farnborough, Hants., England, Gregg International Publishers, 1969. (Repr. of 1865 ed.). 2v. £21.50. LC 76-437979. ISBN 0-576-79203-9. DS 207.P162. DDC 915.3'04'4.

An extremely detailed, very well-written account of everything learned and observed by the author, as well as his personal experiences. Palgrave was a long-time resident of the Arab world who made the trip in disguise. He records his conclusions about what he saw, with much appreciation for his Bedouin companions and the Arabs in general. There is much description, history, and disapproving comments on the Wahhabi (Muslim puritan) ruling sect of the country, as well as ironic comments on Islam as a barrier to civilization—which, he says, keeps the Arabs from reaching their considerable potential. He describes the land, Arab society and way of life, including the use of drugs; Arab medicine; flora and fauna; personalities, antiquities. He covers Nejd and Riad, Bahrayn and Qatar, Oman, Sharjah and Muscat in some detail. Perhaps the most useful of the Arabian narratives, and extremely interesting to read.

625. Thesiger, Wilfred. **Arabian Sands.** London, Longmans, 1964. 326p. illus. index. £3.50. LC n.a. ISBN 0-582-10516-1. DS 208.I48. DDC 915.3.

Thesiger, a former British Foreign Officer, is a civilization-hating adventurer. His escapades in Ethiopia and the Sudan, and his five years of crossing and recrossing Arabia's Empty Quarter, living as a Bedouin, are recounted in this book. The entertaining and interesting narrative is packed with information on the men of the desert and their ways.

Additional works on the Arabian Peninsula are:

Abu Hakimah, Ahmad Mustafa. **History of Eastern Arabia, 1750-1800: The Rise and Fall of Bahrain and Kuwait.** Beirut, Khayats, 1965. 213p. bibliog. illus. index. LC NE66-1345. DS 326.A27. DDC 953.604.

Albaharna, Husain M. **The Legal Status of the Arabian Gulf States: A Study of Their Treaty Relations and Their International Problems.** Manchester, Manchester University Press; distr. Dobbs Ferry, N.Y., Oceana Publications, 1968. 351p. LC 68-57676. ISBN 0-7190-0332-6. JX 4084.P4A7. DDC 341'.0264'53.

The Arabian Peninsula, Society and Politics. Ed. by Derek Hopwood. Totowa, N.J., Rowman and Littlefield, 1972. 320p. LC 72-170849. ISBN 0-87471-122-3. DS 202.A68 1972b. DDC 309.1'53'05. Papers by various specialists on the history, politics, international relations, and society of the Peninsula. Some are for specialists, but many are of more general interest.

Kelly, John Barrett. **Eastern Arabian Frontiers.** New York, Praeger, 1964. 319p. LC 64-13137. DS 227.K4. DDC 953.8. The history of the delimitation of the eastern frontier of Saudi Arabia with her neighbors: Qatar, the Trucial states, Muscat and Oman. Half the book concerns the Buraimi Oasis dispute between Saudi Arabia and Britain.

Sanger, Richard Harlakenden. **The Arabian Peninsula.** Freeport, N.Y., Books for Libraries Press, 1970. (Repr. of 1954 ed.). 295p. bibliog. illus. LC 76-117891. ISBN 0-8369-5344-4. DS 207.S3 1970. DDC 915.3'03'5. A general survey.

Kiernan, Reginald Hugh. **The Unveiling of Arabia: The Story of Arabian Travel and Discovery.** New York, Arno Press, 1975. (Repr. of 1937 ed.). 359p. bibliog. LC 70-180353. ISBN 0-404-56285-X. DS 204.5.K5. DDC 915.3.

Wahbah, Ḥāfiẓ. **Arabian Days.** London, A. Barker, 1964. 183p. LC 65-2917. DS 223.W3.

B. BAHRAIN

626. Belgrave, James Hamed Dacre. **Welcome to Bahrain.** 8th ed. Manama, Bahrain, Augustan Press, 1973. 207, 49p. bibliog. illus. LC 74-173075. DS 247.B2B4 1973. DDC 915.3'.65'045.

Covers systematically all aspects of the country's existence: history, government, business, commerce, industries, antiquities, natural history, religion, stamps, recreation, oil, roads. A useful introduction to the country, despite the fact that it is of official inspiration.

C. UNITED ARAB EMIRATES
(TRUCIAL STATES, PERSIAN GULF STATES)

627. Hawley, Donald. **The Trucial States.** New York, Twayne Publishers, 1971. 379p. bibliog. index. $10.00. LC 75-178766. ISBN 0-04-953005-4. DS 247.T87H38 1971. DDC 953'.5.
[P1, P2, C2, S1] A former British official of the Trucial States provides the information that most people would need about the small shaykhdoms on the Persian Gulf, which in 1970 became the United Arab Emirates. It includes history, foreign relations, the British relationship, and information on specific topics such as the economy, oil, development, Buraymi Oasis conflict, etc., with appendices of miscellaneous information. It is a reference book rather than an integrated narrative (except for the historical section), even though the appendices are the only parts actually organized for ready reference. It does not contain as much on the British role and British history in the area as would be desirable. A basic book.
See also:
Hay, Sir Rupert. **The Persian Gulf States.** Washington, D.C., Middle East Institute, 1959. 160p. illus. LC 59-4460. DS 326.H35. DDC 915.383.

628. Mann, Clarence C. **Abu Dhabi: Birth of an Oil Shaikhdom.** 2nd ed. Beirut, Khayats, 1969. 141p. bibliog. index. LC 73-156966. DS 247.A18M3 1969. DDC 953'.6.

Beginning with a brief general description of the Shaykhdom, it surveys the history from the mid-eighteenth century to 1962. Includes relations with Britain, the Saud family, oil, Buraymi Oasis dispute (with Saudi Arabia, which claims the oil-rich oasis). A useful addition to comprehensive collections.
See also:
Daniels, John. **Abu Dhabi: A Portrait.** New York, Longman, 1975. 102p. $14.50. LC 73-93277. ISBN 0-582-78043-8. DS 247. A18 D3. Essentially an "official" exposition, of the sort that the embassy would put out. A useful orientation, but no one should pay the price of $14.50, which is exorbitant.

al-Otaiba, Mana Saeed. **The Economy of Abu Dhabi: Ancient and Modern.** Beirut, printed by Commercial and Industrial Press, 1971? 247p. LC 73-170408. HC 497. A62A286. DDC 330.9'53'5. A systematic topical survey, mainly general in nature, with recommendations made by various organizations on improving the economy. Government structure and policy, financial structure, oil facts and figures. Not much hard data; a government insider's view.

629. **Qatar into the Seventies.** Doha, Qatar Ministry of Information; distr. by Embassies, 1973. 143p. DS 247.Q3Q38 1973. DDC 953.'63'05.

A general survey that is a mine of information. Another useful work is Gerard, Bernard, *Qatar: A Forward Looking Country with Centuries Old Traditions* (Paris, Editions Delroisse, for the Qatar Ministry of Information, 1974. 144p. LC cataloging n.a.). Colored photos of all aspects of the country; many of the photos are interesting and informative.

630. Sadik, Muhammad T., and William P. Snavely. **Bahrain, Qatar, and the United Arab Emirates: Colonial Past, Present Problems and Future Prospects.** Lexington, Mass., Lexington Books; distr. Lexington, Mass., D. C. Heath, 1972. 255p. bibliog. stat. tables. index. $12.50. LC 72-5306. ISBN 0-669-84517-5. JQ 1825.P4S23. DDC 309.1'53'6.

[P1, C1] A comparative general study, topically arranged, each topic being subdivided by Emirate. Includes discussion of economy; social development (including education, housing and health); political systems, administrative structures and problems; the United Arab Emirates and the problems, prospects, costs, and benefits of integration; the costs of non-integration. It contains a wealth of statistical data and much analysis. It does not replace Hawley (item 627), which is more systematic and has more historical data, but it complements it with up-to-date information and a different approach. If faced with a choice, select Hawley, as it is more comprehensive and will remain useful longer for most libraries.

Other works are:

Gerard, Bernard. **Les Emirats Arabes Unis=The United Arab Emirates.** Boulogne, Editions Delroisse, 1973. 144p. LC 74-186593. DS 247. T82G47. DDC 915.35. Colored plates; captions in English and French.

Fenelon, Kevin Gerard. **The United Arab Emirates: An Economic and Social Survey.** London, Longman, 1973. 145p. LC 73-85895. ISBN 0-582-78041-1. HC 497.T8F46 1973. DDC 330.9'53'5. A supplementary source of statistical and general information.

D. KUWAIT

631. Hewins, Ralph. **A Golden Dream: The Miracle of Kuwait.** London, W. H. Allen, 1963. 317p. illus. o.p. LC 63-24761. DS 247.K85H4 1963. DDC 953.87.

The most detailed history available of the important oil shaykhdom, covering the period from the seventh century to the 1960s. Unfortunately, it is undocumented. Probably too much for most college libraries, but worthwhile for larger collections.

632. International Bank for Reconstruction and Development. **The Economic Development of Kuwait: Report of Missions Organized by the International Bank for Reconstruction and Development at the Request of the Government of Kuwait.** Baltimore, Johns Hopkins Press, 1965. 194p. index. $10.00. LC 65-11664. ISBN 0-8018-0290-3. HC 497.K8I5. DDC 338.95387.

A survey of the economy, all sectors, government organization and public finance, potential for future development and proposals for specific action. Informative on the economy in general, with discussion and proposals concerning public health and welfare, education, etc. A basic work despite its age, simply because there is little else.

633. Winstone, Harry Victor Frederick, and Zahra Freeth. **Kuwait, Prospect and Reality.** New York, Crane, Russak, 1972. 232p. bibliog. illus. index. $20.50. LC 72-80110. ISBN 0-8448-0020-1. DS 247.K88W5 1972b. DDC 915.3'67'03.

A general work covering the history of the shaykhdom and the history of its oil industry, with facts and figures on oil production, and a brief discussion of its economics and politics. At present the best single work for most libraries, but for the quantity and quality of information, the price is too high.

See also:

Freeth, Zahra (Dickson). **A New Look at Kuwait.** London, George Allen and Unwin, 1972. 196p. illus. LC 72-194827. ISBN 0-04-953008-9. DS 247.K82F73. DDC 915.3'67'035. HRP and Victoria Dickson's daughter compares past and present Kuwait.

Freeth, Zahra (Dickson). **Kuwait Was My Home.** London, George Allen and Unwin, 1956. 164p. LC 56-2451. DS 247.K82F7.

Kuwait (State). Wizarat al-Irshad wa-al-Anba'. **Kuwait Today: A Welfare State.** Written for the Ministry of Guidance and Information by Quality Publications. Nairobi, Quality Publications; distr. New York, W. S. Heinman, 1963. 191p. LC 64-1414 rev. DS 247. K8A37. DDC 309.15387.

E. OMAN

634. Landen, Robert Geran. **Oman Since 1856: Disruptive Modernization in a Traditional Arab Society.** Princeton, N.J., Princeton University Press, 1967. 488p. bibliog. index. $17.50. LC 66-21835. ISBN 0-691-03040-5. DS 247.O67L3. DDC 953'.5.

A scholarly study. Its "modernization" slant is one that often affects selection of materials but that makes a contribution by drawing attention to important aspects of the country's history and that gives to a collection of facts a meaningful orientation. There is a highly interesting account of the British system of indirect rule and its mode of operation. Oman's history during this period (through the early 1960s) is given in the broader context of Persian Gulf developments. There is also a 75-page chapter on economic changes during the century. For college libraries.

635. Phillips, Wendell. **Oman, A History.** Beirut, Librairie du Liban; distr. Mystic, Conn., Lawrence Verry, 1971. (Repr. of 1967 ed.). 246p. illus. index. $8.50. LC n.a. DS 247.O 65.P5. DDC 953'.5.

An interesting popular history, one of the first in English, of this obscure corner of Arabia, by the then Economic Advisor to the King of Oman. A chatty, anecdotal treatment from ancient times, with emphasis on the nineteenth and twentieth centuries.

636. Phillips, Wendell. **Unknown Oman.** Beirut, Librairie du Liban; distr. Mystic, Conn., Lawrence Verry, 1972. (Repr. of 1966 ed.). 319p. bibliog. illus. index. $8.50. LC n.a. DS 247.O 6.P48. DDC 915.35035.

The author's travels, with descriptions of life and the country, much history, lore and many anecdotes, and discussions of the region's medicine, slavery, women and marriage, and antiquities. The author went there as an archaeologist and became an advisor to the government. This is an interesting, informative book, enriched by the results of the author's research while he was writing his history of Oman.

Other works of interest:

Skeet, Ian. **Muscat and Oman: The End of an Era.** London, Faber and Faber, 1974. 224p. LC 74-171461. ISBN 0-571-10476-2. DS 247.062S5. DDC 915.3'5'045.

Morris, James. **Sultan in Oman: Venture in the Middle East.** New York, Pantheon, 1957. 146p. LC 57-7169. DS 247.O68M6 1957a. DDC 915.35.

Oman in Color. Oman, Ministry of Information and Tourism, 1974. 166p. LC cataloging n.a. Eighty-three beautiful colored photos depicting Oman's landscape, buildings, arts, people, modernization; most of the photos are fascinating.

F. SAUDI ARABIA

637. Alireza, Marianne. **At the Drop of a Veil.** Boston, Houghton Mifflin, 1971. 275p. $5.95. LC 70-144077. ISBN 0-395-12090-X. DS 215.A43. DDC 915.38'03'50924.

The delightfully written adventures of an American woman who married a Saudi Arabian in 1945 and lived in Arabia until 1957, when he divorced her. A splendid account and unusual picture of women's lives and problems in a traditional Arab society. It features a highly amusing description of culture shock and her experiences abroad when travelling with her husband, an Arabian official. It is concluded by a cloak-and-dagger story of how she spirited her five children away, to gain legal control of them. Included also is a very different portrait of the late King (then Prince) Faisal, who visited the author's home several times.

638. **Area Handbook for Saudi Arabia.** [Walpole, Norman C.]. 1971. 373p. (DA PAM 550-51). $5.85. LC 74-614218. DS 204.W34 1971. DDC 309.1'53'805.

[B, C1, S1] See the annotation at the head of Section II (page 30).

Another general work is:

Assah, Ahmad. **Miracle of the Desert Kingdom.** London, Johnson, 1969. 330p. LC 73-434960. ISBN 0-85307-073-3. DS 204.A813. DDC 953'.8. In essence an official Saudi view of the kingdom under Faisal. Includes history, political events, foreign (including inter-Arab) relations, policy and views, government and administration. Covers oil and the economy, social institutions, and programs and policy. A useful, if rosy, view.

639. Hirashima, Hussein Yashio. **The Road to Holy Mecca.** Tokyo, Palo Alto, Kodansha International, 1972. 129p. illus. (This Beautiful World, Vol. 31). $2.75pa. LC 70-174212. ISBN 0-87011-162-0. DS 208.H55. DDC 915.38'04.

A Japanese journalist, a convert to Islam who took the "lesser pilgrimage," provides a travelogue and dozens of color photos of Arabia in general and especially Mecca. Criticisms might be made of the book, but it is interesting to the Westerner and a bargain at the price. (The most favored time to take the pilgrimage is during the prescribed "month of the pilgrimage," when most of the pilgrims come. However, if one cannot come during this month, the "lesser" pilgrimage may be made at any time during the year.)

640. Howarth, David Armine. **The Desert King: Ibn Saud and His Arabia.** New York, McGraw-Hill Book Company, 1964. 307p. illus. $6.50. LC 64-16472. ISBN 0-07-030548-X. DS 244.53.H6. DDC 953.8.

[P2, C1] A journalistic account, insufficiently but not badly researched, of the Arabian King's life and times. While weak in spots, speculative, opinionated and often erroneous in its statements concerning the international background and diplomacy, it is sympathetic and supplies many useful and interesting details. Howarth tries to put Ibn Saud's escapades, extravagance, and sex life in objective perspective, intelligently confronting Western value judgments on such matters. A useful, fascinating work for anyone interested in the subject.
See also:

Armstrong, Harold Courtenay. **Lord of Arabia: Ibn Saud, An Intimate Study of a King...** London, A. Barker, 1934. 306p. LC 34-12986 rev. DS 244.A7 1934. DDC 923.153.

641. Hurgronje, Christiaan Snouck (1857-1936). **Mekka in the Latter Part of the 19th Century: Daily Life, Customs and Learning; the Moslims of the East-Indian-Archipelago.** Tr. from Dutch. Leiden, E. J. Brill, 1970. (Repr. of 1931 ed.). 309p. illus. index. LC 73-509848. DS 248.M4H933 1970. DDC 309.1'53'8.

The Dutch Orientalist lived incognito in Mecca for six months and describes life there in much detail (212 pages). The second part of the book describes the life of the Malay Archipelago Muslim pilgrims living and travelling in Mecca. An interesting work for gaining insight into the times and Arab life.

642. Monroe, Elizabeth. **Philby of Arabia.** London, Faber and Faber, 1973. 332p. bibliog. illus. index. £4.50. LC 73-180796. ISBN 0-571-09464-3. DS 244.5.P45M66. DDC 915.3'04.50924 [B].

An interesting biography of the Englishman who became a Muslim and chief advisor to Ibn Saud of Arabia. Beginning with his Indian service, it traces his World War I duty in Mesopotamia, his service in Jordan, his extensive travels across the Arabian deserts, his pilgrimage to Mecca, and his service to the King. While the man always remains the center of attention, the work is valuable for its contextual material on British politics and policies in the area, its history of the regime, and its view of the personality of King Saud. A useful and entertaining addition to larger collections. Readers wishing to go further are referred to Philby's many books, such as *Arabian Jubilee* and *A Pilgrim in Arabia.*

643. Philby, Harry St. John Bridger (1885-1960). **Saudi Arabia.** New York, Arno Press, 1972. (Repr. of 1955 ed.). 393p. index. (World Affairs: National and International Viewpoints). $20.00. LC 72-4289. ISBN 0-405-04581-6. DS 244.53.P48 1972. DDC 935.8. (Also, Beirut, Librairie du Liban, 1972; repr. of 1958 ed. Distr. Mystic, Conn., Lawrence Verry. $8.50.)

[P1, C1, S1] A detailed history of the last 200 years, in greatest detail for the period through the 1930s, carrying on to 1953 with the death of King Abdul Aziz Ibn Saud. Philby, who has his own view of things, was a Britisher who served Ibn Saud for years (cf. Monroe, item 642).

The account is undocumented but is the standard history for the time being. Smaller libraries that purchase this book do not need Howarth's *Desert King* (item 640) because it duplicates much of Philby's material.

Two more informative books by Philby are:

Arabia of the Wahhabis. New York, Arno Press, 1973. (Repr. of 1928 ed.). 422p. LC 73-6297. ISBN 0-405-05355-X. DS 207.P52 1973. DDC 915.3'04'4.

Arabian Highlands. Ithaca, N.Y., published for the Middle East Institute by Cornell University Press, 1952. 771p. illus. LC 52-7239. DS 207.P48. DDC 915.3.

See also:

De Gaury, Gerald. **Faisal, King of Arabia.** New York, Praeger, 1966. 191p. LC 67-15606. DS 244.6.D4 1967. DDC 953'.8'050924. Very unsatisfactory journalistic account which, however, sheds some additional light on the late king.

De Gaury, Gerald. **Rulers of Mecca.** London, Harrap, 1954. 317p. LC 52-427. DS 248.M4D4. DDC 953.2.

644. Polk, William Roe, and William J. Mares. **Passing Brave.** New York, Alfred A. Knopf, 1973. 206p. illus. $7.95. LC 72-11524. ISBN 0-394-47893-2. DS 208.P65 1973. DDC 915.3'8.

Two madmen, o e a leading Arabist, take a 1300-mile camel trip across the Arabian desert, including the dreaded Great Nefud. The reader will be shocked to find, as they were, that camels and saddles, etc., were hard to come by, as were Bedouin guides—the guides they found had not been camel-riding nomads for a decade and more. The account of the trip is amusing and thoroughly entertaining, as well as informative on the Bedouins.

645. Winder, R[ichard] Bayly. **Saudi Arabia in the Nineteenth Century.** New York, St. Martin's Press, 1965. 312p. bibliog. illus. index. o.p. LC 65-14359. DS 241.W5. DDC 953.804.

A very detailed history, based on original sources, by an Arabist. It includes the British involvement and discusses directly relevant international aspects as they related to Arabian and British politics. For more comprehensive collections.

G. SOUTH ARABIA

646. Allfree, P. S. **Hawks of the Hadhramaut.** London, Robert Hale, 1967. 192p. illus. o.p. LC 67-113526. DS 247.A22 A6. DDC 915.3'35.

The reminiscences of a former mercenary in the army of Muscat and Oman who became Assistant Advisor, Northern Deserts, Protectorate of Aden. The author's experiences are truly fascinating and give an excellent picture of life there, law and politics, the implementation of British policy, and how the British agents worked their areas, while also providing a description of the country and its people. Only larger collections would need its particular information, but most readers will enjoy it thoroughly.

See also:

Ingrams, Doreen. **A Time in Arabia.** London, John Murray, 1970. 160p. LC 74-503287. ISBN 0-7195-2050-9. DS 247.A14I5. DDC 915.3'35. Fascinating memoirs of experiences in South Arabia by the wife of a British official. Includes material on women's life.

647. Bujrah, Abdulla S. **The Politics of Stratification: A Study of Political Change in a South Arabian Town.** Oxford, Clarendon Press, 1971. 201p. bibliog. illus. index. $9.00. LC 78-25586. ISBN 0-19-823157-1. DS 247.A14B8. DDC 320.9'53'35.

Hureidah, located exactly in the middle of the former Protectorate of South Arabia, has 2,000 people. Their social structure is based on a complex stratification system that is typical for the Hadramawt. The three mutually exclusive religious and kinship strata pervade all aspects of social life, and the system is reaffirmed in semi-annual rituals. Bujrah describes in detail each stratum, its role, origin, life, position maintenance, education, religious life; rules of behavior and the economic role. Also, the economy of the town, the vital role that migration plays in the economy and system; and the marriage system. Also, the transformation of the political system and the status of the present structure and dynamics as the outside world has increasingly impinged on it; the internal politics of the classes and inter-class relations; the contradictions between theory and reality of socio-political relations and inter-class mobility, etc. A useful and very interesting book for large collections and advanced students.

648. Ingrams, William Harold. **Arabia and the Isles.** 3rd ed. New York, Praeger, 1966. 102, 400p. illus. index. o.p. LC 64-25589. DS 207.I65 1966a. DDC 915.3045.

A description of Zanzibar, and especially of Aden and the Aden protectorates: the people and their lives, places, society, British policy and its implementation. The author is a highly successful British official who lived in the region for years. His style is brilliant, and the detailed account of his fascinating experiences is unfailingly interesting. The period covered is mainly the 1930s. His experiences in Zanzibar during the 1920s take up the first 70 pages of the main text, which was first published in 1942; a second edition, published in 1952, contained additional information on his life in the Hadramaut in the 1940s, after he left British service. This edition has a 102-page introduction, written in his retirement, which analyses the British methods of handling the Arabs and offers advice concerning future action and means for dealing with nationalist South Arabia—which the British left in 1970. The best book on the subject.

649. Little, Tom. **South Arabia, Arena of Conflict.** New York, Praeger, 1968. 196p. index. $5.00. LC 68-19644. DS 247.A14L5 1968b. DDC 953'.32.

[P1, C1, S1] After a brief historical introduction, it treats the nineteenth and twentieth centuries and the British role there, all as background to the main interest of the book, the period of the 1950s and 1960s. It is mainly a political history, with a brief survey of information vital to understanding the situation in the region and the creation of the Republic of South Yemen. Much has happened since the book was written, but it has not been superseded; it provides good background for current events.

650. Trevaskis, Sir Gerald Kennedy Nicholas. **Shades of Amber: A South Arabian Episode.** London, Hutchinson, 1968. 256p. illus. index. o.p. LC 68-97688. ISBN 0-09-08741-02. DS 247.A14T7. DDC 953'.35.

The account of a Colonial officer and British agent in the Western Protectorate of the Aden Protectorate, 1951-1967. An advisor to Arab sultans, Trevaskis reveals much about the history of the Protectorate and British government, as well as the background of British withdrawal in 1967 and the creation of the now defunct South Arabian Federation. He includes but little description of the country; rather, he recounts personal experiences, reflects a bit, and provides much information on and a feel for the politics of the area. Not an official, apologetic perspective, but an independent, often critical, view of British policy, with much on the Arab view of British rule and the failure of colonialism. One of the best books on the subject.

H. YEMEN

651. O'Ballance, Edgar. **The War in the Yemen.** Hamden, Conn., Archon Books, 1971. 218p. bibliog. index. $7.00. LC 79-21058. ISBN 0-208-01038-6. DS 247.Y48 O2 1971. DDC 953'.32'05.

[C1, S2] The most comprehensive book in English on the Yemen War, 1962-1969. It was a civil war between the traditional tribal structure, led by the new Imam, and "Republican" forces, which took over the country just after the old Imam died and sought to create a modern nation and new power structure. The civil war got caught up in the "conservative"-"revolutionary" inter-Arab rivalry between Saudi Arabia and Egypt, and it was ultimately somewhat internationalized as the U.S. and Russia came to exert influence through military, economic, and political aid. The U.N. became involved, and Egypt contributed massive forces to the Republican side. When Egypt was defeated in the June 1967 War with Israel, partly because so much of its best manpower and armaments were committed to a grueling stalemate in Yemen, it had to reduce its commitment (on which the Republicans depended) and it ultimately withdrew when an agreement was reached. O'Ballance devotes the first 64 pages to the period 1948-1962 as vital background, then traces the political and military struggle on its local, regional, and international levels. An interesting, very useful book. Read item 653 first. See also:

> Ingrams, Harold. **The Yemen: Imams, Rulers and Revolutions.** New York, Praeger, 1964. 164p. LC 64-16679. DS 247.Y45I5. DDC 953.32. Yemen since Independence; personal observations.

> Schmidt, Dana Adams. **Yemen: The Unknown War.** New York, Holt, Rinehart and Winston, 1968. 316p. LC 68-24747. DS 247.Y48S3. DDC 953'.32. The former *N. Y. Times* reporter writing about his visit to the Royalist forces and the war in general.

> Somerville-Large, Peter. **Tribes and Tribulations: A Journey in Republican Yemen.** London, Robert Hale, 1967. 187p. LC 67-73944. DS 247.Y48S6. DDC 915.3'32'045. Fascinating description of the country, political situation, the civil war, Egyptian intervention; his adventures with the Royalists and tribesmen.

652. Tarcici, Adnan. **The Queen of Sheba's Land: Yemen (Arabic Felix).** Beirut, Nowfel Publishers, 1971? 296p. bibliog. illus. stat. tables. $12.50. LC 74-173454. DS 247. Y4T28. DDC 915.3'32'03.

[B, P1, C1] A useful introduction to the country for the general reader. It treats the people and their life; history from ancient times to 1972; antiquities; economy, education, physical geography; foreign relations. There is an extensive bibliography of books and articles in various languages, and a 21-page chronology of events from 1961 to 1972. The many illustrations, a great number of which are in color, are most interesting and informative. Another excellent collection of photographs, of much better color reproduction, is: Gérard, Bernard, *Yemen* (Paris, Delroisse, 1974? 128p. 63 F. LC cataloging n.a.). Brief text and captions in Arabic, French, and English.

Other works are:

> Gerlach, Richard. **Pictures from Yemen.** Leipzig, Edition Leipzig; distr. New York, W. S. Heinman, 1960. LC 62-1797 rev. DS 247.Y42G413. DDC 915.332. Useful collection of photographs.

> Macro, Eric. **Yemen and the Western World Since 1571.** New York, Praeger, 1968. 150p. LC 68-17558. DS 247.Y45M3. DDC 327.53'32.

> Tritton, Arthur S. **Rise of the Imams of Yemen.** London, Oxford University Press, 1925. 141p. bibliog. LC 45-40092. DS 247.Y4T7 1925.

> Fayein, Claudie. **A French Doctor in the Yemen.** London, Robert Hale, 1957. LC cataloging n.a. Especially valuable for details on life in Yemen under Imam Ahmad.

653. Wenner, Manfred W. **Modern Yemen, 1918-1966.** Baltimore, Johns Hopkins Press, 1967. 257p. bibliog. index. (The Johns Hopkins University Studies in Historical and Political Science, Ser. 85, No. 1). $9.00. LC 67-12420. ISBN 0-8018-0668-2. H31.J6 ser. 85, no. 1. [DS 247.Y48W38]. DDC 953'.3'205.

[B, P1, C1, S1] Beginning with a general description of the country and its peoples, the government (military and civilian organization) and administration, and legal codes, the book studies the history of Yemen and its foreign relations to mid-1966. Based on Arabic sources. A good introduction and basic work for students and college collections. To be read before O'Ballance (item 651).

XVII. ARMENIA

654. Boyajian, Dickran H. **Armenia: The Case for a Forgotten Genocide.** Westwood, N.J., Educational Book Crafters, 1972. 498p. $15.00. LC 73-188056. ISBN 0-912826-02-9. DS 195.5.B68. DDC 956.6'2'01.

The most recent English book on the Armenian massacres in Turkey, it is essentially a collection of documents and extracts from reports and books of the times, connected by the author's commentary. It was prepared in support of the Armenians' claim to the land where they once lived (which is now part of Turkey), and their demand for an independent state made on much the same basis as Zionist efforts on behalf of a Jewish state. Most of the documents, from non-Armenian sources, describe the massacres, seek to show that they were part of a Turkish plan, and express the reactions of the West to the massacres and the Armenian claims; they include the Harbard and King-Crane Commissions' reports. The issue is currently of little international significance, but to many Armenians the memories of the horrors are as vivid and important as are Jewish memories of the Nazi Holocaust, and they write books and articles on the subject in Armenian. The issue received wide-spread publicity in the United States, particularly during and after World War I, when immense efforts to aid the victims were made in the United States and the question of a U.S. mandate for Armenia was raised. The issue was also discussed at the Peace Conference, though no meaningful action was taken; Ataturk forestalled the issue when he created the republic of Turkey and made it a viable state, which the war-weary West was unwilling and unable to cope with for Armenian benefit.

655. Lang, David Marshall. **Armenia, Cradle of Civilization.** London, George Allen and Unwin, 1970. 320p. bibliog. illus. index. £6.50. LC 74-596192. ISBN 0-04-956007-7. DS 175.L35. DDC 915.66'2'03.

[C1] This is the only recent general history, and it is one of but a very few written or translated into English during the past century and a half. It is very surprising to the layman that this book is by an Englishman, not an Armenian; in fact, for a people as proud of their heritage as the Armenians, they have done very little to acquaint the English-speaking World with this heritage and their fascinating history, except for the massacres of the World War I era. This is even more surprising considering the fact that there are many general histories and a wealth of more specific works in Armenian that could be translated into English. Lang deals with the period from pre-history to the fourteenth century—i.e., Armenia as an independent state. He devotes 174 pages to the pre-Islamic period, 36 pages to the Islamic era, 70 pages to the arts and learning, while the modern period occupies but 10 pages. It is obvious that we still need a more comprehensive work covering the Islamic and modern period.

Other useful works are:

Atamian, Sarkis. **The Armenian Community: The Historical Development of a Social and Ideological Conflict.** New York, Philosophical Library, 1955. 479p. bibliog. LC 55-14405. DS 175.A77. DDC 956.6.

Der Nersessian, Sirarpie. **The Armenians.** New York, Praeger, 1970. 216p. bibliog. illus. LC 78-92586. DS 171.D43 1970. DDC 915.66'2'03.

Kerr, Stanley Elphinstone. **The Lions of Marash: Personal Experiences with American Near East Relief, 1919-1922.** Albany, State University of New York Press, 1973. 318p. LC 75-38001. ISBN 0-87395-200-6; 0-87395-201-4 microfiche. DS 51.M28K47. DDC 361.5'3'0924.

Kurkjian, Vahan M. **A History of Armenia.** New York, Armenian General Benevolent Union, 1958. 526p. LC 59-2789. DS 175.K8. DDC 956.6.

Morgan, Jacques Jean Marie de. **The History of the Armenian People.** Boston, Hairenik Press, 1965. (Repr. of 1918 ed.). 430p. LC 65-28075. DS 175.M713 1965. DDC 956. 6'2. Two-thirds concerns the period since the seventh century. A standard work.

Sanjian, Avedis Krikor. **The Armenian Communities in Syria under Ottoman Dominion.** Cambridge, Mass., Harvard University Press, 1965. 390p. LC 65-19827. DS 97.5.S2. DDC 956.910097491992.

656. Lynch, Harry Finnis Blosse (1862-1913). **Armenia, Travels and Studies.** Beirut, Khayats, 1965. (Repr. of 1901 ed.). 2v. illus. (Khayats Oriental Reprints, No. 15). LC 66-45223. DS 165.L9 1965. DDC 915.66204.

A typical nineteenth-century travelogue—exhaustively detailed description of the country and the author's experiences; description of antiquities, churches, and main cities such as Erivan and Erzerum. There is relatively little on the people. It covers both Russian and Turkish Armenia. Treatment is inconsistent: sometimes there is a wealth of historical information on a place and description of the people, sometimes none at all on either subject. It is an interesting book, the most extensive in English; it conveys fairly well the atmosphere and appearance of the country in the last decade of the nineteenth century. The many photos contribute greatly to the vividness of the portrayal.

657. Nalbandian, Louise. **The Armenian Revolutionary Movement: The Development of Armenian Political Parties through the Nineteenth Century.** Berkeley, University of California Press, 1963. 247p. bibliog. index. $7.00. LC 63-13806. ISBN 0-520-00914. DS 194.N3. DDC 956.64.

Covers particularly the latter half of the nineteenth century. The 66 pages of background information include a discussion of the Armenian national awakening and its cultural aspects. It is a history of the individual parties, their ideas and activities. Though the book is specialized, it is a source of information on one aspect of Ottoman history. In conjunction with other books on the political struggles of the other minorities and the Turks themselves, it contributes to an understanding of the processes of national and cultural awakening during the period. One of the few books available in English on this period of Armenian history.

658. Surmelian, Leon Z. **Apples of Immortality: Folktales of Armenia.** Berkeley, University of California Press, 1968. 319p. (UNESCO Collection of Representative Works). $7.95. LC 68-12420. ISBN 0-04-398001-5. GR 280.S9 1968. DDC 398.2'09174'91992.

Forty tales collected from peasants in the Mt. Ararat area. The first 24 are "wonder" tales; the remainder concern everyday life and people. A thoroughly enjoyable collection.

XVIII. CYPRUS

659. **Area Handbook for Cyprus.** [Keefe, Eugene K.]. 1971. 241p. (DA PAM 550-22). $4.80. LC 76-610125. DS 54.K4 1971. DDC 915.645'03'4.

[B, P1, C1, S1]   See the annotation at the head of Section II (page 30).

660. Forwood, William. **Cyprus Invitation.** London, Garnstone Press, 1971. 176p. bibliog. illus. index. £1.80. LC 77-861331. ISBN 0-900391-53-7. DS 54.F67. DDC 915.645'04'4.

This travel guide to the island features extensive historical notes, a discussion of the architecture, antiquities, and roads, and a description of the geography. There are also notes on the people and their customs, though not really enough to make it a particularly helpful source of that sort of information; there are no tips on how to conduct personal relations. It makes Cyprus very inviting, but it is not for armchair types.

661. Ierodiakonou, Leontios. **The Cyprus Question.** Stockholm, Almqvist & Wiksell, 1971. 310p. bibliog. (Publications of the Political Science Association in Uppsala). LC 76-886298. DS 54.8.I38. DDC 320.9'5645'04.

Emphasizes the period 1954 to 1959, during which attempts were made to reach a settlement between Greeks, British, and Turks. It discusses U.N. action, British domestic debate and government efforts, and the negotiating conferences. A chapter of 46 pages on the period between 1959-1969 follows, with a 25-page analysis and discussion of prospects. The author uses few Greek and Turkish sources, relying mainly on British documents, Keesings Archives, and the press. There is a useful bibliography and an introductory chapter on the monographic sources, which will be helpful in making further purchases and inter-library loans.

Other useful items:

Mayes, Stanley. **Cyprus and Makarios.** London, Putnam, 1960. 260p. LC 60-50618. DS 54.8.M38. DDC 956.45. Much on the British role; pro-British.

Vanezis, P. N. **Makarios: Faith and Power.** New York, Abelard-Schuman, 1972. 196p. LC 74-166536. ISBN 0-200-71858-4. DS 54.9.V36 1971. DDC 956.4'503'0924. Pro-Makarios.

662. Jenness, Diamond. **The Economics of Cyprus: A Survey to 1914.** Montreal, McGill University Press, 1962. 219p. bibliog. index. $8.75. LC 63-28358. HC 497.C9J4.

A general work with some specific information in non-technical language. The sections get longer and more detailed as the period covered approaches 1914. A basic work. On the modern economy, but much out of date: Meyer, Albert Julius, *The Economy of Cyprus* (Cambridge, Mass., Harvard University Press, 1962. 94p. bibliog. LC 62-8183. HC 496.C9M4. DDC 330.95645). A general survey, problems and prospects, dynamics.

663. Kyriakides, Stanley. **Cyprus: Constitutionalism and Crisis Government.** Philadelphia, University of Pennsylvania Press, 1968. 212p. bibliog. index. $9.00. LC 68-25333. ISBN 0-8122-7567-5. JQ 663 1968.K9. DDC 342'.5645'09.

A history and analysis of Cyprus' constitutional development. The author traces the course of British rule and the evolution of its system in the nineteenth and early twentieth centuries; Enosis movement; British attempts at constitutional self-government in the post World War II era; elections, violence and the 1955 Tri-partite Conference (Greece, Britain, Turkey); events through 1958; the 1960 constitution and independence; the peace treaties; an analysis of major constitutional tension areas: bi-communal problems, political rifts in the Greek community; tensions in public service—the percentage representation provisions, how they were implemented and how they failed; issues causing strife. Also, Makarios' constitutional proposals and Turkish Cypriot reactions; the crisis; views of the respective communities. The author shows how external interests became entrenched and prevented solutions and he discusses the domestic aspects of the Cyprus question in Britain, Greece, and Turkey, and the U.N. role. He discusses the prospects and calls for promotion of communal cooperation. A basic work.

664. Lee, Michael and Hanka Lee. **Cyprus.** Harrisburg, Pa., Stackpole Books, 1973. 208p. illus. index. (The Islands Series). $8.95. LC n.a. ISBN 0-8117-0479-3. DS 54.L47. DDC 916.64'5'03.

[P1] A handy general work, written by a couple who lived on the island. Treats history, life of the people, education, economy, communications, towns and villages, etc. It has a brief section of tourist information, and discusses problems and prospects. An interesting and very well-written armchair evocation of the island is Thubron, Colin, *Journey into Cyprus* (London, Heinemann, 1975. 256p. illus. bibliog. £4.90. LC n.a. ISBN 0-434-77984-9). Thubron is mainly interested in the past, and he provides many historical notes connected with his descriptions of places. The format is that of a walking tour taken in 1971, and he reflects frequently on the people and their lives, Greek-Turkish relations and mutual attitudes, the religious heritage and life, including the popular, pre-Christian essence, and its remnants today.

665. Purcell, Hugh Dominic. **Cyprus.** New York, Praeger, 1969. 416p. bibliog. index. (Nations of the Modern World). $9.00. LC 68-9731. DS 54.5.P8 1969b. DDC 956.45.

[P1, C1, S1] The first 73 pages are a general introduction to the politics, personalities, people, and economics of the island. The rest of the book covers comprehensively the history, in increasing detail as the period advances, from pre-history to the present. The last 100 pages deal with the period of independence, mainly outlining facts and arguments made, emphasizing the Greek-Turkish conflict. The author concludes that integration of Turkish and Greek Cypriots is impossible; he therefore favors a solution based on "repatriation" of the Turkish minority to Turkey. Unfortunately, the author's particular method does not really serve to *explain* developments and help us understand the dynamics of the Cyprus question. However, it does serve as a factual framework on which to build understanding from other works. For college libraries.

666. Stephens, Robert Henry. **Cyprus: A Place of Arms; Power Politics and Ethnic Conflict in the Eastern Mediterranean.** New York, Praeger, 1966. 232p. bibliog. maps. o.p. LC 66-12987. DS 54.5.S68 1966a. DDC 956.45.

[S1] One of the most useful works for understanding the long-term historical perspective and immediate background to the conflict, as well as its development through 1965. Stephens goes back to the Ottoman period and surveys the history of Greek-Turkish strife (of which the Cyprus conflict is but one aspect) in considerable detail before treating the post-World War II era. He then provides a detailed account of the politics of Cyprus' independence, the strife leading to it, conditions after independence, and the crisis of the early 1960s, which was the occasion for writing this book. He discusses fully the significance of Cyprus to Greece and Turkey, and the role of the great powers. It will greatly help the general reader to cut through the propaganda issued by both sides, even a decade later, and to understand generally the type of settlement required. A basic book.

667. Thurston, Hazel. **Cyprus.** Rev. ed. London, Jonathan Cape, 1971. 286p. bibliog. illus. index. (Travellers Guide Series). £1.75. LC 73-159950. ISBN 0-224-00500-6. DS 54.T48 1971. DDC 915.64'5'044.

A typical tourist guide featuring practical information of the *Fodor* variety; general information on the history, people, customs, religion. Then, city-by-city descriptions and other information, with itineraries branching out from each city. Historical notes and lore about each main site, antiquities, excavations. Pocket-sized. For more up-to-date information, refer to *Nagel's Encyclopedia-Guide: Cyprus* (distr. New York, Hippocrene Books. $13.00. ISBN 2-8263-0334-1). Particularly good for its 50 pages of practical information, although this information has probably been rendered obsolete by the events of summer 1974.

XIX. EGYPT

There are virtually no comprehensive works on medieval Egypt. Admittedly, much research remains to be done before the definitive works can be written, but enough material exists to permit the writing of one work on history and another on civilization, or a work that combines these two.

A. GENERAL WORKS

668. **Area Handbook for the United Arab Republic (Egypt).** [Smith, Harvey Henry]. 1970. 554p. (DA PAM 550-43). $6.80. LC 71-608841. DT 107.83. S 59 1970. DDC 916.2'03'5.

[B, P1, C1, S1]   See the annotation at the head of Section II (page 30).

Another general work similar to the **Area Handbook** is:

Wilber, Donald Newton. **The United Arab Republic-Egypt, Its People, Its Society, Its Culture.** New Haven, Conn., Human Relations Area Files Press, 1969. 461p. LC 68-22208. DT 46.W54. DDC 916.2'03'5.

669. Kay, Shirley. **The Egyptians: How They Live and Work.** New York, Praeger, 1975. 152p. bibliog. illus. $8.95. LC AC74-15680. ISBN 0-275-26020-8. DT 48.K36. DDC 916.2'03'5.

[P]   A juvenile work suitable for the totally uninitiated general reader. It covers geography, history, culture, daily lives, occupations (including labor unions, unemployment, women); education, transportation and communications, political system; and recreation, including literature and the press. Read it in conjunction with Mahmoud (item 670).

670. Mahmoud, Zaki Naguib. **The Land and People of Egypt.** Rev. ed. Philadelphia, J. B. Lippincott, 1972. 159p. illus. index. (Portraits of the Nations Series). $3.95. LC 71-37247. ISBN 0-397-31259-8; 0-397-31184-2 lib. bdg. DT 77.M3 1972. DDC 916.2'03'5.

[P]   An interesting introduction to Egypt by an Egyptian. It covers the history from earliest times; Christianity in Egypt, Islam; Egypt as depicted in the Arabian Nights; women and family life; Cairo and Alexandria; agriculture and the countryside, peasant life; education and culture; the nineteenth-twentieth century intellectual awakening. A rather rosy view, but useful for its Egyptian perspective. Should be read in conjunction with Kay (item 669).

B. HISTORY AND POLITICS TO 1800

671. Glubb, Sir John Bagot. **Soldiers of Fortune: The Story of the Mamlukes.** New York, Stein and Day, 1973. 480p. bibliog. maps. index. $12.50. LC 73-80041. ISBN 0-8128-1611-0. DT 96.G57 1973. DDC 962.02.

This is the only recent comprehensive work on the "slave" kings who ruled Egypt and part of Syria from 1250 to 1517, and whose descendants were important in Egypt until the early nineteenth century under Ottoman rule. Of all eras of medieval Islam, this period is richest in documentary and historiographical sources. Those sources are still being studied by scholars and the results have come out only in dribbles; this leaves the field open to Glubb, who is neither a professional historian nor a readable writer. The earlier comprehensive histories of the period are no better, except perhaps in style. This is mainly an account of politics, "musical thrones," and battles, with sketches of the characters and lives of the sultans. Glubb has uncritically gleaned innumerable details and anecdotes—as well as evaluations of the

Sultans—from the medieval Arabic sources. He only briefly discusses, in a most superficial fashion, the economic and social conditions, and he ignores the great cultural activity and arts of the time. Despite its grievous faults, it is a useful source of much basic information; the reader is aided by the many useful maps.

672. Lane-Poole, Stanley. **A History of Egypt in the Middle Ages.** New York, Haskell House, 1969. (Repr. of 1901 ed.). 382p. LC 68-25246. DT 95.L35 1969. DDC 962'.02.

[P1, C1, S1] Despite the age and inadequacies of this work, its uniqueness in the field makes it essential to students. Based on Arabic sources, it is a detailed history, with cultural notes, anecdotes and battles, and material on government and the courts, from the Arab conquest to the Ottoman conquest. Written in a popular style, it will appeal to the general reader.

673. O'Leary, De Lacy Evans. **A Short History of the Fatimid Khalifate.** Wilmington, Del., Scholarly Resources, Inc., 1975? (Repr. of 1923 ed.). 267p. bibliog. index. (Islamic Studies Library). $15.00. LC n.a. ISBN 0-8420-1759-3. DT 173.O5 1975.

This general history discusses Fatimid origins in Shiism and the Isma^{C}ilite branches of Shiism, the Qarmathians, expansion of the sect into North Africa, rise to power as a Caliphate in Kairawan (873-966), and the conquest of Egypt, as well as the history of the Fatimid dynasty there until Saladin finished off the last ruler in 1771. Despite being out of date, it is a useful work for the student, written in semi-popular style and not too technical, but based on original sources.

See also:

Ivanov, Vladimir Alekseevich. **Ismaili Tradition Concerning the Rise of the Fatimids.** London, Oxford University Press, 1942. 337p. LC 53-53243. DT 173.I8. DDC 961.

Vatikiotis, Panayiotis J. **The Fatimid Theory of State.** Lahore, Orientalia Publishers, 1957. 223p. LC 72-201082. JC 49.V38.

C. 1800-1952

674. Dodwell, Henry Herbert (1879-1946). **The Founder of Modern Egypt: A Study of Muhammad ^{C}Ali.** Cambridge, England, Cambridge University Press, 1967. (Repr. of 1931 ed.). 276p. index. o.p. LC n.a. DT 104.D58 1967.

[C1] This as yet unsurpassed work traces the rise and career of the Egyptian ruler, his military activity in Arabia and the Sudan, the Greek War of Independence, Algeria; the conquest of Syria; the government of Egypt, Crete and Syria; the quashing of his second effort in Syria by the great powers; relations with the Ottoman Empire, the British and the French. It also covers Muhammad Ali's efforts to change Egypt, particularly in the realms of agriculture, military forces, education, and trade. This is not a biography but a history of Egypt during his reign; it contains virtually no information on his life. The author used all available sources so judiciously that this will remain the standard work for some time to come, as dated as it is. This work should be followed up by the reader with Rivlin (item 702), which is a good example of the many works that need to be written before Dodwell can be displaced.

675. Kinross, John Patrick Douglas Balfour, baron. **Between Two Seas: The Creation of the Suez Canal.** London, John Murray, 1968. bibliog. illus. index. £2.50. LC 68-142661. ISBN 0-7195-1813-X. TC 791.K5 1968. DDC 386'.43.

This book is to a great extent a diplomatic history of the Canal from the inception of de Lesseps' effort through the British occupation of Egypt in 1882. It provides much on the background: previous interests in building a canal, the commercial and political aspects, and British, French, and Ottoman efforts to frustrate or encourage it. It also covers the long process by which it was financed, de Lesseps' continuing efforts on its behalf; practical problems (including manpower, supplies, communications); Egyptian internal politics as they affected the project; and the men (de Lesseps, the Egyptian Khedives, the diplomats and financiers). It covers in detail the period through the Canal's opening in 1869 and briefly surveys the remaining period, including Disraeli's purchase of the Khedive's shares, and finally the occupation. A well-researched book which is fairly interesting to read, though perhaps a bit much for many readers. Suitable for all libraries. A much more readable, popular work is John Pudney, *De Lesseps's Canal* (London, J. M. Dent, 1968. DT 154.S9P8), which covers basically the same topics, but with less emphasis on diplomatic aspects, and generally in less detail. The most detailed work is D. A. Farnie, *East & West of Suez: The Suez Canal in History, 1854-1956* (Oxford, Clarendon Press, 1969. 860p. $41.00. LC 70-443576. DT 154.S9F375 1969. DDC 962'.15). This is an immense account of the influence of the Canal on world economics and international relations; it contains a wealth of information on a host of topics relating directly and indirectly to the Canal as a key influence in world affairs, but it is probably too much for most users of this *Guide.*

A comprehensive work for the general reader is:

> Schoenfeld, Hugh. **The Suez Canal in Peace and War, 1869-1969.** Rev. ed. London, Vallentine, Mitchell, 1969. LC 74-473467. HE 543.S35 1969b. DDC 386'.43.

See also:

> Wilson, Arnold Talbot. **The Suez Canal: Its Past, Present and Future.** London, Oxford University Press, 1939. 224p. LC 40-4793. TC 791.W5 1939.

676. Marlowe, John. **Cromer in Egypt.** London, Elek, 1970. 383p. bibliog. illus. index. £3.50. LC 75-528810. ISBN 0-236-17656-0. DT 107.6.M2 1970b. DDC 962'.04'0924.

[C2] Based on official British and French documents, this history of the British administration under the autocratic Evelyn Baring, Lord Cromer, should be the standard work for years to come. Described in full are the conditions and events leading to the internationalization of the Egyptian debt in the 1860s and 1870s, European administration of the debt, the Egyptian economy, British-French relations, and the British occupation of 1882; Cromer's rule, his relations with the British government in England as well as the government in Egypt, the economic measures taken, the method of administration; the rise of Egyptian nationalism and its role in the administration and politics; and finally, a summary of the achievement and its real nature. It offers many new insights into the man Cromer, which enhances its value. Perhaps too detailed for most libraries, it certainly belongs in more comprehensive collections.

677. al-Sayyid, Afaf Lutfi. **Egypt and Cromer: A Study in Anglo-Egyptian Relations.** London, John Murray, 1968. 326p. bibliog. index. £2.25. LC n.a. ISBN 0-7195-1810-5. DT 107.6.S37 1968. DDC 962'.04'0924.

[P2, C1, S2] A fascinating, critical, interpretive history of Egypt from 1882 to 1907, with a general epilog covering the period from 1907 to 1952 on Egyptian politics, particularly the nationalist movement. It is less detailed than Marlowe (item 676) and emphasizes Egyptian internal politics. It includes discussion of the nature of the administration, Egyptian nationalism, and key Egyptian political leaders. For the general reader. Another useful work is Robert L. Tignor, *Modernization and British Colonial Rule in Egypt, 1882-1914* (Princeton, N.J., Princeton University Press, 1966. 417p. LC 65-17163. DT 107.T5. DDC 325.3420962).

678. Vatikiotis, Panayiotis J. **The Modern History of Egypt.** New York, Praeger, 1969. 512p. bibliog. index. (The Praeger Asia-Africa Series). $9.50. LC 69-16084. DT 107.V38 1969b. DDC 916.2'03.

[P1, P2, C1, S1] One of the best introductions in English, it covers the nineteenth and twentieth centuries to 1962. While it devotes much space to political and diplomatic history, it is also important for its extensive coverage of Egyptian culture and society, including literature and journalism, Islamic response to Western influence, and the penetration of European ideas into Egyptian society and intellectual life. Unfortunately, the cultural material is treated separately rather than being integrated with political history, where it could serve as an aid in suggesting the flavor of the times. Basic for all collections. To be read after a more general work and matched up with Mansfield, who treats the period since 1952 in much greater detail and for a longer period.

An excellent supplement on the religious, political, and intellectual trends is the following work, whose perspective is that of the change from traditional Islamic to Westernized non-Muslim but still semi-traditional society and political system, is Nadav Safran's *Egypt in Search of Political Community: An Analysis of the Intellectual and Political Evolution of Egypt, 1804-1952* (Cambridge, Mass., Harvard University Press, 1961. 298p. LC 61-13742. DT 107.S2).

Other works basic to studying the nineteenth and twentieth centuries to 1952 are:

Berque, Jacques. **Egypt: Imperialism and Revolution.** Tr. from French. New York, Praeger, 1972. 736p. LC 79-134531. DT 107.B413 1972. DDC 962'.05. An important work comprehensible to advanced students only, because of Berque's style and his assumption of extensive reader background. Greatly rewards careful study.

Ahmad, Jamal Mohamed. **The Intellectual Origins of Egyptian Nationalism.** London, Oxford University Press, 1968. (c. 1960). LC 60-52161. DT 100.A58. DDC 962.

Cromer, Evelyn Baring, 1st Earl of (1841-1917). **Modern Egypt.** New York, Macmillan, 1909. 2v. DT 107.C88 1909. A general discussion of Egypt during his regime, and an account of his activities and administration. A basic source on the period. Larger collections should watch for a reprint.

Lloyd, George Ambrose Lloyd, Baron. **Egypt Since Cromer.** New York, AMS Press, 1970. (Repr. of 1933 ed.). 2v. LC 75-107074. ISBN 0-404-04024-1. DT 107.L552 1970. DDC 962'.04. Lloyd became High Commissioner in Egypt in 1925.

Conference on the Modern History of Egypt, University of London, 1965. **Political and Social Change in Modern Egypt: Historical Studies from the Ottoman Conquest to the United Arab Republic.** Ed. by P. M. Holt. London, Oxford University Press, 1968. 400p. LC 68-121481. DT 43.C63 1965a. DDC 962. Important collection of scholarly essays.

Landau, Jacob M. **Parliaments and Parties in Egypt.** New York, Praeger, 1954. 212p. LC 54-7145. JQ 3854.L3 1954. DDC 328.6209.

Marlowe, John. **Anglo-Egyptian Relations, 1800-1956.** 2nd ed. Hamden, Conn., Archon Books, 1965. 468p. LC 65-10972. DT 82.5.G7M3 1965. DDC 327.42062. Superficially researched but useful summary; mainly from the British perspective, but without editorial viewpoint.

Marlowe, John. **Spoiling the Egyptians.** London, Deutsch, 1974. 277p. LC n.a. ISBN 0-233-96601-3. LC cataloging n.a. Europe's technical and especially economic "colonization" of Egypt, 1798-1882, especially from the 1850s. The financial and diplomatic process by which the Egyptian economy became controlled by Europe, oriented around European needs, and exploited. An evaluation of Khedive Ismail's reign; his deposition; Britain's takeover in 1882. For the educated general reader.

Ziadeh, Farhat Jacob. **Lawyers: The Rule of Law and Liberalism in Modern Egypt.** Stanford, Calif., Hoover Institution on War, Revolution and Peace, 1968. 177p. LC 68-9503. LC class: LAW. DDC 340. Covers the period 1800 to 1960.

See also:

Quraishi, Zaheer Masood. **Liberal Nationalism in Egypt: Rise and Fall of the Wafd Party.** Allahabad, Kitab Mahal, 1967. 245p. LC SA 67-7547. JQ 3898.W3Q7. DDC 320.9'62.

Weigall, A. E. **A History of Events in Egypt from 1798 to 1914.** Edinburgh, W. Blackwood, 1915. LC 15-13679. DT 100.W4.

Zāyid, Maḥmūd Yūsuf. **Egypt's Struggle for Independence.** Beirut, Khayats, 1965. 258p. LC NE 65-1614. DT 107.Z3.

Two works on the Muslim Brotherhood, the conservative, militant religio-political organization that came to prominence in the post-World War II period, are:

Harris, Christina (Phelps). **Nationalism and Revolution in Egypt: The Role of the Muslim Brotherhood.** The Hague, Mouton, 1964. 276p. LC 64-18923. DT 107.H38. DDC 962. The first half gives an interpretation of the history of Egyptian nationalism and Islamic thought that leads to the conclusion that the rise of the Brotherhood or a similar organization was natural, if not inevitable. The rest of the book discusses the ideas, history, and organization of the group.

Mitchell, Richard P. **The Society of Muslim Brothers.** London, Oxford University Press, 1969. 349p. LC 77-115987. DT 107.83.M5 1969. DDC 323'.2'0962. The most detailed study of the history, organization, and ideology of the group, through 1954.

Wendell, Charles. **The Evolution of the Egyptian National Image: From Its Origins to Aḥmad Lutfi al-Sayyid.** Berkeley, University of California Press, 1972. ca.300p. bibliog. LC 72-170724. ISBN 0-520-02111-8. LC cataloging n.a. Development of the concept of the Egyptian "nation," going back to the pre-Islamic, Koranic and medieval usages of the term "ummah" (community) and the concepts involved in it; development in eighteenth century Egypt; nineteenth century and the evolution into an Egyptian nationalist concept. About a third of the book concerns Ahmad Lutfi al-Sayyid's formulation of the latter idea. A significant study of the evolution of Egyptian political thought in the nineteenth century.

A work that caused considerable controversy in its day (1938) is: Taha Husayn, **The Future of Culture in Egypt.** Tr. from Arabic. New York, Octagon Books, 1975. (Repr. of 1954 ed.). 164p. LC 75-14319. ISBN 0-374-94066-5. LA 1646.T3513 1975. DDC 370'.962. In this critique of Egypt's educational system, Husayn said that Egypt belonged to the broader Mediterranean civilization, including Roman and Greek, and the mainstream of Western civilization. He felt that Egypt should emphasize those roots rather than the Near Eastern and Islamic cultural heritage in order to move into the modern world.

Another important work:

Mūsá, Salāmah. **The Education of Salama Musa.** Tr. from Arabic. Leiden, E. J. Brill, 1961. LC cataloging n.a. The memoirs of an important Fabian Socialist Christian Secularist; gives a portrait of pre-World War II Egypt.

D. 1952 TO PRESENT

See also Section XXIII C, "1956 War and Suez Crisis."

679. Abdel-Malek, Anouar. **Egypt: Military Society, the Army Regime, the Left, and Social Change under Nasser.** Tr. from French. New York, Vintage Books, 1968. 458p. bibliog. index. (V 428). $1.95pa. LC 68-14511. ISBN 0-394-70428-2. DT 107.83.A5933 1968. DDC 962'.05.

[P1, C1, C2, S1, S2] The most detailed account of internal Egyptian politics during Nasser's period, it is a heavily documented, interpretive history of the economic and social aspects, the Nasserist search for an ideology, the development effort and the opposition to that effort among various elements, and the activity and repression of the left. The author is a Coptic Marxist who had to leave the country in 1959 and who has made a reputation as an outstanding scholar in France. Also treated are the cultural and intellectual life, neutralism, and Arab nationalism. The author's emphasis, the great amount of specific data, and the stimulating moderate Marxist analysis, which illuminates the dynamics of Egypt's social-economic-political complex during the period, make this must reading for advanced students and a basic work for larger collections.

Other useful works are:

Dekmejian, R. Hrair. **Egypt under Nasir: A Study in Political Dynamics.** Albany, State University of New York Press, 1971. 368p. bibliog. LC 70-152520. ISBN 0-87395-080-1; 0-87395-180-8 microfiche. DT 107.83.D43. DDC 962'.05. One of the better studies of the period: history, structure, development and dynamics of the system, political elite membership, their backgrounds; ideology (socialism, Arabism, Arab nationalism); system during 1967 war. It is often too technical—more so than necessary—for the general reader, but non-specialists will find much of worth in it.

Berger, Morroe. **Bureaucracy and Society in Modern Egypt: A Study of the Higher Civil Service.** New York, Russell & Russell, 1969. (Repr. of 1957 ed.). LC 72-75460. JQ 3847.B4 1969. DDC 354.62'006. Though this book is outdated in some specifics, the dynamics and processes of Egyptian society are basically the same, as are the personnel types making it up.

Two accounts of the 1952 revolution and its aftermath by participants are:

Sadat, Anwar. **Revolt on the Nile.** New York, John Day, 1957. 159p. LC 57-12107. DT 107.83.S3. DDC 962.

Neguib, Mohammed. **Egypt's Destiny: A Personal Statement.** Garden City, N.Y., Doubleday, 1955. LC 55-5271. DT 107.83.N44 1955a. DDC 962.

680. Mansfield, Peter. **Nasser's Egypt.** 2nd ed. Gloucester, Mass., Peter Smith, 197– . $3.50. LC n.a. ISBN 0-8446-2525-6. DT 107.83.M32. DDC 962.05.

[P1, C1, S1] A general work written by a British journalist who knows Arabic and the Arab world well. It covers the background to the 1952 revolution; Egypt's relations with the other Arab states, Russia and the West; human resources; economic, social, and educational policy; agricultural policy; the search for a political system. A sympathetic view, it is a useful introduction which clearly suggests Egypt's problems and needs. Another useful introductory work for the general reader is Tom Little's *Modern Egypt* (New York, Praeger, 1967. LC 67-25303), which devotes 121 of its 300 pages to the period before 1952, particularly the twentieth century.

Some of the best works for the general reader on the period are:

Hopkins, Harry. **Egypt, the Crucible: The Unfinished Revolution in the Arab World.** Boston, Houghton Mufflin, 1969. 533p. LC 69-15016. DT 46.H65 1969. DDC 916.2'03'5. A sympathetic journalistic attempt to suggest the flavor and dynamics of the Nasser period: ideology, theory, changes being made. Touches on many aspects of daily life and culture not usually dealt with. A good supplement to Mansfield.

Lacouture, Jean, and Simon Lacouture. **Egypt in Transition.** New York, Criterion Books, 1958. 532p. LC 58-10614. DT 107.83.L323. DDC 962.

Egypt since the Revolution. Ed. by P. J. Vatikiotis. London, Allen and Unwin, 1968. 195p. LC 75-374558. DT 107.83.E76 1968b. DDC 916.2'03'5. Essays by various authorities on a number of aspects.

Vatikiotis, Panayiotis J. **The Egyptian Army in Politics: Pattern for New Nations?** Westport, Conn., Greenwood Press, 1975. (Repr. of 1961 ed.). LC 72-6216. ISBN 0-8371-6473-7. DT 107.83.V28 1975. DDC 962.05. Much hard data provided, along with pre-1952 background.

Wheelock, Keith. **Nasser's New Egypt: A Critical Analysis.** Westport, Conn., Greenwood Press, 1975. (Repr. of 1960 ed.). 326p. bibliog. LC 75-14708. ISBN 0-8371-8233-6. DT 107.83.W48. DDC 962.05. Much factual information, and a critical analysis.

Wynn, Wilton. **Nasser of Egypt: The Search for Dignity.** Cambridge, Mass., Arlington Books, 1959. 213p. LC 59-8082. DT 107.83.W9. DDC 962.05. A very sympathetic interpretation of Egypt's behavior.

681. Stephens, Robert. **Nasser, a Political Biography.** New York, Simon and Schuster, 1972. 640p. bibliog. index. $12.50. LC 79-183762. ISBN 0-671-21224-9. DT 107.83.S74 1972. DDC 962'.05'0924 [B].

[P1, C1, S1] An interpretive survey, for the general reader, of Egypt's role in world and inter-Arab politics and its relations with Israel, with some information on Egypt's domestic affairs. It contains but little about Nasser, and far too little about internal politics—too little even in relation to the sparse information we do have available. However, it is a very useful orientation on the period. Though it is not comprehensive, its discussion of many key events during the Nasser era will enlighten readers not familiar with them and also those who want to put various events into the broader context of the entire period. For public and college collections.

Other works on Egyptian foreign policy are:

Haykal, Muḥammad Ḥasanayn. **The Cairo Documents: The Inside Story of Nasser and His Relationship with World Leaders, Rebels and Statesmen.** Garden City, N.Y., Doubleday, 1973. 360p. LC 76-182696. ISBN 0-385-06447-0. DT 107.83.H367. DDC 962'.05'0924 [B]. An interesting work by Nasser's confidant, the former editor of *al-Ahram*, Egypt's most important newspaper.

Ismael, Tareq Y. **The U.A.R. in Africa: Egypt's Policy under Nasser.** Evanston, Ill., Northwestern University Press, 1971. 258p. LC 73-126902. ISBN 0-8101-0323-0. DT 82.5.A37 I8. DDC 327.62'06.

E. BIOGRAPHY

682. Gendzier, Irene L. **The Practical Visions of Ya^cqūb Ṣanu^c.** Cambridge, Mass., Harvard University Press, 1966. 175p. bibliog. (Harvard Middle Eastern Monographs, 15). $4.50pa. LC 66-28047. PN 5463.S3G4. DDC 892.78508.

A biography of the founder of the Egyptian theater, journalist, and Egyptian nationalist. In the 1860s he was a famous playwright; in the 1870s, an agitator and organizer-member of secret societies; from the late 1870s on, a journalist, often in Paris and other places outside Egypt; and an anti-establishment and anti-British reformer. Working closely with al-Afghani and Abduh in Paris, he wrote in French as a propagandist on behalf of the Muslim against the British. In the early twentieth century he strove for East-West rapprochement. The book indicates his ideas and provides much illuminating detail on the history and politics of the times. For the reader with some knowledge of nineteenth century Egypt.

683. Lacouture, Jean. **Nasser: A Biography.** New York, Alfred A. Knopf; distr. New York, Random House, 1973. 399p. bibliog. index. $10.00. LC 71-154914. ISBN 0-394-46625-X. DT 107.83.L1713 1973. DDC 962'.05'0924 [B].

[C2] Since we have no documents such as Nasser's correspondence, state papers, personal papers, etc., and since most of the available material from the public domain consists of press reports, articles, and journalistic books, most "biographies" of Nasser or other political figures are essentially political histories of the era, records of speeches, etc. St. John (item 685) served up the most factual details of Nasser's life and regime. Lacouture, a long-time observer of Egypt, whose previous study, *Egypt in Revolution*, was one of the best volumes of the 1950s, provides us with one of the best *analyses* of Nasser's policies and a critique of his successes and failures, attempting to arrive at the essence of his regime, and his particular role in it. There is a stimulating discussion of Nasser's socialism, the rise of a new class of Egyptian bourgoisie, and the role of Egyptian Marxists. A long section discusses the confrontation with Israel, including a detailed treatment of Nasser's shifting attitudes toward peace with Israel, and Israel's frequent misperceptions of Egypt. For college collections.

684. Reid, Donald M. **The Odyssey of Farah Antun: A Syrian Christian's Search for Secularism.** Minneapolis, Bibliotheca Islamica, ca. 1975 (forthcoming). (Studies in Middle Eastern History, 2). $12.50. LC cataloging n.a. ISBN 0-88297-009-7.

A Syrian émigŕe (1874-1922) to Egypt whose secularist views and journalistic activity greatly influenced the Egyptian liberal national movement. He also interpreted and disseminated Western science and other thought to the Egyptian and other Arab publics through his periodical *al-Jami^cah* and novels, and he advocated a vague brand of socialism.

685. St. John, Robert. **The Boss: The Story of Gamal Abdel Nasser.** New York, McGraw-Hill, 1960. 325p. index. o.p. LC 60-14047. DT 107.83. DDC 923.162.

[S1] The best work on Nasser, which supplies the most factual details on his life, up to 1959. He describes the man, Egyptian political history, the "police state" aspects of the government. St. John has a critical eye but is not polemical. Useful as a supplement to a work such as Lacouture (item 683), and for its details on the internal political history.

F. SOCIETY

686. ^cAmmār, Ḥamīd. **Growing up in an Egyptian Village: Silwa, a Province of Aswan.** New York, Octagon Press, 1966. (Repr. of 1954 ed.). 316p. bibliog. index. $12.00. LC 66-22037. ISBN 0-374-90171-6. HN 790.S3A4 1966. DDC 309.162'3.

[C1] This classic work begins with a general survey of the economy, social organization, folk life, and social change of the community. This is followed by a detailed treatment of all aspects of childhood, including education and teaching methods, games; children's tales, presented and analysed as to their meaning and significance; childhood training. Throughout the book, the specific material is related to theoretical considerations, which makes the data more meaningful and useful. One of few works on childhood in the Near East. Basic for college libraries.

687. Ayrout, Henry Habib, S. J. **The Egyptian Peasant.** Tr. from French. Boston, Beacon Press, 1963. 167p. bibliog. illus. (Beacon Books on World Affairs, BP 276). $1.95pa. LC 63-7574. ISBN 0-8070-5997-8. HD 1538.E3A952 1963. DDC 301.444.

[P2, C1, S2] A classic basic work on the fellah, his life, food, psychology, superstitions and religion, social and family organization, health, agricultural methods, village life. Also, irrigation, landowners, government, and the peasants; land administration, living standards, modernization problems; and problems of government planners who are not familiar with the lives and therefore the psychology of the peasants, which ensures inadequately conceived plans and implementation, and therefore the continued frustration of failure. Written in a simple style that the general reader can understand. Basic for most collections and students.

688. Baer, Gabriel. **Studies in the Social History of Modern Egypt.** Chicago, University of Chicago Press, 1969. 259p. index. LC 69-17537. HN 783.B32. DDC 309.1'62.

A collection of the author's groundbreaking studies on fundamental aspects of nineteenth and twentieth century Egypt, including Bedouin settlement, rural disintegration, urbanization, land ownership, slavery, the fellah, guilds, socioeconomic changes. For advanced students. A good source of bibliography and fine examples of methodology.

689. Blackman, Winifred Susan. **The Fellāhīn of Upper Egypt, Their Religions, Social and Industrial Life with Special Reference to Survivals from Ancient Times.** London, Frank Cass; distr. Portland, Ore., International Scholarly Book Services, 1968. (Repr. of 1927 ed.). 331p. 186 illus. index. $11.50. LC 68-86656. ISBN 0-7146-1637-0. DT 70.B6 1968. DDC 390.09'62'3.

[P, C2] This book treats all aspects of the life of the peasant of Northern Egypt: tattoos and jewelry, villages, women and children, marriage, divorce, death and funerals; aspects of economy; harvest rites, magic, medicine, relations between men and women; superstitions such as the evil eye; supernatural beings; festivals, story-tellers, shaykhs and Coptic saints, etc. A fascinating, informative book for any reader, written in non-technical language.

690. Burckhardt, John Lewis (1784-1817). **Arabic Proverbs; Or, the Manners and Customs of the Modern Egyptians Illustrated from Their Proverbial Sayings Current in Cairo.** 3rd ed. Totowa, N.J., Rowman and Littlefield, 1972. (Repr. of 1830 ed.). 283p. $10.00. LC 72-172384. ISBN 0-87471-088-X. PN 6519.A7B8 1972. DDC 398.9'927.

Egyptian colloquial Arabic, in Arabic script, with English translation and, where necessary, the saying's source and/or an explanation of its meaning.

691. Fernea, Robert Alan. **Nubians in Egypt: Peaceful People.** Photos by Georg Gersten. Notes on Nubian architecture by Horst Jaritz. Austin, University of Texas Press, 1973. 146p. bibliog. index. $15.00. LC 73-3078. ISBN 0-292-75504-X. DT 135.N8F47. DDC 916.25'03.

The first 47 pages consist of an ethnological essay by Fernea, followed by a brief discussion of Nubian architecture illustrated with color photos and diagrams. The rest of the book is made up of an excellent collection of about 100 photos, most in black and white, depicting village life and buildings. This book is one result of a study undertaken before the Aswan High Dam was completed. The purposes of the study were to learn about traditional Nubian life, to record it for posterity before the dam's lake destroyed it, and to provide data for use in creating villages in which to resettle the people. An interesting book for the general reader and for students (cf. Elizabeth Fernea, item 705).

See also:

Fernea, Robert Alan, ed. **Contemporary Egyptian Nubia: A Symposium.** New Haven, Conn., 1968. LC cataloging n.a.

692. Harik, Iliya F. **The Political Mobilization of Peasants: A Study of an Egyptian Community.** Bloomington, Indiana University Press, 1974. 309p. bibliog. illus. (Studies in Development, No. 8). LC 73-16535. ISBN 0-253-34535-9. HN 783.5.H37 1974. DDC 301.35'2'0962.

After generalities on various aspects–social, economic, political–of rural community and Egyptian society, the author describes the system in a medium-sized Egyptian rural "village," including the impact of land reform, cooperative societies, and other government intervention, both historically and in the present. He describes village leadership dynamics, its relation to the Arab Socialist Union (the single Egyptian party); ASU's role in the community at large; peasant mobilization organization and the mass media, public opinion formation; village response to official political ideology; relationship of political attitudes, kinship and social mobility; ASU election of 1968; reflections on political change. Has some useful information on the efforts of Nasser's regime at local levels. For more advanced students.

Another source is:

Mayfield, James B. **Rural Politics in Nasser's Egypt: A Quest for Legitimacy.** Austin, University of Texas Press, 1971. 288p. bibliog. index. LC 70-165910. ISBN 0-292-70136-5. HN 783.5.M38. DDC 320.9162. Political history of the Egyptian fellahin, their personality; village politics in rural Egypt; history and ideology of ASU, its functions and structure; political socialization and ASU; structure and functions of local-level ASU organizations and village councils; Egyptian village bureaucracy; the local savings bank.

693. Heyworth-Dunne, James. **An Introduction to the History of Education in Modern Egypt.** London, Frank Cass; distr. Portland, Ore., International Scholarly Book Services, 1968. (Repr. of 1939 ed.). 502p. bibliog. indices. $13.00. LC n.a. ISBN 0-7146-1677-X. LA 1646.H4. DDC 370.962.

The period 1700-1798 is covered in 92 pages; 188 pages cover 1798-1848; the rest of the book covers the period to 1883, divided by Khedival reign. It includes lists of schools and curricula, covering Muslim, Jewish, Coptic, Greek, and other ethnic schools, religious schools, and the important educational missions to Europe. It has some information on the intellectual infrastructure of the country. A very detailed work, probably too detailed for most collections, but one of the few works on the subject, and basic for a rounded picture of nineteenth century Egypt.

694. Lane, Edward William (1801-1876). **Manners and Customs of the Modern Egyptians.** New York, Dover Publications, 1973. 619p. illus. $5.00pa. LC 72-93077. ISBN 0-486-22935-1. DT 70.L27 1973. DDC 916.2. (Also, New York, E. P. Dutton, 1966. $3.50. LC n.a.)

[P1, C1, S1, S3] The "modern Egyptians" in this monumental work were those living in the 1820s and 1830s. Lane "went Egyptian" and wrote a detailed account of all aspects of daily life, including religion, laws, education, government, social usages, domestic life, folkways, and superstitions; the bath, use of tobacco, etc.; games, music, storytelling, public festivals, and funeral customs. A fundamental work written just before the major changes in Egyptian life began in response to Western civilization's penetration; it covers all classes of the population. The basic work on the subject.

695. Leeder, S. H. **Modern Sons of the Pharaohs.** New York, Arno Press, 1973. (Repr. of 1913 ed.). 355p. illus. index. (The Middle East Collection). $21.00. LC 73-6288. ISBN 0-405-05346-X. DT 70.L4 1973. DDC 916.2'03'4.

Half the book describes all aspects of Coptic life, particularly the country folk, both upper and lower classes, including daily life, beliefs, occupations, superstitions, life cycle beliefs and ceremonies; saints; shopkeepers and craftsmen. The second half deals with the

Church–appearance of churches, clergy, theology, sacraments, worship. The author depicts a declined Church lacking in spirituality and sunk in ignorance. The photos are interesting.

G. ECONOMY

697. Hansen, Bent, and Girgis A. Marzouk. **Development and Economic Policy in the UAR (Egypt).** Amsterdam, North-Holland Publishing Company; distr. New York, Humanities Press, 1965. 333p. indices. $13.25. LC 66-41365. HC 535.H37. DDC 330.962.

A general description and analysis of the Egyptian economic system, covering all sectors of the economy: agriculture and prices, value-added, techniques and inputs, productivity, government agricultural policies; industry (capital, prices, wages, profits, industrialization); foreign trade and payments, balance of payments, trade policy; savings, investments, foreign deficit; public finance and fiscal policy; the new economic system; five-year plan; nationalization of industry; labor. A useful addition to larger collections for advanced students, it is not a systematic survey of basic data or a detailed description of economic activity, but a macro-analysis concerned with how the economy operates and the intent, process of creation, implementation, and results of government economic policy, as well as general trends in the various secotrs during Nasser's period. As will be seen from the number of books included in this *Guide*, Egypt has had by far the most scholarly attention of any Near Eastern country, except perhaps Israel.

698. Issawi, Charles Philip. **Egypt in Revolution: An Economic Analysis.** London, Oxford University Press, 1963. 343p. bibliog. tables. index. $8.50. LC 63-6492. ISBN 0-19-214907-5. HC 535.I74. DDC 330-962.

[P1, C1, S1] The basic description of all aspects of Egypt's economy, featuring factual data as well as generalizations, analysis of problems, possible solutions, and prospects for the future. Indispensable, despite being grossly outdated because neither Issawi nor anyone else has seen fit to bring it up to date. It does not describe the planning process.

699. Mabro, Robert. **The Egyptian Economy, 1952-1972.** Oxford, Clarendon Press, 1974. 254p. bibliog. index. $12.75; price n.a. pa. LC 74-188342. ISBN 0-19-877030-8; 0-19-877031-6pa. HC 535.M17. DDC 330.9'62'05.

[P1, C1, S1] This interpretive study of the subject begins with a brief historical background to the economy before 1952, a brief but rigorous discussion of the demography, and an account of the resources and their recent development. The rest treats land reform, the Aswan Dam, and land reclamation; institutional changes and planning process; economic growth and structural changes; employment problem; changes in income distribution. Some background is given in each chapter with an account of actions taken, their theoretical assumptions, the changes that resulted, trends and conclusions about the positive and negative aspects of the changes and trends, and the implications for the future. Treatment is mainly general, with only enough statistical and other information provided to indicate trends and make comparisons; no effort is made to use specific cases to illustrate the author's points, nor to present a factual survey of either the structure or the operation of the economy. Some knowledge of economics and its terminology is useful because the discussion is technical in places. A critical study which takes a constructive, essentially positive attitude.

700. Mead, Donald C. **Growth and Structural Change in the Egyptian Economy.** Homewood, Ill., Richard D. Irwin, 1967. 414p. bibliog. stat. tables. index. (Publications of the Economic Growth Center). $8.50. LC 66-27466. HC 533.M4. DDC 330.962.

[C2] A general description and analysis of the Egyptian economy, problems, policy, and prospects. The discussion is so generalized that the whole process is totally, shockingly depersonalized, as if no people were involved. However, this is not necessarily the fault of this particular book. It gets rather technical at times. It is not a reference work, nor really an introduction, but it is useful as one of our relatively few sources of information. It gives a somewhat different perspective from other works listed in this *Guide*.

701. O'Brien, Patrick [Karl]. **The Revolution in Egypt's Economic System: From Private Enterprise to Socialism, 1952-1965.** London, Oxford University Press, 1966. 354p. bibliog. index. $10.00. LC 66-67381. ISBN 0-19-214949-0. HC 535.02. DDC 338.962.

An economic history with particular emphasis on the developing government role. Mainly a generalized, analytical treatment rather than a detailed factual narrative. It is based on field work and extensive use of Arabic sources, unlike many works on the subject, with much material on the Egyptian form of socialism. It describes the planning system and process in general terms, including problems and the effectiveness of the whole.

702. Rivlin, Helen Anne B. **The Agricultural Policy of Muhammad ᶜAlī in Egypt.** Cambridge, Mass., Harvard University Press, 1961. 393p. bibliog. index. (Harvard Middle Eastern Studies, 4). $11.00. LC 61-5251. ISBN 0-674-01251-8. HD 2123 1961.R5. DDC 338.10962.

Based on primary sources, the book treats changes in land tenure and Muhammad ᶜAlī's administration, its organization, dynamics, and failures. It includes a useful general introduction, followed by a discussion of the administration of the agricultural program. Rivlin also treats the failure of the financial system and agricultural policy, the influence of trade and industry on agriculture, and the influence of the military service on manpower availability; irrigation, its development and organization, and its influence on the agrarian economy. An important book for the history of Egyptian agriculture and the Muhammad Ali regime, on which we have so few books that even though this work is rather specialized it is one of our main sources of information.

703. Saab, Gabriel S. **The Egyptian Agrarian Reform, 1952-1962.** London, Oxford University Press, 1967. 236p. bibliog. index. (Middle Eastern Monographs). $8.50. LC 67-84570. ISBN 0-19-214947-4. HD 976.S2. DDC 333.7'6'0962.

An attempt to "analyse the operation of the Egyptian agrarian reform at close range . . . to appraise the extent to which the various laws and measures had been effectively implemented and to determine the immediate effects." Basing his work on field research, he describes the expropriation and distribution of estates, procedures, structures, practice and problems, as well as the same aspects of the cooperative organizations, including their management. Also, infrastructure problems, including housing and farm buildings, irrigation, types of supervised agrarian credit; production and marketing, use of man and animal power; land distribution and its economic, social, and financial aspects, including farm income and use of added income; vocational training; problems of changes in tenancy and agricultural labor status, as well as problems of cooperative farming, land reclassification, etc. A most useful book for regional and disciplinary collections.

See also:

Abdel-Fadil, Mahmoud. **Development, Income Distribution and Social Change in Rural Egypt (1952-1970): A Study in the Political Economy of Agrarian Transition.** Cambridge, England, Cambridge University Press, 1975. ca. 240p. (University of Cambridge. Department of Applied Economics. Occasional Paper, 45). $16.50; $7.50pa. LC 75-17114. ISBN 0-521-21000-3; 0-521-29019-8pa. LC cataloging n.a.

Baer, Gabriel. **A History of Land Ownership in Modern Egypt, 1800-1950.** London, Oxford University Press, 1962. 252p. LC 62-5229. HD 975.B233. DDC 333.30962. Land ownership patterns, their relation to production and the economy; agricultural credit, government intervention; foreign ownership; land reform. Extremely informative and important.

Crouchly, Arthur Edwin. **Economic Development of Modern Egypt.** New York, Longmans, Green, 1938. 286p. LC 39-16390. HC 533.C7. DDC 330.962.

Hurst, Harold Edwin. **The Nile: A General Account of the River and the Utilization of Its Waters.** London, Constable, 1952. 326p. LC 52-14686. TC 119.N5H8. DDC 627.12.

Landes, David S. **Bankers and Pashas: International Finance and Economic Imperialism in Egypt.** New York, Harper and Row, 1969. 354p. LC 75-3718. HG 3384.L3 1969. DDC 332.1'5'0962. The latter nineteenth century.

Omran, Abdel Rahman R. **Egypt: Population Problems & Prospects.** Chapel Hill, Carolina Population Center, University of North Carolina, 1973. 448p. LC 73-168173. HB 3663.O57. DDC 301.32'9'62.

Rabie, Hassanein. **The Financial System of Egypt, A.H. 564-741/A.D. 1169-1341.** London, Oxford University Press, 1972. LC 72-182840. ISBN 0-19-713564-1. HJ 1861.A3R3. DDC 336.62.

Radwan, Samir. **Capital Formation in Egyptian Industry and Agriculture, 1882-1967.** London, Ithaca Press, 1975 (forthcoming). ca. 320p. (St. Antony's Middle East Monographs). $12.50. LC cataloging n.a. Estimates capital formation for the period, then discusses long-term trends in capital formation and the underlying economic, historical, and institutional factors involved. [Annotation taken from catalog blurb.]

Shaw, Stanford Jay. **The Financial and Administrative Organization and Development of Ottoman Egypt, 1517-1798.** Princeton, N.J., Princeton University Press, 1962. (c. 1958). 451p. LC 61-7412. PJ 25.P7 vol. 19 [HJ 1681.S5].

H. DESCRIPTION AND TRAVEL

704. Brander, Bruce. **The River Nile.** 2nd ed. Washington, D.C., National Geographic Society, 1968. 208p. illus. index. $4.25. LC 68-4434. DT 124.B7 1968. DDC 916.2'03.

[P]   A typical National Geographic book, it is an interesting description of the author's travels and the country, from its sources in the African highlands to the Delta. He discusses the people and the antiquities, and his story is made infinitely more vivid by the excellent, very interesting, and informative color illustrations. For public libraries. Another work featuring an interesting collection of photos is Paul Strand, *Living Egypt*, text by James Aldridge (New York, Horizon Press, 1969. 154p. [An Aperture Book]. LC 74-5902. DT47.S7. DDC 916.2'0022'2). Rural Egypt—landscape, atmospherics, popular architecture, lives of the people, portraits of many individuals illustrating racial types. Marginal for purchase, but useful for readers wanting to get a feel for the country.

705. Fernea, Elizabeth Warnock. **A View of the Nile.** Garden City, N.Y., Doubleday, 1970. 320p. $6.95. LC 71-89130. ISBN 0-385-08545-1. DT 56.F47. DDC 916.2'04'5.

An American woman describes her years of living in Cairo and in a village in Nubia, most of the book concerning the latter. Much of her personal life is recounted, including the birth of her two children and her reactions to giving birth in a strange country. It is not a source of much specifically useful information, but the elements of Nubian village life and the nature of the people emerge vividly, particularly women's life. The portion on Cairo is less useful, except as it suggests what an American woman might experience there. A most interesting book.

706. Johnson, Irving. **Yankee Sails the Nile.** New York, W. W. Norton, 1966. 256p. illus. $7.50. LC 66-18627. ISBN 0-393-03116-0. DT 124.J6. DDC 916.2045.

The author and his wife sailed their sloop up the Nile, took excellent photos, and have very vividly described the sights and lives of the people. A most enjoyable book.
See also:
Marlowe, John. **Four Aspects of Egypt.** London, George Allen and Unwin, 1966. 303p. illus. LC 66-70016. DT 56.M38. DDC 916.2045. For the general reader, a tour of Egypt, with much on antiquities; ancient Egypt, its history and civilization; medieval Cairo; the Nile, its sights and role in agriculture, and agricultural methods; modern Egypt under Nasser.

707. St. John, Bayle. **Village Life in Egypt.** New York, Arno Press, 1973. (Repr. of 1852 ed.). 2v. in 1. (The Middle East Collection). $30.00. LC 73-6298. ISBN 0-405-05358-4. DT 54.S15 1973. DDC 916.2'04'3.

A fascinating, well-written, often humorous, very sympathetic narrative of a 10-month trip. It describes the people, their character, lives, dress, houses, food; their stories, of which several examples are presented at length; government abuse of the peasants and the negative results on the size of the population and productivity; life cycle; superstitions; Cairo; the ruling elite; Bedouins; antiquities; army and conscription; "justice."

708. Sykes, John. **Down into Egypt: A Revolution Observed.** London, Hutchinson, 1969. 190p. o.p. LC 79-449349. ISBN 0-09-098300-9. DT 56.S9. DDC 916.2'03'5.

Sykes, who went to Egypt eight months after the 1967 war, gives us a very interesting account of conversations with members of the Egyptian elite and officials. It reveals the psychology, processes, attitudes, and self-view of the Egyptian government and its ways, and the mind of the transitional elite, both men and women. He also describes a village's relations with the government, and the relations of a member of the elite who was of village origin with his village. A fascinating work for general reader and student alike.

I. GUIDEBOOKS

709. **Nagel's Encyclopedia-Guide: Egypt.** Geneva, Nagel Publishers; distr. New York, Hippocrene Books, 1973. 815p. bibliog. glossary. maps. index. $26.00. LC cataloging n.a.

The first 189 pages of this travel guide, which was prepared by French Egyptologists, with contributions from other specialists, survey the history and civilization of Egypt from earliest times to the present. The book includes a dictionary of archaeology, discussions of the Copts and their arts, Islamic art, etc. The book is organized around itineraries in the main cities and regions beginning with Cairo, each section having an introductory historical survey of the region or city. The sites along each route are described in detail. The ancient antiquities receive by far the lion's share of attention, though Islamic antiquities and sites are not entirely slighted when they are part of itineraries. There is a concluding section of practical information on the climate, clothing, passports, transportation, facilities, and an Arabic glossary, but this section is skimpy and rather general, with no effort made at evaluating facilities. In effect, the book is a handbook of ancient Egyptian antiquities, since it gives the history of the sites and the excavations. The place of each item in Egyptian religion, history and civilization is detailed. Thus anyone interested in ancient Egypt can benefit from the book. Those interested in Islamic antiquities should refer to Russell (item 712).

J. CAIRO

710. Abū Lughd, Jānit. **Cairo: 1001 Years of the City Victorious.** Princeton, N.J., Princeton University Press, 1971. 284p. bibliog. illus. index. (Studies on the Near East). $25.00. LC 73-112992. ISBN 0-691-03085-5. DT 143.A26. DDC 916.2'1603.

A first-rate history and description of the city and analysis of its growth, arrangement, problems, and prospects. Utilizing 156 excellent photos and drawings, plus many maps and tables, the author traces the physical and demographic growth of the city and discusses its quarters, economy, social life, and government, as well as topics such as land use, urban problems, infrastructure, government plans, patterns of growth, etc. It is an urban studies approach that does not cover the city's role in Egypt's history, nor its cultural life. Over half the book deals with the twentieth century. The only major monograph on Cairo, it is one of very few such studies in any language on any city in the Near East-North Africa area, based on over 15 years of study of all available sources and much field work. This oversized, double-columned book is probably too much for college collections unless they are supporting urban studies courses. A good popular work, which should be read by most readers before Abu-Lughd to get a feel for the city, is Aldridge (item 711).

711. Aldridge, James. **Cairo.** Boston, Little, Brown, 1969. 370p. illus. o.p. LC 72-79364. DT 143.A6. DDC 916.2'16'05.

A thoroughly interesting, informative, loving history and description of the city, its role in Egypt's history (which is narrated at length), its growth and physical development; the architecture and antiquities; social and cultural life down through history; the quarters as they developed; the European discovery of Egypt and Cairo. About two-thirds of the book covers the nineteenth and twentieth centuries. The many excellent photos are quite informative. For all types of travellers it is a must, and most readers will find it useful to read before passing on to the formal scholarship of Abu-Lughd (item 710).

712. Russell, Dorothea (Moore), Lady. **Medieval Cairo and the Monasteries of the Wādi Nātrūn: A Historical Guide.** London, Weidenfeld and Nicolson, 1962. 368p. bibliog. illus. index. £2.10. LC 72-200076. ISBN 0-297-16774-X. DT 143.R8 1962. DDC 916.216.

A travel guide with itineraries, descriptions, and historical and socio-cultural notes. While it is mainly for serious tourists, armchair travellers will also find it of interest.

XX. IRAN

A detailed work on the period since 1500 is a must, since that period is vital for understanding modern Iran.

A. GENERAL WORKS

713. **Area Handbook for Iran.** [Smith, Harvey Henry]. 1971. 653p. (DA PAM 550-68). $7.45. LC 73-608678. DS 254.5.S6 1971. DDC 915.5'03'5.
[B, P1, C1, S1] See the annotation at the head of Section II (page 30).

714. **Iran Almanac and Book of Facts.** 11th ed. Tehran, Echo of Iran; distr. New York, William S. Heinman, 1972. 816p. illus. $17.50pa. LC 62-50366. AY 1185.I7.
A yearbook containing an enormous amount of information and statistics on the history and geography of the country; national affairs (including government, politics, armed forces, media, administration, foreign relations); all aspects of the economy; social and cultural life; education; charity and business organizations; sports, etc. The statistics must be taken as suggestive, not definitive.

715. Wilber, Donald Newton. **Iran, Past and Present.** 7th ed. Princeton, N.J., Princeton University Press, 1975. 376p. bibliog. illus. index. $13.50. LC 75-4626. ISBN 0-691-03102-9. DS 272.W49 1975. DDC 955.
[P1, C1, S1] The standard introduction to the country, covering all aspects: history (incorporating cultural notes); ethnology, popular culture, and social life; reflections on the modern Iranian character. Two-thirds of the book deals with the twentieth century: politics, government, economy, and infrastructure. A good bibliography. The first book to get.
Additional works:

Bahrampour, Firouz. **Iran: Emergence of a Middle Eastern Power.** Brooklyn, Theodore Gaus' Sons, 1970. 125p. LC 79-140151. DS 254.5.B33. DDC 327.55'073.

New York University Near Eastern Round Table, 4th, 1970-1971. **Iran: Continuity and Variety.** Ed. by Peter J. Chelkowski. New York, Center for Near Eastern Studies, New York University, 1971. 75p. LC 72-182490. DS 252.4.N48 1971. DDC 915.5.03'5.

B. HISTORY AND POLITICS

716. Armajani, Yahya. **Iran.** Englewood Cliffs, N.J., Prentice-Hall, 1972. 182p. bibliog. index. (The Modern Nations in Historical Perspective. A Spectrum Book, S 629). $6.95; $2.45pa. LC 70-168738. ISBN 0-13-506139-3; 0-13-506121-0pa. DS 272.A9. DDC 955.
[P1, P2, C1, S1, S2] An interesting, often controversial, introductory history of Iran from earliest times. Much space is allotted to the twentieth century. Some of the author's explanations of events and generalizations are unsatisfactory, and his transliteration of Persian words follows Persian pronunciation, rather than standardized systems, and is applied inconsistently. The book complements Bausani (item 717) and Frye (item 718); it is more freely analytical and it does a better job of relating Iranian history to what most readers already know. It is very readable, but more technical and a bit more advanced than Frye. Each of the three books emphasizes certain topics or points that the others do not, but if a choice must be made, either Armajani or Frye will do just as well, except that Frye is somewhat more elementary, for the uninitiated general reader.

Until recently the standard history has been:

Sykes, Sir Percy Molesworth. **A History of Persia.** New York, Barnes and Noble, 1969. (Repr. of 1915 ed.). 2v. LC 79-6457. DS 272.S8 1969. DDC 955. It covers the period from ancient times to the early twentieth century. It is grossly inadequate in many ways but is more detailed than other general surveys for the average reader.

The major work on Iranian history is:

Cambridge History of Iran. Cambridge, England, Cambridge University Press, 1968– . 8v. LC 67-12845. DS 272.C34. DDC 955. To date Volume 1, *Geography*, and Volume 5, *The Seljuq and Mongol Periods*, have been issued. Volume 4, *Arab Invasion to the Seljuqs*, is scheduled for Summer 1975. Each volume consists of essays by various authorities structured to form a systematic, comprehensive survey, which includes culture and other aspects in addition to political history.

More specialized works include:

Lockhart, Lawrence. **Persian Cities.** London, Luzac, 1960. 188p. LC 60-39215. DS 259.L6. DDC 955. Brief histories of 23 main Iranian cities, their significance and history. Many good photos.

Lockhart, Lawrence. **The Fall of the Safavi Dynasty and the Afghan Occupation of Persia.** Cambridge, England, Cambridge University Press, 1958. 583p. LC 58-14843. DS 293.L6. DDC 955.

717. Bausani, Alessandro. **The Persians, from the Earliest Days to the Twentieth Century.** Tr. from Italian. New York, St. Martin's Press, 1971. 204p. bibliog. illus. index. $8.95. LC 71-149313. DS 272.B3813 1971b. DDC 915.5'03.

[B, C1, S2] An introduction which has little on the twentieth century. It includes information on economic history and relates aspects of Persian history and culture to our general knowledge. More scholarly and technical than Armajani (item 716) and more systematic. Much Persian terminology is used. It has a very full 10-page multilingual bibliographical essay, subdivided by chapter. For the beginning specialist and other readers wishing to probe a bit more deeply than they can with Armajani or Frye (item 718).

718. Frye, Richard Nelson. **Persia.** Rev. ed. London, George Allen and Unwin, 1968. 128p. bibliog. index. £1.50; £1.10pa. LC 75-385978. ISBN 0-04-955002-0; 0-04-955003-9pa. DS 254.5.F7 1968. DDC 915.5'03.

[P1, C1, S1] An excellent general introduction, by a renowned specialist, to Iranian history, culture, and religion. One-third of the book concerns the period from 1800. It is well written and can be easily understood by the general reader. The first book for small public libraries, it is less technical than Bausani (item 717) and Armajani (item 716).

719. Frye, Richard Nelson. **The Golden Age of Persia: The Arabs in the East.** New York, Barnes and Noble Books, 1975. 289p. illus. (History of Civilization). $25.00. LC n.a. ISBN 0-06-492288-X.

After a chapter on pre-Islamic Sassanian Iran, this work, a continuation of the author's *Heritage of Persia*, proceeds with a discussion of pre-Arab Central Asia. It covers peoples, government, culture, history; the Arab conquests of Iran and Central Asia in the seventh century; history of the regions through the Abbasid period (thirteenth century); Persian-Arab cultural interaction, religious political history and developments; Iranian contributions to Islamic civilization, the growth of Muslim learning and scholarship, and other cultural activities in the region; arts and crafts; the Iranian dynasties; ascendancy of the Turks in the tenth and eleventh centuries; Arab heritage in Iran, particularly in the fields of religion and linguistics. Throughout, Frye offers his own interpretations and analyses, as well as comments on the state of our knowledge. Not overwhelmingly loaded with details, it is an interesting and informative work for the reader with a basic background.

C. 1800 TO THE PRESENT

720. Avery, Peter. **Modern Iran.** New York, Praeger, 1965. 527p. bibliog. index. (Nations of the Modern World). $11.00. LC 65-14176. DS 307.A95. DDC 955.05. Paperback: London, Ernest Benn, £1.50. ISBN 0-510-37711-4.

[P1, C1, S1] This is the basic work on nineteenth and twentieth century Iran, based on original sources and a deep knowledge of the country and language. It emphasizes political and diplomatic history, with some material on economy and society. The first 125 pages cover the nineteenth century, up to the Constitutional revolution of 1905-1906. More research is needed on the nineteenth century, and some of the research that has been carried out since Avery was published has rendered his account somewhat obsolete; however, the new material has not been synthesized into a monograph, and this is no way detracts from the value of the book as a basic part of any college or larger public library. No other book remotely approaches Avery's treatment of the twentieth century.

Other important works are:

Algar, Hamid. **Religion and State in Iran, 1785-1906: The Role of the Ulema in the Qajar Period.** Berkeley, University of California Press, 1969. 286p. LC 72-79959. ISBN 0-520-01386-7. DS 299.A45 1969. DDC 297'.197'7.

Fasā'ī, Ḥasan ibn Ḥasan (b. 1821 or 1822). **History of Persia under Qajar Rule.** Tr. from Persian by Herbert Busse. New York, Columbia University Press, 1972. 494p. LC 74-183229. ISBN 0-231-03197-1. DS 298.F3713 1972. DDC 955'.04.

Cottam, Richard W. **Nationalism in Iran.** Pittsburgh, University of Pittsburgh Press, 1964. 332p. LC 64-12490. DS 318.C66. DDC 955.

Keddie, Nikki R. **Religion and Rebellion in Iran: The Tobacco Protest of 1891-1892.** London, Frank Cass, 1966. 163p. LC 67-77359. DS 307.K4. DDC 955.04.

Zabih, Sepehr. **The Communist Movement in Iran.** Berkeley, University of California Press, 1966. 279p. LC 66-25348. HX 417.Z3. DDC 329.955.

Maftūn, ʿAbd al-Razzāq Bayg ibn Najaf Qulī Khān Dumbulī (1762 or 1763-1827 or 1828). **The Dynasty of the Kajars.** Abridged tr. from the Persian Maʿāṣir-i Sulṭāniyah, by Sir Harford Jones Brydges. New York, Arno Press, 1973. (Repr. of 1833 ed.). cxci, 448p. maps. LC 73-6272. ISBN 0-405-05327-4. DS 298.M3131973. DDC 955'.04. The work treats in detail the period 1797-1811. The almost 200 pages of "preliminary matter" by the translator provide historical and political background to the events related in the text, including his personal experiences at the court. The text is an official court history; it provides not only a source of the period's history, but a Persian perspective. It is a typical example of Persian historiography and style of writing.

721. Banani, Amin. **The Modernization of Iran, 1921-1941.** Stanford University Press, 1961. 191p. bibliog. index. $6.00. LC 61-5504. ISBN 0-8047-0050-8. DS 317.B3. DDC 955.05.

[C3] This interpretive work deals with Reza Shah's reforms in various fields—in particular, legislative and statutory reform, especially in social organization. There is much on education and the economy, the army, administrative and public health systems, with an analysis of the results of the various measures. This is a general treatment, which notes gaps in the plans and failures in implementation and conception, the lack of understanding of all the implications of individual measures, etc. It includes general historical background and discusses the rise of Reza Shah. For larger collections.

722. Chubin, Shahram, and Sepehr Zabih. **The Foreign Relations of Iran: A Small State in a Zone of Great Power Conflict.** Berkeley, University of California Press, 1975. 384p. bibliog. LC 73-91677. ISBN 0-520-02683-7. DS 274.C48. DDC 327.55.

[B, C1, S1] An interpretive historical survey of Iran's policies and relations with the United States and Russia from World War II on; it covers Egypt, Iraq, and the Persian Gulf, with brief coverage of relations with Afghanistan and Pakistan. Also, the interrelations of Iran's new military and economic importance and its potential roles in Near Eastern politics. Well documented, with a comprehensive bibliography. A basic work.

723. Ramazani, Rouhollah K. **The Foreign Policy of Iran: A Developing Nation in World Affairs, 1500-1941.** Charlottesville, University Press of Virginia, 1966. 330p. index. $7.50. LC 66-12469. ISBN 0-8139-0200-2. DS 274.R33. DDC 327.55.

[P1, C1, S1] The main emphasis of this work, despite its title, is the nineteenth and twentieth centuries; the material on the earlier period merely presents highlights and the broad sweep of events. Basically synthetic and superficial, it is useful mainly in bringing the information together. There are 86 pages that cover 1905 to 1920, and 130 pages that deal with the rise and policy of Riza Shah. The research is not extensive, nor is it a scholarly disciplinary case study, but it is all we have. For most readers, Avery (item 720) and Lenczowski (item 144) are probably sufficient.

Other important works are:

Kazemzadeh, Firuz. **Britain and Russia in Iran, 1864-1914: A Study in Imperialism.** New Haven, Yale University Press, 1968. 711p. LC 67-24501. DS 274.2.R8K36. DDC 327.47'055.

Lenczowski, George. **Russia and the West in Iran, 1918-1948: A Study in Big Power Rivalry.** New York, Greenwood Press, 1968. (Repr. of 1949 ed.). 383p. LC 68-23307. DS 318.L46 1968. DDC 955.05.

Martin, Bradford G. **German-Persian Diplomatic Relations, 1873-1912.** 'S-Gravenhage, Mouton, 1959. 237p. LC A 60-1243. DD 120.I55M3.

724. Ramazani, Rouhollah K. **Iran's Foreign Policy, 1941-1973: A Study of Foreign Policy in Modernizing Nations.** Charlottesville, University Press of Virginia, 1975. bibliog. index. LC 74-16467. ISBN 0-8139-0594-X. DS 274.R3 1975. DDC 327.55.

[P1, C1, S1] This history of Iran's foreign policy emphasizes its relations with the United States, Britain, and Russia. The author's main interest is a running interpretation of policy from Iran's perspective, not a detailed factual diplomatic history. Some relation to local politics is indicated. Even allowing for the fact that much of the requisite documentation is not available, the book is not satisfying. For all its bulk, far fewer facts are included than are available, while much of the interpretation, which occupies a great deal of space, is pure verbiage rather than substance; and one constantly feels that the analysis is superficial. The final chapter, surveying Iran's relations with its Near Eastern neighbors, is too brief, which vitiates the book's usefulness as a basic work. However, as one of but two such works available, it is essential.

725. Ramazani, Rouhollah K. **The Persian Gulf: Iran's Role.** Charlottesville, University Press of Virginia, 1972. 157p. bibliog. index. $7.50. LC 72-77262. ISBN 0-8139-0406-4. DS 274.2.I55.R35 1972. DDC 327.55'0182'4.

Iran's position in the Persian Gulf was the subject of many press articles in 1973-1974. This book surveys briefly, in general terms, the history of Iran's relations with the powers interested in the Gulf, particularly Britain; Reza Shah's rise to power and attempt to reassert Iran's position there. The next three chapters discuss respectively Iran's political, economic and security interests in the Gulf: the Iranian-Arab cold war, the conflict with Iraq over the mouth of the Tigris-Euphrates confluence, Hormuz Island, Bahrein; oil, trade through and with the Gulf, Iran as a leading power in the Gulf; political stability of the various Gulf countries; the superpowers there—the power transition resulting from Britain's withdrawal and the various policy alternatives for Iran; prospects for the future. It is concluded by 27 pages of documents. A useful source of background information, but not a high priority for purchase because it is so superficial and brief.

726. Shuster, William Morgan (1877-1960). **The Strangling of Persia: Story of the European Diplomacy and Oriental Intrigue That Resulted in the Denationalization of Twelve Million Mohammedans; A Personal Narrative.** New York, Greenwood Press, 1968. (Repr. of 1939 ed.). 63, 423p. index. $21.50. LC 69-10154. ISBN 0-8371-0224-3. DS 315.S5 1968. DDC 955.05.

An American financial advisor to the Persian government during the first decade of the twentieth century tried to put the country's financial system into shape, organize taxation and enforce it, and otherwise make considerable changes in the system, which had very strongly entrenched traditions of corruption and tax-evasion that could only strongly oppose Shuster's efforts. At the same time, the British, Russians, and Iranian groups were engaging in a merry-go-round of intrigues and rivalries which in various ways influenced and were potentially influenced by Shuster's efforts. In a bluntly worded account, Shuster details the situation, his experiences in trying to make his program work, and his ultimate ouster from Iran, as the bad guys won. Although quite subjective, the book is an important illustration of the problems of trying to change a traditional system; many readers will find it interesting. Shuster was a typical example of the many successful Americans who, having mastered the American system, its values, procedures, and psychology, go abroad assuming that theirs is the only way. Confronted by a symmetrically complete "Oriental" system, they find that they have to start over as neophytes in learning the new system, and they return home frustrated failures.

See also:

McDaniel, Robert A. **The Shuster Mission and the Persian Constitutional Revolution.** Minneapolis, Bibliotheca Islamica, 1974. 259p. LC 72-96696. ISBN 0-88297-004-6. DS 313.M27. DDC 955'.05.

727. Upton, Joseph M. **The History of Modern Iran: An Interpretation.** Cambridge, Mass., Harvard University Press, 1961. 163p. bibliog. (Harvard Middle Eastern Monograph, 2). $4.50pa. LC 60-7202. ISBN 0-674-39900-5. DS 315.U75. DDC 955.05.

A brief introduction to twentieth century Iran (to 1958). It begins with a historical introduction, followed by an interesting and enlightening chapter on divisive pressures in the country—social, economic, and cultural factors. The next two sections treat the rise of Reza Shah (1921-1941), the impact of his regime, and conditions and life in Iran. It then discusses all aspects of development, including economics, from 1941 to 1958. A final chapter notes the situation as it stood in 1958. An analytical treatment to be read before Avery, though one of the other introductions will do about as well. Upton's value lies in his basically dispassionate analysis and the stimulation of reader thinking; his book provides an orientation to the subject that makes the detailed works more meaningful. For larger collections.

D. BIOGRAPHY

728. Bayne, E. A. **Persian Kingship in Transition: Conversations with a Monarch Whose Office Is Traditional and Whose Goal Is Modernization.** New York, American Universities Field Staff, 1968. 288p. index. $7.50. LC 68-30502. ISBN 0-910116-65-2. DS 318.B34. DDC 320.9'55.

Bayne, a long-term representative of the AUFS and author of many of its reports on Iran, had numerous, lengthy conversations with the Shah, in an attempt at oral history. He probes the Shah's motivations and intentions, his conceptions of the monarchy, Iran's need for him, his role as he conceives it, and his views on national issues. Bayne relates the Shah's words, which are quoted at length, to the broader picture and to political science concepts, and he gives his own analysis of the Iranian situation. The book is not a comprehensive analysis of the Shah's actions and the office, and it has nothing on Iran's political processes, but it is a useful expression of the views of a key regional leader who is receiving much attention.

729. Mohammad Rezā Shāh, Shah of Iran. **Mission for My Country.** New York, McGraw-Hill Book Company, 1961. 336p. illus. index. LC 61-7241. DS 318.M6 1961. DDC 955.05.

The autobiography of the present Shah—after a brief outline of Persian history and a discussion of his father, Reza Shah, and his revolution. The autobiography covers the Shahinshah's childhood, education, and personal view of events and politics from the 1940s on. Then follow discussions of his foreign policy goals, social policy, economic policy, Iran's democracy; agriculture, women, education policy, oil; his daily routine. Strictly an official view, but relevant to the present.

730. Wilber, Donald Newton. **Riza Shah Pahlavi, the Resurrection and Reconstruction of Iran.** Hicksville, N.Y., Exposition Press, 1975. 301p. bibliog. illus. index. (An Exposition-University Book). $15.00. LC 74-34518. ISBN 0-682-48206-4. LC cataloging n.a.

The only serious biography of the present Shah's father, who began the process of modernization after he seized power and became the first Pahlavi Shah. The bulk of the book concerns his reign. The reforms and attempts at Westernization are not dwelt upon at length for their own sake, but as part of the flow of his life, ideas and politics, international relations, etc. Based on Persian language sources, interviews and U.S. diplomatic documents, it is an important contribution to the literature.

Additional biographical works are:

Lockhart, Lawrence. **Nadir Shah: A Critical Study Based Mainly upon Contemporary Sources.** New York, AMS Press, 1973. (Repr. of 1938 ed.). 344p. LC 78-180358. ISBN 0-404-56290-6. DS 294.L6 1973. DDC 955'.03'0924 [B]. A study of the rise to power and reign of the general who became Shah (1736-1747).

Sarwar, Ghulam, historian. **History of Shah Isma^cil Safawi.** New York, AMS Press, 1974. (Repr. of 1939 ed.). 126p. LC 75-180376. ISBN 0-404-56322-8. DS 292.3.S3 1974. DDC 292.3.S3 1975. The first Shah of modern Iran, who made Shiism the official sect.

E. CIVILIZATION

731. Arberry, Arthur John. **The Legacy of Persia.** Oxford, Clarendon Press, 1953. 421p. bibliog. illus. index. $7.50. LC 53-2314. ISBN 0-19-821905-9. DS 266.A7. DDC 915.5.

[P1, C1, S1] As with other volumes of the "Legacy" series, this is a collection of more or less introductory essays by leading authorities. Essays cover aspects of the country's classical civilization (arts, literature, science, language); relations with the ancient world, Byzantium, and the Arabs; and finally the early contacts with the West, including the Persian image in the Western mind. A basic work for colleges and more comprehensive public libraries. Beginning readers should start with one of the basic introductions first, because the experts make many of their essays somewhat detailed and technical.

732. Blunt, Wilfrid, and Wim Swaan. **Isfahan, Pearl of Persia.** New York, Stein and Day, 1966. 208p. bibliog. illus. index. (Centers of Art & Civilization Series). o.p. LC 66-17157. NA 1487.I8B55. DDC 709.5595. (*BIP* lists ed. distr.: New York, International Publications Service, $15.00.)

Emphasizing the period of Shah Abbas, 1587-1629, which was the city's golden age, the book describes in detail the city's architecture, and includes descriptions by writers (including Westerners) from various periods, as well as historical notes. It also describes life in the city, its festivals, Christian residents, the Armenian suburb of New Jolfa, Westerners in Isfahan, the minor arts (painting, gardens, carpets), the city under later rulers through the nineteenth century. The 115 illustrations, many of which are in color, are excellent. It will fascinate the general reader; a low priority book, but it adds a nice touch to any collection. Blunt, *not* the same as Wilfred Scawen Blunt, has written a number of popular works on Near Eastern subjects, to which the general reader is directed.

733. Frye, Richard Nelson. **Bukhara, the Medieval Achievement.** Norman, University of Oklahoma Press, 1965. 209p. bibliog. index. (The Centers of Civilization Series). $3.50. LC 65-24200. ISBN 0-8061-0666-2. DK 876.F7. DDC 958.707.

This interesting volume treats the city in the Islamic period, when the Arabs established their rule there in the seventh-eighth centuries. The city became an important commercial and cultural center in the ninth century and was an important source of the Persian literary renaissance. Frye traces its growth as a power center and capital of the Samanid dynasty. He describes the system of government, civilization, life, Persian writings in various fields; the role of Arabic; the economy; art and architecture; religious sciences. He traces the city's decline and history as the Samanids fell under Turkish domination and Bukhara lost its eminence in the eleventh and twelfth centuries. Unlike other volumes in the series that are listed in this *Guide*, it devotes little space to the physical description of the city. A fairly good background is needed before students can get much out of it.

734. Frye, Richard Nelson. **The Heritage of Persia.** London, Weidenfeld and Nicolson, 1963. 318p. bibliog. illus. index. £4.75. LC n.a. ISBN 0-297-16727-8. DS 275.F7. DDC 935. Paperback: New York, New American Library, 1966. (A Mentor Book, MQ 662). o.p.

[P1, P2, C1, S1] An excellent study and introduction to Iranian civilization before the Islamic era. The final chapter, "The Persian Conquest of Islam," records the retention of Iranian traditions into Islamic times and the linguistic change that led to the blossoming of Persian literature and culture under the Islamic canopy. The book is important because the memory of much of Iran's past is being revived and studied anew in Iran. It is also useful as good general background for the student of the Islamic period, who should know the people that Islam conquered and was partly conquered by in turn. Frye is a top specialist who makes the subject interesting.

735. Gray, Basil. **Persian Painting.** New York, Skira; distr. Cleveland, World Publishing Company, 1961. 191p. bibliog. index. (Treasures of Asia). o.p. LC 61-10169. ND 980.G72. DDC 759.955.

Islamic painting in the Iran-Afghanistan region, thirteenth to sicteenth centuries, consisted mainly of manuscript illuminations. This book traces the history of the art, which was highly developed, its technique, themes and styles, and the painters. It discusses the painting in the historical-cultural context of the times, since painting was one of the court arts. The many illustrations are magnificently reproduced hand-tipped colored plates. Basic for larger collections and students.

736. Pope, Arthur Upham. **An Introduction to Persian Art since the Seventh Century A.D.** Westport, Conn., Greenwood Press, 1972. (Repr. of 1931 ed.). 256p. bibliog. 103 illus. index. $18.75. LC 76-109824. ISBN 0-8371-4315-2. N 7280.P6 1972. DDC 709'.55.

A general introduction treating architecture, ceramics, books and miniatures, carpets, textiles, metalwork, and gardens, with a treatment of general historical trends. It is not really very good, but it does offer some perspectives to bring together and supplement information found in other books. For more comprehensive collections, but not really worth the price.

737. Pope, Arthur Upham. **Persian Architecture: The Triumph of Form and Color.** New York, George Braziller, 1965. 288p. bibliog. 397 illus. index. $25.00. LC 65-10275. ISBN 0-8076-0379-1. NA 1480.P6. DDC 720.955.

[P, C1, S] Seventy-five pages concern the pre-Islamic period; the rest of the book covers the Islamic era to the seventeenth century. It deals mainly with monumental buildings–mosques, palaces, tombs, fortresses–and emphasizes Persian architecture as *art*: thus, no houses, popular architecture, nor modern buildings are included. It goes beyond mere description to artistic appreciation. It discusses some technical details and the development of the techniques of structure and style, relating them to the geographical and cultural milieu. A most interesting and worthwhile book that even the beginner can well appreciate.

738. Wulff, Hans E. **The Traditional Crafts of Persia: Their Development, Technology and Influence on Eastern and Western Civilizations.** Cambridge, Mass., MIT Press, 1966. 404p. bibliog. gloss. 423 illus. $25.00; $7.95pa. LC 66-22642. ISBN 0-262-23025-9; 0-262-73028-6pa. TT 107.W8. DDC 745.5'0955.

[C1] Metallurgy of the various types of metals, including iron, gold, bronze, copper, embossing and engraving; oven-making; gem-cutting; woodworking, including inlay, wheel-wrights, bellowsmaking, and building crafts; ceramic arts; textiles, leathercrafts; agriculture and food treatment, including plow making and mills. Each topic includes a history of the craft and technical details, with drawings of machinery and close-up photos. A fascinating book that even the general reader might enjoy despite its technical information. Many of these crafts are found throughout the region; thus, much of the information can be considered to be of general usefulness, even though the details and individual techniques may differ from locale to locale.

F. SOCIETY

739. Arasteh, A. Reza. **Education and Social Awakening in Iran, 1850-1968.** 2nd rev. and
enl. ed. Leiden, E. J. Brill; distr. New York, W. S. Heinman, 1969. 237p. $20.00.
LC 73-416016. LA 1351.A7 1969. DDC 370'.955.

After chapters on general background and history, the book deals topically with
nineteenth and twentieth century education: training for bureaucracy and civil service;
vocational education and technical change; education for citizenship and literacy; secondary
education and the dilemma of youth; physical education to engender group affiliation; teachers
as agents of change; socio-political education (the media and organized youth activities);
missionary educational efforts; and the role of education in the reconstruction of Iran. The
book includes descriptions of the schools and system but offers relatively few details about any
subject; treatment is usually quite general. One of very few available works on the subject, but
not worth the price for most collections, unless there is specific need for it.

740. Barth, Fredrik. **Nomads of South Persia: The Basseri Tribe of the Khamseh Confederacy.**
New York, Humanities Press, 1965. 159p. bibliog. illus. index. (Series in Anthropology).
o.p. LC 66-67859. DS 269.B36 B3 1965. DDC 915.51035. Paperback: 1968. $2.87.
ISBN 0-316-08245-7.

A typical anthropological study describing the economy, social life and structure, kinship and political relations; camp structure; chieftanship, its origins and dynamics; demographic
aspects; a concluding chapter on Persian nomadic organization; and a longish appendix on ritual
life, from birth through marriage and death.

741. Binder, Leonard. **Iran: Political Development in a Changing Society.** Berkeley, University
of California Press, 1964. 362p. index. o.p. LC 62-14944. DS 318.B5. DDC 955.05.

[P1, C1, S1, S2]   A basic analysis and description of the political processes and socioeconomic structures of Iran, preceded by a 58-page "strategy for the study of a whole political
system." The book presents little specific information; it consists mainly of general statements,
with a few specific examples from history. However, it contains much general political wisdom
and an excellent analysis that is extremely enlightening, especially when read after the other
works in this *Guide.*

Another useful work is:

Bill, James Alban. **The Politics of Iran: Groups, Classes and Modernization.** Columbus,
Ohio, Merrill, 1972. 174p. bibliog. LC 73-187714. ISBN 0-675-09102-0. HN 740.Z9S62.
DDC 301.44'0955.

742. Donaldson, Bess Allen. **The Wild Rue: A Study of Muhammadan Magic and Folklore in
Iran.** New York, Arno Press, 1973. (Repr. of 1938 ed.). 216p. index. $12.00. LC 73-6277.
ISBN 0-405-05332-0. GR 290.D6 1973. DDC 390'.0955.

A detailed study based on research during long years of residence in Iran. It discusses
beliefs, theory, and practice of magic and presents stories about the evil eye, child-birth
practices, the jinn, love and marriage; saints, sayyids, and shrines; pilgrimage, angels, sacrifices;
weather, the heavens; names and numbers; oaths, curses, and blessings; calendar; Koran practices (such as using its verses as amulets); sacred and holy objects such as trees, plants, etc. It
includes stories about animals, insects, snakes, etc.; dreams; body functions; nails, hair and
teeth; talismans, divination, and exorcism. A fascinating basic work.

743. Elwell-Sutton, Laurence Paul. **Persian Proverbs.** London, John Murray, 1954. 103p.
(The Wisdom of the East Series). o.p. LC 55-338. PN 6519.P5E4. DDC 398.9.

Proverbs in English only, with explanations of their meanings, usage, and in many cases
the tale or well-known anecdote from which the proverb is taken and which must be known
before the meaning of the proverb is clear.

744. English, Paul Ward. **City and Village in Iran: Settlement and Economy in the Kirman
Basin.** Madison, University of Wisdonsin Press, 1966. 204p. bibliog. illus. index. LC
66-22856. HN 740.K5E5. DDC 309.1558.

A study of the city and region of Kirman, its various types and sizes of settlements, and the influence (and, indeed, dominance) of the city. It seeks to study the nature of settlement in the Middle East, nature of the region's social and economic organization, and the nature of change—e.g., the impact of technology and modernization. It begins by studying the geography and history of settlement; settlement patterns—relation to water sources; the development of structure and organization of Kirman city, including housing, village composition, field patterns; socioeconomic structure of the city and the surrounding area. Also social classes, occupations, relationship of the villages to the city, including the role of the urban elite in economic control of villages, and patterns of stability and change—social and economic, settlement patterns. The author concludes that the villages are not isolated and self-sufficient, as many have believed, but are dependent on the city. Several appendices provide additional factual data. For more advanced students.

745. Jacobs, Norman. **The Sociology of Development: Iran As an Asian Case Study.** New York, Praeger, 1966. 541p. bibliog. (Praeger Special Studies in International Economics and Development). o.p. LC 66-15743. HN 733.5.A8J3. DDC 309.155.

A description and analysis of various aspects of the Iranian social, political, and economic system, psychology, and values as they relate to Western concepts of development and modernization processes. It is based on personal observation, Iranian press, discussions with Iranians; except for its analyses, most of the book presents the Iranian view. It covers the theory, structure, practice and dynamics of political authority; economy and development; occupations, stratification, kinship; religion and authority, social relations, interpersonal relations; legitimate change—channels, process and limitations; Iranian society vis-à-vis the development model and problems; development myths—a critique. Jacobs seeks to answer the questions "Why have some countries not developed despite extensive aid and resources?" and "How can the situation be improved?" He demonstrates at length that Iranian values are extremely different from ours, and that they often are incompatible with what the West perceives to be the requirements of modernization. 1) Status and self-image values in all their ramifications are of much higher priority than "rational" economic considerations, efficiency, and the practical results of real achievement. 2) Iranian personal relations are totally negative, distrustful, defensive, opportunistic and selfish; cooperation, commitment, and consistency over the long run and often even for the short term are impossible; the personal position of each individual is basically insecure. These factors decisively affect the dynamics of the political system and power structure. 3) The educational system is geared to status, not to knowledge and training; general education is the ideal, not technical specialization or vocational education, which are not valued; a degree unrelated to actual merit or achievement is expected to imply qualification for high position. Jacobs distinguishes between form and function with respect to the adoption of the apparatus of development. Each component of the apparatus has in Western conceptions a rational social and economic result; the Iranians adopt the apparatus for entirely different reasons, such as international status rather than strictly economic reasons, so Western observers must not assume that development is actually occurring merely because they see that all the apparatus is in place: it probably is not working the way they intended it to. The available and useful forms will be adopted, but will also be modified and integrated with preexisting practice to fulfill pre-existing needs and functions. Jacobs seeks to understand the goals, the adaptive mechanisms, and the ground rules for meeting the goals in Iran, to help us realize why Iran has failed to develop and determine whether Iran *can* modernize. He concludes that the values of a rational economy are incompatible with the basic goals of each and all of the institutions in Iran's sociopolitical system; all the aid rendered will achieve nothing until the Iranians want to modernize and change the social system. The long chapter on development myths indicates that many of our key assumptions must be re-examined in light of this study; Jacobs believes most of them to be false, at least for Asian society (he believes that most Asian societies resemble Iran's) and perhaps for other regions as well. Must reading for advanced students. Many of the points made in this study are supported by: Zonis, Marvin, *The Political Elite of Iran* (Princeton, N.J., Princeton University Press, 1971. LC 74-90966. ISBN 0-691-03083-9) which is a technical but extremely informative study, for graduate students. Zonis, however, explores the points from a different perspective, and he includes more specific data.

746. Oberling, Pierre. **The Qashqā'i Nomads of Fars.** The Hague, Mouton, 1974. 277p. bibliog. illus. index. (Near and Middle East Monographs, 6). fl. 90.00. LC 72-94492. DS 269.K3.O.

The Qashqa'i tribal confederacy is one of the largest nomadic groups in Iran. The book begins with an account of their economy and political organization; rather than an ethnological study, however, it is a history of their important role in Iran's politics during the nineteenth and especially the twentieth century. A useful case study of a basic element in Iran's political dynamics, involving not only internal politics per se, but foreign intervention in Iran's politics, since Russia, Germany, and Britain all used the tribes to gain influence, including the Qashqa'i.

747. **Persian Folktales.** London, G. Bell, 1971. Tr. from German. 216p. £1.30. LC 71-871522. ISBN 0-7135-1727-1. GR 290.P4713 1971. DDC 398.2'0955.

A collection of tales for the general reader.

See also:

Lorimer, David Lockhart Robertson. **Persian Tales, Written Down for the First Time in the Original Kermani and Bakhtiari.** Translated by D. L. R. Lorimer and E. O. Lorimer. London, Macmillan, 1919. 354p. LC 20-9724. PZ 8.P432.

748. Rice, Mrs. Clara Colliver (Hammond). **Persian Women and Their Ways; the Experiences & Impressions of a Long Sojourn Amongst the Women of the Land of the Shah with an Intimate Description of Their Characteristics, Customs & Manner of Living.** London, Seeley, Service, 1923. 312p. illus. index. o.p. LC 24-5313. DS 266.R5.

A general description of all aspects of their lives, dress, religion, superstitions, status, with general observations on aspects of the country. Includes treatment by men, domestic life; polygamy; childhood life and child care; marriage customs; education; houses; food and shopping; occupations, "industries," and amusements; fasts and feasts; illness and death. A very interesting book, though not of high priority for purchase (should a reprint become available), unless there is a special interest.

See also:

Kulṣūm Nah'nah. **Customs and Manners of the Women of Persia and Their Domestic Superstitions.** Tr. from Persian. New York, Burt Franklin, 1971. (Repr. of 1832 ed.). 98p. LC 72-164039. ISBN 0-8337-0110-X. DS 266.K8513 1971. DDC 301.41'2'0955.

G. ECONOMY

749. Bharier, Julian. **Economic Development in Iran, 1900-1970.** London, Oxford University Press, 1971. 314p. bibliog. statis. tables. index. $12.75. LC 73-875594. ISBN 0-19-215342-0. HC 475.B5. DDC 330.955'05.

[P1, C1] A reference book of basic statistical, descriptive, and historical information, and an analysis of all aspects of Iran's economy. It includes the government role in the economy, foreign trade, monetary and fiscal policy, agriculture, infrastructure, banking, industry, development policy, etc. The statistical sources are indicated and evaluated as to their accuracy. Written in non-technical language so that the non-specialist who knows a little economics can use it.

See also:

Amuzegar, Jahangir. **Iran: Economic Development under Dualistic Conditions.** Chicago, University of Chicago Press, 1971. 177p. LC 79-153044. ISBN 0-226-01754-0. HC 475.A64. DDC 338'.0955.

Baldwin, George Benedict. **Planning and Development in Iran.** Baltimore, Johns Hopkins Press, 1967. 212p. LC 67-18377. HC 475.B28. DDC 338.955.

750. Issawi, Charles, ed. **The Economic History of Iran, 1800-1914.** Chicago, University of Chicago Press, 1971. 405p. bibliog. index. $17.50. LC 70-153883. ISBN 0-226-38606-6. HC 475.I85. DDC 330.9'55'0408.

[C1] Mainly documents and reports, with some secondary articles, from a wide variety of sources, many translated from various languages. The book is topically divided, each chapter being further subdivided by specific aspects of the topic. Includes material on social structure, population, wages, classes, minorities; foreign trade in Tehran, Tabriz, and the Persian Gulf; slave trade; transportation, agriculture, land tenure; silk and other products; petroleum; industry and guilds, finance, public finance, and other subjects. Each section and each item has an introduction by Issawi. Indispensable as a source for the period and as background to the present economic situation. Includes much on relations with the European powers.

751. Looney, Robert E. **The Economic Development of Iran: A Recent Survey with Projections to 1981.** New York, Praeger, 1973. 199p. bibliog. illus. (Praeger Special Studies). $15.00. LC 73-10946. HC 475.L64. DDC 330.9'55'05.

[P1, C1, S1] Describes the developmental process, problems such as the structural and regional imbalances in the economy, population, statistics and their reliability, projections for the future. Probably the best analysis to date, and a good source of information.

752. Lambton, Ann Katherine Swynford. **Landlord and Peasant in Persia: A Study of Land Tenure and Land Revenue Administration.** London, Oxford University Press, 1953. 459p. bibliog. index. $14.50. LC 53-2458. ISBN 0-19-828162-5. HD 921.L22. DDC 333.

Starting with the pre-Islamic period and the Arab conquest of Iran, the book deals with a myriad of topics: agricultural methods; debt, standard of living, payment of local officials; flocks, pastures; revenue administration, feudal system, financial and other relations between landlord and peasant; law, irrigation methods, responsibilities of various parties; religious endowments; small owners and peasant proprietors; security of tenure; crop division and rents; personal servitudes. A very detailed treatment too specialized for most collections, but it has a wealth of information not found elsewhere, which is based on original sources.

See also:

Lambton, Ann Katherine Swynford. **The Persian Land Reform, 1962-1966.** Oxford, Clarendon Press, 1969. 386p. LC 79-441517. ISBN 0-19-828163-3. HD 926.L3. DDC 333.7'6'0955. An interim report based on personal observations and some documents.

H. DESCRIPTION AND TRAVEL

753. Curzon, George Nathaniel Curzon, 1st marquis (1859-1925). **Persia and the Persian Question.** New York, Barnes and Noble, 1966. (Repr. of 1892 ed.). 2v. illus. maps. index. $35.00. LC 66-6542. ISBN 0-06-491343-0. DS 258.C98 1966. DDC 915.5.

Using his extensive experience and travels in the country as a basis, Lord Curzon describes the geography and provides much information on the politics and inhabitants of the various regions of Iran; history, economy and institutions; the Shah, ministers, government reform efforts; the army. He also describes the main cities and their buildings; conditions for travellers; Persepolis and other main ruins; rivers; the Persian Gulf; industry, resources, revenues, commerce. He also discusses British and Russian interests, which gave rise to the "Persian Question." These two volumes contain a wealth of general information on the country as it stood at the end of the nineteenth century. The book is a must for larger collections.

Travelogues from various periods that are basic sources of information include:

Bell, Gertrude Lowthian. **Persian Pictures.** 3rd ed. London, Ernest Benn, 1947. (c. 1894). 157p. LC 48-16693. DS 258.B4 1947. DDC 915.5.

Browne, Edward Granville. **A Year amongst the Persians.** London, Adam and Charles Black, 1950. (c. 1893). 650p. LC 51-19601. DS 258.B88 1950. DDC 915.5. An account of the famous scholar's travels, containing much observation and comment still relevant today.

Chardin, Sir John (1643-1713). **Travels in Persia.** New York, AMS Press, 1972. (Repr. of 1720 ed.). 287p. LC 76-181928. ISBN 0-404-01449-6. DS 257.C5 1972. DDC 915.5.

Herbert, Thomas (1606-1682). **Travels in Persia, 1627-1629.** Abridged ed. edited by William Foster. Freeport, Conn., Books for Libraries Press, 1972. (Repr. of 1929 ed.). 352p. LC 78-39468. ISBN 0-8369-9912-6. DS 257.H472 1972. DDC 915.5'04'3. The author travelled in the retinue of the first British ambassador to Iran as a youth of

22 years, traversing the country many times. Here he describes everything he saw, including the people, courts, customs; conditions of travel; justice; the ruler Abbas and his family; structure and operation of government; and various cities, etc.

Jackson, Abraham V. W. **From Constantinople to the Home of Omar Khayyam: Travels in Transcaucasia and Northern Persia for Historic and Literary Research.** New York, Macmillan, 1906. 317p. LC 11-29371. DS 49.5.J2.

Layard, Sir Henry. **Early Adventures in Persia, Susiana, and Babylonia, Including a Residence Among the Bakhtiari and Other Wild Tribes before the Discovery of Nineveh.** London, John Murray, 1894. 436p. Abridged edition. Experiences and real adventures in Petra, Jordanian Desert, Palestine, Damascus, Baghdad, and Iran in the 1840s. Full description of the tribesmen. Most interesting, though not very informative.

Malcolm, Sir John (1769-1833). **Sketches of Persia.** London, John Murray, 1861. 287p. LC 49-42258. DS 258.M25 1861. Social life and customs in the early nineteenth century.

754. Freville, Nicholas. **The Bridge of the Maiden.** London, Robert Hale, 1967. 208p. illus. o.p. LC 67-93038. DS 266.F7 1967. DDC 915.5'03'5.

A doctor's three fascinating years in Luristan province, Iran. He describes the people and his dealings with them, relations with officialdom, health problems in a developing society, medical superstitions, etc. A sympathetic book which provides many insights into the country and village society for all readers.

See also:

Harnack, Curtis. **Persian Lions, Persian Lambs: An American's Odyssey in Iran.** New York, Holt, Rinehart and Winston, 1965. 279p. LC 65-10129. DS 266.H35. DDC 915.5. Fascinating memoirs of a professor's stay in Tabriz, which suggest much about the current generation, their lives, thoughts, trials, fears, and character.

Hobson, Sarah. **Through Persia in Disguise.** London, John Murray, 1973. 175p. LC 73-176141. ISBN 0-7195-2911-5. DS 259.H57. DDC 915.5'04'50924.

Stark, Freya. **The Valleys of the Assassins and Other Persian Travels.** London, John Murray, 1934. 364p. LC 34-34964. DS 258.S78.

755. Najafi, Najmeh, and Helen Hinckley. **Reveille for a Persian Village.** New York, Harper, 1958. 273p. illus. o.p. LC 58-8836. HN 740.S3N3. DDC 915.5.

The personal experiences of a Persian woman, well written, interesting, and very informative on Persian village life. She came to help the village of Sarbandan and had great success in changing certain aspects of daily life. She recounts in some detail her problems and methods of operation, as well as the way of life she had to change. A vivid account of an effort to change traditional patterns of thought and behavior; anyone interested in modernization must read it. The general reader who has strong ideas about foreign aid and the modernization efforts that developing countries need to undertake should also read it.

756. Najafi, Najmeh, and Helen Hinckley. **A Wall and Three Willows.** New York, Harper and Row, 1967. 212p. illus. o.p. LC 67-13690. HN 733.5.N3. DDC 309.2'3'0955.

In this volume, the author returns, after a long absence, to Sarbandan, via Bampoor in Baluchistan. She narrates her efforts to introduce new concepts of hygiene, weaving, and childcare to the women of the two villages. In Sarbandan she ultimately sets up a textile factory and other facilities. There is much on Iranian government programs, the problems of reaching and changing life patterns of nomads, and rebuilding efforts after natural disasters. A fascinating book.

757. Somerville-Large, Peter. **Caviar Coast.** London, Robert Hale, 1968. 192p. illus. o.p. LC 68-99914. DS 324.C3S6. DDC 915.5'1.

An interesting taste of what one can expect in the northern Iranian provinces of Gilan and Mazandaran, by a British traveller. He describes the countryside and his experiences, village life, etc., with a bit of history and lore. It has little hard information, but it does include a useful collection of the views of Iranian students and others on U.S. foreign aid operations, including CARE and the Peace Corps, whose volunteers the author visited several times, and on which he presents a British view.

758. Wilson, Samuel Graham (1858-1916). **Persian Life and Customs.** New York, AMS Press, 1973. (Repr. of 1900 ed.). 333p. illus. index. $17.50. LC 76-178305. ISBN 0-404-06996-7. DS 266.W56 1973. DDC 915.5.

A missionary, in the first half of the book, recounts his travels and describes the geography and peoples of the area from Tabriz to Tehran, Georgia, Ararat and the Lake Urmia region. In the second half, he gives a systematic presentation of the religions, social life, and customs of the Tabriz region, as he apparently observed it during his 14 years there. The book is useful for its coverage of conditions before modernization.

I. GUIDEBOOKS

759. Matheson, Sylvia A. **Persia: An Archaeological Guide.** Park Ridge, N.J., Noyes Press, 1973. 330p. bibliog. illus. index. (Archaeological Guides). $20.00. LC 72-85331. ISBN 0-8155-5010-3. DS 261.M38 1973. DDC 913.35'03. Paperback: London, Faber, 1973. o.p. LC 73-152654. ISBN 0-571-10229-8.

The antiquities to the end of the Seljuq period (thirteenth century). It is quite detailed, with brief suggestions for travellers, including facilities, equipment needs for viewing certain sites, degree of accessibility, route suggestions. It describes the museums in detail, gives histories of hundreds of excavations, and provides notes on the historical background. A conventional guidebook is still necessary.

760. **Nagel's Encyclopedia-Guide: Iran.** Genera, Nagel Publishers; distr. New York, Hippocrene Books, 1972. 392p. maps. index. $22.00. LC cataloging n.a.

A typical Nagel guide. The historical section is pitifully inadequate for a country with Iran's long history; it could well have been at least half again as long. It has few real advantages over *Fodor's Islamic Asia* (item 467), and it has an unreasonably high price; nonetheless, most travellers should refer to Nagel in their planning, for whatever additional details it has, as well as to Stevens (item 761).

761. Stevens, Sir Roger. **The Land of the Great Sophy.** 2nd ed. London, Methuen; distr. New York, International Publications Service, 1971. 326p. bibliog. illus. index. $17.50. LC 72-178036. ISBN 0-416-66910-7. DS 254.5.S7 1971. DDC 915.5'04'5.

A general descriptive guide for the tourist. It describes the roads, scenery, and buildings, with comments on what is particularly interesting to see, and a little history and lore. It has but little on the people, and Fodor *et al.*, are still necessary. Not for the armchair traveller.

XXI. IRAQ

A. GENERAL WORKS

762. **Area Handbook for Iraq.** [Smith, Harvey Henry]. 1971. 411p. (DA PAM 550-31). $6.15. LC 72-602177. DS 70.6.S6. DDC 915.67'03'4.

[B, P1, C1, S1] See the annotation at the head of Section II (page 30).
An older general work is:

Harris, George Lawrence. **Iraq: Its People, Its Society, Its Culture.** New Haven, Conn., Human Relations Area Files Press, 1958. 350p. LC 58-14179. DS 70.6.H3. DDC 915.67.

B. HISTORY AND POLITICS

763. Longrigg, Stephen Hemsley. **Four Centuries of Modern Iraq.** Beirut, Librairie du Liban, 1968. (Repr. of 1925 ed.). 378p. bibliog. index. $8.40. LC 79-233766. DS 77.L6 1968. DDC 956.7'03.

[P1, C1, C2, S1] ·The only work in English to deal in detail with the period 1500-1900. Using Arabic sources, it is a factual narrative indispensable for understanding the twentieth century. Its treatment of the nineteenth century has been outdated by recent research but is still useful. Beginners should read first Holt (item 76). A basic book.

C. 1900 TO THE PRESENT

764. Khadduri, Majid. **Independent Iraq, 1932-1958.** 2nd ed. London, Oxford University Press, 1960. 388p. o.p. LC 60-50855. DS 79.K43 1960. DDC 956.7.

[C1] A knowledgeable political history by a scholar of Iraqi origin. It actually deals with the period to 1952-53, providing only the briefest treatment of the later period (to 1958); this is quite unsatisfactory, particularly since the author's work on the 1958 revolution (item 765) does not compensate for this vital gap. For the period covered it is a basic work; the author knew many of the people involved and makes use of inside information not available to other writers. It has very sketchy chapters on foreign policy, constitutional and institutional developments, economic development planning and reform 1953-1958, which in no way help the reader understand events during the period. The author is pro-establishment, which colors his approach and selection of material. To be read in conjunction with Longrigg (item 766).
Additional sources are:

De Gaury, Gerald. **Three Kings in Baghdad, 1921-1958.** London, Hutchinson, 1961. 223p. LC 61-1918. DS 79.D4. DDC 956.7. A most interesting portrait and memoir of Iraq by a witness who was friend to three kings. Events, British policy, Iraqi politics, and many personalities—Faysal I, Ghazi, Faysal II; the regent Abd al-Ilah; Abdullah of Jordan and the Hashemites of Arabia; creation of Iraq; Gertrude Bell, Nuri al-Said. Some notes on local customs. He does not discuss the regime of the 1950s or the nationalist movement but approaches things from the perspective of the royal households and politics. A very useful supplement to the scholarly works.

Sinderson, Sir Harry Chapman. **Ten Thousand and One Nights: Memories of Iraq's Sherifian Dynasty.** London, Hodder & Stoughton, 1973. 287p. LC n.a. ISBN 0-340-1761-0. DDC 915.670340924. Memoirs of the royal family's doctor, with much on the politics and personalities, some material on medical services and education. Interesting and informative.

765. Khadduri, Majid. **Republican Iraq: A Study in Iraqi Politics Since the Revolution of 1958.** London, Oxford University Press, 1969. 318p. index. $9.75. LC 75-447193. ISBN 0-19-214979-2. DS 79.65.K48. DDC 320.9'55.

[P1, C1, S1] This book deals with the regime from 1958 to 1968; most of the material covers the period to 1966, the later period being discussed only briefly. It is mainly a general, descriptive, factual narrative, which does not necessarily help the reader understand why events occurred as they did. It treats in some detail the 1958 revolution. A basic work.
See also:

Dann, Uriel. **Iraq under Qassem: A Political History, 1958-1963.** New York, Praeger, 1969. 405p. LC 68-54317. ISBN 0-269-67064-5. DS 79.65.D35 1969. DDC 320.9'567.

Kimball, Lorenzo K. **The Changing Pattern of Political Power in Iraq, 1958-1971.** New York, Robert Speller, 1972. 246p. LC 79-178827. ISBN 0-8315-0120-0. DS 79.65.K55. DDC 320.9'567'04.

766. Longrigg, Stephen Hemsley. **Iraq, 1900-1950: A Political, Social and Economic History.** Beirut, Librairie du Liban; distr. Mystic, Conn., Lawrence Verry, 1968. (Repr. of 1956 ed.). 435p. bibliog. index. $8.50. LC n.a. DS 79.L6. DDC 956.7.

[P1, C1, S1] A basic work which, while overlapping Khadduri (item 764), is necessary because half of it deals with the pre-1932 period and the rest adds socioeconomic aspects not treated by Khadduri. It illuminates the role in Iraq of the original Iraqis, who deserted the Turks to fight for the Arab revolt in World War I. The author is a former official of mandate Iraq. For much more detail on the establishment and nature of the British administration in Iraq and the Iraqi regime under the 1932 Constitution, see Philip Willard Ireland's *Iraq: A Study in Political Development* (New York, Russell & Russell, 1970. [Repr. of 1937 ed.]. 510p. LC 75-83852. DS 79.17 1970).
See also:

Atiyyah, Ghassan R. **Iraq, 1908-1921: A Socio-Political Study.** Beirut, Arab Institute for Research and Publishing, 1973. 407p. LC 75-502689. DS 77.A85. DDC 956.7'03.

767. Marr, Phebe A. **Modern History of Iraq.** New York, Praeger, 1975 (forthcoming). (Asia-Africa Series). LC 74-33113. ISBN 0-275-33620-4. LC cataloging n.a.

[P1, C1, S1] No information at all available. The author is a younger scholar of the region; the books in this series concerning the Near East have become standard works.

D. BIOGRAPHY

768. Birdwood, Christopher Bromhead Birdwood, baron. **Nuri al-Said: A Study in Arab Leadership.** London, Cassell, 1959. 306p. bibliog. illus. index. LC 59-3307. DS 79.8. N8B5. DDC 923.2567.

al-Said was frequently Prime Minister of Iraq and was a powerful figure even out of office; he was one of the original Arab nationalists, fought in the Arab Revolt, knew Lawrence, and was killed in the 1958 revolution. Birdwood's biography is a sympathetic, even admiring, portrait in which Nuri moves in and out of the heavily padded background material on the events in which he took part. Undocumented and not proportionate in its coverage (about half the book deals with the period 1914-1921), it does present considerable information in readable fashion, including a fair amount on Iraqi politics, which will be of interest to students.
Another source of information:

Gallman, W. J. **Iraq under General Nuri: My Recollections of Nuri al-Said, 1954-1958.** Baltimore, Johns Hopkins Press, 1964. 241p. bibliog. LC 63-19559. DS 79.8.N8 G3. DDC 956.7.

E. SOCIETY

769. Campbell, Charles Grimshaw. **From Town and Tribe.** London, Ernest Benn, 1952. 217p. o.p. LC 52-32473 rev. GR 275.C26.

Entertaining tales and stories from Southern Iraq and the Sultanate of Muscat and Oman, some of which are quite ribald, à la Boccaccio.

See also:

Campbell, Charles Grimshaw. **Tales from the Arab Tribes: A Collection of the Stories Told by the Arab Tribes of the Lower Euphrates.** London, Lindsey Drummond, 1949. 252p. o.p. LC 50-3074. GR 275.C3. DDC 398.21. Translated from Arabic, these are stories of love and heroism, told by Shiite tribes. Arranged by tribe. Entertaining and useful.

770. Drower, Ethel Stefana (Stevens), Lady. **Folk-Tales of Iraq, Set Down and Translated from the Vernacular.** New York, Benjamin Blom, 1971. (Repr. of 1931 ed.). 303p. o.p. LC 73-174391. GR 295.I7D7 1971. DDC 398.2'09567.

Collected from story-tellers by a long-term resident of Iraq, mainly in Baghdad, Mosul, and the desert north of Mosul.

771. Fernea, Elizabeth Warnock. **Guests of the Sheik: An Ethnology of an Iraqi Village.** London, Robert Hale, 1968. 333p. index. o.p. LC 77-427078. ISBN 0-7091-0231-3. DS 70.7.F4 1968. DDC 915.67. Paperback: Garden City, N.Y., Doubleday, 1969. (Anchor Books A 693). $2.50. ISBN 0-385-01485-6.

[P2, C1] A fascinating, truly delightful account of all aspects of the woman's side of life in a small, primitive village where the author and her husband lived while he conducted doctoral research. It is written informally, in the first person, and will entertain the general reader and provide valuable information to the student. It recounts the author's reaction to her being a stranger there, her adjustment problems, her many faux-pas as she worked out her personal life and her relationships with the villagers.

772. Fernea, Robert Alan. **Shaykh and Effendi: Changing Patterns of Authority among the El Shabanah of Southern Iraq.** Cambridge, Mass., Harvard University Press, 1970. 225p. bibliog. index. $8.00. LC 70-88804. ISBN 0-674-80585-2. HN 764.I7F46. DDC 309.1'567.

Concerns the Āl Shabānah, a settled tribe maintaining a tribal type of organization, living near the village of Daghgharah. The first 76 pages give a general description of the area, the tribes, history, economy, ecology, and society of the town and its region (which should be supplemented by Elizabeth Fernea, item 771). It then describes the tribal system and its relation to economic aspects, kinship-family system and structure, land ownership, segmentary aspects. Also, shaykhship (tribal leader) and its power and authority; marriage system; changing local authority patterns as related to the irrigation system, its division, construction, and maintenance; and sharing of water. Also, status system, the relationships between tribal authority and control of irrigation, and the changing situation under the British regime and under independence as that control has become increasingly centralized, to the detriment of tribal power, and importance. For the largest collections only.

773. Jamali, Sarah Powell. **Folktales from the City of the Golden Domes.** Beirut, Khayats, 1965. 110p. LC NE67-1782. GR 295.I7J3.

Tales from Baghdad, mainly of human relationships rather than fairy tales or tales of the supernatural.

774. Thesiger, Wilfred. **The Marsh Arabs.** London, Longmans, 1964. 242p. illus. index. £3.25. LC 64-6741. ISBN 0-582-10517-X. DS 70.7.T45 1964. DDC 915.67.

An exceptionally interesting account, with excellent informative photos, of the author's life among the Arabs of Iraq's southern marsh region, from 1951 to 1958. He has a keen eye for the details of life and customs, which makes the book useful as an informal ethnological study.

See also:

Salīm, Shākir Muṣṭafá. **Marsh Dwellers of the Euphrates Delta.** London, University of London, Athlone Press, 1962. 157p. LC 62-4819. DS 70.7.S3. A scholarly treatment.

F. ECONOMY

There is no general monograph on Iraq's economy. Most readers can be satisfied with the *Area Handbook*. There are, however, a few books that shed light on past conditions.

774a. Adams, Doris Goodrich. **Iraq's People and Resources.** Berkeley, University of California Press, 1958. 160p. LC A58-8963. HC 497.I7A3. DDC 330.9567.

774b. International Bank for Reconstruction and Development. **The Economic Development of Iraq: Report of a Mission Organized by the International Bank for Reconstruction and Development at the Request of the Government of Iraq.** Baltimore, Johns Hopkins Press, 1952. 463p. LC 52-2530. HC 497.I7I65. DDC 330.9567.

774c. Jalal, Ferhang. **The Role of Government in the Industrialization of Iraq, 1950-1965.** London, Frank Cass; distr. Portland, Ore., International Scholarly Book Services, 1972. LC 77-171260. 142p. ISBN 0-7146-2586-8. HD 3616.I72J35. DDC 338'.09567.

774d. Langley, Kathleen M. **The Industrialization of Iraq.** Cambridge, Harvard University Press, 1961. 313p. LC 61-3179. HC 497.I7L3. DDC 338.09567.

G. DESCRIPTION AND TRAVEL

775. Bell, Gertrude Lowthian (1868-1926). **Amurath to Amurath.** London, Macmillan, 1924. 370p. 234 illus. index. LC 26-7604. DS 49.2.B4 1924.

An account of the author's five-month journey in Asia Minor and Iraq. The annotation to item 935 applies equally well to this book.

See also:

Edmonds, Cecil John. **Kurds, Turks and Arabs: Politics, Travel and Research in North-Eastern Iraq, 1919-1925.** London, Oxford University Press, 1957. 457p. LC 58-761. DS 51.M7E4. DDC 956.7.

XXII. ISRAEL AND PALESTINE

We lack a political history of Israel from 1948 to the 1970s.

A. GENERAL WORKS

776. **Area Handbook for Israel.** [Smith, Harvey Henry]. 1970. 457p. (DA PAM 550-25). $6.20. LC 78-607520. DS 126.5.S6. DDC 309.1'5694'05.

[B, P1, C1, S1] See the annotation at the head of Section II (page 30).

777. Eckhardt, Alice, and Roy Eckhardt. **Encounter with Israel: A Challenge to Conscience.** New York, Association Press, 1970. 304p. index. o.p. LC 79-132395. ISBN 0-8096-1783-8. DS 126.5.E27. DDC 915.694.03'5.

A moral approach in favor of Israel. It discusses Israel's origin and achievement, aspects of its life and those factors which contribute to Israel's ethos—polarities in society, integration of its diverse peoples, religious life and the contradictions in the religion-state controversy, political system, kibbutz and other communal movements, economic progress, problems, the meaning of Israel to Jews and the interrelationship of Judaism and Israel, Israel's right to Palestine, anti-Semitism and Western-Christian attitudes toward Israel, a plea for Christian understanding, Israel and the Israeli Arabs. By far the heaviest emphasis is on the Arab-Israeli conflict, from a pro-Israel perspective. It assumes that at no time did the Arabs have a right to oppose the Zionist influx and creation of the Jewish state, let alone try to destroy Israel. It discusses Arab anti-Semitism and violence, the outrageousness and significance of the dual standard the world applies in expecting different behavior on the part of the Arabs and the Israelis, the psychological origins of this dual standard, and Israel's right to acceptance by the world and the Arabs. It expresses and espouses many Zionist points on a variety of matters; but it acknowledges that the Israelis are human and capable of error and occasional wrong-doing and it makes a few critical comments. Unfortunately, it begs rather too many important moral questions, mainly by avoiding them or, in the case of the question of the rights of the Palestinian Arabs, by stating that in a situation of conflicting rights, the Jews have a greater need and right to Palestine; some of the arguments are specious and not entirely honest, and much of its often undocumented factual information comes from pro-Zionist propaganda sources. However, the book contains considerable food for thought for those seeking a balanced perspective because it is somewhat more than mere propaganda. A useful addition to balanced collections.

778. Elon, Amos. **The Israelis: Founders and Sons.** New York, Bantam Books, 1972. 469p. bibliog. index. $1.95pa. LC 75-138887. DS 126.5.E4195. DDC 915.694'03.

[P1, C1, S1] One of the best and most readable works available on Israel, by a well-known Israeli journalist. It is a sober and fair account that provides great understanding of the Israeli psyche and national character, and the circumstances and origins that shaped Israel and conditioned the outlook and behavior of its people. It deals somewhat more with the founders than the sons, and it handles the former in a fashion that is more enlightening to the reader than is the account of the sons. There is a good chapter on Zionist relations with the Arabs. Elon is an independent writer and does not hesitate to manhandle cherished illusions and cliches, but he does it in a responsible and sympathetic manner. At times the book appears to be simplistic and to take a few too many journalistic liberties, but it is an excellent introduction for any reader. The younger generation is emphasized in David Schoenbrun's *The New Israelis* (New York, Atheneum, 1973. 258p. LC 72-94241. DS 126.5.S29), which surveys the views of Israelis under 30 on a wide variety of topics.

779. Karmon, Yehuda. **Israel: A Regional Geography.** New York, Wiley-Interscience, 1971. 345 p. bibliog. illus. index. $12.50. LC 70-116162. ISBN 0-471-45870-8. DS 126.5.K347. DDC 915.694.

[P1, C1] A systematic presentation of the historical, physical, economic and demographic geography of Israel, similar to Orni-Efrat (item 782). However, it has more cultural information and less on the occupied territories, and it is different in its organization, since half the book is devoted to individual treatment of each region. It has more maps and is somewhat more advanced than Orni-Efrat.

See also:

Finbert, Elian J. **Israel.** Tr. from French. London, Kaye & Ward, 1968. 251 p. 157 illus. LC 75-355781. ISBN 0-7182-0781-5. DS 108.5.F513 1968b. DDC 915.694. A physical description with one of the better collections of pictures (mainly black and white). The pictures are more important than the text.

780. Kaufman, Gerald. **To Build the Promised Land.** London, Weidenfeld and Nicolson, 1973. 259 p. bibliog. index. £4.25. LC 73-169794. ISBN 0-297-76509-4. DS 126.5.K365. DDC 915.694.

[P, P1, C1, S1] Interesting essays on aspects of Israel for the general reader. It includes chapters on conditions in and the building of Israel's cities, education, the arts, freedom and censorship, conditions in the diaspora. The chapter on the Israeli Arabs is much better than average. It is quite informative and factual and, while sympathetic, is not uncritical. It covers several topics that are not handled well in other books.

781. Naamani, Israel T. **Israel: A Profile.** New York, Praeger, 1972. 246 p. bibliog. illus. index. (Praeger Country Profile Series). $8.50. LC 78-173284. DS 126.5.N2. DDC 915.694'03.

[P1] A useful, systematic introduction for the general reader on all aspects of the country. A first book.

Other general works:

Prittie, Hon. Terence Cornelius Farmer. **Israel: Miracle in the Desert.** New York, Praeger, 1968. 260 p. LC 68-28337. DS 126.5.P7 1968. DDC 956.94'05.

Safran, Nadav. **The United States and Israel.** Cambridge, Mass., Harvard University Press, 1963. 341 p. bibliog. LC 63-17212. E 183.8.I7S2. DDC 327.7305694. An excellent survey of Israel, with only a few pages on U.S.-Israeli relations, despite the title.

782. Orni, Efraim, and Elisha Efrat. **Geography of Israel.** 3rd rev. ed. New York, American Heritage Press, 1971. 551 p. bibliog. illus. maps. tables. index. $10.95. LC 71-178048. ISBN 0-07-047701-9. DS 107.4.O6813.DDC 915.694. (*BIP* lists: Jewish Publication Society, 1973. $10.95. ISBN 0-8276-0006-2.)

[P1, C1, S1] A systematic presentation, handsomely printed and bound, of the historical, physical, economic, and demographic geography of Israel and the occupied territories. There are special discussions of rural and urban settlements and the roads. It is a topical general treatment of the country as a whole and does not comprehensively treat each region individually as item 779 does. It is a mine of information; the well-chosen illustrations are very useful.

783. Patai, Raphael, ed. **The Encyclopedia of Zionism and Israel.** New York, Herzl Press, McGraw-Hill, 1971. 2 v. illus. $39.50. LC 68-55271. ISBN 0-07-079635-1. DS 149.E597. DDC 956.94'001'03.

[P1, C1, C2] These oversized, double-columned volumes contain most of the facts the average person might need to know about Zionist-Israeli history. The work contains biographies of many individuals and information on many aspects of Israel's existence, including the economy. For statistics one must consult the various Israeli and Zionist yearbooks. The reader must be very much aware that this Zionist-Israeli project tells him only what it is desired that he know and omits anything that goes against the official line. Virtually anything the book says about Israeli relations with the Arabs, the United States, and the U.N. must be treated with suspicion; factual omissions, nuances in wording, and one-sided interpretations abound, whether or not they are deliberate. The facts given are useful for reference, but the articles on the topics mentioned above should be read in conjunction with independent material. Most of the articles, which are by Zionist-Israeli authorities, are signed. Basic for larger collections. Another excellent source of additional material on Israel, Zionism (75 pages), Hebrew literature, biographies, etc., is *Encyclopedia Judaica* (Jerusalem, Encyclopedia Judaica; New York, Macmillan, c. 1971-1972. 16v. LC 72-177482. DS 102.8.E496. DDC 296'.03).

784. Samuel, Edwin, Viscount Samuel. **The Structure of Society in Israel.** New York, Random House, 1969. 184p. bibliog. index. (Studies in Modern Societies). $2.95pa. LC 68-24674. ISBN 0-394-30778-X. HN 761.P32S3. DDC 309.1'5694.

[P1, P2, C1, C2, S1, S2] A general work that covers immigration-emigration, national origins of Israelis, population distribution, and new town development; employment distribution, unemployment, productivity, kibbutzim; the "ultra-orthodox" in Israel; Israeli Arabs; parties, rich and poor, taxation, living standards, industries; education and poor students, brain drain; family, women, generation gap; crime, national integration. A wealth of useful information for all readers and libraries.

785. Vilnay, Zev. **The New Israel Atlas: Bible to Present Day.** New York, McGraw-Hill Book Company, 1969. 112p. $7.95. LC 79-653289. ISBN 0-07-067484-1. G 2235.V52 1969. DDC 912.5694.

A popular work that covers geographical regions, climate, soils, communications, economy, archaeological and Biblical sites, locations of kibbutzim, etc., population, schools; history, including Biblical periods and the Arab-Israeli Wars; the various proposals for a Jewish state. Concluded by a gazetteer. Very useful for public libraries. Larger libraries should consider: Israel. Mahleket ha-Medidot, *Atlas of Israel* (Jerusalem, Survey of Israel, Ministry of Labor; Amsterdam, Elsevier Publishing Company, 1970. G 2235.I82 1970), which covers the same material in much more detail, with more, larger, and better maps.

B. HISTORY

786. Bauer, Yehuda. **From Diplomacy to Resistance: A History of Jewish Palestine, 1939-1945.** Tr. from Hebrew. Philadelphia, Jewish Publication Society of America, 1970. 432p. LC 70-105065. DS 126.3.B363 1970. DDC 956.94'04.

An important work providing new perspectives on the White Paper of 1939, among other topics, including the development of the Zionist military forces—Palmach, I.Z.L., Stern Gang—internal politics, relations with the British, etc.

787. Brecher, Michael. **The Foreign Policy System of Israel: Setting, Images, Process.** New Haven, Yale University Press, 1972. 693p. bibliog. index. $17.50. LC 73-179469. ISBN 0-300-01549-6. DS 119.6.B74 1972b. DDC 327.5694.

787a. Brecher, Michael. **Decisions in Israel's Foreign Policy.** New Haven, Yale University Press, 1975. 639p. bibliog. index. $25.00. LC 73-77143. ISBN 0-300-01660-3. DS 119.6.B73 1975. DDC 327.5694.

The first book describes in detail all aspects of Israel's foreign policy decision-making apparatus, and the factors or environments that influence the decisions: external setting, military and economic capabilities; political structure, interest groups and competing elites (political parties, etc.); the communications network, including role of the media; policy-making elite, its attitudes and perceptions, the views of the policy-makers (Ben-Gurion, Meir, Eshkol, Allon, Eban, etc.); the formulation of decisions; foreign ministry and other agencies influencing policy. Each topic is dealt with at length and an immense quantity of hard information is provided. Extremely valuable for students of Israel and as a model for studies of other countries. The only systematic study of a foreign policy process, whether of Israel or of any other country.

The companion volume offers a "micro" analysis of seven decision series: Jerusalem; German reparations; Korean War and China; Jordan waters; Sinai campaign; Six-Day War; and the Rogers proposals of 1969-1971. For each the author suggests the background factors and events, the factors in the decision-making process, the decisions made, and feedback into the

Israeli system from world and Israeli opinion. Much factual information, some of it new, is presented, based on a thorough study of Israeli sources, including extensive interviews with Israeli officials. However, the information is not presented in narrative form, but in terms of the categories outlined in the first volume. A final chapter compares the results of Brecher's findings in the Israeli case with the hypotheses on international relations expressed by various other theorists, noting the ways in which these hypotheses were or were not supported. For advanced readers with much background on the Arab-Israeli conflict and for students of international relations theory these books are invaluable. The first book is accessible to the general reader who is seeking information, but the second is much harder to follow because Brecher applies his theoretical models.

Other works on aspects of Israel's foreign relations:

Balabkins, Nicholas. **West German Reparations to Israel.** New Brunswick, N.J., Rutgers University Press, 1971. 384p. LC 70-152724. ISBN 0-8135-0691-3. DS 119.8.G4B33. DDC 327.5694'043.

Crosbie, Sylvia Kowitt. **A Tacit Alliance: France and Israel from Suez to the Six Day War.** Princeton, N.J., Princeton University Press, 1974. 280p. bibliog. LC 73-18310. ISBN 0-691-07557-3. DS 119.6.F8C76. DDC 327.44'05694.

Dagan, Avigdor. **Moscow and Jerusalem: Twenty Years of Relations between Israel and the Soviet Union.** New York, Abelard-Schuman, 1970. 255p. LC 73-123210. ISBN 0-200-71691-3. DS 119.8.R9D34 1970. DDC 327.47'05694.

Eytan, Walter. **The First Ten Years: A Diplomatic History of Israel.** London, Weidenfeld and Nicolson, 1958. 219p. LC 58-2981. DS 126.5.E9 1958a. DDC 956.94.

Glick, Edward Bernard. **Latin America and the Palestine Problem.** New York, Theodor Herzl Foundation, 1958. 199p. LC 58-3123 rev. 2. DS 126.4.G53. DDC 327.569408.

Jerusalem. Hebrew University. **Israel and the United Nations: Report of a Study Group Set Up by the Hebrew University of Jerusalem.** Prepared for the Carnegie Endowment for International Peace. New York, Manhattan Publishing Company, 1956. 322p. LC 56-3075. DS 126.4.J38. DDC 327.5694.

Krammer, Arnold. **The Forgotten Friendship: Israel and the Soviet Bloc, 1947-1953.** Urbana, University of Illinois Press, 1974. LC 74-7121. ISBN 0-252-00396-9. DK 68.7.I8K72. DDC 327.47'05694.

Reppa, Robert B. **Israel and Iran: Bilateral Relationships and Effect On the Indian Ocean Basin.** New York, Praeger, 1974. 187p. LC 73-19448. ISBN 0-275-08380-2. DS 274.2.I7R46. DDC 327.5694'055.

788. Hopwood, Derek. **The Russian Presence in Syria and Palestine, 1843-1914: Church and Politics in the Near East.** Oxford, Clarendon Press, 1969. 232p. bibliog. index. LC 70-429795. DS 95.6.H6. DDC 327.47'05691.

Based on Russian, Arabic, and other sources, the book traces imperial Russia's presence—the Church, education, relations of Church and politics in Palestine—and tries to suggest its influence on the people. Background provided includes Russian Middle Eastern interests, the state of the Orthodox Church in Palestine, the Orthodox Arabs. Much of the book is concerned with internal developments of the Russian effort and the establishment of Russian institutions. There is also material on the interaction of Orthodox Arabs with Arab nationalism in Syria, Palestine and Lebanon, and Greek-Arab rivalry for control of the Orthodox Church.

789. Lucas, Noah. **The Modern History of Israel.** New York, Praeger, 1975. 512p. bibliog. (Praeger Asia-Africa Series). $17.50. LC 74-16411. ISBN 0-275-33450-3. DS 126.5.L82 1975. DDC 956.94.

A well-written interpretation and analysis of which about 300 pages concern the nineteenth and twentieth centuries to 1948; nearly 200 pages cover the period 1947 to 1967, followed by an epilog on 1967-1973. It is not a detailed factual narrative history, but largely a series of general statements on various aspects of life, politics, problems, policies, and key events during each of a number of periods. Includes ideology, national identity, economy, society. The author is very free with his opinions, particularly on Israel's policy toward the Arabs after the 1967 war. Based on Hebrew and Western sources, but the useful bibliographic essay includes only English books. We stand in great need of a single work that digests and presents coherently the mass of scattered but currently readily available facts. Nevertheless, this work is an item of low priority because it presents little hard information and it devotes so little space to Israel since 1948. The general reader will, however, find it useful for orientation.

See also:

Rubin, Jacob A., and Meyer Barkai. **Pictorial History of Israel.** New York, Yoseloff, 1968. 329p. LC 68-15197. DS 126.5.R8 1968. DDC 956.94.

Schiff, Zeev. **A History of the Israeli Army (1870-1974).** San Francisco, Straight Arrow Books; distr. New York, Simon and Schuster, 1974. 338p. LC 74-76602. ISBN 0-87932-077-X. DS 119.2.S3413. DDC 355'.0095694. The first 140 pages deal with the pre-1967 era. Includes chapters on training, women, the War of Independence, and the Sinai campaign. Many pictures of actions, leaders, weapons.

Allon, Yigal. **The Making of Israel's Army.** New York, Universe Books, 1970. 273p. LC 73-133424. ISBN 0-87663-137-5. UA 853.I8A65. DDC 355'.00095694. By one of the founders of Palmach and an Israeli political leader.

Luttwak, Edward, and Dan Horowitz. **The Israeli Army.** New York, Harper and Row, 1975. illus. $10.00. LC 73-14270. ISBN 0-06-012723-6. UA 853.I8L87 1975. DDC 355'.0095694. A history and analysis of the concepts, strategies, and tactics of the Israeli army; their origin and development, and the testing of these in the successive wars; relationship to the State; the leaders, organization, training; relations of the various military arms; weaponry; debates on strategy and tactics. Not a systematic military history. Includes a 90-page section on the 1967 War and an analysis of the "failures" of the October 1973 War. A really fascinating book.

790. Sachar, Howard Morley. **The Course of Modern Jewish History.** New York, Dell Publishing Company, 1958. 630p. bibliog. index. (A Delta Book, 1538). $2.65pa. LC n.a. DS 125.S28. DDC 296.09.

[C1, S1] After describing the background to the pre-"Enlightenment" and "Emancipation" era, Sachar in great detail narrates the story of Jewish culture and history in the nineteenth and twentieth centuries, including their impact on Western culture, Jews in America, Israel's creation, etc. A necessary background work to the development of the Palestine problem and the rise of Zionism. The author does not have a specialist's knowledge of the history of East European Jewry, a vital aspect of Israel's background, which vitiates the book's authoritativeness.

791. Tibawi, Abdul Latif. **British Interests in Palestine, 1800-1901: A Study of Religious and Educational Enterprise.** London, Oxford University Press, 1961. 280p. LC 61-66208. DS 125.T5. DDC 956.94.

History of British missionary and educational activities, with much material on political aspects and implications of this activity, also missionary relations with indigenous Christians and the Jews. Little on events and conditions in the country, and nothing on the real influence of the British efforts.

C. ZIONISM

792. Halpern, Ben. **The Idea of the Jewish State.** 2nd ed. Cambridge, Mass., Harvard University Press, 1969. 493p. bibliog. index. $15.00. LC 71-89969. ISBN 0-674-44201-6. DS 149.H34 1969. DDC 956.94'001.

[C2, S2] This excellent book treats the concepts of the Jewish State and their interaction with the historical stages and problems encountered in the development and activities of Zionism; it relates these to Zionist negotiations with various nations and international organizations. Halpern traces the strategies and positions of the supporters of the Jewish State, and the emergent concepts of Jewish sovereignty over the land. The book seeks to explain how circumstances conditioned these concepts, with a discussion of the rise of Zionism, anti-, and non-Zionism. It treats the negotiation of the Balfour Declaration, developments of the Mandate era, Partition Plan; Israeli-U.N. relations; Israel and world politics; and the degree and scope of Israel's sovereignty. Included are discussions of the constant reformulation of Zionist ideology and the ideas of sovereignty to win world Jewish support; Jewish rights and claims in Palestine; the degree of Zionism's international acceptance and rejection. A solid, useful work that reveals much of the history of the Zionist perspective of the Arab-Israeli conflict.

793. Hertzberg, Arthur. **The Zionist Idea: A Historical Analysis and Reader.** New York, Atheneum, 1972. (Repr. of 1959 ed.). 638p. (A Temple Book). $4.95pa. LC 77-90073. DS 149.H4376 1972. DDC 956.94'001. (Cloth repr.: New York, Greenwood Press, 1970. $18.50. LC 70-97312. ISBN 0-8371-2565-0.)

[P1, C1, S1] The best introductory work on Zionist ideology, it includes an excellent 100-page introduction by Hertzberg, who is a top American Zionist leader. This is the best brief treatment of the subject, and it presents the most significant texts, from the earliest expression, through Herzl's *The Jewish State*, to statements made in the latter 1940s by Ben-Gurion and Buber. Each selection has a biographical introduction. A basic work, which should be read before Laqueur (item 794), since Laqueur really deals more with the political and ideological struggles within Zionism.

794. Laqueur, Walter Ze'ev. **A History of Zionism.** New York, Holt, Rinehart and Winston, 1972. 639p. bibliog. illus. index. $10.00. LC 72-78096. ISBN 0-03-091614-3. DS 149.L256 1972. DDC 956.94'001.

[P2, C1, S2] The best book on Zionist history. It treats the ideological and political history of the movement in all its various theories, personalities, parties and sub-movements. After tracing the background and Herzl's forerunners, it discusses Herzl, left-wing Zionism, Zionism and its critics, revisionism, Weizmann's era, the holocaust, and the final struggle for Israel's independence. There is an excellent chapter on Zionist-Arab relations, one of the best treatments available. A well-written, enlightening study, it emphasizes the politics of the movement, rather than the dogmas and ideology, thus complementing Halpern (item 792) and Hertzberg (item 793).

Additional sources:

Cohen, Israel. **A Short History of Zionism.** London, Muller, 1951. 280p. LC 52-1422. DS 149.C544. DDC 956.94.

Goldberg, Israel. **Fulfillment: The Epic Story of Zionism.** Cleveland, World, 1951. 426p. LC 51-14316. DS 149.G539. DDC 296.

Litvinoff, Barnet. **Road to Jerusalem: Zionism's Imprint on History.** London, Weidenfeld and Nicolson, 1965. 311p. LC 66-71472. DS 149.L57 1966. DDC 956.94001.

Sokolow, Nahum. **History of Zionism, 1600-1936.** New York, KTAV Publishing House, 1969. (Repr. of 1919 ed.). 2v. in 1. LC 68-19730. DS 149.S6 1969. DDC 956.94'001.

795. Silverburg, Robert. **If I Forget Thee O Jerusalem: American Jews and the State of Israel.** New York, William Morrow, 1970. 620p. bibliog. illus. index. o.p. LC 70-100558. DS 149.S535. DDC 956.94'001. Paperback: New York, Pyramid Publications, 1972. $1.95. ISBN 0-515-02765-0.

[P1, C1, S] A history of American Zionism and American Jewish support for Israel. It incorporates a vast amount of information on the public politics of support for the Zionist cause before and after Israel's independence, including Zionist activities in garnering support, Congressional resolutions, Presidential support, etc. It is mainly a synthesis of a great number of popular works, articles, interviews, and material from various Jewish and Zionist organizations. It is not an "inside story." It contains all the traditional tales, in detail, about Truman and U.S. recognition of Israel and about diplomacy from World War I to 1967. The author is sympathetic but independent, and not uncritical. Not a scholarly book, but basic.

See also:

Halperin, Samuel. **The Political World of American Zionism.** Detroit, Wayne State University Press, 1961. 431p. LC 61-10126. DS 149.H337. DDC 956.94.

Rosenblatt, Bernard Abraham. **Two Generations of Zionism: Historical Recollections of an American Zionist.** New York, Shengold, 1967. 286p. LC 67-18134. DS 151.R57A3. DDC 956.94'001'0924.

Schechtman, Joseph. **The United States and the Jewish State Movement: The Crucial Decade, 1939-1949.** New York, Herzl Press, T. Yoseloff, 1966. 474p. LC 65-22229. DS 126.3.S3. DDC 327.5694073. A polemical account which, by various means, rather significantly distorts the picture, but it is useful as a cohesive narrative and a source of bibliography.

Urofsky, Melvin I. **American Zionism from Herzl to the Holocaust.** Garden City, N.Y., Anchor Press, 1975. LC 74-19757. ISBN 0-385-03639-6. DS 149.U76. DDC 956.94'001. The nineteenth century through 1942, especially 1914-1942. Has an extensive bibliographical essay.

Snetsinger, John. **Truman, the Jewish Vote, and the Creation of Israel.** Stanford, Calif., Stanford University, Hoover Institution Press, 1974. 208p. bibliog. index. LC 70-187267. ISBN 0-8179-3391-3. A scholarly narrative of events and interpretation on a controversial subject that is usually badly handled. Based on original sources.

D. BIOGRAPHY

796. Avi-hai, Avraham. **Ben-Gurion, State-Builder: Principles and Pragmatism, 1948-1963.** New York, John Wiley, 1974. 354p. bibliog. index. (A Halstead Press Book). $12.50. LC 74-557. ISBN 0-470-03836-5. DS 125.3.B37A97 1974. DDC 956.94'05'0924 [B].

After providing sufficient background on Ben-Gurion's life and basic outlook, the Zionist and Israeli political system and parties, the book deals with aspects of his ideology and ideas on various issues, their interaction with Israel's internal and external policies and politics, and his approaches and strategy. Topics include socialism, and the economy; religious-secular conflict; defense; Arabs in Israel; the Arab-Israeli conflict; arms and the great powers; Israel and the diaspora; Ben-Gurion's attitude toward organized Zionism; and party-state relationships. There are frequent excerpts from his statements, given in their historical and political context. Finally the book traces the process of his withdrawal from top power. Not a systematic biography, this is a useful contribution to our understanding of the man and of Israel's development and politics; its analysis of his ideas, events, the Israeli system, and their interrelationship is enlightening. For the more advanced reader; much more useful than St. John (item 799). For larger collections.

Ben-Gurion's writings are important sources of information, and they provide insight into his approach.

Israel: Years of Challenge. New York, Holt, Rinehart and Winston, 1963. 240p. LC 63-18431 rev. DS 126.5.B44. DDC 959.94.

Israel: A Personal History. New York, Funk and Wagnall's; distr. New York, T. Y. Crowell, 1971. 862p. LC 73-162585. DS 126.5.B44513 1971. DDC 956.94'05. A very disappointing work that reveals few facts and little about internal politics, presenting mainly readily available information; useful, though, for viewing his perspective on a variety of events and issues.

The Jews in Their Land. Garden City, N.Y., Doubleday, 1974. 352p. LC 73-10589. DS 118.B4213. DDC 915.694'06'924.

Memoirs: David Ben-Gurion. Comp. by Thomas R. Bransten. New York, World, 1970. 216p. LC 72-123707. DS 125.3.B37A27. DDC 956.94'05'0924. Not his memoirs, but interviews and recollections.

Letters to Paula. Pittsburgh, University of Pittsburgh Press, 1972. LC 72-164702. ISBN 0-8229-1102-7. DS 125.3.B37A433 1972. DDC 956.94'05'0924 [B]. Very important source of his views on Arabs in Palestine and other matters, included in letters to his wife and children.

My Talks With Arab Leaders. Ed. and tr. from Hebrew by Misha Louvish. New York, Third Press; distr. New York, Viking Press, 1972. 342p. LC 72-94297. ISBN 0-89388-076-0. DS 126.B3933. DDC 301.29'5694'0174927. Mainly 1933-1939, plus items from 1917, 1929, "negotiations" with Nasser, 1954-1956, 1962-1963 via Tito. Useful mainly in studying the dynamics of Ben-Gurion's approach to negotiations, since he does not provide blow-by-blow detail.

Rebirth and Destiny of Israel. New York, Philosophical Library, 1954. 539p. LC 53-13385 rev. DS 126.3.B4. DDC 956.94004. Speeches over several decades.

797. **Chaim Weizmann: A Biography by Several Hands.** Ed. by Meyer W. Weisgal and Joel Carmichael. New York, Atheneum, 1963. 364p. illus. index. o.p. LC 63-7707. DS 125.3.W45C5 1963. DDC 923.15694.

This work consists of eulogistic essays on aspects of the Zionist leader's life. Contributors include Isaiah Berlin, Lord Ritchie Calder, Maurice Samuel, T. R. Fyvel, Abba Eban, Jon Kimche, R. H. S. Crossman, and others. By no means the definitive work, it provides an outline of his life and achievements and describes his significance for Zionism and Israel. His papers are in the process of publication, and the Zionist archives are open to researchers, so perhaps in a few years a good biography will become available.

798. Meir, Golda Mabovitz. **My Life.** New York, G. P. Putnam's Sons, 1975. illus. index. LC n.a. ISBN 0-399-11669-9. LC cataloging n.a.

This autobiography of the former Israeli Prime Minister is not a definitive work, nor even the documented if bowdlerized typical political memoir, but a series of reminiscences and reflections in chronological order, apparently largely from memory. It includes details of her life, her dealings in politics and diplomacy, reflections on people and events, including much on Dayan. It does not reveal extensively the details of Israeli politics, but it is useful for her views, reactions, and life.
See also:

Meir, Golda (Mabovitz). **A Land of Our Own: An Oral Biography.** Ed. by Marie Syrkin. Philadelphia, Jewish Publication Society of America, 1973. 251p. index. $6.95. LC 72-87630. ISBN 0-399-11069-0. DS 126.6.M42 A36. DDC 956.94'05'0924 [B].

799. St. John, Robert. **Ben-Gurion.** Rev. ed. Garden City, N.Y., Doubleday, 1971. 360p. index. $6.95. LC 71-150915. ISBN 0-385-09309-8. DS 125.3.B37S3 1971. DDC 956.94'05'0924 [B].

An informal biography to 1962, using Ben-Gurion's speeches, anecdotes, and interviews, etc., with material on his personal and political life, but little on his ideas and nitty-gritty politicking. It is not overly padded with background and general information as so many biographies are. It is too pro-Israel and obviously anti-Arab. Since Ben-Gurion has died recently, we should expect a number of biographies to appear soon; hopefully one of them will be really worthwhile. Until then, St. John is the best we have, for all its faults. Additional illumination concerning his life and beliefs will be found in Avi-hai (item 796) and in *Ben Gurion Looks Back in Talks with Moshe Pearlman* (New York, Simon and Schuster, 1965. LC 65-25283).
See also:

Litvinoff, Barnet. **Ben-Gurion of Israel.** London, Weidenfeld and Nicolson, 1954. 273p. LC 55-25850. DS 125.3.B37L5. DDC 923.2569. A sympathetic treatment including personal life, leadership, politicking, views and ideology, his conflicts with others, and his dealings with the Arabs. Most of the background material provided is necessary, not padding.

800. St. John, Robert. **Eban.** Garden City, N.Y., Doubleday, 1972. 542p. bibliog. illus. index. $10.00. LC 72-83151. ISBN 0-385-08944-9. DS 126.6.E2S24. DDC 956.94'05'0924 [B].

A very detailed biography, with little or no irrelevant material used for padding. St. John has effectively used Eban's papers, interviews, and other materials to produce a work that gives a better idea of Eban's personality and life history than any other biography of an Israeli leader in English. The detail makes vivid the potentialities and methods of diplomats, and the dynamics of Israel's efforts to garner support for its positions. The many quotations from Eban's writings and statements illuminate his approach to propaganda and other matters, his ideas on the Arabs and international relations, his relations with people, etc. On Israel's relations with the Arabs, the United States, and Britain, St. John is belligerantly pro-Israel. This is not what one would call a "good" biography. It is not just sympathetic, but effusively devotional, and it omits too much of Eban's politicking within Israel. However, the wealth of material presented makes it useful for its own sake, and as a source for other works. Good for public and college libraries, interesting reading for almost anyone.

See also:

Eban, Abba Solomon. **Voice of Israel.** New York, Horizon Press, 1969. 398p. LC 68-23531. DS 102.5.E2 1969. DDC 956.94'05. Speeches.

Eban, Abba Solomon. **My Country: The Story of Modern Israel.** New York, Random House, 1975. LC 74-23729. DS 126.5.E2 1975. ISBN 0-394-47752-X. DDC 956.94'05.

801. Stewart, Desmond Stirling. **Theodor Herzl.** Garden City, N.Y., Doubleday, 1974. 395p. bibliog. illus. index. $12.50. LC 73-83676. ISBN 0-385-08896-5. DS 151.H4S74. DDC 956.94'001'0924.

801a. Elon, Amos. **Herzl.** New York, Holt, Rinehart and Winston, 1975. 448p. bibliog. illus. index. $15.00. LC 74-5128. ISBN 0-03-013126-X. DS 151.H4E57. DDC 956.94'001' 0924 [B].

Either of these biographies will inform the reader adequately about the life of the "father of modern Israel." Both are included here because their emphases are somewhat different. Both treat the main facts of his life using his diaries, papers, and a wide variety of other materials. Stewart, who becomes wordy at times, puts much emphasis on the atmospherics of the times. He interprets and analyses Herzl's psychology and ideas and treats his literary works in some detail, especially as they reflect his life; he deemphasizes the anti-Semitic background and the diplomatic negotiations. Elon is a simply written, more straightforward, smoothly integrated narrative which places less emphasis on the personality and times but goes into the anti-Semitism at considerable length. It discusses Herzl's specific ideas less than Stewart does. Each book deals with issues and events not covered by the other. Stewart, a well-known resident and long-time student of the region, writes for the uninitiated reader and explains everything. Without appearing to cast aspersions on Herzl, he focuses on some of the more sensational aspects of his life. Though appreciative, Stewart is not eulogistic. Elon, a well-known Israeli journalist, is not trying to eulogize; his account is straightforward, and he downplays the negative and sensational without necessarily omitting it. Whereas two-thirds of Elon's work is devoted to events after Herzl's "conversion" to Zionism, only half of Stewart is; Elon details the diplomatic negotiations in the capitals of the East and West, while Stewart mentions them and concentrates on analyzing their importance. Elon also gives much more detail on Herzl's relations with the Zionist movement, the Congresses, etc.; Stewart gives but little information on this aspect. Most readers will probably prefer Elon, particularly since he emphasizes what they will most likely be interested in and what seems most important in the history of Zionism and Israel from a retrospective viewpoint. The standard biography has been Alex Bein, *Theodor Herzl: A Biography* (Cleveland, World, 1962. 557p. LC 62-20753. DS 151.H4 B4 1962. DDC 923.25693).

Herzl's writings translated into English:

Complete Diaries. Ed. by Raphael Patai. Tr. from German. New York, Herzl Press, 1960. 5v. (1961p.). LC 60-8594. DS 151.H4A33. DDC 923.25693.

Diaries. Abridged and tr. by Marvin Lowenthal. New York, Dial Press, 1956. 494p. LC 56-8112. DS 149.H5253. DDC 956.94'296.

The Jewish State (Der Judenstaat). Tr. by Harry Zohn. New York, Herzl Press, 1970. 110p. LC 79-109700. DS 149.H514 1970. DDC 056.94'001.

Old-Newland (Altneuland). Tr. from German. 2nd ed. New York, Bloch Publishing Company, 1960. 295p. LC 60-10757. PZ3.H4484 Ol 5. DDC 833.8.

Zionist Writings: Essays and Addresses. Tr. from German. New York, Herzl Press, 1973– . LC 73-76668. DS 149.H5313 1973. DDC 956.94'001.

802. Syrkin, Marie. **Golda Meir: Israel's Leader.** Rev. ed. New York, G. P. Putnam, 1969. 366p. index. $6.95. LC 76-94238. ISBN 0-399-10346-5. DS 126.6.M42S9 1969. DDC 956.94'05'0924 [B].

Strictly devotional pap, emphasizing Mrs. Meir's strength of character. Most of it deals with aspects and details of her life. Part of it, particularly the post-World War II period, consists of the author's reminiscences of Palestine and Mrs. Meir; the author is a long-time Zionist leader. It will be in demand in public libraries; it is the best thing we have.

803. Teveth, Shabtai. **Moshe Dayan: The Soldier, the Man, the Legend.** Tr. from Hebrew. Boston, Houghton Mifflin, 1973. 372p. illus. $8.75. LC 72-5221. ISBN 0-395-15475-8. DS 126.6.D3T4213 1973. DDC 956.94'05'0924.

Using interviews and Hebrew sources, an Israeli journalist traces the life of the former Israeli general and Defense Minister, his military and political career, with considerable information on his personal life. Unlike most available English language biographies of Israeli personalities, it is no mere devotional bluff but describes the warts and all, analyzing Dayan's failures and errors as well as his successes. It also deals mostly with Dayan, incorporating appropriate contextual material only where useful and needed, unlike some works.

804. Weizmann, Chaim. **Trial and Error: The Autobiography of Chaim Weizmann.** Westport, Conn., Greenwood Press, 1972. (Repr. of 1949 ed.). 498p. index. $17.75. LC 70-156215. ISBN 0-8371-6166-5. DS 125.3.W45A3 1972. DDC 956.94'05'0924 [B]. Paperback: Schocken Books, $3.95. ISBN 0-8052-0116-5.

The memoirs of the Zionist leader constitute a basic source on his life and ideas, his politics, and the history of Zionism. Naturally his account of events is biased, but it is an essential book well worth reading.

E. CIVILIZATION

See also the Hebrew literature section (VIII, K).

805. Tamuz, Benjamin, and Max Wykes-Joyce. **Art in Israel.** Philadelphia, Chilton Book Company, 1967. 298p. 298 illus. o.p. LC 67-20515. N 7277.T29 1967. DDC 709'.5694.

General essays on painting, sculpture, architecture, crafts and design, by four authorities. There are many illustrations; most are in color and most are of paintings.

See also:

Shehori, Ran. **Art in Israel.** Photographs by Israel Zafrir. Tel-Aviv, Sadan Publishing House, 1974. 199p. LC information n.a. Consists of 38 pages of text and 148 pages of plates, some in color.

Dayan, Ruth. **Crafts in Israel.** New York, Macmillan, 1974. 174p. illus. LC 73-10787. ISBN 0-02-534420-X. TT 113.I75D38. DDC 745.5'095694.

F. POLITICS AND GOVERNMENT

806. Arian, Alan. **The Choosing People: Voting Behavior in Israel.** Cleveland, The Press of Case Western Reserve University, 1973. 259p. bibliog. index. $10.95. LC 72-7828. ISBN 0-8295-0249-1. JQ 1825.P365 A748. DDC 324'.2.

An interesting general discussion of the nature of elections in Israel, the relation of the masses to the political system (which, he says, is relatively little); how electoral choice is influenced; religious factors in political behavior; the four main political party blocs; public opinion and politics; voting and modernization of the various types of groups in Israeli society. For comprehensive collections.

807. Badi, Joseph. **The Government of the State of Israel: A Critical Account of Its Parliament, Executive and Judiciary.** New York, Twayne Publishers, 1963. 307p. bibliog. index. $5.00. LC 63-17404. JQ 1825.P3 B2. DDC 354.95694.

[P1, C1, S1] This is a systematic, factual, descriptive presentation of Israel's institutions. Each of the four Knessets is described, including its organization, legislation, composition, major issues, etc. Also treated are the cabinet structure and the various governments (including the Provisional Government), and the cabinets of the first three Knessets, their changes, make-up, and main issues. The book includes discussions of the Civil Service, Presidency, Ben-Gurion's role in the government as Prime Minister. Coverage of the Judiciary includes the issue of legal continuity, the courts, and laws, followed by a chapter setting forth the author's conclusions. Though out of date, it is useful for comparative and historical studies, particularly because, for the period it covers, it provides details that are not readily available elsewhere.

808. Bernstein, Marver H. **The Politics of Israel: The First Decade of Statehood.** New York, Greenwood Press, 1969. (Repr. of 1957 ed.). 360p. index. $15.25. LC 69-13825. SBN 8371-2036-5. JQ 1825.P3 B4 1969. DDC 320.9'5694.

[P1, C1, S1] This is the standard work on the subject; for some time it was the only work. It is a formal, systematic, topical survey of the parties, institutions, procedures and dynamics, administration and civil service; economy, methods of financing growth, planning and economic development, budgetmaking; government-Knesset relationships, the dynamics of coalition government, the welfare state, and local government. A good survey of the early period, useful for comparison with other works in this *Guide.*

809. Birnbaum, Ervin. **The Politics of Compromise: State and Religion in Israel.** Rutherford, N.J., Fairleigh Dickinson University Press, 1970. 348p. bibliog. index. $10.00. LC 70-92557. ISBN 0-8386-7567-0. DS 126.5.B57. DDC 320.9'5694.

This is an excellent study of the interaction and the dynamics of the political system and the religious establishment; it supplies information not only on the role of religion and the religious parties in Israel but on the cabinet system itself. This gives the book a broader appeal and usefulness than otherwise might be the case, particularly since the author provides much background material wherever needed to clarify and explain what is happening. Both theory and practice are examined fully, utilizing case studies.

810. Deshen, Shlomo A. **Immigrant Voters in Israel: Parties and Congregations in a Local Election Campaign.** Manchester, England, Manchester University Press; distr. New York, Humanities Press, 1970. 239p. bibliog. index. $10.00. LC 70-555883. ISBN 0-7190-0421-7. JQ 1825.P365D46. DDC 329'.023'569405.

" . . . how religious parties fought an election campaign in an Israeli development town . . . ." This is an anthropoligical study of the North African immigrants to Israel. First Deshen studies the material—the demographic and economic setting, the political setting (voting procedures, parties, etc.). He describes the candidates and their nomination. He lived for several years in the town and joined a party, actively participating and even becoming a leader. Thus, he can take a personal, detailed look at the process, the appeals used, the nomination procedures, and the means and channels of campaigning, including use of synagogues. He studied the ethnic factors and methods of religious and ethnic propagandizing. One of a series of excellent studies on Israel published by Manchester University Press, based on Ph.D. dissertations written at the University. It is probably too specialized for most college collections, but advanced students will find it fascinating and informative.

811. Elizur, Yuval, and Eliahu Salpeter. **Who Rules Israel.** New York, Harper and Row, 1973. 342p. index. $7.95. LC 73-5460. ISBN 0-06-011164-X. JQ 1825.P3S2713. DDC 320.9' 5694'05.

A description of the "control system," or power elite, in Israel: about 200 people. It describes how they got to power, their positions, their interrelationships, personal lives, and patterns of contact (including protektzia), which make this small group so powerful. Also covered are contrasts in leadership and personal styles (e.g., between Dayan and Allon); personal relationships of members with other members. Includes Histadrut, Mapai, Mapam, and other party leaders, in addition to the top few such as Mrs. Meir, Dayan, etc., plus officials in the Prime Minister's office and Foreign Ministry, particularly those who have access to top information; leaders who have contact with the Diaspora; government agency heads and top administrators; generals. Also, economic enterprise heads and managing technocrats; leaders in agriculture; the scientific, artistic, and public-opinion-molding community leaders. There is a concluding chapter on the "Changing of the Guard." A very interesting book that offers insights into Israel's government and politics, though it is not the definitive work.

812. Israel. Laws, Statutes, etc. **Fundamental Laws of the State of Israel.** Ed. by Joseph Badi. New York, Twayne Publishers, 1961. 451p. bibliog. index. $15.00. LC 61-8605. LC class: LAW. DDC 340.095694.

[C2] Since Israel does not have a constitution, the Fundamental Laws serve this purpose. The 138 items (1948-1958) in this book concern everything: aspects of the transition to independent state and the establishment of a regular government after the Provisional Government; elections to Constituent Assembly, courts, flag and holidays; Knesset and its members; Law of Return; Nazi and Nazi collaborators punishment law; property, including Arab property; defense services; education; religious courts, etc. There is an appendix listing all laws of Israel in order of adoption, 1948-1958. A useful work for larger collections; initiated readers can benefit from it since the language of the translations is generally not technical. It reveals many of Israel's special concerns.

813. Kraines, Oscar. **Government and Politics in Israel.** Boston, Houghton Mifflin Company, 1961. 246p. bibliog. index. pa. o.p. LC 61-19908. JQ 1825.P3K. DDC 354.5694.

[P1, C1, S1] The best systematic survey: the institutions, systems and citizenship, civil rights, administration, local government, foreign policy, Knesset, parties, cabinet, president, judicial and electoral system, etc. It provides some historical background and traces the development of each facet of the system. Out of date but indispensable. A formal, systematic, detailed survey of the structures and their rules of operation from a legal perspective is Yehoshua Freudenhim, *Government In Israel* (Dobbs Ferry, N.Y., Oceana Publications, 1967. LC 66-17246. JQ 1825.P3F713); it provides references to specific laws, etc.

See also:

Medding, Peter Y. **Mapai in Israel: Political Organization and Government in a New Society.** Cambridge, England, Cambridge University Press, 1972. 326p. LC 75-184900. ISBN 0-521-08492-X. JQ 1825.P373P65. DDC 329.9'5694. A general analytical study (rather than straight history) of the processes and organization of Israel's largest party. One of few such studies.

Perlmutter, Amos. **Military and Politics in Israel: Nationbuilding and Role Expansion.** London, Frank Cass, 1969. 161p. LC 75-409540. ISBN 0-7146-2392-X. DS 126.5.P44. DDC 320.9'5694.

Zohar, David M. **Political Parties in Israel: The Evolution of Israeli Democracy.** New York, Praeger, 1974. 193p. LC 73-15201. ISBN 0-275-28814-5. JQ 1825.P37Z64 1974. DDC 329.9'5694.

Naamani, Israel T., comp. **Israel: Its Politics and Philosophy.** New York, Behrman House, 1973. 447p. LC 73-15645. ISBN 0-87441-249-8. DS 126.5.N22 1973. DDC 915.694'05'08. Contains 36 essays by Israeli leaders from the left to the right which suggest much about their attitudes and beliefs on a variety of issues—rebirth: why?; Israel's Jewishness; religion and state; social messianism; in-gathering; securing the future; Arab relations.

814. Lissak, Moshe, and Emanuel Gutmann, comps. **Political Institutions and Processes in Israel.** Jerusalem, ACADEMON, 1971. 619p. LC 72-950558. JQ 1825.P3L57. DDC 320.9'5694.

[C2] A collection of previously published articles and book extracts, all but four in English, on aspects of Israeli political history, processes, and institutions. It includes the nature of the relations between the Mandate administration and Yishuv; Yishuv institutional development, elite, and leadership; ideology and voting; parties, campaigning; the Knesset; Mapai Party; the Army in politics; role of religion; law and religion in Israel, etc. A useful supplement to the systematic works listed in this *Guide*.

815. Segre, V. D. **Israel: A Society in Transition.** London, Oxford University Press, 1971. 227p. index. $9.95. LC 70-21515. ISBN 0-19-215172-X. DS 126.S38 1971. DDC 915.694'06'924.

[C2, S2] The theme is the modernization of Israel. It is a useful and stimulating analysis of the basic elements of Israel's political culture and consciousness, including ideological trends and conflicts and the interaction of economic, social, political, and international developments and conditions with the political climate. It deals with the fundamental structures and their dynamics and with specific issues that govern the reactions of the various forces within Israel. Included are some very interesting discussions and perceptions of the fundamentals of the Arab-Israeli conflict. While not all of these topics are dealt with explicitly as such, the material is to be found herein, and the reader can fairly readily determine the factors that were operating during specific periods and those that carried over into succeeding periods. For more knowledgeable readers.

816. Zidon, Asher. **Knesset: The Parliament of Israel.** Tr. from Hebrew. New York, Herzl Press, 1967. 342p. o.p. LC 67-20569. JQ 1825.P36Z4813. DDC 328.5694.

[C1] A general description of the development, structure, rules, and operation of the Knesset; privileges of members; officials; Knesset record, politicking, debates; relation to and with the public and various branches and agencies of government; legislative process, committees; Constitution question. Concluded by a 40-page section of facts and figures—cabinets, members, election statistics. A basic work.

G. SOCIETY

1. General

817. Cohen, Abner. **Arab Border Villages in Israel: A Study of Continuity and Change in Social Organization.** Manchester, England, Manchester University Press; distr. New York, Humanities Press, 1972. (Repr. of 1965 ed.). 194p. bibliog. index. $7.75. LC n.a. ISBN 0-7190-0251-6. DS 113.7.C6 1972. DDC 309.15694.

A general discussion of economic, social, and political changes in the villages of the Arab Triangle in Israel (roughly the region between Tel-Aviv and Haifa, and between the Mediterranean and the border of the occupied West Bank region of Jordan). It includes the change from agricultural to non-agricultural occupations by the inhabitants of the area; the transition to a cash economy, changes in land ownership and economic relations, and resulting changes in power structure and social status; social classes and increasing egalitarianism; changes in marriage systems and parent-children relationships. Also, the relationship between border tension and family structures and the political system; Israeli social legislation and village structures; family cleavages and national politics. It is descriptive and analytical, using many case studies as examples. A fascinating book.

818. Eisenstadt, Shmuel Noah, Rivkah Bar Yosef, and Chaim Adler, eds. **Integration and Development in Israel.** New York, Praeger, 1970. 703p. bibliog. $20.00. LC 75-109470. SBN 269-02690-8. HN 761.P3E36. DDC 309.1'5694.

[C2] A collection of 28 previously published articles which complements Eisenstadt's *Israeli Society* (item 819) by offering more data and different approaches and by amplifying his ideas and generalities. It is a systematic selection, emphasizing "analysis of the crystallization of Israeli social structure as the continuous interplay among the parts within the structure" of the society, including the economic, social, political, and educational "institutional spheres" of Israel.

819. Eisenstadt, Shmuel Noah. **Israeli Society.** New York, Basic Books, 1968. 451p. bibliog. (Publication Series in the History of Zionism and the Yishuv). $10.95. LC 67-16886. ISBN 0-465-03615-5. HN 761.P282E4 1967b. DDC 309.1'5694.

[P1, C1, S1] This is the basic work on Israel. The author is a widely respected Israeli authority who is, indeed, founder of the main school of Israeli sociology. This is a formal sociological presentation and analysis of the country's social, economic, and political structures treated as interrelated parts of the whole. Most other general works in essence expand on and emphasize, over-emphasize, or de-emphasize various topics found herein (which is not to charge that they are derived from it) in more or less dramatic tone. It presents a wealth of basic information and discusses problems in fairly understandable, if slightly technical, language; it is dry and uninspiring in its style. It is solidly researched and generally neutral. Unfortunately, it has nothing on the Israeli Arabs. Most of the other works listed in this *Guide*, however well researched, are less "scientific" and less solidly based, actually being more like interpretations of the author's personal and secondhand knowledge. They all provide food for thought, but they should be read after Eisenstadt.

Other sources:

Israel: Social Structure and Change. Ed. by Michael Curtis and Mordechai S. Chertoff. New Brunswick, N.J., Transaction Books, 1973. 443p. LC 73-78696. ISBN 0-87855-080-1; 0-87855-575-1pa. HN 761.P32I83. DDC 309.1'5694'05.

Segal, Ronald. **Whose Jerusalem?** London, Jonathan Cape, 1973. 284p. LC n.a. ISBN 0-224-00880-3. LC cataloging n.a. A critical view of Israel, with 75 pages on Egypt and other Arab belligerents. A moderate leftist view.

Zweig, Ferdynand. **Israel: The Sword and the Harp; The Mystique of Violence and the Mystique of Redemption—Controversial Themes in Israeli Society.** Rutherford, Fairleigh-Dickinson University Press, 1970. 326p. LC 74-86291. ISBN 0-8386-7534-4. DS 126.5.Z85 1970. DDC 301.29'5694.

820. Kleinberger, Aharon Fritz. **Society, Schools and Progress in Israel.** New York, Pergamon Press, 1969. 337p. LC 73-92460. ISBN 0-08-006494-0. LA 1141.K54. DDC 370'.90694.

Begins with a 115-page introduction on the history (to 1948), society, politics, and economy of Israel, which offers a blunt critique of many aspects of Israeli life, including problems of the whole structure, treatment of Oriental Jews, kibbutzim, and prospects for the future. Next come chapters on the legislation and politics of education, including ideological and philosophical aspects: educational structure and the role of parties in its development in Israel; the schools, including school day, demographic aspects, class size, curriculum, and problems; teachers (training, quality of teaching, social position of teachers); higher education (the system, structure, finance, relation to aspects of life, student demographics, dropout rates, social and economic background of students, problems); and education of non-Jewish minorities, including the problems of Arab education. Generally the book concentrates on problems and pays little attention to achievements. The footnotes are useful as sources of bibliography, including Hebrew sources. Good as a source of perspectives on Israel as a whole aside from the system of education.

See also:

Bentwich, Joseph Solomon. **Education in Israel.** Philadelphia, Jewish Publication Society of America, 1965. 204p. LC 65-3111. LA 1441.B43. DDC 370.95694.

Burstein, Moshe. **Education in Israel.** Jerusalem, Youth and Hechalutz Department of the Zionist Organization, 1957. 179p. LC 58-791. LC 1441.B8. DDC 370.95694.

Tadmor, Shlomo. **Education in Israel: Towards a New Society.** New York, Appleton-Century-Crofts, 197– ? LC cataloging n.a.

Rabin, Albert J., and Bertha Hazan, eds. **Collective Education in the Kibbutz, from Infancy to Maturity.** New York, Springer Publishing Company, 1973. 184p. bibliog. illus. $6.95. LC 73-80602. ISBN 0-8261-1470-9. Eight essays on the theory and practice of Israeli kibbutz education: methods, subjects taught, integration of education with kibbutz life, children's life in the kibbutz. Includes early childhood education and parental roles, youth society, special education and the childhood guidance clinic. Written by kibbutz educators, it treats the subjects in general terms, rather than providing information on specific kibbutzim.

821. Leslie, Samuel Clement. **The Rift in Israel: Religious Authority and Secular Democracy.** New York, Schocken Books, 1971. 185p. index. $7.50. LC 76-150986. ISBN 0-8052-3410-1. BM 390.L44 1971b. DDC 915.694'03'5.

A compassionate, stimulating, interpretive essay on the problems of the role of religion in Israel. It discusses the implications of the concept of a *Jewish* state–application of religious law and the question of "who is a Jew?" in its theoretical and practical ramifications; segregation in the schools, its operation and results, as well as the differences between Israeli secular and religious education; the meaning of "religious" in a modern state and its relation to Orthodoxy and secularism; Judaism and the "Land"; non-religion and non-Jewishness on the part of Israelis, especially the younger generation; the religious aspects of Zionism; and the "pragmatic interrelationships" of religion and nationalism. Leslie analyses effectively and perceptively aspects and the character of the political system and their implications; the role and character of the military and kibbutzim; in-gathering; the Arab problem in relation to the Jewish nature of Israel; sovereignty based on theocratic principles; and Israel-Diaspora relations. Much of the book's value lies in its treating frequently discussed topics from a somewhat different perspective, in Leslie's objectivity, and in his vivid portrayal of the dynamics of the situation's contradictions.

822. Patai, Raphael. **Israel between East and West: A Study in Human Relations.** 2nd ed. Westport, Conn., Greenwood Press, 1970. 394p. LC 70-98711. ISBN 0-8371-3719-5. DS 113.P38 1970. DDC 956.94.

Covers ethnic make-up of Israel, integration of the diverse groups (particularly with regard to integrating the "Oriental" Jews from the Middle Eastern countries) and the non-Jewish minorities. Describes Oriental and minority life and values, problems of integration. Includes religious and cultural problems.

823. Weintraub, Dov, M. Lissak, and Y. Azmon. **Moshava, Kibbutz and Moshav: Patterns of Jewish Rural Settlement and Development in Palestine.** Ithaca, Cornell University Press, 1969. 360p. bibliog. illus. index. LC 69-18362. ISBN 0-8014-0520-3. HD 1491.P3W38. DDC 335'.9'5694.

A comparative analysis of the three main types of agricultural settlements. It treats Petach Tikva, Ein Herod, and Nahalal as an example of each type; gives a history of the movement and development of each type, its aims, operation, etc., to 1948; then compares them. The general reader can understand it.

See also:

Leon, Dan. **The Kibbutz: A New Way of Life.** New York, Pergamon Press, 1969. 206p. bibliog. LC 69-12386. ISBN 0-08-013356-8. HX 765.P3L4 1969. DDC 335'.9'5694.

824. Willner, Dorothy. **Nation-Building and Community in Israel.** Princeton, N.J., Princeton University Press, 1969. 478p. LC 68-20884. HD 1516.P18W55. DDC 335'.9'5694.

Rural land settlement program and its implementation in Israel, and the social transformations made as a result, with an analysis of the process, in the context of society as a whole. Kibbutzim, moshavim, immigrant villages. Government activities, integration of the communities into the Israeli government system. Special attention is given to the Atlas Mountain (Moroccan) immigrants, their pre- and post-immigration life.

See also:

Deshen, Shlomo A., and Moshe Shokeid. **The Predicament of Homecoming: Cultural and Social Life of North African Immigrants in Israel.** Ithaca, N.Y., Cornell University Press, 1974. 288p. LC 74-4902. ISBN 0-8014-0885-7. DS 113.8.N6D47. DDC 301.29'5694.

Shokeid, Moshe. **The Dual Heritage: Immigrants from the Atlas Mountains in an Israeli Village.** Manchester, England, Manchester University Press; distr. New York, Humanities Press, 1971. 245p. bibliog. index. $11.00. LC 70-881442. ISBN 0-7190-0451-9. HN 761.P32S48. DDC 301.29'5694'9. Shokeid describes the moshav of "Remema": its Moroccan cultural and sociological heritage and the people's consciousness of their Israeli-Jewish heritage, which in various ways clashed and led to conflicts in the village; the mutual influencing of Israeli immigrant settlement authorities and the immigrant community; the process of integrating a new group. After presenting the original Moroccan community and its immigration-settlement process, which had considerable problems, the author describes the Moshav community itself, its geography, structure, and farm planning. He discusses the principles of organization of groups of relatives in the moshav, their dynamics in conflict and cooperation, economy, political dynamics and administration, decision-making and adjustments, marriage and the position of women. A fascinating book written in non-technical language.

2. Arabs in Palestine and Israel

See also Palestinian Refugees and Guerrillas (XXIII, F).

825. Bowen, Mrs. Barbara (Macdonald). **The Folklore of Palestine.** Grand Rapids, Mich., William D. Eerdmans, 1940. 103p. LC 40-36115. GR 285.B6. DDC 398.09569.

Folklore and tales of the peasants and townspeople, Jewish tales, children's tales, tales about animals. A discussion of sacred trees and plants, magic and cures (including tales about cures and instances of magical workings), superstitions. A very interesting popular work.

826. Granqvist, Hilma Natalia. **Birth and Childhood among the Arabs: Studies in a Muham-madan Village in Palestine.** New York, AMS Press, 1975. (Repr. of 1947 ed.). 289p. $17.50. LC 72-9643. ISBN 0-404-57447-5. HQ 792.P3G7 1975. DDC 392. (*BIP* lists orig. ed.: Helsingfors, Soderstrom; distr. New York, International Publications Service, 1947. $9.50. LC 48-23783.)

This widely quoted book is one of only a few on the subject. Studying the village of Artas, south of Bethlehem, the author describes pre-natal customs, birth, post-natal celebra-tions and other customs; child care, children's games and duties; education and character train-ing; circumcision. Treatment includes discussions of attitudes, religious beliefs and other aspects, superstitions. Also pregnancy, midwife, delivery beliefs; nursing and weaning; character formation; man-earth-god relations and their effect on attitudes and practices. The author lets the people speak for themselves. It includes 76 pages of detailed, informative notes and commentary on the text, with suggestions of Biblical parallels with modern practice and beliefs in a separate appendix. The text is non-technical and can be comprehended by most readers.

827. Granqvist, Hilma Natalia. **Child Problems among the Arabs: Studies in a Muhammadan Village in Palestine.** Helsingfors, Soderstrom, 1950. 336p. bibliog. indices. LC 52-32979. HQ 792.P3G72.

Like the previous item (826), this is a widely cited book that is almost unique in the field. It treats problems of childhood such as health and welfare. It discusses names and their importance to the individual, superstitions about names; child mortality; twins, orphans, illegitimate children; barrenness and impotency; diseases and their treatment; portection from dangers, which include evil influences; vows with regard to children; emotional life of children; values concerning children—in the family and in a patriarchal society; relations of parents, parent-children relations, children's relations with other adults; home, siblings, other aspects of the milieu; religious aspects and customs, curses concerning other people's descendants, prayers about children. Concludes with 87 pages of notes and commentary, and a very detailed index of Biblical parallels covering both this and the preceding item.

828. Granqvist, Hilma Natalia. **Marriage Conditions in a Palestinian Village.** New York, AMS Press, 1975. 2v. bibliog. illus. index. LC 72-9644. ISBN 0-404-57450-5. HQ 689.I8 G73. DDC 392'.5'095694.

Age of marriage, choice of bride; marriage by consideration (exchange, as compensation for wrong done, purchase, etc.); customs; betrothal ceremonies, marriage ceremonies; married life; polygyny; the married woman and her relations with her father's house, including living there away from her husband; relations with her husband's family; divorce; widower and widow. General statements, detailed description and specific examples, and analysis of the customs, with very full references to and quotations from other writings in the extensive footnotes. Unlike the author's other books, this one has no section of specific references to the Bible.

829. Granqvist, Helma Natalia. **Muslim Death and Burial: Arab Customs and Traditions Studied in a Village in Jordan.** Helsinki, Societas Scientiarum Fennica; distr. New York, International Publications Service, 1965. 287p. bibliog. index. (Commentationes Humanarum Litterarum, Vol. 34, No. 1). $12.50. LC 76-650681. P9.F5 t.34, no. 1.

As in her other works, Granqvist has provided data from Artas, which she studied in the 1920s and revisited in 1959 to confirm her data. In this discussion she notes the many changes she found. Treats the factors affecting death and mortality, the impact of death on society; the feeling that a man is alive only when he is among his own people (when he leaves the village he is thought of as dead); sickness and religious attitudes toward it; faith healing and protection against various evils; religion and hygiene; exorcism. Beliefs concerning death, its time and place; afterlife, the soul at death; last wills, debts; grief and funeral ceremonies, last farewells, burial clothes. Also, widows, family members, role of the community in the process; paradise, folk-lore of graveyards; dead appearing in dreams; murder, revenge, and blood-money. The villagers express themselves, and the author describes events she witnessed. Includes translations of many "wailing songs," extensive notes, and an index of Biblical parallels.

830. Landau, Jacob M. **The Arabs in Israel: A Political Study.** London, Oxford University Press, 1969. 300p. bibliog. index. LC 70-392686. ISBN 0-19-214977-6. DS 113.7.L3. DDC 323.1'19'2705694.

After a general introduction, the book describes Israeli-Arab political organization, participation and role in Israeli politics, including the courting of the Arabs by Israeli parties in parliamentary elections, local and trade-union elections; the parties the Arabs adhere to and other political organizations; Arab leadership. Generally Landau minimizes Arab discontents. A Palestinian Arab view is presented in Sabri Jurays, *The Arabs in Israel, 1948-1966.* Tr. from Arabic (Beirut, Institute for Palestine Studies, 1969. 180p. LC cataloging n.a. DS 113.7.J812. [Arabic version]).

Jiryis (correct pronunciation) was a lawyer under the Mandate and an Israeli citizen who now is associated with the IPS in Beirut. His book, which is based on Hebrew documents but not adequately footnoted, presents the case against Israeli treatment of its Arab citizens: the Military Government of the areas of Israel where 75 percent of its Arabs lived, which had wide powers, acted, he says, against the Arabs in an arbitrary fashion; expropriation of Arab land and establishment of Jewish colonies on it; the massacre of Arabs at Kfar Qasim in 1956, of which an extensive account is given; Arabs as second-class citizens; repression of independent political and other organizational activity, etc. While these two books differ greatly in their coverage and intent, one can readily and legitimately compare them as excellent examples of the wide divergences between the Israeli and Arab perspectives, even allowing for the fact that they both represent, at least in part, attempts to influence public opinion. This is particularly true of Jiryis, whose book is written specifically to accomplish that; sometimes it is hard to decide to what extent Landau is propagandizing and to what extent he is simply incapable of understanding the Arabs, or even of empathizing intellectually, if not emotionally.

See also:

Schwartz, Walter. **The Arabs in Israel.** London, Faber and Faber, 1959. 172p. LC 60-1436. DS 126.5.S33. DDC 956.94.

Stock, Ernest. **From Conflict to Understanding: Relations between Jews and Arabs in Israel since 1948.** New York, Institute of Human Relations Press, American Jewish Committee, 1968. 103p. LC 70-4857. DS 113.7.S7. DDC 309.1'5694.

831. Marx, Emanuel. **Bedouin of the Negev.** New York, Praeger, 1967. 260p. bibliog. illus. index. $8.50. LC 67-19214. DS 113.7.M3. DDC 301.451'93'505694.

The 22,000 Israeli Bedouins are, for the most part, farmers who raise camels and sheep and do wage labor; they live mainly in the lower half of the Hebron-Beersheba-Dimona triangle. Marx names the tribes and surveys their ecology and environment, economy, health, etc. He describes the administrative environment—their relations with the succession of rulers (including the Israeli military administration) and the Israelis' handling of relations; changes in Bedouin economy under that administration; land ownership and regulation of pastoral movement; Part II describes in detail kinship and corporate groups—tribes, camps and movements, marriage patterns, personal and joint interests in marriage; political structure and its relation to the kinship system; political and economic aspects of marriage; cooperation levels and relation to genealogy; status aspects; effects on the structures of demographic changes; and relations between groups. An interesting work that offers insights into the workings of traditional Near Eastern society and politics.

H. ECONOMY

832. Halevi, Nadav, and Ruth Klinov-Malul. **The Economic Development of Israel.** New York, Praeger, 1968. 320p. bibliog. stat. tables. index. (Praeger Special Studies in International Economics and Development). o.p. LC 68-17557. HC 497.P2H33. DDC 330.95691.

Covers population dynamics; the labor force (its characteristics, structure, education, etc., and changes); growth and distribution of products and resources of the economy; makeup of the product in its various sectors; sectoral structure of the GNP; income distribution; capital and productivity growth; international transactions, sources of funds from the U.S. government and the Diaspora; economic policy; public finance, budget changes; redistribution of income; fiscal policy; foreign exchange and trade policy; inflation, money supply, wage policy. Treatment is mainly general, historical, and comparative, rather than a detailed description of all sectors of the economy; it seeks to indicate the essence of the structure and its dynamics. It complements Horowitz (item 834). For advanced students and large collections.

833. Himādah, Sa'īd, ed. **Economic Organization of Palestine.** Beirut, printed at the American Press, 1938. 602p. (American University of Beirut. Social Science Series, No. 11). LC 41-4875 rev. H 31.A6 no. 11 [HC 497.P2H5]. DDC 330.9569.

A survey of the entire economy by various authorities. Has many statistical tables. Does not seem to have any particular bias or intention in its selection—and interpretation of facts with regard to the Zionist-Arab conflict in Palestine.

834. Horowitz, David. **The Economics of Israel.** New York, Pergamon Press, 1967. 193p. index. (The Commonwealth and International Library. Social, Administration, Training, Economics and Production Division). $6.50; $4.75pa. LC 66-29588. ISBN 0-08-013450-5; 0-08-012206-Xpa. HC 497.P2H613 1967. DDC 330.95694.

A general discussion and analysis for advanced students covering basic trends and tendencies—agriculture, economic growth, living standards, industrialization, labor supply, building, services. Also, consumption and employment, cost of living, balance of payments and international trade, inflation; investment and capital formation, public and private finance, money supply, economic policy, GNP. Many statistical tables, but minimal specific factual data on the economy, stressing dynamics, objectives, problems. For larger collections.

Other sources:

Kanovsky, Eliyahu. **The Economy of the Israeli Kibbutz.** Cambridge, Mass., Harvard University Press, 1966. 169p. LC 66-18097. HX 765.P3K3. DDC 335.95694.

Preuss, Walter. **The Labour Movement in Israel, Past and Present.** 3rd ed. Jerusalem, Rubin Maas, 1965. 239p. LC HE66-432. HD 6851.P3P713. The pre-1948 labor movement, and Histadrut.

Zweig, Ferdynand. **The Israeli Worker.** New York, Herzl Press, 1959. 305p. LC 59-9714. HD 8761.P3Z9. DDC 331.095694.

Horowitz, David. **The Enigma of Economic Growth: A Case Study of Israel.** New York, Praeger, 1972. 157p. LC 77-184338. HC 497.P2 H616. DDC 338'.095694.

Pack, Howard. **Structural Change and Economic Policy in Israel.** New Haven, Yale University Press, 1971. 273p. bibliog. LC 75-140536. ISBN 0-300-01415-5. HC 497.P2P24. Description and analysis of the growth process, including government activity and policy. Rather technical. Includes many statistical tables. Analytical, with generalizations of trends, etc.

835. Rubner, Alex. **The Economy of Israel: A Critical Account of the First Ten Years.** New York, Praeger, 1960. 307p. bibliog. stat. tables. index. o.p. LC 60-7760. HC 497.P2R78 1960a. DDC 330.95694.

A survey and analysis of the economy and its development, 1948-1958 (119 pages). The second part deals with specific topics: five standards for the Israeli pound, foreign currency controls, exchange rates, costs and protection of Israeli entrepreneurs, imports and exports, devaluation, Israel and other underdeveloped countries. A basic work for the period by an expert who worked in and out of the government in Israel during the period covered. One of the few general works on the economy.

I. DESCRIPTION AND TRAVEL

836. Green, Gerald. **The Stones of Zion: A Novelist's Journal of Israel.** New York, Hawthorne Books, 1971. 386p. bibliog. illus. index. o.p. LC 72-130718. DS 107.4.G68 1971. DDC 915.694'04'5.

[P] A delightful description of the places, people, and antiquities of Israel by the well-known Jewish writer. It is extremely well written, with reflections on Israel's history and current society by one who loves the country. Green is sceptical at times and has some devastating comments on tourists he has observed. Probably the best of the travelogues, it is sheer entertainment for prospective and armchair travellers, and fairly informative, though information is not its prime objective.

837. Le Strange, Guy (1854-1933). **Palestine under the Moslems: A Description of Syria and the Holy Land from A.D. 650-1500, Tr. from the Mediaeval Arab Geographers.** New York, AMS Press, 1975. (Repr. of 1890 ed.). 604p. index. $40.00. LC 70-180356. ISBN 0-404-56288-4. DS 124.L6 1974.

Very extensive extracts from the classical Arab geographers linked with commentary and introductions by the editor. Includes mainly physical description of the places, with notes on conditions and the history of Syria and Palestine, their territorial divisions, rivers, mountains, with much emphasis on Jerusalem, including very extensive accounts of the Dome of the Rock and al-Aqsa Mosque. Also includes materials on the Damascus region, legends, marvels, notes on provincial capitals and chief towns. Included is a 172-page gazetteer of places identified by the geographers. Valuable as a source on Muslim attitudes toward Palestine and Jerusalem. For the most comprehensive collections.

838. Wright, Thomas, comp. (1810-1877). **Early Travels in Palestine, Comprising the Narratives of Arculf, Willibald, Bernard, Saewulf, Sigurd, Benjamin of Tudela, Sir John Mandeville, De La Brocquière, and Maundrell.** New York, AMS Press, 1969. (Repr. of 1848 ed.). 517p. index. $10.00. LC 77-84863. ISBN 0-404-50026-9. DS 105.W9 1969. DDC 915.694'04'3.

The accounts date from 700 A.D. to 1699; they usually include descriptions and experiences through other lands on the way to Palestine. They are useful not only for their descriptions of the country and Jerusalem, but also for their reflections on what they saw and their attitudes, which illuminate their outlook as representatives of their eras.

J. GUIDEBOOKS

839. **Fodor's Israel, 1974.** New York, David McKay Company, 1974. (Annual.) 448p. illus. index. $7.95. LC 75-5266. ISBN 0-679-00044-5. DS 103.F62 1974. DDC 915.694'04'5.

The first half consists of general material—history, culture, food and drink, arranging one's trip, transportation, etc. The rest treats individual cities and regions, with descriptions of sights and historical notes, detailed lists of facilities, and extensive descriptions of life in each area to be visited. Vilnay (item 842) totally omits the latter, and his shopping tips and list of facilities are quite inadequate. Fodor and Rand (item 841) are sufficient for most tourists; Vilnay will be useful for those planning a long stay, with exploration; armchair travellers will find Vilnay useful for taking a systematic, vicarious tour. A series of guidebooks that blanket the entire country is the *Weidenfeld Colour Guides to Israel* (London, Weidenfeld and Nicolson, 1973). They are paperbacks, well illustrated (half the pictures being in color), and organized in itineraries; they cost £1.00 each.

Haim, Hadassah Bat. **Galilee and Golan.**

Kohansky, Mendel. **Tel Aviv and Environs** (ISBN 0-297-76630-9. DS 110.T33K63).

Mann, Sylvia. **Jerusalem, Judea and Samaria.**

Samuel, Rinna. **The Negev and Sinai** (ISBN 0-297-76627-9. DS 110.N4S25).

840. **Nagel's Encyclopedia-Guide: Israel.** 4th ed. Geneva, Nagel Publishers; distr. New York, Hippocrene Books, 1971. 430p. maps. index. $17.50. LC cataloging n.a.

The usual Nagel, it features much more detailed descriptions of sights, particularly antiquities, than Fodor (item 839), but not as much material as Vilnay (item 842). A good combination of books to carry might be Nagel and Rand (item 841).

841. Rand, Abby. **The American Traveler's Guide to Israel.** New York, Charles Scribner's Sons, 1972. 296p. illus. index. $8.95; $4.50pa. LC 70-37228. ISBN 0-684-12765-2; 0-684-12838-1pa. DS 103.R35. DDC 915.694'04'5.

An interesting, chatty guidebook geared to the first-time traveller. It provides much more useful information and tips on planning, behavior, shopping, prices, what to expect, and sightseeing procedures than do Fodor *et al.* It has much less detail on the sights than Fodor, so both books should be carried along.

842. Vilnay, Zev. **The Guide to Israel.** 15th ed. New York, International Publications Service, 1972. 720p. illus. maps. $7.50. LC 56-25288. DS 103.V475. DDC 915.694'04'5.

After a general survey of the country, this standard guidebook is organized around itineraries, with detailed descriptions, historical notes, and popular lore on each place; Biblical references; and an indication of the importance of each site throughout history, including the role, if any, in Zionist-Israeli history in the twentieth century. There are innumerable drawings of buildings, antiquities, artifacts, inscriptions, diagrams of buildings, and photographs. The most detailed available. Other than an extensive list of facilities, organizations, institutions, etc., at the end of the book (listed according to city or region), the practical tourist information is lacking, so Fodor or another guide is a necessary supplement (cf. item 839).

XXIII. ARAB-ISRAELI CONFLICT

This topic is especially problematic for librarians and readers. In the first place, there is so much material that it is extremely difficult to choose; in the second place, the vast majority of the works are polemics for one side or the other, or are profit-seeking works pandering to a particular audience. We still lack a comprehensive, documented, systematic, neutral recital of "all" the facts for the various periods. The majority of the works are pro-Israel, as that attitude is the dominant view among the reading public, and most of the works are partisan to the extent that they suppress negative facts and exaggerate the positive. It is only since 1967 that a significant number of books expressing a different viewpoint have appeared, but most of these are unfortunately as rabidly partisan and worthless as the pro-Israeli books. The selections in this *Guide*, taken as a whole, seek to offer the reader a reasonably fair, comprehensive body of facts, analysis, opinion, and propaganda, which should provide him with some basis for developing an independent, balanced view of the conflict. It is emphasized that because of the quantity of and gaps in the literature, this can only represent a beginning, an overview. Many of the general works on Israel have material on the conflict. The general bibliographies in this *Guide*, and listings in the various general and specific works, will guide the reader further. Librarians should constantly check *LJ*, *Choice*, and *PW* (all of which at the present time provide fairly reliable reviews of the latest books on the subject); before buying works on the subject, it would also be wise for librarians to check the *Middle East Journal* for longer reviews. Unless there is strong reader demand for a particular book, the object is to build a rounded collection.

A. GENERAL

843. Alexander, Yonah, and Nicholas N. Kittrie, comps. **Crescent and Star: Arab & Israeli Perspectives on the Middle East Conflict.** New York, AMS Press, 1973. 486p. bibliog. $25.00; pa. price n.a. LC 72-5797. ISBN 0-404-10522-X; 0-404-10523-8pa. DS 119.7. A642. DDC 301.29'17'492705694.

[P1, C1, C2, S1, S2] A useful collection of Arab publications (mainly from the Palestine Liberation Organization Research Center, plus similar materials by a variety of Arab spokesmen) and official Israeli government statements on various aspects of the conflict. Topics include the rights of the Palestinians, refugees, Arabs in Israel, Jews in Arab countries, international legal aspects; guerrillas; economic warfare; Jerusalem, etc. The book concludes with 50 pages of basic historical documents and a useful bibliography. There is an Arab and an Israeli position paper for each topic or subtopic. The papers deal with outstanding issues, rather than with aspects of history. For larger collections.

844. Allen, Richard. **Imperialism and Nationalism in the Fertile Crescent: Sources and Prospects of the Arab-Israeli Conflict.** London, Oxford University Press, 1974. 686p. bibliog. index. $15.95; ca. $4.95pa. LC 73-90373. ISBN 0-19-501782-X; 0-19-501781-1pa.

[P1, C1, S1] A comprehensive history of the conflict in historical context, for the general reader. The first 105 pages treat the history from Biblical times to 1800. The rest of the book deals with the remaining period, emphasizing the twentieth century (through early 1974). It concludes with the author's thoughts on the prerequisites for a settlement. This is not the meticulously researched piece of in-depth scholarship one normally would expect from Oxford; in fact, the research as footnoted is ludicrous. The author's historical knowledge and treatment are quite inadequate for the early period, and he includes much extraneous material or fails to relate much of it emplicitly to the conflict *per se*; many of his individual statements are questionable. It offers nothing new, relying on pitifully few sources, many of which hardly meet good standards of scholarship. But somehow he has chosen and used his material in such a way as to produce an adequately written, judicious, balanced account that suggests well the dynamics of the conflict and that provides the reader with a most useful outline of the facts.

845. Bell, J. Bowyer. **The Long War: Israel and the Arabs since 1946.** Englewood Cliffs, N.J., Prentice-Hall, 1969. 467p. bibliog. illus. index. o.p. LC 68-30968. SBN 13-540617-X. DS 119.7.B38. DDC 956.

[P1] For the general reader, this is the best single book on the whole conflict since World War II. It covers in its main text the period to 1966, with a rather long epilogue on the 1967 War. The narrative is exciting, detailing at length the battles and politics in as fair a manner as is possible for one man. In the main, it is thoughtfully and judiciously written, and the author puts himself, in turn, in the shoes of each party, giving praise and criticism when each is due. Any emphasis on the Israeli side, such as when Bell describes details of battles, is due to the fact that the Arabs have not written much in Arabic, let alone in English, that has much or any value, and very few details are ever provided. Thus the scholar, not to speak of the general writer, has the choice of ignoring some of the facts we have or giving more material on the Israeli side. Bell wrote the book mainly from public, secondary materials and the press; he did not go deeply into each war and topic, as Collins and Lapierre or Kurzman did (in items 862 and 864) for the 1948 War, but his book is most informative.

846. Bovis, H. Eugene. **The Jerusalem Question, 1917-1968.** Stanford, Calif., Hoover Institution Press, 1971. 176p. bibliog. index. (Hoover Policy Study, No. 1). $4.95. LC 73-149796. ISBN 0-8179-3291-7. DS 109.93.B68. DDC 320.9'5694'4.

An excellent history and summary of the various plans for the protection and disposition of the Holy City, from the time of its capture from the Turks during World War I. Includes the international diplomacy, the interests of the various parties (including the multitude of religious groups and denominations inside and outside of Palestine), and the politics involved as each party jockeyed to secure the most favorable position in the City. The Christian, Jewish, and Muslim interests in Jerusalem are neatly summarized. A most useful source of background information.

847. Cohen, Aharon. **Israel and the Arab World.** Tr. from Hebrew. New York, Funk and Wagnalls, 1970. 576p. index. o.p. LC 68-29460. DS 119.7.C6213 1970b. DDC 301.29'174'9240174927.

[C1, S2] A Mapam (leftist Israeli party) Arab expert traces and analyzes Jewish-Palestinian Arab relations and Jewish-Arab diplomacy. The material on the period before 1947 (400 pages) is much more extensive than that on the later period and is the most detailed study available on the subject. It includes attempts of some Zionists to spark a positive attitude toward their Arab neighbors and the attempts to build a foundation for long-term, constructive relations. The final part of the book covers the period through 1967, with an interesting concluding section on the problems of peacemaking. The section on the period 1947-1967 is brief and polemical, being ideological and belligerent toward the Arabs; it is not to be taken seriously as history. When the pre-1947 section is read in conjunction with the section on Jewish-Palestinian relations in Laqueur (item 794), and Sykes (item 860), the reader comes away with a reasonably good notion of the dynamics of the conflict and why it became intractable.

848. Douglas-Home, Charles. **The Arabs and Israel: A Background Book.** Rev. ed. London, Bodley Head, 1970. 128p. (A Background Book). £0.90. LC 73-151560. ISBN 0-370-00469-8. DS 119.7.D68 1970. DDC 956'.04.

[P1, C1, S1] Perhaps the best short introduction. Dealing with the post-1948 period, it is an often pithy exposition and analysis of events, the issues and problems involved, both in general terms and with regard to specific incidents. Probably as fair in its attitude and approach as it could possibly be. It examines the conflict from both perspectives, dealing with such topics as the frontiers; terrorism and propaganda; refugees; Jordan River division; Arab nationalism; Israel; the 1967 War, both prelude and aftermath; the future. A first book.

849. Hadawi, Sami. **Bitter Harvest: Palestine between 1914-1967.** New York, New World Press, 1967. 355p. index. $6.00. LC 67-28543. DS 119.7.H3. DDC 956.94.

[P2, C2, S2] A systematic presentation of the Arab version by a Palestinian: history and specific topics. It makes a deliberate attempt to counter many Zionist positions and to list Zionist and Israeli offenses against the Palestinians, as well as to present the Arab views. Strictly a polemic, but one of the best in English. It belongs in any balanced collection as an authentic expression of the Arab view. Another version of the Arab view is Henry Cattan's *Palestine, the Arabs, and Israel: The Search for Justice* (London, Longmans, 1969. 381p. £2.25. LC 71-432183. ISBN 0-582-78021-7. DS 119.7.C38). Cattan, a Palestinian, covers the usual historical aspects and spends much time on International legal aspects, including Israel's illegitimate existence, offenses against the Palestinians, U.N. condemnations and other resolutions, and the "just" solution: Israeli evacuation from territories in excess of the 1948 Partition boundaries and further relinquishing of land if she will not repatriate Arabs who fled the areas allotted under Partition. Also, de-Zionization of Israel. He says that since Israel will not give up its basic Zionist aims, the U.N. and the United States, who have prime responsibility, must force Israel to act.

850. Hodes, Aubrey. **Dialogue with Ishmael: Israel's Future in the Middle East.** New York, Funk and Wagnalls, 1968. 258p. index. $5.95. LC 68-28245. ISBN 0-308-70259-X. DS 119.7.H6. DDC 327.5694'0174'927.

This is a thoughtful exposition of the Arab-Israeli conflict, a critique of the positions, behavior, and policies of Israel and the Arab governments, and a comprehensive series of suggestions for creating a climate in which peace efforts might be made. Hodes says that since Arab society is basically inert (i.e., a society that perpetuates problems by accepting and living with them) and Israel society is dynamic (i.e., one that considers solving problems to be a challenge), Israel is the party that should and could take the initiative. Hodes, an Israeli, lays out numerous steps that he believes Israel could take unilaterally, including many regarding the refugees and Palestinian Arabs. One of the more worthwhile books on how to solve the conflict, though it is at times naive. A similar work is Uri Avnery, *Israel without Zionists: A Plea for Peace in the Middle East* (New York, Macmillan Company, 1968. 215p. LC 68-25221. DS 119.7.A9 1968); it is much more sharply polemical, particularly with regard to Israeli internal politics on the conflict and especially the roles of Ben-Gurion and Dayan. Avnery is a well-known, leftist former member of the Knesset. The latest exposition by an Israeli "dove," billed as a member of the Establishment, is Arie L. Aliav (ex-cabinet member, MK), *Land of the Hart: Israelis, Arabs, the Territories and a Vision of the Future* (tr. from Hebrew. Philadelphia, Jewish Publication Society, 1974. 381p. $6.95. LC 73-21170. DS 126.5.E416 1974). When it was originally published in Hebrew in 1972, it caused an uproar because it so sharply varied from the conventional approach to dealing with the Palestinians, as well as because of its views on Israeli society and Israel's relations with the rest of the world. Its summary of the creation of the Jewish community in Palestine and the development of the conflict with the Arabs is strictly conventional and very nicely capsulizes the Zionist-Israeli view of history; it beautifully exemplifies the Israeli self-view and psychology. Much of the book is concerned with Israel's relations with the U.S., USSR, Europe, the Third World, and the Diaspora; concluding chapters treat Israeli social problems and means of solving them and Eliav's hopes for the future. For all readers and larger collections.

851. Hurewitz, Jacob Coleman. **The Struggle for Palestine.** New York, Greenwood Publishers, 1968. (Repr. of 1950 ed.). 404p. bibliog. index. $16.00. LC 68-28594. ISBN 0-8371-0111-5. DS 126.H87 1968. DDC 956.94'04.

[P1, C1, S1] This is the standard work on the Palestine conflict, 1936-1948. After a rather long introduction on the previous decade, it details the structures, institutions, and dynamics of the Arab and Jewish communities and traces the political history, including the international diplomacy, of the period. It is based on Hebrew, Arabic, and Western sources of various kinds. Although additional research has been done recently, and a new work is in order, Hurewitz has not been superseded. There is no comparable work for the period 1918-1936, and even the Arabs have not produced any decent works on their side of the hill for the period.

852. John, Robert, and Sami Hadawi. **The Palestine Diary.** Beirut, Institute for Palestine Studies, 1970. 2v. bibliog. index. $6.95/vol. LC 73-286232. DS 126.J552. DDC 956.94'04.

A narrative survey of the Palestine problem—*not* a chronology or narrative of the authors' lives, etc.—using almost exclusively Western sources. The aim is to demonstrate the truth of the Arab version of history by showing that many Western officials and other writers hold the same views as the Arabs on the Palestine conflict. This is accomplished by using these sources to weave the story. This is not to deny the truth of part of the account, but it is incomplete even if one does not take into account the fact that no Arabic or Hebrew archives are used. It is not even a piece of biased research, but a synthesis of the public record. However, it does represent an authentic, widely held view and is a basic book for balanced collections. Volume 1 covers 1917-1945; Volume 2, 1945-1948; additional volumes are promised for the later period. Volume 2 is particularly useful since it uses mainly U.N. documents and press accounts and gives a very detailed account of the U.N. debates.

853. Khalidi, Walid. **From Haven to Conquest: Readings in Zionism and the Palestine Problem until 1948.** Beirut, The Institute for Palestine Studies, 1971. 914p. index. (Anthology Series, No. 2). $12.50. LC 73-161566. DS 149.K55. DDC 956.94'001.

The main theme of these 80 previously published readings by European and American writers is the process by which Palestine was lost to the Arabs: the growth of Zionism; the nature of Zionist measures to win support abroad, increase their control over the land and build a viable community in Palestine. It covers the period from 1897, with preliminary excurses on the period before—the Biblical era, through the Middle Ages (to demolish Zionist Biblical claims to Palestine and establish Muslim attachment to Jerusalem) through the first Arab-Israeli War in 1948. There are discussions of British and U.S. policies and how they evolved, U.N. intervention, Count Bernadotte's assassination by terrorists in 1949. A well-selected, useful source book that reflects Arab and much Western opinion. A volume on the post-war period is promised.

854. Khouri, Fred John. **The Arab-Israeli Dilemma.** Syracuse, N.Y., Syracuse University Press, 1968. 436p. bibliog. index. $10.00; $4.25pa. LC 68-20483. ISBN 0-8156-0063-1; 0-8156-0066-6pa. DS 119.7.K48. DDC 956.

[B, P1, C1, S1] The most useful work on the conflict from 1948-1967. Using U.N. and other sources, it provides much more factual data, names, dates, and sources than other books. Dealing with each war, it also treats topics such as the Arab refugees, Jerusalem, peace efforts, armistice problems. It also attempts much analysis, which is often so simplistic and superficial that it cannot be taken seriously; this in no way vitiates its usefulness as a basic work. To most readers who are acquainted with other works on the period it will seem anti-Israeli. It often appears to be mainly a catalog of Israeli misdeeds (contradicting most of our conventional wisdom about who is to blame) and it does not provide the same degree of information about Arab misdeeds. However, Khouri is trying to pack a great deal of information into one book, and is apparently trying to balance the record, which usually emphasizes negative aspects of Arab actions and positive aspects of Israeli actions. Khouri is sympathetic to the Arabs but is not anti-Israel; he tries to be fair. His main emphasis is U.N. activity. A thoroughly researched and documented book.

See also:

Bar-Yaacov, Nissim. **The Israel-Syrian Armistice: Problems of Implementation, 1949-1966.** Jerusalem, Magnus Press, 1967. 377p. LC HE 68-988. DS 126.98.B36. DDC 956.

Gabbay, Rony E. **A Political Study of the Arab-Jewish Conflict: The Arab Refugee Problem (A Case Study).** Geneva, Librairie E. Droz, 1959. 611p. LC A60-2555. HV 640.5.A6G3 1959. DDC 361.53. One of the most detailed and most thoroughly documented/footnoted studies available, tracing the conflict from December 1947 to the late 1950s, with much emphasis on the refugee problem but much material on other aspects as well. Based on Western, Arabic, and Hebrew sources; the notes and the 32-page bibliography are extremely helpful to students. An essential work for all serious readers.

855. Laqueur, Walter Ze'ev. **The Israel-Arab Reader: A Documentary History of the Middle East Conflict.** Updated and expanded ed. New York, Bantam Books, 1970. 511p. bibliog. (Bantam Matrix Editions, BM 5640). $1.65pa. LC n.a. DS 119.7.L3 1970. DDC 956.

[P1] Contains 71 documents and articles—official items from governments and organizations—from Herzl through the 1948 period, including the Balfour Declaration, the Mandate, 1939 White Paper, U.N. Partition Resolution. Post-1948 items include Israel's Declaration of Independence, the Law of Return, Arab documents and speeches, and many articles, both analytical and polemical, by well-known Western writers on various aspects of the conflict, particularly on the post-1967 period. Many are commonly available elsewhere, but are widely scattered. For the public and smaller college collection this is a basic work.

Other collections of documents and articles:

Avineri, Shlomo, comp. **Israel and the Palestinians.** New York, St. Martin's Press, 1971. 168p. LC 70-145690. DS 119.7.A87. DDC 327.5694'0174927. By Israelis, mainly establishment figures, and two Israeli Arabs on past, present, and future relations with the Palestinians. A variety of perspectives and some disagreements on how to approach the problem.

Bober, Arie, comp. **The Other Israel: The Radical Case against Zionism.** Garden City, N.Y., Doubleday, 1972. 264p. (Anchor Book A 860). pa. LC 72-76225. ISBN 0-385-01467-8. DS 126.5.B67. DDC 956.94'001. Includes much on Israel apart from the conflict. Statements by the Israeli Socialist Organization.

Hadawi, Sami, comp. **United Nations Resolutions on Palestine, 1947-1966.** Beirut, Institute for Palestine Studies, 1967. 203p. LC 70-10757. JX 1977.2.P34H32. DDC 341.13'9'5694. Watch for a new edition in 1975.

Howe, Irving, and Carl Gershman, eds. **Israel, the Arabs and the Middle East.** New York, Quadrangle Books, 1972. 440p. LC 72-75043. DS 126.5.H66. DDC 320.9'56'04. Pro-Israel.

Ingrams, Doreen. **Palestine Papers, 1917-1922: Seeds of Conflict.** New York, George Braziller, 1973. 198p. LC 72-87221. ISBN 0-7195-2638-8. DS 126.I45 1973. DDC 956.94'04. British Foreign Office Documents, connected by the compiler's notes, relating to the early development of the conflict as viewed by policy makers. They show clearly how the Arabs and Zionists reacted to each other.

Khadduri, Majdia D., comp. **The Arab-Israeli Impasse.** Washington, Robert B. Luce, 1968. 223p. LC 68-55364. DS 119.7.K42. DDC 956. A moderately pro-Arab, or at least non-Israeli, orientation, by non-Arabs. It focuses on the 1967 War and its implications.

The Arab-Israeli Conflict. Ed. by John Norton Moore. Princeton, N.J., Princeton University Press, 1975. 3v. LC 72-39792. ISBN 0-691-05648-X. DS 119.7.A6718 1975. This is the largest collection of materials. The first two volumes contain articles on various issues, particularly the international legal and political aspects, both polemical and scholarly, emphasizing the period 1967-1972; alternatives for a peaceful solution. Volume 3 contains 175 documents, all but 42 of which date from 15 May 1948 to April 1973.

Sheffer, Gabriel, comp. **Dynamics of Conflict: A Reexamination of the Arab-Israeli Conflict.** Atlantic Highlands, N.J., Humanities Press, 1975. bibliog. LC 73-85041. ISBN 0-391-00379-8. DS 119.7.S4665. DDC 327.5694'017'4927.

Taylor, Alan R., and Richard N. Tetlie, comps. **Palestine, a Search for Truth: Approaches to the Arab-Israeli Conflict.** Washington, D.C., Public Affairs Press, 1970. 284p. LC 77-132105. DS 119.7.T38. DDC 301.29'174'9240174927. Anti-Zionist, pro-Arab, to a great extent.

856.   Polk, William Roe, David W. Stamler, and Edmund Asfour. **Backdrop to Tragedy: The Struggle for Palestine.** Boston, Beacon Press, 1957. 399p. bibliog. index. o.p. LC 57-12743. DS 123.P68. DDC 956.94.

One of the best general introductions to the Palestine problem before 1948, with some information on the aftermath of the 1948-1949 War. Polk commences with a 130-page historical introduction, which goes back to Babylonian times, then discusses Islam and the Jews, nineteenth and twentieth century history, great power intervention in the region, the Mandate, and partition. Stamler deals with Zionism and the development of Jewish interests in Palestine; politics, religion, and other aspects of Israel. Polk follows with the Arab interests in Palestine— the communities and society, Arabism, Islam, Arab reaction to Zionism, Pan-Arabism, and the refugees. Asfour concludes with an analysis of the economic framework—alienation of the Arabs from their lands, land purchases by the Zionists, Mandate period capital formation and income distribution; Israel's economy. While dated, and to some extent inadequately researched, it is a good basic work that clearly delineates key aspects in a generally dispassionate fashion; it is sympathetic to the Arab position as well as to the Jewish vision.

857. Porath, Yehoshua. **The Emergence of the Palestinian Arab National Movement, 1918-1929.** London, Frank Cass; distr. Portland, Ore., International Scholarly Book Services, 1974. 406p. bibliog. index. £7.50. LC 72-92976. ISBN 0-7146-2939-1. DS 126.P6313 1974. DDC 320.5'4'095694.

A thoroughly researched, objective study of Palestinian politics. The author, an Israeli scholar, discusses the origins and early manifestations of Palestinian anti-Zionism before World War I, the development of Palestinian consciousness—Arab nationalism, Palestinian nationalism, the organization of the Palestinian elite and youth, diffusion of ideas, organization of action against the mandate and the Jewish influx; interrelations of Palestinian and Pan-Arab movements; British policy; the politics of these aspects. The 1929 Wailing Wall incident is given careful treatment. The book makes clear the process by which national consciousness and anti-Zionism emerged, and the rise of al-Hajj Amin al-Husayni, the Grand Mufti of Jerusalem; it clears up innumerable misconceptions concerning the situation in Palestine during the period. While much of its detail is too specialized for the less initiated reader, it is an outstanding contribution to understanding the Palestine conflict. All serious students of the question must read it, particularly in conjunction with Hurewitz (item 851).

See also:

Abu-Ghazaleh, Adnan Mohammed. **Arab Cultural Nationalism in Palestine During the British Mandate.** Beirut, Institute for Palestine Studies, 1973. 114p. LC cataloging n.a. Poorly done, but the only work we have on Arab culture in Palestine.

858. Roberts, Samuel J. **Survival or Hegemony? The Foundations of Israeli Foreign Policy.** Baltimore, Johns Hopkins Press, 1973. 163p. bibliog. (Washington Center of Foreign Policy Research. Studies in International Affairs, No. 20). $7.50; $2.95pa. LC 73-8134. ISBN 0-8018-1541-X; 0-8018-1543-6pa. DS 119.6.R6. DDC 327.5694.

A good general interpretive essay on Israeli-Arab relations, which sets forth and analyzes basic factors and policies. It includes some discussion of Israel's relations with the U.N., the United States and the Diaspora, all in the context of the conflict with the Arabs. It does not mention Israel's relations with Africa or Europe.

859. **Search for Peace in the Middle East: A Report Prepared for the American Friends Service Committee.** Rev. ed. New York, Hill and Wang, 1971. 126p. $4.50. LC 75-148238. ISBN 0-8090-8573-9. DS 119.7.S38 1971. DDC 956'.04.

After two years of research here and in the Near East, a Quaker study group (which included two professional area experts) produced this analysis of the Arab-Israeli conflict, its causes, the positions and fears of the parties; the role, positions and policies of outside parties (the great powers and the U.N.); views on negotiations of the various parties and interests (including world Jewry, oil companies, etc.); and finally, what the study group believes to be the basic elements necessary for peace, and the steps that each side must take to begin and maintain the momentum of the process. It seeks to identify the attitudes, statements, and acts on the part of *both* sides that have led to and have continually inflamed the conflict, and to work toward squelching these factors. Despite the fact that it was written before the October 1973 War, most of the book is not dated. It stands out as one of the best works, attempting to go beyond history and polemic in order to start a psychological process that could contribute to a final settlement. It proposes interim measures to prevent further conflict while other means are used to achieve final settlement. The serious general reader as well as the student will find in it much food for thought, even if he does not agree with all of its conclusions. A Zionist response to this book is found in Arnold M. Soloway, *Truth and Peace in the Middle East: A Critical Analysis of the Quaker Report* (New York, published by Friendly House Publishers for the American Jewish Congress and the Anti-Defamation League of B'nai B'rith, 1971. 100p. $1.25. LC 78-172532. ISBN 0-87068-175-3); the importance of the Quaker report is indicated by the virulence of the widespread attack on it even as late as 1975 by Zionist publicists and periodicals, and even in the *Encyclopaedia Judaica Yearbook.*

Worthwhile books relating to the dynamics of settling the conflict:

Elon, Amos, and Sana Hassan. **Between Enemies: A Compassionate Dialogue between an Israeli and an Arab.** New York, Random House, 1974. 151p. LC 74-9077. ISBN 0-394-49514-4. DS 119.7E5. DDC 327.5694'0171'4927. The famous Israeli journalist and the wife of an Egyptian diplomat (who is studying international relations in the U.S.) engage in a dialogue that suggests some bases of understanding and some conflicts between the parties. This dialogue was widely covered in the media. Perceptive readers will find exemplified some of the problems that will arise in personal contacts and in the negotiating process between the parties.

Fisher, Roger. **Dear Israelis, Dear Arabs: A Working Approach to Peace.** New York, Harper and Row, 1972. 166p. index. LC 74-181618. ISBN 0-06-011274-3. DS 119.7.F57. DDC 327.5694'017'4927. Letters and draft documents sent by Fisher to the parties suggesting ways for working out a settlement: very clearly delineates basic issues, legitimate concerns and rights of the parties, the real self-interest of the parties as divorced from arguments about the past. A very enlightening work for all readers, containing much food for thought.

Rikhye, Indar Jit, and John Volkmar. **The Middle East & the New Realism.** New York, International Peace Academy, 1975- . 99p. $2.65pa. LC 75-13733.

The normal view advocated by Zionist publicists has been that the Arabs are totally incapable of reconciling themselves with Israel; due in part to their usual presentation, it is fairly easy for non-Zionists and pro-Arab partisans to dismiss, at least to some extent, the more extreme implications and expressions of this perspective, and of course the Quaker report quite rejects the view. A well-known proponent of the Zionist view is Yehoshafat Harkabi (cf. his book on the Palestinians, supplementary citation to item 876), whose book *Arab Attitudes toward Israel* (New York, Hart Publishing Company, 1972. 527p. bibliog. ISBN 0-8055-1027-3. DS 119.7.H7213) quotes extensively from Arabic books to illustrate what Arabs say to other Arabs about Zionism, Israel, and the Jews. His selections are generally fairly representative, not only for the period until 1967, which the book covers, but for the period thereafter. However, his analyses of the Arab psyche and reasons behind their writings are so convoluted, obviously biased, and tortured that they would convince only the ignorant and the biased. The book of another writer who has been very active in advocating this view is: Gil Carl AlRoy, *Behind the Middle East Conflict: The Real Impasse between the Arab and the Jew* (New York, G. P. Putnam's Sons, 1975. 317p. bibliog. index. [Capricorn Books]. $9.95). He argues that hostility to Israel is a basic part of the Arab psyche, and that a final settlement including a commitment by the Arabs to really accept and recognize Israel's existence is not possible. This point is not recognized by most of the sincere peace seekers, he says, be they Israelis or Westerners, including Americans, journalists, religious figures and organizations, politicians or diplomats. Because of a basic lack of understanding of the place of Israel in the Arab mind, and in Arab character and thought process as they relate to the Arab approach to the conflict, he says, peace efforts at all levels actually *inhibit* the process by which the Arabs might ultimately come to adjust to Israel's existence. The argument is very carefully and cogently developed through an examination and refutation of the views and approaches of the various non-Arab observers and participants in peace efforts, including the Zionists in Palestine and the Israelis; a study of Arab perceptions of Israel; Arab character, religion, and culture; means of expression and the present state of Arab existence in relation to Westernization and modernization, as well as differences in the attitudes of various Arab sects, classes, and the individual countries; Arab views of their history and glories of the past; psychological processes, attitudes toward the Jews before the conflict developed and since the introduction of Zionism; the reasons for the violence of the Arab reaction to Zionism; indeed, it covers much of the material discussed in all books cited in item 428. AlRoy eschews polemic tones and expertly uses his wide variety of (non-Arabic) sources, both original and secondary. He does not cloth his work with "scientific" disciplinary apparatus, but develops a straightforward, very closely reasoned, and very convincing analysis that is by far superior to any full-length discussion of any aspect of the subject yet available from any author, whatever his basic views. There is much room for disagreement with particular points and with some of his argument, but AlRoy offers a first-class, well-written, understandable presentation that provides much food for thought. Partisans of both sides will find something to object to, particularly pro-Arab ovservers, but the latter will find much that is useful in a reexamination of their approach, if not of their basic views (though they will have to do a great deal of careful rethinking, digging, and reformulating to respond effectively to this book!). A must for every somewhat knowledgeable reader interested in the conflict.

860. Sykes, Christopher. **Crossroads to Israel, 1917-1948.** Bloomington, Indiana University Press, 1973. (c. 1965). 404p. (A Midland Book, MB 165). $3.50pa. LC 72-93912. ISBN 0-253-20165-9. DS 125.S86 1973. DDC 956.94'04.

[P1, C1, S1] The best book on the Palestine conflict to 1948. Well-written for general readers, it is very judicious in its statements, expression, and conclusions, and it should be read by any-one interested in the subject. The main emphasis is on British-Zionist relations and the British policy perspectives that explain the course of those relations. Sykes is rather more sympathetic to the Zionists than to the Arabs. He includes but little on events on the Arab side, but what he has is carefully thought out and written and shows considerable understanding. He is not mindlessly pro-Zionist, and he has a critical eye.

See also:

ESCO Foundation for Palestine, Inc. **Palestine: A Study of Jewish, Arab and British Policies.** New Haven, Conn., Yale University Press, 1947. 2v. LC 47-2569. DS 126.E8. DDC 956.9. A standard work for decades, even though it is not trustworthy and is undocumented; useful for orientation in many topics, but not as a prime source.

Hyamson, Albert Montefiore. **Palestine under the Mandate, 1920-1948.** London, Methuen, 1950. 210p. LC 50-11871. DS 125.H95. DDC 956.9. A pro-Zionist account.

Jeffries, Joseph Mamy Nagle. **Palestine, the Reality.** New York, Longmans, 1939. 728p. LC 39-17705. DS 126.J37 1939. A very detailed account of the diplomatic process by which Palestine came to be put under the Mandate on behalf of the Zionists. Bitterly against Zionist expansion in Palestine at the expense of the Arabs, but provides a detailed, if undocumented, account. Attacks British duplicity vis-à-vis the Arabs. Many quotations from documents. Covers much the same ground as Antonius (item 117) on the subject, but in more detail.

Marlowe, John. **The Seat of Pilate: An Account of the Palestine Mandate.** London, Cresset Press, 1959. 289p. LC 59-2513. DS 126.M34. DDC 956.94.

861. Whetten, Lawrence L. **The Canal War: Four-Power Conflict in the Middle East.** Cambridge, Mass., M.I.T. Press, 1974. 520p. bibliog. index. appendices. LC 74-11424. ISBN 0-262-23069-0. DS 119.7.W47. DDC 327.5694'017'4927.

A useful narrative history, interpretation, and analysis of the Egyptian-Israeli conflict 1967-1974, and the roles and influence of the United States and Russia in the past, present, and future. It seeks to prove the nature and dynamics of the confrontation as a case study in the relationship of politics and the use of armed strength. Considerable attention is given to Soviet policy, less emphasis on U.S. policy. There is some discussion of aspects of a settlement. Whetten finds that Israel's policy in the conflict is unrealistic because its actions have not responded to the changes in conditions the author believes to have occurred in U.S.-U.S.S.R. relations and in the nature of their interests in the region. He also finds U.S. policy unrealistic and dwells on both themes at some length. While the book is obviously the product of ivory tower academic scholarship and is based on secondary sources, it has much food for thought for students of the region and of international relations, and it is quite useful for its continuous narrative history of this aspect of the conflict.

B. 1948 WAR

862. Collins, Larry, and Dominique Lapierre. **O Jerusalem.** New York, Simon and Schuster, 1972. 637p. bibliog. illus. index. $10.00. LC 77-185063. SBN 671-21163-3. DS 126.99.J4C63. DDC 956.94'405. Paperback: Pocket Books, $1.95.

Based on interviews, the secondary and monographic literature, and a wealth of original (and, in some cases, previously unutilized) sources—Jewish, Arab, American and British—this is one of the best books on the 1948 War. It is not comprehensive in its coverage. It seeks to recreate the atmosphere and events in the words of participants, from interviews and diaries, focusing on the vital struggle for Jerusalem, which covered much of the war zone. There is material on the diplomacy in Washington and New York. It deals not only with the Jewish side but, as much as possible, with the Arab participants, about which not much material is available; it is remarkably fair. Excellent reading.

863. Kimche, Jon, and David Kimche. **A Clash of Destinies: The Arab-Jewish War and the Founding of the State of Israel.** New York, Praeger, 1960. 287p. index. (Books That Matter). o.p. LC 60-6996. DS 126.9.K5. DDC 956.94.

The most interesting book on Israel's War of Independence. It attempts to probe events and problems on the Arab as well as Israeli side, and it treats diplomatic aspects, especially British-Arab policy, as well as the battles. It is definitely pro-Israel and sometimes twists or omits facts, but no one has as yet done any better in as comprehensive a manner.

864. Kurtzman, Dan. **Genesis, 1948.** New York, World Publishing Company, 1970. 750p. bibliog. illus. (An NAL Book). o.p. LC 77-96925. DS 126.9.K87. DDC 956. Paperback: New York, New American Library. (Signet Book J 5174). $1.95.

Basing his work on interviews and much secondary and source material, award-winning newsman Kurzman seeks to recreate the 1948 Israeli-Arab war in much the same way as Collins/ Lapierre (item 862), using the same techniques: recreation of the scene as seen by individual participants. He is about as fair as Collins/Lapierre. He tries to be comprehensive and deal with the entire war. However, he is less successful somehow in transporting the reader. He does provide some new material, which makes the book useful. The scattered diplomatic, U.N., and U.S. political episodes are quite incomplete and are hardly the main interest of the book.

865. Lorch, Netanel. **The Edge of the Sword: Israel's War of Independence, 1947-1949.** 2nd rev. ed. Hartford, Conn., Hartmore House, 1968. 579 columns. illus. maps. $12.50. LC 71-4189. ISBN 0-87677-011-1. DS 126.9.L613`1968b. DDC 956.

The most detailed English military history of the first Arab-Israeli War, by an Israeli officer. Written from an Israeli perspective, it frequently is not objective, particularly with regard to the Arabs and the U.N. O'Ballance (item 866) offers a corrective because of his critical eye and greater objectivity. The many illustrations and maps are splendid.

866. O'Ballance, Edgar. **The Arab-Israeli War, 1948.** New York, Praeger, 1957. 220p. maps. o.p. LC 57-6649. DS 126.4.O2 1957. DDC 956.

A good, critical military history of the first Arab-Israeli war for the general reader; it details the battles, comments on the strategy and tactics of both sides, and compares the various armed forces involved as to numbers, quality, and armaments.

C. 1956 WAR AND SUEZ CRISIS

867. Love, Kennett. **Suez: The Twice-Fought War, a History.** New York, McGraw-Hill Book Company, 1969. 767p. bibliog. index. $10.00. LC 76-81913. ISBN 0-07-038780-X. DT 107.83.L6. DDC 956.

[P1, C1, S1] The best single-volume work on the 1956 War, its background and development. Love, who was the *New York Times* reporter on the scene and who knows Arabic, used the press of several countries, including the Arab press, the secondary literature, Dulles papers, and Egyptian military archives, as well as interviews. He minutely details events and gives an exhaustive account of the general and immediate background to trace the confluence of events that led to the War, including the development of the roles in the region and psychology of the participants—Israel, Egypt, Britain, France, Russia, the U.S.—and their leaders, and the diplomatic history of the entire period. It is the most complete account and will likely remain the standard work. Unfortunately, it is marred, some would say seriously, by a seemingly unabashed sympathy for Nasser, which may cloud the author's judgments. The brief final chapter on the 1967 War is of little importance.

An important work that provides much additional detail is Herman Finer's *Dulles Over Suez: The Theory and Practice of His Diplomacy* (Chicago, Quadrangle Books, 1964. 538p. o.p. LC 64-10924). A vituperative attack on Dulles and others, but it has so much information that it is essential for researchers.

See also:

Calvocoressi, Peter. **Suez Ten Years Later.** New York, Random House, 1967. 160p. LC 67-23530. DT 107.83.C27 1967. DDC 962'.05. The war as seen through the eyes of key leaders and participants: Eban, Pineau, Dayan, etc.

Childers, Erskine B. **The Road to Suez.** London, MacGibbon and Kee, 1962. 416p. LC 62-5649. DS 63.C475. A stimulating and controversial pro-Arab view of the Suez crisis and events leading up to it, sharply critical of Britain and France.

Nutting, Anthony. **No End of a Lesson: The Story of Suez.** New York, C. N. Potter, 1967. 205p. LC 67-27355. DT 107.83.N8 1967b. DDC 962'.15'05. Inside story of British role; Nutting, a high official in the British Government, resigned over Suez. Disappointing, but useful.

Robertson, Terence. **Crisis: The Inside Story of the Suez Conspiracy.** London, Hutchinson, 1965. 349p. LC 66-351261. DT 107.83.R6. Unfootnoted but important account emphasizing the role of late Canadian Prime Minister Pearson.

Thomas, Hugh. **Suez.** New York, Harper and Row, 1967. 261p. LC 67-15506. DT 107.83.T42 1967a. DDC 962'.15'05. Deals mainly with British perceptions and decision-making prior to the War, and the reaction to the War of British opinion, but has nothing on post-War events and diplomacy.

A useful collection of documents is:

U.S. Department of State. **The Suez Canal Problem, July 26-September 22, 1956: A Documentary Publication.** Washington, D.C., 1956. 370p. LC 56-62403. JX 1403.U5. DDC 386.43.

868. O'Ballance, Edgar. **The Sinai Campaign of 1956.** New York, Praeger, 1959. 223p. maps. index. o.p. LC 60-8717. DS 110.5.O2 1960. DDC 953.1.

After 77 pages of background (and particularly the history, organization, armaments, and comparative strengths of the Egyptian and Israeli forces), the author describes the Israeli War plan and the campaign in detail, with critical comments on the strategies and tactics of both sides. Most of the details, such as unit actions, deal with Israeli forces, since at the time little or no comparable material was available for the Egyptian side. An interesting useful work, but not of high priority.

D. 1967 WAR

869. Churchill, Randolph Spencer, and Winston S. Churchill. **The Six Day War.** London, Heinemann; distr. Baltimore, Penguin Books, 1968. 250p. index. $1.25. LC 67-112865. ISBN 0-14-009999-9. DS 127.C48 1967b. DDC 956.

A journalistic account of the June 1967 War, almost entirely from the Israeli perspective. The first 78 pages survey the pre-War period and build-up of arms and tension. Virtually all the action described in detail is that of the Israeli forces; the authors' basic attitude toward the Arabs is negative, while many Israeli viewpoints are accepted uncritically. The diplomatic fronts are treated in varying amounts of detail, while battles are given somewhat more emphasis. A final section discusses the immediate post-War period and prospects for the future, as well as prospects for changes in the Arab world and in Israeli-Arab relations. Not a very good book, but as good as or better than most; certainly most readers will enjoy it.

870. Howard, Michael Eliot, and Robert Hunter. **Israel and the Arab World: The Crisis of 1967.** London, Institute for Strategic Studies, 1967. 51p. maps. (Adelphi Papers, 41). o.p. pa. LC 68-82311. U162.A3 no. 41. DDC 956.

The best short treatment of the 1967 War and the events leading up to it. The book's general survey and analysis of the political, international, and military events are quite objective. A good orientation and introduction for any reader; to be read before other works. No really good general works have been written on the War, its origins, and its aftermath using even the material we have available; most existing works are either too specialized or essentially worthless. A few that are particularly useful are: Walter Laqueur, *The Road to Jerusalem: The*

Origins of the Arab-Israeli Conflict 1967 (London, Weidenfeld and Nicolson, 1968. 358p. LC 68-92253. DS 127.L38. [also in Penguin paperback, LC 70-508385]), which is basically diplomatic history; Nadav Safran, *From War to War: The Arab-Israeli Confrontation, 1948-1967* (New York, Pegasus, 1969. LC 68-27991. DS 119.7.S32), a politico-military interpretation-analysis, with much on the War; *Middle East Record, v. 3, 1967* (Jerusalem Universities Press, 1971. LC 63-48859. DS 63.M58), the single most important book on the period; it has much factual data and documentation, but it is too much for most collections.

Additional works are:

International Documents on Palestine, 1967. Ed. by Faud Jabber. Beirut, Institute for Palestine Studies, 1970. 748p. LC 72-223758. DS 119.7.I494. DDC 327.5694. Much stress on Arab statements, U.N. documents and speeches, communiqués, etc.

Lall, Arthur Samuel. The UN and the Middle East Crisis, 1967. Rev. ed. New York, Columbia University Press, 1970. 350p. LC 70-114179. ISBN 0-231-08635-0. JX 1977.2.N4L35 1970. DDC 341.13'9'56.

871. Kimche, David, and Dan Bawley. The Sandstorm: The Arab-Israeli War of June, 1967, Prelude and Aftermath. New York, Stein and Day, 1968. 319p. illus. index. $6.95. LC 68-25637. ISBN 0-8128-1159-3. DS 127.2.K5 1968b. DDC 956.

Beginning with Yassir Arafat, the Palestinians, and inter-Arab politics, the authors develop the background to the War, including great power involvements, Israeli politics after Ben-Gurion, and conditions in Israel; the Fedayeen terrorism and escalation of tensions in Spring 1967 (156 pages). The War itself and the immediate prelude, with a comparison of forces, take up but 47 pages. The aftermath in Israel and the occupied territories, the Arab countries, and the international political struggle, and thoughts on the future occupy the rest. A journalistic treatment, mainly from the Israeli perspective (and bias). It is not particularly good, but even with its decided faults it is one of the more comprehensive popular works, and it is more interesting than most.

872. O'Ballance, Edgar. The Third Arab-Israeli War. Hamden, Conn., Archon Books, 1972. bibliog. $10.00. LC 72-1059. ISBN 0-208-01292-3. DS 127.O23. DDC 956'.046.

After tracing the political escalation in May 1967, the author discusses the forces of the countries involved, including their structure and weaponry. He "walked" the battlefields and had access to Israeli participants, but he had no cooperation from the Arabs. As usual with his works, the book is undocumented and relatively informal. This one sticks to the military side of the War; it is a fairly well-written, detailed, judicious, and critical account, with analyses of tactics, strategies, and battle actions. It appears to have been more hastily written than some of his other books, but it is still probably the best on the subject and should be a standard work for some time.

E. 1973 WAR

873. The Yom Kippur War. By the Insight Team of the London *Sunday Times.* Garden City, N.Y., Doubleday, 1974. 514p. illus. index. $10.00. LC 74-2719. ISBN 0-385-06738-0. DS 128.1.I57 1974. DDC 956'.048.

The only really worthwhile book in English on the October 1973 War to date. Emphasis throughout is on the military campaigns, battles, weaponry, and the decision-making and preparations of both sides. Includes Israel's intelligence errors, why Israel let the Arabs strike first, why the Arabs went to war, the roles of the United States and the U.S.S.R.; the arms airlifts and the calculations of the two great powers which led to them; the truce; Kissinger's role; the oil weapon; the U.S. nuclear alert; Israeli politics; rescue of Egypt's third army; lessons and implications of the War, both politically and militarily; the military leaders, their backgrounds, strategies and tactics, and rivalries. More detail is given on Israel's side concerning the battles and internal politics, since more information is available. An extremely interesting book for all readers.

See also:

Barker, A. J. Yom Kippur War. New York, Ballantine Books, 1974. 159p. illus. (Ballantine's Illustrated History of the Violent Century: BB Campaign Book, No. 29). $2.00pa. LC 75-307177. ISBN 0-345-24295-5. DS 128.1.B37. DDC 956'.048.

Laqueur, Walter Ze'ev. **Confrontation: The Middle East and World Politics.** New York, Quadrangle, 1974. 308p. $8.95. LC 74-79438. ISBN 0-8129-0454-0. LC cataloging n.a. An analysis of the causes of the 1973 War; diplomatic history; aftermath and results, significance and lessons to be drawn from the War, including its relation to "detente," European politics, and the Arab-Israeli conflict. It is not a survey or narrative of the military actions, and therefore it is complementary to the Insight Team book.

F. PALESTINIAN REFUGEES AND GUERRILLAS

874. Peretz, Don. **Israel and the Palestine Arabs.** Washington, D.C., Middle East Institute, 1958. 264p. bibliog. index. o.p. LC 58-2533. DS 126.5.P4. DDC 956.94.

A scholarly survey of the Palestinian refugee problem based on U.N., Hebrew, and other sources. Background on the origins; approaches made by the West and the U.N. to encourage resettlement; Arab government-refugee relations and policies; early repatriation efforts; U.N. and Israeli policies; Arab positions; Israeli domestic politics concerning refugee repatriation and compensation. Then, the shift in interest to an economic solution: proposals for economic projects and aid to Arab countries for refugee resettlement and regional development proposals; the problem of the linkage between territorial questions and the refugee problem, clashing Arab-Israeli views and vain efforts at mediation; the Israeli shift from favoring repatriation to favoring compensation, as well as problems of calculating compensation and the problem of absentee Arab property; Israel's Arab minority and the security issue, internal politics on that question, problems of social integration of Israeli Arabs; the issue of blocked Palestinian accounts in Israeli banks. A basic work for understanding a number of key issues in the Arab position, the Israeli response to these issues, and the dynamics of the conflict.

875. Pryce-Jones, David. **The Face of Defeat: Palestinian Refugees and Guerrillas.** New York, Holt, Rinehart and Winston, 1973. 179p. $5.95. LC 72-89908. ISBN 0-03-006906-8. DS 119.7.P79. DDC 322.4'2'095694.

One of the best recent books on the Palestinian situation, by a British journalist. He suggests perceptively and with reasonable objectivity the origin and dynamics of the problem and then describes his visits during and just after the 1967 War and continuously through 1971. He visited the battle fronts, Jerusalem and the West Bank, Lebanon, Jordan and Syria, and Israeli prisons. He also met with the Arab leadership of the occupied territories, and their names flow endlessly through the narrative along with information on individuals. He describes the refugee camps, lives of the refugees, their hopes and despair. He suggests the nature of the interaction between Israelis and Arabs better than most, giving one a feel for the situation. His discussion of the propaganda question is one of the best: the origin of the Arab points, their provision or lack of evidence to prove their contentions, and the evidence itself; why they approach propaganda as they do and how the particular views held and positions taken spread among the Palestinians. He makes vivid the terrible contradictions felt by the Palestinians—their hopes versus reality, personal lives versus the need to struggle for the cause, their being pressed between the Arab governments and the Fedayeen. A must for larger collections.

Other works include:

Association of Arab American University Graduates. **The Palestinian Resistance to Israeli Occupation.** Ed. by Naseer Aruri. Wilmette, Ill., Medina University Press International, 1970. 171p. LC 74-141033. DS 119.7.A74 1970. DDC 327.5694'017' 4927.

Chaliand, Gérard. **The Palestinian Resistance.** Tr. from French. Baltimore, Penguin Books, 1972. 190p. LC 72-192317. ISBN 0-14-021503-4. DS 119.7.C4613. DDC 322.4'2'095694.

Cooley, John K. **Green March, Black September: The Story of the Palestinian Arabs.** London, Frank Cass; distr. Portland, Ore., International Scholarly Book Services, 1973. 263p. LC 73-175832. ISBN 0-7146-2987-1. DS 119.7.C66 1973. DDC 301.45'19' 275694. The last two books are sympathetic journalistic accounts by long-time Middle East hands.

Turki, Fawaz. **The Disinherited: Journal of a Palestinian Exile.** New York, Monthly Review Press, 1972. 156p. LC 78-178970. ISBN 0-85345-210-5. DS 119.7.T83. DDC 915.694'06'9270924. A "moderate" Palestinian view of how Palestinians should approach the conflict and deal with Israel.

O'Ballance, Edgar. **Arab Guerilla Power, 1967-1972.** Hamden, Conn., Archon Books, 1974. 246p. LC 74-4306. ISBN 0-208-01436-5. DS 119.7.O22 1974. DDC 322. 4'2'09174927.

876. Quandt, William B., Faud Jabber, and Ann Mosely Lesch. **The Politics of Palestinian Nationalism.** Berkeley, University of California Press, 1973. 234p. bibliog. index. $6.95; $2.95pa. LC 72-89791. ISBN 0-520-02336-6; 0-520-02372-2pa. DS 119.7.Q7 1973. DDC 320.9'56'04.

[P1, C1, S1] Lesch surveys the background and early development of Palestinian Arab nationalism under the Mandate. Quandt deals with the history and the political and military aspects of the revival, political organization, and military organization and activity of the Fedayeen groups, as well as their ideology and objectives. Jabber describes and analyses the relations of the commandos and Arab governments. By far the best book on the subject, it is based on Arabic and other sources. Quandt's presentation and analysis are affected by his presupposition that a compromise settlement with Israel is desirable—he speaks of progress being made and a trend toward moderation, a perspective many Palestinians reject.

Other works:

Buehrig, Edward Henry. **The United Nations and the Palestinian Refugees: A Study in Non-Territorial Administration.** Bloomington, Indiana University Press, 1971. 215p. LC 71-160124. ISBN 0-253-39603-4. HV 640.5.A6B8. DDC 361.5'3.

Harkabi, Yehoshafat. **Palestinians and Israel.** New York, Halstead Press, 1975. 295p. LC 74-23800. DS 119.7.H37544 1975. DDC 327.5694'017'4927. The author's articles, mainly translated from Hebrew, 1967-1974. The ex-head of Israeli intelligence is an Arab expert, a "hard-liner" on the Palestinians; his work is of considerable importance despite its jaundiced view.

Peretz, Don, Evan M. Wilson, and Richard J. Ward. **A Palestine Entity?** Washington, D.C., Middle East Institute, 1970. 119p. LC 73-139243. DS 119.7.P45. DDC 320.1'58'095694. Three articles on the idea and economics of a Palestinian state.

Bull, Vivian A. **The West Bank—Is It Viable?** Lexington, Mass., Lexington Books, 1975. LC 74-33978. ISBN 0-669-99142-0. DS 127.6.O3B84. DDC 956.95'04. A socioeconomic study. Surveys various economic sectors and some social problems to ascertain the potential viability of a Palestinian entity on the West Bank region of Palestine, now occupied by Israel.

The Palestinians: People, History, Politics. Ed. by Michael Curtis. Prepared under the auspices of the American Academic Association for Peace in the Middle East. New Brunswick, N.J., Transaction Books, 1975. 277p. $4.95pa. LC 74-32601. ISBN 0-87855-112-3; 0-87855-597-8pa. LC cataloging n.a. Conference papers, some of which are fairly straightforward, some of which are strictly polemical. The intended cumulative effect of the whole is to disprove Palestinian claims to Palestine and to prove Israeli contentions that there is neither a need of nor a place for a separate Palestinian state.

XXIV. JORDAN

Recent general works are pitifully few. Very much needed is a detailed work on the country's history from 1914-1951; also needed is more on the period up to the present, which is inadequately covered by available books.

A. GENERAL WORKS

877. **Area Handbook for the Hashemite Kingdom of Jordan.** [Nyrop, Richard F.]. 1974. (DA PAM 550-34). DS 153.N93 1974. DDC 915.695'03'4.

[B, P1, C1, S1]   See the annotation at the head of Section II (page 30).

Two general works covering an earlier period:

Harris, George Lawrence. **Jordan: Its People, Its Society, Its Culture.** New Haven, Conn., HRAF Press, 1958. 246p. LC 58-12701. DS 153.H3.

Patai, Raphael. **The Kingdom of Jordan.** Princeton, N.J., Princeton University Press, 1958. 315p. LC 58-6107. DS 153.P32. DDC 956.95.

B. HISTORY AND POLITICS

878. Abidi, Aqil Hyder Hasan. **Jordan, a Political Study, 1948-1957.** New York, Asia Publishing House, 1965. 251p. bibliog. index. o.p. LC 65-6501. DS 154.5.A54. DDC 320.95695.

[P1, C1, S1]   One of the most detailed and best-documented studies of the country's political history during the period. It covers the negotiations before and after the 1948 War between the Zionists and King Abdullah; Jordan's part in the War; the problem of the Palestinian Arabs and Jordan's annexation of the West Bank; Jordan under Talal and Hussein; the internal struggle of 1956; problems of the political system and political socialization and integration. A basic book.

879. Shwadran, Benjamin. **Jordan, a State of Tension.** New York, Council for Middle Eastern Affairs Press, 1959. 436p. bibliog. illus. index. o.p. LC 59-11043. DS 154.15.S4. DDC 956.95.

[P1, C1, S1]   The first 101 pages cover the history of Jordan from earliest times to World War I; the rest treats 1914-1958. The most detailed work in English, it does not cover the internal politics as thoroughly as one could wish, though that fault is to a great extent a function of limited source materials. It includes a great deal of material on the international and regional politics of Jordan's creation and its continuing controversial existence.

Other works:

Aruri, Naseer. **Jordan: A Study in Political Development (1921-1965).** The Hague, Martinus Nijhoff, 1972. 206p. LC 72-192707. ISBN 90-247-1217-3. DS 154.5.A78. DDC 320.9'5695'04. A general treatment of the various factors, internal (economy, society) and external, plus aspects of the political system. Extremely superficial, but it brings together information otherwise scattered.

Faddah, Mohammad Ibrahim. **The Middle East in Transition: A Study of Jordan's Foreign Policy.** New York, Asia Publishing House, 1974. 339p. LC cataloging n.a. ISBN 0-210-22387-1. Covers 1947-1967, Jordan-Zionist relations, relations with Arab countries, Britain and the United States. These topics are not dealt with consistently or completely, and some important subjects are virtually ignored. It is included because it is all we have.

Glubb, John Bagot. **The Story of the Arab Legion.** London, Hodder and Stoughton, 1948. 371p. LC 49-1942. DS 110.4.G5. DDC 956.9.

Peak, F. G. **A History of Jordan and Its Tribes.** Coral Gables, Fla., University of Miami, 1958. LC 58-14059. DS 153.P4. DDC 956.95.

Vatikiotis, Panayiotis J. **Politics and the Military in Jordan: A Study of the Arab Legion, 1921-1957.** New York, Praeger, 1967. 169p. LC 67-28182. DS 154.5.V3 1967b. DDC 956.95'04.

C. BIOGRAPHY

880. Abdallāh, King of Jordan (1882-1951). **Memoirs of King Abdullah of Transjordan.** Tr. from Arabic. New York, Philosophical Library, 1950. 278p. LC 51-103. DS 154.52. A3A27. DDC 956.95.

My Memoirs Completed (al-Takmilah). Tr. from Arabic. Washington, D.C., American Council of Learned Societies, 1954. 121p. LC 55-1012. DS 154.52.A3A32.

881. Hussein, King of Jordan. **Uneasy Lies the Head: The Autobiography of His Majesty King Hussein I of the Hashemite Kingdom of Jordan.** New York, Bernard Geis Associates; distr. New York, Random House, 1962. 306p. o.p. LC 62-11165. DS 154.55.H8A3. DDC 923.15695.

[C1] Covers the King's days from his early years at Harrow through 1961, the year of his marriage to Princess Muna. Most of the book deals with his reign and includes his relations with other countries, internal politics, the Palestine problem, events in 1956, and the various attempts on his life. It has the usual characteristics of an official biography. Nevertheless, it is quite useful as a basic document that illustrates the King's views and outlook, and it is most interesting to read. A basic book. Another worthwhile book is the King's *My "War" with Israel*, as told to and with additional material by Vick Vance and Pierre Lauer (New York, William Morrow, 1969. 170p. o.p. LC 78-79099. DS 127.9.J6H83), which is Hussein's version of the June 1967 War and its background, aftermath, and inter-Arab politics of the time.

882. Snow, Peter [John]. **Hussein, a Biography.** Washington, D.C., Robert B. Luce, 1972. 256p. bibliog. index. $7.95. LC 72-85018. DS 154.55.S62 1972b. DDC 956. 95'04'0924 [B].

[P1, C1, S1] A British journalist has written a useful outline of the King's life to 1954, including his schooling, marriages, aspects of his personal life, etc. However, most of the book deals with two periods: 1955-1964, when Hussein was hotly involved in inter-Arab politics and maturing, focusing on his struggle with Nasser; and 1965-1972, stressing Hussein's relations with the Palestinians. The rise of the Fedayeen is described, their dominance in Jordan, and the June 1967 War. Jordan's defeat of the Palestinians, 1970-1972, is narrated in great detail, more so than in most works and more than any other topic in the book. This is basically a political history of the kingdom, with useful information on the Fedayeen. Useful but superficial, and not the inside story, even though the author is well acquainted with the area and the actors. It is listed because it is probably the best currently available source, and one of very few recent works on the country.

D. SOCIETY

883. Gubser, Peter. **Politics and Change in al-Karak, Jordan: A Study of a Small Arab Town and Its District.** London, Oxford University Press, 1973. 189p. bibliog. index. $14.50. LC 73-173423. ISBN 0-19-215805-8. DS 154.9.K35G8. DDC 301.5'92'0956956.

A comprehensive study of the town and the region it dominates. It traces the environmental, historical, and economic factors influencing its existence, describes traditional society and ethnology, the various social groups, tribes and religious groupings. It also deals with the government offices in the area and their influence on the town; people's problems with the government; the town's political history and tribal politics; local government and socio-economic institutions; and social and economic mobility. An interesting, if scholarly, work for college collections.

884. Hacker, Jane M. **Modern ͨAmmān: A Social Study.** Durham, Durham Colleges in the University of Durham, 1960. 144p. illus. (Research Papers Series, No. 3). LC 74-184149. HN 761.J63A553. DDC 309.1'5695'804.

The growth and development of Jordan's capital city: physical description, population and demographics, ethnic makeup; communications; social survey of the city; living standards, recreation, occupations and business, employment, industry, wages; social classes. One of few studies of any Arab city, virtually unique for Amman.

885. Lutfiyya, Abdulla M. **Baytin, a Jordanian Village: A Study of Social Institutions and Social Change in a Folk Community.** The Hague, Mouton; distr. New York, Humanities Press, 1966. 202p. bibliog. (Studies in Social Anthropology). $13.50. LC 65-27400. HN 761.J62L8. DDC 301.35095695.

A general study of this village's daily life and popular culture; Islam, popular religion, and rituals; government, politics, and the process of settling disputes; economy, marriage customs, family structures. Baytin is the author's native village, a Palestinian community on the West Bank. An interesting account written in non-technical language.

See also:

Antoun, Richard T. **Arab Village: A Social Structural Study of a Transjordanian Peasant Community.** Bloomington, Indiana University Press, 1972. 182p. LC 70-633555. ISBN 0-523-38429-X. DS 154.9.K3A7.

E. DESCRIPTION AND TRAVEL

886. Randall, Rona, pseud. **Jordan and the Holy Land.** London, Frederick Muller, 1968. 243p. illus. index. o.p. LC 68-141460. DS 153.2.R3. DDC 915.695'03'4.

An interesting travelogue-guidebook. A little more than half of it is physical description of the area; the rest concerns the people, including their customs and much on the role of women. The author discusses the Samaritans and Bedouins and recalls her visit with Princess Muna, recently divorced wife of King Hussein. She also describes her visit with Musa Alami, the Palestinian Arab whose boys' farm is a well-known example of Arab refugee self-help. Includes tips for travellers.

887. Wolf, Betty Hartman. **Journey through the Holy Land.** Garden City, N.Y., Doubleday, 1968. 267p. (Waymark Books). o.p. LC 68-5522. DC 153.2.W6 1968. DDC 915.695'04'.

A fairly interesting guidebook and travelogue on Jordan and the Old City of Jerusalem by an American who spent a year there before the June 1967 War. She has many observations and notes on the people, antiquities, and history; there is nothing on Israel. She has no strong religious interest and writes in a straightforward manner, with a sympathetic but not uncritical eye. Good reading for the armchair traveller.

F. GUIDEBOOKS

888. Harding, George Lankester. **The Antiquities of Jordan.** Rev. ed. Guilford, England, Lutterworth Press, 1967. 216p. illus. index. £1.75. LC 67-105050. ISBN 0-7188-0025-7. DS 153.3.H3 1967b. DDC 913'.3.

Jordan's Chief Director of Antiquities from 1936 to 1956, lovingly presents brief historical notes and descriptions of each site. For tourists only.

889. Nelson, Nina. **Your Guide to Jordan.** London, Alvin Redman, 1966. 247p. illus. LC 66-70962. DS 153.2.N5. DDC 915.695044.

One of the very few English guidebooks exclusively devoted to Jordan. Contains the usual information on sites and historical and other background, as well as much practical information, though a lot of this is, of course, out of date. Still, useful as orientation for the general tourist.

890. Sanger, Richard Harlakenden. **Where the Jordan Flows.** Washington, D.C., The Middle East Institute, 1963. 397p. bibliog. illus. index. $5.75. LC 63-5019. DS 117.S36. DDC 956.94.

A history and travel guide of the Jordan River region, arranged chronologically for systematic continuity, which has accounts of most of the significant archaeological discoveries. It also has notes on twentieth century Jordan and Bedouin life, to 1956. A well-written, very interesting book for the prospective and armchair traveller.

XXV. LEBANON

We need a more detailed and expert history of the country during the Ottoman period, as well as a good political history for the nineteenth and twentieth centuries, especially the latter.

A. GENERAL WORKS

891. **Area Handbook for Lebanon.** [Smith, Harvey Henry]. 25, 352p. 1974. (DA PAM 550-24). LC 74-13241. DS 80.S63 1974. DDC 915.692'0344.

[B, P1, C1, S1]   This is a reprint of the 1969 edition, with a 25-page summary of trends and events from 1969 to 1973. See the annotation at the head of Section II (page 30).
   An older work:

   Patai, Raphael. **The Republic of Lebanon.** New Haven, Conn., HRAF Press, 1956. 2v. (639 p.). LC 57-42962. DS 80.P3. DDC 956.9.

892. Winder, Viola H. **The Land and People of Lebanon.** Rev. ed. Philadelphia, J. B. Lippincott, 1973. 159p. illus. index. (Portraits of the Nations Series). $4.95. LC 72-13164. ISBN 0-397-31407-8. DS 80.W5 1973. DDC 915.692'03'4.

[P1]   Half the book traces Lebanon's history from Ancient times. The rest describes the country and its people today, concluding with an interesting chapter on Lebanese in the United States. A sympathetic but perhaps overly rosy view. A first book, not necessarily just for juvenile readers.

B. HISTORY

893. Hitti, Philip Khûri. **Lebanon in History from the Earliest Times to the Present.** 3rd ed. New York, St. Martin's Press, 1967. 550p. illus. index. $17.50. LC 67-21542. DS 80.9.H5 1967. DDC 956.92.

[P1, C1]   The basic history of Lebanon for the college library. It is probably too detailed for most readers, but it contains a wealth of information on the culture, antiquities, religion, and economy of the country. It covers the period to 1952; the twentieth century material is far too brief to meet the needs of most readers, so Salibi (item 895) is needed to fill this gap.
   See also:

   Beirut—Crossroads of Cultures. Beirut, Librairie du Liban, 1970. 220p. LC 76-278257. DS 89.B4B4. Slightly more than half of the book consists of black and white photographs, most of which are of pre-Islamic antiquities. Most of the text concerns the pre-Islamic period. The same publisher has similar items on Tyre, Sidon, and Byblos.

894. Hitti, Philip Khûri. **A Short History of Lebanon.** New York, St. Martin's Press, 1965. 248p. index. $7.50; text ed. $6.50. LC 64-25714. DS 80.9.H52. DDC 956.92.

[P1]   A general survey in a flowing popular style, from ancient times through the early independence period. Abridged from item 893, and preferable to the longer version for smaller collections.

895. Salibi, Kamal Suleiman. **The Modern History of Lebanon.** New York, Praeger, 1965. 227p. (The Praeger Asia Africa Series). $8.50. LC 65-14186. DS 84.S25. DDC 956.92.

[P1, P2, C1, S1]   Coverage extends from the early seventeenth century to 1958, with the brief background notes on the earlier period. A general descriptive history, with some interpretation, which provides basic information and perspective in non-technical language for the uninitiated reader and student. Unfortunately, it suffers from a number of weaknesses including inadequate scholarship and analysis, so it should be replaced by a better work when one becomes available. Until then, it is a basic book.

Other works:

Agwani, Mohammed Shafi, ed. **The Lebanese Crisis, 1958: A Documentary Study.** New York, Asia Publishing House, 1965. 407p. LC 65-16070. DS 86.A68. DDC 956.9204.

Churchill, Charles Henry Spencer (1828-1877). **The Druzes and Maronites under the Turkish Rule from 1840-1860.** New York, Arno Press, 1973. (Repr. of 1862 ed.). 300p. LC 73-6273. ISBN 0-405-05329-0. DS 97.5.C49 1973. DDC 956.92'08. The background to and narrative of the Druzes' and Maronites' 1860 massacres of each other; includes coverage of local politics and Western involvement.

Harik, Iliya F. **Politics and Change in a Traditional Society: Lebanon, 1711-1845.** Princeton, N.J., Princeton University Press, 1968. 324p. LC 67-21024. DS 84.H3. DDC 915.6'92'03'3.

Meo, Leila M. **Lebanon, Improbable Nation: A Study of Political Development.** Bloomington, Indiana University Press, 1965. 246p. LC 65-63610. DS 86.M4. DDC 320.95692. Stresses the more recent period of the twentieth century, with nineteenth century background.

Polk, William Roe. **The Opening of South Lebanon, 1788-1840: A Study of the Impact of the West on the Middle East.** Cambridge, Mass., Harvard University Press, 1963. 299p. LC 63-13815. DS 84.P6 1963. DDC 956.92.

Qubain, Fahim Issa. **Crisis in Lebanon.** Washington, D.C., Middle East Institute, 1961. 243p. LC 61-19686. DS 86.Q8. DDC 956.92. Conditions and events leading to the Lebanese civil war of 1958, U.N. debates, landing of U.S. Marines, and aftermath; inter-Arab political aspects. The basic work on the subject.

C. POLITICS AND GOVERNMENT

896. Binder, Leonard, ed. **Politics in Lebanon.** New York, John Wiley, 1966. 345p. index. $13.25. LC 66-13524. ISBN 0-471-07302-4. DS 86.B5. DDC 320.95692.

[P1, C1, S1] These essays by various authorities cover economic and social factors; institutions, administration, and parties; Lebanon's international and inter-Arab political status and relations; problems of intellectuals; the interrelationship of traditional elements and sociopolitical change as they influence each other. A basic work for larger collections and more advanced students.

897. Hudson, Michael C. **The Precarious Republic: Political Modernization in Lebanon.** New York, Random House, 1968. 364p. bibliog. index. $8.95. LC 68-25341. ISBN 0-394-30287-7. DS 87.H8. DDC 320'.095692.

[B, C] An analysis of the dynamics and structure of the political system, emphasizing the question of the system's adequacy for the future, in light of the political implications of increasing social and thus political mobilization of Lebanon's increasingly educated population. Based on interviews and a wide range of secondary material, and utilizing tabular information, the book consists mainly of generalizations. It has much on the sources of pressure for political change, including new political forces as well as the external pressures, but it includes little discussion of the *formal* structure. It provides much *feel* for what is happening. The bibliography of works on Lebanon and general disciplinary works is quite useful.

Other works:

Entelis, John Pierre. **Pluralism and Party Transformation in Lebanon: al-Kata'ib, 1937-1970.** Leiden, E. J. Brill, 1974. 227p. LC cataloging n.a. History, ideas, organization, membership, activities of the Phalangists, "rightists," Lebanon's largest, best-organized party. Also its role in Lebanon's system.

Koury, Enver M. **The Operational Ability of the Lebanese Political System.** Beirut, Catholic Press, 1972. 456p. LC 75-131973. JQ 1825.L4K68. DDC 320.9'5692'04.

Salem, Elie Adib. **Modernization without Revolution: Lebanon's Experience.** Bloomington, Indiana University Press, 1973. 174p. LC 72-85854. ISBN 0-253-33870-0. JQ 1825.L4S33. DDC 309.2'3'095692.

Suleiman, Michael W. **Political Parties in Lebanon: The Challenge of a Fragmented Political Culture.** Ithaca, Cornell University Press, 1967. 326p. LC 67-14604. JQ 1825.L4S8. DDC 329.9'5692.

D. SOCIETY

898. Furayḥah, Anis. **A Dictionary of Modern Lebanese Proverbs.** Beirut, Librairie du Liban, 1974. 748p. LC 75-319588. PN 6519.A7F9. DDC 398.9'927.

English and Arabic arranged by the Arabic alphabet, with explanation of usage and meaning, by a foremost scholar of Arab folklore and ethnology.

899. Gulick, John. **Social Structure and Culture Change in a Lebanese Village.** New York, Wenner-Gren Foundation for Anthropological Research, 1955. 191p. bibliog. illus. (Viking Fund Publications in Anthropology, No. 21). LC 55-1698. HN 761.L492 M84. DDC 309.1569.

A socio-anthropological study of al-Munsif. The study covers the material culture, subsistence, occupational and residence patterns and types; formal institutions (stores, olive presses, church, schools, government); socio-religious behavior and customs; secular recreations; kinship structure and marriage patterns; patterns of change, values, stability patterns. A general description not at all detailed. Some analysis. Not a sophisticated disciplinary work, so it can be fairly readily understood by the general reader.

A similar work is:

Fuller, Anne H. **Buarij: Portrait of a Lebanese Muslim Village.** Cambridge, Mass., Harvard University Press, 1961. 98p. LC 61-14633. DS 80.4.F8. DDC 915.692.

900. Gulick, John. **Tripoli, a Modern Arab City.** Cambridge, Mass., Harvard University Press, 1967. 253p. bibliog. illus. index. $8.50. LC 67-14340. ISBN 0-674-90915-1. DS 89.T7G8. DDC 915.692'03'4.

An excellent social-anthropological description and analysis of the Lebanese city: physical description, economics, administration, politics, and much on all aspects of social life. It is useful for its generalizations, which are applicable to Lebanon and many Near Eastern cities.

901. Khalaf, Samir, and Per Kongstad. **Hamra of Beirut: A Case of Rapid Urbanization.** Leiden, E. J. Brill, 1973. bibliog. illus. LC 73-164077. ISBN 90-04-03548-6. HT 178. L42B44. DDC 301.36'3.

Hamra is a central zone of the Ras-Beirut section of Beirut. The book begins with a history of Beirut and a survey of its recent (post-World War II) rapid urbanization and growth. Hamra became "the dominant urban center of Beirut." The building, settlement, and patterns of socioeconomic structure, land-use, and development are examined in detail. Also, demography, households, the influence of American University, occupational structure, literacy and educational levels, ethnic-religious composition, socio-ecological features, ecological mobility; daily routines. Includes much basic information, methodology, and analysis of data, which were gleaned from city records and house-by-house surveys. For advanced students.

902. Khuri, Faud I. **From Village to Suburb: Order and Change in Greater Beirut.** Chicago, University of Chicago Press, 1975. 272p. bibliog. illus. index. $19.50. LC 74-75613. ISBN 0-226-43471-0. HN 761.L43B454. DDC 301.36'2'095692.

[P1, C1, S2]   Based on a detailed household survey and other material, and computer manipulation of the data, this is a study of the Beirut suburbs of Chiyah and Ghobeire, their history and development, many aspects of their social, political, and economic organization and life (including settlement patterns, occupational and income structure, leadership selection, marriage and family, voluntary organizations, etc.); the phenomenon of suburbanization, the relations of the suburbs to Beirut and the hinderlands; relations between natives and migrants,

with comparisons of their life, organizational and interaction patterns; and the pervasive role
of confessional life in the community, with comparisons of the Muslim and Christian patterns
in all phases of life, and notes on significant differences between the sects of each religion.
Throughout the book Khuri characterizes the interrelationships of all of these factors, instead
of treating them in isolation, as many books do. Rather than overwhelm the reader with a
minutely detailed description of the two communities, Khuri intersperses much information
about them with hundreds of general statements, analyses, and conclusions concerning the two
communities, Lebanon, and the Arab world as a whole; most of these are very useful as working
hypotheses for most readers. The result is one of the most useful books available on the
dynamics of Arab life, a real contribution to our understanding. Furthermore, Khuri relates
his findings to the existing literature, with which he often explicitly disagrees. The book's style
makes most of it accessible to the knowledgeable general reader. A basic work for understanding
Arab affairs and events such as the civil violence in Lebanon in 1975 (of which Chiyah was one
of the centers).

903. Prothro, Edwin Terry. **Child Rearing in the Lebanon.** Cambridge, Mass., Harvard University Press, 1961. 186p. bibliog. (Harvard Middle Eastern Monographs, 8). $4.50pa.
LC 61-18039. ISBN 0-674-11500-7. HQ 771.L43P7. DDC 301.427.

A study of several hundred mothers and children in parts of Lebanon, 1959. It discusses
demographic aspects of the studied families; infant indulgence and maternal warmth; feeding,
weaning, and toilet training; aggression, discipline, and conscience; sex and sex roles; dependence
and achievement; patterns in child-rearing practices. Includes infant care, attitudes toward boys
and girls, reward and punishment; sex-differences in upbringing; and role of father. Comparison
of U.S. and Lebanese mothers and families are made throughout the book. One of but a few
existing works on this subject.

904. Williams, Judith R. **The Youth of Haouch el-Harimi, a Lebanese Village.** Cambridge,
Mass., Harvard University Press, 1968. 146p. bibliog. (Harvard Middle Eastern Monographs). $4.50pa. LC 68-23032. ISBN 0-674-96675-9. HQ 792.L4W5. DDC
301.43'1'095692.

After describing the village and aspects of its changing situation, the author discusses
infancy and childrearing, attitudes towards boy and girl children, feeding, care, sanitation,
hygiene, games, parent-children relations, etc., and provides statistics on adolescence in the
village. It then treats subjects such as education and sex-differences in education; economic
status and education; work patterns of youth and relation of work patterns to economic status;
mobility and contact of youth and other people of the village with urban centers (the village
is a two-hour drive from Beirut), including transportation, emigration, and sex differences in
mobility as related to family structure. Also, friendship patterns and their significance; courtship and marriage; ideals of the good man and good woman; views of adolescents concerning
their past, present and future, including aspirations, fatalism, hopes, dissatisfaction and contentment levels. One of few works on the subject.

An additional work on Lebanese society is:

Sabri, Marie Aziz. **Pioneering Profiles: Beirut College for Women.** Beirut, Khayats, 1967.
314p. LC 68-2215. LG 357.B4S3. DDC 378.5692.

E. ECONOMY

904a. Ṣa'igh, Yūsuf ᶜAbd Allāh. **Entrepreneurs of Lebanon: The Role of the Business Leader
in a Developing Economy.** Cambridge, Mass., Harvard University Press, 1962. 181p.
LC 62-11404 rev. HD 70.L4S3. DDC 658.

F. DESCRIPTION AND TRAVEL

905. Sykes, John. **The Mountain Arabs, a Window on the Middle East.** London, Hutchinson, 1968. 224p. o.p. LC 68-1165820. DS 57.S95 1968. DDC 915.692'03'4.

A splendid, beautifully written, vividly striking evocation of half-Maronite Christian, half-Muslim Lebanon, which absorbs the reader into it. Sykes is interested in the people, not the places, and he narrates at length accounts of his political discussions with Lebanese of all types and tendencies. These accounts reveal the workings of Lebanese political dynamics more comprehensibly than do most scholarly works by political scientists. To some, it will seem unfortunate that most of his talk is with members of the upper class; however, these are the people who run the country. Sykes was in Lebanon in June 1967, and the last third of the book consists of a diary of the Six-Day War. One of the better books on an Arab country.

906. Thubron, Colin. **The Hills of Adonis: A Quest in Lebanon.** Boston, Little, Brown, 1968. 179p. bibliog. illus. index. o.p. LC 69-13574. DS 80.2.T45 1969. DDC 915.692'04'4.

A walking tour of Lebanon in search of the love goddess Astarte-Aphrodite. It contains descriptions of antiquities, religions, and mythical lore, the country's ancient and Hellenistic heritage, and with observations on the people. It will be fascinating for those who have read Hitti on Lebanon's history, and who have at hand a well-illustrated tourist guide. The nineteenth century situation is described in Charles Henry Spencer Churchill, *Mount Lebanon: A Ten Years Residence, from 1842-1852* (London, Saunders and Otley, 1853. 3v. LC 5-3527. DS 99.L4C5).

G. GUIDEBOOKS

907. Nelson, Nina. **Your Guide to Lebanon.** London, Alvin Redman, 1965. 228p. bibliog. illus. LC 66-1930. DS 80.A5N4. DDC 915.692044.

One of the few guidebooks devoted exclusively to Lebanon. The usual information, historical notes, etc., plus much practical information, which is not out of date. Useful as a supplement to works covering several countries.

XXVI. SUDAN

A. GENERAL WORKS

908. **Area Handbook for the Democratic Republic of Sudan.** [Nelson, Harold D.]. 1973.
351p. (DA PAM 550-27). $5.50. LC 72-600260. DT 121.N44. DDC 916.24'03'4.
[B, P1, C1, S1] See the annotation at the head of Section II (page 30).

909. Barbour, Kenneth Michael. **The Republic of the Sudan: A Regional Geography.** London,
University of London Press, 1961. 292 dbl.-col. pages. bibliog. illus. index. o.p.
LC 61-65685. DT 124.B28. DDC 916.24.
[P1, C1, S1] A general, comprehensive treatment: relief, drainage, geology, climate; deserts
and tropical soils; vegetation; peoples and demographic trends; the waters of the Nile and their
control. Then follows treatment by main region; the chapter on each region discusses the
people, economy, development, farming, industries, employment, infrastructure, communications. Although some of the specific information and figures are out of date, this is still an
extremely useful book and a basic work on the country.

910. University Press of Africa. **Sudan Today.** Nairobi, University Press of Africa; distr. New
York, International Publications Service, 1971. 234p. illus. index. $12.50. LC 72-183900.
DT 121.U5. DDC 916.24'03'4.
[C2] Produced by the UPA for the Sudan Ministry of Information and Culture, this is a most
useful handbook on the country, covering all aspects—history, economics, government structure, development projects—and providing a wealth of information in a reasonably objective
fashion. Most collections can be satisfied with the *Area Handbook* . . . (item 908), but for
larger collections this volume will be useful as a source of additional detail.

B. HISTORY AND POLITICS

911. Abdel-Rahim, Muddathir. **Imperialism and Nationalism in the Sudan: A Study in Constitutional Development, 1899-1956.** Oxford, Clarendon Press, 1969. 275p. bibliog.
index. (Oxford Studies in African Affairs). $13.75. LC 75-455729. SBN 19-821648-3.
JQ 3981.S8 A42. DDC 320.9'624.
[P1, C1, C2, S1, S2] Treats the institutional history of the Sudan, covering the Anglo-Egyptian Agreement of 1899; administrative development to 1936 and its politics; the rise of Sudanese
nationalism and the relations of the Anglo-Egyptian government with the Sudanese people and
local politics; how nationalism was aroused and communicated to the people and to the government; political movements; the Advisory Council as British reaction to internal events and
Sudanese demands; the Legislative Assembly (its origin, duties, powers, structure, parties and
dynamics); local government after 1937; the transfer of power in the 1950s. A good history
and analysis for larger collections.

912. Collins, Robert O., and Robert L. Tignor. **Egypt and the Sudan.** Englewood Cliffs,
N.J., Prentice-Hall, 1967. 180p. bibliog. index. (The Modern Nations in Historical
Perspective. A Spectrum Book, S 623). $1.95pa. LC 67-14846. ISBN 0-13-246603-1.
DT 77.C6. DDC 962.
[P1, C1, S1] The first two sections (50 pages) deal with the ethnology, human geography,
and history of the two countries, which have been linked variously for millenia, to the nine-
teenth century. The rest surveys and analyzes the history, politics, society, and modernization
of the two countries to the mid-1960s. A useful orientation for the general reader.

913. Henderson, Kenneth David Druitt. **Sudan Republic.** New York, Praeger, 1965. 256p. bibliog. index. (Nations of the Modern World). o.p. LC 62-27084. DT 108.H4. DDC 309.1624.

[S1] Covers mainly the twentieth century, the bulk of the book dealing with the independence period; emphasis is on internal politics. Complementary to Holt (item 915). Because it is so out of date, a later edition should be watched for and perhaps matched with Holt, depending on the coverage of the new edition.

914. Holt, Peter Malcolm. **The Mahdist State in the Sudan, 1881-1898: A Study in Its Origins, Development and Overthrow.** 2nd ed. Oxford, Clarendon Press, 1970. 295p. bibliog. index. $10.50. LC 70-523419. ISBN 0-19-821660-2. DT 108.3.H6 1970. DDC 962.4'03.

[C1, S3] The best work so far on this important period in the history of the Anglo-Egyptian Sudan, which featured the battles of Khartum and Omdurman and made household words of the names Gordon and Kitchner. Holt has done much work in the Sudanese archives and uses them to good effect. A scholarly work for colleges.

915. Holt, Peter Malcolm. **A Modern History of the Sudan, from the Funj Sultanate to the Present Day.** 2nd ed. London, Weidenfeld and Nicolson, 1965. 247p. bibliog. illus. (Asia-Africa Series). o.p. LC 72-291794. DT 108.H72 1965. DDC 962.4'03.

[C1, S1] Covers mainly the period 1820 to 1962. By a leading expert. The chapters are evenly balanced in their coverage. Complementary to Henderson (item 913); Holt is a more workmanlike straight history. A basic book. Watch for another edition.

Other works:

Abbas, Mekki. **The Sudan Question: The Dispute over the Anglo-Egyptian Condominium, 1884-1951.** London, Faber and Faber, 1952. 201p. bibliog. LC 52-2963. DT 108.A48 1952. DDC 962.4.

Albino, Oliver. **The Sudan, a Southern Viewpoint.** London, Oxford University Press, 1970. 132p. LC 70-482995. ISBN 0-19-218187-4. DT 108.7.A63 1970. DDC 916.29'03.

Beshir, Mohamed Omer. **Revolution and Nationalism in the Sudan.** New York, Barnes and Noble, 1974. 314p. LC n.a. ISBN 0-06-490378-8.

Beshir, Mohamed Omer. **The Southern Sudan: Background to Conflict.** New York, Praeger, 1968. 192p. LC 68-17559. DT 108.B4 1968b. DDC 962.9. Includes 70 pages of documents. Examines the political and social aspects of the history of Southern Sudan that led to the conflict between north and south. The author, a Northerner, tries to be fair, and often succeeds. Much on the Christian missionaries and their role in the conflict.

Beshir, Mohammed Said. **The Sudan, Crossroads of Africa.** Chester Springs, Pa., Dufour Editions, 1965. 238p. LC 66-10826. DT 108.6.S3. A Northerner's viewpoint on the conflict.

Churchill, Sir Winston Leonard Spencer. **The River War.** 3rd ed. London, New English Library, 1973. (Repr. of 1933 ed.). LC 74-188321. DT 108.5.C56 1973. DDC 962.4'03. War against the Mahdi. A fascinating account.

Collins, Robert O. **King Leopold, England and the Upper Nile, 1899-1909.** New Haven, Yale University Press, 1968. 346p. LC 68-27750. DT 108.6.C6. DDC 325.3'493'09624.

Collins, Robert O. **The Southern Sudan, 1883-1898: A Struggle for Control.** New Haven, Yale University Press, 1962. 212p. LC 62-8240. DT 108.3.C6. DDC 962.403.

Collins, Robert O. **Land beyond the Rivers, the Southern Sudan, 1898-1918.** New Haven, Yale University Press, 1971. 368p. LC 77-140523. ISBN 0-300-01406-6. DT 108.6.C62 1971. DDC 962.9'03. Western imperialism in the upper reaches of the Nile.

Gray, Richard. **A History of the Southern Sudan, 1835-1889.** London, Oxford University Press, 1961. 219p. LC 61-66800. DT 108.G7 1961. DDC 962.403.

Hill, Richard Leslie. **Egypt in the Sudan, 1820-1881.** London, Oxford University Press, 1959. 188p. LC 59-861. DT 108.2.H5. DDC 962.403.

Shibeika, Mekki. **British Policy in the Sudan, 1882-1902.** London, Oxford University Press, 1952. 439p. LC 53-766. DT 108.3.S4. DDC 962.4.

Sanderson, George Neville. **England, Europe and the Upper Nile, 1882-1899: A Study in the Partition of Africa.** Edinburgh, Edinburgh University Press, 1965. 456p. LC 65-15642. DT 117.S3. DDC 320.962.

Wai, Dunstan M., ed. **The Southern Sudan: The Problem of National Integration.** London, Frank Cass, 1973. 255p. LC 72-92980. ISBN 0-7146-2985-5. DT 108.7.W33 1973. DDC 320.9'629.

916. Marlowe, John. **Mission to Khartoum: The Apotheosis of General Gordon.** London, Victor Gollanz, 1969. 324p. bibliog. index. £2.10. LC 74-413427. ISBN 0-575-00247-6. DT 108.3.M3. DDC 962.4'03'0924.

Gordon's biography is briefly presented (60 pages), followed by the background to Gordon's mission, the siege of Khartoum, and the relief expedition. Using official records and all other material, Marlowe treats in detail the British government discussions and policies that belatedly led to the relief expedition. Not a literary or romantic work, but a solid factual treatment.

917. Moorehead, Alan. **The Blue Nile.** New York, Harper and Row, 1972. 336p. bibliog. illus. index. $15.00. LC 73-186776. ISBN 0-06-013011-3. DT 115.M6 1972. DDC 962. Paperback: Dell. $0.60.

[P] This and the following item are a beautifully produced pair of matched volumes containing innumerable illustrations—paintings, drawings, photos, maps, and diagrams (many in color) of the places, events, and individuals mentioned in these fast-moving, well-written, interesting books. They trace in an impressionistic manner the history of the exploration of the Nile Valley and its two sources, and the role of these sources in the history of the region during the nineteenth century. *Blue Nile*, which begins with the eighteenth century explorer James Bruce and his efforts in Central Africa, covers the coming of the French to Egypt under Napoleon, French exploration of the Nile, and finding of the Rosetta Stone; expulsion of the French and the rise of Muhammad Ali, who sought to expand his empire into the Sudan; Europeans in the Upper Nile (Lady Duff Cooper, Baker); explorers in the Abyssinia of Emperor Theodore and the role of the British there, as well as the influx of missionaries; the destruction of the region's isolation. The more knowledgeable reader will be dissatisfied with the book's episodic, unsystematic coverage, but the general reader will be delighted.

See also:

Moorehead, Alan. **The White Nile.** New York, Harper and Row, 1971. 368p. $15.00. LC 78-160663. ISBN 0-16-013049-0. DT 117.M6 1971. DDC 962.9'3. This volume treats the period 1856-1900: the further exploration and exploitation of the Nile Valley and its other source; Richard Burton and Speke, Baker, Stanley and the books and controversies that revolved around the "source" of the Nile and who should get credit for its discovery, with extracts from the accounts; Suez Canal and European domination; military penetration into Central Africa; slavery; Gordon and the Mahdi; Anglo-Egyptian domination of the Sudan; missionaries and Emin Pasha.

Additional works on history and politics are:

Hasan, Yūsuf Fadl Hasan. **The Arabs and the Sudan from the Seventh to the Early Sixteenth Century.** Edinburgh, Edinburgh University Press, 1967. 298p. LC 67-17614. DT 108.1.H3. DDC 962.4'02.

Macmichael, Harold Alfred. **A History of the Arabs in the Sudan.** New York, Barnes and Noble, 1967. 2v. LC 67-7677. GN 652.A7M3 1967. DDC 572.9'624.

al-Mahdi, Mandour. **A Short History of the Sudan.** London, Oxford University Press, 1965. 154p. LC 66-38246. DT 108.M35. DDC 962.4.

C. BIOGRAPHY

918. Badri, Babakr. **Memoirs of Babikr Bedri.** Tr. from Arabic. London, Oxford University Press, 1969. 250p. LC 70-434386. ISBN 0-19-211194-9. LA 2389.B3A313. DDC 370'.924[B].

This book is a translation of the first of the four Arabic volumes. The author, an outstanding Sudanese educator, opened the first girls' school in the Sudan in 1906; he died in 1958 at age 94. This volume treats his life, mainly that portion between the siege of Khartoum, in which he took part and which he describes, and the battle of Omdurman, where he was living at the end of the book. He describes his fighting with the Mahdist forces; his personal (including marital) life; life as a saddle maker and his shop in Aswan, Egypt; his life as a gum trader; life in Omdurman. Virtually unique in the Western language literature, the book gives much insight into nineteenth century lower class Muslim life in the country as viewed by an insider.

919. Hill, Richard Leslie. **A Biographical Dictionary of the Sudan.** 2nd ed. London, Frank Cass, 1967. 409p. LC 67-94080. DT 108.05.A2H5 1967. DDC 920.0624.

[P1, C1] Virtually unique among the English books on individual countries in the region, it consists of short notices ranging from a few lines to (in a few cases) a page, depending on the available information and the importance of the individual. It covers dead individuals important in the history, politics, exploration, and culture of the Sudan, including many Europeans, down through the mid-twentieth century.

D. SOCIETY

Most works on Sudanese ethnology deal with the black African tribes and peoples—the Nuer, Azande, etc. However, although these tribes are vital to Sudan's existence, as the books on the war between the Arab North and black South in the history section make clear, they are outside the culture area covered by this *Guide*. A list of works on the Southern peoples is found in item 17 in the **Bibliography** section.

920. Asad, Talal. **The Kababish Arabs: Power, Authority and Consent in a Nomadic Tribe.** New York, Praeger, 1970. 263p. bibliog. illus. index. LC 74-100929. DT 132.A8 1970. DDC 301.29'624.

A typical anthropological study of a Sudanese tribe, emphasizing the sources, types, and institutions of power, including household structures and patterns, laws, and economics.

A similar work on another tribe is:

Cunnison, Ian George. **Baggara Arabs: Power and the Lineage in a Sudanese Nomad Tribe.** Oxford, Clarendon Press, 1960. 233p. LC 66-75687. DT 132.C8. DDC 390.09624.

921. Barclay, Harold B. **Buuri Al Lamaab, a Suburban Village in the Sudan.** Ithaca, N.Y., Cornell University Press, 1964. 296p. bibliog. illus. index. (Cornell Studies in Anthropology). $9.75. LC 64-11188. ISBN 0-8014-0026-0. DT 124.B29 1964. DDC 572.96262.

A traditional ethnological study, based on field work, of a suburb of Khartoum; the study searches for the "kinds of changes which this village at the edge of a major urban center is undergoing." It deals with family and kinship patterns and organization, religion, the economic and political structure, social groups, life cycle, and the Hindiyah order of Islam, which is the dominant religious organization. It contains much of interest on popular Islam and is one of the only studies we have on a Near Eastern suburb.

922. Beshir, Mohamed Omer. **Educational Development in the Sudan, 1898-1956.** Oxford, Clarendon Press, 1969. 276p. bibliog. index. (Oxford Studies in African Affairs). $11.25. LC 76-427016. ISBN 0-19-821649-1. LA 1646.B4 1969. DDC 370'.9624.

This book concerns the relationship of educational change to economic, political, and administrative changes under the Anglo-Egyptian Condominium. It includes history, some information on individual schools, government educational policy, and examples of progress made. It is based on extensive research in unpublished sources and is one of very few available works on Sudanese education, as well as an important source on the period as a whole.

XXVII. SYRIA

A. GENERAL WORKS

923. **Area Handbook for Syria.** [American University, Washington, D.C. Foreign Area Studies Division]. 1971. 357p. (DA PAM 550-47). $5.55. LC 75-177250. DS 93.A65 1971. DDC 915.691'03'4.

[B, P1, C1, S1] See the annotation at the head of Section II (page 30).

924. Copeland, Paul W. **The Land and People of Syria.** Rev. ed. Philadelphia, J. B. Lippincott, 1972. 160p. illus. index. (Portraits of the Nations Series). $4.95. LC 77-37732. ISBN 0-397-31208-3 (lib. bdg.). DS 93.C6 1972. DDC 315.691.

[P1] An interesting, if at times overdone and irreverent, generally sympathetic description of Syria's customs and daily life, games, recreation, antiquities, and history. The historical section was obviously not prepared by an expert, but it is more or less indicative of the situation; Copeland's discussion of Islam, however, is much too simplistic even for a book of this type. Still, it is a useful introduction for the general reader.

B. HISTORY AND POLITICS

925. Hitti, Philip Khuri. **History of Syria, Including Lebanon and Palestine.** 2nd ed. New York, Macmillan, 1957. 750p. illus. index. LC 59-3552. DS 95.H5. DDC 956.9.

[P1, C1, S1] The first 406 pages cover the pre-Islamic period; the rest of the book covers the period to the eighteenth century A.D. Hitti is not an expert on the pre-Islamic period, and the book is quite out of date in light of more recent research. However, his effort, written in an easy-to-read, comprehensible style, puts the whole history together as no one else has, and makes it meaningful. An interesting book for the general reader. If the choice must be made, select this book over his *History of Lebanon* (item 893); there is much overlap between the two books, and this one is broader.

See also:

Ziadeh, Nicola A. **Damascus under the Mamluks.** Norman, University of Oklahoma Press, 1964. 140p. LC 64-11330. DS 99.D3Z5. DDC 915.691. Extensive quotations from contemporary travellers, including Europeans. All aspects of the city.

926. Hitti, Philip Khuri. **Syria, a Short History: Being a Condensation of the Author's History of Syria, Including Lebanon and Palestine.** New York, Macmillan, 1959. 270p. index. o.p. LC 59-8223. DS 95.H52. DDC 956.9.

[P1] An interesting popular treatment from earliest times through the early independence period.

927. Longrigg, Stephen Hemsley. **Syria and Lebanon under French Mandate.** New York, Octagon Books, 1972. (Repr. of 1958 ed.). 404p. bibliog. index. $12.50. LC 72-8940. ISBN 0-374-95088-1. DS 98.L6 1972. DDC 956.91. (Also: Beirut, Librairie du Liban; distr. Mystic, Conn., Lawrence Verry, 1972. $8.50.)

[P1, C1, S1] History and analysis of French rule from 1920 to 1945, when the two countries became independent. It traces the events and discusses French attitudes and institutions; French-Arab relations; administration; domestic Lebanese-Syrian politics. Includes a full discussion of the Mandate period and the origin of the regime, Faysal's brief monarchy, the independence process. The only English language work on the subject and a must for larger collections.

928. Ma'oz, Moshe. **Ottoman Reform in Syria and Palestine, 1840-1861: The Impact of the Tanzimat on Politics and Society.** Oxford, Clarendon Press, 1968. 266p. bibliog. index. $13.75. LC 68-100226. ISBN 0-19-821537-1. DS 97.5.M35 1968. DDC 309.1'569.

Covers in detail the Turkish administration of Syria and Palestine during the period of Ottoman administrative reform. It describes and analyzes the administration, with information on economic and political affairs, including European activity there, Muslim-Christian and Muslim-Jewish relations, etc. In a field where the research is just beginning, it presents basic, essential information, based on Arabic, Turkish, and British documentary sources. For larger college libraries.

929. Petran, Tabitha. **Syria.** New York, Praeger, 1972. 284p. bibliog. illus. index. (Nations of the Modern World). $11.00. LC 72-88257. DS 98.2.P47 1972b. DDC 956.91'04.

[P1, C1, S1]   The best history of modern Syria, emphasizing the period since 1946, with 79 pages of historical, economic, social, and institutional background. Two chapters on Syria's economic and social development present a rare view that progress is being made despite the country's many problems, which are also discussed. A final chapter deals with the present regime. This sympathetic perspective serves as a much-needed corrective to the more usual image of a backward nation mired in chaotic cycles of corrupt reactionism and mindless radicalism. Complements Tibawi (item 931), which devotes relatively little space to the post-World War II era.

Other important works:

Abu Jaber, Kamal S. **The Arab Ba'th Socialist Party: History, Ideology, and Organization.** Syracuse, Syracuse University Press, 1966. 218p. LC 66-25781. JQ 1825.S8A67. DDC 329.956.

Hourani, Albert Habib. **Syria and Lebanon: A Political Essay.** Beirut, Lebanon Bookshop, 1968. 402p. LC 77-250942. DS 98.H65 1968. DDC 956.91'04.

Zuwiyya-Yamak, Labib. **The Syrian Social Nationalist Party: An Ideological Analysis.** Cambridge, Mass., Harvard University Press, 1966. 177p. LC 66-24812. JQ 1825.S8Z8. DDC 329.95691.

930. Seale, Patrick. **The Struggle for Syria: A Study of Post-War Arab Politics, 1945-1958.** London, Oxford University Press, 1965. 344p. bibliog. index. $8.00. LC 65-4920. ISBN 0-19-214927-X. DS 98.2.S4. DDC 327.5691.

[P1, P2, C1, S1]   The British Near East correspondent for *The [London] Observer*, an Arabist, has written a superb narrative account of inter-Arab politics and Arab political ideology as it influenced and was influenced by the "struggle." The emphasis and perspective lie in Syrian domestic politics interacting with inter-Arab politics; Syria was the focus of inter-Arab politics during this period because of its location and because Syrian intellectuals formulated and set the tone of Arab ideology and ideological activism. The extensive detail on the inter-Arab aspect makes this book the basic work on the period; there is a great deal of material on Syrian politics, which makes it the basic book on that subject as well. A joy to read, most informative for any reader. It is based on the author's personal knowledge, interviews, and research into Arabic sources.

931. Tibawi, Abd al-Latif. **A Modern History of Syria, Including Lebanon and Palestine.** New York, St. Martin's Press, 1969. 441p. bibliog. index. $10.95. LC 73-93539. ISBN 0-333-10066-2. DS 95.T5. DDC 956.91.

[P1, C1, S1]   A rather contentious history which covers Syria-Lebanon-Palestine from the late eighteenth century to 1921, and Syria alone from 1921 to 1967. It is anti-British and anti-French, but not to such an extent that it is utterly irresponsible; the author does not hesitate to express his own opinions, particularly when he discusses, as he does in some detail, the World War I and Mandate periods. Whatever its faults, which include lack of documentation, it is useful. It is based on the author's considerable researches on the nineteenth century, to which period half the book is devoted. There is relatively little material on the post-World War II period, which is covered in Petran (item 929). A basic book.

Additional works of importance:

al-Ḥuṣarī, Abū Khaldūn Ṣātiᶜ. **The Day of Maysalun, a Page from the Modern History of the Arabs; Memoirs.** Tr. from Arabic. Washington, D.C., Middle East Institute, 1966. 187p. LC 66-29228. DS 98.H813. DDC 956.9104.

Zeine, Zeine N. **The Struggle for Arab Independence: Western Diplomacy & the Rise and Fall of Faisal's Kingdom in Syria.** Beirut, Khayats, 1960. 297p. LC A 61-142. DS 98.Z4.

932. Torrey, Gordon H. **Syrian Politics and the Military, 1946-1958.** Columbus, Ohio State University Press, 1964. 438p. bibliog. index. o.p. LC 64-63089. DS 98.2.T6. DDC 956.91.

A strictly factual, chronological political history using Arabic sources, especially the press, with almost no analysis. For most readers Seale (item 930) is quite sufficient and much more informative on the feel of the times. Torrey is included in this *Guide* because he provides documentation lacking in Seale.

C. SOCIETY

933. Bliss, Frederick Jones. **The Religions of Modern Syria and Palestine.** New York, AMS Press, 1972. (Repr. of 1912 ed.). 354p. LC 76-39454. ISBN 0-404-00897-6. BL 2340.B6 1972. DDC 200'.9569.

A very useful work on Christianity and Islam in the Levant, their sects, doctrines, history, organization, liturgies, and customs.
Another work is:

Haddad, Robert M. **Syrian Christians in Muslim Society: An Interpretation.** Princeton, N.J., Princeton University Press, 1970. 118p. LC 75-113002. ISBN 0-691-03086-3. BR 1110.H33. DDC 301.45'28'095691. Their intellectual, social, and political role.

934. Sweet, Louise. **Tell Toqaan: A Syrian Village.** Ann Arbor, University of Michigan, 1960. 280p. LC A 60-9787. GN 2.M5 No. 14. DDC 301.35095691.
An anthropological study.

D. ECONOMY

934a. Asfour, Edmund Y. **Syria: Development and Monetary Policy.** Cambridge, Mass., Harvard University Press, 1959. 158p. LC 59-13357. HG 1311.S95A8. DDC 332.495691.

934b. Himadeh, Saᶜid B., comp. **Economic Organization of Syria.** New York, AMS Press, 1973. (Repr. of 1936 ed.). 466p. bibliog. index. LC 73-180346. ISBN 0-404-56276-0. HC 497.S8H5 1973. DDC 330.9'5691'04.

A useful systematic survey, each topic by a different authority, on the economy of Mandate Syria.

934c. Shair, Khaled Abdo. **Planning for a Middle Eastern Economy: Model for Syria.** London, Chapman and Hall, 1965. 118p. LC 66-2614. HC 497.S8S5. DDC 339.35691.

E. DESCRIPTION AND TRAVEL

935. Bell, Gertrude Lowthian (1868-1926). **The Desert and the Sown.** New York, Arno Press, 1973. (Repr. of 1907 ed.). 347p. illus. index. (The Middle East Collection). $22.00. LC 73-6270. ISBN 0-405-05325-8. DS 94.B42 1973. DDC 915.691'04'3.

A description of the intrepid lady Orientalist's trip through Syria, in which she depicts the country, its antiquities, and the people she met in the desert, cities and villages, both common and noble. While not specifically informative about the country, it is interesting reading and it imparts the flavor of the area and the nature of human relations there. It describes the people's existence and world view, the minority peoples and their problematic relations with the Muslim majority, and people-government relations. The reader should have a detailed map at hand. The innumerable photos are most informative. This is the type of book that anyone studying the region should read as an orientation immediately before commencing detailed studies of documents and treatises on anthropology and politics, if one cannot visit the area for a first-hand view. Students specializing in it should immerse themselves in good travelogues as part of their studies, because any conclusions they reach in their formal studies must take into account the human factor and its dynamics; such travelogues should be read before the students encounter the theories that will bias their perspective.

936. Thubron, Colin. **Mirror to Damascus.** Boston, Little, Brown, 1968. 226p. bibliog. illus. o.p. LC 68-11518. DS 99.D3T5 1967b. DDC 915.691.

A chatty description of Damascus as seen through the author's eyes as he wanders around the city and its environs. The physical city, its people, and an infinite variety of history and legend from Biblical, classical, Islamic, and modern times are suggested in a way that vividly conveys the flavor of this ancient place across its myriad ages. Useful in conjunction with a guide book, to be read before travelling or for pleasure. The map, photos and bibliography are excellent.

937. Richer, Xavier. **Syrie.** Textes, Antoine Guiné; photographies, Xavier Richer. Boulogne, Delroisse, 1975. 190p. LC 75-504141. DS 94.R5. DDC 915.691'04'42.

Colored photographs of various cities, towns, and regions of Syria depicting places, buildings, landscapes and people, arts. Not an outstanding collection, but many of the pictures are interesting and informative. Captions are in French and English.

F. GUIDEBOOKS

938. Fedden, Henry Romilly. **The Phoenix Land: The Civilization of Syria and Lebanon.** By Robin Fedden. New York, George Braziller, 1966. 276p. bibliog. illus. index. $6.50. LC 66-20190. ISBN 0-8076-0380-5. DS 94.F4 1965. DDC 915.6903.

[P1] This fascinating historical guidebook (which omits all practical information for travellers) describes the towns and presents the author's reflections and interpretations of the essence and role of Lebanon's main cities. Little information is provided on the people. A first book. Much more useful than Thubron (items 906, 936). Excellent for armchair travellers.

939. Nelson, Nina. **Your Guide to Syria.** London, Alvin Redman, 1968. 244p. bibliog. illus. LC 79-355494. DS 94.N38. DDC 915.691'04'4.

The only recent English guidebook exclusively devoted to Syria. A typical example of the type devoted to the general tourist, it has the usual information, historical notes, etc., and much practical information, most of which is out of date. Still, most people will find it useful for orientation in conjunction with one of the more comprehensive works.

XXVIII. TURKEY

A. GENERAL WORKS

940. **Area Handbook for the Republic of Turkey.** [Roberts, Thomas Duval]. Prepared by Systems Research Corporation. 1973. 438p. (DA PAM 550-80). $6.05. LC 76-607576. DR 417.R54. DDC 309.1'561.

[B, C1, S1] See the annotation at the head of Section II (page 30).

941. Dwedney, John C. **Turkey.** New York, Praeger, 1971. 214p. bibliog. maps. (Praeger Introductory Geographies). $7.50. LC 79-101658. DR 417.D48 1971. DDC 915.61.

[P1, C1, S1] A somewhat technical geography of Turkey which deals with the physical, human, economic, historical, political, and demographic aspects. It covers these subjects for the country as a whole and then for the main regions of the country individually. For college libraries.

B. HISTORY (GENERAL)

942. Davison, Roderic H. **Turkey.** Englewood Cliffs, N.J., Prentice-Hall, 1968. 181p. bibliog. index. (The Modern Nations in Historical Perspective. A Spectrum Book). $1.95pa. LC 68-14470. DR 441.D24. DDC 956.1.

[P1, C1, S1] A general history from the pre-Ottoman Turks, through the Ottoman Empire, to the late 1960s. It discusses society, political systems, culture and education, economics, and Islam. Throughout it emphasizes internal history, without the long excurses on international diplomatic history found in most works. It also treats problems of Turkey's immediate future. A good general introduction.

943. Mango, Andrew. **Turkey.** New York, Walker, 1968. 192p. bibliog. index. (New Nations and Peoples). $8.50. LC 68-13999. ISBN 0-8027-2119-2. DR 590.M35 1968b. DDC 956.1'02.

[P1, C1] A very well-written, interesting, thoughtful, sympathetic introduction to modern Turkey, beginning with the sweep of history and Turkey's relations with the West, followed by an attempt to convey the social and political processes operating in the nineteenth and twentieth centuries. More detailed is the treatment of the political and diplomatic history of the post-World War II period. The latter half of the book describes and analyzes the basic socioeconomic and other forces interacting in the country, while offering much basic information and describing the geography of Turkey as well. For the more educated uninitiated reader. Though easy to read, it requires some concentration to benefit fully from it. Read Davison (item 942) first.

C. OTTOMAN EMPIRE

944. Busbecq, Ogier Chiselin de (1522-1592). **The Turkish Letters of Ogier Chiselin de Busbecq, Imperial Ambassador at Constantinople, 1554-1562.** Tr. from Latin. Oxford, Clarendon Press, 1968. (Repr. of 1927 ed.). 265p. index. (Oxford Reprints). $6.00. LC 75-397638. ISBN 0-19-821473-1. DR 423.B8 1968. DDC 915.6'04'01.

[P, C2] The book consists of four long, extremely fascinating letters from a Flemish diplomat and scholar who describes his interesting experiences, places he visited, the Ottoman court, the various classes of Turks he met, and the events of the time he was there. It is a basic source for the period, and a thoroughly enjoyable book for general readers.

945. Cahen, Claude. **Pre-Ottoman Turkey: A General Survey of the Material and Spiritual Culture and History, c. 1071-1330.** Tr. from French. New York, Taplinger Publishing Company, 1968. 458p. bibliog. illus. index. $12.95. LC 68-24744. ISBN 0-8008-6500-6. DR 481.C3313 1968b. DDC 915.61'03'1.

[C2] Beginning with the rise of the Seljuq Empire and its institutions and civilization, Cahen traces the development of the Seljuq Kingdom of Rum in Asia Minor; the Crusades; Rum's relations with Byzantium; society, institutions, economy, administration and culture before the Mongol period. He then provides systematic treatment of the same topics for the Mongol era, when Rum was a protectorate of the Mongols. This is the basic work on the period. Although it becomes technical and overly detailed at times for the non-specialist, it is essential as background to the rise of the Ottoman Empire, as well as for the material it contains on its period; it is not incomprehensible for the reader who has acquired a good background from the works listed in this *Guide.* Of similar value is a work on the subject from the Byzantine perspective: Speros Vryonis, *The Decline of Medieval Hellenism in Asia Minor and the Process of Islamization from the Eleventh through the Fifteenth Century* (Berkeley, University of California Press, 1971. 532p. illus. LC 75-94984. ISBN 0-520-01597-5. DF 545.V78. DDC 913.3'95'08). Begins with a summary of Byzantine Anatolian religious and sectarian, political, social, and economic conditions just before the Turkish conquest, and the story of the conquest (to page 142)—including the decline of Byzantine power, its reasons, the infiltration of Turkish tribes, etc. The author then deals with the Islamization of Anatolia: Turkish invasion, pillage and destruction, population displacements, intermarriage and the mixed generation, Muslim cultural domination, Church organization; Christian participation in Turkish administration and Turkish absorption of Christian youth into their system; economic influence and results; Turkish settlement, Turkish customs and life, both pagans and Muslims; fourteenth century decline of the Church there, including conversion to Islam, Turkish appropriation of Church properties for Muslim religious uses (mosques, schools, etc.); Sufi orders and Futuwwah organizations of the Turks; Greek reaction to the loss of Anatolia, including religious polemics against Islam; Christian residue in Turkish Anatolia (population, administration, institutions, Turkish customs, economic institutions, terminology, etc.). An important, scholarly, well-footnoted work based on a vast array of sources, including Greek and Turkish documents.

946. Creasy, Sir Edward Shepherd (1812-1878). **History of the Ottoman Turks.** Beirut, Khayats, 1966. (Repr. of 1878 ed.). LC [for 1961 printing] NE 65-981. DR 440.C91 1878b.

[P1, C1, S1] This greatly outdated work has not been replaced as the only detailed one-volume history of Turkey from the fourteenth century on (to 1878). Its closely printed pages feature wars, battles, and atrocities, as well as international diplomacy and intrigues. It is based mainly on the 10-volume German work of von Hammer-Purgstall. Creasy is quite opinionated and makes the value judgments his times required, but he attempts to do so in a fair manner, finding much good in the Turks as well as much that is unspeakable. Despite being outdated by more recent research in many of its details and matters of interpretation and emphasis, the chronology and facts are still useful for their convenient and sometimes entertaining presentation (especially if one likes battles). By no means light reading, it is not for the uninitiated. The later period of Turkish history, nineteenth and twentieth century, is well covered by Lewis (item 963).

Other useful works:

Coles, Paul. **The Ottoman Impact on Europe.** London, Thames and Hudson, 1968. 216p. LC 68-118905. D 231.C6. DDC 940. The impact on Europe as it is described by Coles is mainly political: the interaction of Turkey and Europe until 1699, with some information on economic relations provided. Most space is devoted to the history, institutions, and socioeconomic dynamics of the Ottoman Empire rather than to relations with Europe. By no means expertly done, it is useful for the general reader as an orientation. Many illustrations.

Eversley, George John Shaw-Lefevre, baron, and Valentine Chirol. **The Turkish Empire from 1288-1922.** And from 1914-1924 by Sir Valentine Chirol. New York, Howard Fertig, 1969. (Repr. of 1924 ed.). 478p. LC 68-9623. DR 441.E75 1969. DDC 956.1.

Kortepeter, C. Max. **Ottoman Imperialism during the Reformation: Europe and the Caucasus.** New York, New York University Press, 1972. LC 72-75005. ISBN 0-8147-4552-0. DR 511.K67. DDC 946.6.

Lane-Poole, Stanley. **Turkey.** With a chapter by E. J. W. Gibb and A. Gilmen. Beirut, Khayats, 1966. (Repr. of 1908 ed.). 393p. LC 66-6754. DR 441.L3 1966. DDC 956.101. History to 1878. Gibb's chapter is on Ottoman literature. Material on institutions, the court, etc. Written for the general reader.

Susa, Nasim. **The Capitulatory Regime of Turkey, Its History, Origin and Nature.** Baltimore, Johns Hopkins Press, 1933. 378p. LC 33-28950. JX 1568.S8 1933. DDC (308.2)341.7. A survey from 1535 to 1923.

947. Davison, Roderic H. **Reform in the Ottoman Empire, 1856-1876.** New York, Gordian Press, 1973. (Repr. of 1963 ed.). 483p. bibliog. index. $15.00. LC 73-148618. ISBN 0-87752-135-2. DR 569.D3 1973. DDC 956.1'01.

[B, C2] The definitive work (until much more research is done in the Turkish Archives) on the Tanzimat, the period of conscious multifaceted administrative and legal change in the Ottoman Empire. The book discusses in great detail the various reform measures, the key personalities, and the extremely intense internal and international politics involved—international because the reforms were forced partly by French, British, and Russian diplomats in Istanbul; Western-influenced, and sometimes Western-educated, modernizers also sought the reforms, over the intense resistance of traditionalist and vested interests, in order to centralize and galvanize a corrupt, moribund system. This reprint edition has a supplementary bibliography of sources published between 1962 and 1972. The bibliographies are annotated. A very detailed work, it is probably too much for most students, but it is basic to the study of the nineteenth century Near East and should be included in more comprehensive collections.

See also:

Devereux, Robert. **The First Ottoman Constitutional Period: A Study of the Midhat Constitution and Parliament.** Baltimore, Johns Hopkins Press, 1963. 310p. LC 63-9741. H 31.J6 ser 81, no. 1. DDC 342.561.

948. Evliya, Efendi (ca. 1611-ca. 1682). **Narrative of Travels in Europe, Asia and Africa in the Seventeenth Century.** Tr. from Turkish by Joseph van Hammer-Purgstall. New York, Johnson Reprint, 1969. (Repr. of 1834 ed.). 2v. in 3. (713p.). $30.00. LC n.a. DR 730.E823.

Evliya Efendi toured parts of the Ottoman Empire several times (except for Tunis, Algeria and Tripoli), and went on diplomatic and economic missions to Europe for the Otto-man government. These volumes are his utterly fascinating accounts of his travels in the Empire, describing the places and their buildings; city administration; the organization of the administration and government of the Empire; and the statistical code of the Empire, which is given in great detail in the form of tables of tribute, fees and other regular revenue of the Empire, such as customs. Istanbul is described in very extensive detail—most of the first two volumes is devoted to Istanbul and the history of the Empire. He describes Istanbul's shops, tradesmen, food, and dervishes, and provides a detailed list of the trade guilds—their numbers, products and services, special holidays, processions, and other activities. Volume 3 describes his trips to Anatolia, Georgia, the Crimea, and Iran, with descriptions of the people of each place. A basic source for larger collections. Unfortunately, there is nothing on his travels to Western Europe.

Other sources for the early period:

Katib Çelebi (1608 or 1609-1657). **The Balance of Truth.** Tr. from Turkish by G. L. Lewis. London, George Allen and Unwin, 1957. 160p. LC cataloging n.a. Written in 1656. The author was one of the first Turks to see the inadequacy of Muslim education as a cause of the Turkish loss of military supremacy against Europe. He criticized the lack of science and rational thought among Muslims and describes the origins of these characteristics. Discusses various controversial issues in theological disputes of his time, particularly aspects of religious practice and ethics.

Naima, Mustafa. **Annals of the Turkish Empire, from 1591 to 1969 of the Christian Era.** Tr. from Turkish by Charles Fraser. New York, Arno Press, 1973. (Repr. of 1832 ed.). 467p. LC 73-6294. ISBN 0-404-05352-5. DR 485.N3132. DDC 956.1'01. A year-by-year account. Only one volume of the translation was published, covering the first 26 years of the period. Mainly military history and major changes of officials, with some long passages on internal politics. Too detailed for such a short period, but it offers insight into the government, foreign relations, and naval affairs.

949. Gibb, Sir Hamilton Alexander Rosskeen, and Harold Bowen. **Islamic Society and the West: A Study of the Impact of Western Civilization on Moslem Culture in the Near East. Vol. 1: Islamic Society in the Eighteenth Century.** London, Oxford University Press, 1962-63. 2v. $8.50/vol. LC 50-9162. ISBN 0-19-214528-2 (pt. 1); 0-19-214529-0 (pt. 2). DS 38.G485. DDC 949.6.

[P1, C1, S1] This book was intended to be the prolegomenon to a larger study, which was never published. A systematic study of Ottoman society, it stands alone in the field. It covers the Ruling Institution—government, military, administration of provinces; government of the Arab provinces; peasantry and urban population; taxation and finance; the Religious Institution and the Ulema; administration of justice; education; religious endowments; dervishes; millets (non-Muslim religious communities, which had their own system of government and laws). Though research has modified some of its statements and conclusions, it is unlikely to be surpassed in the near future. A basic book.

950. Inalcik, Halil. **The Ottoman Empire: The Classical Age, 1300-1600.** Tr. from Turkish. New York, Praeger, 1973. 257p. bibliog. illus. index. $15.00. LC 76-187274. DR 486.I5 1973b. DDC 914.96'1'031.

[B, P1, C1, S1] The first good English book on the subject. The first 52 pages are a history of the period. The rest of the book consists of essays on the government institutions, law, and class system; economic and some social life; religion and culture. It is an authoritative source for a wealth of information and a most useful introduction, based on considerable research. Unfortunately, the style is terrible, and the facts in the various topical chapters are not integrated with the others, so that the reader is unable to construct readily a comprehensive view of the whole. Nearly a fifth of the book consists of notes and bibliography, which makes it useful as a handbook for further research.

Other works:

Kritoboulos (15th century). **History of Memed the Conquerer.** Tr. from Greek by Charles T. Riggs. Westport, Conn., Greenwood Press, 1970. (Repr. of 1954 ed.). 222p. LC 79-90541. ISBN 0-8371-3119-7. DR 501.K713 1970. DDC 949.6.

Stripling, George William Frederick. **The Ottoman Turks and the Arabs, 1511-1574.** Urbana, University of Illinois Press, 1942. 136p. LC 42-36863. H31.I4 vol. 26, no. 4. (DS 239.S7). DDC (308.2)953.

Vaughan, Dorothy Margaret. **Europe and the Turk: A Pattern of Alliances, 1350-1700.** Liverpool, England, Liverpool University Press, 1954. 305p. LC A56-4710.

Witteck, Paul. **The Rise of the Ottoman Empire.** New York, Burt Franklin, 1971. 54p. LC 70-153023. ISBN 0-8337-3855-0. DR 481.W5 1971. DDC 956.1'01. A classic, essential for the student with some background; stimulating reading.

951. Lybyer, Albert Howe. **The Government of the Ottoman Empire in the Time of Suleiman the Magnificent.** New York, Russell and Ruseell, 1966. (Repr. of 1913 ed.). 349p. bibliog. glossary. index. o.p. LC 65-17908. DR 507.L8 1966. DDC 320.9561.

[C1] Though out of date, this book remains unbettered as the standard survey of the Turkish ruling and religious institutions in the Ottoman Empire's Golden Age, when it was at the height of its power. It discusses the palace organization, education, the army, nobility, court ceremonies, court structure, and legislation. A basic work.

952. Mardin, Serif Arif. **The Genesis of Young Ottoman Thought: A Study in the Moderniza-tion of Turkish Political Ideas.** Princeton, N.J., Princeton University Press, 1962. 456p. bibliog. index. (Princeton Oriental Studies, V. 21). $14.50. LC 61-7420. ISBN 0-691-03018-9. DR 557.M3. DDC 320.9561.

[C3] Utilizing the literary artifacts of Turkish intellectual life, Mardin studies the development of the political concepts of a group of Turkish intellectuals in the third quarter of the nine-teenth century. He presents first a long and extensive discussion of the ideas that the Young Ottomans worked with and their Western origins, their penetration into the Ottoman Empire, the process of percolation and absorption by the intellectuals, and the context of contempor-ary history in which the process occurred. A first-class work that constitutes an important source on the impact of the West and the reaction of Muslim intellectuals as Turkey "awoke" and struggled to resist European encroachments. For larger collections.

953. Mehmed, pasha (d. 1717). **Ottoman Statecraft: The Book of Counsel for Vezirs and Governors. [Nasā'iḥ ül-Vüzera ve'l-Ümera]** of Sari Mehmed Pasha, the Defterdar. Turkish text, with introd., tr. and notes by Walter Livingston Wright, Jr. Westport, Conn., Greenwood Press, 1971. (Repr. of 1935 ed.). 172, 135p. index. $13.00. LC 79-141262. ISBN 0-8371-5825-7. JN 9718.M4. DDC 320.9'561'01.

The author served the Ottoman Empire for nearly 50 years, working his way up from the ranks to become Treasurer of the Empire. This book was written in the early eighteenth century. There is a 50-page introduction that describes the Ottoman System and discusses the author and the book. The book describes theory and practice of the system, its structure and dynamics, both directly and indirectly through the advice he gives. Living in turbulent times, and personally embroiled as a victim of the system's negative aspects, he shows us what was happening through his instructions on how to operate and what not to do. He also suggests what should be the ideal personal characteristics of officials. The introduction and copious notes are useful for understanding the text and for their factual data.

954. Pitcher, Donald Edgar. **An Historical Geography of the Ottoman Empire from Earliest Times to the End of the Sixteenth Century.** Leiden, Brill; distr. New York, Humanities Press, 1973. 171p. 29 folded maps. bibliog. index. $110.00. ISBN 90-04-03828-0.

The text is a history of the changing political map of the Empire; it outlines the con-quests and defeats of the Turks from the immediate pre-Ottoman period to 1606. (It must be remembered that the Turks we call Ottoman were originally only one of many tribes who came West from Central and East Asia, in a succession of waves, and that the great Empire which we think of mainly in its late fifteenth and sixteenth century glories—the fall of Constantinople through the reign of Sulayman the Magnificent—took a couple of centuries to develop.) This summary is quite handy. The multicolored fold-out maps are essentially outline maps similar in their degree of detail to those in Palmer's *Rand McNally Atlas of World History*. There are maps of individual regions of the Empire and its frontier area, including Central Asia, Europe and the Balkans, the Arab regions, etc. Unfortunately, it is unspeakably expensive for its limited coverage and for the elementary quality and the paucity of the maps. For most libraries and students Hazard (item 51) will suffice.

955. Ramsaur, Ernest Edmondson. **The Young Turks: Prelude to the Revolution of 1908.** New York, Russell and Russell, 1970. (Repr. of 1957 ed.). 180p. bibliog. index. $9.00. LC 79-81456. ISBN 0-8462-1372-9. DR 572.R3 1970. DDC 956.1'01.

A detailed history of the Committee of Union and Progress and the revolutionary and reform movement, 1889-1908, including the revolution; it is based on Turkish and other sources. It discusses the conditions that generated the movement, internal politics, ideas and goals, propaganda, Ottoman politics during the period, structure and dynamics of the move-ment. A basic book for larger collections.

956. Shaw, Stanford Jay. **Between Old and New: The Ottoman Empire under Sultan Selim III, 1789-1807.** Cambridge, Mass., Harvard University Press, 1971. 535p. bibliog. index. (Harvard Middle Eastern Studies, 15). $15.00. LC 74-131465. ISBN 0-674-06830-0. DR 559.S5. DDC 949.6.

The first detailed scholarly work on this brief period of Turkish history, which was important as a transitional era worth study for other than purely historical reasons. It was the first reform period in the Empire, and a period in which conditions developed that ultimately allowed further, more drastic changes in the Empire in response to contact with the West, despite Selim's defeat and overthrow. Shaw, the foremost American specialist on the Empire, has used Turkish primary sources to write this account, which covers the military, political, and diplomatic history, the reform efforts and the triumph of reaction, the interaction of Western influence and the reform attempt. Most subjects are treated topically, but not in isolation from each other. A basic work for more comprehensive collections.

957. Vucinich, Wayne S. **The Ottoman Empire: Its Record and Legacy.** Princeton, N.J., Van Nostrand, 1965. 192p. (An Anvil Original, 80). $1.95pa. LC 65-1585. ISBN 0-442-00080-4. DR 422.V8. DDC 914.96.

[P1, C1, S1] There are 123 pages of history, description, and analysis, utilizing and explaining much Turkish terminology. This section covers the institutions, culture, and society. The rest of the book consists of illuminating readings—selections from various books and a few documents. A useful introduction. A first book to read on the Empire.

See also:

Itzkowitz, Norman. **Ottoman Empire and Islamic Tradition.** New York, Alfred Knopf; distr. New York, Random House, 1972. 117p. LC 79-1914. ISBN 0-394-31718-1. DR 445.I8. DDC 949.6.

D. 20TH CENTURY

958. Ahmad, Feroz. **The Young Turks: The Committee of Union and Progress in Turkish Politics, 1908-1914.** Oxford, Clarendon Press, 1969. 205p. bibliog. index. $9.00. LC 70-436940. ISBN 0-19-821475-8. DR 584.A6. DDC 956.1'01.

A detailed scholarly study based on original sources, emphasizing the period after the revolution of 1908 and the establishment of the Constitution. It treats the constitutional regime and the reorganization of the government under the young Turks; the counter-revolution of 1909, its origins, the opposition to the young Turks; the military-CUP relations and the politics of the whole period; CUP consolidation of power; the wars of 1911-1912 and the question of the non-Turkish nationalities, Ottomanism, pan-Turanianism and Turkism; CUP internal politics. The book concludes with a useful appendix of 15 biographies. Rather too detailed for smaller collections and beginning students, but the basic work on the period. The author promises a further work on the CUP in the World War I period; when it is published, it should be a good addition to the literature.

959. Gökalp, Ziya (1875-1924).[Türkçülüğün esaslari]. **The Principles of Turkism.** Tr. from Turkish by Robert Devereux. Leiden, E. J. Brill, 1968. 141p. index. LC 68-137023. DR 476.G613.

[C3] If Ataturk was the "creator of modern Turkey," Gökalp, as Devereux says in his introduction, was the Ataturk revolution's "philosopher," the father of "Turkism" (Turkish ethnic nationalism). This particular book summarizes most of his ideas and is "the most significant volume published by Gökalp." It is source material for the nationalist version of history and culture and for the vision of what they should be. It discusses also Turkish ideology in the world of nations and the Turkish ethical system. Necessary for larger collections.

A biography and discussion of Gökalp is found in:

Heyd, Uriel. **Foundations of Turkish Nationalism: The Life and Teachings of Zia Gökalp.** London, Luzac, 1950. 174p. LC 50-14637. HM 22.T92G645. DDC 301.

960. Gökalp, Ziya (1875-1924). **Turkish Nationalism and Western Civilization.** Tr. from Turkish by Niyazi Berkes. New York, Columbia University Press, 1959. 336p. index. o.p. LC 59-65081. DR 405.G613 1959a. DDC 915.61.

[C2] A selection of the Turkish thinker's writings: autobiographical items; values and ideals, nationalism, culture and civilization; evolution of society (nationhood, Turkey as a nation); social values and institutions; religion, education, and family; Turkism. Gökalp sought to discover what the Turkish essence was, what was wrong and right with Turkey, what the Turks needed to do and what the State should do to bring Turkey into the modern world as it was perceived by Asians at the time. He sought to define the new Turkey, to determine what was uniquely Turkish, and to decide which of the Old World, Islamic, and Turkish traditions should be retained in a modern national Turkish state. He found Turkey's essence conducive to civilization and modernization. In order to do all this, he had to go into the processes and concepts of civilization, society, history, etc., in general terms, defining them so that he had a yardstick against which to measure his Turkish subject. A basic source book for the ideas of the Ataturk period.

962. Karpat, Kemal H. **Turkey's Politics: The Transition to a Multi-Party System.** Princeton, N.J., Princeton University Press, 1959. 522p. bibliog. indices. $13.50. LC 58-10051. JN 9798.A1K3. DDC 329.9561.

The book first surveys the background of the development of twentieth century Turkey, from the nineteenth century; the establishment of the Republic and its ideology, reforms, new political culture, problems, party development and government system; internal politics; economic and social transformation and its process; social classes and World War II developments—peasants, land ownership, industrial workers, middle classes (to page 133). Part II treats the liberalization of the political system and the reintroduction of political parties; political history and issues 1945-1950, including party rivalries, legislative programs and their politics, and finally the process by which the Democratic Party took power from the long-entrenched Republican Party. Part III deals with the transformation of Turkey after 1946 (ideological, behavioral, and other aspects); party structure, society and economics, in terms of Ataturk's basic principles (nationalism, secularism, etatism in economics; republicanism, populism, revolutionism); communism, the political regime, and the continued development of the parties, with elements of the political history to 1958, though throughout this part the emphasis remains the 1946-1950 period. Includes the role of the intellectuals and their ideas, debates on philosophy, and discussions of the individual parties. The immensely detailed notes are highly informative. A useful work which, however, neglects the aspects of self-interest in political behavior. A basic book.

963. Lewis, Bernard. **The Emergence of Modern Turkey.** 2nd ed. London, Oxford University Press, 1968. 524p. bibliog. index. (Oxford Paperbacks, No. 135). $3.95pa. LC 68-139021. ISBN 0-19-500344-6. DR 583.L48 1968. DDC 956.1.

[P1, P2, C1, S1] The best single work on the Ottoman Empire in decay and collapse, from the eighteenth century, and the creation of modern Turkey, to 1950. Events are dealt with chronologically in 319 pages, while the rest of the book treats the problems of the creation of a comm nity and nationalism; the government and how it developed; the conscious creation of a new religion and culture; the remnants of old Turkey; changes in the elite and class system, including new political and economic elites. It treats in detail the influx and influence of Western ideas and how they occurred. A truly fascinating book packed with information, it is a must for all collections and students.

A very important work for the advanced student:

Berkes, Niyazi. **The Development of Secularism in Turkey.** Montreal, McGill University Press, 1964. 537p. LC 64-8158. DR 557.B4. DDC 320.9561.

A brief work for the general reader:

Bahrampour, Firouz. **Turkey: Political and Social Transformation.** Brooklyn, Theo. Gaus' Sons, 1967. 100p. LC 67-14175. DR 590.B28. DDC 320.9'561.

964. Lewis, Geoffrey L. **Modern Turkey.** 4th ed. New York, Praeger, 1975 bibliog. index. (Nations of the Modern World). LC 73-15170. ISBN 0-02-751468-4. DR 441.L45 1975. DDC 956.1.

[P1, C1, S1] No specific information available on this edition, but the third edition was a straight history of the twentieth century, much more detailed than Mango (item 943), which it complements, or Davison (item 942), and less sweepingly analytical. A standard work.

Other works:

Frey, Frederick W. **The Turkish Political Elite.** Cambridge, Mass., M.I.T. Press, 1965. 483p. LC 65-13834. DR 590.F7. DDC 956.102.

Harris, George Sellers. **The Origins of Communism in Turkey.** Stanford, Calif., Hoover Institution on War, Revolution and Peace, 1967. 215p. LC 67-26980. HX 357.H36. DDC 335.43'09496'1.

Weiker, Walter F. **Political Tutelage and Democracy in Turkey: The Free Party and Its Aftermath.** Leiden, E. J. Brill, 1973. 317p. LC 74-18184. ISBN 90-04-03818-3. JN 9798.S4W44. DDC 329.9'561.

Weiker, Walter F. **The Turkish Revolution, 1960-1961: Aspects of Military Politics.** Washington, D.C., Brookings Institution, 1963. 172p. LC 63-17303. DR 590.W4. DDC 956.101.

Ozbudun, Ergun. **The Role of the Military in Recent Turkish Politics.** Cambridge, Mass., Center for International Affairs, Harvard University, 1966. LC 66-28533. JN 9720.C5 O3. DDC 320.94961.

965. Robinson, Richard D. **The First Turkish Republic: A Case Study in National Development.** Cambridge, Mass., Harvard University Press, 1963. 367p. bibliog. index. (Harvard Middle Eastern Studies, 9). $9.50. LC 63-17210. ISBN 0-674-30450-0. DR 590.R62. DDC 956.102.

[P1, C1, S1]   This is the best treatment of the economic, social, and foreign policy aspects of Turkey throughout the twentieth century, to the revolution of 1960. It discusses the village culture and system and its problematic existence vis-à-vis the modernization effort; traditional town society; Ataturk's political and other reforms; economic development to 1956; Turkey in global politics and her foreign policy. Also, Turkey's problems on the eve of the 1960 Revolution, including education, social and economic tensions, religion, etatism and administration; army development after World War II; the Revolution itself; and the new constitution. Includes a 40-page chronology (1919-1961). A useful general work that still has validity and utility despite its age. Written in non-technical language.
  See also:

Bisbee, Eleanor. **The New Turks: Pioneers of the Republic, 1920-1950.** Westport, Conn., Greenwood Press, 1975. (Repr. of 1951 ed.). LC 74-23411. ISBN 0-8371-7868-1. DR 590.B5 1975. DDC 956.

966. Vali, Ferenc Albert. **Bridge across the Bosporus: The Foreign Policy of Turkey.** Baltimore, The Johns Hopkins Press, 1971. 410p. bibliog. index. $12.50. LC 79-123197. ISBN 0-8018-1182-1. DR 471.V3. DDC 327.561.

[P1, C1, S1]   Beginning with background chapters on Turkish history, ideology and the foreign service, political parties and their views, public opinion and foreign policy, the author then deals with specific topics: relations with the United States, NATO, Western Europe; relations with Russia, the Balkan countries; the Straits question; Greece and Cyprus; relations with other Near Eastern countries; development as a basic foreign policy goal (i.e., aid from abroad, EEC membership). The main interest of the book is the post-World War I period. This is not a systematic factual narrative but a general discussion of key issues, trends, influences on and basic features of the foreign policy, with attention given to some key episodes; even in the latter case, however, treatment is general rather detailed diplomatic history. The emphasis on generality rather than detail vitiates the book's value, especially since the interrelatedness of many topics is inadequately shown. However, this is the only comprehensive work we have; thus, it is a basic book for college collections.
  See also:

Weisband, Edward. **Turkish Foreign Policy, 1943-1945: Small State Diplomacy and Great Power Politics.** Princeton, N.J., Princeton University Press, 1973. LC 72-7801. ISBN 0-691-05653-6. DR 477.W44. DDC 327.561.

967. Vali, Ferenc Albert. **The Turkish Straits and NATO.** Stanford, Calif., Hoover Institution Press, 1972. 348p. bibliog. index. (Hoover Institution Studies, 32). $9.50; $6.95pa. LC 70-170205. ISBN 0-8179-7321-2. JX 1383.S8V34. DDC 341.44'6.

A history of the Turkish Straits problem from the nineteenth century, when it was a vital aspect of the Eastern Question, to the present. The book places particular stress on the period since the Montreux Convention of 1936, including the Convention itself, World War II, Soviet efforts to seize control of the Straits; Turkey in NATO and the strategic importance and role of the Straits; Russian Near Eastern policy and the Straits; current issues (revision of the Montreux Convention, defense of the Straits, U.S. interests); policy options and the Straits aspect of the NATO policy of containment of Russia. This useful summary makes up half the book. The rest consists of documents, such as treaties and diplomatic notes, concerning the Straits. For larger collections.

E. BIOGRAPHY

968. Adivar, Halidé Edib. **Memoirs of Halidé Edib.** New York, Arno Press, 1972. (Repr. of 1926 ed.). 472p. illus. (World Affairs: National and International Viewpoints). $24.00. LC 72-4272. ISBN 0-405-04568-9. DR 592.A4 A3 1972. DDC 956.1'02'0924 [B].

The author was a well-known, Western-educated woman educator and journalist in Turkey. Half the book covers her childhood, to 1908 (the year of the Turkish revolution); the rest deals with her experiences and Turkey in a more general way, from 1908 to 1922. Her interesting memoir reveals life in old Turkey; besides treating her life in Syria (1916-1918), she describes Turkey under the revolutionary regime to 1916 and its politics, Turkish nationalism, the transfer of modern ideas into Turkey, the role of Ziya Gökalp (cf. items 959, 960) and others in the culture of her time. The author, as a member of the elite, knew many people and had many fascinating experiences. An informative book that is enjoyable to read. Unfortunately, for the amount of hard information it contains, the price is far too high.

969. Bradford, Ernle Dusgate Selby. **The Sultan's Admiral: The Life of Barbarossa.** New York, Harcourt, Brace and World, 1968. 224p. bibliog. illus. index. $5.75. LC 68-24384. ISBN 0-15-186635-X. DR 509.B22B7. DDC 961'.02'0924 [B].

A popular treatment of the life of the Turkish sea raider, Sulayman the Magnificent's high admiral, who was the scourge of the Western Mediterranean and who secured North Africa for the Ottoman Empire in the first half of the sixteenth century. The author describes the ships, the battles, and the historical context in a smooth style. Good entertainment for the general reader with little background.

970. Haslip, Joan. **The Sultan: The Life of Abdul Hamid II (1842-1918).** New York, Holt, Rinehart and Winston, 1973. (c. 1958). 320p. bibliog. illus. $7.95. LC 72-91568. ISBN 0-03-006936-X. DR 571.5.H3 1973. DDC 923.1496.

[P2, C1] A popularly written, decently (if thinly) researched, and undocumented biography of the Ottoman Sultan, who reigned during the final decades of the Empire's decline and fall. By no means a scholarly work, and sometimes simplistic, it intelligently provides a fascinating inside view of the man who usually is only a name or the stereotype of the "terrible Turk" in most books on the period. The portrait is highly sympathetic, crashing through the stereotype to provide even the specialist with a faulted but very useful caricature, and showing that even tyrants are people. Haslip's theory is that the Red Sultan was an insecure ugly duckling who remained that way and came to the throne by chance. A pathologically fearful man, his calm, courteous, self-possessed demeanor and his rages of unleashed tyranny masked a pathetic, even pitiable figure. A thoroughly enjoyable approach to history that has not been balanced by a scholarly biography based on Turkish archival sources.

971. Kinross, John Patrick Douglas Belfour, baron. **Ataturk, the Rebirth of a Nation.** New York, Morrow, 1965. 615p. bibliog. index. $10.00. LC 65-11486. DR 589.K54 1965. DDC 923.1561.

[P2, C1, S1] The most authoritative, standard biography of the Turkish leader; it is based on extensive research in Turkish and other sources, and on many interviews, but it is undocumented throughout. The first 159 pages deal with the period up to the beginning of the independence struggle. The rest of the book covers the period to Ataturk's death, with the main emphasis on the period through the late 1920s. The book sticks pretty much to his life, ideas, and activities; his method of operation and the internal politics of his regime; the battles he took part in; his reforms, love life, etc. Contains a minimum of material on events in and outside of Turkey as background, and only a little on the implementation of the reforms. Popularly written, with only a readily manageable amount of factual material, it is a basic work for all collections, and the only one needed.

Another work for the general reader, with a critique:

Orga, Irfan, and Margaret Orga. **Atatürk.** London, M. Joseph, 1962. 304p. LC 63-1719. DR 592.K4 068. DDC 923.1561.

972. Merriman, Roger Bigelow. **Suleiman, the Magnificent, 1520-1566.** New York, Cooper Square Publishers, 1966. (Repr. of 1944 ed.). 325p. bibliog. index. $6.00. LC 65-25497. ISBN 0-8154-0152-3. DR 506.M4 1966. DDC 956.1'01'0924.

A general semi-scholarly work by an author who did not know Turkish and therefore could not use Turkish sources. Despite being based mainly on secondary works, it has become the standard biography because it provides a useful, unromanticized outline. Actually, it is mainly a work of military and diplomatic history rather than a description of the Sultan's personal life, and it has little on the internal politics of the period. When a biography based on Turkish archives becomes available, it should be acquired.

F. CIVILIZATION

973. Aslanapa, Oktay. **Turkish Art and Architecture.** New York, Praeger, 1971. 422p. bibliog. illus. index. $50.00. LC 72-144222. N 7161.A87 1971b. DDC 720'.561.

[P1, C1] A major book that includes the works of pre-Islamic Turks, the Karakhanids, Ghaznevids, Seljuqs, Zengid architecture in Syria and Iraq, Tulunid and Mamluk art in Egypt; Turkish art in India, pre-Ottoman art in Anatolia; and, finally, the Ottoman period. The first 260 pages deal mainly with architecture (palaces, mosques, tombs, caravanserais, fortifications, monuments), with separate sections thereafter on the minor arts (ceramics, tiles, carpets, books and calligraphy, painting, etc.). An excellent introduction for the more advanced reader who has acquired background from one or more of the general works listed in this *Guide.* An oversized book, illustrated with 32 color and 250 black and white illustrations, maps, and 53 plans.

974. Goodwin, Godfrey. **A History of Ottoman Architecture.** Baltimore, The Johns Hopkins Press, 1971. 511p. bibliog. 606 illus. index. $30.00. LC 79-124947. ISBN 0-8018-1202-X. NA 1364.G6 1971b. DDC 720'.9561.

This is the definitive work on the subject. It covers mosques, palaces, tombs, gates, kiosks, schools, khans and houses of various kinds and sizes, and popular architecture. It includes detailed descriptions and histories of the buildings.

975. Lewis, Bernard. **Istanbul and the Civilization of the Ottoman Empire.** Norman, University of Oklahoma Press, 1963. 189p. bibliog. index. (The Centers of Civilization Series). $3.50; $2.50pa. LC 63-17161. ISBN 0-8061-0567-4; 0-8061-1060-0pa. DR 726.L4. DDC 914.961.

The author opens with the origins and eventual conquest by Turks of Asia Minor, including general notes on the civilization and religion, institutions, society, and the palace; the city as the Turks and European visitors saw it; and its life, economy, goods, foods, religion, and learning. The book makes the general subject more vivid and is a worthwhile supplement to the more general works. (Some works in this series are fairly successful, and this is one of them. Other items are definitely not worth having, and librarians must be careful in their selection. Several works on Near Eastern cities have been excluded from this *Guide* for that reason.)

976. Vogt, Ulya (Göknil). **Living Architecture: Ottoman.** Text by Ulya Vogt-Göknil. Photos by Eduard Widmer. New York, Grosset and Dunlap, 1966. 192p. bibliog. plans. $7.95. LC 66-9833. ISBN 0-448-00694-0. NA 1364.V613 1966a. DDC 720.9561.

The text discusses the principles of the science and the techniques involved and describes the various buildings. The many excellent photos, diagrams, and plans nicely illustrate the many types of buildings found: mosques, schools, and other religious buildings, houses, baths, caravanserais, etc. An interesting and enlightening book.

G. POLITICS AND GOVERNMENT

977. Conference on Political Modernization in Japan and Turkey, Gould House, 1962. **Political Modernization in Japan and Turkey.** Ed. by Robert E. Ward and Dankwart A. Rustow. Princeton, N.J., Princeton University Press, 1964. 502p. bibliog. index. (Studies in Political Development, 3). $10.00; $3.45pa. LC 63-16238. ISBN 0-691-07516; 0-691-00004-2pa. JQ 1622.C6 1962. DDC 351.

Essays by various authorities on the following topics, one for each country per topic: traditional society; environmental and foreign contributions; economic and political modernization; education, mass media; civil bureaucracy, the military; political leadership and political parties. Most of the papers, which are written in non-technical language, are historical and interpretive treatments rather than technical analyses. They duplicate much of the information found in other works listed in this *Guide*, but the variety of approaches and perspectives and the additional data make this a useful supplement for most collections and most students.

978. Dodd, Clement Henry. **Politics and Government in Turkey.** Berkeley, University of California Press, 1969. 335p. bibliog. index. $9.25. LC 78-85453. ISBN 0-520-01430-8. JN 9715 1965.D6. DDC 309.9'561.

[C2] A general discussion and analysis of the development, operation and problems of the current system and institutions, with a brief background section on the history and system to 1960, including the 1960-1961 revolution. After the background material, there is a 52-page section tracing and analyzing the political history from 1961 to 1965. The next 120 pages discuss the political system—the Constitution of 1961, its drafting and main features; political parties, their ideologies, constituents and leaders, and their role in government; pressure groups (the military, students, trade unions); elections (system and campaigns); Parliament and its organization, legislative process and members; the Council of Ministers and the Presidency. Part II (80 pages) treats the administration—its organization and functions; departmental functions and operation, and performance; Central Administration in the provinces; the civil service and civil servants, including a profile of members, their backgrounds and career patterns, general characteristics, problems and the prospects for the civil service. Each topic is treated in general terms, with comment and analysis but with a minimum of factual data; this limits the book's usefulness, especially since it is out of date. Its suggestion of the problems and prospects is still valid. Necessary for larger collections since it is all we have. It will orient the reader when read in conjunction with one of the introductions in this *Guide*, such as when studying problems of Near Eastern governments, etc., but it is of little use as specific background to current newspaper articles, etc.

See also:

Roos, Leslie L., and Noralou P. Roos. **Managers of Modernization: Organizations and Elites in Turkey (1950-1969).** Cambridge, Mass., Harvard University Press, 1971. 292p. LC 76-162855. ISBN 0-674-54762-4. JN 9715. 1965.D6. DDC 309.9'561.

The effects of modernization and political change on the administration and administrators and elite composition in Turkey. Has much on the nature of Turkish bureaucracy; particular attention is paid to the increased *rural* participation in the political-administrative system. Strictly for advanced readers.

979. Karpat, Kemal H. **Social Change and Politics in Turkey: A Structural-Historical Analysis.** Leiden, E. J. Brill, 1973. 375p. (Social, Economic and Political Studies of the Middle East, V. 7). fl. 88.00. LC 74-164470. ISBN 90-04-03817-5. HC 407.T9K37. DDC 309.1'561'03.

Nine important essays on the middle class, labor as a moving force for change, the Free Boarding Schools; integration of villagers into national life; provincial political parties; historical perspective of the modernization process in Turkey; structural change, modernization, roles of social groups, ideology. A useful mix of analysis and hard information. Some of the information is out of date, since the papers were originally delivered at a conference in 1965 and not all of them were updated for this book.

H. SOCIETY

980. Başgöz, M. Ilhan, and Howard E. Wilson. **Educational Problems in Turkey, 1920-1940.** Bloomington, Indiana University Press, 1968. 268p. bibliog. index. (Uralic and Altaic Series, V. 86). $7.00. LC 67-65317. LA 941.8.B3 1968. DDC 370'.9561.

Covers the history and development of Turkish educational philosophy and the education system during the Ataturk period, with a discussion of the problems encountered, the structures, legislation and reform, new schools, etc., with some analysis. Although more general than factual in its treatment, it is useful as one of the few available works in English on Turkish education.

981. Cohn, Edwin J. **Turkish Economic, Social and Political Change: The Development of a More Prosperous and Open Society.** New York, Praeger, 1970. 196p. bibliog. (Praeger Special Studies in International Economics and Development). $12.50. LC 70-108749. DC 405.C57. DDC 301.1'561.

Based on the literature and on the author's long-time personal experience in Turkey, this is a general discussion of Turkish economic development efforts in their political context, with a brief discussion of aspects of their social implications. It covers education, urbanization, population policy, expanded freedom of discussion, and the resulting intensification of extremist activities of various kinds. Cohn also treats what he believes to be the main problems in the past, present, and future: elite-villager gap, bureaucracy, and the educational system; he takes a hopeful view of future prospects. A general analytical treatment, with relatively few facts, though there are a number of statistical tables. It is too brief and superficially researched and it has far too many undocumented statements, but it offers a useful perspective. As with many works in the Praeger Special Studies series, this work should have been published as a $2.00-$3.00 paperback; it certainly is overpriced at $12.50, as are most of the others on the Middle East in this particular series. Borrow, don't buy.

982. Hinderink, Jan, and Mübeccel B. Kiray. **Social Stratification as an Obstacle to Development: A Study of Four Turkish Villages.** New York, Praeger, 1970. 248p. (Praeger Special Studies in International Economics and Development). $15.00. LC 73-119027. HD 2037.H55 1970. DDC 309.1'564.

A study of the interdependence of social and economic factors in development. After a description of the physical environment of the four villages, there is a chapter indicating changes in farming patterns and land tenure and their impact on people's lives and livelihoods. Other chapters cover present farming patterns, farm populations, types of farms and techniques, farm size, degree of modernization, wage labor and labor conditions. Also, income patterns, living standards and life styles, spending patterns; subjective evaluation of actual life conditions; population characteristics, migration; family as a mechanism of adjustment to socioeconomic change and composition of households, intra-family authority patterns and lineage; changes in social differentiation as the economy changed; religiosity and fatalism, and other values as they relate to development; attitudes toward the media. Also, achievement need, degree of orientation toward the future; literacy and desire for education; power relations and social stratification. The book nicely illustrates the interdependence of these elements. For large collections.

983. Johnson, Clarence Richard. **Constantinople Today; Or, the Pathfinder Survey of Constantinople, a Study in Oriental Social Life.** New York, Macmillan, 1922. 418p. LC 22-24790. HN 620.C7J6.

Social and economic aspects by various writers: history, civic administration, community organization; industry and business life, refugees, orphanages; recreation and school activities; widowhood; adult delinquency; native schools. Mostly generalities rather than bodies of factual data, though there is much useful information on aspects of life not usually dealt with in the available monographs.

984. Kazamias, Andreas M. **Education and the Quest for Modernity in Turkey.** Chicago, University of Chicago Press, 1966. 304p. index. $6.75. LC 66-20585/CD. ISBN 0-226-42866-4. LA 941.K3 1966a. DDC 370'.9561.

The first 112 pages treat in general terms the pre-Republic background: the palace schools, religious schools, nineteenth century efforts to change education, the new schools;

changes during the Tanzimat period and the emergence of new elites; post-Tanzimat era; the millet schools of the Greeks, etc., missionary schools, and Ziya Gökalp's influence. Part II covers the system under the Republic, its structure, the responsibilities of the various administrative levels, local administration; curriculum; types of schools, their roles, social status; objectives of Turkish education. It also treats the problems of educating the masses and mass attitudes toward education, village versus urban attitudes, with comparisons between Turkey and other developing areas. Part III deals with the schools and aspects of socio-cultural change, including secularization of education, laicization of education, the process by which this was accomplished, its implications, degree of progress; education and ideological-cultural-institutional changes; education and political culture; elite and education; the lisés and social changes; differences in generational attitudes toward education; modernism versus traditionalism in Turkish education. An interesting book; the best we have, though it is not up to date.

985. Kunos, Ignácz. **Turkish Fairy Tales and Folk Tales.** Tr. from Hungarian. Magnolia, Mass., Peter Smith, 1969? (Repr. of 1896 ed.). 275p. $4.00. LC n.a. ISBN 0-8446-0751-7. GR 245.K823. DDC 398.2'09561.

A delightful collection suitable for all ages.

986. Lewis, Raphaela. **Every Day Life in Ottoman Turkey.** New York, G. P. Putnam's Sons, 1971. 206p. illus. index. $5.00. LC 75-597129. ISBN 0-399-20067-3. DR 432.L46 1971. DDC 915.61'03'1.

[P1, C1, S1] This interesting, obviously well-researched (but undocumented) book treats all aspects of daily life: institutions and how they work (including administration of justice); religion and superstitions, festivals, religious customs; family life, houses and furnishings, as well as other buildings such as baths; costumes; health and medicine; and occupations. There is also a portrait of life in Istanbul, Anatolia, and the provinces. It discusses in rich detail the lives of both the masses and the elite. The many illustrations are helpful but have not been selected systematically enough to provide the reader with a full visual image of the country. To be read before going to the pre-twentieth century travel books. A basic work.
See also:

White, Charles (1793-1861). **Three Years in Constantinople; Or, Domestic Manners of the Turks in 1844.** London, H. Colburn, 1845. 3v. LC 5-10693. DR 726.W58.

987. Miller, Barnette. **Beyond the Sublime Porte: The Grand Seraglio of Stambul.** New York, AMS Press, 1970. (Repr. of 1931 ed.). 281p. illus. $10.50. LC 79-111774. ISBN 0-404-04329-1. DR 736.M5 1970. DDC 949.6.

A historical sketch of the Palace of the Ottoman Sultans, its buildings and institutions; the ideas, moods, influences, and human elements operating within its environment; the nature of the regime and life inside the Palace, which was largely closed off from the world. Includes discussion of the schools and harem; the administration of the Palace regime; personnel and officials; ceremonies. The detailed description is interesting for its own sake, and it also gives the reader a much more vivid awareness of the life and system of the court. The many illustrations are particularly useful in helping the reader imagine the scene.
See also:

Penzer, Norman Mosley. **The Harèm: An Account of the Institution As It Existed in the Palace of the Turkish Sultans, with a History of the Grand Seraglio from Its Foundation to the Present Time.** New York, AMS Press, 1974. (Repr. of 1937 ed.). 276p. LC 77-180304. ISBN 0-404-56316-3. DR 736.P4 1974. DDC 916.96'1. The buildings, officials and servants, eunuchs; lives of women and their influence; organization.

988. Miller, Barnette. **The Palace School of Muhammad the Conqueror.** New York, Arno Press, 1973. 226p. index. (The Middle East Collection). $12.00. LC 73-6291. ISBN 0-405-05349-5. LF 5321.I7S454 1973. DDC 371.9'62'094961.

A description of the training school for government and military officers, courtiers, and administrators established by Muhammad II. It was located in the Grand Seraglio's inner palace. For several centuries its rigorous courses trained the top leadership and middle bureaucrats who kept the Ottoman Empire functioning even in the period of decline, until the school lost its discipline and vitality. Its origin, history, and physical plant are described, as are the personnel, curriculum and textbooks used, the other schools in the system; the slave system, which constantly infused new blood into the government system and provided the student body; daily life; positions to which students were appointed and names of famous graduates; the school's decline. A valuable source of information on the Ottoman government. For larger collections. To be read after Lybyer (item 951) and a book on Islamic education.

989. Pierce, Joe E. **Life in a Turkish Village.** New York, Holt, Rinehart and Winston, 1964. 102p. (Case Studies in Anthropology). $2.50pa. LC 64-18755. DR 432.P5. DDC 915.63. ISBN 0-03-046135-9.

A brief study of the small village of Demirciler, seen first through the eyes of a hypothetical male child in all its daily activities, customs, stages of life. It is partly a composite view of many villages, partly about this individual village. Part II, about half the book, is a traditional ethnology of the village. The approach used in the first half makes things quite vivid for the general reader and beginning student, while the standard second part (covering kinship and social structure, language, religion, education and the economy) fills in the general aspects not amenable to the fictionalized treatment.

990. Stirling, [Arthur] Paul. **Turkish Village.** New York, John Wiley, 1966. 316p. bibliog. index. (Science Editions). pa. o.p. LC 66-1526. HN 613.5.S8. DDC 309.1564.

A comprehensive, general ethnological study of a small, grubby village. It includes the economy, social and family life and relationships, kinship system, politics, feuds, and relations with the outside world. Not overly technical, and generally fairly interesting.

991. Szyliowicz, Joseph S. **Political Change in Rural Turkey: Eredemli.** The Hague, Mouton; distr. New York, Humanities Press, 1966. 218p. bibliog. index. (Columbia University Publications in Near and Middle East Studies, Ser. A., 8). $12.75. LC 66-15856. HN 613.5.S9. DDC 320.9561.

This study based on field work stresses political modernization. A settlement with a recent nomadic heritage, Eredemli is located on the Southern coast of Turkey, opposite Cyprus. Two parts of the book compare the village as it was in 1941 and in 1957, discussing government policy and relations with the village, the market economy, population, tradition, and the change in village life as it became an administrative center. It includes discussions of courtship and marriage, religious change; finance and structure, political and administrative leadership and its achievements; municipality-government relations; political parties and affiliations, elections, etc. One of only a very few books dealing with the subject at the village level.

992. Walker, Warren S., and Ahmet E. Uysal. **Tales Alive in Turkey.** Cambridge, Mass., Harvard University Press, 1966. 310p. bibliog. index. $8.00. LC 66-21348. ISBN 0-674-86775-0. GR 245.W3. DDC 398.2.

A wide variety of stories and anecdotes, drawn from the oral tradition of all of Turkey: supernatural tales, perplexities and ingenious deductions, humorous tales; moralistic tales; Köroghlu, the chivalrous outlaw; anticlerical tales and anecdotes. Each section is preceded by an introduction on the origin, types, and themes of the tales in the section. A scholarly, informative, but most enjoyable book, made more useful by the extensive notes.

I. ECONOMY

993. Hershlag, Zvi Yehuda. **Turkey: The Challenge of Growth.** 2nd completely rev. ed. of **Turkey, an Economy in Transition.** Leiden, E. J. Brill, 1968. 406p. bibliog. index. LC 68-110442. IIC 405.H4 1968. DDC 330.9561.

[P1, C1, S1] After setting the scene at independence—including the population exchange with Greece and the implications of the Lausanne Treaty, Hershlag details the history of the economy during the 1920s through World War II, and the 1960s (to page 263). Part six, to the end of the book, takes up the problems and the economic and social implications of the growth process, including inflation, real income and standard of living, growth rate and mixed economy. A final chapter deals with manpower, labor, and labor relations. Included throughout the book are discussions of the role of the state and the results of its efforts in all sectors, including policies, goals, the change from an agricultural to a rounded economy; the various measures taken during the Ataturk period; etatism, its origins, and the USSR's influence on it; post-World War II foreign aid. The state of the economy in general is presented throughout the book for each period discussed. A basic work.

See also:

Shorter, Frederic C. **Four Studies on the Development of Turkey.** London, Frank Cass, 1967. 145p. LC 68-80183. HC 405.S47. DDC 330.9561.

Thornburg, Max Weston, Graham Spry, and George Soule. **Turkey, an Economic Appraisal.** New York, Greenwood Press, 1968. (Repr. of 1949 ed.). 324p. LC 68-8074. HC 405.T46. DDC 330.9561.

J. DESCRIPTION AND TRAVEL

994. Lister, Richard Percival. **A Muezzin from the Tower of Darkness Cries: Travels in Turkey.** New York, Harcourt, Brace and World, 1967. 271p. index. o.p. LC 67-20313. DR 429.L5 1967b. DDC 915.61'04'3.

A delightful, utterly irreverent, highly opinionated view of a non-tourist who dislikes much, greatly appreciates much, and thinks much is silly, especially the usual tourist sights. Much simplistic history is interspersed with a full share of ascerbic comment. He sees the funny side of life, its contrasts and contradictions, and he chortles at the legends and myths connected with the places he visits. A nice change for the reader who has had his fill of the other books in this *Guide*, even though it is not very informative about the Turks.

See also:

Hills, Denis Cecil. **My Travels in Turkey.** London, George Allen and Unwin, 1964. 252p. LC 64-54921. DR 429.H5. Extremely jaundiced view, with comments and value judgments, by one who "roughed it"—camping, walking, bus trips. A balancing perspective since most books are more laudatory. Fairly represents at least part of the reaction of many tourists, especially the less sympathetic and more fussy types, who should read this book as well as others before going to Turkey.

995. Marriner, John. **Journey Into the Sunrise.** London, William Kimber, 1970. 253p. illus. index. £3.50. LC 79-512639. ISBN 0-7183-0421-7. DR 429.M35. DDC 915.61'04'3.

A yachtman's view of the Turkish coasts, with much description and historical background. It is not particularly evocative of Turkey, but it does present in interesting fashion a rather different perspective of the country, since he deals mainly with places that can be reached by boat.

996. Namikawa, Ryō, and Banri Namikawa. **Istanbul: Tale of Three Cities.** Tokyo and Palo Alto, Kodansha International, 1972. 142p. maps. illus. (This Beautiful World, Vol. 30). $2.75pa. LC 77-174211. ISBN 0-87011-161-2. DR 723.N3. DDC 914.96'1'043.

[P1] Brief historical notes and marvelous, well-chosen color photos of people, sights, and art. The book gives the traveller a good idea of what the city might be like.

997. Pereira, Michael. **Istanbul: Aspects of a City.** London, Geoffrey Bles; distr. New York, International Publications Service, 1968. 300p. bibliog. illus. index. $12.50. LC 70-359709. ISBN 0-7138-0228-6. DR 723.P47. DDC 914.96'1.

A travelogue and evocation of the great city, with much description and innumerable notes on all periods of its long history, including much on recent eras. Pereira describes each section, with an eye for the humorous, letting the people speak for themselves in his many conversations with them. He provides histories and descriptions of the buildings, the people and their houses, stores, tea rooms, etc. Most sympathetic, with interesting illustrations. It avoids politics, for the most part. An excellent work for both prospective and armchair travellers, but not a guidebook. The author has written other travelogues on Turkey that are fun to read, though not particularly informative.

One guidebook is:

Sumner-Boyd, Hilary. **Strolling through Istanbul: A Guide to the City.** 2nd ed. rev. and corr. Istanbul, Redhouse Press, 1973. 537p. illus. $15.00. LC 74-164342.

998. Slade, Sir Adolphus. **Records of Travels in Turkey, Greece, &c. and of a Cruise in the Black Sea with the Capitan Pasha, in the Years 1829, 1830 and 1831.** London, Saunders and Otley, 1833. 2v. LC 5-8190 rev. DR 425.S64.

A marvelously written, witty, and very perceptive account of the Ottoman Empire at the time of the Greek rebellion, written by a British naval officer. He describes his experiences on Turkish naval vessels; his dealings with the Turks; the life of Turkish sailors, officials, and the elite; Turkish manners; methods by which Christians should deal with Turks; the Greek revolt itself; and the dynamics of the Empire. The account is extremely illuminating. It provides historical notes and descriptions of the political structures and processes; the reign of Mahmud II; justice; foreign advisors; Mahmud's reform efforts and British policy toward the Empire. It also contains a detailed description of Constantinople and its life; the Russian-Turkish War; minorities in the Empire; Greece; Western Christian missionaries in the Near East; Smyrna. One of the best of the nineteenth century travel books, it is a fascinating basic source.

999. Sykes, John. **A Summer in Turkey.** London, Hutchinson, 1970. 166p. o.p. LC 79-529031. ISBN 0-09-104050-7. DR 432.S94. DDC 915.64.

An in-depth account of his experiences and particularly his conversations with a wide variety of people, since people interest him more than places. He gives a considerable feel for the country, presenting a wide range of public opinion on society and politics, and comparing the old and new generations. A fascinating, well-written book.

K. GUIDEBOOKS

1000. Bean, George Ewart. **Aegean Turkey, an Archaeological Guide.** London, Ernest Benn, 1966. 288p. bibliog. illus. index. LC 66-71191. DS 156.I6B4. DDC 913.392303.

Pergamum, Smyrna, Ephesus, Miletus, Sardis—names we know from ancient history and the Bible; they are located on Turkey's West Coast and their ruins stir the imagination of travellers and armchair types. Bean tries to let the prospective tourist know what is to be seen and all he might be interested in knowing about each main site, to 300 A.D., in an area "roughly that which is in comfortable reach from Smyrna." Rich in history, well-written, and presented so that even non-travellers will enjoy much of it, aided by the excellent photos. The same general remarks hold true for his other works: *Turkey's Southern Shore, an Archaeological Guide* (New York, Praeger, 1968. $7.95. LC 68-31439). Covers areas comfortably reachable from Antalya, regions that are little known to the general reader, but that are interesting nonetheless; and *Turkey beyond the Meander, an Archaeological Guide* (Totowa, N.J., Rowman and Littlefield, 1971. $11.00. LC 77-872116. ISBN 0-87471-038-3). Covers Mugla Province.

1001. Denham, Henry Mangles. **Southern Turkey, the Levant and Cyprus: A Sea-Guide to the Coasts and Islands.** London, John Murray, 1973. 124p. illus. maps. index. LC 73-165800. ISBN 0-7195-2721-X. DS 43.D43. DDC 915.6'04'3.

This yachtsman's guide describes the ports that will accommodate yachts; their facilities, formalities and customs; mail, conditions, currencies used, vernacular terms for foods, nautical terms; weather; sites; sailing approaches and anchorages. Detailed maps of the ports and marinas are provided, with some historical notes on the areas covered. A regular guidebook is still needed to supplement this book.

1002. **Fodor's Turkey, 1974.** New York, David McKay Company, 1974. Annual. 414p. illus. index. $7.95. LC 76-3702. ISBN 0-679-00055-0. DR 416.F62. DDC 915.61.

The usual travel guide, with the necessary practical information, including advice on trip-planning, facilities and various points of interest at each site, routes for getting there, history and description of major sights, road conditions, recreation and entertainment (besides sight-seeing). Unlike Nagel (item 1003), it is not limited to antiquities. Includes campgrounds and tourist information sources, with general chapters on the country as a whole, then sections on main regions and big cities, descriptions of towns and the life one will observe there.

1003. **Nagel's Encyclopedia-Guide: Turkey.** Geneva, Nagel Publishers; distr. New York, Hippocrene Books, 1972. 799p. maps. index. $22.00. LC cataloging n.a. ISBN 0-88254-134-X.

The Nagel guides have a common organization. They begin with a section of general information on the country: geography, people, economy, history, art, languages and literature, and anything else appropriate (including, at times, a bibliography). They conclude with a section of practical information, consisting of lists of tourist facilities, information agencies, embassies, money tables, brief glossaries of important words in local languages, etc. The bulk of the book consists of itineraries centered around main cities and regions, which include histories of the towns and notes on the peoples of each main area; detailed descriptions and histories, folklore, archaeological notes, etc., of key sites, particularly antiquities; transportation, road conditions, mileages, scenery, etc.; and minor sites to be noted in passing. The emphasis in each volume varies depending on what the authors, most of whom are French scholars, think is important, and on the kinds of sites available in each country. Generally they are books for permanent reference that should be read by all travellers who want to make a serious educational tour. For most countries, the *Fodor* guides are essential. They are updated annually, and they contain very extensive practical information on all aspects of a traveller's life in the country; in fact, they should be taken along on the trip. Nagel's "practical information" is incomplete and not updated. However, Nagel's descriptions and other information on the sights and sites are much more detailed than Fodor. This volume on Turkey is a mine of information on that country's antiquities through millennia of succeeding civilizations, from ancient times through the Ottoman period. Most users will want to begin with Williams (item 1005) for orientation and fill in details with Nagel; the serious traveller will want to buy Nagel along with Fodor.

Also, for more up to date information:

Schneider, Dux. **Turkey.** London, Jonathan Cape, 1975. 621p. bibliog. illus. (Travellers' Guide). £4.95. LC n.a. ISBN 0-224-00989-7. Organized around itineraries, it includes up-to-date practical information, descriptions of sites, historical notes, and general essays on various aspects of the country.

1004. Williams, Gwyn. **Eastern Turkey, a Guide and History.** London, Faber and Faber, 1972. 355p. bibliog. illus. index. £4.90. LC 72-188346. ISBN 0-571-09342-6. DS 51.E27W54. DDC 915.66'04'3.

The book deals with Anatolia east of longitude 36.5, an area Williams views as a major focal point of Western history and civilization in their formative stages, and a great place to visit. A mountainous region featuring a pastoral life, it has been occupied by the Hittites, Urartians, Persians, Armenians, Greeks, Kurds, Nestorians, Romans, Byzantines, Seljuq Turks, and Mongols. The book traces the history from earliest times and discusses the peoples now inhabiting the region, as well as the Muslim architecture found there. The bulk of the work describes a series of itineraries, offering historical and cultural notes and reflections on the importance of each place, as well as aids and suggestions for travellers. An informative and most interesting book for prospective and armchair travellers.

1005. Williams, Gwyn. **Turkey: A Traveller's Guide and History.** London, Faber and Faber, 1967. 318p. bibliog. illus. index. £3.25. LC 67-101521. ISBN 0-571-08458-3. DR 429.W5. DDC 915.61.

After 113 pages of history and civilization, the book consists of itineraries that tell the traveller what to see, inspire him to see it, and show him why it is important or otherwise noteworthy. Williams seeks to give the prospective and armchair traveller a feel for what he will see, while leaving the practical details up to Fodor, *et al.*, one of which will still be essential for the tourist. Each site is described, with historical background. A useful source of information and good reading.

XXIX. NORTH AFRICA

Very few aspects are covered adequately enough for anybody's purposes, at least in English. A more detailed history of the period down to the early nineteenth century is needed; also needed are a good history of the period thereafter, a history of North African civilization, a social history, etc. Serious study of the region, except for Libya, requires a good knowledge of French, in which language there is a wealth of material already in existence and continuously being published.

A. GENERAL WORKS

1006. Amin, Samir. **The Maghreb in the Modern World: Algeria, Tunisia, Morocco.** Tr. from French. Baltimore, Penguin Books, 1970. 256p. bibliog. index. (Penguin African Library, AP 29). $2.25pa. LC 71-25840. ISBN 0-14-041029-5. DT 185.A6313. DDC 309.1'61.

[P1, C1, S1, S2] An excellent comparative study and interpretation of the process and impact of French colonialism: the economy, the transformation of society; the birth of nationalism and the independence movements; the processes by which colonial rule was ended and the forms of socialism that the new states developed; transitional changes after independence—decolonization and the new economy and society. A constructive Marxist approach by an Algerian, it is quite enlightening and provides much basic information not available in other English language books. A useful complement to the listed histories and political treatises.

1007. Barbour, Nevill, ed. **A Survey of North West Africa (The Maghrib).** 2nd ed. London, Oxford University Press, 1962. 411p. bibliog. index. o.p. LC 62-51256. DT 185.B3 1962. DDC 916.1.

[P1, C1, S1] A general work on Morocco, Algeria, Tunisia, Libya, Spanish West Africa and Tarfaya, Mauritania, Spanish Sahara, and Meulla. It includes history, geography, the populations, government and political life, social and economic conditions. A general descriptive reference work that is gravely out of date; libraries that do not have the *Area Handbooks*, however, will find it still useful and all collections should purchase the new edition that is supposedly being written.

1008. Kittler, Glenn D. **Mediterranean Africa: Four Muslim Nations.** Camden, N.J., Thomas Nelson, 1969. 224p. bibliog. illus. index. (World Neighbors). $5.95; $5.80 lib. bdg. LC 69-15224. ISBN 0-8407-7040-5; 0-8407-7041-3 (lib. bdg.). DT 185.K5. DDC 916.1.

[P1] A general work for younger and less educated general readers concerning the history, religion, daily life, culture, modern history, and politics of Algeria, Morocco, Libya and Tunisia, as well as the activities of the Peace Corps in North Africa. It has many useful illustrations. Quite elementary and often simplistic, but good for public libraries.

1009. Zartman, I. William. **Government and Politics in Northern Africa.** New York, Praeger, 1963. 205p. LC 63-10828. DT 176.Z35 1963. DDC 961.

[P1, C1, S1] Brief surveys of political history, development and organization of Sudan, Egypt, Somalia, Ethiopia, Libya, the Maghreb. One of few such works. A useful introduction for the general reader despite being out of date.

1010. Zartman, I. William. **Man, State and Society in the Contemporary Maghrib.** New York, Praeger, 1973. 531p. bibliog. index. $13.50; $5.95pa. LC 68-16096. DT 204.Z37. DDC 301.29'61.

[B, C1] Forty essays, many translated from French, on various aspects of North Africa (including Libya), grouped under the following rubrics: values and attitudes, leaders and personalities, change and environment, forces and institutions. They discuss forces and groups in society, institutions and political systems, politics, bureaucracy, the military, aspects of economics and their social implications. An excellent resource collection, which includes statements of leaders. The bibliographical section is most useful. For more advanced students. Basic for college collections.

See also:

Brown, Leon Carl, ed. **State and Society in Independent North Africa.** Washington, D.C., Middle East Institute, 1966. 332p. LC 66-20316. HC 545.B7. DDC 916.1033. Fifteen papers, most of which have bibliographies in addition to their notes; they deal with politics, culture, economics, oil, foreign policy. Some are ephemeral, but many are solid and of long-term value; most are informative, many are mainly interpretive and analytical. Useful for most students with basic background.

B. HISTORY

1011. Abun-Nasr, Jamil M. **History of the Maghrib.** 2nd ed. Cambridge, England, Cambridge University Press, 1975. 422p. bibliog. maps. index. $7.95pa. LC 74-25653. ISBN 0-521-20703-7; 0-521-09927-7pa. DT 194.A63 1975. DDC 961.

[P1, C1, S1] A general history from ancient times, covering Libya, Tunisia, Algeria and Morocco; the study becomes more detailed as it approaches the modern period—the nineteenth and twentieth centuries occupy almost half the book; it does not cover the post-independence period of any country. It is mainly political history; although other aspects are not ignored (particularly for more recent periods), they are not given due weight. At least one specialist has labelled it "a total bust"; it was not written by a specialist; the author more or less chopped and pasted together his material without having a thorough mastery of his sources, while his scholarship is inadequate; many of his statements regarding cause and effect are unreliable; he mixes up conflicting interpretations of events, while many of his generalizations cannot be taken seriously; there are many errors of fact. However, it is the only such comprehensive work we have; despite its many faults (it is also deadly dull) it is useful as an overview, orientation, and outline of basic facts. The general reader will find it hard going because innumerable names flow by, and the text is overly concise, sometimes to the point of obscurity; the author often fails to explain himself sufficiently. In addition, many of the facts provided burden the reader unnecessarily; they seem to have been chosen uncritically and haphazardly.

At the opposite extreme is the only other general work on North Africa:

Welch, Galbraith. **North African Prelude: The First Seven Thousand Years.** Westport, Conn., Greenwood Press, 1972. (Repr. of 1949 ed.). 650p. bibliog. index. LC 76-143313. ISBN 0-8371-5969-5. DT 167.W4 1972. DDC 961. This is another cut-and-paste job for the uninitiated reader, written in a chatty popular style with no real pretense at scholarship. Covering the Maghrib and Libya, and more sketchily Egypt, the Sudan, and Saharan West Africa from ancient times, it is episodic and often sensational, featuring well-known incidents and less-known events that will interest the reader, including the Western discovery and exploration of Africa, European relations, etc. It is pretty bad, but it is not without some virtues, in that it will orient the reader and even stimulate many. It utilizes to fair advantage the early travel books, and provides some atmosphere— life and society, etc.—that is totally lacking in Abun-Nasr.

Most readers would benefit from reading these two books in conjunction with Julien (item 1020) to gain the necessary functional (if inadequate) introduction; after this introduction, the reader can proceed to the other books on the region listed in this *Guide.*

1012. Bovill, E. W. **The Golden Trade of the Moors.** 2nd ed. London, Oxford University Press, 1968. 293p. bibliog. index. $10.25; $2.25pa. LC 68-92645. ISBN 0-19-215630-6; 0-19-501294-1pa. DT 356.B6 1968. DDC 382'.0966.

[P2, C1] An exceptionally interesting and readable history of the North-South Sahara trade from Roman times through the nineteenth century, and the history of the Saharan peoples bound up with it. A useful and stimulating introduction, with adventure, some mystery, romance, and a sweep and style that keeps the book from being dull. A first-rate example of good "amateur" scholarship.

1013. Brace, Richard Munthe. **Morocco, Algeria, Tunisia.** Englewood Cliffs, N.J., Prentice-Hall, 1964. 184p. bibliog. index. (The Modern Nations in Historical Perspective. A Spectrum Book, S-604). $1.95pa. LC 64-23571. ISBN 0-13-60154-7. DT 194.B79. DDC 961.

[C1, S1] A general survey of the history of the three countries, emphasizing the twentieth century. Not very good, but one of the few such works we have. In some ways it supplements Gallagher (item 1017), which is the first book to read or purchase.

1014. Chouraqui, Andre. **Between East and West: A History of the Jews of North Africa.** Philadelphia, The Jewish Publication Society of America, 1968. 376p. index. $6.00. LC 68-19610. DS 135.A25C383. DDC 301.451'924'061. Paperback: Atheneum, 1972. (Temple Books, T 26). $4.95.

This interesting book for the general reader is by a Jew originally from Morocco. It covers mainly the Islamic period, with a brief background account of the pre-Islamic era. Slightly more than half the book concerns the French occupation and independence periods, with a substantial chapter on the North African Jews in Israel. A synthetic work, not deep original scholarship, it includes an analysis of French-Jewish relations and concludes that the Jews would have had to leave North Africa even if the Arab-Israeli conflict had not existed, because Jewish socioeconomic well-being coincided with—and, indeed, was tied to—the French presence in twentieth century North Africa. For public and college libraries. For a scholarly work, see item 1018.

1015. Conference on the Western Mediterranean, Palma, Majorca, 1972. **The Western Mediterranean, Its Political, Economic and Strategic Importance.** Ed. by Alvin J. Cottrell and James Daniel Theberge. New York, Praeger, 1974. 256p. index. (Praeger Special Studies in International Politics and Government). LC 73-29. DE 100.C66 1972. DDC 320.9'182'2.

A useful collection of interpretive and analytical essays on French, Spanish, and Italian policy toward North Africa; the importance of the North African countries, and their political and economic conditions; oil in North Africa; the relationship of North Africa to Middle Eastern and Eastern Mediterranean politics; U.S.-Russian rivalries and the policies of the two great powers in the region; the significance of Gibraltar and Malta. There is not much factual data in the essays, but they provide students of European and U.S.-Russian policies and of the Near East-North African region with essential perspectives on the international politics of the area.

1016. Fisher, Sir Godfrey. **Barbary Legend: War, Trade and Piracy in North Africa, 1415-1830.** Westport, Conn., Greenwood Press, 1974. (Repr. of 1957 ed.). 349p. bibliog. index. LC 74-9166. ISBN 0-8371-7617-4. DT 201.F5 1974. DDC 961.

The main topic of this work is British relations with the "corsair" states. It contains a discussion of the literature and previous judgments, and it uses the available material critically. It describes pre-Turkish North Africa, the coming of the Turks and the development of Western relations with the region; Western-Turkish relations; conditions in the "regencies," as the corsair states were called; and the Mediterranean region in general during the seventeenth century. Treatment emphasizes the period to 1712, with an epilogue covering 1712-1830. There is much on French-British-Near Eastern relations, with various informative appendices. An interesting book providing details and a clear picture of the period and of the origins of British policy there, as well as other background useful to the student.

1017. Gallagher, Charles F. **The United States and North Africa: Morocco, Algeria and Tunisia.** Cambridge, Mass., Harvard University Press, 1963. 275p. bibliog. index. (The American Foreign Policy Library). $8.00. LC 63-20766. ISBN 0-674-92670-6. DT 194.G15.

[P1, C1, S1] As with other books in the series, this volume is chiefly a history and description of the region; emphasis is on the twentieth century, and particularly the immediately post-independence period, with a final chapter on North Africa and the world. There are only a few pages on U.S. relations with the region. A good introduction but unfortunately very much out of date. Watch for a new edition.

See also:

Brunschwig, Henri. **French Colonialism, 1871-1914: Myths and Realities.** New York, Praeger, 1966. 228p. LC 65-20084. JV 1817.B743 1966a. DDC 325.344. Very useful as background to French interest in North Africa.

Le Tourneau, Roger. **L'evolution politique de l'Afrique du Nord Musulmane, 1920-1961.** Paris, Armand Colin, 1962. 503p. LC 65-74729. DT 204.L4. The best survey of recent history. Since there is nothing even faintly equal to it in English, it is basic for all students. Written by a long-time observer, it is based on the best scholarship and intensive personal experience.

1018. Hirschberg, Haim Zeev. **A History of the Jews in North Africa.** Tr. from Hebrew. 2nd ed. Leiden, E. J. Brill, 1974- . V. 1: "From Antiquity to the Sixteenth Century." fl. 144.00. LC n.a. ISBN 90-04-03820-5.

A detailed history of economic, social, spiritual, and communal conditions and organization, and life of the Jews. Based on a wide variety of documents such as responsa, other Hebrew writings, and the secondary literature, it is a scholarly treatment that carefully draws its conclusions only as the sources allow. In addition to providing the material on the Jews, the book greatly enriches our knowledge of the general history and conditions of the region; it gives added sources of information, details, and clues basic to our understanding of the periods covered.

1019. Hopkins, J. F. P. **Medieval Muslim Government in Barbary until the End of the Sixth Century of the Hijra.** London, Luzac, 1958. 169p. bibliog. index. o.p. LC 59-26683. JQ 3200.H6. DDC 354.61.

A detailed survey of the administration of medieval North Africa based on primary sources. Includes discussion of the functionaries of government—wazirs, chancery secretaries, chamberlains, intelligence officials; revenue and its sources, collection, and disbursement; the treasury; religious minorities. It treats the position of Qadi and the administration of justice; law enforcement; theory, functions, and practice of various officials, changing roles and conditions, and institutions, under the various dynasties. The book is quite technical, with many gaps in coverage due to the inadequacy of the sources; for the same reason, it deals mainly in generalities. The only book we have on the subject. For the most comprehensive collections only.

1020. Julien, Charles André. **History of North Africa: Tunisia, Algeria, Morocco, from the Arab Conquest to 1830.** Tr. from French. Ed. and rev. by Roger Le Tourneau. New York, Praeger, 1970. 446p. bibliog. index. $13.50. LC 79-104771. ISBN 0-7100-6614-7. DT 194.J82213. DDC 961.

[P1, P2, C1, S1] The standard work, being one of very few that exist in any language, and by far the best. A survey and analysis stated in general terms, it includes political, social, cultural and economic aspects, as well as relations with Europe. It is scholarly but quite intelligible to the general reader with some background; the quantity of facts is manageable. Though it has been outdated by recent research, the new material has not yet been synthesized into an acceptable work.

C. CIVILIZATION

1021. Gordon, David C. **North Africa's French Legacy, 1954-1962.** Cambridge, Mass., Harvard University Press, 1962. 121p. bibliog. (Harvard Middle Eastern Monographs, 9). $4.50pa. LC 62-21836. ISBN 0-674-62650-8. DT 204.G65. DDC 327.44061.

These essays deal with the cultural impact of the French presence in the Maghrib, discussing the *mission civilisatrice*; Algerian colons, their negative attitudes toward the natives, their attempts to maintain their superiority in all fields, and their fears as to their fate in an independent Algeria; French cultural oppression of Algerians and the rejection of assimilation by Muslims; anti-French literature in French written by Algerians and colons such as Camus and Memmi; the problem of the Frenchified Algerians and their crisis of identity, including a discussion of key Algerian writers of French works; French interest in maintaining bilingualism; native education—the debate on it, Muslim education and culture, and the search for Muslim self-identification, including Arabization in education and modernization; Tunisian and Moroccan educational policy; the role of the war in creating an Algerian national identity. The book does not deal with continuing economic and other ties with the French. Although it is not systematic and it stresses mainly problem areas, it still has considerable relevance today because some of the problems and debates continue, despite the absence of direct French presence. It is valuable as a source on the particular period covered.

1022. Hanna, Sami A. **Modern Intellectual and Literary History of North Africa.** ca.4v. forthcoming. LC has a photocopy of a manuscript labelled v. 1, Tunisia. LC 72-190885. DT 192.H352. DDC 916.1'03'3.

[C1, S1]   An immense, very detailed work that promises to be of fundamental importance to the study of the region.

D. POLITICS AND GOVERNMENT

1023. Hermassi, Elbaki. **Leadership and National Development in North Africa: A Comparative Study.** Berkeley, University of California Press, 1972. 241 p. bibliog. index. $8.50. LC 70-182279. ISBN 0-520-02170-3. JQ 3189.A2H47. DDC 301.5'92.

This is a stimulating exploration and analysis of the development of Moroccan, Algerian, and Tunisian societies, political culture, leadership elites and the regimes; their formation as distinct national societies; the patterns of colonial domination and colonial change; the ways in which their formation and French domination have influenced North African institutions; and the postures of their elites toward the basic problems of their nations, as well as the strategies and costs of the particular choices made. The book evaluates their successes and failures in structure building and suggests future prospects, including the potential effectiveness or lack thereof of their economic planning. It offers a critique of current development theory, past and present social anthropological explanations, and various theories of Maghribi dynamics. It suggests areas and approaches for future research. Should be read after the other works listed in this *Guide.* Perhaps too advanced for all but advanced college students, but it is mind-stretching.

1024. Moore, Clement Henry. **Politics in North Africa: Algeria, Morocco, and Tunisia.** Boston, Little, Brown, 1970. 360p. index. (The Little, Brown Series in Comparative Politics. A Country Study). $4.50pa. LC 78-106493. ISBN 0-316-58000-7. JQ 3189.A3 1970. DDC 320.9'61.

[P1, C1, C2, S1, S2] A formal political study by a specialist. After an introduction on the pre-colonial systems, it treats the colonial system, in general terms: the old elites, political struggle and anti-colonialism movements, their objects and ideology, relations between French and native elites; key figures; the stage of political development reached at independence. Then, the founding, building and stabilizing of the new political systems, their characteristics and problems. There are several chapters on specific topics: scope and effectiveness of government in development and regulation of national life and nation-building; distributive capability (jobs, services, etc.); their symbolic capabilities vis-à-vis the masses (interest articulation—i.e., demands—by unions, student groups, etc.); interest aggregation (congealing of groups to present proposals for action on their demands); interrelations of lower levels of government; comparative development strategies; political socialization and recruitment of cadres; Greater Maghreb. A technical and not comprehensive work, it is basic for colleges because there is virtually nothing else. A typical case in which the author has chosen to neglect the interests of the many for the satisfaction of a few, when he could have met the needs of both. We totally lack a satisfactory work on the politics and government of the three countries. If the present work is valid, then the author must have collected enough data to produce a work for students that would be infinitely better than anything now available, into which he could incorporate the technical discussion without too much trouble, written in non-technical language.

See also:

Ashford, Douglas Elliott. **National Development and Local Reform: Political Participation in Morocco, Tunisia and Pakistan.** Princeton, N.J., Princeton University Press, 1967. 439p. LC 66-14307. JS 7809.2.A88. DDC 320.3.

E. SOCIETY

1025. **Arabs and Berbers: From Tribe to Nation in North Africa.** Ed. by Ernest Gellner and Charles Micaud. Lexington, Mass., Lexington Books; distr. Lexington, Mass., Heath and Company, 1973. 448p. index. $15.00. LC 79-15180. ISBN 0-699-83865-9. DT 313.2.A7 1973. DDC 301.29'64.

The 23 essays in this volume include six ethnological studies on the Berbers and their social, religious, and political institutions and organization; eight on the relations of the Berbers to and with the State, both the French colonial regime in Morocco and the present Moroccan government, and the role of the Berbers in the Algerian political elite; five on social change and its manifestations in Morocco and Mauritania; the Berbers in the Moroccan Coup of July 1971. The North African countries of Tunisia, Morocco, and Algeria, being relatively more open to scholars than the increasingly "closed" Eastern Arab states, and having inherited a strong and productive French tradition of ethnology, have begun to yield some outstanding, stimulating studies—in this instance, by a group of mainly younger Anglo-American scholars who appear to be on the verge of making great contributions to the field. While this example of their work is too specialized for most collections and college students, libraries with strong anthropology collections will find it useful, particularly since it brings to bear a number of different approaches on a relatively limited topic, which is instructive for budding specialists.

1026. Berque, Jacques. **French North Africa: The Maghrib between the Two World Wars.** Tr. from French. New York, Praeger, 1967. 422p. indices. $12.50. LC 65-20083. DT 204. B433 1967b. DDC 916.1'03.

This is a profound evocation of the dynamics of North Africa (excluding Libya) under the French colonial system; it is not a systematic factual survey, though it does cover all aspects of North African life: human ecology, physical aspects of life; politics, economy, social life, religion, the quality of Muslim life; the operation and daily as well as long-term impact of the French colonial system on the indigenous population; and the latter's reaction to that impact at all levels of society. The author uses a wide range of source materials and topics, as well as his personal experience, to provide the reader with one of the best works on the region. However, it is a most difficult work which presupposes a considerable reader background; it should cap the student's reading of the appropriate works in this *Guide.* Careful study of this demanding work is immensely rewarding.

1027. Briggs, Lloyd Cabot. **Tribes of the Sahara.** Cambridge, Mass., Harvard University Press, 1960. 295p. bibliog. illus. $8.50. LC 60-7963. ISBN 0-674-90870-8. DT 337.B7. DDC 572.96611.

[C1] An outstanding general description of the Saharan peoples, based on years of first-hand experience. The author traces briefly the history of the Sahara from earliest times, then treats in general terms aspects of life—settlement patterns, crafts, social systems, and the other main features of Saharan culture. He discusses specifically the Tuaregs, Teda, Chaamba, and Moors, covering health and disease, food taboos, birth control, diet, etc. An extremely interesting account with good illustrations and a critique of the previous literature. A basic work.

See also:

Slavin, Kenneth, and Julie Slavin. **The Tuareg.** London, Gentry Books, 1973. 142p. LC 74-155787. ISBN 0-85614-033-3. DT 346.T6 S57. DDC 916.5'06'933. The authors' experiences, with interesting descriptive notes on the lives, poverty, customs, etc., of the famous nomads. Many excellent photos. For the general reader.

F. ECONOMY

1027a. Robana, Abderrahman. **The Prospects for an Economic Community in North Africa: Managing Economic Integration in the Maghreb States.** New York, Praeger, 1973. 206p. bibliog. (Praeger Special Studies in International Economics and Development). $15.00. LC 72-92465. HC 545.R6. DDC 338.91'6.

A comparative analysis of various aspects of the economies of Tunisia, Algeria, and Morocco, with a special chapter on Libya, to explore the structural bases, possibilities, and problems of closer economic cooperation and eventual union. The main use for most readers is in its up-to-date information provided on the state of the economies and approaches of each country.

G. DESCRIPTION AND TRAVEL

1028. Powell, Edward Alexander. **In Barbary: Tunisia, Algeria, Morocco and the Sahara.** New York, Century, 1926. 483p. illus. LC 26-19742. DT 190.P6.

A general description—places, people, buildings—with historical notes, comments on the French presence, and excellent photographs.

XXX. ALGERIA

A. GENERAL WORKS

1029. **Area Handbook for Algeria.** [Nyrop, Richard F.]. 1972. 401p. (DA PAM 550-44). $5.75. LC 72-600149. DT 275.N9 1972. DDC 916.5'03'5.
[B, P1, C1, S1]   See the annotation at the head of Section II (page 30).

B. HISTORY AND POLITICS

1030. Behr, Edward. **The Algerian Problem.** New York, W. W. Norton, 1962. 260p. bibliog. illus. o.p. LC 62-9687. DT 295.B38 1962. DDC 965.04.

This journalistic account is one of the best books available on the conflict. Behr begins with the French conquest and administration and the rise of Algerian nationalism. He then covers the Algerian underground; Jacques Soustelle's administration; French politics; the FLN and its politics; negotiations, the Evian Accords, and the *colon* reaction; de Gaulle; the Algiers rising; the Algerian economy and the impact of the rebellion, including a description of the economy and a discussion of the changes in the Muslim sector. Basically a chronological treatment, it has many more details than Kraft (item 1036) concerning both the French and Muslim sides. A final chapter offers an interpretation. Extremely interesting.

1031. Brace, Richard Munthe, and Jean Brace. **Ordeal in Algeria.** Princeton, N.J., D. Van Nostrand Company, 1960. 453p. index. $7.95. LC 60-53318. ISBN 0-442-01005-2. DT 295.B64. DDC 965.04.

A general treatment of the Algerian rebellion, which begins with an 80-page background section. Two-thirds of the book treats the period 1958-1960. It covers French actions and politics in France, the international politics of the Algerians and French as they sought to gain support, and the reaction of the world; de Gaulle's rise to power and his election; the *colon* rebellion of 1960, as well as the negotiations between the French and Algerians, 1958-1959. Less material is provided on internal Algerian politics during and after the war. One of the few useful English works we have, it complements Behr (item 1030) and Kraft (item 1036).

1032. Confer, Vincent. **France and Algeria: The Problem of Civil and Political Reform, 1870-1920.** Syracuse, N.Y., Syracuse University Press, 1966. 148p. bibliog. index. $5.00. LC 66-24455. ISBN 0-8156-2099-3. DT 294.C74. DDC 320.965.
[B]   The question of the native Algerians was a disruptive issue in French politics, and more so in Algeria, which was considered by Frenchmen to be part of France. The *colons*—French settlers—intended to control the country, over all objections of the indigenous population. But enough Frenchmen raised the question of the role that the natives should play in the administration under French rule to cause considerable commotion. Confer deals with the debates in France and Algeria over the alternatives of economic justice or exploitation; Muslim participation in the administration; the motivations of the Frenchmen; conditions in Algeria; and the various arguments propounded by the parties. The whole is discussed from the French perspective only; it is a contribution to understanding the nature of French rule in North Africa and the Near East and French reaction to local nationalism. We still need a good comprehensive study that will explain the *mission civilisatrice*—one of the driving motivations and rationalizations for French colonization; and an explanation of the viciousness and violence of French reactions to Arab nationalism.

1033. Gillespie, Joan. **Algeria, Rebellion and Revolution.** New York, Praeger, 1961. 208p. bibliog. index. (Nations of the Modern World). o.p. LC 60-14956. DT 295.G5 1960. DDC 965.04.

A straight narrative history from the early nineteenth century through independence, almost half of which treats the pre-1954 period.

1034. Gordon, David C. **The Passing of French Algeria.** London, Oxford University Press, 1966. 265p. bibliog. index. $8.50. LC 66-2149. ISBN 0-19-215629-2. DT 295.G58 1966. DDC 965.

[P1, C1, S1] One of the best books on twentieth century Algeria (to 1962). It is in effect a series of essays rather than a systematic history. Chapter one treats the French regime, 1830-1935; chapter two, 1936-1954; chapter three, the Algerian revolution, 1954-1962. Other chapters deal with the men of the revolution and their ideals; the early independence years; the cultural question (education and the French-Arabic-Islamic interaction); the end of the French human presence and the departure of the *colons*; post-independence relations with France; and the issue of Algerian identity. It gives a broad overview and discusses aspects of history and the problems of nationalism, the revolution's growth, success, and aftermath, but it offers so little specific information that some readers will be disappointed. The definitive work is yet to come, but this is a basic work of particular use to the reader with some background.

1035. Heggoy, Alf Andrew. **Insurgency and Counter-Insurgency in Algeria.** Bloomington, Indiana University Press, 1972. 327p. bibliog. index. (Indiana University International Studies). $10.00. LC 74-180487. ISBN 0-253-33026-2. DT 295.H4 1972. DDC 320.9'65'04.

[C2, S2] A carefully researched and documented history and analysis of the Algerian revolution, 1954-1958, with considerable background material and much material on the organization of the various groups, both Algerian and French. It also discusses the internal politicking, methods of operation of the parties; communism; the U.N. and the revolution; and the relations of the revolutionaries with the population. It concludes by relating the Algerian experience to the study of insurgency and counter-insurgency. Despite its somewhat specialized emphasis, as one of the few serious works on the revolution—and a good work, at that—it is basic for collections on Algeria.

1036. Kraft, Joseph. **The Struggle for Algeria.** Garden City, N.Y., Doubleday, 1961. 263p. o.p. LC 611-15519. DT 295.K68. DDC 965.04.

One of the best accounts of the 1954-1958 War, by a syndicated columnist. He gives some background, trying to suggest the essence of the feelings, interests, and lives of the various parties: the native Algerians, *colons*, and their societies and role in the country; *colon* attitudes toward the Muslims, and the reasons for their bitter reactions and violent behavior. Also, the development of the rebellion and the rise of the rebel leaders. Kraft outlines the history of the war, the FLN and its organization, and the methods used by both sides. Also, French politics and the atmosphere of France at the time, its weakness in a period of decline, the declining French system; de Gaulle's takeover; the Secret Army Organization and its activities; peace negotiations. More evocative than factual, it is one of our few decent books on the period; it complements Behr (item 1030) and Brace (item 1031).

1037. O'Ballance, Edgar. **The Algerian Insurrection, 1954-1962.** Hamden, Conn., Archon Books, 1967. 231p. bibliog. index. $7.00. LC 67-2184. DT 295.O343 1967. DDC 965'.04.

[P1, C1, S1, S2] A military history with some political background, including French Secret Army Organization terrorism, and the final settlement. Besides being an informed military description and analysis, the book is useful for showing the interrelation of military and political considerations in this type of insurrection.

1038. Ottoway, David, and Marina Ottaway. **Algeria, the Politics of a Socialist Revolution.** Berkeley, University of California Press, 1970. 322p. bibliog. index. $9.75. LC 70-83210. ISBN 0-520-01655-6. DT 295.O8. DDC 320.9'65.

[P1, C1, S1] A narrative treatment and analysis of Algeria's political history from independence (1962-1969), including the political struggles, the system, formation and operation of institutions, foreign policies. The first 50 pages suggest the main factors and diversities among Algerians and other conditions bearing on the country's prospects. Includes material on the operation of the economy and the "socialist" measures, French-Algerian relations, and oil policy; the indication is that some of the seeming contradictions in Algeria's politics and foreign relations are not really contradictions if one knows more about trends in Algeria. A good general discussion based on field research, it will help the reader understand some of what is happening today. The biographical appendix is quite useful.

See also:

Humbaraci, Arslan. **Algeria: A Revolution That Failed: A Political History since 1954.** New York, Praeger, 1966. 308p. LC 66-21783. DT 295.H8 1966a. DDC 965.05. A left-wing Turkish journalist's stinging critique of various aspects of the post-independence regime's policies and politics. Neither systematic nor consistently factual, but it has much information that should be checked and coordinated with other works.

Joesten, Joachim. **The New Algeria.** Chicago, Follett, 1964. 258p. LC 64-15333. DT 295.J58. DDC 965. A brief orientation for the general reader: background to independence; Ben Bella's life and rise to power; post-independence politics and policies in various fields; social problems; cooperation with France. In the nature of an interim report.

1039. Quandt, William B. **Revolution and Political Leadership: Algeria, 1954-1968.** Cambridge, Mass., M.I.T. Press, 1969. 313p. bibliog. index. $8.95. LC 71-87302. ISBN 0-262-17002-7. DT 295.Q3. DDC 320.9'65.

[P1, C1, C2, S1, S2] This example of the application of political science approaches to a country's recent history contains much political history, analysis of the revolution and structure of the Algerian political elite, and material on the characteristics, roles, and interrelations of the men who comprise it (but little on their personal lives and careers). It is based on field research. Quandt uses theoretical methods and statistical charts to structure his approach, which is more formal and selective than Ottaway (item 1038). It therefore will be of much less general interest than Ottaway. However, it is quite informative, and in various ways it supplements Ottaway. Because we have so few books on Algeria in English, this is a necessary work, particularly as it covers the broader period.

C. BIOGRAPHY

1040. Merle, Robert. **Ahmed Ben Bella.** Tr. from French. New York, Walker, 1967. 160p. LC 66-22513. DT 295.3.B4 M473 1967a. DDC 965'.04'0924.

Written in the form of an autobiography based on taped conversations with the former Algerian President. Discusses his early life and his role in the Algerian revolution.

D. SOCIETY

1041. Bourdieu, Pierre. **The Algerians.** Tr. from French. Boston, Beacon Press, 1962. 208p. bibliog. index. o.p. LC 62-15064. DT 283.B623. DDC 916.5.

[P1, C1, S1, S2] The best work of its kind in English, this book discusses the family and social structures and organization of the various peoples of Algeria—the Berber Kabyles, Shawia and Mozabites, and the Arabic-speaking groups. It includes city, rural, and nomadic life and society, land structure and the peasantry; there are general discussions of the aspects of culture common to the different groups, economy, attitude toward life, religion; the disintegration of society under the French colonial system and the impact of Western civilization, economic and political structures, as well as European colonization of the land. The effect of the 1954-1958 revolution, including its cultural aspects and disruption of values, is also discussed. A sociological analysis and interpretation stated mainly in general terms. For colleges and more advanced readers.

See also:

Pavard, Claude. **Lumières du M'zab.** Boulogne, Delroisse, 1974? 165p. LC cataloging n.a. Excellent color photos of this Algerian village nicely suggest the nature of any North African village–its form, housing, life, subsistence, landscape. Text in English, French, and Arabic.

1042. Gordon, David C. **Women of Algeria: An Essay on Change.** Cambridge, Mass., Harvard University Press, 1968. 98p. (Harvard Middle Eastern Monographs, 19). $4.50pa. LC 68-21889. ISBN 0-674-95505-6. HQ 1804.A4G6. DDC 301.41'2'0965.

Essays treating the traditional position of women in Algeria; the emancipation movement, in the Near East in general (particularly Egypt), and in Algeria; position of women under the French regime, including legal status, polygamy trends, reaction of the Frenchified Algerian women like Assia Djebar, the writer; women during the revolution; all aspects of the problem during the early independence period (social, economic, political, and educational); the traditionalist reaction. The book is suggestive and impressionistic rather than comprehensive. The author's generalities and conclusions also illuminate the problem of women in the entire region in a time of transition. For larger collections.

1043. Miner, Horace, and George de Vos. **Oasis and Casbah: Algerian Culture and Personality in Change.** Ann Arbor, University of Michigan Press, 1960. 236p. bibliog. LC A 60-9819. GN 2M5 no. 15. DDC 916.5.

The basic aim is to explore the relationship between culture and personality, using a case study based on interviews and Rorschach tests. It compares Arabs raised and living in an oasis with some who moved to Algiers from the oasis. It describes village life and discusses cultural attitudes, including sex, childhood, superstitions, culture change due to contact with the French. It suggests psychological characteristics of the Algerian Arabs, including emotions, perceptions, and adjustment patterns. One of few works in English on Algerian ethnology.

E. ECONOMY

1043a. Blair, Thomas L. V. **The Land to Those Who Work It: Algeria's Experiment in Worker's Management.** Garden City, N.Y., Doubleday, 1969. 275p. LC 69-10953. HD 5660.A4B55. DDC 658.31'52'0965.

1043b. Clegg, Ian. **Worker's Self-Management in Algeria.** New York, Monthly Review Press, 1971. 249p. LC 73-178709. HD 5660.A4C56. 1972. DDC 331'.0965.

F. DESCRIPTION AND TRAVEL

1044. Isnard, Hildebert. **Algeria.** Tr. from French. Paris, Arthaud; distr. Fairlawn, N.J., Essential Books, 1955. 235p. 156 illus. index. o.p. LC 56-2624. DT 288.I82. DDC 916.5.

A geographical description, region by region, with notes on the history and the people. The information is useful, though out of date. Its main value for the purposes of this *Guide* is the large number of excellent rotogravure photos, which help the reader visualize the country.

1045. Marriner, John. **Sailing to Timbuctoo.** London, Kimber, 1973. 278p. illus. index. £3.95. LC 74-159956. ISBN 0-7183-0063-7. DT 280.2.M37. DDC 916.5'7'045.

After skirting along the Algerian coast, the yachtsman-author took to a range-rover and crosses the Algerian Sahara (this part of the trip is the main concern of this book). He travelled through Niger and Mali to Timbuctoo, and back through Algeria. He describes his experiences, the land, and the buildings, and includes interesting notes on the history, antiquities, legends and lore, and the people and their lives as he experienced them, as well as his experiences with officials and notes on the Western explorers and other characters who enliven Algeria's history–e.g., Isabel Eberhardt, Charles de Foucauld, Aurélie Picard, etc. A fascinating medium for armchair escapism.

1046. Morell, John Reynell. **Algeria: The Topography and History, Political, Social and Natural.** London, Nathaniel Cooke, 1854. 490p. illus. LC 1-5500. DT 275.M87.

Part I treats the topography and the history of exploration of the country; political divisions of Algeria under the successive Arab, Turkish and French regimes; descriptions and statistics of the French Algerian provinces and their subregions, including ethnology, sites, historical notes; agriculture, climate, fortifications, roads, towns, etc. Part II contains a systematic history, statistics, and ethnology—the Kabyles and their lives, customs, sayings, legends, economy, institutions; similar information on the Arabs, both peasants and nomads, including mores and values, tents; Turks, Jews, Negroes; slavery. He describes fully the European population; colonization of land, decrees, organization of the administration and *colons*, with a survey of the individual colonized areas and farms; civil and religious governments, justice, the French army. Concludes with appendices on Algerian antiquities, languages, commerce, natural history, and geology. A mine of information, though probably too much for most collections.

See also:

Blofeld, J. H. **Algeria, Past and Present . . . with a Review of Its History from the Earliest Periods to the Present Time.** London, T. C. Newby, 1844. LC 5-9835. DT 275.B65.

Crawford, Mabel Sharmon. **Through Algeria.** London, Richard Bently, 1863. 362p. LC 5-9827. DT 279.C89. A well-written travelogue describing the people and the French colonists.

Prus, Mme. Laure. **A Residence in Algeria.** London, W. Pickering, 1852. 332p. Tr. from French. LC 5-12866 rev. DT 279.P97.

G. GUIDEBOOKS

1047. **Nagel's Encyclopedia-Guide: Algeria.** Geneva, Nagel Publishers; distr. New York, Hippocrene Books, 1973. 543p. bibliog. maps. index. $22.00. LC cataloging n.a.

The first 105 pages contain generalities on Algerian life, history, arts, religion. The only recent English guidebook to Algeria, it is organized like the others in the series (cf. item 1003). It is unique among the *Nagel's* on the region covered by this *Guide* in that it features a considerable amount of information on the country's economy and geography, treats factories, etc., as significant attractions, and has much on the modern history of main cities, towns, and regions. Road conditions are noted in detail. Antiquities play a relatively minor role in this book, for while there are some interesting remains, they are not the main feature of the country, and most are not discussed at length, though they get the usual treatment. Algeria's main interests for tourists are its climate as a resort area, its interesting geography and scenery, and its people, accented by the antiquities that dot the landscape, especially in the coastal regions.

XXXI. LIBYA

A. GENERAL WORKS

1048. **Area Handbook for Libya.** [Nyrop, Richard F.]. 2nd ed. Prepared by Standord Research Institute. 1973. 317p. (DA PAM 550-85). $5.30. LC 72-600386. DT 215.S73 1973. DDC 309.1'61'2.

[B, P1, C1, S1] See the annotation at the head of Section II (page 30).
> See also:
>
> Hajjaj, Salem Ali. **The New Libya: A Geographic, Social, Economic and Political Study.** Tripoli, 1967. LC cataloging n.a.

1049. Copeland, Paul W. **The Land and People of Libya.** Philadelphia, J. P. Lippincott, 1974. (Portraits of the Nations Series). LC 78-37735. ISBN 0-397-31203-2. DT 215.C6 1972. DDC 916.1'2.

[P1] A typical volume in the series: a general survey, for the totally uninitiated, of the history, social life, religion, economy, politics and government, etc., with the author's personal notes describing the countryside and towns.
> See also:
>
> Blunsum, Terence. **Libya, the Country and the People.** London, Queen Anne Press, 1968. 117p. LC 68-101155. DT 215.B55. DDC 916.1'2.

1050. First, Ruth. **Libya: The Elusive Revolution.** New York, Africana Publishing Company, 1975. bibliog. index. LC cataloging n.a. ISBN 0-8419-0211-9. Paperback: Hammondsworth, Baltimore, Penguin Books, 1974. 294p. bibliog. index. (Penguin African Library). $2.95pa. DT 236.F57. ISBN 0-14-040140-6. DDC 961.204.

[P1, C1, S1] The first 96 pages deal with the history to 1969, mainly the twentieth century. The rest treats the period of Qadhdhafi's regime: political history, foreign policy, Islam as ideology, the economic situation; oil; Arab politics. Based on the relatively few sources available and on visits to the country and interviews, the book assembles the extant information in a coherent fashion and offers interpretations of events, comments on problems and prospects. The only book in English on the current era, it is basic for all readers.
> See also:
>
> Ansell, Meredith O., comp. **The Libyan Revolution: A Source Book of Legal and Historical Documents.** Stoughton, Wis., Oleander Press, 1972- . LC 73-170464. ISBN 0-902675-10-7. DT 236.A7. DDC 961'.204. Volume 1 covers 1 September 1969-30 August 1970.

B. HISTORY AND POLITICS

1051. Evans-Pritchard, Sir Edward Evan. **The Sanusi of Cyrenica.** Oxford, Clarendon Press, 1949. 240p. bibliog. illus. index. $8.50. LC 49-10261. ISBN 0-19-823107-5. DT 238.C8E85. DDC 961.4.

The history and an anthropological study of the Islamic religious order-tribal grouping that ultimately seized power in Libya. It traces the order's historical and political role and its relations with the other tribes and the Italians, with a discussion of Italian rule and colonization efforts. The main emphasis is political, not anthropological.
> See also:
>
> Ziadeh, Nicola. **Sanūsiyah: A Study of a Revivalist Movement in Islam.** Leiden, E. J. Brill, 1958. 148p. LC 60-33897. BP 187.7.S4Z5. DDC 297.8.

1052. Khadduri, Majid. **Modern Libya, a Study in Political Development.** Baltimore, The Johns Hopkins Press, 1963. 404p. appendices. index. o.p. LC 62-18509. DT 236.K5. DDC 961.204.

[C1, S2] A superficial political history from World War II through 1961. The author worked there in 1957 and knew many of the political actors. It contains a detailed discussion of the U.N.-directed creation of the State, the writing of the constitution, and the political structure, followed by a history of the cabinets and foreign relations, development laws, parliament sessions, etc. It is basically a routine survey of the externals, with little in-depth perception or analysia and it is definitely not a study of political development in the current sense of the word. It also presents a rosy view of things from an establishment perspective. Whatever its faults, it is the most detailed treatment available and it serves as a useful introduction.

See also:

Khalidi, Ismail R. **Constitutional Development in Libya.** Beirut, Khayats, 1956. LC 57-26411. JQ 3592.K5. DDC 342.6109.

Norman, John. **Labor and Politics in Libya and Arab Africa.** New York, Bookman Associates, 1965. 219p. LC 65-14415. HD 6879.L5N6. DDC 961.204.

Pelt, Adrian. **Libyan Independence and the United Nations: A Case of Planned Decolonization.** New Haven, Yale University Press, 1970. 1016p. LC 72-99836. ISBN 0-300-01216-0. DT 236.P44 1970. DDC 341.13'9'612. The creation of the independent state of Libya after World War II by the U.N. The author was the U.N. commissioner in charge of the operation.

Rivlin, Benjamin. **The United Nations and the Italian Colonies.** New York, Carnegie Endowment for International Peace, 1950. LC 50-13070. JV 2218.R5. DDC 325. 345096.

Villard, Henry Serrano. **Libya, the New Arab Kingdom of North Africa.** Ithaca, N.Y., Cornell University Press, 1956. 169p. LC 56-13846. DT 236.V5. DDC 961.2. The first U.S. minister to Libya describes the country and narrates some of his personal experiences. A general interim report for the general reader.

1053. Wright, John L. **Libya.** London, Ernest Benn, 1969. 304p. bibliog. index. (Nations of the Modern World). £2.25. LC 70-424023. ISBN 0-510-39521-X. DT 224.W7 1969. DDC 961.2.

[P1, C1, S1] The only comprehensive history of Libya in any European language, from ancient times to the last years of the monarchy. The last 50 pages outline the history of the independence period and the discovery of oil and its importance to the country; it discusses very briefly general aspects of development, including the economy, infrastructure, human resources, etc. A basic book.

See also:

Cachia, Anthony Joseph. **Libya under the Second Ottoman Occupation, 1835-1911.** Tripoli, Government Press, 1945. 197p. LC 48-1207. DT 215.C3. DDC 961.2.

Sègre, Claudio. **Fourth Shore: The Italian Colonization of Libya.** Chicago, University of Chicago Press, 1975 (forthcoming). Other information n.a.

C. SOCIETY

1054. Abdelkafi, Mohamed. **One Hundred Arabic Proverbs from Libya.** London, Vernon and Yates, 1968. 100p. £0.75. LC 74-490342. SBN 900776-00-5. PN 6519.A7 A36. DDC 398.9'927.

Arabic proverbs with English translations, explanations, and equivalent English proverbs. Some are quite entertaining.

D. ECONOMY

1054a. Allan, John Anthony, K. S. McLachlan, and Edith T. Penrose, eds. **Libya: Agriculture and Economic Development.** London, Frank Cass; distr. Portland, Ore., International Scholarly Book Services, 1973. 214p. LC 73-160841. ISBN 0-7146-2946-4. HD 2139.L5A7. DDC 338.1'0961'2.

Physical geography and climate; land use and crop patterns, 1911-1950; present use and cropping patterns, a systematic survey; investment in Libyan agriculture. Notes on employment and wages. Specialized, but useful.

1054b. Farley, Rawle. **Planning for Development in Libya: The Exceptional Economy in the Developing World.** New York, Praeger, 1971. 349p. LC 76-126777. HC 567.L5F3. DDC 330.9612'04.

A survey of the resources and economy, and history of government plans and policy, including manpower resources. Ignores the planning *process*.

E. DESCRIPTION AND TRAVEL

1055. Furlonge, Sir Geoffrey Warren. **The Lands of Barbary.** London, John Murray; distr. Levittown, N.Y., Transatlantic Arts, 1966. LC 66-71448. DT 190.2.F8. DDC 916.1.

A travelogue and historical notes on Italian-occupied Libya, discussing the antiquities of the area and relating the author's personal experiences. Although it is not very informative, it is interesting for the uninitiated armchair traveller.

1056. Tully, Miss. **[Narrative of a Ten Years' Residence at Tripoli in Africa]. Letters Written during a Ten Years' Residence at the Court of Tripoli.** New ed. with introd. and notes by Seton Dearden. London, Arthur Barker, 1957. 381p. LC 58-21791. DT 218.T92 1957. DDC 961.2.

Miss Tully, the sister of the British Consul, Richard Tully, lived at the Consulate from 1783 to 1793. She describes all aspects of life and politics in the "letters," which were first published in 1816. A truly fascinating, very detailed account that is a basic source of our knowledge of the era. Interesting for students of North Africa and for the general reader who is familiar with the romance of Barbary.

F. GUIDEBOOKS

1057. Williams, Gwyn. **Green Mountain: An Informal Guide to Cyrenaica and Its Jebel Akhdar.** London, Faber and Faber, 1963. 136p. bibliog. illus. index. o.p. LC 63-6111. DT 238.C8W5. DDC 961.4.

An interesting description of Libya's Green Mountain region, which discusses the numerous antiquities and the author's experiences there, with anecdotes and many quotations from classical authors. It is not very informative, but it is good reading for the armchair traveller.

1058. Ward, Philip. **Touring Libya: The Southern Provinces.** London, Faber and Faber; distr. Levittown, N.Y., Transatlantic Arts, 1968. 103p. bibliog. illus. index. LC 74-372116. DT 220.2.W3. DDC 916.1'2'044.

Touring Libya: The Eastern Provinces. London, Faber, 1969. 102p. illus. LC 79-461583. ISBN 0-571-09099-0. DT 238.C8W3. DDC 916.14'04'4.

Touring Libya: The Western Provinces. London, Faber, 1967. 102p. illus. LC 67-114584. DT 238.T8W3. DDC 916.1'22'044.

A series of travel guides that blanket the country. Includes description of the country and the author's experiences. They lack practical information, but they are virtually unique and are interesting for armchair travellers.

XXXII. MAURITANIA

1059. **Area Handbook for Mauritania.** [Curran, Brian Dean]. Prepared by The American Institutes for Research. 1972. 185p. (DA PAM 550-161). $4.25. LC 72-600188. DT 553.M2 C87. DDC 916.61'03'5.

[B, C1] See the annotation at the head of Section II (page 30).

1060. Gerteiny, Alfred G. **Mauritania.** New York, Praeger, 1967. 243p. bibliog. index. (Praeger Library of African Affairs). o.p. LC 67-23574. DT 553.M2G4. DDC 916.6'1.

[C1, S1] A general work, the first and still the only one in English, covering the historical background, society, mores and manners; folk-lore, including magic and superstitions, language and literature; the French administration, independence, political parties and politics; the economy, industrial planning, and development; foreign relations. A basic work on the nineteenth member of the League of Arab States.

XXXIII. MOROCCO

A good general history is needed, as well as a comprehensive general work on the French occupation period, a systematic political history of the independence era, and a good general work covering history, culture, society, etc.

A. GENERAL WORKS

1061. **Area Handbook for Morocco.** [Nyrop, Richard F.]. 1972. 403p. (DA PAM 550-49). $6.15. LC 72-600025. DT 305. A74 1972. DDC 309.1'64'05.

[B, P1, C1, S1] See the annotation at the head of Section II (page 30).
See also:
Barbour, Nevill. **Morocco.** New York, Walker, 1965. 239p. LC 65-19258. DT 305.B33.

1062. Cohen, Mark I., and Lorna Hahn. **Morocco: Old Land, New Nation.** New York, Praeger, 1966. 309p. bibliog. index. (Nations of the Modern World). $8.00. LC 65-14062. DT 314.C58. DDC 964.

[C1, S1] After a 54-page historical introduction emphasizing the French protectorate (1912-1952), and 40 pages on the 1953-1955 period (the independence struggle), the book deals topically with aspects of Morocco's post-independence existence: social problems and cultural affairs, including women, labor, and education; politics and foreign affairs, with a concluding chapter on U.S.-Moroccan relations. It is superficial and deeply faulted in various respects, but it is useful nonetheless as a systematic introduction to the country. The political history is brought up to date by Waterbury (item 1075), who gives it much more meaning. The topical subdivision serves to disintegrate the discussion of basically interrelated factors, which should be discussed together at least somewhere in the book. Soon after reading this book as an orientation, proceed to Willcox (item 1089).

1063. Spencer, William. **The Land and People of Morocco.** Rev. ed. Philadelphia, J. B. Lippincott, 1973. 160p. illus. index. (Portraits of the Nations Series). $4.95. LC 73-4906. ISBN 0-397-31481-7. DT 324.S6 1973. DDC 916.4.

[P1] A sympathetic description of the country, its people, history, architecture, and main cities, with sidelights from the author's experiences. As with the rest of the books in this series, the history is often simplistic, but this does not detract from the book's utility for upper juvenile and less educated readers.

B. HISTORY

1064. Bidwell, Robin Leonard. **Morocco under Colonial Rule: French Administration of Tribal Areas, 1912-1956.** London, Frank Cass; distr. Portland, Ore., International Scholarly Book Services, 1973. 349p. bibliog. index. £7.50. LC 72-92959. ISBN 0-7146-2877-8. DT 324.B48 1973. DDC 325'.344'0964.

This is not a systematic narrative history of the French occupation, but a topical study of various aspects of the administration outside the central power area—i.e., the rural and mountain regions, where the social organization was primarily tribal. It begins with the first administration under Lyautey, "pacification" of the tribes, the Berber policy; the Sultan's role; use of Pashas and Caids (local tribal leaders); use of religious leaders; the various French officials in the local regions; land policy; agricultural policy and achievements; education, health, justice, local tribal councils; Moroccans as French soldiers and workers; and the effect of French rule on the tribes. While the book assumes a fair degree of knowledge on the part of the reader, who should read the more general works as background, and is probably too much for most students, it is quite useful for the great deal of information it contains about Moroccan society, the philosophy of French rule, colonial processes and institutions, and their implications.

1065. al-Fāsī, 'Allāl. **The Independence Movements in Arab North Africa.** Tr. from Arabic. New York, Octagon Books, 1970. (Repr. of 1954 ed.). 414p. $13.00. LC 70-96201. ISBN 0-374-90095-7. DT 204.F323 1970. DDC 320.1'59'61.

[C2, S2] The first 78 pages deal with the twentieth century nationalist movements in Algeria and Tunisia, and the rest of the book treats the Moroccan movement to 1948, the year in which the Arabic original was published. al-Fasi was a leader of the movement, head of the Istiqlal (Independence) Party. This is the movement as he saw it and as he wanted others to see it; it is part history, part memoir. A most interesting book as well as a basic source for the period; it is one of the more detailed works in English.

1066. Halstead, John P. **Rebirth of a Nation: The Origins and Rise of Moroccan Nationalism, 1912-1944.** Cambridge, Mass., Harvard University Press, 1967. 323p. bibliog. (Harvard Middle Eastern Monograph Series, 18). $4.50. LC 67-31566. ISBN 0-674-75000-4. DT 324.H24. DDC 964'.04.

[P1, C1, S1] An excellent detailed history of Moroccan politics during the period of the French occupation, up to the evolution of a separatist doctrine by the Istiqlal Party. It discusses the protectorate system and Moroccan interaction with it; the impact of external factors, including the Arab awakening and Muslim Salafiyah movement; European impact; the rise of nationalism. A systematic history of the parties, personalities, and ideas. A basic book.
Also, for the later period:

Bernard, Stephane. **The Franco-Moroccan Conflict, 1943-1956.** Tr. from French. New Haven, Yale University Press, 1968. 680p. bibliog. LC 67-24490. DT 317.5.F7 B43. DDC 301.15'3. The first part (to page 372) of this important study details the history of the political conflict and negotiations, particularly French policy and actions. The second part is a methodological study—theory, model, and application to the conflict. For advanced students.

1067. Hoffmann, Eleanor. **Realm of the Evening Star: A History of Morocco and the Lands of the Moors.** New York, Chilton Books, 1965. 307p. bibliog. illus. index. o.p. LC 65-11483. DT 314.H6. DDC 964.

[P, C1, S1] Except for a brief introductory section on the background, this book is concerned with the Islamic period down to the mid-1960s. One-third of the book covers the twentieth century. It is a systematic survey that includes in the narrative references to scenes the modern traveller will see, such as important buildings and tombs of important personages. Also covers Muslim Spain, the history of the African empires of Ghana, Mali, and Songhai (ninth-sixteenth centuries), Timbuctoo, and Moroccan efforts in the south, relations with Europe, the Barbary pirates, U.S. relations 1727-1822, nineteenth and twentieth centuries. Popularly written and quite interesting. The author is no professional historian, but the book is useful as an initiation.

1068. Landau, Rom. **Moroccan Drama, 1900-1955.** London, Robert Hale, 1956. 430p. bibliog. index. o.p. LC 56-14687. DT 324.L35 1956a. DDC 964.

[C1, S1] After a general introduction on the situation in 1912 and the tendencies in Moroccan society, politics, and international diplomacy that led up to it, the book treats the history of the country more or less from the perspective of French administration activities and policies and their implementation, and the native Moroccan reaction to this. It covers some aspects of Muslim politics and protectorate administrative structure; the rise and progress of Moroccan nationalism; French government policy; U.S.-Moroccan relations; events in Spanish Morocco; the process by which independence was achieved; the U.N. role. A very useful general narrative, although it lacks extensive detail of native politics; it is a convenient introduction for any reader.

1069. Le Tourneau, Roger. **Modern History of Morocco.** New York, Praeger, 1975 (forthcoming). LC 75-165854.

[P1, C1, S1] No specific information on this book is available. However, Le Tourneau, who died recently, was one of the top experts on North Africa. His books are basic. Since we lack a good history of the country in English, it should become an essential work for most libraries and all readers.

1070. Scham, Alan. **Lyautey in Morocco: Protectorate Administration, 1912-1925.** Berkeley, University of California Press, 1970. 272p. bibliog. index. $8.75. LC 74-92680. ISBN 0-520-01602-5. DT 324.S36. DDC 325.3'44'0964.

A systematic study of the system and issues of the French administration and its development from the inauguration of the protectorate to the end of Lyautey's regime. It begins with a biography of Lyautey and portrait of the man and his career. Scham then details the establishment and structure of the administration and discusses key topics: property administration, tenancy changes, government handling of various types of land, expropriation, etc.; colonization of the land as official policy and how it was implemented. Also, French-Muslim education—structure, policy and implementation; new institutions and curriculum. Also, judicial structure, including Muslim courts and procedures, Jewish courts. It concludes with an assessment of Lyautey's regime, followed by 40 pages of documents. Too specialized for most collections, but basic for systematic comprehensive collections; necessary for understanding the French regime and Moroccan reactions to the occupation.

1071. Woolman, David S. **Rebels in the Rif: Abd el Krim and the Rif Rebellion.** Stanford, Calif., Stanford University Press, 1968. 257p. bibliog. index. $6.95. LC 68-12333. ISBN 0-8047-0664-6. DT 324.W6. DDC 964'.2'04.

A scholarly, interesting, readable account of the rebellion of Spanish Moroccan Rifians against Spanish rule, 1921-1926. It includes the background to Spanish rule and anthropological notes on Rifian social and political structure. Abd al-Krim became a worldwide legendary hero for his long fight against a European power; his exploits were publicized by newsmen on the scene.

C. BIOGRAPHY

1072. Maxwell, Gavin. **Lords of the Atlas: The Rise and Fall of the House of Glaoua, 1893-1956.** London, Longmans, 1966. 318p. bibliog. illus. index. £6.50. LC 66-66631. ISBN 0-582-10761-X. DT 324.M38 1966. DDC 964.04. Paperback: Pan Books, 1970. £0.40. ISBN 0-330-02436-1.

The biography of T'hami Glaoui, warlord of Southern Morocco, who became a major force in Morocco's politics, cooperating with the French during the occupation (1912-1956) and seeking to become ruler of the entire country. It is a truly fascinating book that contains much information on the history and dynamics of Moroccan politics: the interaction of traditional politics, the modernist and independence movements, and the French colonial regime as they impinged on each other. One of few works available that examines in detail the lives of individuals.

See also:

Blunt, Wilfrid. **Black Sunrise: The Life and Times of Mulai Ismail, Emperor of Morocco, 1646-1747.** London, Methuen, 1951. 294p. LC 57-35357. DT 323.5.B55.

D. CIVILIZATION

1073. Le Tourneau, Roger. **Fez in the Age of the Marinids.** Tr. from French. Norman, University of Oklahoma Press, 1961. 158p. bibliog. index. (The Centers of Civilization Series). $2.50pa. LC 61-6496. ISBN 0-8061-1114-3. DT 329.F4L423. DDC 964.31.

A well-written and most interesting description and history of the Moroccan city; it treats officials and administration, economy, and intellectual and religious life during the fourteenth to the sixteenth centuries. It discusses the construction of the city, its importance, population, occupational and class structures, markets, daily life, housing, clothing, customs, marriage and family, recreation, etc., as well as court life and education. One of the best Near East-North Africa volumes in the series.

E. POLITICS AND GOVERNMENT

1074. Ashford, Douglas Elliott. **Political Change in Morocco.** Princeton, N.J., Princeton University Press, 1961. 432p. bibliog. index. o.p. LC 61-6285. DT 324.A777. DDC 964.04.

The politics of independent Morocco, 1955-1959, are surveyed and analyzed in this useful study which is based on field work, interviews, etc. Claiming that Morocco has "successfully created a nation," Ashford is mainly interested in political behavior. He discusses the institutions, government and administration (including the names of chief officials, with their party affiliations), political tendencies, administrative problems, lines of power; loyalty question, purges, political and other privileges of the elite; party-government interrelations; civil rights; violence and coercion; rural administration and the tribes. Also, the Istiqlal Party and its role in the independence period, its organization, etc.; the labor movement; opposition parties; representative government; interest groups. It should be read with Waterbury (item 1075).

See also:

Zartman, I. William. **Morocco: Problems of New Power.** New York, Atherton Press, 1964. LC 64-10961. DT 324.Z3. DDC 964.04. Decision-making and approaches to problems in Morocco as applied to specific topics, to "elucidate the nature of Moroccan government and politics between 1956 and 1961."

1075. Waterbury, John. **Commander of the Faithful: The Moroccan Political Elite—A Study in Segmented Politics.** New York, Columbia University Press, 1970. 367p. bibliog. index. $10.50. LC 76-108417. ISBN 0-231-03326-5. DT 324.W35 1970b. DDC 320.9'64.

[P1, C1, S1, S2]   The best single work on Morocco, it describes and analyzes the structure and dynamics of Morocco's socio-political system. It outlines the social, historical, and political background, and presents much on the political history of the independence period. It is important not only as one of our only books on the period and as a view of the little-understood dynamics of the anthropological concept of segmentation and how it applies to politics, but also because it may be used as a tool for studying the other countries of the Near East and North Africa, which appear to operate in pretty much the same way, at various levels. Though intended for the advanced student, it is a basic work for college collections and students with a general background on the country.

F. SOCIETY

1076. Chimenti, Elisa. **Tales & Legends of Morocco.** Tr. from French. New York, Ivan Obolensky, 1965. 155p. (An Astor Book). $3.95. LC 65-20804. ISBN 0-8392-3049-4. GR 360.M6C53. DDC 398.20964.

Most of these stories were collected in Tangier and are different from those of the rest of Morocco. Their ultimate origins go back to earliest antiquity, the Islamic period, Sephardic Jewish and Christian sources (e.g., the appearance of Christ in Morocco), and the black slaves who were imported into the country. The author collected them in the markets, from storytellers. An excellent selection of fascinating tales beyond description in their breadth and variety.

1077. Crapanzano, Vincent. **The Hamadsha: A Study in Moroccan Ethnopsychiatry.** Berkeley, University of California Press, 1973. 258p. bibliog. illus. index. $12.00. LC 72-75529. ISBN 0-520-02241-6. BP 189.7.H342C72. DDC 297'.65.

The Hamadsha are a "loosely and diversely organized religious brotherhood, or confraternity" that is Sufi in origin. Their mission is not union with God, but exorcising devils. They use a variety of methods and ceremonies to cure non-organic ills, relieving the anxieties common to primitive societies. Their organization is multi-faceted, being on a kinship as well as a spiritual basis. The book details their origins, organization and institutions, society, behavior, beliefs and theory, practice and method, with a full explanation of the theory. The latter topic occupies half the book. A fascinating work on a rarely treated subject; it is important for the study of ethnopsychiatry as well as Moroccan society. For comprehensive collections and more advanced students.

1078. Gellner, Ernest. **Saints of the Atlas.** London, Weidenfeld and Nicolson, 1969. 317p. bibliog. illus. LC 71-439405. ISBN 0-297-1779-6. DT 313.G4. DDC 301.29'174'933.

The dynamics of a system of "government . . . by hereditary saints in a near anarchic tribal environment." In this case, the Zawiyah Ahansal, in a Berber region in the High Atlas of Morocco. It discusses the general Moroccan background, the concept of segmentation in social organization and its dynamics; the nature of sainthood, its functions in the environment; the political system and role of lineage. Then the village itself, its social-lineage structure, organization and socio-political dynamics, families, individuals and their lines in Zawiyah Ahansal; other Ahansal settlements; other saints in the region. Most of the book consists of general statements and close analysis. For advanced students a most interesting book.

Another interesting book dealing with Moroccan sainthood is Paul Rabinow, *Symbolic Domination: Cultural Form and Historical Change in Morocco* (Chicago, University of Chicago Press, 1975. 107p. illus. LC 74-7565. ISBN 0-226-70148-4. DT 329.Z36R3. DDC 301.29'64). Zawiyah Sidi Lahsene is a community of descendants of a Sufi saint whose *baraka*, or religious power and authority, was held to be inherited by those descendants; this *baraka* was a basic value in their self-identity. Social, political, and economic conditions changed, but the community's response to change was prescribed by its close relation to the old, traditional symbols. The result was that the matrix of their culture became outmoded because the response, which was tied to the symbols and with which the symbols became identified, was inadequate to meet the needs of the community. Therefore the symbols themselves became less and less relevant, resulting in alienation from those symbols, and a loss of cultural and thus psychological coherence and meaningfulness. The book traces the development of the symbols and the community, the function and meaning of the symbols, their significance in relations between those possessing *baraka* and those not having it, and their relevance in daily life; the relationship to political power and order, which is traced from the nineteenth through the twentieth centuries, with much attention given the French protectorate period; economic and the resulting social and political changes; description of the political changes, their history in the community, and their implications; relations of the community to the larger nation. Treatment is mainly general and all too brief, but it is suggestive and quite interesting for more advanced readers. For larger collections only.

1079. Kramer, Jane. **Honor to the Bride Like the Pigeon That Guards Its Grain under the Clove Tree.** New York, Farrar, Straus and Giroux, 1970. 211p. $5.95. LC 78-122828. ISBN 0-374-17757-9. PZ 4.K89626 Ho. DDC 813'.5'4.

The marvelous, hilarious true story of the search for Khadijah, a Moroccan girl of marriageable age who is kidnapped and raped, and her ultimate marriage. A portrait of poor, ignorant, semi-urbanites caught up in the disruption of traditional ways brought about by modernization; traditional Moroccan life and society; lower level civil servants; and marriage customs, as well as the unfavorable position of women in the old society. Informative and very entertaining. For all libraries.

1080. Legey, Françoise. **The Folklore of Morocco.** Tr. from French. London, George Allen and Unwin, 1935. 277p. illus. index. o.p. LC 36-9336. GR 360.M6L4.

A general survey of the superstitions and practices of Moroccans, with stories illustrating and explaining them, collected by a French woman doctor who lived there for 15 years. It encompasses the life cycle and daily life, and includes magic and cures for illness. It covers much the same material as Westermarck (item 1084), but is written for the general reader.

1081. **Living on the Edge of the Sahara: A Study of Traditional Forms of Habitation and Types of Settlement in Morocco.** By Kasba 64 Study Group: A.L.M.T. Nijst and others. The Hague, Government Publishing Office, 1973. 357p. bibliog. illus. ISBN 90-12-00105-6.

A discussion of the history, development, social context, environmental and functional aspects, and structures of the various types of dwellings in Morocco, including tents of the nomads, houses, kasbahs, fortresses, and traditional quarters of the cities. The innumerable photographs and diagrams, even without the text, give an excellent portrayal of the living environment and atmosphere of Morocco and its lower classes. Although structures such as the kasbahs are virtually unique to Morocco, much of the book is valid for the other countries of the region. A basic work for larger college collections.

1082. Montagne, Robert. **The Berbers, Their Social and Political Organization.** Tr. from French, with an introd. by David Seddon. London, Frank Cass; distr. Portland, Ore., International Scholarly Book Services, 1973. 44, 160p. bibliog. index. $8.50. LC 72-92972. ISBN 0-7146-2968-5. DT 313.2.M6613 1973. DDC 309.1'64.

[C1, S2]   A general description, interpretation, and analysis of the history, economy, and particularly the social-religious-political structure of the Moroccan Berbers at various levels, by the late French scholar who studied them intensively under and as part of the French administration. The long introduction is quite useful in explaining Montagne's errors in light of recent disciplinary and regional studies and approaches; it covers Montagne's life, work, and ideas and provides a critique of French theories on Moroccan politics and society. The bibliography contains both disciplinary and specifically relevant works. This is an extremely stimulating and interesting book for more advanced students, basic for college collections.
See also:

Vinogradov, Amal Rassam. **The Ait Ndhir of Morocco: A Study of the Social Transformation of a Berber Tribe.** Ann Arbor, University of Michigan, Museum of Anthropology, 1974. 121p. bibliog. illus. (Anthropological Papers, No. 55). $4.00pa. LC 75-622029. GN 2.M5. History of the tribe, relations with the political system, including French; ecology, economic organization, socio-political organization; land tenure, both traditional and under the French, and its relationship to tribal organization; results of French land seizures. A supplementary, not a basic, work providing further data, questions, and conclusions for use with Montagne and other materials. The bibliography is useful.

1083. Waterbur,, John. **North for the Trade: The Life and Times of a Berber Merchant.** Berkeley, University of California Press, 1972. 226p. bibliog. index. $10.75. LC 70-174453. ISBN 0-520-02134-7. HF 3931.M62W38. DDC 381'.0964.

Most books in political science, sociology, anthropology, and their hyphenated disciplines focus on groups. They describe the groups, or break them down statistically and rebuild them for analysis, or otherwise treat them in an impersonal manner, however many individuals they may discuss. Although the basic approach may be valid, the individual is often lost sight of to such an extent that the conclusions and, worse still, the theories derived from general analyses of data bodies are quite irrelevant to most of the individuals in those groups. The theories go too far and the investigators cannot empathize with the individuals sufficiently to understand their behavior—mainly, it would seem, because they have not studied the individual in enough depth. This book goes the other route, treating the life of one man as an individual, and as an example and member of his group. Waterbury lets the man speak for himself at length. Hajj Brahim is a grocer from the Sous region in Southwest Morocco. He works part of the year in the city, and during the rest lives in his home valley. His good status and well-off life style in the valley are the *raison d'être* for a grubby, frugal life in the city. The book describes the trade, and its family, kinship, social, economic, and political processes and implications. Brahim is the vehicle through which the reader learns much of the social and economic dynamics of a country of inadequate, overburdened resources, as well as the problems of a labor overintensive economy entering the modern world, the degree of adequacy or inadequacy of modern efficiency for handling problems in an underdeveloped country. Also, Islam's relevance to Brahim's class, his outlook on life, and the differences (and sources of those differences) between his life, his attitudes, and his conceptions of society, business and politics, and those of the West, which has formulated the modern theories. Included is a critique of Western assumptions made when analyzing the Near Eastern world. The critique is especially strong in the final chapter, where Waterbury compares various theories of achievement motivation, native capital formation, entrepreneurship and economic take-off of developing countries, by searching them for an explanation of Brahim's behavior—a vain search. A fascinating, important, nontechnical book for any educated reader.

1084. Westermarck, Edvard Alexander. **Ritual and Belief in Morocco.** New Hyde Park, N.Y., University Books, 1968. (Repr. of 1926 ed.). 2v. illus. index. $25.00. LC 66-27623. GR 360.M6W4 1968. DDC 390'.0964.

Based on seven years of field work over a 28-year period, this is an excellent, exhaustively detailed description of all aspects of popular religion and superstition and all their concomitant customs. It includes *barakah* (holiness or blessed virtue), saints and other persons, objects endowed with powers; the jinn, their nature and doings; propitiation; individual spirits, evil eye, curses and oaths, witchcraft; dreams; calendar rites, beliefs, and festivals; solar year rites and beliefs; agricultural beliefs and rites; weather influencing; animals; childbirth and early childhood; death. So immensely detailed that it is probably too much for most collections unless they have a special emphasis, but it is a most valuable work that has much relevance for modern Morocco, as well as for comparative studies of popular religion and folk society in the other countries of the region. Another work is the author's *Wit and Wisdom in Morocco: A Study of Native Proverbs* (London, George Routledge, 1930. 448p. PN 6519.A7W4), a collection of 2,013 Arabic proverbs with translations and explanations of their usages and meanings, topically arranged. The third volume of the trilogy is his: *Marriage Ceremonies in Morocco* (Totowa, N.J., Roman and Littlefield, 1972. [Repr. of 1914 ed.]. 422p. LC 73-160530. ISBN 0-87471-089-8. HQ 703.M7W4 1972. DDC 392'.5'0964). Far too detailed for most readers, since he discusses minute local variations.

An additional work on Moroccan society is:

Stuart, Graham Henry. **The International City of Tangier.** Stanford, Calif., Stanford University Press, 1955. 270p. LC 55-9694. DT 329.T16S7 1955. DDC 964.2. Geographical, financial and political problems.

G. ECONOMY

1085. International Bank for Reconstruction and Development. **The Economic Development of Morocco: Report of a Mission Organized by the International Bank for Reconstruction and Development at the Request of the Government of Morocco.** Baltimore, The Johns Hopkins Press, 1966. 356p. $10.00. LC 66-24215. ISBN 0-8018-0292-X. HC 591.M8I55. DDC 330.964.

A general description of the infrastructure and economic dynamics of the country, with considerable discussion of the country's needs and proposals for developing the economy, including areas for concentrated attention. Due consideration is given to human needs. The only comprehensive work on the subject, which includes all sectors of the economy. The IBRD has produced similar works for Syria, Jordan, and other countries; except for the one on Kuwait, however, they are hopelessly out of date and useful mainly for an indication of the situation during the early mid-1950s and comparison with the present.

1086. Stewart, Charles F. **The Economy of Morocco, 1912-1962.** Cambridge, Mass., Harvard University Press, 1964. 234p. bibliog. (Harvard Middle Eastern Monographs). $4.50pa. LC 64-8716. ISBN 0-674-23600-9. HC 591.M8S8. DDC 330.964.

[P1, C1, S1] The first 53 pages survey the economy, government and administration, and society before the protectorate, and the process of the French takeover in 1912. The rest treats topically various aspects of the economy, politics, and society: population and society; agriculture, including land tenure and use, crops; rural life; industry and labor; the Jews; transport, trade and public finance; a summary of the assets and liabilities inherited by the Moroccans at independence, their use of this heritage, national economic integration, emigration of the French and Jews; problems and prospects in each sector and related areas such as education, etc. Throughout, the author notes changes made, the means used to initiate changes, and the implications of these changes. A work basic to the study of twentieth century Morocco. While a little too detailed at times, it is written in non-technical language. To be read after more general works.

H. DESCRIPTION AND TRAVEL

1087. Meakin, Budgett. **The Moors, a Comprehensive Description.** London, Swan Sonnenschein, 1902. 503p. illus. index. o.p. LC 2-12000 rev. DT 312.M48. DDC 916.4.

A general systematic treatment of Morocco which covers life, society, dress, houses, etiquette, food, slavery, trade and commerce, arts and manufactures; musical instruments; health, ethics, religion, education; marriage, saints, funerals, etc. There are separate descriptions of the Berbers and Jews covering the same topics, though in somewhat less detail. This book is by a journalist who edited a newspaper in Morocco for some years and who sought in this and other books to write a complete account of the country. A very detailed, comprehensive eye-witness description that is basic for larger collections.

Also, Meakins's companion volumes:

Life in Morocco and Glimpses Beyond. New York, Dutton, 1906. 400p. LC 49-32766. DT 312.M475.

The Moorish Empire, a Historical Epitome. New York, Macmillan, 1899. 576p. LC 1-12652. DT 314.M48. History from ancient times, emphasizing the Islamic period, including foreign relations, especially with Europe.

The Land of the Moors, a Comprehensive Description. London, S. Sonnenschein; distr. New York, Macmillan, 1901. 464p. LC 2-21002. DT 305.M48. A geography, including descriptions of the cities and their history, and the author's travels around the country.

See also:

Chenier, Louis de (1722-1795). **The Present State of the Empire of Morocco.** New York, Johnson Reprint Company, 1967. (Repr. of 1788 ed.). 2v. LC cataloging n.a. DT 314.C52 1967.

Grey-Jackson, J. **An Account of the Empire of Morocco and the Districts of Sus and Tafilelt.** Philadelphia, 1810. LC cataloging n.a. Grey-Jackson was the English Consul at Mogador.

1088. Saltman, David. **The Marrakech Express: A Train of Thought.** Photos by Paul Hyman. New York, Links, 1973. 179p. $3.95pa. LC 72-94091. ISBN 0-8256-3006-1. DT 310.2.S3. DDC 916.4'04'5.

A serious travel book by a member of the "pot" generation, with obscene language but a very interesting, different perspective. There is much on the Berbers, whom the author idealizes, including their supernatural arts, and a number of their traditional stories are told at length. For larger public libraries.

1089. Willcox, Faith Mellen. **In Morocco.** New York, Harcourt, Brace, Jovanovich, 1971. 295p. bibliog. illus. index. $12.50. LC 74-142101. ISBN 0-15-144410-2. DT 310.2.W54. DDC 916.4'04'5.

[P1, C1, S1] One of the most interesting and effective travel books read in the course of preparing this *Guide*. The author thoughtfully combines a description of the country with closely delineated and carefully written observations on the people (common people, officials, intellectuals, youth) which note the patterns of their lives, beliefs, and reactions to a changing (or, in some cases, seemingly unchanging) world. She relates her personal experiences in the markets and countryside, records of conversations, and historical and political notes. A truly memorable book that evokes a feeling of past, present, and future Morocco, it is one of the best introductions to be found to any country in the region; one can only wish she would write such a book for each.

Another interesting travelogue that is informative is:

Fernea, Elizabeth Warnock. **A Street in Marrakesh.** Garden City, N.Y., Doubleday, 1975. LC 74-12686. ISBN 0-385-00096-0. LC cataloging n.a. As in Ms. Fernea's other books, she suggests with feeling the dynamics and vitality of life.

1090. Wright, Thomas E. **Into the Moorish World.** London, Robert Hale, 1972. 236p. illus. index. £2.90. LC 72-172196. ISBN 0-7091-3420-7. DT 310.2.W75 1972. DDC 916.4'04'5.

A travelogue of Southern Spain and Morocco in which the author creates a pleasant, romantic evocation of his experiences and the sights, feelings, and atmosphere of the places he visits. He describes the scenery, utilizing tale and local lore effectively to absorb the reader into a different world. It is not terribly informative for the student or traveller, but it is extremely interesting reading.

See also:

Landau, Rom. **Morocco: Marrakesh, Fez, Rabat.** Photos by Wim Swaan. New York, Putnam, 1967. 160p. LC 67-23125. NK 1270.L3 1967. DDC 916.4'03. The life and history of Morocco's key native cities, their people, and architectural monuments and other arts. The text mainly covers history and architecture. The 105 plates, many of which are colored, are excellent. For the most part, they feature exteriors and interiors of buildings, though some depict people and the minor arts. Most readers will enjoy it.

I. GUIDEBOOKS

1091. **Fodor's Morocco, 1974.** New York, David McKay, 1974. (Annual). 346p. illus. index. $7.95. LC 70-649469. ISBN 0-679-00048-8. DT 309.M652. DDC 916.4'04'5.

Typical travel guide for tourists, with all the usual practical information, plus history, culture, arts, folk culture. It is divided by region and chief cities, with itineraries, sites and sights, and the background and description of each; transportation, facilities, recreation.

1092. **Morocco.** Paris, Hachette, 1966. 460p. index. (Hachette World Guides). (*Br. BIP* lists £3.00.) LC 67-75467. DT 304.M313. DDC 916.4'045.

A typical guidebook, the best in English. It provides practical traveller's information from visas to hotels and shops, both in general and for specific places. Besides considerable historical background, there are descriptions of each site and monument and a number of itineraries. Fodor (item 1091) is probably more useful to the average tourist because its information is updated annually, but it has less information.

XXXIV. TUNISIA

Just about *everything* is lacking!

A. GENERAL WORKS

1093. **Area Handbook for the Republic of Tunisia.** [Reese, Howard C.]. Prepared by Systems
Research Corporation. 1970. 415p. (DA PAM 550-89). $5.90. LC 70-607904.
DT 245.R4. DDC 309.1'61'1.

[B, P1, C1, S1] See the annotation at the head of Section II (page 30).

1094. Knapp, Wilfred. **Tunisia.** New York, Walker, 1970. 224p. bibliog. illus. index. (Nations
and Peoples). $8.50. LC 68-13998. ISBN 0-8027-2118-4. DT 245.K59 1970b. DDC
309.1'61'1.

[B, P1, S1] A general work, half of which is history from ancient times. Knapp discusses
Tunisia's politics, Bourguiba's role, the Destour Party, foreign relations, and the country's
development problems and prospects. Includes biographical notices of current figures. Useful
particularly for public libraries.

1095. Spencer, William. **The Land and People of Tunisia.** Philadelphia, J. B. Lippincott, 1972.
160p. illus. index. (Portraits of the Nations Series). $4.95. LC 74-39818. ISBN
0-397-31209-1 (lib. bdg.). DT 245.S6 1972. DDC 916.1'1.

[P1] A sympathetic general introduction for the upper juvenile or general reader. It is mostly
a history from Roman times to the present, with some description of the country. Rather too
often it is overly simplistic, rash, or just wrong in some of its statements, but it is still useful.

1096. Sylvester, Anthony, pseud. **Tunisia.** Chester Springs, Pa., DuFour Editions, 1969.
221p. illus. index. $7.75. LC 73-77232. ISBN 0-8023-1217-9. DT 245.S9 1969b.
DDC 916.11'03'5.

[P] A general introduction by a journalist, with sections on history and politics. It describes
Tunisia's development and problems, Bourguibism in the villages, agriculture and its problems,
industry, and foreign relations. The author recounts trips he took around the country, describing the places and people.

B. HISTORY

1097. Brown, Leon Carl. **The Tunisia of Ahmad Bey, 1837-1855.** Princeton, N.J., Princeton
University Press, 1974. bibliog. index. $20.00. LC 73-16770. ISBN 0-691-03100-2.
DT 264.B76. DDC 961'.1'03.

This book is valuable in various respects: 1) It provides a detailed description of
Tunisian history, society, and government structures and dynamics during this period and is
one of but a very few studies of any period in Tunisian history. 2) It clearly illustrates the
process by which Europe came to dominate the country. 3) It outlines the process and problems of Westernization. 4) It is a basic source for comparative study of the last item, and in
fact refers to reform efforts in Egypt under Muhammad Ali and in the Ottoman Empire in the
nineteenth century. 5) Much of what the author says of Tunisia's system and structures can be
applied to the other Near Eastern countries. It is not a systematic history but a topical portrayal
of the country and Ahmad Bey's attempts to change aspects of the situation; it explains how he
had to operate within the realities of that situation in order to attempt what he did. The military
reforms are discussed, and the failure of the reform effort is thoroughly analyzed. Some attention
is paid to education and economics. The bibliography is annotated.

1098. Ling, Dwight L. **Tunisia, from Protectorate to Republic.** Bloomington, Indiana University Press, 1967. 237p. bibliog. index. (Indiana University International Studies). $8.50. LC 67-63013. ISBN 0-253-18990-X. DT 264.L5. DDC 961'.1.

[P1, C1, S1] A general mainly political history from 1882 to the present. Not really very good, but it is about all we have; it will serve acceptably for the general reader and beginning student. A basic work.

1099. al-Tūnisī, Khayr al-Dīn (d. 1890). **[Aqwām al-Masālik fī Ma^crifat Aḥwāl al-Mamālik].** The Surest Path, the Political Treatise of a Nineteenth-Century Muslim Statesman; a tr. of the introduction to the Surest Path to Knowledge Concerning the Condition of the Countries.** Tr. by Leon Carl Brown from Arabic, with introd. Cambridge, Mass., Harvard University Press, 1967. 182p. bibliog. (Harvard Middle Eastern Monographs, 16). $4.50pa. LC 67-25399. ISBN 0-674-85695-3. JC 49.T8. DDC 320.9'176'7.

One of only a few existing nineteenth century political treatises, by a Tunisian official. It illuminates beautifully the impact of Western influence and education and the process of change, as seen by a participant and mover who sought to deal with the problems faced during the Tanzimat period of Ottoman reform. Khayr al-Din was highly educated and tried to introduce reforms in Tunisia. The 64-page introduction is extremely useful to the student of the nineteenth century. For larger collections.

1100. Ziadeh, Nicola A. **Origins of Nationalism in Tunisia.** Beirut, Librairie du Liban; distr. Mystic, Conn., Lawrence Verry, 1969. (Repr. of 1962 ed.). 196p. bibliog. index. $5.00. LC 70-961281. DT 264.Z48 1969. DDC 961'.1.

A summary discussion of the French occupation in 1881, its administration, colonization of the land, economic changes (including the introduction of various new industries), agricultural change, commerce, roads, and a new educational system, and the Tunisian reaction, which was an accelerating opposition and ultimately a resistance movement that pushed for and won various reforms in the post-World War I period. The book discusses the opposition movement, its organization, publications, internal politics, French reactions, and the resulting reform legislation, through 1925. Basically a superficial treatment, but one of few books we have, therefore basic.

An additional work on Tunisian history is:

Marsden, Arthur. **British Diplomacy and Tunis, 1875-1902: A Case Study in Mediterranean Policy.** New York, Africana Publishing Company, 1971. 276p. LC 71-180671. ISBN 0-8419-0110-4. DT 257.5.G7M37. DDC 327.42'061'1.

C. POLITICS AND GOVERNMENT

1101. Micaud, Charles Antoine, Leon Carl Brown, and Clement Henry Moore. **Tunisia: The Politics of Modernization.** New York, Praeger, 1964. 205p. index. o.p. LC 64-13384. DT 264.M5. DDC 961.104.

[P1, C1, S1, S2] A general treatment of late nineteenth century and twentieth century history, and particularly the politics of Tunisia. It emphasizes the awakening of national consciousness and the creation of the organizational and intellectual infrastructure that led to native Tunisian political movements under the French regime and that ultimately culminated in independence. Half the book concerns the building of the Neo-Destour Party of Habib Bourguiba and its increasing dominance until it became the main power at the time of independence; the structure, philosophy and activities of the Party; the state it built after independence, its institutions, role of the Party, various organizations (including unions and student organizations); how the Party mobilizes and organizes the masses; the new society; degree of democracy; local government and party systems, government-party relations, etc. Efforts at economic and social change occupy the last third of the book: modernization strategy and reforms in education and agriculture, economic planning. A very inadequate book that displays much naiveté and deals mainly in generalities, but one of few we have. To be read with Ling (item 1098).

Other works:

Beling, Willard A. **Modernization and African Labor: A Tunisia Case Study.** New York, Praeger, 1965. 259p. LC 65-21101. HD 88609.T8 B4. DDC 331.8809611.

Rudebeck, Lars. **Party and People: A Study of Political Change in Tunisia.** London, C. Hurst, 1969. LC 74-452235. ISBN 0-900966-13-0. DT 264.R8. DDC 320.9'61'1.

D. SOCIETY

1102. Duvignaud, Jean. **Change at Shebika: Report from a North African Village.** Tr. from French. New York, Pantheon Books, 1970. 303p. $6.95. LC 68-26042. ISBN 0-394-41888-3. HN 810.T82S513. DDC 309.1'61'1. Paperback: Vintage Book V749. $1.95. ISBN 0-394-71749-X.

One of the most compellingly written and interesting ethnographies listed in this *Guide.* It is a scholarly work based on field study. Rather than being a formal systematic treatment, however, it seeks not to provide the standard structured information but to *evoke* a feeling of the dynamics of change in this particular village in a most sympathetic manner. It describes the people and their lives, how they reacted to the researchers, and how, in turn, the researchers were influenced by their experience. The book also discusses the people's reaction to government intervention and illustrates the weaknesses of government efforts that are planned and executed by men who do not and cannot understand the people, their needs, and their desires. Though the village is in Tunisia, it might be anywhere in the region. The student and general reader will thoroughly enjoy it.

E. ECONOMY

1102a. Duwaji, Ghazi. **Economic Development in Tunisia: The Impact and Course of Government Planning.** New York, Praeger, 1967. 222p. LC 68-14157. HC 547.T8D8. DDC 330.961'1.

F. DESCRIPTION AND TRAVEL

1103. Hesse-Wartegg, Ernst von. **Tunis, the Land and the People.** Tr. from German. New York, Dodd, Mead, 1882. 302p. LC 3-13404 rev. DT 249.H57.

Tunisia before the French; a description.

1104. Marriner, John. **The Shores of the Black Ships.** London, William Kimber, 1971. 256p. illus. index. £3.50. LC 72-300352. ISBN 0-7183-0812-X. DT 250.2.M31. DDC 916.1'1'045.

An interesting Yachtsman's tour of Tunisia, featuring the author's personal experiences and reflections; it has notes on history, antiquities, and life of the people, and descriptions of the cities and countryside. It includes travellers' hints scattered throughout the text, as well as nautical notes on ports and facilities. Not a basic source of information, but good reading for prospective and armchair travellers.

G. GUIDEBOOKS

1105. **Fodor's Tunisia, 1974.** New York, David McKay Company, 1974. (Annual). 263p. illus. index. $8.75. LC 73-640761. ISBN 0-679-00054-2. DT 244.F63 1974. DDC 916.1'1' 04505.

A typical Fodor guide. Very little on the people.

1106. Thurston, Hazel. **Tunisia.** London, Jonathan Cape, 1972. 412p. bibliog. illus. index. (Travellers Guides). £3.50. LC 73-174608. ISBN 0-224-00803-X. DT 244.T5. DDC 916.1'1'045.

A typical travel guide: itineraries, transportation, facilities, practical information; history and the people; government. The cities are described in some detail: their appearance and sights, museums, roads, etc., with brief historical notes on sites and buildings, and suggestions on how best to use one's time at each place.

SPECIAL LISTS

SMALL PUBLIC LIBRARIES

These are works for uninitiated readers with less than a college education who want a brief general orientation as a background to the news.

57	795
61	844
65	882
69	891
71	892
76	912
77	926
86	929
94	940
105	942
117	986
130	1008
133	1029
134	1048
144	1049
168	1061
213	1063
218	1094
220	1164
224	
226	
262	
330	
419	
424	
433	
435	
487	
490	
491	
502	
509	
510	
511	
601	
619	
638	
664	
668	
669	
670	
694	
715	
767	
779	
781	
784	
790	

MEDIUM PUBLIC LIBRARIES

These basic works, mainly for beginners at various levels of education, provide essential information for reference and understanding. This list includes all items on the list for **Small Public Libraries.**

4	208	602	892
6	213	619	893
32	215	627	895
47	218	638	908
57	220	643	911
58	224	649	912
59	226	652	923
60	231	659	925
61	261	664	926
65	262	668	929
66	325	669	930
69	330	670	931
71	367	672	940
72	395	678	942
73	418	680	943
74	419	681	946
76	424	694	957
77	433	715	963
86	435	716	964
88	437	720	966
94	446	722	973
97	452	731	986
105	454	762	1006
111	472	767	1007
112	480	776	1008
117	483	778	1009
123	484	779	1011
125	487	780	1017
127	488	781	1020
130	490	783	1029
132	491	784	1034
133	494	790	1037
134	498	793	1038
136	502	795	1048
138	504	807	1049
141	505	813	1050
143	509	819	1053
144	510	844	1061
156	511	854	1063
157	536	860	1069
159	545	867	1089
161	557	876	1093
168	565	877	1094
199	597	879	1098
201	599	882	1121
204	601	891	1160
			1164

SMALL COLLEGE

The works on this list provide basic information and a general survey of the region's history, culture and politics for reference and collateral reading.

4	437	925
6	446	929
32	480	930
47	487	931
52	488	940
57	491	942
61	498	957
65	502	963
66	504	964
71	505	986
73	509	1006
74	510	1007
76	511	1009
77	536	1011
88	539	1017
97	540	1020
105	545	1029
111	549	1034
112	597	1038
117	599	1048
123	619	1050
125	638	1061
127	643	1067
130	659	1069
133	668	1093
134	672	1098
136	678	1160
138	680	
141	694	
144	715	
156	716	
157	720	
158	731	
159	762	
199	767	
201	776	
213	778	
218	779	
220	784	
224	790	
226	793	
255	795	
262	813	
325	819	
330	844	
367	854	
395	876	
418	877	
419	891	
424	895	
433	908	
435	912	
	923	

MEDIUM COLLEGE

These works provide basic information, trends, and concepts on all aspects of the region for reference, collateral reading, and support for general courses on the region. There is some duplication in coverage to permit orientation by the totally uninitiated and growth in depth of knowledge. Acquisition of the documentary sources is highly recommended, as is a generous selection of individual literary works, anthropoligical-sociological studies, and some travel books. Mastery of the core collection in various fields is necessary for using the source materials and preparing for advanced graduate study.

4	132	424	601	776	941	1159
6	133	427	602	778	942	1160
15	134	431	603	779	943	1166
31	136	433	604	780	946	
32	138	435	608	782	949	
47	140	437	609	783	950	
48	141	444	619	784	957	
52	143	446	627	790	963	
53	144	447	630	793	964	
57	146	454	638	795	965	
58	156	471	643	807	966	
59	157	472	649	808	973	
60	158	480	652	813	986	
61	159	483	653	819	993	
65	161	484	659	843	1006	
66	165	487	665	844	1007	
67	168	488	668	851	1009	
71	199	491	672	854	1011	
73	201	494	678	860	1017	
73	203	497	679	867	1020	
74	204	498	680	876	1024	
75	208	502	681	877	1027	
76	213	504	694	878	1029	
77	214	505	698	879	1034	
88	215	509	699	882	1037	
94	219	510	713	891	1038	
97	220	511	715	893	1039	
101	224	513	716	895	1041	
104	225	514	720	896	1048	
105	226	517	722	902	1050	
111	231	525	723	908	1053	
112	255	536	724	911	1061	
117	261	539	731	912	1066	
120	262	540	734	919	1069	
121	325	545	741	923	1075	
123	326	549	749	925	1086	
125	330	557	751	927	1089	
126	367	558	762	929	1093	
127	368	565	763	930	1098	
130	395	571	765	931	1101	
131	418	597	766	937	1122	
	419	599	767	940	1151	

THE SERIOUS READER

This list will give the serious general reader a start at systematic study of the region, its people, and individual countries. Though they are not included, perusal of the *Area Handbooks* is a useful first step in dealing with individual countries, unless another general work is available.

65	261	665	913
66	262	668	915
69	325	672	925
71	326	678	927
73	367	679	929
74	395	680	930
75	418	681	931
76	419	694	941
77	424	698	942
88	427	699	946
94	431	715	949
105	433	716	950
112	435	720	957
117	437	722	963
120	438	723	964
121	444	724	965
123	446	731	966
125	447	741	986
126	452	751	993
127	454	763	1006
130	472	765	1007
131	480	766	1009
132	483	767	1011
133	484	778	1017
134	488	780	1020
136	491	782	1024
138	497	784	1034
141	498	790	1037
143	502	793	1038
144	505	795	1039
146	509	807	1041
156	510	808	1050
157	511	813	1053
158	513	819	1066
159	514	843	1069
161	539	844	1075
165	545	851	1086
168	549	854	1089
199	558	860	1094
201	565	867	1098
204	571	876	1101
208	599	878	1122
213	603	879	1151
219	604	882	1159
220	627	895	1160
224	638	896	1166
225	643	902	
226	649	909	
231	653	911	
255	659	912	

BASIC STUDENT LIBRARY
(p = paperback)

32	923
47p	929
61p	930
72p	931
73	940
74	942p
76p	946
77p	957p
88p	963p
117p	964
121p	1009p
123	1011p
130	1017
138p	1020
131p	1024p
143p	1029
144	1048
159	1050p
199p	1061
208p	1069
226p	1093
262p	
419p	
424	
427p	
431	
437p	
446p	
454	
487p	
488p	
497	
498p	
505	
511p	
539p	
597	
599	
619	
638	
668	
678	
680	
713	
716p	
720p	
762	
767	
776	
844p	
854p	
877	
891	
895	
908	
912p	

BUSINESSMEN

A brief overview of the historical, political,
social, and cultural background, and basic
information on key countries likely to be of
interest to businessmen. These works also
provide quick reading on basic issues, acquaintance with which might be relevant to improving a businessman's ability to get along with
his Arab and other Near Eastern counterparts.

57
58
69
86
94
117
123
127
130
132
144
156
157
168
213
418
419
433
438
446
480
487
490
619
627
630
638
668
713
715
844
848
891
923
929
1007
1029
1048
1050

ADDENDUM

The items below represent the most useful works published, announced, or cataloged in LC (some from CIP data, and not all of this information was adequate for annotating) from the time the main list was completed in mid-summer of 1975, until early February 1976. Several older items that are of particular value to the general reader but that were overlooked previously are now included.

A word of caution to users: Whereas numbered works in the main list are considered to be basic items, the importance of *Addendum* items to core collections will have to be ascertained from the annotations, because all items, even those supplementary to numbered works in the main list, had to be numbered consecutively for convenience in indexing.

All *Addendum* items are included in the indexes; appropriate items were incorporated in the special lists.

I. BIBLIOGRAPHIES

1107. Emanuel, Muriel. **Israel: A Survey and Bibliography.** New York, St. Martin's Press, 1971. 309p. LC 77-166526. DS 126.5.E44 1971b. DDC 915.694'03'5.

Twenty-five chapters by various authorities; each chapter has a long bibliography. Topics covered include history, Zionism, politics, law, defense, economy (including individual industries), education, arts, literature, minorities; mainly English language books.

1108. Geddes, Charles L. **An Analytical Guide to the Bibliographies on the Arab Fertile Crescent, with a Section on the Arab-Israeli Conflict.** Denver, American Institute of Islamic Studies, 1975. 131p. (Bibliographical series, no. 8). LC n.a. Z 7835.M6A54 No. 8. [Z3013] [DS 44].

1109. Hussaini, H. I. **The Palestine Problem: An Annotated Bibliography, 1967-1974.** New York, Arab Information Center, 1974. 81p. LC n.a.

Fully annotated list of mainly pro-Arab and non-Zionist books on the Arab-Israeli conflict. Each note includes a description, an evaluation, a discussion of the particular view represented in the book, and an indication of how pro-Arab each item is.

1110. King, Russell, and J. H. Stevens. **A Bibliography of Oman, 1900-1970.** Durham, University of Durham, Centre for Middle Eastern and Islamic Studies, 1973. 28p. (Occasional papers series, no. 2). $3.00. LC 75-327973. ISBN 0-903011-03-4. Z 3028.O5K56 [DS 247.O6]. DDC 016.953'5.

1111. **Near East and North Africa: An Annotated List of Materials for Children.** New York, Information Center on Children's Culture, 1970. 98p. index. LC 77-29227. Z3454.N4. DDC 016.9156'03.

This very useful guide has 502 numbered items, a few of which actually represent sections, listing several books on specific topics not reviewed for the list. The list is said to include all English books in print on the region in 1970. Arranged by country, with subdivisions for fiction, folklore, and items specifically not recommended. Each item has several lines of annotation evaluating the text as to factual reliability, readability and grade level, the illustrations, the author's attitude toward the people, and, in the case of fiction, plot summaries.

1112. Tronik, Ruth. **Israeli Periodicals & Serials in English and Other Western Languages: A Classified Bibliography.** Metuchen, N.J., Scarecrow Press, 1974. 193p. LC 73-14901. ISBN 0-8108-0682-7. Z 6958.I8T76. DDC 016.15.

III. GENERAL WORKS

1113. Bucher, Henry. **The Third World: Middle East.** West Haven, Conn., Pendulum Press, 1973. 149p. bibliog. pa. LC 72-93316. ISBN 0-88301-063-1. DS 58.B83. DDC 915.6'03.

[P1] After a general and historical orientation (to p. 51), this book deals with five peoples of the region: the Copts, Shiite Muslims, Jews, Armenians, and Palestinians. A successful effort to illuminate for the general reader (high school level and above) problems of the region's minorities; also gives salient points of history and specific information about each group. It features an annotated list of introductory works, bibliographies, organizations from which materials are available, teaching guides, reference books and records, and audiovisual aids.

1114. Vicker, Ray. **The Kingdom of Oil; the Middle East: Its People and Its Power.** New York, Charles Scribner's Sons, 1974. 264p. index. LC 73-19654. ISBN 0-684-13728-3. HD9576.N36V52. DDC 338.2'7'2820956.

[P] Interweaves the history of Near Eastern oil with descriptions of Iran, Israel, and the Eastern Arab countries, including Egypt, Syria, Lebanon, Arabia, and Iraq. Contains anecdotes and interviews with officials and others, vignettes from history, and notes on the people, particularly tradition and change. A very interesting, sympathetic book which gives the general reader a good idea of the currents operating there, and comments on future prospects and problems, including U.S.-Arab relations.

IV. HISTORY AND POLITICS

B. TO 1800

1115. Shaban, M. A. **Islamic History A.D. 750-1055 (A.H. 132-448): A New Interpretation.** Cambridge, Eng., Cambridge University Press, 1976. bibliog. $18.00. LC 75-39390. ISBN 0-521-21198-0. DS 38.6.S48.

For advanced students. Supplementary to item 105.

C. MEDIEVAL SPAIN UNDER THE MUSLIMS

1116. Read, Jan. **The Moors in Spain and Portugal.** Totowa, N.J., Rowman and Littlefield, 1975. 268p. bibliog. illus. index. $12.00. LC 75-312213. ISBN 0-87471-644-6. DP 102.R4 1975. DDC 946'.02.

[P] A well-written general work for all readers, with a useful annotated bibliography. See also:

Stewart, Desmond Stirling. **The Alhambra.** New York, Newsweek, 1974. 172p. illus. (Wonders of Man). LC 73-87152. ISBN 0-88225-087-6. LC cataloging n.a. Magnificent colored illustrations with a lengthy text by Stewart on the history and civilization of Islamic Spain, much broader in scope than the title indicates.

Another popular work:

Sordo, Emrique. **Moorish Spain: Cordoba, Seville, Granada.** Photos by Wim Swaan. New York, Crown, 1963. 223p. illus. LC 63-21116. DP 302.A5S613. DDC 914.68. Many excellent illustrations.

D. 1800 TO THE PRESENT

Only a few popular works on the region have been published since the main list was compiled. The works in the main list and below are the best currently available and are sufficient for most needs.

1117. Hassouna, Hussein A. **The League of Arab States and Regional Disputes: A Study of Middle East Conflicts.** Dobbs Ferry, N.Y., Oceana Publications, 1975. bibliog. LC 75-33041. ISBN 0-379-00290-4. DS 36.2.H35. DDC 341.24'77.

Supplement to item 129.

1118. McKinley, Webb. **Trouble in the Middle East.** New York, Franklin Watts, 1972. 202p. illus. index. LC 74-189119. ISBN 0-531-02582-9. DS 62.8.M33. DDC 320.9'56'04.

[P] A general introduction to the history and particularly to twentieth century politics of the region, for upper juvenile and less-educated general readers. Well written and fair, it provides basic facts and a useful overview.

1119. Malone, Joseph J. **The Arab Lands of Western Asia.** Englewood Cliffs, N.J., Prentice-Hall, 1973. 269p. bibliog. (The Modern Nations in Historical Perspective series). LC 73-5948. ISBN 0-13-043968-1; 0-13-043950-9pa. DS 62.8.M344. DDC 320.9'174'927.

[P1] Brief histories, emphasizing twentieth century and especially post-World War II era of Lebanon, Syria, Iraq, Jordan, and the various states of the Arabian Peninsula. For the totally uninitiated.

V. INTERNATIONAL RELATIONS

E. UNITED STATES RELATIONS

1120. Nakhleh, Emile A. **Arab-American Relations in the Persian Gulf.** Washington, American Enterprise Institute for Public Policy Research, 1975. 52p. (Foreign Affairs Study, 7). $3.00pa. LC 75-4005. ISBN 0-8447-3154-4. JX 1428.A68N33. DDC 327.73'017'4927.

Covers the period 1971 to date and includes discussion of the interrelations of economic and social change, ideological currents, internal politics, etc., of the Gulf states.

1121. Stookey, Robert W. **America and the Arab States: An Uneasy Encounter.** New York, Wiley, 1975. 298p. bibliog. index. LC 75-25874. ISBN 0-471-82975-7; 0-471-82976-5pa. DS 63.2.U5S76. DDC 327.73'017'4927.

[P1] A useful, generalized, interpretive treatment for the general reader which, although it goes back as far as the nineteenth century, emphasizes the post-World War II era and includes some critique of U.S. policy. It would have been more useful had it included more hard data such as names of ambassadors and other key individuals, details of negotiations and agreements, etc., but it is a good synthesis of U.S. policy and relations, in the context of Arab political history and conditions.

VII. CIVILIZATION

A. GENERAL

1122. Lombard, Maurice. **The Golden Age of Islam.** Tr. from French. Amsterdam, North-Holland; New York, American Elsevier, 1975. 259p. illus. (North-Holland Medieval Translation, v. 2). ISBN 0-444-10788-6. LC cataloging n.a.

An interpretation for the general and serious reader with some background of the dynamics of the creation and life of the Islamic world in the Middle Ages: creation of the Empire, its place in the continuum of history, evolution over time, etc., emphasizing the economic and commercial basis of the process, and the interrelations of economic, social, and political conditions, movements of people, relations with Europe, Africa and the Orient, civilization, and the *urban* origin, nature, and orientation of the whole. There are separate chapters on the linguistic and social dynamics, economics, commerce—products traded, trade routes, etc. The first 87 pages treat the individual regions (geography and natural conditions, economy, peoples, political situation). Very little attention is paid to the cultural artifacts of civilization. The book is quite helpful in understanding the context in which Islamic civilization developed, aided by excellent maps and diagrams. Read before Hodgson and Peters (items 75 and 497).

B. ART

1123. Blunt, Wilfrid. **The Splendours of Islam.** New York, Viking Press, 1976. bibliog. (A Studio Book). $10.95. LC 75-41335. ISBN 0-670-66443-X. N 6260.B58. DDC 709'.1'7671.

VIII. LANGUAGE AND LITERATURE

B. ARABIC LANGUAGE (GENERAL)

1124. Bateson, Mary Catherine. **Arabic Language Handbook.** Washington, Center for Applied Linguistics, 1967. 124p. bibliog. (Language Handbook series). LC 67-26367. PJ 6095.B3. DDC 492.7.

Basic information on Arabic: the characteristics and dynamics of grammatical and other aspects of the language described for linguists and others who want to know *about* the language for the sake of making comparisons, etc., but who do not want to study the language itself. Also covers the history of the language, its development, use in history, literature, science, etc. Also the current situation (where it is spoken, the dialects, their characteristics, uses, etc.), and the relation between written and colloquial Arabic. It is concluded by a brief annotated bibliography. A brief introduction worth reading for anyone intending to study Arabic; supplementary to item 231.

See also:

I͡Ushmanov, Nikolaĭ Vladimirovich. **The Structure of the Arabic Language.** Tr. from Russian. Washington, Center for Applied Linguistics of the Modern Language Association, 1961. 86p. LC 78-269168. PJ 6095.I813 1961. DDC 492.75.

C. ARABIC WRITTEN LANGUAGE

1125. Abdel-Massih, Ernest T. **A Sample Lexicon of Pan-Arabic.** Ann Arbor, Center for Near Eastern and North African Studies, University of Michigan, 1975. 157p. LC 75-18985. LC cataloging n.a.

A very useful English-Arabic dictionary of some 5,000 standard modern Arabic vocabulary items readily understood by the educated in most Arab countries. Basic vocabulary found in written sources, such as the press and popular works, and in radio broadcasts. It includes items in a wide variety of fields. The first 109 pages are an alphabetical listing. The rest consists of a categorical list including topics such as colors and directions, home, furniture, trades, government agencies, religion, health, food, education, social life, numbers, names of countries and capitals—i.e., the terms most likely to be used by anyone needing to communicate. This is a preliminary work in a project compiling comprehensive lists—one a three-volume categorical list, the other a comprehensive alphabetical list.

1126. **Elementary Modern Standard Arabic.** By Peter Abboud, *et al.* Ann Arbor, University of Michigan, Department of Near Eastern Studies, 1975. 2v. in 3. LC n.a. PJ 6111.E4 1975. DDC 492.7'88'42.

Grammar and drills. Tapes available. Teacher desirable.

1127. Wehr, Hans. **A Dictionary of Modern Written Arabic.** Ed. by J. Milton Cowan. Ithaca, N.Y., Spoken Language Services, 1976. ?p. $7.50. LC 75-24236. ISBN 0-87950-001-8. PJ 6640. W43 1976. DDC 492.7'321.

Cf. annotation for item 240.

D. ARABIC SPOKEN DIALECTS

1. Egyptian

1128. Berberi, Dilaver. **Arabic in a Nutshell.** Montclair, N.J., Institute for Language Study; paperback distr.: New York, Funk & Wagnalls, 1975. 251p. (A Funk & Wagnalls paperback. F 106/ILS 409). $2.95. LC 74-17006. PJ 6779.B4. DDC 492.'79.

Forty units containing functional dialogues printed in Arabic script, each with romanization, literal translation and grammatically correct translation, plus grammar, notes, and vocabulary lists. No glossary or index. This pocket-sized item is reliable and is particularly helpful when used in conjunction with item 241.

5. Arabian Peninsula

1129. Omar, Margaret K. **Saudi Arabic, Urban Hijazi Dialect: Basic Course.** Washington, Foreign Service Institute, Department of State; for sale by the Superintendent of Documents, U.S. Government Printing Office, 1975. 288p. (Foreign Service Institute Basic Course series). $3.65. (Stock no.: 044-00-01592-1). LC 75-602812. LC cataloging n.a.

One of very few texts on the dialect, by an FSI Arabic expert. Classroom oriented: grammar and drills.

1130. Qafisheh, Hamdi A. **A Basic Course in Gulf Arabic.** Tucson, University of Arizona Press, 1975. 482p. $7.95. LC n.a. PJ 6853.Q3 1975.

Typical oral-aural approach, with dialogue, grammar, and many drills. The dialect is that of the Persian Gulf sheikhdoms, particularly the largest, Abu Dhabi.

E. ARABIC LITERATURE

1. History and Criticism

1131. Badawi, Muhammad Mustafa. **A Critical Introduction to Modern Arabic Poetry.** Cambridge, Eng., Cambridge University Press, 1975. 289p. index. LC 75-9279. ISBN 0-521-20699-5; 0-521-29023-6pa. LC cataloging n.a.

The first significant work in English on the subject for the non-specialist. It deals with key poets, some of whom are represented in this *Guide*, their place in the development of modern poetry, their innovations, views on poetry, themes, genres, Western and early Arab literary influences on their works, with positive and negative critical comments by the author. The author also compares and contrasts their work with Western literature and ideas, and discusses the place of individual poets in their own social and cultural milieux, as well as their lives and times. Included also are notes on other critics' views of these poets, with some of whom Badawi disagrees. It has a chapter on Arab immigrants to North and South America. The problem for the non-Arabist is that Badawi does not include extensive extracts from the poems he discusses, and most of the poems are not readily available, if at all, in English. Although it is interesting by itself, until Badawi or someone else publishes a companion anthology of translations, it will be useful mainly in larger collections. If an anthology is published, most libraries will want both books.

2. Collections

1132. **Modern Arab Poets, 1950-1975.** Ed. and tr. by Issa J. Boullata. Washington, Three Continents Press, 1976. $16.00; $10.00pa. LC n.a. ISBN 0-914478-37-0; 0-914478-38-9pa.

Bilingual, parallel texts; includes key poets from various countries, but excludes North Africa.

4. Modern Authors since 1800

1133. Nijland, C. **Mikha'il Nu'ayma: Promotor of the Arabic Literary Revival.** Leiden, Instanbul, Nederlands Historisch-Archaeologisch Instituut, 1975. 131p. (Uitgaven, 39). LC cataloging n.a.

A literary-critical discussion of the prose, poetry, criticism, and biography of Gibran by the leading Arab author.

F. PERSIAN LITERATURE

1134. Bashiri, Iraj. **Persian 70 Units.** Minneapolis, Manor House, 1975. 3v. bibliog. LC 75-5088. LC cataloging n.a.

Volume 1 consists of grammar lessons for both the spoken and written language, with many drills of various kinds. The script is introduced only late in the volume. Volume 2 continues the spoken Persian and also has 40 units in the Persian script, with reading texts on culture, history, travel, etc. Volume 3 has two-way glossaries, plus such handy material as how to write a letter, topical lists of vocabulary, etc. Evaluation by a specialist is not available, but this work appears to be a basic text containing just about anything the serious beginner would need.

K. HEBREW LITERATURE (ISRAELI)

2. Collections

1135. **New Writing in Israel.** Ed. by Ezra Spicehandler. New York, Schocken Books, 1976. LC 75-36497. ISBN 0-8052-3625-2. LC cataloging n.a.

Translations of prose, poetry, drama, and essays by 31 contemporary writers.

IX. SOCIETY

A. GENERAL

1136. Gulick, John. **The Middle East: An Anthropological Perspective.** Pacific Palisades, Calif., Goodyear Pub. Co., 1976. ? p. bibliog. index. (Goodyear Regional Anthropology series). LC 75-26052. ISBN 0-87620-578-3; 0-87620-577-5pa. DS57.G84. DDC 956.

1137. Hazen, William Edward, and Mohammed Mughisuddin. **Middle Eastern Subcultures: A Regional Approach.** With George N. Atiyeh, Abdul Aziz Said, and Alan R. Taylor. Lexington, Mass., Lexington Books, 1975. 215p. bibliog. index. LC 75-21786. ISBN 0-669-00198-8. DS 62.8.H4. DDC 301. 2'2'09174927.

After general surveys of Arab regionalism, pan-Arabism and nationalism, Islam's cultural aspects, and modern ideologies in the region (their history, role and dynamics, and a general chapter on various subcultures–in this book, the modern functional elite groups), there are separate treatments of each group. They include the military, Western-educated elites, bureaucracy, students, professionals, communicators (press, theatre, cinema, writers, TV-radio). The history and development of each group, and particularly its dynamics and role in politics and society, are given, with material on selected individual countries. Though some factual data are provided, treatment is mainly general; the conclusions and interpretations are really hypotheses for further investigation, since much of the basic research remains to be done. For more advanced students as a supplementary reading and source of ideas, providing coverage of some topics not dealt with elsewhere. A useful stimulus to thinking. Main emphasis is on the Arab countries.

1138. Mernissi, Fatima. **Beyond the Veil: Male-Female Dynamics in a Modern Muslim Society.** Cambridge, Mass., Schenkman Publishing Co.; distr.: New York, Halsted Press, a division of John Wiley, 1975. ? p. LC 75-29283. HQ 1170.M46. DDC 301.41'2' 0917671.

Appears to be a significant addition to the sparse literature on the subject.

1139. **Political Elites and Political Development in the Middle East.** Ed. by Frank Tachau. Boston, Schenkman Publishing Co.; distr.: New York, Halsted Press, 1975. 310p. bibliog. index. (States and Societies of the Third World). $17.50; $6.50pa. LC 75-13176. ISBN 0-470-84314-4; 0-470-84315-2pa. JQ 1758.A3 1975 P 64. DDC 320.9'56'04.

Eight essays on how the elites have adapted to change; their paths (evolution and revolutions); the effect of modernization on the elites and their countries. Covers Turkey, Iran, Egypt, Syria, Saudi Arabia, Algeria, Israel. A supplementary work for more advanced students.

1140. **Political Elites in the Middle East.** Ed. by George Lenczowski. Washington, American Enterprise Institute for Public Policy Research, 1975. 227p. (United States Interests in the Middle East). (Foreign Affairs study, 19). $9.50; $3.50pa. LC 75-10898. ISBN 0-8447-3164-1; 0-8447-3163-3pa. DS 63.1.P66. DDC 301.5'92'0956.

Essays by various authorities taking a variety of approaches. Several of these, notably those on Egypt, are of considerable importance because they break new ground.

XI. ECONOMY

B. OIL

1141. Klebanoff, Shoshana. **Middle East Oil and U.S. Foreign Policy, with Special Reference to the U.S. Energy Crisis.** New York, Praeger, 1974. 288p. bibliog. (Praeger Special Studies in International Economics and Development). $12.50. LC 73-17727. ISBN 0-275-08530-6. HD9576.N36K57. DDC 338. 2'7'2820956.

Interpretive study of the energy crisis, foreign relations with the region after World War II, the Soviet factor, oil history and its influence in the future, policy alternatives, problems and prospects. Supplementary to item 452.

See also:

Sampson, Anthony. **The Seven Sisters: The Great Oil Companies and the World They Made.** New York, Viking Press, 1975. LC 75-20268. ISBN 0-670-65591-X. HD 9560.5.S24 1975 DDC 338.2'7'28209.

Rand, Christopher T. **Making Democracy Safe for Oil: Oilmen and the Islamic East.** Boston, Little, Brown, 1975. 422p. bibliog. index. LC 75-1426. ISBN 0-316-73331-8. HD 9578.N36R35. DDC 338.2'7'282.

XIV. ISLAM

A. GENERAL WORKS

1142. **Islam: Its Meaning and Message.** Ed. by Khurshid Ahmad. London, Islamic Council of
Europe; distr.: London, News and Media, Ltd., 1975. LC cataloging n.a.

A very useful compendium of writings by well-known Muslim writers, translated from
various languages, dealing with key aspects of Islam; organized to be a systematic introduction.
Followed by a good annotated bibliography of works in English by Muslims, including translations from other languages.

H. SHIITES

1143. Lalljee, Yousuf N. **Ali, the Magnificent.** Bombay, Lalljee, 1973? 279p. illus. LC
cataloging n.a.

A devotional biography, panegyric, and documentation of the caliphate and religious
position of Ali, the first Imam, with excerpts from his sayings.

1144. Sarfaraz Ali Khan, Syed. **Insaan-e-kamil.** Tr. from Hindi. Karachi, Peer Mahomed
Ebrahim Trust, 1971. 161, 71p. LC cataloging n.a.

Shiite view and version of the martyrdom of Husayn ibn Ali, the third Imam. Cf. annotation to item 566.

1145. **Tehzibul Islam.** Karachi, Peer Mahomed Ebrahim Trust, 1973. 2v. LC cataloging n.a.

A very detailed exposition of Shiite religious etiquette and practice. It covers every
facet of life from prayer and behavior in the mosque to clothing, sex life, and toilet practices;
includes prayers to be recited on various occasions. The Trust has published several dozen of
these translations from Urdu and other works on Shiism, which may be considered to be
representative works, at least of the Indo-Pakistani variety, which is one of the more
important outside of Iran.

I. REGIONAL

1146. Eickelman, Dale Floyd. **Moroccan Islam: Tradition and Society in a Pilgrimage Center.**
Austin, University of Texas Press, 1976. ? p. LC 75-45136. ISBN 0-292-75025-0.
BP 64.M62B653. DDC 297'.0964.

This important work discusses the role of the marabouts in Moroccan popular Islam,
the role and significance of Bujad, the site of maraboutic activity and thus pilgrimage; the
processes by which Islam as symbol system and field of social action has been reinterpreted
and modified to reflect and influence new socio-economic realities; the problems and implications of these changes. Eickelman traces the history of the processes from the nineteenth
century, then generalizes from these data about Moroccan perceptions and conceptions of
their society. He seeks an anthropological understanding of Islamic civilization and complex
societies, contrasting popular with formal Islam, and concluding that the former is indeed a
vital force. A basic work for advanced students of Islam and Morocco.

J. BIOGRAPHY

1147. Husaini, Abdul Qadir, Saiyid. **The Pantheistic Monism of Ibn al-'Arabi.** Lahore,
Sh. Muhammad Ashraf, 1970. 250p. bibliog. index. Rs 20.00. LC cataloging n.a.

Most of the book consists of excerpts from a number of Ibn al-'Arabi's works in
Arabic, with English translation, each with commentary by Husaini. Supplementary to
item 588.

1148. Quasem, Mohammad Abul. **The Ethics of al-Ghazali: A Composite Ethics in Islam.** Petaling Jaya, Selanger, Malaysia, Quasem, 1975. 273p. LC cataloging n.a.

A Ph.D. dissertation which was supervised by W. Montgomery Watt, a leading British scholar. Physical production of the book is fully up to Western standards. A useful addition to the literature on al-Ghazali. Supplementary to item 592.

1149. Rahman, Fazlur. **The Philosophy of Mullā Ṣadrā (Ṣadr al-Dīn al-Shirāzī).** Albany, State University of New York Press, 1976. ? p. (Studies in Islamic Philosophy and Science). LC 75-31693. ISBN 0-87395-300-2; 0-87395-301-2 (microfiche). B 753.M84R3. DDC 181'.07.

A topical treatment of this important Iranian figure: his ideas and system, with notes on his sources and a critique.

XV. AFGHANISTAN

A. GENERAL WORKS

1150. Hanifi, Mohammed Jamil. **Historical and Cultural Dictionary of Afghanistan.** Metuchen, N.J., Scarecrow Press, 1976. ? p. (Historical and Cultural Dictionaries of Asia, no. 5). bibliog. LC 75-40249. ISBN 0-8108-0892-7. DS 351.H36. DDC 958.1'003.

XVI. ARABIAN PENINSULA

A. GENERAL WORKS

1151. Anthony, John Duke. **Arab States of the Lower Gulf: People, Politics, Petroleum.** Washington, Middle East Institute, 1975. 273p. bibliog. illus. index. (The James Terry Duce Memorial Series, v. 3). $10.95. LC 75-24890. LC cataloging n.a.

[B, C1, S1] Covers Bahrain, Qatar and the United Arab Emirates. Based on extensive field work, interviews with key figures, etc., it discusses in an initial chapter elements of society, economy, politics, their dynamics and interrelationship; the nature, roles, and conditions of the various population elements; relations between the states and foreign relations. Following a general chapter on the UAE as a whole, the author then discusses the individual shaykhdoms: society, economy, political systems and their dynamics and aspects of change; recent political history, education, foreign relations; government efforts for change, ruling families and elites. It concludes with a chapter suggesting the main factors that influence political behavior. The 24-page bibliography is quite useful. There is a reasonable balance between hard fact and generality. It is essentially an interim report rather than a systematic comprehensive work of permanent value, but it is likely to be a standard work for some time to come. Essential for larger collections and anyone interested in the current situation, particularly since the trends discussed at length are unlikely to change for a while. A good supplement to item 627, of higher priority than item 630.

B. BAHRAIN

1152. Nakhleh, Emile A. **Bahrain: Political Development in a Modernizing Society.** Lexington, Mass., Lexington Books, 1976. ? p. LC 75-37374. ISBN 0-669-00454-5. DS 247.B28N34. DDC 301.5'92'095365.

G. SOUTH ARABIA

1153. Fiennes, Ranulph, Sir, bart. **Where Soldiers Fear to Tread.** London, Hodder and Stoughton, 1975. 256p. illus. index. £3.95. LC n.a. ISBN 0-340-14754-7.

Memoirs of a British mercenary's experiences fighting for the Sultan of Oman against guerrillas in Dhofar, 1967-1969. He describes the origin and training of the Marxist guerrillas, who were instigated and supported by South Yemen and Russia, the efforts to indoctrinate the Dhofari bedouins and townspeople and terrorize them into supporting the cause. He details his operations against them. The account, which is very well written, describes the incredibly bad conditions under which he and his bedouin men fought, and the unspeakable cruelty of the war. Included are many descriptions of the lives, customs, beliefs, and mores of the men and women of the country, the villages and towns, the desert; the brutality of their lives is unbelievable. A fascinating expose which is a counterperspective to that of item 622, because Fiennes is totally opposed to the Dhofar rebels, whose movement he says constitutes a great threat to Near Eastern oil and Western interests. Not for the weak-stomached! The only book-length treatment of the Dhofar war in English, it does not treat the 1970s at all.

1154. Gavin, R. J. **Aden under British Rule, 1839-1967.** New York, Barnes and Noble, 1975. 472p. illus. index. $35.00. LC 75-5387. ISBN 0-06-492337-1. LC cataloging n.a.

A detailed history of British policy and administration, relations with Arab tribes, etc., with some indication of the broader context of British Near Eastern policy and activities in neighboring areas, including India, Red Sea, etc. A very useful contribution for more advanced readers, it fills a significant gap in the field.

XIX. EGYPT

D. 1952 TO THE PRESENT

1155. Haykal, Muhammad Hasanayn. **The Road to Ramadan.** New York, Quadrangle, 1975. 285p. illus. index. $8.95. LC 75-8287. ISBN 0-8129-0567-9. DT 107.83.H375. DDC 320.9'56'04.

Egyptian politics during the period leading up to the 1973 war. The author is the former editor of *al-Ahram* and confidant of Nasser and Sadat. Much on foreign policy.

XX. IRAN

G. ECONOMY

1156. **Iran–Past, Present, and Future: Papers and Proceedings from the Aspen Institute-Persepolis Symposium.** Ed. by Jane W. Jacqz. New York, Aspen Institute for Humanistic Studies, 1976. ? p. index. $10.95; $4.95pa. LC 75-45315. ISBN 0-915436-10-8; 0-915436-09-4pa. HC 475.I737. DDC 330.9'55.

Papers, mostly by Iranian officials and scholars, on Iranian economic and social policy, development plans and philosophy, economic conditions, and international economic situation of Iran, with items on political development and culture. Useful as an expression of Iranian ideas on the present situation, plans, outlook, and hopes for the future.

XXII. ISRAEL

F. POLITICS AND GOVERNMENT

1157. Abramov, Shene'ur Zalman. **Perpetual Dilemma: Jewish Religion in the Jewish State.**
Cranbury, N.J., Associated University Presses, 1975. ? p. bibliog. $15.00. LC 74-
5897. ISBN 0-8386-1687-9. BM390.A4. DDC 296'.095694.

　　History of the religious parties and issues in Israel from the nineteenth century to the
present, particularly the political aspect.

XXIII. ARAB-ISRAELI CONFLICT

E. 1973 WAR

1158. Herzog, Chaim. **The War of Atonement, October, 1973.** Boston, Little, Brown, 1975.
ca.300p. illus. LC 75-16118. ISBN 0-316-35900-9. DS 128.1.H467 1975. DDC
956'.048.

　　The most extensive account of the 1973 war from the Israeli perspective.

XXV. LEBANON

B. HISTORY

1159. Salibi, Kamal Suleiman. **Crisis and Civil War in Lebanon.** Delmar, N.Y., Caravan Books,
1976. ? p. LC 75-45397. ISBN 0-88206-010-4. DS 87.S2. DDC 956.92'04.

[P2, C1, S1] A history of Lebanon, 1958-1975, with considerable emphasis on the Christian-
Muslim conflict. A basic work providing background to the civil war which, as of January
1976, had almost torn the country apart.

XXVIII. TURKEY

B. HISTORY (GENERAL)

1160. Shaw, Stanford Jay. **A History of the Ottoman Empire and Turkey.** Cambridge, Eng.,
Cambridge University Press, 1976 or 1977. (forthcoming). 2v. Other information n.a.

[P1, C1, S1] When published, this work by perhaps the foremost Western Ottomanist will be
the standard book on the subject, and a must for all but small collections and the casual reader.

　　See also:

　　Parry, V. A. **The Military History of the Ottoman Empire.** 1976? (forthcoming). No
other information available.

C. OTTOMAN EMPIRE

1161. **History of the Ottoman Empire to 1730: Chapters from the Cambridge Modern History.**
By V. J. Parry [*et al.*] Ed. by M. A. Cook. Cambridge, Eng., Cambridge University Press,
1976. 233p. bibliog. $18.00; $6.00pa. LC 75-38188. ISBN 0-521-20891-2; 0-521-
09991-9pa. DR 486.H57. DDC 949.6.

　　One chapter from the *Cambridge History of Islam*, and one chapter each from volumes one
through six of the *New Cambridge Modern History*. Together, these chapters form a more or
less systematic history of the Empire, based on the latest scholarship, for most libraries.

Save money by purchasing the paperback, then purchase Shaw (item 1160), which will be the standard work for the foreseeable future.

G. POLITICS AND GOVERNMENT

1162. Landau, Jacob A. **Radical Politics in Modern Turkey.** Leiden, E. J. Brill, 1974. 316p. bibliog. index. LC 75-316463. ISBN 90-04-04016-1. DR 593.L36. DDC 320.9'561'03.

Based on Turkish language sources–press and political literature–it covers the period 1960-1971: background, key personalities, the political literature, events, groups and parties, ideas espoused. A topical, not chronological, treatment, it includes Islam in Turkish politics, pan-Turkism, the activities of the right and the leftists. Will help more advanced readers understand aspects of current events and political problems.

H. SOCIETY

1163. Magnarella, Paul J. **Tradition and Change in a Turkish Town.** Boston, Schenkman Publishing Co.; distr.: New York, Halsted Press, 1974. 199p. bibliog. illus. $10.00; $4.95pa. LC 74-14927. ISBN 0-470-56338-9; 0-470-56339-7pa. DS 51.S94M3. DDC 309.1'562.

Change in a neglected community, Susurluk, Turkey.

XXX. ALGERIA

A. GENERAL WORKS

1164. Spencer, William. **The Land and People of Algeria.** Philadelphia, J. B. Lippincott, 1969. 156p. illus. (Portraits of the Nations series). LC 77-82396. DT 275.S65. DDC 916.5'03.

A typical example of the works in the series, for all readers; a sympathetic portrayal.

B. HISTORY

1165. Spencer, William. **Algiers in the Age of the Corsairs.** Norman, University of Oklahoma Press, 1975. ? p. bibliog. (Centers of Civilization series). LC 75-38728. ISBN 0-8061-1334-0. DT 299.A5S67. DDC 965'.3.

Describes the government, history, civilization, and economy of the city. One of only a few serious works available in English on a North African city.

XXXI. LIBYA

B. HISTORY AND POLITICS

1166. Habib, Henri Pierre. **Politics and Government of Revolutionary Libya.** Montreal, Le Cercle du Livre de France, 1975. v.1 (385p.) pa. LC n.a. ISBN 0-7753-6010-4. LC cataloging n.a.

After introductory chapters on the historical and political background from early times, Habib sets forth the ideals of the revolution and the political and administrative structure of the new government, including individual ministries, local government, and Libya's foreign relations. A more or less straightforward, factual presentation to be used with caution, since its main concern is the "ideal" and formal structure rather than actual dynamics and analysis of the system. The author is definitely pro-Libya. A useful supplement to item 1050. Since it is the only such work, it must be considered essential for large collections and students.

AUTHOR INDEX

Abadir, A., 309
Abbas, M., 915n
Abboud, P., 1, 1126
Abd al-Hamid. *See* Abdul Hamid.
Abd al-Rahman Khan, 610
Abd al-Sabur, S., 297
Abd al-Wahhab, F., 264
Abdallah, King of Kordan, 880
Abdel-Fadil, M., 703n
Abdel-Malek, A., 679
Abdel-Massih, E.J., 248, 1125
Abdel-Rahim, M., 911
Abdelkafi, M., 1054
Abduh, Muhammad. *See* Muhammad Abduh.
Abdul Hamid II, Sultan of Turkey, 970
Abidi, A.H.H., 878
Abir, M., 149
Abramov, S.Z., 1157
Abu al-Ala, al-Ma'arri, 228, 279, 280, 281
Abu Hakimah, A.M., 625n
Abu-Ghazaleh, A.M., 857n
Abu Jaber, K.S., 929n
Abu-Lughod, I.A., 121n
Abu-Lughod, J.L., 710
Abu Nuwas, 282
Abu Tammam al-Ta'i, 265, 283
Abun-Nasr, J.M., 548, 1011
Adam, A., 2
Adamec, L.W., 599n, 603, 609
Adams, C.C., 583
Adams, C.J., 3
Adams, D.G., 774a
Adelson, R., 171
Adivar, H.E., 968
Adler, C., 818
Adler, R., 412
Adonis. *See* Sa'id, Ali Ahmad.
Affifi, A.E., 584
al-Afghani, J. al-Din, 180
Afifi, M.H., 144n
Afnan, S.M., 585
Agnon, S.J., 405-407
Agrali, S., 365
Agwani, M.S., 124n, 895n
Ahmad, Aziz. *See* Aziz Ahmad.
Ahmad, B.M., 510n
Ahmad, F., 958
Ahmad, J.M., 678n
Ahmad, K., 1142
Ahmad Shah Durrani, 611
Akrawi, M., 443
Al Ahmad, J., 336
Alatas, H.S., 478n

al-'Alawi, A., 589
Albaharna, H.M., 625n
Albino, O., 915n
Alcalay, R., 386
Alderson, A.D., 360
Aldington, R., 186
Aldridge, J., 704n, 711
Alexander, L.T., 444
Alexander, S.S., 131, 445
Alexander, Y., 4, 31n, 843
Algar, H., 272, 720n
Ali ibn Abi Talib, 490, 1143
Ali, Ameer, 478
Ali, Muhammad, of Egypt. *See* Muhammad
   Ali, of Egypt
Ali, M., prof. of history, Habiba College,
   Kabul, 612
Ali, S.A., 478
Ali-Shah, O., 356n
Aliav, A.L., 850n
Alireza, M., 637
Allen, J.A., 1054a
Allen, R., 844
Allen, R.M.A., 309, 312
Allfree, P.S., 646
Allon, Y., 789n
AlRoy, G.C., 859n
Alter, R., 401
Alwan, B., 26n, 299
American Friends Service Committee, 859
American University, Washington, D.C.
   Foreign Area Studies Division, 923.
   See also Area Handbook . . . entries in
   title index.
American University of Beirut. Economic
   Research Institute, 16n
Amin, G.A., 450
Amin, S., 1006
Amine, R.G., 438a
Amirie, A., 16
Ammar, H., 686
Amuzegar J., 749n
Anderson, J.N.D., 540n
Anderson, M.S., 138
Andrae, T., 506
Andrews, W.G., 366
Ani, M., 254
Ansell, M.O., 1050n
Antara ibn Shaddad, 284
Anthony, J.D., 1151
Antonius, G., 117
Antoun, R.T., 11n, 434, 885
Antun, F., 684

TITLE INDEX

Abbasid Revolution, 105n
Abu Dhabi, A Portrait, 628n
Abu Dhabi, Birth of an Oil Shaikhdom, 628
Account of the Empire of Morocco, 1087n
Account of the Kingdom of Caubul, 614
Acrophile, 410
Adam Resurrected, 410
Aden under British Rule, 1154
Aegean Turkey, 1000
Afghanistan, 599, 601, 602, 605n, 616
Afghanistan: A Study in International
  Political Developments, 604n
Afghanistan: A Study of Political Develop-
  ments in Central and Southern Asia, 604
Afghanistan and British India, 604n
Afghanistan: Cockpit in High Asia, 615
Afghanistan, Highway of Conquest, 604n
Afghanistan in the 1970's, 600
Afghanistan, 1900-1923, 603n
Afghanistan, Some New Approaches, 599n
Afghanistan's Foreign Affairs to Mid-
  Twentieth Century, 603
Agricultural Policy of Muhammad Ali in
  Egypt, 702
Agricultural Potential of the Middle
  East, 444
Ahmad Shah Durrani, 611
Ahmadiyah Movement, 578
Ahmed Ben Bella, 1040
Ait Ndhir of Morocco, 1082n
Akhlak-i-Jalali, 523
Akhlaq-i Nasiri, 544
Alchemy of Happiness, 530
Alfarabi's Philosophy of Plato and
  Aristotle, 526
Algeria, 1044
Algeria: A Revolution That Failed,
  1038n
Algeria, Past and Present, 1046n
Algeria: Rebellion and Revolution, 1033
Algeria: The Politics of a Socialist Revolu-
  tion, 1038
Algeria: Topography and History, 1046
Algerian Insurrection, 1037
Algerian Problem, 1030
Algerians, 1041
Algiers in the Age of the Corsairs, 1165
Alhambra, 1116n
Ali the Magnificent, 1143
Allah's Commonwealth, 497
America and the Arab States, 1121
America and the Mediterranean World, 161

American Approach to the Arab World,
  156
American Doctoral Dissertations on the
  Arab World, 30n
American Interests and Policies in the
  Middle East, 159
American Interests in Syria, 166
American Philanthropy in the Near East, 158
American Relations with Turkey, 167n
American Traveler's Guide to Israel, 841
American Zionism, 795n
Amurath to Amurath, 775
Analytical Guide to the Bibliographies on
  Islam, 3n
Analytical Guide to the Bibliographies on
  Modern Egypt and the Sudan, 18
Analytical Guide to the Bibliographies on the
  Arab Fertile Crescent, 1108
Analytical Guide to the Bibliographies on the
  Arabian Peninsula, 40n
Anglo-Egyptian Relations, 678n
Annals of the Turkish Empire, 948n
Annotated Bibliography of Afghanistan, 45
Anthology of Islamic Literature, 224
Anthology of Modern Arabic Poetry, 272
Anthology of Modern Hebrew Poetry,
  398, 402
Anthropology of the Middle East, 11n
Antiquities of Jordan, 888
Apples of Immortality, 658
Aqwam al-Masalik, 1099
Arab-American Relations in the Persian
  Gulf, 1120
Arab Attitudes Toward Israel, 859n
Arab Awakening, 117
Arab Ba'th Socialist Party, 929n
Arab Bloc in the United Nations, 144n
Arab Border Villages in Israel, 817
Arab Civilization, 203n
Arab Civilization to A.D. 1500, 203n
Arab Cold War, 125
Arab Contemporaries, 181
Arab Cultural Nationalism in Palestine, 857n
Arab Culture and Society in Change, 6n
Arab Discovery of Europe, 121n
Arab Genius in Science and Philosophy,
  192
Arab Guerilla Power, 875n
Arab Heritage, 203n
Arab Historians of the Crusades, 84
Arab Intellectuals and the West, 135
Arab-Israeli Conflict, 855n

U.S. Security Interests in the Persian Gulf, 168n
United States Response to Turkish Nationalism and Reform, 167
Unity and Variety in Muslim Civilization, 203n
Unknown Oman, 636
Unveiling of Arabia, 625n
Usfur min al-Sharq, 303
Ushshaq-nama, 348

Valleys of the Assassins, 754n
Venture of Islam, 75
View of the Nile, 705
Village Life in Egypt, 707
Vis and Ramin, 340
Visions of Life, 302n
Voice of Israel, 800n
Voice of the Master, 302n

Wall and Three Willows, 756
War and Peace in the Law of Islam, 540n
War in the Yemen, 651
War of Atonement, 1158
Washiyyat al Hamasa al Sugra, 265
Way of the Pathans, 613
Way of the Sufi, 562
Wedding of Zein and Other Stories, 316
Week-End Caravan, 222
Welcome to Bahrain, 626
West Bank–Is It Viable, 876n
West German Reparations to Israel, 787n
Western Civilization in the Near East, 127n
Western Mediterranean, 1015
What Is the Christian Orient, 472
When the Candle Was Burning, 415
Where Soldiers Fear to Tread, 1153
Where the Jordan Flows, 890
White Nile, 917
Whither Islam, 499n
Who Rules Israel?, 811
Whose Jerusalem?, 819n

Wild Rue, 742
Winds from the Plain, 385
Wisdom of Gibran, 302n
Wisdom of Omar Khayyam, 356n
Woe to the Victor, 411n
Women and the New East, 438(j)
Women of Algeria, 1042
Women of Egypt, 438(b)
Worker's Self-Management in Algeria, 1043(b)
World of Islam, 213
World of the Crusaders, 103
Worship in Islam, 531n
Written Arabic, 233

Ya Talic al-Shajarah, 306
Yankee Sails the Nile, 706
Yawmiyat Na'ib fi al-Aryaf, 305
Year Amongst the Persians, 753n
Yemen and the Western World, 652n
Yemen: Imams, Rulers and Revolutions, 651n
Yemen: The Unknown War, 651n
Yom Kippur War, 873
Young Hearts, 413
Young Turks: Prelude to the Revolution of 1908, 955
Young Turks: The Committee of Union and Progress, 958
Your Guide to Jordan, 889
Your Guide to Lebanon, 907
Your Guide to Syria, 939
Youth of Haouch el Harimi, 904

Zionist Idea, 793
Zionist Writings, 801n
Zuqqaq Midaq, 310

SUBJECT INDEX

Land. *See* Agriculture.
Languages. *See also* Arabic language;
   Hebrew language; Persian language;
   Turkish language.
   bibliography, 24
Latin America
   Israel-Palestine, 787n
Law, 56, 68
   See also Islamic law.
   Egypt, 678n
   Israel, 812
League of Arab States. *See* Arab League.
Lebanon, 891-907
   bibliography, 35, 891
   economics, 904(a)
   foreign relations
      France, 927
      United States, 895n
   guidebooks, 907, 938
   history, 893-895, 925
   politics and government, 895-897,
      905, 1159
   reference, 891
   society, 897-904
   travel books, 905-906
Libya, 1048-1058
   bibliography, 21, 39, 1048
   economy, 1054(a)-(b)
   guidebooks, 1057-1058
   history, 1051-1053
   politics and government, 1052, 1166
   reference books, 1048
   society, 1054
   travel books, 1055-1056
Literature, 220-416, 558
   See also Arabic literature; Hebrew
   literature; Persian literature; Turkish
   literature; Folk literature and folklore; Literature sections under
   individual countries.
   collections, 204, 220, 222, 224,
      225, 229
   reference books, 59

Mahdi (Sudan), 914
Mamlukes, 671, 925n
Mapai (Israeli party), 813n
Maps
   See also Atlases.
   bibliography, 20
Marrakesh, Morocco, 1090n
Marriage
   Morocco, 1084n
   Palestine, 828
Mauritania, 1059-1060
Mecca, 482, 639, 641
Medina, 482

Military in politics, 112, 118
   Egypt, 679, 680
   Israel, 813n
   Jordan, 879n
   Syria, 932
   Turkey, 964n
Minorities, 67, 1113
   See also Christianity and Christians;
   Copts; Jews and Judaism; Kurds;
   Nestorians.
Mocha, Yemen, 28
Mongols, 106
Morocco, 1061-1092
   bibliography, 2, 1061
   biography, 1072
   civilization, 1073n
   economy, 1083, 1085-1086
   foreign relations
      France. *See* Morocco, History
         section.
      United States, 163
   guidebooks, 1091-1092
   history, 1064-1071
   politics and government, 1068, 1074-
      1075, 1078
   reference books, 1061
   religion, 1078, 1084, 1146
   society, 438(d), 1075-1084, 1146
   travel books, 1087-1090
Muhammad, the prophet, 506-509
al-Munsif, Lebanon, 899
Muslim Brotherhood, 678n
Mzab, Algeria, 1041

Nationalism, 124, 127, 133, 134
   Arab countries, 117, 120, 136
   Egypt, 678n
   Iran, 720n
   Morocco, 1066
   Sudan, 911
   Tunisia, 1100
   Turkey, 959, 960
Near East, 62-70, 1114
   bibliography, 6, 8, 15, 16, 30-33, 36,
      1108, 1111
   biography. *See* Biography.
   civilization. *See* Civilization.
   economics. *See* Economics.
   education. *See* Education.
   foreign relations. *See* International
      relations.
   guidebooks, 466-468
   history, 71-137
      bibliography, 27, 38, 74
      reference, 47, 48, 51, 55, 60, 61
      to 1800, 79-116, 497
      1800 to the present, 117-170, 1117,
         1118, 1119